AN INTRODUCTION TO
DEVELOPMENTAL
PSYCHOLOGY

Edited by
ALAN SLATER AND GAVIN BREMNER

Blackwell
Publishing

© 2003 by Blackwell Publishing Ltd
except for editorial material and organization © 2003 by Alan Slater and Gavin Bremner

BLACKWELL PUBLISHING
350 Main Street, Malden, MA 02148-5020, USA
9600 Garsington Road, Oxford OX4 2DQ, UK
550 Swanston Street, Carlton, Victoria 3053, Australia

The right of Alan Slater and Gavin Bremner to be identified as the Authors of the Editorial Material in this Work has been asserted in accordance with the UK Copyright, Designs, and Patents Act 1988.

First published 2003 by Blackwell Publishing Ltd

4   2006

Library of Congress Cataloging-in-Publication Data

Introduction to developmental psychology / edited by Alan Slater and Gavin Bremner.
   p. cm.
   Includes bibliographical references and indexes.
   ISBN 0-631-21395-3 (hbk.) ISBN 0-631-21396-1 (pbk. : alk. paper)
   1. Developmental psychology. I. Slater, Alan. II. Bremner, J. Gavin, 1949–

BF713 .I54 2003
155—dc21   2002151999

ISBN-13: 978-0-631-21395-6 (hbk.) ISBN-13: 978-0-631-21396-3 (pbk. : alk. paper)

A catalogue record for this title is available from the British Library.

Set in 10/12½ pt Photina
by Graphicraft Ltd, Hong Kong
Printed and bound in the United Kingdom
by TJ International, Padstow, Cornwall

The publisher's policy is to use permanent paper from mills that operate a sustainable forestry policy, and which has been manufactured from pulp processed using acid-free and elementary chlorine-free practices. Furthermore, the publisher ensures that the text paper and cover board used have met acceptable environmental accreditation standards.

For further information on
Blackwell Publishing, visit our website:
www.blackwellpublishing.com

Brief Contents

Contents

Contributors

Robert Atkins, Rutgers University, USA.

Tanya Bergevin, Concordia University, Canada.

Gavin Bremner, Lancaster University, UK.

Peter Bryant, Oxford University, UK.

William M. Bukowski, Concordia University, Canada.

Debra Burock, Rutgers University, USA.

Stephen J. Ceci, Cornell University, USA.

Alyson Davis, University of Surrey, UK.

William P. Fifer, New York State Psychiatric Institute and Departments of Psychiatry and Pediatrics, Columbia University, USA.

Stanka A. Fitneva, Cornell University, USA.

Alejo Freire, Queen's University, Canada.

Livia L. Gilstrap, Cornell University, USA.

Elena L. Grigorenko, Yale University, USA, and Moscow State University, Russia.

Daniel Hart, Rutgers University, USA.

Heather M. Hill, University of Southern Mississippi, USA.

Ian Hocking, University of Exeter, UK.

Stan A. Kuczaj II, University of Southern Mississippi, USA.

Kang Lee, Queen's University, Canada.

Vicky Lewis, The Open University, Milton Keynes, UK.

Bonita London, Rutgers University, USA.

Jon Loose, University of Exeter, UK.

Elizabeth Meins, University of Durham, UK.

Richard Miners, Concordia University, Canada.

Peter Mitchell, University of Nottingham, UK.

Christine Moon, Department of Psychology, Pacific Lutheran University, Tacoma, Washington, USA.

Darwin Muir, Queen's University, Canada.

Dan Olweus, University of Bergen, Norway.

H. Rudolph Schaffer, University of Strathclyde, UK.

Michael Siegal, University of Sheffield, UK.
Alan Slater, University of Exeter, UK.
Peter K. Smith, Goldsmiths College, University of London, UK.
Robert J. Sternberg, Yale University, USA.

Preface

Our aim in producing this textbook is to offer a representative, comprehensive and completely up to date "state of the art" account of human development from conception to adolescence. We appreciated that this needed to be an edited book rather than one written by the two editors, since one can be an expert in one or two fields of study, but not all! By making it an edited book that fulfilled our aims of a comprehensive textbook, we first decided the areas that needed covering, specified in detail the topics for each chapter, and then invited some of the world's leading experts to write the chapters. Our invitations were received with enthusiasm, and we have been extremely gratified at the ways in which our authors have responded to our suggestions. The dangers of uneven writing levels and possible lack of integration of the chapters were dealt with in two ways. First, we gave clear and extensive instructions to our authors as to content and style, and of course carefully edited the chapters. Second, the copy editors and production staff at Blackwell have gone through each chapter to ensure that the book reads well and coherently as a whole, and is well and appropriately illustrated.

The book is organized chronologically and also thematically, into five parts, each concerned with different aspects of development and each containing three or more chapters. Here are brief comments on each part.

 ## *Part I: Introduction*

In order to put child development into its modern context the student needs to be aware of the many ways that have been devised to explore development, and the theories that have emerged from and have guided this research. These are described in chapters 1 and 2. One major topic that pervades almost all areas of development is the nature–nurture issue – to what extent do our genetic inheritance and our experiences across the life span influence and determine our development? This topic is explored in detail in chapter 3.

Part II: Infancy

The Latin term "infans" can be literally translated as "the period without speech." It is the development of the infant during this period, which we know as infancy, that is the starting point of child development. It is becoming increasingly recognized that developments prior to birth have considerable psychological implications and in chapter 4 we have an account of biological and psychological development from conception to birth. Once born, in order to act upon the world infants have to have functioning sensory systems, have to acquire knowledge of the people, objects and events in their world, and they have to convert this growing knowledge into action. Chapter 5 describes how this development takes place, while chapter 6 begins the story of the infant's development into a social world and considers the development of emotions, with a particular emphasis on the formation of attachments with others. The theme of social development is continued in chapter 7 with an account of how the infant's early exchanges with others gradually turn into effective communication.

Part III: Childhood

The period of infancy draws to a close around the end of the second year, but early competencies continue to develop and many new aspects of development begin to make their appearance. These many developments are charted in part III, which is thematically organized from cognitive to social developments. According to "the giant of developmental psychology," Jean Piaget, a new stage of thinking emerges around ages 6 to 7 years. The preceding cognitive abilities that lead to these changes, the changes themselves, and alternative accounts of them, are given in chapter 8.

Language development, probably a uniquely human accomplishment, is the focus of chapter 9, and chapter 10 describes how it is that children learn that others have thoughts, ideas, feelings and beliefs that are often different from their own – that is, how they develop a "theory of mind."

In western societies it is vital that children learn to read and write. How they do so, and the complexities of the task facing the child, is the focus of chapter 11. In chapter 12, the development of memory, a vital cognitive ability that underlies all development, is discussed along with its social implications – how reliable is memory, how truthful are children, how suggestible are they, and do they make reliable eye witnesses?

Development takes place within the social network that surrounds the child, and as childhood progresses beyond infancy peer groups and peer relations become of great importance. Chapter 13 considers the topic of play and how it develops in the context of peer relations. Chapter 14 continues the theme of social interactions and asks how prosocial and antisocial development takes place, and how the child's understanding of moral issues and concerns develops.

Part IV: Adolescence

The two chapters in part IV give an account and overview of the major cognitive and social changes that take place in adolescence. In chapter 15 the authors describe developments in perception and attention, memory, intelligence, and reasoning. Piaget presented evidence that a major change in thinking develops in adolescence, known as *formal operational reasoning*. The authors describe and evaluate Piaget's account, and go beyond his theory to give alternative accounts of adolescent reasoning and thinking.

Adolescence is often thought of as a period of turmoil as the individual copes with raging hormones and the changes that accompany the transition from child to adult. Chapter 16 considers the many aspects of social development that accompany adolescence, including such themes as storm and stress, the role of the family and of peer groups, developing independence, and romantic relationships.

Part V: Practical issues

There are, of course, many practical issues that accompany child development, and three of these important issues are considered here. Chapter 17 discusses the educational implications of what we have learned about children's development. Two major theoreticians whose work has had a major impact on educational thinking – Jean Piaget and Lev Vygotsky – are discussed in detail, and many other issues which include peers, educational practice, and the role of the parents.

One of the major social problems that can dramatically affect children's school experiences is that of bullying. It is, sadly, all too common for children who are bullied to experience great misery, and we have long been aware that programs are necessary in order to reduce the effects of bullying. Chapter 18 describes bullies and their victims, and outlines an effective school-based intervention program which can help to overcome some of the problems.

Many of the chapters in this book focus exclusively on "normally developing" children, that is, those who are following a typical pattern of development. However, we can learn much by studying the development of children with disabilities. Chapter 19 considers three disabilities – profound visual impairment, autism, and Down's syndrome – each of which leads to different courses of development. Such studies tell us that there is a range of different processes underlying development. Such understanding is particularly important on two counts – it impacts on practice and intervention with children with disabilities, and it has implications for our understanding of development in general.

Pedagogical features and dedicated website

The book comes with a range of pedagogical features that contribute to students' learning experience. Each chapter begins with an overview and the key concepts that are highlighted in the text. The chapters end with discussion points that focus on the important issues that have been raised, and with suggestions for further reading for those who wish to expand and develop their knowledge of the area. The book has a dedicated website (http://www.blackwellpublishing.com/slater), which features author details, sample chapters, a glossary, contents listings, and figures from the text that can be downloaded for PowerPoint presentations. For instructors who adopt the text there is password-protected access to 475 multiple-choice questions – 25 for each chapter. For students a sample of 5 of these multiple-choice questions from each chapter is given in interactive format on the website.

Overview

In summary, *Introduction to Developmental Psychology* has been written by a group of internationally known and respected authors who are at the forefront of research, and they give an unrivalled high level of expertise and insight across all topics. The result is an outstanding and authoritative "state of the art" chronicle of human development from conception to adolescence, which gives a stimulating account of theories, findings, and issues in this fascinating area. The text is designed for a broad range of readers, and in particular those with little prior exposure to psychology. The comprehensive coverage and emphasis on core topics in human development make it an excellent text for introductory students. We owe enormous thanks to our authors, and to Blackwell Publishing – especially Martin Davies who helped initiate the project and Sarah Bird who saw it through to completion.

Alan Slater and Gavin Bremner

Acknowledgments

The editors and publishers gratefully acknowledge the following for permission to reproduce copyright material:

Bagwell, C. L., Newcomb, A. F., Bukowski, W. W. (1998). Preadolescent friendship and peer rejection as predictors of adult adjustment. *Child Development*, 69, 140–53. Reprinted by permission of the Society for Research in Child Development.

The poem "Children Learn What They Live" © Dorothy Law Nolte. Excerpted from the book *Children Learn What They Live* © 1988 by Dorothy Law Nolte and Rachel Harris. Used by permission of Workman Publishing Co., Inc., New York. All rights reserved.

Dockett, S. (1998). Constructing understandings through play in the early years. *International Journal of Early Years Education*, 6, 105–16. Reprinted by permission of Taylor & Francis http://www.tandf.co.uk.

The publishers apologize for any errors or omissions in the above list and would be grateful to be notified of any corrections that should be incorporated in the next edition or reprint of this book.

part I

Introduction

CONTENTS

chapter 1

The Scope and Methods of Developmental Psychology

Darwin Muir and Alan Slater

KEY CONCEPTS

AFFECT	DEVELOPMENTAL FUNCTIONS	OBSERVATIONAL STUDIES
BABY BIOGRAPHIES	ECOLOGICAL VALIDITY	ORGANISMIC WORLD VIEW
BEHAVIORISM	EVENT SAMPLING	PARADIGM
CATHARSIS HYPOTHESIS	EXPERIMENTAL GROUP	PERSONALITY TRAIT
CLINICAL METHOD	EXPERIMENTAL METHODS	PSYCHOLOGICAL TESTS
COHORT	EXTRAVERSION	SEQUENTIAL DESIGN
CONTINUOUS FUNCTION	FOLK THEORIES OF	SOCIAL POLICY
– DECREASING ABILITY	DEVELOPMENT	STAGE-LIKE CHANGES IN
CONTINUOUS FUNCTION	HEAD START	DEVELOPMENT
– INCREASING ABILITY	INDEPENDENT VARIABLE	STAGES OF MORAL
CONTROL GROUP	INTELLIGENCE QUOTIENT (IQ)	REASONING
CORRELATIONAL STUDIES	INTROVERSION	STRUCTURED OBSERVATION
CROSS-SECTIONAL	IQ TEST	SURE START
DESIGN	LONGITUDINAL DESIGN	THEORY OF MIND
DEPENDENT VARIABLE	MATURATION	TIME SAMPLING
DEPRIVATION DWARFISM	MECHANISTIC WORLD VIEW	U-SHAPED FUNCTIONS

OVERVIEW

The evidence base is the bedrock of the science of psychology, and developmental psychology is no exception. This chapter outlines the questions to which developmental psychologists seek answers, and shows that folk theories of development often contradict one another or find little support when research is done to test them.

The authors go on to present the different world views that form the basis for evidence-based accounts of human development, contrasting organismic and mechanistic views. This leads on to a discussion of the research designs: longitudinal and cross-sectional designs are compared and the advantages and disadvantages of each are clearly stated.

The authors also discuss the pros and cons of the different forms of evidence that arise from observation, experimentation, psychological testing, and correlational studies, respectively. Their argument is that in the case of many questions, experimental research is more likely to yield results that can be interpreted in terms of cause and effect.

Having provided a comprehensive summary of research methodologies, the authors show how well-carried-out research has radically changed our views about various aspects of development. Finally, they turn to a discussion of the different developmental curves that are detected. Not all development is gradual and continuous: it can be step-like, or show reversals and U-shaped or inverted U-shaped profiles.

Throughout the chapter, the authors illustrate their points with fascinating examples drawn from current literature.

Introduction

Developmental psychology can be defined as the discipline that attempts to describe and explain the changes that occur over time in the thought, behavior, reasoning, and functioning of a person due to biological, individual, and environmental influences. Developmental psychologists study children's development, and the development of human behavior across the lifespan, from a variety of different perspectives. Thus, if one is studying different areas of development, different theoretical perspectives will be important and may influence the ways psychologists and students think about, and study, development.

In this chapter we first discuss the role of age-related factors in affecting development. Then we describe different *concepts of human development* and human nature that have helped to shape people's thinking about development. The issues raised in these sections will recur later in the chapter as we present psychological evidence relating to them. Next we will give an account of some of the *research designs* used to explore development, followed by a description of different *developmental methods*. Finally, we will present some of the *developmental functions* that have emerged from the research.

Studying Changes with Age

The newborn infant is a helpless creature, with limited means of communication and few skills. By 18 months – the end of the period of infancy – all this has changed. The child has formed relationships with others, has learned a lot about the physical world, and is about to undergo a vocabulary explosion as language development leaps ahead. By the time of adolescence the child is a mature, thinking individual actively striving to come to terms with a rapidly changing and complex society.

It is tempting to think that the many developments we find as childhood progresses are a result of age, but in this we must be careful. Increasing age, *by itself*, contributes nothing to development. What is important is the **maturation** and experience that intervene between the different ages and stages of childhood: the term maturation refers to *those aspects of development that are primarily under genetic control, and which are relatively uninfluenced by the environment.* We would not, for instance, expect a particular 4-year-old child to be more advanced in language development than a 2-year-old if, from the age of 2, the child had not been exposed to language at all. The normal 4-year-old will have been exposed to a multiplicity of agents, forces, and events in the previous two years, and will have had the opportunity actively to explore and experiment with the world.

Developmental psychologists study *age-related changes* in behavior and development, but underlying their descriptions of these changes is the clear understanding that increasing age by itself causes nothing, and so we always need to look for the many factors that cause development to take place.

 ## *Concepts of Human Development*

The assumptions and ideas we have about human nature will affect how we rear our own children and how we interpret the findings from studies of children. Our implicit, lay, or **folk theories of development** often reflect the issues that psychologists investigate, with the aim of putting our understanding on a firmer, more scientific footing. We will begin by discussing two such views – "punishment or praise?" – and then we will discuss some of the theoretical views that have influenced psychologists' thinking about development.

FOLK THEORIES OF DEVELOPMENT: PUNISHMENT OR PRAISE?

We all of us have theories and views on how children should be reared. These views result from our own upbringing, our peers' experiences (and shared with us), our parents' ideas, the media, and many other sources. These views will often influence how we bring up our own children and there is often *intergenerational continuity* of childcare practices. For example, there are several ways in which children become attached to their caregivers (see chapter 6) and these "styles of attachment" show continuity and stability across generations – from grandparents to parents to children (e.g., Benoit & Parker, 1994).

Here are two opposing views about the usefulness of physical punishment – see which one you agree with!

Spare the rod and spoil the child

The dauphin, Louis, was born to King Henri IV of France in 1601 ("dauphin" means the eldest son of the king, and he became King Louis XIII at the age of 9). The king wrote to Louis' governess:

> I command you to whip him every time that he is willful or naughty, knowing by my own experience that nothing else did me so much good.
>
> *(from Wallace, Franklin, & Keegan, 1994, p. 4)*

John Wesley (1703–91) was the founder of the religious Evangelical movement known as Methodism. He was the fifteenth of 19 children born to Samuel
and Susanna Wesley. Here is part of a letter from Susanna Wesley (a woman of great
piety) to her son John about how to rear children (cited in Sants & Barnes, 1985,
p. 24):

> Let him have nothing he cries for; absolutely nothing, great or small; else you undo your
> own work . . . make him do as he is bid, if you whip him ten times running to effect it. Let
> none persuade you it is cruelty to do this; it is cruelty not to do it. Break his will now, and
> his soul will live, and he will probably bless you to all eternity.

At that time infant mortality was very high (why else have 19 children?), and Susanna
Wesley's views originate from a belief that children are born in a state of sin and it is
therefore necessary to use all means to save their souls, almost from birth. A similar
view was expressed by Theodore Dwight (1834, *The Father's Book*) – "No child has
ever been (born) destitute of an evil disposition – however sweet it appears."

All sweetness and light: like begets like

Compare these views with the following: "Your baby is born to be a reasonable,
friendly human being" (Benjamin Spock, from his book *Baby and Child Care*, 1946,
cited in Sants & Barnes, 1985). Spock's book had a huge impact on American parents'
rearing of their children. Here is an extract from the famous poem "Children Learn
What They Live" by Dorothy Law Nolte (the complete poem can be found at http://
www.oswego.org/staff/sbernreu/PoemChildLives.html):

> *If children live with criticism they learn to condemn*
> *If children live with hostility they learn to fight*
> *If children live with approval they learn to like themselves*
> *If children live with acceptance, they learn to love*

In this and the previous section we have two opposing lay, or folk, theories about
childrearing: (1) children need to be punished regularly in order to develop as pleasant, law-abiding citizens – failure to use harsh physical punishment carries with it the
possibility, if not the certainty, that the child will grow up to be disobedient, and his/
her very soul may be at risk; (2) the contrary view is that children are born inherently
good, a view that carries the implication that the use of physical punishment might be
unnecessary, perhaps even harmful.

We shall see later that research has given strong support to the latter view,
but clearly the views and theories that parents and guardians have about childrearing will influence their own childrearing practices. In much the same way that
parents will be influenced by their folk theories, developmental psychologists will
be influenced by their theoretical leanings (which are not always based on a fully
objective appraisal of the evidence!), and we discuss two of the most important of
these next.

DEFINING DEVELOPMENT ACCORDING TO WORLD VIEWS

Psychologists, and others who study children's development, also have different views of development. The manner in which development is defined, and the areas of development that are of interest to individual researchers, will lead them to use different methods of studying development. We will describe two such different views of development that have been offered by psychologists holding different *world views*.

The eminent developmental psychologist Richard Lerner defines a world view (also called a **paradigm**, *model*, or *world hypothesis*) as "a philosophical system of ideas that serves to organize a set or family of scientific theories and associated scientific methods" (1986, p. 42). They are beliefs we adopt, which are often not open to empirical test – that is, we simply believe them!

Lerner and others note that many developmental theories appear to fall under one of two basic world views: *organismic* and *mechanistic*. Only a superficial description of these two world views will be presented here (Lerner, 1986, chap. 2, gives a detailed discussion, and Hultsch & Deutsch, 1981, give a concise summary). In chapter 2 we describe some of the theories of development that "fit into" these theoretical views.

Organismic world view

According to the **organismic world view** a person is represented as a biological organism which is *inherently active and continually interacting with the environment, and therefore helping to shape its own development*. This world view emphasizes the interaction between maturation and experience which leads to the development of new internal, psychological structures for processing environmental input.

As Lerner states: "The Organismic model stresses the integrated structural features of the organism. If the parts making up the whole become reorganized as a consequence of the organism's active construction of its own functioning, the structure of the organism may take on a new meaning; thus qualitatively distinct principles may be involved in human functioning at different points in life. These distinct, or new, levels of organization are termed stages" (p. 57). An analogy is the qualitative change that occurs when molecules of two gases, hydrogen and oxygen, combine to form a liquid, water. Other qualitative changes happen to water when it changes from frozen (ice) to liquid (water) to steam (vapour). Depending on the temperature, these qualitative changes in the state of water are easily reversed, but in human development the qualitative changes that take place are rarely, if ever, reversible – that is, each new stage represents an advance on the preceding stage and the individual does not regress to former stages.

The point is that the new stage is not simply reducible to components of the previous stage; it represents new characteristics not present in the previous stage. For example, the organism appears to pass through structural stages during fetal development. In the first stage (Period of the Ovum – first few weeks after conception) cells multiply and form clusters; in the second stage (Period of the Embryo – 2 to about 8 weeks) the major body parts are formed by cell multiplication, specialization, and migration as well as cell death; in the last stage (Period of the Fetus) the body parts mature and begin to operate as an integrated system (e.g., head orientation toward and away from stimulation, arm extensions and grasping, thumb sucking, startles to loud noises, and so on). Similar stages of psychological development beyond birth are postulated to occur as well.

Piaget is perhaps the best example of an organismic theorist, and his views are discussed in the next chapter. In brief, Piaget suggested that cognitive development occurs in stages and that the reasoning of the child at one stage is qualitatively different from that at the earlier and later stages. The job of the developmental psychologist subscribing to an organismic viewpoint is to determine *when* (i.e., at what ages) different psychological stages operate and *what* variables, processes, and/or laws represent the differences between stages and the transitions between them.

Mechanistic world view

According to the **mechanistic world view** a person can be represented as being like a machine (such as a computer), which is inherently passive until stimulated by the environment. Ultimately, human behavior is reducible to the operation of fundamental behavioral units (e.g., habits) which are acquired in a gradual, cumulative manner. According to this view the frequency of behaviors can increase with age due to various learning processes, and they can decrease with age when they no longer have any functional consequence or lead to negative consequences (such as punishment). The developmentalist's job is to study the environmental factors, or principles of learning, which determine the way organisms respond to stimulation, and which result in increases, decreases, and changes in behavior.

Unlike the organismic view development is reflected by a more continuous growth function, rather than occurring in qualitatively different stages, and the child is passive rather than active in shaping his/her own development. **Behaviorists** represent this world view, and their views are discussed in chapter 2.

 ## *Ways of Studying Development*

Developmental psychologists have a variety of strategies with which to study development. These various strategies can be subdivided into two broad categories – designs that enable us to study age-related changes in behavior, and the research methods that are used to collect the information or data about development. These are discussed under the next two broad headings – *Designs for studying age-related changes* and *Research methods*.

 ## *Designs for Studying Age-Related Changes*

In all studies that describe behavioral changes with age, one of two general developmental designs, either the *cross-sectional* or the *longitudinal*, is used. Here we discuss the strengths and weaknesses of these designs. Many examples of research using these designs are presented later in this chapter, and throughout this book. There is a third approach – the *sequential design* – which often gives a partial solution for the limitations imposed by the use of only one method.

CROSS-SECTIONAL DESIGNS

In a **cross-sectional design** people of different ages are tested once; thus, each point on the X-axis (the horizontal axis of graphs, such as those shown in figures 1.1, 1.2, 1.6, and 1.7) is represented by a different age group. This is the most common method employed by developmental researchers because it is the least time-consuming and provides a quick estimate of changes with age. However, it only describes age differences. There is no way to derive an estimate of the continuity or discontinuity of various processes over age (e.g., stability of personality; sudden shifts in language comprehension or production) because performance is averaged over *different* individuals at each age.

LONGITUDINAL DESIGNS

In **longitudinal designs** people are tested repeatedly as they grow older. This method is powerful because each individual's development is measured over time, allowing one to assess *within-person* changes with age and *between-person* differences in age changes. In many cases the data are summarized by plotting the group average as a function of age; but, by looking at each individual's data, we can determine if there is a gradual change with age or a sudden shift in performance more characteristic of stage-like development (these and other types of developmental change are discussed later under *developmental functions*).

Unfortunately, there are several problems with longitudinal designs as well! The cost is very high in several respects. They are time-consuming, it may be difficult to schedule repeated visits of the same children, and the drop-out rate can be very high. If those who find the task difficult withdraw from the study, this *participant attrition*, with the accompanying *selective survivorship* of the remaining children in the sample, can produce a population bias which can give a misleading impression of development and may limit the generality of the results.

Perhaps the biggest problem is the time it takes to complete a study – it equals the age span being tested. If, for example, the task is to map changes in performance on **IQ tests** between age 20 and 80, it would take 60 years to complete the study! And, after all that work, the results may only be true for the particular age **cohort** studied (those born at about the same time), producing yet another population bias. There is one final problem we can mention, which is the possible effects of repeated testing – children might get better over age simply because they have more practice on the tasks they are given!

WHEN LONGITUDINAL AND CROSS-SECTIONAL RESULTS TELL A DIFFERENT STORY

Usually researchers try to obtain both longitudinal and cross-sectional data on any topic. In general, we expect to obtain similar developmental functions from cross-sectional and longitudinal data, and generally this is the case. However, this does not always happen, and the two designs can sometimes give us dramatically different results. Two instances of conflicting results will be discussed; the first concerns the *length of time between measures* (the age scale), and the second concerns *cohort effects*.

Time between measures

In designing a developmental study one must decide what intervals to use on the X-axis, i.e., at what ages the children are to be tested or how often repeated tests will be administered. When studying infants, it is common to test them monthly or bi-weekly in longitudinal studies, depending on when we expect to see an age difference in performance appear. The transition point for changes in performance with age can be estimated using cross-sectional data. While this may be appropriate in most cases, sometimes different distances between test ages can result in very different developmental functions.

An interesting example involves physical growth, which usually is represented as a continuous, increasing growth curve. This is shown in figure 1.1, where the filled circles connected by a solid line have been estimated from a normative study by Babson and Benda (1976) that is based on a combination of cross-sectional and longitudinal data. The function looks continuous, and the shape matches the monthly longitudinal data they reported for a few "normally" growing individual infants. By contrast, a discontinuous step-like function was found by Lampl, Veldhuis, and Johnson (1992) when they made daily or weekly measures of the growth in the length of a small number of infants during the first 21 months from birth. Lampl et al. analyzed

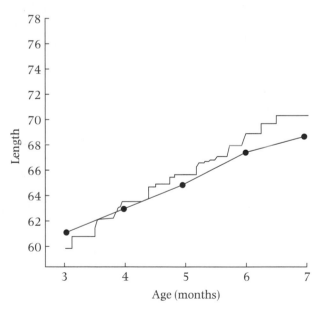

Figure 1.1 A comparison of the continuous-growth function for length/height derived from averaged data from cross-sectional studies (the solid line connected by the filled circles) with the step-like function (sudden increases in length followed by periods of no growth) derived from daily measures on an individual infant.

individual growth functions and discovered that the main change in length occurred in sudden bursts followed by longer periods of no change. Indeed, in daily measures, children were found to grow substantially, as much as 1 centimeter, in a sudden burst, in many cases overnight, and then not change for an average of 12 days. This is shown in figure 1.1 where a summary of the growth pattern of one infant in Lampl et al.'s study is pictured by the thin line overlaying Babson and Benda's normative curve.

This may come as no great surprise to some parents who report that their babies seemed suddenly to outgrow their sleeper (or "babygrow") overnight! The main point is that according to Lampl et al. changes in size occur in a stage-like progression, with the most common state being "no change" at all. This developmental function is not revealed unless frequent measures are taken on individuals. It should be noted that if all of Lampl et al.'s data were collapsed across individuals and plotted as a function of monthly age groups, the curve probably would look like Babson and Benda's continuous age function.

Cohort effects

A serious design problem, which is particularly relevant for studies covering a large age range, involves cohort effects. This is where there are changes across generations in the characteristic one is interested in. Here are a few examples of such effects.

Height: The average height of the western 20-year-old male has risen from around 5'7" in the early 1900s to around 6'0" at the turn of the twenty-first century. This has resulted from gradual improvements in diet which make fetal life in the womb and postnatal life healthier.

Attitudes: There have been many changes in important psychological characteristics over generations. Consider, for example, current attitudes toward homosexuality – how do you think they have changed over the last 50 years?

Leisure activities: Western children spend much more time in sedentary activities such as watching television, playing video games, and surfing the web than their counterparts of 50 or 60 years ago, for whom such activities were not available.

Everyday life: Huge changes have occurred in everyday life in recent generations which combine to produce substantial intergenerational psychological changes. In addition to changes in leisure activities, consider the impact of better, more affordable cars and better transport in general, household appliances such as washing machines, computers – the luxuries of yesteryear become today's necessities.

Intelligence: In much the same way that height has increased over generations, so too has measured intelligence (**intelligence quotient** or IQ as measured by intelligence tests). This means that the findings from early cross-sectional and longitudinal studies gave a different account of the development of intelligence across the lifespan than more recent studies – these findings are described in the next section.

SEQUENTIAL DESIGNS

One possible way of investigating the different findings that might result from longitudinal and cross-sectional designs is with the use of what are called **sequential** or **age/**

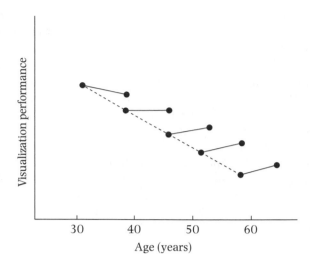

Figure 1.2 The use of a sequential design with an intelligence test demonstrates that different results can emerge from cross-sectional findings (the cohort effect shown by the downward-sloping dotted line) and longitudinal findings (the solid lines).

cohort designs. These studies involve a combination of designs, and are fairly rare (in large part because of the costs and time involved). We will illustrate this design with a schematic drawing of performance on one intelligence test (known as *visualization performance* – the precise details of the test are not important for our purposes), adapted from Nesselroade, Schaie, and Baltes (1972), which is shown in figure 1.2. In this figure, adults in five different age groups (30, 37, 44, 51, and 58 years – the *cross-sectional* aspect of the study) were tested twice (7 years apart – the *longitudinal* part), giving us overlapping age groups.

The results show two effects. There is a *cohort effect*, resulting from testing different adults of different ages at about the same time: this is the lower performance by the older age groups, illustrated by the dotted line connecting the cross-sectional data. There is also a contrasting, *longitudinal effect*, where the same individuals tested at two ages show a slight improvement in performance over age, illustrated by the solid lines connecting each pair of longitudinal points for the five age groups.

Although sequential designs are not used often, when they are used they provide a measure of individual differences and reveal whether or not longitudinal and cross-sectional results agree. We now turn to an account of the different *research methods* that are used to collect data on children's development.

Research Methods

The research designs that we have discussed are always used in combination with one or more developmental *research methods* in order to investigate development.

Developmental psychologists employ a variety of methods, and here we will discuss some of the most important: **observational studies**, **experimental methods**, **psychological testing**, and **correlational studies**.

OBSERVATIONAL STUDIES

Baby biographies

Perhaps the simplest in form is the case study, which involves repeated observations of the same person over time. These observations are usually of infants, and are made by the parents or caregivers who are close to the child. These are often called baby diaries, or **baby biographies**.

A famous example is Charles Darwin's (1877, reprinted in Slater & Muir, 1999) delightful biographical sketch of the development of his first-born son – William Erasmus Darwin. William Erasmus (nicknamed "Doddy") was born on December 27, 1839, but Darwin's account of his development was not published until 1877, by which time Charles and his wife Emma had had another nine children, five boys and four girls: thus Darwin was able to compare his eldest child with his others. We will give four extracts from this account in order to illustrate some of the strengths and weaknesses of such biographies:

Seeing: "With respect to vision, – his eyes were fixed on a candle as early as the 9th day, and up to the 45th day nothing else seemed thus to fix them; but on the 49th day his attention was attracted by a brightly coloured tassel . . ."

Hearing: "Although so sensitive to sound in a general way, he was not able even when 124 days easily to recognize whence a sound proceeded, so as to direct his eyes to the source . . ."

Anger: "When two years and three months old, he became a great adept at throwing books or sticks, etc., at anyone who offended him; and so it was with some of my other sons. On the other hand, I could never see a trace of such an aptitude in my infant daughters; and *this makes me think that a tendency to throw objects is inherited by boys.*" (italics added)

Moral Sense: (When 2 years and 7.5 months) "I met him coming out of the dining room with his eyes unnaturally bright, and an odd unnatural or affected manner, so that I went into the room to see who was there, and found that he had been taking pounded sugar, which he had been told not to do. As he had never been in any way punished, his odd manner certainly was not due to fear and I suppose it was pleasurable excitement struggling with conscience. . . . *As this child was educated solely by working on his good feelings, he soon became as truthful, open, and tender, as anyone could desire.*" (italics added)

While such case studies provide a rich source of ideas and insights, they have many obvious weaknesses. Despite the fact that Darwin was one of the finest observers of natural behavior who has ever lived, we now know that his account of the development of vision and hearing is wrong. As is described in chapter 5, we know from

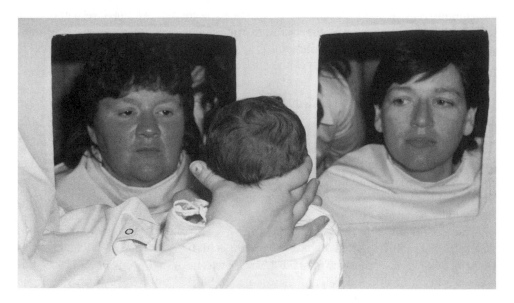

Plate 1.1 Which one is mother? A few hours after birth newborn infants prefer to look at their mother's face. Photograph by Ian Bushnell.

careful experimentation that although vision at birth is poor, it is sufficient for the infant to begin learning about the visual world: for instance, within hours from birth infants will prefer to look at their mother's face when hers is shown paired with that of a female stranger (Bushnell, Sai, & Mullin, 1989; see plate 1.1). We also know that newborn infants can localize sounds at birth, an ability that Darwin was unable to detect in his son, even at 124 days (4 months). We will discuss auditory localization later (under *Developmental functions*).

We can notice weaknesses in the italicized extracts from *Anger* and *Moral Sense*: in both of these Darwin is expressing untested theoretical views which are derived either from observations of just a few children or from a folk theory of development of the sort we discussed earlier. With respect to *Anger* Darwin suggests that there may be inherited gender differences in acts of aggression, and indeed there is clear evidence that the majority of physically aggressive acts are committed by males. With respect to the *Moral Sense* note that Darwin is assuming that children brought up in the absence of physical punishment will display less antisocial behavior in later life. We will comment on this later, in the section on *Experimental methods*, but it turns out that Darwin was right: that is, the use of punishment is not a good way of changing behavior, and children disciplined with the use of physical punishment are more likely to misbehave and become aggressive.

The weaknesses of such accounts include problems of generalization – one or two children hardly constitute a representative sample of the population. Also, the observations tend to be unsystematic, and in many cases are retrospective – i.e., events described long after their occurrence. Baby biographers may have strong theoretical biases which lead them to note anecdotes supporting their own theories.

The strengths of such accounts are primarily twofold: (1) the biographer can give a detailed account of subtle changes in behavior because of his/her intimate knowledge of the child; (2) the observations can lead to the production of theories of child development, which can then be given a more systematic (often experimental) test.

Time and event sampling

Time sampling is an observational method in which individuals are studied over a period of time, and at frequent brief intervals during this period a note is made – usually by an observer but sometimes by the individuals themselves – of whether or not certain behaviors of interest are occurring. For example, a researcher might watch a child over a 20-minute play period, noting every 30 seconds for a 5-second interval whether the child is playing alone, playing with others, not playing, being aggressive, and so on.

Here is one study to illustrate the use of this method. Lee and Larson (2000) sampled 56 high school seniors (17–18-year-olds) in Korea and 62 seniors (17-year-olds) in the United States. Each student was studied for one month and was provided with an electronic timer which gave a beep 7 times a day at randomly spaced intervals over the period between approximately 7.00 a.m. to 11.30 p.m. Every time the beeper sounded the student was asked to note down (a) what they were doing and (b) their **affect state** (i.e., whether they were happy, sad, etc.) as it was just before the beeper sounded. What they found was that the Korean students recorded many more times spent in schoolwork and much less time in other (e.g., recreational) activities than the American students. They also found that the Korean students experienced many more negative affect states (i.e., they were more depressed) than their American counterparts. This suggests that the Koreans' ordeal of studying in preparation for the competitive college entrance examinations was causing them considerable distress and depression.

This, and other time sampling studies, records the participants' behavior at frequent intervals over a period of time, and simply notes what is happening at each recording period. The aim is to get an idea of how frequently different behaviors occur during the total observation period. However, there are two interrelated criticisms of time sampling. One is that the researcher may not get an accurate record of the amount of time spent in different behaviors – quite simply, many naturally occurring behaviors may not be happening when each behavior sample is taken! The other is that many behaviors of interest may simply not occur, or might be missed, during the period that recording is taking place.

Event sampling is an alternative method that avoids these problems. As the name suggests, in this procedure the researchers actively select the type of event that they want to observe. This event is then recorded, usually *throughout* its time period (rather than at intervals, as would be the case for time sampling), on a continuous basis – for this reason this type of event sampling is also known as *continuous sampling*, and it is the most common observation method used in child development research. There are innumerable events that are of interest to child psychologists. The following list, while long, is not exhaustive!

quarrels, anger episodes, fear episodes, frustration, success episodes, failure episodes, competition episodes, cooperation episodes, problem-solving, prosocial episodes, antisocial times, play with pets, play with others, solitary play, school recitations, toilet-training, discipline periods, first school day, bedtime activities, reading with mother, weaning, feeding, illness, vaccinations, school leisure times, mother–infant social engagements . . .

A final point to note is that the baby biographies, referred to earlier, used both time and event sampling procedures, but not in a particularly systematic fashion.

The clinical method

The greatest developmental psychologist of all time, Jean Piaget, studied the development of his three children during their infancy. He kept very detailed records of their development, but instead of simply recording their development, which is typical of the baby biographers, he would note an interesting behavior and then, in order to understand it better, he varied the task to note any changes in the infant's response. This technique, which is a combination of observation and loosely structured experimentation, is known as the **clinical method**. Piaget also used this method extensively with older children in order to develop his theory of the growth of intelligence. Here is a brief extract (Piaget, 1954, pp. 177–8) to illustrate the procedure – Piaget observed his son Laurent (aged 6 months 22 days) when reaching for objects:

> Laurent tries to grasp a box of matches. When he is at the point of reaching it I place it on a book; he immediately withdraws his hand, then grasps the book itself. He remains puzzled until the box slides and thanks to this accident he dissociates it from its support.

Piaget's reasonable interpretation of this observation is that when one object is on top of, and hence touching, another object, his infant did not realize that there were two objects. In fact, it was not until he was 10 months old that he

> immediately grasps matchboxes, erasers, etc., placed on a notebook or my hand; he therefore readily dissociates the object from the support. (p. 178)

EXPERIMENTAL METHODS

The majority of investigations of child behavior and development are experimental in nature. Behavior does not occur, and development does not take place, without a *cause*. The aim of the experimenter is to specify, in as precise a manner as possible, the causal relationships between maturation, learning and experience, and behavior. The essential aspect of experimental techniques is *control*. A situation is constructed which enables the experimenter to exert control over the causal variables that influence the behavior of interest. One of these factors, which is called the **independent variable**, is varied in a systematic fashion, and objective measurements are made of any changes in the child's behavior. The behavior that is measured is called the **dependent variable** since (if all goes well!) changes in this behavior are dependent upon, that is, caused by, changes in the independent variable.

Why do infants grasp pictures of objects?

To illustrate the experimental method we will describe a series of interrelated experiments by Judy Deloache and her colleagues (e.g., Deloache, Pierroutsakos, Uttal, Rosengren, & Gottlieb, 1998). The famous Belgian experimental psychologist Albert Michotte (1881–1965) discussed the meaning of objects and the way in which a picture of an object represents the real object. Note that adults do not confuse objects with pictures except under special viewing conditions – perhaps looking with one eye, or being given *binocular stereoscopic images* (these are where slightly different images are presented to the two eyes so that they give the illusion of solidity and three-dimensionality). If someone were to ask us to pick up a pictured object we'd think them very strange! However, Deloache and her colleagues have reported that young infants *will* try to pick up a pictured object.

In their most recent experiment they tested 9-month-old infants and their *independent variable* was the extent to which the objects depicted in pictures looked like the real thing. They had four versions of pictorial representations, which were, in order of realism: (1) a highly realistic colored photograph of real objects (such as a toy car); (2) a black-and-white photograph; (3) a colored line drawing of the object; and (4) a black-and-white line drawing. All of the depicted objects measured approximately 3 cm × 3 cm, a size that matches the size of the infants' grasp. A black-and-white photograph and line drawing are shown in figure 1.3. Their dependent variable was the amount of manual investigation of the depicted objects, which included attempts

Figure 1.3 An example of a photograph and a line drawing of the same object, to explore children's grasping and reaching behaviors.

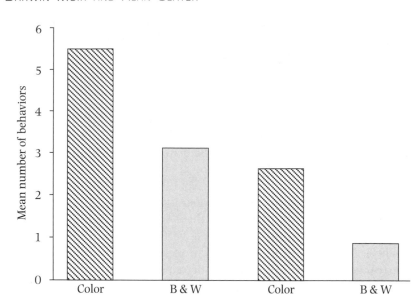

Figure 1.4 Grasping and reaching behaviors were clearly related to how realistic the pictures were; the more the pictures looked like a real object, the more exploration they evoked.

at grasping them. The results are shown in figure 1.4 and clearly show that the closer the depicted object is to the real object, the greater the amount of manual exploration. Sometimes, the pictured object is just too enticing (plate 1.2)!

Deloache et al. had other experimental conditions. Their 1998 paper describes two experimental findings: a *cross-cultural* comparison – 9-month-old infants from two extremely different societies (the United States and the West African republic of the Ivory Coast) produced the same reaching and grasping behavior; a *cross-sectional* study, where different infants were tested at three different ages (9, 15, and 19 months) – the younger infants reached and grasped, by 15 months this behavior was rare, and by 19 months of age they merely pointed at the pictures. Note that in this instance the independent variable is the age of the infants. In a further experimental condition 9-month-olds were presented with the realistic picture and the real object – in this condition none of the infants reached for the picture!

Deloache et al. interpret their intriguing results as indicating that the younger 9-month-olds do not understand the ways in which depicted objects are both similar to and different from real objects: when the real object is not present they treat the pictures as if they were real objects because in many ways they *look* like real objects. As they gain experience the infants develop a more sophisticated understanding of the relationship between the pictures and the objects they depict, and learn that pictures are *representations* of objects.

Deloache et al. are able to tell a convincing developmental story of the nature and development of infants' understanding of pictures and objects. In these experiments the independent variables – such as the realism of the pictorial representations and the

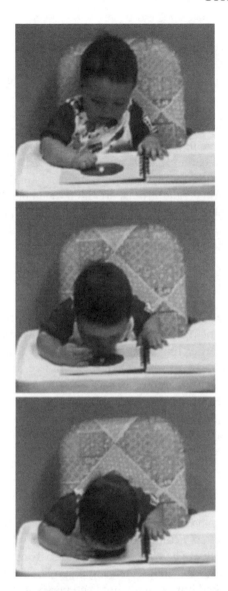

Plate 1.2 A 9-month-old infant as he grasps and mouths a photograph of a baby bottle – the picture is just too enticing! Photographs by Sophia Pierroutsakos, reprinted with permission.

age of the infants – were systematically varied, and the experimenters then carefully observed the babies' reaching responses. Sometimes this sort of experiment is called a **structured observation**, and there are those who would distinguish between this sort of experiment and those involving more formal or precise measures of the dependent variable. There is clearly an element of observation in many, perhaps most, experimental studies of children's development.

Psychological testing

Psychological tests can be defined as *instruments for the quantitative assessment of some psychological attribute or attributes of a person.* The developmental psychologist has available a wide variety of tests for measuring psychological functioning at all ages of childhood. These include tests of motor development, personality development, aptitudes (perhaps mechanical or musical or scholastic achievement), achievement, motivation, self-esteem, reading ability, general intelligence, and many others.

Such tests are usually carefully standardized on large samples of children of the appropriate age groups, and norms (i.e., average scores and the range or spread of scores) for various age and gender groups are often available. Researchers, or testers, can compare their sample of children (or individual children) against the appropriate norms. Clear and precise instructions for administering and scoring the test items are usually included with the published test.

Types of test items

The type of item included in a particular test will depend both on the age group it is intended for and what is being measured. Tests of infant development usually consist of careful observations of the child when confronted with a number of standard situations: Can he stand alone? Can she build a tower of five bricks? and so on. Beyond about 2 years of age tests make increasing use of children's ability to use language, and the instructions given to the child are typically in a verbal form. Thus, in a test of intelligence the child might be asked to solve problems, to give the meanings of words, to say in what way(s) two or three words are similar in meaning, to trace a pathway through a maze, and so on.

Can test scores predict later development?

Tests of ability and intelligence become increasingly accurate in predicting later behavior (for example, school achievement) as children get older (chapter 15 presents findings on the predictability of IQ scores in adolescence from scores obtained in earlier childhood). However, attempts to predict adult personality from measures of personality in earlier childhood have usually not been very successful. There are a couple of exceptions: children who are shy or bold as infants tend to become adults who are shy or bold; the child who fights with other children a lot is likely to become the adolescent who is judged by peers to be aggressive (see chapter 14). In fact, aggression shows greater continuity across childhood and adolescence than any other facet of personality.

However, the term *personality* is extremely difficult to define, and **personality traits** are difficult to measure precisely. One problem with measuring personality is that the most important personality traits – such as **extraversion**, **introversion**, sociability, suggestibility – are *social* in nature and may vary depending on the different types of social settings individuals find themselves in. Thus, although there may be some underlying stability of a shy/bold personality, the child who is sociable and outgoing with his/her family and friends may be shy and withdrawn in the classroom. Furthermore, changing life experiences alter behavior and attitudes: an adolescent will be treated differently than a 7-year-old, and this will affect the way the individual behaves and responds.

Uses of tests

The uses of tests by developmental psychologists are many and varied. Tests are regularly used in *clinical* and *educational assessment*, to gain an understanding of an individual child and to see how he/she compares with others of the same age and gender.

Another use is to select groups of children for participation in an experiment, and then to evaluate the results of the experiment. Suppose a researcher is interested in evaluating a new scheme for teaching children to read. She may then wish to divide children into two groups of equal reading ability: to select these groups she will give the children a standardized test of reading ability, and will perhaps also administer a test of general intelligence. On the basis of the test scores the children would be matched in terms of ability, usually in pairs. One of the matched pair will then be randomly assigned to the experimental and the other to the control group, resulting in two groups of children who are equated on the two variables of reading ability and intelligence. In this sort of experimental situation the group of children who receive the new reading scheme are often known as the **experimental group** (since they are to be experimented on!), and the other group, which simply receives the usual, "old" reading scheme, are the **control group**. When the two groups have had their different reading experiences they would then be assessed again on a standardized reading test: if the children in the experimental group now have higher reading scores than those in the control group, we can perhaps conclude that the new reading scheme is a success!

CORRELATIONAL STUDIES

Let us begin with a definition: a *correlation coefficient* is *a statistic between +1 and −1 which indicates the extent to which two variables tend to be related or to vary together.* A value close to +1 is a high positive correlation which tells us that the two variables are closely related. There are many instances of naturally occurring positive correlations: between height and weight (taller people tend to weigh more); between math and English (students tend to be good, bad, or indifferent at both!). There are innumerable instances of correlations that are close to zero (indicating no relationship): height is not correlated with academic performance; IQ is not correlated with sports achievement.

A correlation coefficient close to −1 is a high negative correlation which tells us that two variables are inversely related. There are fewer instances of negative correlations – perhaps amount of time spent watching television and school grades!

There are primarily two types of correlational studies that are of interest to the developmental psychologist, *concurrent* and *predictive*.

Concurrent studies

A *concurrent* correlational study is where we are interested in the relationship between variables that are measured *at the same time*. An example of such a study would be to find out how similar the IQs of identical twins are. In this study we would give intelligence tests to pairs of identical twins and, if the correlation is high (which it almost certainly would be), this would tell us that if one twin had a high IQ the other one would also be bright; if one had a low IQ we could predict a low IQ for the other twin.

Predictive studies

A *predictive* correlational study is one where we are interested in finding whether individuals retain their relative standing, or rank order, relative to others, over time. For example, does the bright child at age 5 turn out to be the gifted student at age 20? Does the outgoing child become an extraverted teenager? Here is one example of a predictive correlational study, asking the question "can we predict IQ in 3-year-olds from problem-solving in infancy?"

This is a study carried out by Peter Willatts, a developmental psychologist at Dundee University, Scotland, UK. It begins with 9-month-old infants who were tested on what is called a *means-ends* problem-solving task. Each infant was shown an attractive toy which was placed out of reach on a cloth, and their job was then to grasp the cloth, pull it toward them – the means – in order to take the toy – the end. This doesn't sound too difficult, but babies only begin to string behaviors together to solve such tasks around 7 or 8 months – at 9 months many can do it expertly, but others are lagging behind. Willatts then gave the same infants the *British Picture Vocabulary Test (BPVT)* when they were 3 years 3 months old (the *BPVT* is the British version of the well-known American test, the *Peabody Picture Vocabulary Test, PPVT*, which is a test of intelligence).

What Willatts found was that those 9-month-old infants who were best at the means-ends task tended to become the 3-year-olds with the higher IQs. The correlation was 0.64, and the relationship between the infants' scores at 9 months and their scores as children is shown in figure 1.5. This figure is called a scattergram and is a graphical way of showing a correlation.

Correlational studies are thus important in telling us what sorts of abilities or psychological characteristics tend to go together (concurrent studies) and what abilities and characteristics predict later occurring behaviors (predictive studies).

Choosing the method of study

It will be apparent that psychologists have available a great many research strategies and methods for observing, classifying, testing, and studying children's development. There are no hard and fast rules for determining which method should be used at a particular time, and the decision will depend on a number of considerations: the

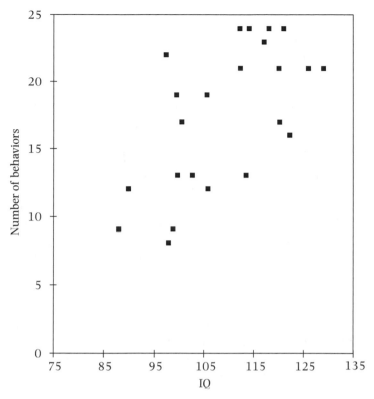

Figure 1.5 Scattergram to show the relationship between the number of successful reaching behaviors at 9 months (vertical axis) and 3-year IQ (horizontal axis). The most successful infants turned out to be those with the higher IQs. Reprinted with permission from Peter Willatts, Dundee University (p.willatts@dundee.ac.uk).

problem being investigated, the availability of participants, individual preferences of the researcher, and so on. In this section we will present the case for observation and the case for experimentation.

Observation versus experimentation

As we have seen, observational studies are ideal for discovering questions to ask about various phases and aspects of children's development. Such studies can often lead to answers and theories, and they are often critical in allowing the researcher to generate hypotheses about aspects of development. We need always to remember that the child has a vast repertoire of behaviors that occur in natural settings. We can conclude that observational studies are ideal in studying children's behavior and development in its natural context.

A common argument against the use of experimentation is that it often takes place in a highly controlled and unnatural setting: while experimental studies tell us a great deal about behavior in such settings, it sometimes happens that experimental findings have little bearing on real life – that is, it is often claimed that many experimental studies lack **ecological validity**. Typically, however, a great deal can be learned from experimental studies even when the experimental setting seems rather distant from real life. Additionally, it is clear that observational studies are less powerful than experimental studies when it comes to understanding the *causes* of development, or in testing hypotheses. To illustrate this point, we may find that children who are aggressive watch more violence on television. However, we cannot therefore infer that watching TV violence causes violent behavior – it is possible that the relationship is the other way round, i.e., that aggressive children seek out violence. To tease out the real cause–effect relationship we would need careful experimental studies in which the relevant variables were systematically varied.

Critical to the research process is the generation of hypotheses that can be systematically tested: hypotheses can be defined as *testable suppositions about the nature of reality*. In the example given above, one of the hypotheses tested by Judy Deloache and her team was "infants will grasp more at pictured objects the more they resemble real objects," and this was tested by careful experimentation.

The well-controlled experiment allows relatively precise statements to be made about cause and effect. The degree of control required is often not easily attained in a natural setting, and experiments are often laboratory-based, where a laboratory has no essential characteristics other than being a place in which the experimenter can exercise control over the relevant variables more easily than elsewhere. A laboratory may simply be a quiet room in a school or nursery, or it might be a purposely designed suite of rooms equipped with sophisticated equipment for measuring precise aspects of behavior.

Experimentation allows us to explore avenues of research that could not easily be investigated by the use of observation alone. We have seen that Charles Darwin was quite wrong in his suggestion that the young infant's vision and hearing are extremely poor and our understanding of infants' development has only begun to emerge because of careful experimental findings – an account of some of these findings is given in chapter 5.

Beyond Common Sense: The Importance of Research Evidence

Sometimes when psychologists publish their findings we hear remarks like, "What a waste of money! Everybody knows people behave like that!" Such comments assume that common observation is an adequate substitute for controlled observation and experimentation. However, everyday observation of human behavior and folk theories of development are notoriously unreliable, and in our impressions and interpretations of behavior we are often unaware of the controlling and causative variables. We should also remember that there are often different and diametrically opposed folk theories of development – see earlier in the chapter – and appropriate research evidence is needed to choose between them, or to show that they are all wrong!

Here are a few examples, some drawn from the accounts given earlier, which serve to convince us that systematic investigations are necessary to help us to understand human behavior and development.

- We now know that babies can see reasonably well at birth, and that they can hear speech and other sounds even while in the womb. To paraphrase an eminent developmental psychologist, Annette Karmiloff-Smith: "When two heavily pregnant women are talking to each other there are four people listening to the conversation." Compare our current knowledge with Charles Darwin's assumption (given at the beginning of this chapter) that vision and hearing are almost nonfunctional at birth.

- Everybody "knows" that a child is more likely to do something for which he/she has been rewarded than *not* to do something for which he/she has been punished: we now know, from many experiments both with animals and humans, that punishment is a very ineffective way of controlling behavior (Mazur, 1990). Contrast this view with the view implied by the expression discussed earlier – "Spare the rod and spoil the child." Psychological findings have influenced governments such that physical punishment of children in schools is banned by many states and countries, and some countries (e.g., Sweden) have banned parents from smacking their children.

- It has been widely held that a child's aggressive behaviors may be reduced by observing aggression through television programs, movies, and the like. This view has been called the **catharsis hypothesis**, the notion being that aggressive tendencies would be "drained off" by the vicarious act of observing aggression. However, several decades of carefully designed experiments with children and adolescents have shown that observing aggression is likely to *increase* rather than decrease children's tendencies to behave aggressively toward others.

- We all know that tender loving care (TLC) is just as important as good nutrition in promoting favorable child development, but this was not always the case. In the 1920s and 1930s there was puzzlement as to why it was that children reared in orphanages, with a lack of care and attention, but with adequate nutrition, were "failing to thrive": there were many cases of what we now call **deprivation dwarfism** (a failure to develop physically), and high infant mortality rates.

- No one is surprised that the young child performs rather poorly on many tests of memory when compared with older children. The obvious reasons for the younger children's poorer performance is that they simply have a more limited memory capacity – that they have fewer "slots" in which to put new information. Research has shown this view to be false: older children's better performance results from what they *do* to try to remember, and not from an increased memory capacity (chapter 12 gives a detailed account of memory development).

- In the past it has often been assumed that infants almost exclusively needed their mother's care, and that alternative caregiving (fathers, older siblings or other relatives, childminders, day care) would have adverse effects on their development. We now know that infants' development can proceed normally if they have multiple caregivers, so long as they receive consistent and predictable care. This understanding was only recently established: for example, we know that infants can form multiple attachments, and that the mother is not necessarily the one with whom the infant has its closest bond. Many studies have demonstrated that adequate day care has no damaging effects on development.

SOCIAL POLICY IMPLICATIONS OF CHILD DEVELOPMENT RESEARCH

In the latter part of the twentieth century, and with increasing emphasis in the twenty-first, developmental researchers have applied their vast store of knowledge to the implementation of **social policies** which are intended to improve children's well-being and to help them achieve their full potential. This is a worldwide endeavor, assisted by such bodies as the international *Society for Research in Child Development*. In the previous section we have seen that child development research has implications for early visual development, discipline procedures, day care, and the provision of adequate psychological care.

Other social policy implications abound and include: the implementation, provision, and assessment of early intervention schemes (such as **Project Head Start** in the United States and its counterpart, **Sure Start**, in the UK – these are schemes aimed at alleviating the worst social and cognitive deficits that result from neglect and poverty in early childhood); programs to reduce the amount of bullying in the school and its effects on the bullied; early detection and treatment of childhood disorders such as autism, dyslexia, and many others; combating the potential negative effects of parental divorce on children; detection and effective intervention in cases of child abuse and neglect; provision of effective health care for pregnant mothers-to-be and for young infants and children.

You will be able to think of many other areas of concern relating to children's development. The essential point is that research into children's development is not simply the accumulation of information: it has a practical purpose, which is to understand better the development of the child in order to provide better attention to the requirements of children and families.

 ## *Developmental Functions: Growing and Changing*

From the data that developmental psychologists collect, analyze, and interpret, it is possible to describe a number of **developmental functions**, or developmental trends – that is, the ways in which humans typically grow and change with age. Developmental functions are presented in graphs similar to those in figure 1.6. Usually, the measure of behavior (or behavioral change) is represented on the vertical, Y-axis, and age or time is on the horizontal, X-axis. The practical value of such functions is that they allow us to detect unusual developmental patterns (e.g., developmental delays) and to intervene with treatment as and when appropriate. The theoretical value is that the data can be used to evaluate hypotheses derived from various theoretical perspectives by comparing *theoretical* schematic plots such as those in figure 1.1 with *empirically derived* functions, where the latter are the data that are collected. Human development of course is extremely complex, and different aspects of development grow and change in different ways. Figure 1.6 shows five of the most commonly found functions, and we will give examples of development that match each of them.

CONTINUOUS FUNCTION (A) – INCREASING ABILITY

Perhaps the most common developmental function found in textbooks is the one shown in figure 1.6(a) in which we simply get better, or increase in an ability or quantity with age. Examples include the negatively accelerating change in the height and weight of children which increase rapidly during the first few years of life, more gradually during childhood, and level off after adolescence. We should note that although height and weight are typically considered to be *continuous* in their development, research by Lampl et al. mentioned earlier (see figure 1.1) suggests that changes in height might be *discontinuous* at times. Another example with a shorter time scale is the precision in reaching for and grasping an object which gradually increases during the first year of life as infants practice and receive feedback from their errors. Intelligence is another example – as children grow older they become more intelligent, and this levels off during adolescence. We will return to the development of intelligence (and whether its development is continuous or discontinuous!) when we compare developmental functions.

CONTINUOUS FUNCTION (B) – DECREASING ABILITY

It seems odd to think of aspects of development where we get *worse* rather than *better* as we grow up! As you can imagine, there are few of these developmental functions. The clearest example is found in speech perception in early infancy (language development is discussed in detail in chapter 9).

Research by Janet Werker and her colleagues has demonstrated that young infants, around 6 months of age, are able to discriminate almost every slight variation in sound (that is, the phonetic contrast between different phones, however similar-sounding they seem), but that this broad-based sensitivity declines by the time the infant is around 1 year old (the time babies produce their first meaningful word). That is, as a result of their experience with their native language, and particularly as they begin to utter meaningful words, infants *lose* the ability to make many phonetic discriminations that are not used to differentiate between words in their native language.

For example, both the [k] sound in "key" and the [k] sound in "ski" are different phones, but members of the same phoneme in English, and English speakers hear them as the same sound. In contrast, the two [k] sounds are members of different phonemes in Chinese. As a result, speakers of Chinese can readily discriminate the two sounds. Conversely, the [r] sound as in "very" and the [l] in "loud" are different phones in English but not in Chinese or Japanese, so that Chinese and Japanese people from about 1 year of age are unable to discriminate, for example, between "berry" and "belly." Thus, speakers of English and speakers of Chinese differ in terms of their ability to discriminate sounds. As Werker (1989) puts it, infants become exquisitely tuned to the properties of the native language – they are "becoming a native listener."

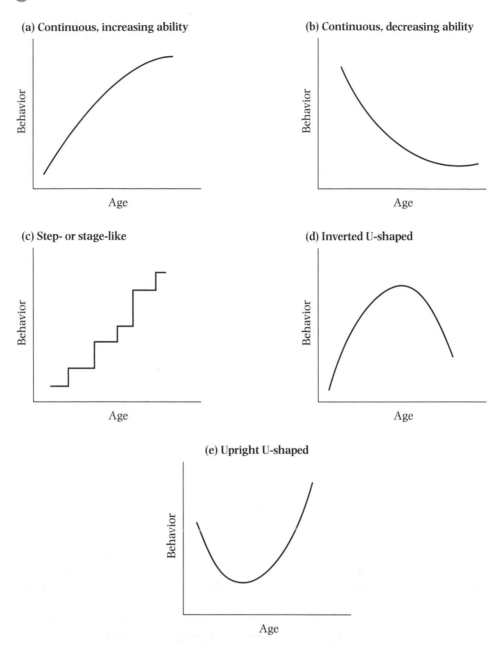

Figure 1.6 Five of the most common developmental functions, illustrating the ways in which people typically grow and change with age: (a) continuous, increasing ability; (b) continuous, decreasing ability; (c) step- or stage-like; (d) inverted U-shaped; and (e) upright U-shaped. Usually (as here), the measure of behavior, or changes in behavior, is represented on the vertical, Y-axis, and age or time is on the horizontal, X-axis.

Discontinuous (step) function

A second, common function is where development takes place in a series of stages, where each new stage appears to be *qualitatively* different from the preceding (and following) stages (figure 1.6(c)). It is easy to describe different major stages in the human lifespan such as infancy, preschool childhood, middle childhood, adolescence, adulthood, and old age: thus, infancy is the period "without language," there are clear biological changes occurring at puberty, and so on. Stages of development are found in many areas of development. Piaget's theory (which is discussed in detail in chapters 2, 8, and 15) is the most famous example of a stage theory of development. In his theory the child's thinking from one stage to the next involves different structures, and undergoes qualitative change: the young child will believe in Santa Claus, but this belief disappears around age 7; the adolescent, but not the younger child, is capable of abstract thought.

A stage-like progression of specific skills or processes also exists, such as in the development of mobility in the infant. Here the vertical, Y-axis on a graph could be distance traveled by an infant, which suddenly accelerates at different points in time matching the onset of various mobility accomplishments. Infants are relatively immobile during the first few months of life, begin to crawl around 6–8 months of age, stand up and toddle around furniture a few months later, and begin to walk on their own between 12 and 18 months of age (the time at which parents move all small objects out of the infant's reach!).

The onset of these mobility milestones seems to occur rather abruptly, and each one represents a qualitatively different type of locomotion suggesting a stage-like progression. Another example is the development of speech – an initial period of no word production is followed by a period of babbling beginning around 6 months of age when infants make speech-like sounds in a flowing "conversation" that contains no words. Infants begin to use single words around 12 months of age, produce two to three word phases at about 1.5 years of age, and finally, produce complex grammatical sentences. These major milestones, which appear to be qualitatively different, also have been conceptualized as stages.

Many other step-like functions have been described, for example in the child's acquisition of a **theory of mind** (chapter 10), in the **stages of moral reasoning** (chapter 14).

U-shaped functions

Two other types of developmental functions are inverted and upright **U-shaped functions**. When we consider development across the lifespan, an *inverted U-shaped developmental function*, illustrated in figure 1.6(d), is commonly observed. One example is the development of visual acuity, which is poor at birth, increases rapidly during the first few months of life, and diminishes during the latter part of the lifespan. Inverted U-shaped functions can also be found during shorter time periods. For example, babbling emerges around 6 months of age, and disappears without a trace a few months later (see chapter 9). Of course, some might argue that it does emerge again during adulthood – perhaps during university lectures!

Inverted U-shaped functions are extremely common in development – we improve in the early years, stabilize or level off in adulthood, and get worse as we get older! Biological as well as psychological development often shows this function: thus, we reach our muscular and athletic peak in adolescence and early adulthood, and from about 30 years of age or thereabouts our abilities decline.

The other U-shaped function, shown in figure 1.6(e), involves abilities which may be present early in life and disappear to reemerge at a later age. One example is the ability of newborn infants to turn their heads and eyes toward sounds. This dramatic auditory localization response diminishes or disappears at around 6 weeks of age and reappears again around 4 months of age (Muir, Humphrey, & Humphrey, 1994). Another example is the common observation that infants will display coordinated alternating step-like movements at birth, if they are supported in an upright position and held so that the soles of their feet are touching a solid surface. This amazing ability seems to disappear when infants are a few months old and reappears again when they begin to stand and walk, around 12 months of age.

This "stepping reflex" gives the impression that the baby is "walking" (Zelazo, 1983), and it was only a few years ago that some "experts" were encouraging parents to keep exercising this stepping response in very young infants with the assumption that they would then learn to walk earlier. In fact, it turns out that the stepping reflex is the remains of the kicking movements that appear near the end of pregnancy, and these serve two vital functions: (1) they prevent the legs from becoming locked or stiffened in the cramped space in the womb, and (2) they reposition the fetus so that it can be delivered in the normal manner. Although the stepping reflex, and later walking, use the same muscles, it turns out that they are qualitatively different, both in the underlying brain systems that control them and in the patterns of muscular coordination.

Comparing developmental functions

It can be useful to plot more than one developmental function on the same graph. Possible causal relationships may be suggested by doing so. In the case of the U-shaped auditory localization function, Humphrey, Dodwell, Muir, and Humphrey (1988) compared the developmental functions for auditory localization responses and orientation to schematic faces, from birth to 5 months of age, shown in figure 1.7(a). When there is a minimum in the performance of headturning to off-centered sounds (i.e., it is very difficult to elicit), there is a maximum in looking time at the faces. They speculated that competition between the two stimulus-response systems occurred, with the most rapidly changing system, visual attention, predominating.

Uttal and Perlmutter (1989) provide a number of comparisons between developmental functions for older children and adults which illustrate possible causal relationships. One example has to do with the maintenance of typing speed by professional typists as they age. The developmental function tends to be flat over much of the lifespan. This is a puzzle because it is well known that as people age they have a slower reaction time, which should therefore slow down the typist's keystroke speed. It turns out that as keystroke speed declines, older typists increase their letter span (the number of words they code as a unit, which are then run off automatically by the fingers).

This cognitive skill, which increases with practice, may compensate for the loss of keystroke speed.

We will make one final comparison, to do with the development of intelligence. Sometimes it is useful to think of intelligence as developing in a qualitative, stage-like manner (as in figure 1.6(c)). However, sometimes it is convenient to think of intelligence as growing in a quantitative manner. This is the assumption that underlies most intelligence tests – as children get older they become able to solve, or answer, more and more of the items in the tests. With this latter assumption we find that children's measured intelligence (the raw scores they obtain on IQ tests) increases until adolescence, and then it levels off or stabilizes. And then what happens? In the 1940s and 1950s there were many cross-sectional studies in which people of different ages, from young adults to the very elderly, were given the same intelligence tests. The clear finding was that the development of intelligence followed an inverted-U function (as in figure 1.6(d)) – people simply got less intelligent as they approached middle and old age.

However, during the 1950s and 1960s the findings from longitudinal studies, in which the same people had been tested over many years, began to emerge. These findings were that intelligence did not decrease as people got older so that the development of intelligence was now best described as being the continuous function shown in figure 1.6(a). The classic work on changes in performance on IQ tests as a function of age and cohort was reported by Schaie and his co-workers (e.g., Schaie & Strother, 1965). An idealized drawing of typical results derived from their work is shown in figure 1.7(b) (Flynn, 1998, gives an up-to-date account of this research). This figure

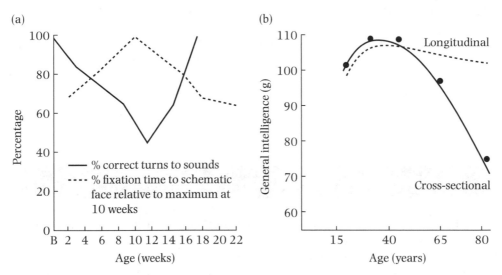

Figure 1.7 Comparing developmental functions. (a) compares the developmental course of the U-shaped auditory localization response function with that of the inverted U-shaped function for interest in a schematic face (reported in Humphrey et al., 1988). (b) shows the results from longitudinal (continuous function) and cross-sectional (inverted U-shaped function) studies of intellectual growth across a wide age span. (a) Copyright 1988. Canadian Psychological Association. Reprinted with permission.

illustrates the finding that the developmental functions of intellectual performance derived from *cross-sectional studies* decrease with age, while those derived from *longitudinal studies* may show little change with age.

One explanation for these apparently contradictory results is the existence of cohort differences in cultural experiences, attributable to improvements in both diet and education (both of which are correlated with performance on intelligence tests). Certainly, the older subjects will, on average, have had fewer years of education than the younger ones. This is a clear example of *intergenerational changes* and an indication that cross-sectional and longitudinal studies can often tell a different developmental story.

Summary and Conclusions

Human development is extremely complex and multifaceted. Not surprisingly, therefore, there are many ways of studying development and many different types of developmental functions that emerge from the research as scientists try to understand the ways in which children grow and change. Sometimes the story that is told gets confusing. For instance, we have seen that the development of intelligence can be described as a continuously increasing function (the child simply gets better with age) – this is the assumption underlying intelligence tests. But sometimes it is better to think of the child's thinking as changing in a step-like, qualitative fashion, a view that is central to Piaget's theory of development. We have also seen that early research suggested that intelligence declined with age, but now we think that it doesn't (which is encouraging news for us all!).

As you read the remainder of the book you will find innumerable examples of longitudinal and cross-sectional studies, of the different developmental methods that are used, and of the different developmental functions that are found. It will be helpful to have a clear idea of these different designs, methods, and functions. This basic understanding will help you understand better the ways in which researchers are gradually unlocking the secrets of children's development.

Discussion Points

1   Think of the differing views that parents have about rearing their children. Is there scientific support for these folk theories?
2   Consider the difference between organismic and mechanistic theories of development. How might these different perspectives be helpful in understanding different areas of development?
3   What are the important differences between longitudinal and cross-sectional studies of development?
4   Why is it important to have both observational and experimental studies of development?
5   Think of ways in which the findings of developmental psychology go beyond common sense.
6   Consider the different developmental functions that describe how children grow and change. Why is it necessary to have these different functions?

SUGGESTIONS FOR FURTHER READING

Christensen, P., & James, A. (1999). *Research with children*. London: Routledge-Falmer.

Greig, A. D., & Taylor, J. (1998). *Doing research with children*. Newbury Park, CA: Sage.

Haslam, S. A., & McGarty, C. (1998). *Doing psychology*. Newbury Park, CA: Sage.

McNaughton, G., Rolfe, S., & Siraj-Blatchford, I. (2001). *Doing early childhood research: Theory and practice*. Milton Keynes: Open University Press.

chapter 2

Theories and Issues in Child Development

Alan Slater, Ian Hocking, and Jon Loose

KEY CONCEPTS

ACCOMMODATION
ANIMISM
ASSIMILATION
BEHAVIOR GENETICS
BEHAVIORISM
CASTRATION COMPLEX
CENTRATION
CEPHALOCAUDAL TREND
CHROMOSOME
CLASSICAL CONDITIONING
COGNITIVE ADAPTATIONS
CONCRETE OPERATIONS STAGE
CONNECTIONISM
CONSERVATION TASKS
CONSTRUCTIVIST THEORY
CONTINUITY VERSUS
   DISCONTINUITY
CRITICAL PERIOD
DYNAMIC SYSTEMS THEORY
EGO
EGOCENTRIC THOUGHT
ELECTRA COMPLEX
EMOTION
ETHOLOGICAL APPROACHES
FORMAL OPERATIONS STAGE

FUNCTIONAL INVARIANTS
GENDER CONSTANCY
GENDER DEVELOPMENT
HARDWARE
HIERARCHY OF NEEDS
HUMANISTIC THEORIES
ID
IMPRINTING
INFORMATION PROCESSING
INTROSPECTIONISM
LAW OF EFFECT
MATURATION
MECHANISTIC WORLD VIEW
MICROGENETIC STUDIES
MONOTROPY
MOTOR MILESTONES
NATURE–NURTURE ISSUE
NEURAL NETWORKS
OBSERVATIONAL LEARNING
OEDIPUS COMPLEX
ONE-TO-ONE
   CORRESPONDENCE
OPERANT CONDITIONING
ORGANISMIC WORLD VIEW
PRECOCIAL SPECIES

PREOPERATIONAL STAGE
PRIMARY CAREGIVER
PRIMARY DRIVES
PROXIMODISTAL TREND
PSYCHOANALYSIS
PSYCHOANALYTIC THEORY
PSYCHOSEXUAL STAGES
PSYCHOSOCIAL STAGES
REACTION FORMATION
REDUCTIONISM
SCHEMA
SECONDARY DRIVE
SELF-ACTUALIZATION
SENSITIVE PERIOD
SENSORIMOTOR STAGE
SOCIAL LEARNING THEORY
SOFTWARE
STABILITY VERSUS CHANGE
STAGE-LIKE CHANGES IN
   DEVELOPMENT
STRANGE SITUATION
SUPEREGO
THEORY OF DEVELOPMENT
ZONE OF PROXIMAL
   DEVELOPMENT

OVERVIEW

This chapter sets the theoretical background for the material in the chapters to follow. The coverage of theoretical approaches is broad, and will give the reader a good introduction to the diversity of explanations of children's development.

First, different theories of motor development are outlined, and the authors point to the advantages of dynamic systems theory according to which motor development is a product of the interplay between brain structure, the structure and dynamics of the body, and the structure of the environment.

Next, the chapter considers theories of cognitive development. Piaget's stage theory is central here, and receives a thorough treatment. His theory is contrasted with the information-processing account. Whereas Piaget's theory treats early deficits in thought as due to lack of logical ability, information-processing accounts identify processing deficits as the problem, in particular, limitations in memory.

A large number of theoretical approaches stress the social environment in some way or other. Vygotsky's theory treats higher cognitive structures as coming from the social world, becoming internalized as a result of interactions with knowledgeable others. Behaviorist theories are all based on the principle that the social world, and in particular the parents, shape the behavior of the individual, and the best example of application of these accounts to child development is the social learning theory of Albert Bandura.

Other theories have their origins in evolutionary theory, and the best example in developmental psychology is attachment theory, originally formulated by John Bowlby, according to which formation of a secure emotional attachment between infant and caregiver is a vital prerequisite for emotional stability. Attachment theory is closely related to psychoanalytic approaches, the prime example being Freud's theory of psychosexual development, according to which emotional problems in adulthood can be traced to problems the child encountered in one of the psychosexual stages. Humanistic theories bear certain similarities to psychoanalytic theory. For instance, Maslow's account proposes a hierarchy of needs that humans must achieve to reach a satisfactory adult state.

The authors summarize the sections on theories by pointing out, through examples, the fact that different theories are not necessarily mutually exclusive. Often, one theory explains some aspects of behavior, while another theory fills in more of the story.

The chapter ends by summarizing some key issues that will reappear in the pages that follow, namely the nature–nurture issue, stability versus change, and continuity versus discontinuity in development. Different theories very clearly say different things with respect to these distinctions, and the challenge for developmental psychology is to weigh these different accounts against each other.

THEORIES IN CHILD DEVELOPMENT

"Es gibt nichts Praktischeres als eine gute Theorie" – Immanuel Kant (1724–1804)

or . . .

"There is nothing so practical as a good theory" – Kurt Lewin (1944, p. 195)

Introduction

Human development is rich, varied, and enormously complex. We should not expect, therefore, that any single theory of development will do justice to this complexity, and indeed no theory attempts to do this. Each theory attempts to account for only a limited range of development and it is often the case that within each area of development there are competing theoretical views, each endeavoring to account for the same aspects of development. We will see some of this complexity and conflict in our account of different theoretical views, and in chapter 1 we have seen that different ways of studying children lead to different developmental functions, and these are linked with different theoretical views.

Before beginning our account of theories of development it is helpful to say what we mean by a theory, since this is a term that has many definitions. For our purposes a **theory of development** is *a scheme or system of ideas that is based on evidence and attempts to explain, describe, and predict behavior and development.* From this account it is clear that a theory attempts to bring order to what might otherwise be a chaotic mass of information – for this reason we can see that "there is nothing so practical as a good theory"!

In every area of development there are at least two kinds of theory, which we can call the minor and the major. What we are calling *minor* theories are those which deal only with very specific, narrow areas of development. So, for example, there are theories about the way in which eye movements develop, about the origins of pointing, and so on. *Major* theories are those which attempt to explain large areas of development, and it is these that are the focus of this chapter.

To make our account of theories more orderly and understandable, we have divided them into six broad groups:

- Motor development
- Cognitive development
- Social-cognitive development
- Evolution and ethology
- Psychoanalytic theories
- Humanistic theory

Motor Development

One of the most obvious signs of development in infancy is the baby achieving the various **motor milestones**. Parents are very proud of these acquisitions and they are a focus of parental conversations about their infants – "Billy can sit now," "Helen has just started to crawl," "Jimmy can walk without help," "Rachel loves to climb up stairs." The development of motor skills has very important implications for other aspects of development. The ability to *act* on the world affects all other aspects of development, and each new accomplishment brings with it an increasing degree of independence. For example, when infants begin to crawl they become independently mobile and one of the major transitions in early development begins. These changes affect emotional and social development, communication, appreciation of heights, and an understanding of distance and space (Campos, Anderson, Barbu-Roth, Hubbard, Hertenstein, & Witherington, 2000).

Table 2.1 charts the sequence of development of various motor milestones during infancy. At birth the infant has a number of well-developed motor skills, which include sucking, looking, grasping, breathing, crying – skills that are vital for survival. However, the general impression of the newborn is one of uncoordinated inability and general weakness. Movements of the limbs appear jerky and uncoordinated, and it takes a few weeks before infants can lift their head from a prone position. The muscles are clearly unable to support the baby's weight in order to allow such basic activities as sitting, rolling over, or standing. By the end of infancy, around 18 months, all this has changed. The toddler can walk, run, climb, communicate in speech and gesture, and use the two hands in complex coordinated actions.

The questions that a theory of motor development needs to explain include the following: Do the early motor activities prepare the way for the more complex voluntary activities that follow, and if so, how do they do it? How do new motor patterns (such as pointing, running, speaking, tool use) develop since they appear to be qualitatively different from earlier patterns? As we shall see, the answers to these questions are complex.

If you look at table 2.1 two things will become apparent. First is that the different motor milestones emerge in a regular sequence – sitting with support, sitting unaided, crawling, standing, walking, and climbing appear almost always in this order. The second is that there is a considerable age range in which individual infants achieve each skill – e.g., some infants crawl at 5 months while others are as late as 11 months. These two aspects of motor development give separate support to the two major theories of motor development that we will discuss here – *maturational theories* and *dynamic systems theory*.

MATURATIONAL THEORIES

One of the first psychologists to investigate human motor development was Arnold Gesell, who studied hundreds of hours of films of motor activity in longitudinal studies of children from birth to 9 years (e.g., Gesell & Ames, 1940). He concluded that motor development proceeded from the global to the specific in two directions. One direction is called the **cephalocaudal trend** and is from head to foot along the length of the body – that is, control of the head is first, then the arms and trunk, and finally control of the legs. The other direction of development is what is called the **proximodistal trend**, which is that motor control is from the center of the body outwards to more peripheral segments – that is, the head, trunk, and pelvic girdle are brought under control before the elbow, wrist, knee, and ankle joints, which in turn lead to finer control over hands and fingers.

These two invariant sequences of development, together with the regular sequence with which the motor milestones are achieved, led Gesell to the view that **maturation** alone shapes motor development – development is controlled by a maturational

Table 2.1 The development of motor skills in infancy

Age	Gross motor skills	Fine motor skills
1–3 months	Stepping reflex, lifts head, sits with support.	Grasps object if placed in hand, sucks, control of eye movements, the first smile.
2–4 months	When prone lifts head and uses arms for support.	Grasps cube when placed near hand.
5–8 months	Sits without support.	Reaches for and grasps object, using one hand.
5–10 months	Stands with support, and pulls self to stand.	Points at object of interest, grasps with thumb and finger ("pincer grip").
5–11 months	Crawls.	Grasps spoon, gradually learns to direct food to mouth!
10–14 months	Stands alone, and walks alone.	Puts objects into small containers, builds "tower" of cubes. Produces first meaningful word.
13–18 months	Walks backwards and sideways, runs, climbs, walks up stairs.	Holds crayon with fingers, scribbles energetically.
18–30 months	Runs easily, jumps, skips, rides and steers tricycle, walks on tiptoe.	Vocabulary and articulation increases rapidly, picks up small objects (e.g., candy/sweets).

timetable linked particularly to the central nervous system and also to muscular development. Each animal species has its own sequence, and experience has little, if any, effect on motor development.

One of the first researchers to question Gesell's hypothesis was Myrtle McGraw (1945). She tested pairs of twins where one member of each pair received enriched motor training (in reaching, climbing stairs, and other motor skills) and found that in the trained twin motor development was considerably accelerated when compared with the "untrained" twin.

In addition to McGraw's findings there are other considerations which suggest that a purely maturational account of motor development can be largely dismissed. Here are just two such considerations. First, the fact that motor skills develop in a regular sequence does not prove a genetic cause. Consider advanced skills such as learning to play a sport, typing, driving, playing the piano. In these instances we can see an invariant sequence of development, as we progress from simple actions to more complex integrated skillful behavior, but nobody would suggest that these skills are genetically determined! Second, a maturational theory does not account for the considerable individual differences in the acquisition of various motor skills.

Clearly, a different theoretical account of motor development is needed, and here we describe one of the most recent of these, known as the **dynamic systems theory** of motor development.

DYNAMIC SYSTEMS THEORY

What has become apparent is that infants (and children) develop skills in different ways. As an example, there are infants who simply do not like to crawl, and they will often stand and walk before they crawl. Those infants who do crawl will acquire the skill in their own individual ways – some will shuffle on their bellies before crawling on hands and knees, others will skip the belly-crawling stage, and still other infants will forgo the crawling stage entirely, and after several months of sitting and shuffling may stand and then walk (Adolph, Vereijken, & Denny, 1998). In addition to these observations there are what are called **microgenetic studies** of motor development in which experimenters observe individual infants or children from the time they first attempt a new skill, such as walking or crawling, until it is performed effortlessly. From these studies it becomes clear that infants' acquisition of a new motor skill is much the same as that of adults learning a new motor skill – the beginnings are usually fumbling and poor, there is trial and error learning and great concentration, all gradually leading to the accomplished skillful activity, which then is usually used in the development of yet new motor skills.

According to the dynamic systems theory all new motor development is the result of a dynamic and continual interaction of three major factors: (1) nervous system development; (2) the capabilities and biomechanics of the body; (3) environmental constraints and support (Thelen & Spencer, 1998). We can illustrate this dynamic interplay by considering three separate studies on infant kicking, crawling, and walking.

Infant kicking

Esther Thelen (1999) tested 24 3-month-olds on a foot-kicking task in which each infant was placed in a crib in a supine (lying on their back) position and a soft elastic ankle cuff was attached to one leg, and the cuff, in turn, was attached by a cord to a brightly colored overhead mobile. By kicking the leg the babies could make the mobile dance around and they quickly learned to make this exciting event happen. In this condition the *other* leg – the one that was not connected to the mobile movements, either moved independently or alternately with the attached leg.

Then Thelen changed the arrangement by yoking the legs together. She did this by putting ankle cuffs on both legs, and joining the two together with a strip of Velcro. What happened then was that the infants initially tried to kick the legs separately – since moving the legs alternately is the more natural action – but gradually learned to kick both together to get the mobile to move.

This study shows that the infants were able to change their pattern of interlimb coordination to solve a novel, experimentally imposed task.

Infant reaching

Thelen and Spencer (1998) followed the same four infants from 3 weeks to 1 year (a longitudinal study) in order to explore the development of successful reaching. Their aim was to look at the interrelationship between different motor systems. What they found was that infants acquired stable control over the head several weeks before the onset of reaching, then there was a reorganization of muscle patterns so that the infants could stabilize the head and shoulder. These developments gave the infants a stable base from which to reach, and successful reaching followed. This is an indication that infants need a stable posture before they can attain the goal of reaching successfully, and is a clear demonstration that new motor skills are learned through a process of modifying and developing their already existing abilities.

Infant walking

Newborn infants are extremely top heavy, with big heads and weak legs. Over the coming years their body weight is gradually redistributed and their center of mass gradually moves downwards until it finishes slightly above the navel. Adolph and Avolio (2000, p. 1148) put it rather nicely – "It is as if infants' bodies are growing to fit their comparatively large heads"! This means that as infants and children grow they need constantly to adjust and adapt their motor activities to accommodate the naturally occurring changes to their body dimensions. There can be few clearer demonstrations that the motor system is dynamic and constantly changing than this simple fact.

Adolph and Avolio give a good demonstration of the way in which infants can make adjustments over a very short period of time. They tested 14-month-olds by having them wear saddlebags slung over each shoulder. The saddlebags increased the infants' chest circumference by the same amount in each of two conditions: *feather-weight* – filled with pillow-stuffing, weighing the negligible amount of 120 g, and *lead-weight* – the not so negligible amount of between 2.2 and 3.0 kg, which increased their body weight by 25 percent and raised their center of mass (raising the center of mass leads to increased instability and is similar to a backpacker carrying a heavy pack). They found that the lead-weight infants were more cautious, and made prolonged exploratory movements – swaying, touching, and leaning – before attempting to walk down a slope. That is, these infants were testing their new-found body dimensions and weight, and adjusted their judgments of what they could and could not do. These findings are again in support of a dynamic systems approach to motor development – infants do not have a fixed and rigid understanding of their own abilities, and have the dynamic flexibility to adjust their abilities as they approach each novel motor problem.

Summary

Despite the apparent appeal of maturational theories of motor development, research over the last 20 years has demonstrated that motor skills are learned, both during infancy and throughout life. The apparently invariant ordering of the motor milestones is partly dictated by logical necessity – you can't run before you can walk! – and is not necessarily invariant (you *can* walk before you can crawl!). From a consideration of the studies described above it becomes clear that motor development cannot be accounted for by any maturational theory. These and other findings contribute to the "emerging view of infants as active participants in their own motor-skill acquisition, in which developmental change is empowered through infants' everyday problem-solving activities" (Thelen, 1999, p. 103).

The emphasis on children as active participants in their own development is an essential characteristic of the theoretical views offered by "the Giant of Developmental Psychology," Jean Piaget, whose claim was that children's ability to act on the world underlies their cognitive development, and we now turn our attention to his views.

Cognitive Development: Piaget's Theory of Development

> Everyone knows that Piaget was the most important figure the field has ever known . . . (he) transformed the field of developmental psychology. *(Flavell, 1996, p. 200)*

> Once psychologists looked at development through Piaget's eyes, they never saw children in quite the same way. *(Miller, 1993, p. 81)*

Piaget's contribution to our understanding of children's development has been quite extraordinary, and his influence is reflected in this book – in particular chapters 5 (infancy), 8 (early and middle childhood), 15 (adolescence), and 17 (education). In order to see why he had such an impact we will first outline the state of developmental psychology before Piaget, and then outline some of the fundamental aspects of human development that he described which changed our view of development. We follow this with a brief account of the **stages of development** that he described, and finally give an overview of his enormous contribution to developmental psychology.

DEVELOPMENTAL PSYCHOLOGY BEFORE PIAGET

Before Piaget revolutionized our understanding of children's development, psychology was dominated by the influence of the two diametrically opposed theoretical views of **behaviorism** and **psychoanalysis**. Both of these views are discussed later, and for the moment we will restrict our comments to note that, despite the fact that they are strikingly opposed, they share one essential feature, which is that the child is seen as the passive recipient of his or her upbringing – development results from such things as the severity of toilet training and of rewards and punishments. Neither approach gives much credit to the child in shaping his or her own course of development. With Piaget, all this changed.

FUNDAMENTAL ASPECTS OF HUMAN DEVELOPMENT, ACCORDING TO PIAGET

Children are active agents in shaping their own development, they are not simply blank slates who passively and unthinkingly respond to whatever the environment offers them. That is, children's behavior and development are motivated largely *intrinsically* (internally) rather than *extrinsically*.

For Piaget, children learn to adapt to their environments and as a result of their **cognitive adaptations** they become better able to understand their world. Adaptation is something that all living organisms have evolved to do and as children adapt they gradually construct more advanced understandings of their worlds.

These more advanced understandings of the world reflect themselves in the appearance, during development, of new stages of development. Piaget's theory is therefore the best example of the **organismic world view** that we discussed in chapter 1, which portrays children as inherently active, continually interacting with the environment, in such a way as to shape their own development.

Since children are active in developing or constructing their worlds, Piaget's theory is often referred to as a **constructivist theory**. In the next sections we will first discuss the ways in which children adapt to their environments, and next give an account of the stages of development that Piaget put forward.

Adaptation: assimilation and accommodation

In order to adapt to the world two important processes are necessary. **Assimilation** is what happens when we treat new objects, people, and events as if they were familiar – that is, we *assimilate* the new to our already-existing schemes of thought. Examples would be: we meet a new policeman (or doctor, professor, etc.) and treat them as we habitually treat policemen, doctors, or professors. Assimilation occurs from the earliest days – the infant is offered a new toy and puts it in his or her mouth to use the familiar activity of sucking; the child meets a new teacher and treats her in the same way he or she treats teachers.

Accommodation is where individuals have to modify or change their **schemas**, or ways of behaving and thinking, in order to adjust to a new situation. For example: the infant might be presented with a toy that is larger than those she has previously handled, and so will have to adjust her fingers and grasp to hold it; when the child meets a new teacher who is different from her previous teachers she has to adjust her way of thinking to understand the new person. It is worth stressing that assimilation and accommodation always occur together during infancy and the examples given above are both cases of assimilation and accommodation occurring together.

Throughout life the processes of assimilation and accommodation are always active as we constantly strive to adapt to the world we encounter. These processes, therefore, are what can be called **functional invariants** in that they don't change during development. What do change are the cognitive structures (often called schemas) that allow the child to comprehend the world at progressively higher levels of understanding. According to Piaget's view, there are different levels of cognitive understanding that take the child from the activity-based sensorimotor functioning in infancy to the abstract levels of thought found in adolescence.

THE FOUR STAGES OF COGNITIVE DEVELOPMENT

Children move through four broad stages of development, each of which is characterized by qualitatively different ways of thinking (Piaget, 1962). These stages are the **sensorimotor stage** of infancy, the **preoperational stage** of early childhood, the **concrete operations stage** of middle childhood, and the **formal operations stage** of adolescence and beyond. We will give a brief account of each of these stages, together with the approximate ages at which they are found – note that these ages are only approximate and individual children's development will often be slower or quicker.

Sensorimotor period (birth to 2 years)

This is one of the most impressive and dramatic areas of development. The child changes from the helpless newborn to the thinking and knowing toddler, that is, to the cognitive individual with a "mind." These changes take place as a result of the infant's actions on the objects and people in its environments, and this stage is the development of *thought in action*. As a result, infants learn to solve problems, like pulling a cloth to obtain an out-of-reach toy (plate 2.1), and they learn that objects continue to exist even though they cannot be seen or heard. As the stage draws to a close the infant, now a toddler whose language is developing rapidly, is able to reason through thought as well as through action.

Preoperational stage (2 to 7 years)

Preschool children can solve a number of practical, concrete problems by the intelligent use of means-ends problem-solving, the use of tools, requesting objects, asking for things to happen, and other means. They can communicate well and represent

Plate 2.1 Around 9 months the infant is able to pull a cloth (a) in order to retrieve an out-of-reach toy (b), and therefore shows efficient means-ends problem-solving.

information and ideas by means of symbols – in drawing, symbolic play, gesture, and particularly speech.

These abilities continue to develop considerably during the preoperational stage, but there are some striking limitations to children's thinking during this period. Children tend to be **egocentric** (find it difficult to see things from another's point of view). They display **animism** in their thinking (they tend to attribute life and lifelike qualities to inanimate objects, particularly those that move and are active, such as the wind and the clouds, and sometimes trees and other objects). Here is Piaget asking a child about the sun, which follows you around as you move: *Piaget* – "Is it alive?" *Child* – "Of course, otherwise it wouldn't follow us, it couldn't shine" (Piaget, 1960, p. 215). Their thinking tends to be illogical, and at times seems quite magical – it is at this stage that children believe in Santa Claus! What underlies children's thinking during the preoperational stage is the lack of a logical framework for thought, and this appears during the concrete operations stage.

Concrete operations stage (7 to 11 years)

One major characteristic of preoperational thought is called **centration** – the focusing or centering of attention on one aspect of a situation to the exclusion of others. This is clearly demonstrated in Piaget's **conservation tasks**. A typical conservation problem, known as conservation of number, is shown in plate 2.2. In this version of the problem the child is shown two rows of candies/sweets, such as M & Ms or Smarties, in **one-to-one correspondence** and with each having six candies. The child is simply asked "Look what I do" and is not questioned about the number in each row. Then, while the child watches, one M & M or Smartie is added to one row so that it has seven. Next, the other row is stretched out so that it *looks* as though it has more, but in reality it has less.

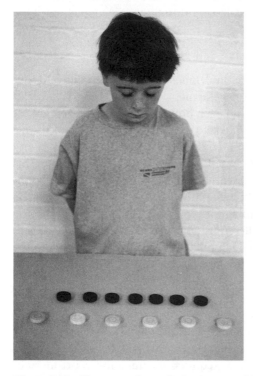
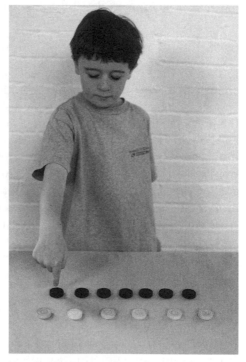

Plate 2.2 Conservation of number – which row contains more?

Then the child is asked "Which row would you like?" Preoperational children will usually ask for the longer row – they focus on the increase in length and ignore the addition of one candy/sweet to the other row. However, the child at the concrete operations level knows that one has been added to the shorter row, and since nothing has been subtracted by the action of stretching out the other row, knows that the shorter row contains more – and will therefore ask for the shorter row. If you have access to a 4- and a 7-year-old and are allowed to give them candies/sweets, then this is an interesting experiment to do with both of them – the younger child will want the longer row, and the older child the shorter, and neither understands the reasoning of the other!

The concrete operational child becomes better at a number of tasks, in addition to conservation, and these are discussed in detail in chapter 8.

The formal operations stage (from about 11 years)

The concrete operational child becomes able to solve many problems involving the physical world, but the major limitation in his or her thinking is to do with the realm of possibilities. When children enter the final stage of cognitive development – the formal operations stage – this limitation is removed. The adolescent now becomes able to reason in the way that scientists do – to manipulate variables to find out what causes things to happen – and is also introduced to the realm of possibilities and hypothetical thought. Adolescents (and adults) spend many hours discussing abstract matters – Does God exist? – Why do we need politics? – Should abortion be allowed? – What is the meaning of life? A more detailed account of adolescent thinking is given in chapter 15.

Summary

In Piaget's theory we have a comprehensive and detailed account of cognitive development from birth to adulthood. Cognitive development proceeds through a series of stages, each more complex than the last, and each building on the achievements of the previous. In many respects, aspects of Piaget's theory seem obvious – of course children are active in shaping their own development. But it was many years before his theories began to make an impact on American and British psychology. This was primarily due to three factors. First, American and British psychology was dominated by the theoretical school of thought known as behaviorism, which offered the **mechanistic world view** that the child is inherently passive until stimulated by the environment, and so the opposing view offered by Piaget took time to be accepted. Second, Piaget only ever wrote in French, which made his work less accessible to the English-speaking psychologists. And third, while Piaget was a brilliant thinker, his writings are often extraordinarily complex and difficult to understand!

Piaget's full impact awaited the arrival of one man who could summarize, synthesize, and present his theoretical views in a way that was comprehensible and available to the English-speaking world. This was John H. Flavell, whose *The Developmental Psychology of Jean Piaget* appeared in 1963 (and in the foreword to this book Piaget wrote, "I am not an easy author; hence it must have required an immense effort at comprehension and intellectual empathy to have produced the clear and straightforward presentation that is found here"). Recently, Flavell (1996) wrote an assessment of Piaget's contribution, entitled "Piaget's legacy," and quotes an anonymous reviewer of his article – "The impact of Piaget on developmental psychology is . . . too monumental to embrace and at the same time too omnipresent to detect," to which Flavell simply adds the words "I agree."

Cognitive Development:
Information-Processing Approaches

Information-processing approaches view the human mind as a complex system through which information flows. There is not one single, unified theory, but most theoretical views that adopt this approach suggest that there are at least three components of the mental system. First, information is received from the environment and *encoded* in some form. Next, a variety of internal processes, such as memory storage, problem-solving strategies, or relating new information to existing knowledge, act on the information and transform it. Finally, the individual is able to change their cognitive structures in order to act on the information. Thus, as development progresses children's knowledge of the world advances, their awareness of their own abilities and limitations increases, and they develop increasingly improved ways of acting on the world.

As a consequence of these activities two broad aspects of the mind change with age – the **hardware**, that is, the size or capacity of its processing units, allowing the child to comprehend more information at a time, and the **software**, that is, the variety and effectiveness of the strategies and action capabilities that allow more efficient use of the information. The terms *hardware* and *software* are an indication that information-processing accounts of cognitive development are based, at least loosely, on computer programming models.

The notion of information flow suggests that information passes smoothly through the mind (or the cognitive system), rather than in discrete or separate steps or stages. Many complex activities illustrate this continual flow – when we are riding a bicycle perceptual, memory, balance, and motor information operate in synchrony to keep us on the road or track, and this is done effortlessly by the skilled rider. Other tasks also illustrate this continual flow of information – reading, playing soccer or basketball, holding a conversation, typing.

Information-processing accounts of human cognition include current views of memory formation, with terms such as *encoding, storage, retrieval, strategies,* and *metamemory,* and this account is given in chapter 12. A brief account of information-processing explanations of cognitive changes in adolescence is given in chapter 15.

COMPARING INFORMATION-PROCESSING APPROACHES WITH PIAGET'S APPROACH

Piaget's theory and information-processing approaches have quite a lot in common. Both attempt to specify children's abilities and limitations as development proceeds, and both try to explain how new levels of understanding develop from earlier, less advanced ones.

However, they differ in several important ways. Information-processing approaches place great importance on the role of processing limitations (another computing analogy) in limiting children's thinking and reasoning at any point in time, and also emphasize the development of strategies and procedures for helping to overcome these limitations – clear accounts of these with respect to memory development are given in chapters 12 and 15. Piaget's theory does not discuss processing limitations, but rather discusses developmental changes in terms of the child gradually constructing logical frameworks for thought, such as *concrete operations* and *formal operations.*

Another important difference is that information-processing accounts see development as unfolding in a continuous fashion, rather than in qualitatively different stages as Piaget suggested. To see how this difference might work, consider the child who moves from Piaget's *preoperational stage* to the *concrete operations stage.* When presented with a conservation of number task, the preoperational child centers attention on one aspect of the changed array – the increase in length – and ignores the other, equally important, aspect, which is that in the example given above a candy/sweet has been added to the smaller row. When the child is able to overcome this limitation, he or she moves to the qualitatively different level of thinking that characterizes the stage of concrete operations. An information-processing account, on the other hand, would simply say that the child's processing capacity has increased so that he or she is now able to hold two things in mind simultaneously, so that what underlies the apparently *qualitative* change in thinking is actually a *quantitative* change in processing capacity.

CONNECTIONISM

Connectionism is a modern theoretical approach, which developed from information-processing accounts and uses computer programs to test models of development. It combines biological and computational knowledge. Computers are programmed to simulate the action of the brain and nerve cells (neurons). The programs often create so-called artificial **neural networks** and, although there is an enormous number of such networks in existence, they all have three things in common.

First, the network is given some initial constraints or guides to learning. This is typically a starting point that represents innate abilities or a particular level of development. Second, the network is given an *input* that represents the experiences a child might have. Third, the neural network acts on the input in order to produce an *output,* which should resemble the sort of learning seen in real life.

Through the construction of such models, connectionists (advocates of connectionism) hope to gain insights into the way in which learning and development take place in the real world, and how the physiological processes taking place in the brain result in a given behavior, or in changes of behavior. Connectionist models have been applied to many areas of child development, e.g., perception, attention, learning, memory, language, problem-solving, and reasoning. Readable accounts of these complex models and their application to children's cognitive development are given by Karmiloff-Smith (1999), Mareschal (2000), and Plunkett (2000).

Social-Cognitive Development

Whereas Piaget tended to focus on the individual child attempting to make sense of the world (given some basic tools), other researchers have been interested in the interaction between the child and his or her community – the social environment.

Vygotsky

The Russian psychologist Lev Semenovich Vygotsky (1896–1934), born in the same year as Piaget, was one of the first to recognize the importance of knowledgeable adults in the child's environment. For him, the development of intellectual abilities is influenced by a *didactic* relationship (one based on instructive dialogue) with more advanced individuals. One fascinating facet of his work is the claim that higher mental abilities are first encountered and used competently in social interactions, only later being internalized and possessed as individual thought processes. For instance, language is used socially to quite a level of competence before it is internalized, reorganizing thought in the process.

Thus, a major theme in Vygotsky's theories is that social interaction plays a fundamental role in cognitive development. He argued that there is a gap between what the child knows and what he or she can be taught. At a given stage of development the child has a certain level of understanding, a temporary maximum. A little beyond this point lies the **zone of proximal development**. This zone can be seen as representing problems and ideas that are just a little too difficult for the child to understand on his or her own. It can, however, be explored and understood with the help of an adult. Thus the adult can guide the child because he or she has a firmer grasp of the more complex thinking involved.

Vygotsky died young (from tuberculosis) but he left an impressive amount of work (over 100 published articles and books) which continues to have an impact on developmental psychology. His contribution to education is discussed in detail in chapter 17.

Behaviorism and social learning theory

Early behaviorism

Toward the end of the nineteenth century, psychology experienced a swing away from the subjective perspective of **introspectionism** (the analysis of self-reported perceptions) toward a more objective method. This scientific approach to psychology had its roots in the work of Vygotsky's countryman, Ivan Petrovich Pavlov (1849–1936). Pavlov developed a grand theory of learning called **classical conditioning**. According to this theory, certain behaviors can be elicited by a neutral (normally unstimulating) stimulus simply because of its learned association with a more powerful stimulus. For example, when food was presented to dogs at the same time as a bell, the bell would eventually cause a salivation response when presented on its own. The dogs learned an *association* between the two. This principle of conditioning is applicable to much human behavior – you might find yourself salivating when the dinner bell sounds, or when you smell the cooking!

Many psychologists seized upon his ideas. Because of its fundamental nature, Pavlov's work had the potential to explain all forms of human behavior and its development. It was combined with other theoretical notions such as Thorndike's **law of effect** (the likelihood of an action being repeated is increased if it leads to reward, and decreased if it leads to punishment), and **behaviorism** was born. With this, the pendulum swing toward objectivity was complete. In its most radical form – as espoused by early behaviorist John Watson (1878–1958) – behaviorism denies the role of the mind as an object of study and reduces all behavior to chains of stimuli (from the environment) and the resulting response (the behavior). Some took this very seriously indeed, and ascribed the mind's "inner voice" to a subvocal tremor of the larynx. One behaviorist administered himself a muscle-relaxing nerve toxin in order to find out, but, despite his condition, his mind remained active along with his scientific zeal.

The early behaviorists' view of child development is quite simple. The infant is born with little more than the machinery of conditioning, and infancy and childhood consists of constant warping and molding under pressure of the environment. The child is passive and receptive and can be shaped in any direction. This view was clearly expressed by Watson (1970, p. 94):

> Give me a dozen healthy infants, well-formed, and my own specified world to bring them up in and I'll guarantee to take any one at random and train him to become any type of specialist I might select – doctor, lawyer, merchant-chief and yes, even beggar-man and thief, regardless of his talents, penchants, tendencies, abilities, vocations, and race of his ancestors.

Any behaviors – even the most elaborate, like language – are towers built upon the foundations of very simple, repeated connections between a stimulus and its response. This has been termed a **reductionist** perspective because it reduces ostensibly complex phenomena to simpler core processes.

B. F. Skinner's behaviorism

Any discussion of behaviorism would not be complete without the inclusion of Burrhus Frederic Skinner (1904–90). He had an effect on his area of psychology perhaps greater than any other individual (and during his lifetime was regularly in the list of the ten most famous Americans). Whilst the early behaviorists emphasized the passive nature of the child, Skinner envisioned a more active role. **Operant conditioning** differs from *classical conditioning* because children operate (emit behaviors) on their environments. It is still the case that the child's development is dominated by his or her environment, but Skinner's viewpoint allowed for more flexible and generative patterns of behavior. According to Skinner's view, it is possible to shape the animal's or child's behavior by manipulating the reinforcement received.

We can see the role of reinforcement in this brief account of infant behavior (Skinner, 1961, p. 418):

One reinforcer to which babies often respond is the flashing on and off of a table lamp. Whenever the baby lifts its hand, flash the light. In a short time a well-defined response will be generated. (Human babies are just as "smart" as dogs or pigeons in this respect.) Incidentally, the baby will enjoy the experience.

It is certainly the case that our behavior is guided by reward and punishment, and behaviorism continues to be used in the control of behavior. Skinner gave an account of how parents may unwittingly promote undesirable behaviors, such as aggression, crying, or shouting in their children. If, for example, the mother only gives the child attention when he or she is misbehaving, then the mother's positive reinforcement of attention is likely to promote the very behavior she does not want! The remedy is this (Skinner, 1961, p. 419):

> The remedy in such a case is simply for the mother to make sure that she responds with attention and affection to most if not all the responses of the child which are . . . acceptable . . . and that she never reinforces the annoying forms of behavior.

Social learning theory

Whereas behaviorism had important but rather vague things to say about the child's acquisition of behavior patterns, the work of Albert Bandura (1925–) examined particular behaviors in more detail. His behaviorism was less mechanistic than that of Skinner. He did not focus only on observable behavior, but posited processing that occurred within the mind – a construct specifically denied by his behaviorist colleagues. His approach was initially named *sociobehaviorism*, then *social cognitive theory*, and finally **social learning theory**.

During the 1960s Bandura carried out a series of experiments on childhood aggression. In one, some children were divided into two groups. The first ("control") group saw a film of an adult playing with toys, one of which was an inflatable "Bobo" doll. The second ("experimental") group saw a film of the same adult, this time playing aggressively with the toys, hitting the doll with a hammer. When allowed to play individually, Bandura observed that children from the experimental group behaved in a more aggressive way toward their own Bobo doll.

So, without obvious reinforcement, a particular aggressive behavior had been reinforced. Bandura termed this **observational learning** or "vicarious conditioning." In some sense, the child had *mentally* assumed the role of the observed person and taken note of any reinforcement. Bandura concluded that children imitate the actions of others, based on perceived reinforcement. He followed up the Bobo-doll experiment with investigations into cartoon and film violence. The findings were clear: children imitated the aggressive behavior.

Bandura's approach kept the essential components of behaviorism – that we learn by reinforcement and punishment of behavior, in accord with the law of effect – and added the important dimension of learning by observation. Adults and others in the child's life provide models, and learning by imitation is extremely common in all areas of social and cognitive development.

Evolution and Ethology

EVOLUTION

The theoretical basis of any evolutionary theory of development is, of course, evolution itself. The present form of the theory is largely identical to that developed by its founder, Charles Robert Darwin (Darwin was born on February 12, 1809 – the same day as Abraham Lincoln – and died on April 19, 1882). Perhaps the most important unit in evolution is the *gene*, which is the basic genetic material out of which **chromosomes** are formed. The term gene is also used in a vague way when talking about any heritable characteristic of an organism: eye color, intelligence, or an inherited behavior. When a set of genes leads to an overall advantage for an organism, the organism tends to produce more copies of itself. Those genes, therefore, will become more frequent in the *gene pool*. When a set of genes leads to an overall disadvantage, those genes will become less frequent. This means that as evolution proceeds any gene still in the gene pool will tend to be advantageous. The difficult concept to master is to remember that this should apply to behaviors as well as physical characteristics.

Evolutionary theories of child development that emphasize the genetic basis of many behaviors, and point to the adaptive and survival value of these behaviors, are known as **ethological approaches**.

THE ETHOLOGICAL APPROACH

The origins of ethology can be traced back to Darwin, and its modern foundations were laid by two European zoologists, Konrad Lorenz (1903–89) and Niko Tinbergen (1907–88), who pioneered the genetic analysis of development. They reasoned that certain behaviors in the young of many species would be genetic in origin because they (1) promote survival and (2) are found in many species, including humans. One such behavior is **imprinting**, which refers to the tendency of the newborn or newly hatched of **precocial species** of animals (which includes ducks, geese, sheep, horses) to follow the first moving objects they see. This behavior involves the formation of an attachment between the infant and the mother. Clearly, imprinting is *adaptive* (adds to survival value) because it leads to a physical proximity between parent and offspring. As a consequence, the parent is always at hand to feed, give warmth, protect from predators, and generally attend to the offspring.

Lorenz is famous for his experiments with young geese (goslings). He demonstrated that if the first moving object they saw after hatching was him, then the unwitting goslings would imprint on him and follow him around (and even, as adults, attempt to mate with him!).

There are two implications of ethology's conception of behaviors. The first is that, for the most part, they require an external stimulus or target. For example, imprinting needs a target "parent" – if this target does not exist, imprinting will either not take place, or will take place with an inappropriate target (cf. Lorenz's goslings). The second implication is one of time. Originally, ethologists envisioned a **critical period**, this being the length of time for the behavior to grow to maturity in the presence of the right conditions (e.g., language developing in a rich linguistic environment). When this critical period expires, the behavior cannot develop. These days, the evidence points toward a **sensitive** rather than critical period; behaviors may take root beyond this sensitive time period, but their development may be difficult and ultimately retarded.

EMOTIONAL DEVELOPMENT

Attachment theory – John Bowlby and Mary Ainsworth

Mother love in infancy and childhood is as important for mental health as are vitamins and proteins for physical health. *(Bowlby, 1952)*

The British physician and psychoanalyst John Bowlby was inspired by observations of imprinting, and was one of the first to offer an ethological and evolutionary interpretation of human development. His contribution to our understanding of attachment formation in infancy and childhood continues to have an immense impact, and here we will give a very brief account of his views, and those of his American colleague, Mary Ainsworth.

Prior to Bowlby the prevailing belief, stemming from behaviorism, is that the attachment of infants to their caregivers was a **secondary drive**, that is, because the mother (or **primary caregiver**) satisfies the baby's **primary drives** (these include hunger, thirst, and the need for warmth), she acquires secondary reinforcing properties. However, Bowlby pointed out that the need for attachment was itself a primary drive (as the quote given above indicates, which is the conclusion to his 1952 report to the World Health Organization).

Several lines of evidence have since supported this conclusion. In the 1950s and 1960s Harry Harlow and his colleagues (e.g., Harlow & Zimmerman, 1959) separated baby monkeys from their real mothers and offered them two surrogate (substitute) "mothers." One of these was made of wire, but had a nipple attached which provided food (and hence satisfied the primary drives of hunger and thirst). The other was made of soft cloth and provided no nutrition. What they found is that the baby monkeys fed from the "wire mother," but cuddled up to the "soft cloth mother," and ran to "her" when frightened by loud sounds. It therefore seemed reasonable to conclude that the "soft cloth mother" provided what we can call *contact comfort*, and satisfied a basic or primary need.

Bowlby argued that there is an innate, instinctual drive in humans to form attachments that is as strong as any other primary drive or need. He put forward the principle of **monotropy**, which is the claim that the infant has a need to form an attachment with one significant person (usually the mother). This claim was later found to be overstated, because Rudolph Schaffer (the author of chapter 7 of this book) and Peggy Emerson (1964) found that infants often formed multiple attachments, and that in some cases their strongest attachment was to people such as the father,

Plate 2.3 Infants will usually form multiple attachments.

a grandparent, or peers, who did not fulfill basic caregiving activities, but who did engage in satisfying interactions ("quality time") with them (see plate 2.3).

Bowlby believed that the attachment system between infant and caregiver became organized and consolidated in the second half of the infant's first year from birth, and became particularly apparent when the infant began to crawl. At this time, infants tend to use the mother as a "safe base" from which to begin their explorations of the world, and it then becomes possible to measure how infants react to their mother's departure and to her return. For these measures we are indebted to Mary Ainsworth, who trained with Bowlby and who invented what is commonly called the **strange situation**. In this situation a baby (usually around a year old) and his or her mother enter an experimental room in which there are several toys. The mother sits on a chair and after a short while a stranger enters, at which point the mother leaves, only to return a few minutes later. An observer then notes the infant's response to several events – when the stranger enters, when the mother leaves, and when she returns.

Using the strange situation, Ainsworth discovered that there are several attachment "styles" that differ in degree of security. A detailed account of these attachment styles and of Bowlby's and Ainsworth's contribution in developing what is called *attachment theory* is given in chapter 6. For the moment we can conclude that their significance has been in demonstrating the importance of early secure attachments and showing that these attachments are as basic and necessary as any other human drive or motivation.

Psychoanalytic Theories

Sigmund Freud: The founder of psychoanalysis

For generations almost every branch of human knowledge will be enriched and illuminated by the imagination of Freud.
(Jane Harrison, 1850–1928)

His place is not, as he claimed, with Copernicus and Darwin, but with Hans Christian Anderson and the Brothers Grimm, tellers of fairy tales.
(Hans Eysenck, 1916–97)

As will be apparent from the above, not everyone agrees that Freud's contribution to knowledge has been entirely positive! Freud claimed that much of our behavior is determined by unconscious forces of which we are not directly aware. In presenting his **psychoanalytic theory**, he suggested that there are three main structures to personality, which are the **id**, the **ego**, and the **superego**. The id is present in the newborn infant and consists of impulses, **emotions**, and desires. It demands instant gratification of all its wishes and needs. Since this is impractical, the ego develops to act as a practical interface or mediator between reality and the desires of the id. The final structure to develop is the superego, which is the sense of duty and responsibility – in many ways the conscience.

The ego and the superego develop as the individual progresses through the five **psychosexual stages** – oral, anal, phallic, latency, and genital – and these are described next.

The five psychosexual stages

Oral stage (approximately birth to 1 year)

The infant's greatest satisfaction is derived from stimulation of the lips, tongue, and mouth. Sucking is the chief source of pleasure for the young infant.

Anal stage (approximately 1 to 3 years)

During this stage toilet or potty training takes place and the child gains the greatest psychosexual pleasure from exercising control over the anus and by retaining and eliminating feces.

Phallic stage (approximately 3 to 6 years)

This is the time when children obtain their greatest pleasure from stimulating the genitals. At this time boys experience the **Oedipus complex**. This expression derives from the Greek myth in which Oedipus became infatuated with his mother. In the Freudian account the young boy develops sexual feelings toward his mother but realizes that his father is a major competitor for her (sexual) affections! He then fears castration at the hands of his father (the **castration complex**) and, in order to resolve this complex, he adopts the ideals of his father and the superego (the conscience) develops. If we return to Greek mythology, the noblewoman Electra remained obsessively bound or fixated to the memory of her father Agamemnon. In the Freudian account, for little girls the **Electra complex** is when they develop feelings toward their father and fear retribution at the hands of their mother. They resolve this by empathizing with their mother, adopting the ideals she offers, and so the girl's superego develops.

Latency and genital stages (approximately 6 years to adolescence)

From around 6 years the torments of infancy and early childhood subside and the child's sexual awakening goes into a resting period (*latency*, from around 6 years to puberty and adolescence). Then, at adolescence, sexual feelings become more apparent and urgent and the genital stage appears. In the latter "true" sexual feelings emerge and the adolescent strives to cope with awakening desires.

Problems with Freudian theory

One of the main claims of Freudian theory is that much of what motivates us is determined unconsciously. By their very nature unconscious processes cannot be measured, and so it is often claimed that belief in Freudian ideas is precisely that – beliefs and not facts. It is certainly the case that Freud's views are almost impossible to test. To illustrate this, consider the Freudian notion of **reaction formation**. If you are harshly toilet trained as a child then the Freudian prediction would be that you become "anally retentive," that is, you become excessively neat and tidy. However, if in some way you recognize this in yourself (maybe even unconsciously), then you can react against it (i.e., *reaction formation* occurs) and you actively become very untidy! What this means is that you can react against your upbringing and reverse the effects, which means in turn that it is impossible to predict the child's development despite the fact that the first 6 years from birth are supposedly critical in determining later personality formation.

Psychoanalysis, then and now: An overview

Freudian theory has been of immense importance in telling us two things. One is that early childhood can be tremendously important in affecting and determining later development (a position also adopted by people such as Bowlby, whose views are given above), and the other is that we can be driven by unconscious needs and desires of which we are not aware. Thus, if we did not go through one of the childhood psychosexual stages very well, then this could reflect itself in later adult disorders such as neurotic symptoms, but we would not be aware of the causes of the problem. The only way to come to terms with this would be intensive sessions of psychoanalysis in which the analyst tries to discover what it is that went wrong in your childhood that is causing your current problems.

The theory is largely unsupported by scientific evidence. Thus, there is little evidence that the Oedipus and Electra complexes occur. Additionally, if events occurring in early childhood can have different outcomes (as a result of reaction formation), then it is impossible to make clear predictions about the effects of early experiences. Nevertheless, there are many who believe that psychoanalytic theories are important in understanding human development, and there have been many theoreticians who have offered variations and alternatives to Freud's proposals. We briefly consider two of these next, Anna Freud and Erik Erikson (for a full treatment of psychoanalytic accounts of adolescence, see chapter 16).

MODERN PSYCHOANALYSTS: ANNA FREUD AND ERIK ERIKSON

Anna Freud (1895–1982) was the youngest of Sigmund Freud's children. She grew up with an interest in psychoanalysis, and is often referred to as "the founder of child psychoanalysis." She felt that adolescence and puberty presented a series of challenges. During this period of ego struggle, through meeting these challenges the ego matures and becomes better able to defend itself. For Erik Erikson (1902–94), like Anna Freud, personality formation was not largely complete by age 6 or 7 as Sigmund Freud suggested. Rather, stages of psychological conflict and adjustment occur throughout the lifespan. Whereas Freud felt that the child's personality was determined largely by parents and by unconscious forces, Erikson gave much greater emphasis to the role of the broader social world which includes relatives, friends, society, and culture. For this reason Erikson's stages are called **psychosocial** rather than *psychosexual*. The work of Anna Freud and Erikson as it applies to adolescent development is discussed in more detail in chapter 16.

 ## *Humanistic Theory: Abraham Maslow*

Humanistic theories focus on the individual's own subjective experiences, motives, and desires. In general, they differ from psychoanalytic views in putting much less emphasis on the role of the unconscious in determining behavior. Humanists argue that we are not driven by unconscious needs, neither are we driven by external environmental pulls such as reinforcement and rewards. Rather, humans have free will and are motivated to fulfill their potential. The inner need or desire to fulfill one's potential is known as **self-actualization**. The drive for self-actualization is not restricted to childhood but is applicable across the lifespan, and a leading proponent of the humanistic view was Abraham Maslow (1908–70).

ABRAHAM MASLOW'S HIERARCHY OF NEEDS

Maslow suggested that there is a **hierarchy of needs** or motives that determine our behavior. The hierarchy is given in figure 2.1 and extends from the basic needs for survival through the search for self-actualization. One interesting and unusual aspect of his

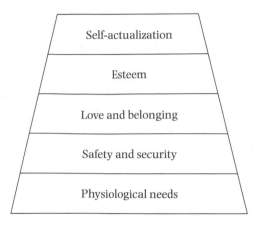

Figure 2.1 Maslow's hierarchy of needs.

 theory is that it was based on data collected only from women – unusual in that Maslow was only 24 years old at the time and he quizzed 140 young women (from 18 to 28 years) about the intimate details of their sex lives (Alimo-Metcalf, 2001, pp. 179–80):

> The subject of the interview included: sex drive; presence or absence of technical virginity; history of promiscuity; frequency and intensity of climax in heterosexual relations; ease of excitability; number of everyday objects regarded as sexual stimuli; and so on.

From these structured interviews Maslow was able to relate the women's experiences to self-actualizing behaviors. To see how Maslow's hierarchy might work, imagine the following scenario (based on Dworetsky, 1995, p. 43). A young man arrives as an emigrant/immigrant to a foreign country, broke and homeless. His first aim would be to ensure that his basic physiological needs for food, water, and warmth were satisfied. Next would be finding a place where he felt safe and secure. He is then able to begin to search for ways of satisfying his psychological needs, to develop relationships with people so he feels that he belongs. His sense of self-esteem develops as he feels needed by others, and his final goal would be to attain self-actualization – this is equivalent to achieving his full potential, perhaps in education, sport, music, rearing children, and many other types of activity and attainment.

Maslow's theory was not intended as a theory of children's development – the hierarchy of needs is applicable at all ages from early childhood on, and children achieve goals and fulfill their potential as do adults. It is worth noting that, sadly, there are over 100 million child slaves in the world today – children who work in the fields, in domestic slavery, in bars, restaurants, on building sites, in sweatshops perhaps making expensive (or cheap) clothes and shoes for western consumption, and in many countries the prettiest children are raised in brothels. For third world countries child slave labor makes good sense – children are a renewable resource, they don't form unions, they are cheap and trainable. These children enter a lifetime sentence of hard labor and ill health for the "crime" of poverty – their needs lower in Maslow's hierarchy are met but self-actualization is a myth, not an attainable possibility.

Putting it All Together: Different Theories for Different Needs

In this chapter we have given a sample of the many different theories that have been advanced to explain human development. As is abundantly obvious, child development is enormously complex, and we should not expect any theory, however "grand," to attempt to account for more than one or two selected areas of development. Thus, there are theories that focus specifically on motor, perceptual, cognitive, emotional, social, or personality development.

However, it is important to remember that in the child him/herself, all aspects of development are interrelated. For example, each new motor acquisition in infancy opens up new ways of exploring the world, which in turn affects infants' awareness of the world and their cognitive and social development. New cognitive achievements affect the child's social development since they allow the child to interact with others at an increasingly more sophisticated level of understanding. Cognitive and social developments give increased opportunities for children to develop their potentials, and hence allow for the possibility of self-actualization.

The essential point is that theories have to focus on specific areas of development, but development itself is multifaceted and all aspects of change are integrally linked. To illustrate this interrelatedness of different aspects of development, we will focus on one area of development where different theoretical views make their own different contributions, the topic of **gender development**.

GENDER DEVELOPMENT

Gender development concerns the important question of how it is that children grow up knowing that they are either a boy or a girl. Psychologists from several different theoretical traditions have offered accounts of how this happens, and here we give very brief accounts of cognitive, behaviorist/social learning, psychoanalytic, and biological explanations.

A cognitive account

A cognitive view of gender development was offered nearly 40 years ago by the American psychologist Lawrence Kohlberg (1966; see also chapter 14 for his theory of the development of moral reasoning). According to Kohlberg's account of gender development the child gradually comes to realize that he or she is a boy or a girl and that this is unchangeable – once a girl (or boy) always a girl (or boy), a realization that is known as **gender constancy**. Most children come to this realization some time after 3 years, and almost all know it by age 7 (Wehren & De Lisi, 1983). Kohlberg's theory suggests that once children understand which gender they are, they will develop appropriate gender-role behaviors. That is, knowing he or she is a girl or a boy helps the child to organize his or her behavior to be gender-appropriate.

A social learning account

Social learning accounts of gender development are based on the work of Albert Bandura, whose views we discussed earlier, and these in turn are developed from behaviorist theories of learning. In this account the child is reinforced for what the parents and others perceive as being gender-appropriate behavior (girls play with dolls, boys don't cry). Additionally, children imitate significant others and learn to observe same-gender models to see how to behave. In this way, through observation, imitation, and reinforcement, children's gender roles are shaped.

A psychoanalytic view

In the Freudian version of psychoanalytic theory a girl's identification with her mother, and a boy's with his father, develop from the resolution of the Electra and Oedipus complexes, as described above. As a result of this identification girls and boys form female and male identities (respectively!) and take on their same-gender parent's views and behavior as their own.

Biological determinants

The accounts described so far all emphasize the role of *nurture* in promoting gender development. But remember that the physical aspects of gender are biologically determined by the type of chromosomes we inherit at conception (see chapter 4). Here we will describe a case history to highlight the role of *nature* (genetic and biological) in gender determination.

This concerns one of a set of normal male twins born in 1966, whom we will call Jim. The twins developed urinary problems and at 8 months Jim (and his twin brother) were taken to a clinic for circumcision. What happened to Jim was that he "had his penis accidentally burned to ablation during phimosis repair by cautery" (Diamond & Sigmundson, 1999, p. 58). What this medical terminology means is that the incompetent physician destroyed Jim's penis.

At the time one of the most influential views on gender development was expressed by the psychologist John Money (e.g., Money & Ehrhardt, 1972) and was that individuals are psychosexually and gender neutral at birth, and that experience (*nurture*) is the sole determinant of their development. A decision was therefore made to carry out gender-reassignment surgery (to create a vagina and female genital appearance), and to rear Jim as Joan. This case is described in earlier textbooks on child development as clear evidence that nurture determined gender roles, and Money's theoretical views achieved widespread acceptance, even to the point that some were arguing that if a genetic male had a small penis (in extreme instances this is referred to as a *micropenis*), then "Often it is wiser to rear a genetic male as a female" (Donahoe & Hendren, 1976, p. 396).

But it all went drastically wrong. Even soon after the operation "Joan" began rejecting girl things, like refusing to wear dresses. Somewhere between the ages of 9 and 11 Joan "figured that I was a guy." At school "she" persisted in standing up to urinate in the girls' bathroom. She made several suicide attempts and finally, in adolescence, learned the truth. At this time "Joan" refused to carry on as a female and insisted on gender reassignment (which included a mastectomy and phallus reconstruction) to his biologically determined gender. He later married an older woman and adopted her children. A fuller account of this case is given by Diamond and Sigmundson (1999).

Summary

These different accounts of gender development all have their appeal. It is clear that social influences and children's cognitive awareness influence their gender-related behavior. But it is also clear that biological (genetic/hormonal) influences are important. Many, perhaps most, *transsexuals* (those who elect for gender reassignment, often through surgical procedures) will say that they have felt that they were a girl in a boy's body (or vice versa) for as long as they can remember, and even though they have never been reinforced for gender-inappropriate behavior. What is clear is that we have different theoretical views and there are multiple causes of gender development in children. Perhaps biological factors provide the basic differences, and cognitive and social factors add the fine detail to create behavioral differences.

ISSUES IN CHILD DEVELOPMENT

There are many issues, controversies, and debates in the study of child development, and we will see the most important of these in the pages of this book. Many of these topics are specific to a particular area or areas of development, but there are others that affect almost all aspects of growth. Here we briefly describe three of these: the **nature–nurture issue**, **stability versus change**, and **continuity versus discontinuity**.

The Nature–Nurture Issue

We are all of us a product of the *interaction* of the two broad factors of *nature* – inheritance or genetic factors – and *nurture* – environmental influences. For example, it is argued that humans are genetically predisposed to acquire language, but which language we acquire is determined by the language(s) we hear and learn. It is important to note that without both factors no development could occur! Nevertheless, people differ in their abilities, temperaments, personalities, and a host of other characteristics, and psychologists and **behavior geneticists** have attempted to estimate the relative contributions of nature and nurture to these individual variations between people – are certain behavioral characteristics such as gender development (as discussed in the previous section), intelligence, and personality more influenced by heredity or by the environment? A detailed account of these attempts, and of the nature–nurture issue in general, is given in chapter 3.

Stability versus Change

It is often claimed that "the child is father to the man" (or "the child is mother to the woman"), meaning that early experiences influence current and later development. This view suggests that certain aspects of children's development display stability, in the sense that they are consistent and predictable across time. It turns out that development is characterized by both stability and change – for example, personality characteristics such as shyness and the tendency to be aggressive tend to be stable, while others such as *approach* (the tendency to extreme friendliness and lack of caution with strangers) and *sluggishness* (reacting passively to changing circumstances) are unstable (as discussed in chapter 14).

Continuity versus Discontinuity

In chapter 1 we described two "world views" which are called **organismic** and **mechanistic**. Organismic theories, such as Piaget's, emphasize that some of the most interesting changes in human development – such as those that accompany major changes in thinking, puberty, and other life transitions such as first going to school, going to college, getting married, etc. – are characterized by discontinuity, by qualitatively different ways of thinking and behaving. Mechanistic theories, as exemplified by behaviorist views, emphasize continuity – that development is reflected by a more continuous growth function, rather than occurring in qualitatively different stages. What complicates things is that, as we have seen, it is often possible to think of the same aspect of development (such as intelligence) as being both continuous and discontinuous. Sternberg and Okagaki (1989, p. 158) state the case as follows:

> as it stands, the continuity-discontinuity debate is largely misconceived and . . . we should . . . be thinking in terms of ways in which development is simultaneously continuous and discontinuous with respect to different dimensions of analysis.

SUMMARY AND CONCLUSIONS

Although these three issues will appear regularly in the chapters of this book, it is important to keep in mind that human development requires both nature and nurture, it displays aspects of stability and also change, and it is both continuous and discontinuous.

In the rest of this book you will find many examples of theories and theoretical approaches – mostly the ones that we have described in this chapter, but also a few new ones. Always remember that a theory has specific applications – that is, a limited *range of convenience* – and we should not ask too much of any one. It would be a mistake to criticize Piaget, Freud, and Bowlby for paying too little attention, respectively, to social development, the role of conscious awareness, and cognitive development, since this was not their aim! All of these theoreticians, the others described here, and yet others whose work will appear in later chapters, have helped to mold our understanding of children's development and make it the exciting, dynamic topic of enquiry that it is today.

DISCUSSION POINTS

1 Considering the evidence presented here, list as many aspects of motor development (a) that may not depend on experience, (b) that probably do depend on experience.
2 Discuss ways in which Piaget's account of development differs from (a) maturational accounts, and (b) accounts that portray development as molded by the environment.
3 Think of differences between Piaget's theory and information-processing theories of development.
4 Skinner's theory of learning through reinforcement seems quite plausible in many ways. Think about what makes the account plausible, and also about the aspects of development that it does not explain.
5 Taking account of the evidence presented here and adding your own arguments, consider the factors likely to lead to secure attachment.
6 Is the psychoanalytic approach to development a theory or just a compelling story?
7 How plausible is it that Maslow was able to establish a hierarchy of needs simply from interviews about sexuality?
8 The view presented here is that different theoretical approaches to development can exist side by side, complementing each other. Consider whether there are limits to this view. For instance, are there some approaches that are so opposed that they cannot coexist?

SUGGESTIONS FOR FURTHER READING

Bremner, G., & Slater, A. (2003). *Theories of infant development*. Cambridge, MA, & Oxford: Blackwell.

Fancher, R. E. (1990). *Pioneers of psychology* (2nd ed.). New York & London: W. W. Norton.

Miller, P. H. (1993). *Theories of developmental psychology* (3rd ed.). Englewood Cliffs, NJ: Prentice-Hall.

Thomas, R. (2000). *Comparing theories of child development*. Belmont, CA: Wadsworth.

Thomas, R. M. (2000). *Recent theories of human development*. Newbury Park, CA: Sage.

chapter 3

The Nature–Nurture Issue

Elena L. Grigorenko and Robert J. Sternberg

KEY CONCEPTS

ALLELES
AUTOSOMES
BEHAVIOR GENETICS
CHROMOSOME
CHRONOLOGICAL AGE
(CA)
COGNITIVE FUNCTIONING
COHORT
CRYSTALLIZED
  INTELLIGENCE
DIFFERENTIAL PSYCHOLOGY
DIZYGOTIC (FRATERNAL)
  TWINS

EMPIRICISM
ENVIRONMENTALISM
ENVIRONMENTALITY
FAMILIAL RESEMBLANCE
FLUID INTELLIGENCE
G
GENE–ENVIRONMENT
  CORRELATION
GENETIC DETERMINISM
GENOTYPE
HERITABILITY
INTELLIGENCE QUOTIENT
(IQ)

IQ TEST
LONGITUDINAL DESIGN
MATURATION
MENTAL AGE (MA)
META-ANALYSIS
MONOZYGOTIC (IDENTICAL) TWINS
NATIVISM
NATURE–NURTURE ISSUE
NURTURE
PHENOTYPE
SOCIOECONOMIC STATUS (SES)
STANDARDIZED TEST

The work described in this chapter was supported by government grants under the Javits Act Program, grant No. R206A970001 and R206R00001, as administered by the Office of Educational Research and Improvement, US Department of Education. Grantees undertaking such projects are encouraged to express freely their professional judgment. This chapter, therefore, does not necessarily represent the positions or the policies of the US government, and no official endorsement should be inferred.

BOX 3.1 INTELLIGENCE AND INTELLIGENCE TESTS: A PRECHAPTER INTERLUDE

Alan Slater

THE START OF IT ALL: THE FIRST INTELLIGENCE TEST

The first intelligence test along modern lines was created by the Frenchman Alfred Binet in 1905. Binet had been set the task by the Parisian school authorities of devising a test that would select those children who were unlikely to learn much from being in ordinary schools, so that they could then be given special education. Binet's test gave different questions to children of different ages and was based on their general knowledge, and their ability to reason and solve problems. His test consisted of some 30 items, ranging from the ability to touch parts of one's face to more abstract concepts. It was sufficiently successful that it correlated well with teachers' estimates of children's ability such that those who scored highly were judged to be "bright," whereas those who did poorly were judged "dull" or retarded. A modern version of Binet's test is still much used today – the Stanford-Binet test.

MENTAL AGE AND INTELLIGENCE QUOTIENT (IQ)

Binet introduced the concept of **mental age (MA)**, which can be defined as *an individual's level of mental ability relative to others*. If a child with a real or **chronological age (CA)** of 5 years succeeded at problems usually solved by 7-year-olds, her MA would be 7 while her CA is 5 and the child is judged to be bright. Conversely, if a 5-year-old succeeded only at the level of a 3-year-old his MA is below average and he is likely to have learning difficulties at school.

A few years later (1912), William Stern introduced the term **intelligence quotient (IQ)**, and in its original formulation it was simply calculated as a child's MA divided by the child's CA multiplied by 100:

$$IQ = \frac{MA}{CA} \times 100$$

We can see from this formulation that those children who are exactly average for their age have an IQ of 100; if MA is below CA then the IQ is below 100; if MA is above CA then the child is bright and IQ is above 100.

INTELLIGENCE TESTS

There are four important things to note about IQ tests and IQ scores. (1) The simple formula given above is no longer used, but the purpose of IQ tests is always to compare people's (children's or adults') scores with those from people of the same population and of approximately the same age. (2) The average IQ at a given time is always 100. To ensure this it means that tests are carefully **standardized** every few years to ensure that the population varies around this mean. This means that test makers provide a conversion chart so that an individual's raw score (i.e., the number of items passed) can be expressed as an IQ score. (3) Children's and adults' raw scores tend to increase from one generation to the next, hence the need for regular standardization of tests – a fuller discussion of this, and the possible reasons for the changes, is given in chapter 1. (4) The items on IQ tests invariably proceed from the simple to the complex, so that an individual's raw score (and hence their IQ) is derived from the number of items passed before they make mistakes.

There are now several widely used IQ tests, and hundreds of tests of specific abilities. Three well-known tests are: (1) the *Stanford-Binet* for the ages of 2 to adulthood; (2) the Wechsler scales (the *Wechsler Preschool and Primary Scale of Intelligence – WPPSI –* for ages 4 to 6.5; the *Wechsler Intelligence Scale for Children – WISC –* 6 to 16 (see table 15.1, p. 368); the *Wechsler Adult Intelligence Scale – WAIS*); (3) the *Differential Ability Scales – DAS –* from infancy to adolescence.

WHAT IS INTELLIGENCE – ONE ABILITY OR SEVERAL?

To a large extent how intelligence is defined determines how it is measured. We can probably agree that intelligence involves verbal abilities, memory, problem-solving skills, and the ability to adapt and change to meet life's demands. Unfortunately, however, the agreement stops there! The concepts of mental age and IQ suggest that intelligence is a single general ability, and there are those who argue that a general intelligence ability (often referred to simply as "**g**") underlies performance on all intelligence tests. Others suggest that intelligence is made up of a number of specific abilities or subskills. Still others have argued that performance on intelligence tests is unrelated to our ability to "live our lives intelligently." One commentator has remarked: "Tests have very modest correlations with performance in skills that society deems important" (Deese, 1993, p. 113).

In line with this view, Steve Ceci and Jeff Liker (1986) tested 30 "avid racetrack patrons" for their ability to use a sophisticated multiplicative model to handicap races – an important ability if you make a living from horse races! They found no relationship (correlation) between this ability and IQ (the handicappers' IQs ranged from 83 to 130), leading them to the conclusion that "IQ is unrelated to real-world forms of cognitive complexity" (p. 255). In additional research Steve Ceci found little relationship between IQ and income, leading him to the reasonable conclusion that "it's better to be born rich than smart"!

Nevertheless, we have known for many years that occupation is related to IQ: teachers, doctors, accountants, pharmacists, lawyers, and those in similar occupations have a mean IQ above 120; people in semi- or low-skilled occupations such as barber, farmhand, or laborer have a mean IQ below 100. Perhaps we can conclude that intelligence, as measured by intelligence tests, is genuinely measuring something that is worthwhile, and there are many who would argue that "intelligence is a useful and powerful construct" (Kline, 1991, p. 145).

INTELLIGENCE TEST ITEMS

The inability of psychologists and others to agree on a definition of intelligence has led some to produce the circular definition that "intelligence is what intelligence tests measure" – at least this avoids a lot of controversy! So, how do intelligence tests measure intelligence?

Many tests divide intelligence into two broad abilities, verbal and performance subscales. You would be likely to find the following sorts of items.

Verbal subscales

Similarities. The child is asked to say in what way things might be similar. For example, "In what ways do blue, green, and yellow go together?" and (an item suitable for an older child) ". . . justice, democracy, freedom."

Comprehension. This subscale measures the child's common sense and understanding. For example: "Why do people need to pay taxes?"

Recall of digits. The tester reads out sequences of digits and after each sequence the child calls it back. For example: "6 – 9 – 4" and later (much later!) "4 – 7 – 8 – 5 – 1 – 7 – 2 – 4 – 8 – 3." The average digit span for adults is about seven items (so very few people would give perfect recall of the second list of digits), and it increases during childhood.

You might wonder why this item is given under the heading "verbal subscales"! This is simply because digit span correlates well with verbal rather than performance subscales – the child with the higher digit span is likely to have the greater verbal skills.

Performance subscales

Block design. The child is given a set of blocks with colored patterns on them, and asked to use them to make patterns that the tester shows.

Copying. The child is shown a drawing and asked to copy it on a sheet of paper. The drawings are initially simple (perhaps an outline of a triangle, or three vertical lines) and become progressively more complex geometric shapes.

CONTROVERSIES AND ISSUES IN INTELLIGENCE

We have seen some of the controversies already: How many types of intelligence are there? How useful is what intelligence tests measure? Here we will consider one more controversial issue: How much of our intelligence is shaped by genetic factors and how much by our environment?

In fact, it has long been recognized that genes and environment are not additive, in the sense that x percent of intelligence is caused by genes and y percent by the environment. Rather, they *interact* with each other in causing the development of all human characteristics, including intelligence. Accordingly, scientists try to produce estimates of **heritability**, which is asking the question *how much of the variation in intelligence between individuals in a population is caused by genetic factors?*

The importance of this issue lies in its societal, racial, economic, and political implications. If heritability is high, then some racial groups and classes of children who score poorly, on average, on IQ tests might be thought to do so for reasons that are primarily of genetic origin. Conversely, if heritability is low, these differences in IQ scores may be primarily environmentally determined and it becomes important to enhance the cognitive environment of the disadvantaged in order to provide an intellectually stimulating environment.

A detailed account of the nature–nurture issue and estimates of heritability is provided in this chapter.

Plate 3.1 A child taking an intelligence test.

OVERVIEW

For centuries philosophers, scientists, and others have speculated on how it is that we become the people we are, and there has long been debate and controversy regarding the ways in which two factors – our genetic inheritance and our environment – combine to cause development. This is the nature–nurture issue, and, as we see in this chapter, the answers are not simple. It is now widely acknowledged that these factors *interact* in causing development, but we are only now coming to an understanding of *how* they interact. The nature–nurture issue affects all aspects of development, but it has been most researched with respect to cognitive development, and this is the focus of this chapter. Amongst other things the authors consider:

- The behavior-genetic approach to studying individual differences.
- Phenotypes and genotypes and causes of variations in these.
- The forces determining individual differences in cognitive abilities.
- The concepts of heritability and environmentality.
- The use of family, twin, and adoption studies.
- What we know about the heritability of general and specific cognitive abilities.

An important point is that estimates of the contributions of genes and environments to individual variations in abilities refer to a given population at a given time, and these estimates will vary from population to population, and from time to time. It appears that in current western societies about 50 percent of interindividual variation in IQ (a measure of general cognitive ability) can be explained by genetic influences. Another 50 percent of the variation is accounted for by environmental factors. At the current time the search is on to find the specific genes and environmental influences that determine development, and in particular *how* they do it.

Why Do People Differ in the Way They Think?

Why do people differ in the way they think? Why are some people smarter than others? Why do children's abilities resemble their parents' abilities? Why do children in one family differ in the way they learn compared with children in another family and, moreover, compared with each other? Why do people vary in intelligence? Why do people's levels of intelligence vary as they develop? These are the kinds of questions we address in this chapter.

The observation of differences in cognitive abilities between people has many explanations, depending on the context and goal of a given discussion. For example, consider how different professionals might seek to understand differences in two people's performance on an **IQ test**. Nutritionists might inquire whether both people have been well nourished over the course of their lifetime; the nutritionists even might ask if both people had breakfast on the day of the test, and if so, what it was. Psychophysiologists might think of differences in nerve conduction velocities. Psychologists might seek to understand previous learning experiences, motivation, and genetic endowments. In this chapter, we will speak from a **behavior-genetic** point of view, considering both genetic and environmental sources of individual differences in **cognitive functioning**.

The goal of this chapter is to explore sources of observed differences in cognitive functioning as informed by behavior-genetic research. The design of the chapter is as follows. First we describe the phenomenon of individual differences in cognition. We then show how this phenomenon is studied in the behavior-genetic approach. Finally, we summarize the current state of knowledge regarding understanding the sources of individual differences in cognition.

The Behavior-Genetic Approach to Studying Individual Differences

THE CONCEPT OF INDIVIDUAL DIFFERENCES

If we enter a randomly selected classroom in any nonspecialized school in any corner of the world and look at the children in this classroom, at first glance we will notice how different these children are. They are different in height and weight, their bodies are formed differently, and their noses and eyes have different shapes. Then, if we look at the class yearbook or talk to a teacher, we will discover that all of these children differ as well in terms of their academic performance and abilities. In other words, in any randomly chosen group of children (or adults, for that matter), we will find a significant amount of variation in virtually any trait we observe. Almost everything that can be measured or counted in human beings demonstrates variation around the mean (average) value in a given population. The concept traditionally used to refer to such variation in human traits (height, weight, facial features, academic performance, etc.) is that of *individual differences*.

The existence of individual differences in the ways people think and learn attracted the attention of philosophers many centuries ago. These philosophers proposed theories to account for the sources of variation between people. The assumption made was quite simple: If people vary in the way they think, there should be some natural explanation of this variation. Two hypotheses dominated philosophical thinking and still dominate much thinking today: (1) People are born to be the way they are (**genetic determinism**) or (2) people learn to be the way they are (**environmentalism**).

There have been many attempts to verify both hypotheses, both philosophical and scientific. In this chapter, we concentrate on the scientific endeavors. As a result of massive scientific efforts, much information has been accumulated. The consensus today, however, is that there is not just a single source of individual differences. Rather, the appearance of variation between people (sometimes called *interindividual variation*) in any population is the product of a complex interplay of two forces, which are globally referred to as genes and environment.

GENES AND ENVIRONMENT

The paradigm

How did the idea come about that genes and environments may be relevant to cognition? The idea to look for links of genes and environment to cognitive functioning is relatively new, but its philosophical framework was formulated many centuries ago. The roots of this idea are in the well-known **nature versus nurture controversy** that has been around for ages. The main idea (albeit a misformulated one) underlying this controversy is that genes and environment act separately. Within the framework of the nature–nurture controversy, genes and environments are viewed as independent forces; the extreme polar examples of this controversy are the assumptions that genes determine one's fate or that environments completely shape one's individuality.

The nature–nurture controversy has many faces, including the **nativism–empiricism** issue in the psychology of sensation and perception, the issue of **maturation** versus learning in developmental psychology, and the issue of environmental equipotentiality (i.e., we all have the same potential to learn and benefit from environmental experiences) versus biological preparedness (i.e., we are genetically different in our ability to learn from our environments) in the psychology of learning and cognition (for more details, see Kimble, 1994). At the end of the nineteenth century, a British scientist, Francis Galton (1869), narrowed the nature–nurture controversy down to an opposition between heredity and environment. With the discovery of genes as units of heredity, the controversy took its current form of the "genes versus environment" debate. The motivation for formulating such an opposition is obvious – knowing that people differ in the ways they think, scientists wanted to understand *why* they differ and, subsequently, what (if anything) can be done to minimize (or maximize) these differences. In other words, knowing that there is variation in cognitive functions between people, scientists want to understand the sources of this variation and how to control them.

Studies investigating sources of variability in behavioral traits presently are being conducted in different fields, among which are developmental psychology, **differential psychology** (that branch of psychology which deals with individual differences between people), quantitative genetics, molecular genetics, psychiatric genetics, behavior genetics, and others. For the sake of brevity, in this chapter we will refer to all these studies as *behavior-genetic* studies. Such studies are the focus of attention in this chapter.

DEFINITION OF TERMS

Four definitions are essential at the outset for the terms *phenotype, genotype, components of the phenotypic variance,* and *familial resemblance.*

Phenotype

One of the most important concepts for this chapter is the concept of **phenotype**. *Phenotype* refers to *apparent, observable, measurable characteristics of the individual.* Behavior is a phenotype. Cognition is a phenotype. When a given phenotype (e.g., IQ) is measured in a population of individuals and characteristics of the distribution of this measure are obtained, the variance of this distribution is referred to as *phenotypic variance.* The concept of phenotypic variance as a behavior-genetic concept is analogous to that of individual differences used in psychology.

Genotype

Another important concept is the concept of **genotype**. *Genotype* refers to *the genetic composition of the individual.* At the present time, there are no known genes that have been definitively identified as contributing to normal interindividual variation in cognition, although research is being carried out in this regard (see, e.g., Ball et al., 1998; Daniels et al., 1998; Petrill et al., 1998; Plomin, McClearn, & Smith, 1994, 1995; Skuder et al., 1995). Therefore, in the context of this chapter, we will refer to the genotype as an unobservable, latent characteristic of the individual that manifests itself in cognitive phenotypes.

Causal components of the phenotypic variance

The importance of the phenotype–genotype distinction is that it depicts the relation between the observable and unobservable characteristics: an observable trait (phenotype) is not a perfect indicator of the individual's latent qualities (genotype).

Plate 3.2 Frances and Philippa are identical (monozygotic or MZ) twins and share the same genes. Identical twins who are reared in the same home have their genes and environments in common, and an important comparison is between the similarities in IQ (or other measure of phenotypic variation) between identical twins reared together and those reared apart. Nonidentical (dizygotic, fraternal, or DZ) twins have half of their genes in common.

These differences between the phenotype and the corresponding genotype can be accounted for by environmental influences. For example, **monozygotic (identical) twins** have identical genotypes, yet one might have a higher IQ than the other because of differences in environment.

An individual has a given genotype and is exposed to a given environment at a given point of time, so that a person has one "overall" phenotype at any given time. The phrase "at any given time" implies that the individual's environment varies over time. The degree to which environmental changes would influence the phenotypic value depends on what is being measured. For example, whereas the outcome of a measurement of a person's height does not depend on daily environment, the outcome of a measurement of a person's verbal ability might vary daily, depending on the person's mental alertness or general state of mind.

In its somewhat more sophisticated form, this model may also include an inter-active term, referring to possible interactions (combinations) of genetic and environmental effects. For example, suppose that parents who have a medium to high genetic endowment provide children with a strong environment that nurtures the children's cognitive abilities, whereas parents with a low genetic endowment provide only a weak environment. Then genetic and environmental factors, as mediated by the parents, are interacting in the children's cognitive development. It is important to realize that attempts to quantify gene–environment interaction can be made only for groups of individuals. We have no way of quantifying the interaction for individuals.

The model may also involve gene–environment covariation, which means that some-times, genes and environment produce effects that are indistinguishable from each other (this effect is discussed later, under the heading of *gene–environment correlation*). To take a simplified case, suppose that children with a certain set of genes that predispose them to musical talents all beg their parents to buy them instruments and music lessons, whereas children without this set of genes do not. The parents agree to the request. Is the effect genetic or environmental? Well, in a certain sense, it is both. The genes led the children to behave in a certain way that encouraged the parents to allow the children to play instruments. But the buying of the instruments and lessons was certainly environmental; without it, no musical skills would have come to fruition. Genes and environment covaried to produce a given effect.

The reader might ask why ideas about genetic and environmental effects, as well as their interaction and covariation, apply at the population level and not at the individual level. The answer to this question is provided in the next section.

Familial resemblance

There are two methods for determining each of the components of the phenotypic variance: (1) measuring response to genetic selection, and (2) assessing resemblance between relatives (**familial resemblance**). The first method assumes the breeding of organisms selectively for a given trait and then measuring the outcome of the genetic experiments. The structure of modern human society is such that, due to our ethical norms and values, we do not wish to do such breeding with humans. What we can do, however, is utilize the second method. We can benefit from so-called natural experiments and assess resemblances between relatives, finding spontaneously occurring situations in which (a) genetic influences are either controlled or randomized so that the effects of the environment can be studied or (b) environmental influences are controlled so that the effects of genes can be studied. So, what is the rationale behind quantifying familial resemblance?

We start with the fact that relatives share genes. *Monozygotic* (identical) twins share all of their genes. A parent and his or her offspring have half of their genes in common. Two siblings share, on average, half of their genes. **Dizygotic (fraternal) twins**, like regular siblings, also share half of their genes. Half-siblings have a quarter of their genes in common, on average, and so on. Moreover, relatives who live in one home share the family environment. Thus, both genetic and environmental hypotheses predict similarity between relatives living together. This similarity is usually measured by covariance or correlation on a given trait between relatives.

For example, the correlation of IQs between pairs of unrelated individuals picked at random is about 0. This absence of a positive correlation makes sense because such individuals share neither genes nor environment, and hence their scores do not resemble each other. Other relationships, however, yield both genes and environment in common. For example, in one analysis, the correlation for IQ between identical twins reared together is 0.86 and between fraternal twins reared together is 0.60. The correlation between the IQs of siblings reared together is 0.47, and the correlation between cousins is 0.15 (Chipuer, Rovine, & Plomin, 1990). In other words, for a given trait (e.g., IQ), the correlation between relatives could be explained by the genetic variance and the environmental variance resulting from genetic and environmental influences shared between relatives.

The simplest illustration of how components of phenotypic variance can be determined from studying relatives comes from studying identical and fraternal twins. Identical twins reared together share 100 percent of their genes and 100 percent of their family environment. Fraternal twins reared together share only 50 percent of their genes and close to 100 percent of their family environment.

Thus, the components of phenotypic variance can be determined by combining various types of relatives and comparing the measures of their similarity on the trait. Behavior-genetic studies use a variety of methods (e.g., the family method, twin method, adoption/separation method) in which the degree of resemblance between relatives of different degrees is assessed.

In this section, we defined the fundamental terms of the chapter. In addition, we summarized the reasoning behind quantifying phenotypic variance and stated that the components of the phenotypic variance could be estimated based on the assessment of trait similarity in relatives who share various degrees of genetic similarity. Now, with the necessary background reviewed, the rest of the discussion will center around the following questions:

- What are the factors that determine interindividual variation in cognitive functioning?
- What are the major concepts used to study these factors?
- What is the current state of knowledge regarding the relative contributions of genes and environments to variation in cognition?

The Forces Determining Individual Differences in Cognition

Current behavioral-genetic conceptualizations of the forces determining individual differences in cognition distinguish three major groups of factors: genetic, environmental, and interactional. Let us consider each of them separately.

GENETIC INFLUENCES (G): TYPES AND EFFECTS

Every normal human cell has two copies of each **chromosome**, one inherited from the mother and one from the father. Chromosomes are made of genetic material, called

DNA, organized into genes, which are templates for the synthesis of the proteins crucial in the functioning of our organism. There are 23 pairs of chromosomes in all human cells, except for sperm or egg cells, where this number is halved, so that each egg and each sperm receives only one copy of each chromosome. Twenty-two chromosomal pairs are identical in male and female organisms; these chromosomes are called **autosomes**. Autosomes look similar in males and females. The twenty-third pair determines sex. Sex chromosomes in men and women are very different. Females have two (large) X chromosomes; males have a single X and a (smaller) Y. Every gene exists in two copies, maternal and paternal (with the exception, of course, of the Y chromosome), as is the case for chromosomes. These gene copies (gene instantiations) are referred to as **alleles**.

Additive genetic effects

Additive genetic effects refer to the combined effects of alleles both within and between genes. If a trait is controlled by a number of genes, the additive genetic effect is calculated as a sum of contributions from every allele, each of which independently contributes a small amount to phenotypic diversity. When alleles do not interact, their joint effect on a trait is equal to a simple sum of their individual effects. Today most behavior geneticists believe that human intelligence relies on the effects of the alleles at dozens of genes; thus, many different genes of fairly small effects contribute to the trait of intelligence.

Nonadditive genetic effects

The two main types of genetic nonadditivity are *dominance* and *epistasis*. Dominance refers to types of interactions between alleles within a gene, whereas epistasis refers to types of interactions between different genes. As we will show below, both dominant and epistatic effects appear to be important in determining variation in cognitive abilities, in general, and in IQ, in particular.

ENVIRONMENTAL INFLUENCES (E): TYPES AND EFFECTS

Behavior-genetic researchers divide environmental variance into *shared* (between-family) and *nonshared* (within-family) components (see Note 1, p. 90).

Shared environmental effects

All children in a family share the same environment to the degree that, on average, psychosocial environmental characteristics (e.g., social class and parenting styles) differ from those in other families. Shared environmental effects make children reared in the same family more similar than children reared in different families. Scarr (1997) has suggested viewing between-family differences as differences in opportunities. For example, children from low **socioeconomic status (SES)** class are thought of as having fewer opportunities to develop higher cognitive abilities than do children from higher

Plate 3.3 Children raised in disadvantaged circumstances, such as this orphanage in Karachi, have fewer opportunities to develop higher cognitive abilities than do children brought up in a more stimulating and enriched home environment. Photograph © Chris Steele-Perkins/ Magnum Photos.

SES class as a result of both more stimulating home environment and the correlated school and after-school activities experienced by the higher SES children.

Nonshared environmental effects

Nonshared environmental variance refers to those aspects of the environment that make children in the same family different. Parents, no matter how hard they try, do not treat all their children in exactly the same way. Examples of within-family environment variance include a wide range of conditions, from prenatal to psychosocial events that affect one sibling differently than another sibling.

WHEN THE TWO ARE BROUGHT TOGETHER: GENE–ENVIRONMENT EFFECTS (G × E)

It long has been realized that any model sharply distinguishing between effects of "genes" and of "environments" is a simplified model that ignores several processes that are important in the appearance of variation between individuals. Two concepts depicting these processes have been suggested.

Gene–environment correlations

In most cases (with the exception of children given up for adoption or adverse social circumstances that result in externally caused family destruction), parents bestow upon their children not only their genes but also their related immediate environments and experiences. This phenomenon is referred to as *passive* **gene–environment correlation** (or covariance), as discussed earlier. One example of evidence supporting passive gene–environment correlation is the finding that social disadvantage tends to correlate with lower levels of IQ. To take the example a step further, consider the child who inherits the genes that predispose him to high IQ and who may also experience the stimulating influence of a family environment that promotes reading. Possibly, the tendency of parents to read to the child a lot may be associated with the same genes that control high IQ.

There are also other types of gene–environment correlations. *Evocative* correlations arise due to the fact that the ways in which people respond to children are influenced by the children's own characteristics (Plomin, DeFries, & Loehlin, 1977). It is possible that high-IQ children elicit different responses from their caregivers than do children of low intelligence. The example given earlier in this chapter – of children begging their parents for a musical instrument – is an example of evocative gene–environment correlation (covariation).

Active correlations arise as a result of the increased control over the environment that is experienced by growing children. Children themselves shape and organize their environments. For example, children with lower levels of intelligence tend to spend less time engaged in activities that would further stimulate their intellectual development.

Scarr and McCartney (1983) hypothesized that the roles of *passive*, *evocative*, and *active* correlations shift in their significance over the course of development, with the effects of the passive type declining, of the active type increasing, and of the evocative remaining equally important throughout the lifespan. Effects that are outcomes of gene–environment correlations are bidirectional – the observed differences, resulting from differential levels of intelligence, may in turn influence the child's later development.

Detection of genotype–environment correlations requires large sample sizes. As of today, only one **meta-analysis**, combining data from five adoption studies, has sufficient power for an analysis of the importance of passive genotype–environment correlation for IQ (Loehlin & DeFries, 1987). It was concluded that passive correlation may account for as much as 30 percent of the overall variance in IQ. However, none of the subsequent behavior-genetic studies has yet replicated this finding.

Genotype × environment interaction

Gene–environment interaction, mentioned earlier, refers to conditions in which genetically influenced characteristics mediate individual responsiveness to the encountered environment. $G \times E$ refers to the genetic control of sensitivity to environmental differences (Neale & Cardon, 1992). For example, individuals who are genetically susceptible to a disease will be free of the condition as long as the environment does not contain the pathogen; resistant individuals, those individuals who do not have the mutant gene, will be free of the disease even in a pathogenic environment. Thus, the appearance of the pathogen in the environment will have a very different impact on the phenotype of susceptible individuals as compared with its effect on the phenotype of resistant individuals. In the context of our discussion, if it were found that genetic predispositions for higher levels of cognitive abilities were actualized to a greater extent in some environments than in others, this finding would be interpreted as indicative of a genotype–environment interaction.

Although there are many examples of gene–environment interactions in biology and medicine (Rutter & Pickles, 1991), there has been little evidence of G × E interactions for variation in cognitive abilities within the normal range. For example, using data from the classic adoption study (Skodak & Skeels, 1949), Plomin et al. (1977) compared general cognitive ability scores for adopted children whose biological parents were high or low in level of education (a genotype index) and whose adoptive parents were high or low in level of education (an environment index). The level of education of the biological parents showed a significant effect on the adopted children's general cognitive ability; however, neither environmental effect for adoptive parent's education nor genotype–environment interaction was statistically significant. Similarly, the attempts to find genotype–environment interaction for cognitive ability in the Colorado Adoption Project, a large longitudinal study of adoptive families, have not been successful (Plomin, DeFries, & Fulker, 1988).

There are three possible explanations for this observation. First, most designs have rather weak power for detecting interactions, which may be small compared to the main effects of genes and environment (Wahlsten, 1990). In other words, the interactions may have been there, but undetectable by the research. Second, genotype–environment interactions for cognitive abilities, if they existed, might not be linear and might be localized in their effects. In other words, these interactions might be important at the extremes of the range of environments, but not in the typical range of environments (Turkheimer & Gottesman, 1991). For example, genotype–environment interactions might be significant within the range of environments that are thought to impede intellectual development (e.g., undernutrition, poverty, abuse, highly authoritarian parenting), but would be virtually undetectable in average nonproblematic families. Most behavior-genetic studies done to date involve middle-class families in which such disadvantaged environments are underrepresented. Third, our statistical apparatus may not be sufficiently developed to detect these interactions (Molenaar, Boomsma, & Dolan, 1999).

In previous sections we introduced the concept of individual differences, translated this concept into the behavior-genetic concept of phenotype, showed how phenotypic variation on a trait in a population could be described in terms of genetic, environmental, and interactive factors, and described all of these factors. In the next section, we discuss two other important concepts, heritability and environmentality.

 ## *Major Concepts Utilized in Behavior-Genetic Research*

The concepts of *heritability* and **environmentality** (Plomin, DeFries, & McClearn, 1990) are used in behavior-genetic studies to quantify the relative contribution of genes and environment to the observed variation on a studied trait in a given population.

WHAT HERITABILITY AND ENVIRONMENTALITY ARE . . .

Heritability

The concept of heritability (h^2), or the proportion of trait variance (phenotypic variance) due to genetic factors, is used to quantify the genetic contribution to phenotype. Heritability is the ratio of genetic variation to total variation in the trait under consideration.

Environmentality

Environmentality (e^2) is defined as the aggregate estimate of the proportion of environmental variance in the phenotype (or $1 - h^2$). Thus, heritability plus environmentality sum to 1.

. . . AND WHAT THEY ARE NOT

Both the heritability and environmentality statistics have a number of properties that are frequently misunderstood (Plomin et al., 1990; Sternberg & Grigorenko, 1997). In considering the value of these statistics, it is important to remember several things.

Heritability and environmentality are estimated variance-components, not measured effects

Neither heritability nor environmentality estimates point to measurable genetic or environmental effects. In other words, h^2 does not translate into an understanding of the biological mechanisms underlying it; obtaining a global estimate of the genotypic effect that is reflected by h^2 does not buy us an understanding of the biological mechanisms behind intellectual development. The same is true for e^2: the estimate of environmentality has yet to be linked to measured characteristics of environment that can explain observed variation in cognition.

Heritability and environmentality are not constants, and their estimates are not precise

Both heritability and environmentality refer to a particular phenotype measured in a given population at a given time. These estimates may vary from population to population and from time to time. Both h^2 and e^2 values vary across age: h^2 generally increases with age, whereas e^2 declines with age, reflecting both changes in the age-specific breakdown of genetic/environmental influences on the trait and changes in age-to-age genetic effects. Both h^2 and e^2 are estimated with a certain degree of precision involving a range of error that is a function of both sample size and type of relatives from which the estimate is obtained.

Heritability and environmentality apply to a population, not to one individual

These concepts apply to populations, not to individuals; hence, they do not say anything regarding the strength of either genetic or environmental effects in an individual's intellectual functioning. If we state that IQ has a heritability of 0.50, we mean that 50 percent of the variation in IQ observed in a given population at this time in the population's history is accounted for by genetic differences among the population's members. We do not mean that an individual whose IQ is 110 got 55 IQ points as a result of her genes and the other 55 as a result of the influences of her environment. However, if an individual from this population were about 20 IQ points smarter than the average, one could estimate (roughly) that about 50 percent of this deviation would be explainable by genetic effects and the other 50 percent due to the influence of the environment.

Heritability and environmentality do not say much about means

Almost every result and conclusion obtained in the field of behavior-genetic research relates to the *causes* of human *differences* and does not deal with the processes that account for the development of the typical expression of a trait in a particular population. Behavior-genetic research is concerned with what makes people vary around the mean of the group, population, race, or species from which they are sampled, not with what makes people score at a given level.

Suppose, for example, it were found that differences in the ability to write poetry had a significant component only of genetic (and not environmental) variation among citizens of the country Ursulandia. What would this finding tell us about the role of Ursulu culture in determining this ability? This finding could suggest two different things. It might suggest that the culture was uniform for everyone (e.g., poetry education is either compulsory and equal for everybody or absent for all), so that only genetic effects could account for variability in the ability to write poetry. Or it might mean that cultural changes were adopted by everyone so rapidly that environmental effects were not apparent. For example, let us assume that Ursulandia has undergone a war resulting in the simultaneous worsening of the living standards of most of the population; the rapid nature of this change might result in a leveling of the profile of various environments. Perhaps instead of teaching children how to write poetry, schools, due to societal hardship, a lack of financial support, and a shortage of teachers, might be forced to concentrate on teaching grammar. In other words, differential levels of poetry education as a source of environmental variability in the ability to write poetry would be absent.

Taking into account the above, it is important to understand the incorrectness of such statements as "The ability to write poetry is genetic," because the precise correct statement based on behavior-genetic analysis would instead be "Individual differences in the ability to write poetry, in this population at this point in time, are mainly genetic." It is crucial to be aware of which conclusions are justified and which are not on the basis of behavior-genetic data.

Heritability and environmentality do not refer to modification and intervention

In early behavior-genetic work, it was assumed that the degree to which a studied trait was inherited carried important implications for the quantification of the impact of environmental interventions (Jensen, 1969). Today, it is recognized that this assumption is wrong. First, intervention influences the mean of the observed variable and can raise the mean and the scores going into it. The mechanism controlling the appearance of individual differences for a given trait might not be altered, however. In other words, effects on means are independent of effects on correlations.

Second, the causes of variation derived from behavior-genetic studies relate to a particular population of individuals at a given time. Results of these studies might change as a result of the influence of factors altering the gene frequencies in the population, the expression of genes in the population, or frequencies and structures of different environments. In any case, then, any conclusions pertain only to a given population at a given time. This logic can be easily illustrated by an example from the evolutionary history of the human species. In a given population, gene frequencies have been altered multiple times due to rapid decreases in the size of a population owing to wars, hunger, or epidemics. The relocation of a population or rapid changes in climate resulted in changed expressions of genes. Cultural developments led to better schooling, reflecting a structural environmental change. This schooling gradually became accessible to the majority of populations, reflecting a change in the frequency of schooling.

Third, even when it is shown that genetic effects are important, the possibility of the existence of a rare crucial environmental factor cannot be entirely excluded. An example of such a factor is a brain injury that could result in severe mental retardation in an individual with a normal genetic endowment for intelligence. Similarly, a rare gene with a major effect may hold the key to understanding cognitive development. Due to its rarity, this gene might account only for a relatively small amount of the *total* variation in cognition, but, when present in an individual, might *almost completely* determine the course of cognitive development for that individual.

 ## *What Do We Know Today About Causes of Variation in Various Cognitive Abilities?*

So far in this chapter most of the examples have pertained to general cognitive ability as measured by IQ. There is certainly more to cognitive functioning than the functioning measured by the IQ score alone. Although there are significant correlations between most specific cognitive abilities, the levels of correlations are different enough to require a more detailed analysis of cognitive functioning than is permitted by IQ alone. Even though the number of studies of the heritability of IQ is magnitudes larger than the number of studies of the heritability of more specific cognitive abilities, there have been a few studies of the heritabilities of these specific cognitive abilities. In the following section we provide a brief overview of the behavior-genetic findings regarding heritabilities (and indirectly environmentalities) of (1) general cognitive ability and (2) specific cognitive abilities.

WHAT HAVE WE LEARNED FROM BEHAVIOR-GENETIC STUDIES ABOUT THE HERITABILITY OF GENERAL COGNITIVE ABILITY (AS APPROXIMATED BY IQ)?

The heritability and environmentality estimates of IQ have been obtained by comparing the degree of resemblance among different types of relatives. Three main methodological approaches – family, twin, and adoption/separation methods – have been utilized in behavior-genetic research.

Family studies

Since the late 1920s, when the first studies regarding familial resemblance for IQ were conducted, dozens of studies have been published (for a review, see Bouchard & McGue, 1981). There is a consensus that the data can be divided into two groups, the so-called older (conducted prior to 1980) and the so-called newer (conducted after 1980) studies. The older studies had relatively small samples, were less sophisticated methodologically, and provided rather high estimates of heritability (for a review, see Erlenmeyer-Kimling & Jarvik, 1963). The newer studies are characterized by larger sample sizes and more sophisticated methodology, and have produced lower estimates of heritability (for a review, see Plomin, 1999, 2001; Plomin & McClearn, 1993; Plomin & Petrill, 1997).

Three explanations of the differences in results have been suggested. First, the mismatch between the old and the new data may be attributable to environmental and genetic changes in the studied populations that occurred in the time frame between the new and the old studies. This explanation seems plausible for environmental effects (life has changed dramatically since the 1930s), but unlikely for genetic components (genetic changes within a population take many generations to take effect). Second, there may be a restriction of range in the new data (Caruso, 1983). The newer data have been collected primarily from middle-class white families, which offer somewhat less variation in IQ than is observed in a normal population, and limit the current findings to a group with IQs that are above average. The third and most plausible explanation highlights the role of methodological differences between the old and new studies. The methodological procedures in the newer studies are more nearly standardized. Moreover, while the older studies were extended for a longer period of time, the newer studies involved tests administered to many families at the same time in the same testing facilities.

Twin studies

The first behavioral-genetic twin study focusing on IQ was conducted by Merriman (1924). Since then, many thousands of twins around the world have served as recruits in studies of general and specific cognitive abilities. Meta-analyses of these data (Bouchard & McGue, 1981; Loehlin & Nichols, 1976) suggest a heritability of about 0.50 for general cognitive ability.

A detailed review of twin studies of cognitive abilities is beyond the scope of this chapter. However, a number of these studies have addressed specific issues that are of interest to our broad discussion. For example, **cohort changes** in the heritability of IQ were investigated in a large Norwegian study of approximately 2,000 twin pairs born from 1930 through 1960 (Sundet, Tambs, Magnus, & Berg, 1988). The question addressed was whether the implementation of the more egalitarian social and educational policies that took place in Norway after World War II influenced the degree of resemblance between monozygotic (MZ) and dizygotic (DZ) twins. No clear changes were observed: The correlations for MZ and DZ twins born from 1931 to 1935 were 0.84 and 0.51, respectively; after the war, the correlations were 0.83 and 0.51, that is, almost identical to the earlier estimates. This study is an illustration of the point made above – global societal changes typically tend to influence the *mean* of a trait rather than the mechanism for explaining individual differences.

Another important finding resulted from a study of approximately 300 pairs of same-sex MZ and DZ twins evenly distributed by gender and ages (from 5 to 23). The pairs were oversampled at the low and high ends of the IQ distribution (Thompson, Detterman, & Plomin, 1993). This study indicated, among other findings, no significant differences in heritability at either the high or the low end, although a trend toward higher heritability for children of higher ability is evident.

Yet another very important line of research originates from cognitive functioning very late in life in pairs of old (65+ years of age) and old-old (80–96 years old and older) twins. This research has been carried out in Sweden for the last 15 years and produced many interesting findings. One of these findings indicates that, although the entire range of cognitive functioning shows moderate genetic influence, the high end of the distribution appears to be highly heritable, whereas the heritability of the low end appears to be low (Petrill et al., 2001).

Among the twin studies, those carried out with MZ and DZ twins reared apart have a special value – they provide direct estimates of heritability. Bouchard (1998) has recently summarized the results of these studies. The correlations between adult MZ twins reared apart are consistently high (weighted mean = 0.75) in samples obtained from a number of western industrialized countries (United States: Bouchard, Lykken, McGue, Segal, & Tellegen, 1990; Newman, Freeman, & Holzinger, 1937; United Kingdom: Shields, 1962; Denmark: Juel-Nielsen, 1980; Sweden: Pedersen, Plomin, Nesselroade, & McClearn, 1992). The correlations (weighted mean = 0.38) between adult DZ twins reared apart (Newman, Tellegen, & Bouchard, 1998; Pedersen et al., 1992) are close but somewhat lower than the frequently reported values for same-age, first-degree relatives reared together (excluding twins, Bouchard & McGue, 1981). When doubled, the DZ correlations (see Note 2, p. 91) yield a heritability estimate close to that obtained through the correlations for MZ twins reared apart.

Adoption/separation studies

Most adoption studies, like family and twin studies, have also investigated the heritability of IQ. The range of obtained estimates of correlations between biological relatives, although broad (ranging from 0.22 to 0.72), results in a mean heritability score of about 0.50, meaning that genetic differences among individuals account for about half of the variation in their performance on IQ tests.

The bulk of the adoption studies have gathered data in *childhood* (Burks, 1928; Freeman, Holzinger, & Mitchell, 1928; Horn, Loehlin, & Willerman, 1979; Leahy, 1935; Scarr & Weinberg, 1977; Skodak, 1950); these data result in a variety of correlations between the adopted children and their adoptive (foster) parents, ranging from about .00 to about .60 (Bouchard, 1998). These data (age range in the studies is 4–16+ years) result in estimates of environmentality of about 0.28. In contrast, the environmentality estimate obtained from the *adult* data (i.e., when the adopted children are now adults: Loehlin, Horn, & Willerman, 1997; Scarr & Weinberg, 1978; Scarr, Weinberg, & Waldman, 1993; Teasdale & Owen, 1984) is virtually 0 (0.04).

Some interesting findings regarding the links between IQ and environmental influences were obtained by French researchers. These researchers found that the mean IQ of adoptees reared by parents of high SES was higher than that of children adopted by low-SES parents (Capron & Duyme, 1989). Moreover, children whose biological parents were of high SES scored higher than did children of parents of low SES, and school failures of adoptive children were associated with the SES of the adoptive rather than of the biological parents (Duyme, 1988). Thus, the results of the French studies point to the importance of shared environment in variation in IQ. Speculating about these and other similar findings, Loehlin (1989) suggested that significant increases in average IQ might occur as a result of radical environmental changes due to adoption. However, individual differences remain large and they appear to be mostly genetic in origin. Moreover, a recent review of adoption studies (Locurto, 1990) concludes that these studies provide modest evidence, at best, for environmental effects on cognitive abilities.

Importance of age and developmental genetic analyses

The striking effect of age on both heritability and environmentality estimates, which escaped the attention of Bouchard and McGue (1981) in their review of the world's IQ kin correlations, is considered now one of the most interesting discoveries of the past decade. Genetic influences on intelligence are not homogeneous across the lifespan (McGue, Bouchard, Iacono, & Lykken, 1994; Plomin, 1986). Heritability increases from about 40 percent in childhood to about 60 percent in early adulthood to about 80 percent in later life, dropping somewhat (to 60–70 percent) in the very late life (Bouchard, 1998; McClearn et al., 1997; Plomin & Petrill, 1997). These findings appear to be somewhat counterintuitive – the change occurs at about the time young people leave their parental homes, effectively minimizing the importance of shared environment as a source of relative resemblance. The nature of these findings is unclear. One of the working hypotheses is that genetic endowment drives us to select environments in which our genetic potentials, in turn, become accentuated (Plomin & Petrill, 1997).

The accumulation of the data stresses the importance of considering the age factor in quantifying contribution of genes to individual differences in general cognitive ability, leading to the appearance of studies introducing **longitudinal design** into behavior-genetic research. Longitudinal design allows researchers to investigate the importance of genes for age-to-age change and continuity. First longitudinal behavior-genetic analyses suggest some genetic involvement in transition from early to middle childhood (Fulker, Cherny, & Cardon, 1993) and from middle childhood to late adolescence (Loehlin, Horn, & Willerman, 1989). Thus, it is possible that individual differences in cognitive abilities attributable to genetic influences result not only from variation in genes working throughout the lifespan, but also from variation in genes turning on and off only at certain developmental stages.

SUMMARY COMMENTS

Four comments should be made regarding the findings resulting from the studies of the heritability of general cognitive ability. First, numerous family, twin, and adoption studies have been combined into global analyses using a model-fitting approach (Chipuer et al., 1990; Loehlin, 1989). This approach allows one to analyze simultaneously the data collected in different studies and to obtain more elaborate and precise estimates of genetic and environmental contributions than is possible by comparing simple correlations. The outcome of these analyses places the estimate of heritability of intelligence at 50–51 percent (Plomin & Neiderhiser, 1991), placing it midway between 0.1 and 0.9 and indicating approximately equal effects of both genetic and nongenetic influences.

Second, heritability estimates vary depending on the method by which they were obtained. In particular, h^2 appears to be higher when it is obtained by comparing the resemblance between individuals reared apart than when it is obtained by comparing the similarity of individuals reared together.

Third, along with the importance of additive genetic components arising from summative main effects of a number of genes, researchers (Chipuer et al., 1990) have demonstrated the contribution of nonadditive genetic effects, pointing to the importance of allele–allele and gene–gene interaction (i.e., dominance and epistasis).

Finally, behavior-genetic studies of intelligence have revealed a number of findings regarding environmental influences. For example, it has been found that shared and nonshared environmental influences account for approximately the same amount of variance (10–30 percent), with the percentage of the *shared* environmental contribution higher for closer relatives (35 percent for twins, 22 percent for siblings, 11 percent for cousins) and, symmetrically, the percentage of *nonshared* environmental contribution higher for more distant relatives (38 percent for cousins, 27 percent for siblings, and 14 percent for twins).

These conclusions have been challenged, however, by both those who question the underlying theory and those who question the nature of the data. Theoretical challenges of the global heritability estimates come from (1) those who deny the importance of genetic effects (Schiff & Lewontin, 1986); (2) those who suggest that the magnitudes of environmental effects are almost negligible within the normal range of environments (Rowe, 1994; Scarr, 1992, 1997); and (3) those who question the generalizability of these findings (Waldman, 1997).

Those who deny the importance of genetic effects

Researchers who deny the importance of genetic effects point to various inconsistencies in the evidence accumulated from different studies. However, supporters of heritability studies counter that, when considered as a whole, the evidence is unequivocal in pointing to a substantial genetic effect (Plomin & Neiderhiser, 1991; Rutter & Madge, 1976). Though individual studies are often controversial, and the range of heritability estimates is enormous – between 0.1 (Matheny, Wilson, Dolan, & Krantz, 1981) and 0.9 (Iskol'dsky, 1988) – if one "mixes" them together and estimates the heritability of IQ based on weighted correlations, the estimate comes out to be around 0.5.

Those who suggest that the magnitudes of environmental effects are almost negligible

Those researchers who doubt the importance of environmental effects point to the following two lines of reasoning. First, they refer to the failure of research to account for the 50 percent of nongenetic effects when researchers attempt to assign the estimated environmental variance to specific measured environmental variables (Cherny, 1994). Thus, even though we have an estimate of the nongenetic effect for IQ, we have no idea what concrete environmental forces are reflected in this estimate. The second point of argument is the "purity" of environmental measures. In particular, researchers have found that many environmental measures, ranging from SES to parenting styles, are still partially under genetic control, and therefore not purely environmental (Plomin, 1994, 1995; Plomin & Bergeman, 1991; Posner, Baker, & Martin, 1994). In other words, many of those variables that were taken in the past to be measures of shared environment appear to be, at least in part, influenced by genes, as when parents with genes for high intelligence are "led" by these genes to provide good environments for their children.

Those who question the generalizability of the findings

A serious concern regarding the generalizability of findings on the heritability of intelligence arises from the fact that most of the data have come from predominantly white, middle-class, North American and European populations. Therefore, the generalizability of these findings is quite limited. Very few "other" populations have been studied (e.g., Lynn & Hattori, 1990; Moore, 1986; Nathwar & Puri, 1995; Pal, Shyam, & Singh, 1997; Scarr & Weinberg, 1977; Scarr et al., 1993). As has been pointed out earlier, heritability estimates are population-specific, and extreme caution is necessary when extending the current knowledge to different populations. Moreover, the vast majority of the correlations for relatives have been derived from samples of individuals between 9 and 20 years of age (Bouchard & McGue, 1981; McGue et al., 1994). There are very few studies addressing the issues of heritability of general cognitive ability outside of these age ranges, but these studies, as mentioned earlier, suggest that heritability estimates vary at different developmental stages. The mechanism of this variability is as yet unclear.

WHAT HAVE WE LEARNED FROM BEHAVIOR-GENETIC STUDIES ABOUT THE HERITABILITY OF SPECIFIC COGNITIVE ABILITIES?

As much as behavior-genetic ideas influence psychology (Waldman, 1997), psychological theories penetrate the field of behavior genetics and influence the heritability-based studies. Even though **g** (general cognitive ability, usually approximated by IQ) remains the king or queen ruling the kingdom of h^2 (heritability) research, attempts have been made to introduce some other cognitive abilities into the kingdom. Although scant, some attention has been given to studying specific cognitive abilities, especially verbal and nonverbal abilities. The general conclusion today is an expected one – specific abilities are differentially heritable (e.g., Cardon & Fulker, 1994; Grigorenko, in press).

The first assessment of heritabilities of specific cognitive abilities was conducted by Vandenberg (1968a, 1968b). In his twin studies, Vandenberg obtained evidence for genetic influences on some abilities (verbal, spatial, and language), but not on others (memory, numerical, reasoning skills). This result has been interpreted as evidence that genetic factors play a more significant role in determining individual variation in some cognitive domains than in others. In an attempt to expand these findings, Vandenberg formulated a hypothesis that what is heritable in specific cognitive abilities is the variance that is accounted for by the g factor. In other words, he suggested the presence of a genetic g with environmental contributions determining a specific h^2/e^2 ratio of various cognitive abilities. A series of Vandenberg's studies was designed to verify this hypothesis. The results yielded evidence both for and against this hypothesis, indicating both a genetic endowment of the correlated components of cognitive abilities (Bock & Vandenberg, 1968; Loehlin & Vandenberg, 1968) as well as unique genetic contributions to various abilities (Vandenberg, 1968a).

Unfortunately, subsequent studies have not much clarified the picture. A number of twin studies (Loehlin & Nichols, 1976; Martin & Eaves, 1977; Martin, Jardine, & Eaves, 1984; Plomin & DeFries, 1979), family studies (DeFries et al., 1979; Spuhler & Vandenberg, 1980), and adoption/separation studies (Horn, Loehlin, & Willerman, 1982; Plomin, 1988) have presented results suggesting the presence of genetic factors for some specific abilities (most consistently, verbal and/or spatial), but not for others. For example, Scarr and Weinberg (1978), in their adoption study, found significant correlations between biological relatives, whereas the correlations between adoptive parents and their adopted children on virtually all studied measures of specific cognitive abilities were mostly not statistically significant. The exception is vocabulary scores, which appear to be influenced by shared environment in addition to genes. In addition to the ongoing debate regarding which specific abilities are controlled by genes and which are not, little agreement is present on the magnitude of genetic influence.

Horn (1988) reported results from a behavior-genetic study of eight mental measures mapping Cattell's higher-order factors of **fluid** and **crystallized** abilities. According to Cattell (1941), variability in fluid ability is due primarily to genes, whereas variability in crystallized ability is due primarily to environmental factors. In contrast, Horn found that variation in both abilities is approximately 60 percent heritable, but that the genetic variance shared between these abilities is only about 14 percent, suggesting that, most likely, the abilities are influenced by different sets of genes.

One of the largest studies of specific cognitive abilities, the Hawaii Family Study of Cognition (DeFries et al., 1979), fanned another controversy. Fifteen different cognitive tests were administered to over 6,000 individuals. Factor analysis yielded four groups of factors: (1) verbal (vocabulary and fluency), (2) spatial (visualizing and rotating objects in space), (3) perceptual speed (simple arithmetic and number comparison), and (4) visual memory (short- and long-term recollection of line drawings). In addition to differences in heritabilities for the four factors, it was found that tests within each factor also demonstrated a wide range in familial resemblance. For example, one spatial test, requiring cutting a figure to yield a certain pattern, showed a heritability of about 0.60. On the contrary, another spatial test, involving drawing one line and connecting as many dots as possible, showed the lowest familial resemblance (about 0.27), and thus the lowest heritability.

Based on the findings of the Hawaii study, researchers involved in the Colorado Adoption Project (Alárcon, Plomin, Fulker, Corley, & DeFries, 1999; Plomin et al., 1988), an ongoing study of specific cognitive abilities, assessed four broad cognitive domains: verbal comprehension, spatial visualization, memory, and perceptual speed. The results (Cardon & Fulker, 1994) showed that these different abilities are influenced, in part, by the same genes, and, in part, by separate genes acting independently from each other. Due to the longitudinal nature of their data, the researchers have successfully demonstrated that the ability-specific genes are pervasive in their effects throughout young childhood. However, the presence of novel genetic influences was detected for 7-year-olds in the study. These influences have been shown to continue to affect variation in ability for 9-year-olds. The environmental analysis showed a large role of nonshared environmental factors, which were found to be important at each age and which exhibited lasting effects throughout childhood. This finding has been interpreted as an indicator that childhood experiences may play an important role for a specific ability at the time of their occurrence, as well as perhaps having a generalized effect on all mental skills. These results suggest that educational or childrearing changes that might influence verbal learning at a given age might also influence both verbal and performance abilities in later childhood.

Although recent studies of twins reared apart generally have supported the findings from other studies indicating that heritabilities of major mental abilities cluster around .50, recent studies of twins reared apart suggest somewhat lower heritabilities for memory abilities (Finkel & McGue, 1993; Finkel, Pedersen, McGue, & McClearn, 1995). Similarly, although somewhat variable in their magnitude, heritability estimates from different memory tests administered to twins reared together are rather low (Thapar, Petrill, & Thompson, 1995).

Another dimension of cognition that has been studied is creativity. Creativity demonstrates little genetic influence. A review of ten studies of twins (Nichols, 1978) presented mean correlations for creativity of 0.61 for identical twins and 0.50 for fraternal twins. However, when controlled for IQ, twin correlations for creativity tests become indistinguishable from zero (Canter, 1973). Thus, it appears that the heritability of creativity, estimated at 20 percent, is primarily due to existing correlations between creativity and IQ.

There also have been a few studies of specific cognitive abilities carried out in countries outside of Western Europe and North America. A recent study of Croatian adolescent twins yielded heritability estimates for verbal and spatial abilities similar to those found in the United States (Bratko, 1996). An Egyptian study, however, reported lower heritabilities (Abdel-Rahim, Nagoshi, & Vandenberg, 1990).

The heritability of specific abilities: A summary

In summary, tests of some cognitive abilities, primarily verbal and spatial, demonstrate significant and often substantial genetic influence throughout the lifespan. In contrast, it appears that memory abilities, perceptual speed, and creativity are influenced by heredity less (if at all). In concluding this discussion, we would like to make four comments.

First, whereas the number of behavior-genetic studies of IQ is exceedingly high, there is only a handful of studies on specific cognitive abilities. These studies are characterized by heterogeneity of both underlying theoretical models (e.g., Cattell, 1971, versus Thurstone, 1938) and of the assessment instruments used. Thus, the observed apparently contradictory nature of findings might change when more data are accumulated.

Second, a special concern in interpreting these studies is the diversity of definitions and operationalizations of constructs utilized in the studies. For example, in studies of creativity, the indicators range from the measures obtained from the *Torrance Test of Creative Thinking* to raters' evaluations of creativity in the subjects' writings. When there is no agreement on the definition of the studied trait at the phenotypic level, it is unlikely that the results of heritability studies will arrive at a consensus.

Third, lower heritability estimates, obtained for specific cognitive abilities, might reflect inadequate redistribution of the phenotypic variance due to considerably less reliable measures used for assessment of these abilities. For example, the fact that behavior-genetic studies of creativity utilize measures whose test-retest reliability is quite (often unacceptably) low might result in attenuation of the genetic factor estimates.

Fourth, a distinct characteristic of specific-abilities studies is the gap between the richness of psychological theories of cognition existing in modern cognitive psychology and their oversimplified applications in behavior-genetic studies. Thus, the findings might have been more homogeneous were the data obtained in correspondence with modern theories of cognitive abilities.

SUMMARY AND CONCLUSIONS

To understand why people vary in cognitive abilities, one must know what sources contribute to individual differences and what the magnitudes of these contributions are. Hence, the problem of heredity and environment and their co-contribution to variation in cognitive functioning has always attracted and will always attract the attention of many psychologists and cognitive scientists.

Many and varied attempts have been made to understand and to theorize about the sources of individual differences in cognition. This chapter presented an overview of only one of those traditions striving to solve the puzzle of individual differences in cognition, the *behavior-genetic approach*. According to this approach, the phenomenon of individual differences on a studied ability might be translated into the phenotypic variance that can be decomposed into genetic, environmental, and interactive components. These components can be estimated by means of comparing relatives of various degrees of genetic similarity. When phenotype is measured in relatives, those who are more closely related genetically are expected to be more similar on the studied ability than those who are genetically more distant.

Behavior-genetic studies of cognitive functioning have investigated both general and specific cognitive abilities. Almost 50 years of intensive research of general cognitive ability (approximated by IQ) have revealed a robust estimate of its heritability. It appears that about 50 percent of interindividual variation in IQ can be explained by genetic influences. Another 50 percent of the variation is accounted for by environmental factors. Today researchers try to extend their findings beyond the estimates of heritability and environmentality to find specific genes and specific measurable environmental factors that contribute to these estimates.

Specific cognitive abilities, however, have been significantly less explored. Not enough work has been done to warrant firm conclusions concerning the relative contributions of genes and environment to phenotypic variance for specific cognitive abilities. As of today, it appears that variation in verbal and spatial abilities might be largely under genetic control; however, the significance of nonshared environmental influences also appears to be crucial. Much as with IQ research, even though it has been suggested that the environment plays a significant role in such specific cognitive abilities as perceptual speed and memory, specific environmental components that influence this variation have not yet been identified.

Recent behavior-genetic studies apply sophisticated methodologies in order to go beyond initial heritability and environmentality estimates and to (1) sharpen the existing estimates by minimizing the measurement error, (2) explore sex differences in the ways genes and the environment operate, (3) detect both genetic and environmental influences that will "fit" in the estimated portion of variance, and (4) explore the role of both genotype–environment correlations and interactions. Fifty years of behavior-genetic studies of cognitive functions have brought us to believe that genes are important for virtually every measured cognitive ability. And when genes are secondary, the leading role belongs to environment. We know that both genes and environments are responsible for individual differences. The next task is to address the questions of *which* (which genes and which environments) and *how* (what biological and social-cultural pathways determine mechanisms of cognitive development). Both are exciting tasks that will be in the center of behavior-genetic research for the next decade or more.

NOTES

1   Note that these distinctions are relevant only for pairs of relatives. In other words, when data collected for relatives of a given degree (e.g., identical twins reared together) are subjected to behavior-genetic analyses, the shared environment variance-component is that component which describes the variance attributable to environmental influences shared between given relatives (e.g., identical twins reared together, while staying in their parents' house, experience the SES level of their parents to the same degree – they *share* the wealth (or

the lack of it) of their parents), whereas the nonshared environment variance-component describes the variance attributable to influences specific to each twin (e.g., different friends, different schools).

2   The most frequently used method in the twin literature is that utilizing the formula $2(r_{MZT} - r_{DZT})$ (Falconer, 1990). The reasoning behind this formula is this: Given that the environments of MZ and DZ twins are equal, their respective correlations reflect the difference in the proportions of genes they share (MZ share 100 percent of the genes and DZ share 50 percent of the genes). This way of calculating h^2 makes two assumptions, the assumption of the equal environment of MZ and DZ twins and the assumption of the additive nature of all genetic variance, both of which have been questioned in the literature (e.g., Grigorenko & Carter, 1996; Chipuer et al., 1990, respectively).

DISCUSSION POINTS

1   The concepts of heritability and environmentality are vitally important in an understanding of the nature–nurture issue. Consider how they reflect genetic and environmental contributions to individual differences.
2   Why are twin studies important in gaining an understanding of the contributions of genes and environment to human development?
3   Think of ways in which heritability (genetic contribution to individual differences) can be high for a particular ability, but the ability is still highly influenced by the environment.
4   Consider why it is that the causes of genetic variation (heritability) derived from behavior-genetic studies only relate to a particular population at a given time.
5   Consider some of the ways in which genetic and environmental factors can interact in causing development.
6   What do we know about the heritability of general versus specific cognitive abilities?

SUGGESTIONS FOR FURTHER READING

Ceci, S. J., & William, W. M. (1999). *The nature/nurture debate: Essential readings.* Cambridge, MA, and Oxford: Blackwell.

Plomin, R. (1994). *Genetics and experience: The developmental interplay between nature and nurture.* Newbury Park, CA: Sage.

Plomin, R., & McClearn, D. L. (Eds.) (1993). *Nature and nurture.* Washington, DC: American Psychological Association.

Sternberg, R. J., & Grigorenko, E. L. (Eds.) (1997). *Intelligence, heredity, and environment.* New York: Cambridge University Press.

Sternberg, R. J., & Grigorenko, E. L. (Eds.) (2001). *Environmental effects on intellectual functioning.* Mahwah, NJ: Erlbaum.

part II

Infancy

Contents

chapter 4

Prenatal Development

William P. Fifer and Christine Moon

KEY CONCEPTS

- AUTOSOMAL GENETIC DISORDERS
- AXON
- CEREBRAL CORTEX
- CHEMOSENSORY DEVELOPMENT
- CHROMOSOMES
- CIRCADIAN RHYTHM
- COCHLEA
- EMBRYO

- FETUS
- MEIOTIC CELL DIVISION
- MYELIN
- MYELINATION
- NEURON
- ONTOGENY
- POSTNATAL DEVELOPMENT
- PRENATAL DEVELOPMENT
- PRETERM

- RODS AND CONES
- ROOTING REFLEX
- SYNAPSE
- SYNAPTOGENESIS
- TRANSNATAL LEARNING (PERINATAL LEARNING)
- TRIMESTER
- VESTIBULAR SYSTEM

OVERVIEW

There is a tendency to treat psychological development as something that begins at birth, and yet an enormous amount takes place before birth, and it is vital that we understand the fetal period if we are to put infant development in a proper context.

Investigations of development of the brain and spinal cord reveal fascinating self-organizing processes through which nerve cells grow, migrate, and become appropriately interconnected, forming pathways between the brain and peripheral organs. A major change within the brain concerns the development of the cerebral cortex, which is fairly mature by 27 weeks and exerts an increasing control over the fetus's activities.

Early in development, the fetus is engaged in almost constant movement. Later in development, however, clear sleep–wake cycles become established and behavior comes more under cortical control. Many of the movements that the fetus engages in are likely to be important for the development of motor systems. For instance, approaching term, fetal breathing becomes increasingly frequent and is probably important for lung development in preparation for birth.

The senses become functional between 8 and 26 weeks, with touch developing first, followed by taste and smell, the vestibular sense, hearing, and finally vision. It is interesting to note that development of most sensory systems is likely to be influenced by sensory input arising in the uterine environment. However, the exception is vision, for which there is no significant sensory input prior to birth. And yet, by the time of birth the visual system is remarkably well developed. This can be contrasted with the case of the auditory system, which, prior to birth, is exposed to auditory input, particularly from the mother's voice. There is striking evidence that the fetus actually learns about his or her mother's voice prior to birth.

The chapter then addresses risks to fetal development. These include both genetic and environmental factors. In the first category, chromosomal defects lead to problems such as Down's syndrome. In the environmental category, heavy maternal alcohol intake can have dramatic effects on fetal development and may lead to cognitive and behavioral impairments in the child. Maternal smoking can also have detrimental effects, particularly on fetal growth rate, and adequate nutrition is important for normal physical and psychological development.

The chapter ends by pointing out the important continuities that exist between developmental processes prior to and following birth. For instance, it seems likely that individual differences in temperament are to a large extent established before the infant is born. Continuing developments in technology for measuring fetal behavior are liable to uncover progressively more of the detail regarding relationships between fetal development and infant behavior.

Introduction

The roots of child development are being uncovered by investigating neurobehavioral development during the fetal period. The identification of fetal phenotypes, i.e. characteristics, capacities, and patterns of activity, and the underlying brain–behavior relationships, is a critical step toward understanding the origins of normal and abnormal developmental trajectories. As is the case throughout infancy, normal development demands constant and complex interactions between genes, environment, and the emerging organism. Fuller appreciation now exists regarding the long-term implications of the fetal adaptation to a changing uterine environment that is unique for each maternal/child dyad. The impact of prenatal experience occurs on multiple levels, from biochemical factors influencing gene expression in the fetus's neuronal circuitry to characteristics of the mother's lifestyle affecting the fetal environment. More specifically, cells acquire identities; nerve fibers, i.e., **axons**, are guided from the periphery to target, connections between some cells are induced and reinforced, and other cells are programmed to die based on and shaped by exquisitely timed, complex interactions between the genes and environmental input. At another level, sensory systems are being sculpted by environmental input. The complexity and need for intrauterine stimulation is just beginning to be appreciated. In what follows, we describe fetal neurobehavioral development throughout gestation and, in particular, focus on the role of the *in utero* environment in facilitating and directing fetal growth and behavior.

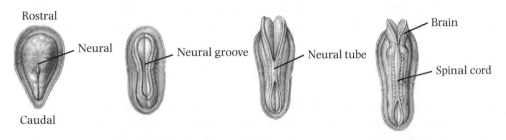

Figure 4.1 The development of the neural tube into the spinal cord and primitive brain. Adapted from J. H. Martin, *Neuroanatomy Text and Atlas*, 2nd ed. (Stamford, CT: Appleton & Lange, 1996). Reproduced with permission of the McGraw-Hill Companies.

 ## *The Brain, the Spinal Cord and the Emergence of Mind*

Early in the second month of pregnancy, the fetal nervous system begins to develop. This will be the future control center for all of the child's thoughts, actions, and emotions. Despite the immense complexity of the adult nervous system, its initial development is simple and very rapid. The outer layer of the **embryo** thickens lengthways to form two folds with a groove running between them. The folds grow toward each other and the groove becomes a tube. The top of the tube then swells to form a primitive brain, while the rest of the tube becomes the spinal cord.

There is a hierarchy of control systems within the nervous system which basically determine what the **fetus** is doing and when. The hierarchical structure becomes more complex as the unborn infant develops. The larger the repertoire, the greater the need for organization by the nervous system. Initially, behaviors are of a reflexive nature, and the circuitry controlling them may consist only of a few sensory cells directly connected to some motor cells – these may be found in the spinal cord and work independently of the brain. The spinal cord is made up of nerves that carry messages back and forth from the trunk and limbs to the brain. The types of behavior mediated by the spinal cord are likely to be the early movements seen starting around 7–8 weeks of pregnancy.

SUBDIVISIONS OF THE PRIMITIVE BRAIN

The primitive brain is divided into three basic parts, forebrain at the front, midbrain, and hindbrain. By 9 weeks, the forebrain subdivides: two cerebral hemispheres are formed at the front; the outer layer of these later forms the **cerebral cortex**. The cerebral cortex is the area of the brain that is associated with complex tasks such as memory, language, and thought, and the control and integration of movement and the senses. The area of the forebrain behind the cerebral hemispheres serves as the relay center for the brain, passing sensory information to the cerebral cortex, and translating nerve impulses into conscious sensations. The midbrain is the control center for reflexes such as blinking in response to an approaching object. The hindbrain also further separates into areas responsible for muscle coordination and body equilibrium, and regulators for vital involuntary processes such as breathing and circulation.

Pʀᴏᴄᴇssᴇs ᴀɴᴅ sᴇǫᴜᴇɴᴄɪɴɢ ᴏғ ʙʀᴀɪɴ ᴅᴇᴠᴇʟᴏᴘᴍᴇɴᴛ

Developmental neurobiologists have begun to discover the intricate intracellular processes, including complex gene–environment interactions, leading to cell birth, differentiation, and survival as well as the pathways by which axons reach their target **neurons** and how **synapses** are formed and elaborated (Kandel, Schwartz, & Jessell, 2000). Despite their ultimate high level of specialization, all the billions of nerve cells that will comprise the nervous system originate from one single layer of identical cells in the wall of the neural tube. The cells multiply and after only 8 weeks of pregnancy, they begin to migrate, making small swimming movements until the neural tube has very distinctive layers. This process of migration continues right up to about the sixth month of pregnancy. This is followed by extensive changes in individual cells, programming them for the myriad tasks awaiting the emerging brain.

Dᴇᴠᴇʟᴏᴘᴍᴇɴᴛ ᴏғ ᴛʜᴇ ᴄᴇʀᴇʙʀᴀʟ ᴄᴏʀᴛᴇx

In terms of memory, language, and thought, the control and integration of movement and the senses, the primary part of the brain responsible is the cerebral cortex, the outer crust of the hemispheres. For the first two or three months of pregnancy there is relatively little development in this "crust." It is not surprising therefore that behaviors emerging before this time, e.g., early fetal movements, are largely reflexive and probably controlled via simpler circuits that arise in the midbrain.

The cerebral hemispheres develop from the forebrain at about 9 weeks and rapidly increase in size, expanding to form different regions that will later become highly specialized. By mid-pregnancy, the cerebral hemispheres have expanded to cover the rest of the brain. By the fourth month of pregnancy, the cells in the cerebral hemispheres begin to proliferate and migrate. As the higher centers of the brain develop, and more neural inputs become active, increasingly sophisticated messages can be sent from the brain. Particularly important at this time is that the process of inhibition becomes functional. This means when the fetus's brain sends a nerve impulse to the muscles, instead of only being able to cause movement, it can now begin to modify it. Consequently, this eventually leads to better control and refinement of movement. A by-product of this process is that at about 15 weeks there is a bit of a lull in activity. This is followed by a period of reorganization of behaviors, reflexive circuits are still in place, but these are now "controlled" by more sophisticated nerve cells in the new "higher" brain centers.

By 27 weeks, the cell numbers in the cerebral cortex are thought to be mature. However, the fetal nervous system is far from adult-like. Two major processes, **synaptogenesis** and **myelination**, are still necessary for a mature nervous system. Synaptogenesis involves the building of circuits between cells. As the circuits become more complex, larger numbers of nerves may be called into play and the fetal behavior becomes more

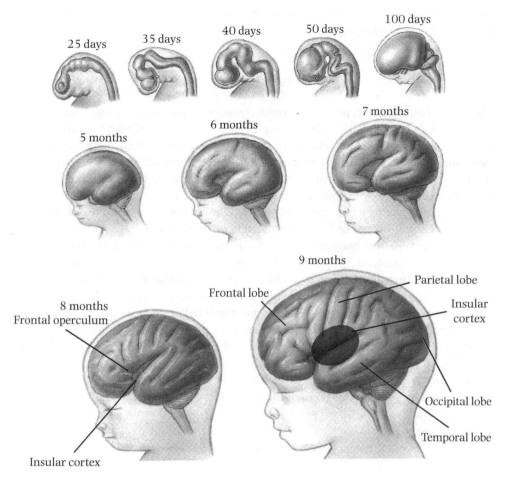

25 days   35 days   40 days   50 days   100 days

5 months   6 months   7 months

9 months

Parietal lobe
Insular cortex
Frontal lobe
8 months
Frontal operculum
Occipital lobe
Temporal lobe
Insular cortex

Figure 4.2 Development of the human fetal brain. Adapted from J. H. Martin, *Neuroanatomy Text and Atlas*, 2nd ed. (Stamford, CT: Appleton & Lange, 1996), p. 51. Reproduced with permission of the McGraw-Hill Companies.

sophisticated and coordinated. The formation of **myelin**, a fatty insulator, around the nerve fibers is also important in neural development. The myelin prevents leakage of the messages traveling along the nerve and speeds their way to and from the brain. Myelination begins in the sixth month of fetal life but continues through childhood.

Despite the immaturity of the fetal nervous system, by about 24 weeks the fetus does have a limited capacity to learn (see *Transnatal auditory learning*). The fetus responds to her environment and begins to show a very basic "memory," e.g., habituation of responding will occur to repeated auditory stimulation. By birth, the cerebral cortex consists of a large number of well-defined primary motor and sensory zones. The frontal lobe is generally thought to be associated with movement. The parietal lobe is concerned with sensation. The temporal lobe is important for hearing, memory, and a sense of self and time. The occipital lobe is the visual center of the brain. The association areas surround these, and their development is much longer since they are concerned with higher cognitive and integrative functions that develop with experience and with the emerging mind.

Behavioral Organization

The fetus's behavior is becoming progressively more organized as she approaches term. She is no longer the continually moving creature of 5 months ago; instead she has distinct patterns of rest and activity. In fact, two dominant patterns of behavior have now emerged. The fetus will spend most of her time either in active sleep or quiet sleep. By this stage, the fetus will only be spending about 20 to 30 percent of her time in a quiet sleep-like state, where she will remain motionless, her heartbeat steady and her breathing movements when they occur are rhythmic. For most of the rest of the time the fetus will not be awake but in a state similar to neonatal active sleep. The fetus initiates many different body movements in this sleep state and the eyes move rapidly back and forth and open periodically. Heart rate and breathing patterns will tend to be irregular and she will be responsive to the sensory stimuli that she is naturally exposed to in her uterine environment. During periods of active sleep the fetus may be more reactive to sounds and touch. Early neuronal networks are being stimulated or "exercised." It is thought that this level of activity is probably necessary for adequate development and further maturation of the vital organs and the nervous system. The fetus is making fewer general body movements now – these movements probably only occur about 15 percent of the time. The fetus is also making breathing movements fairly frequently (about 30 percent of the time), which are important for lung development in readiness for birth.

In contrast to 1 month ago, the 9-month-old fetus no longer spends quite as much time in a state of active sleep. In active sleep, the fetus makes general body movements,

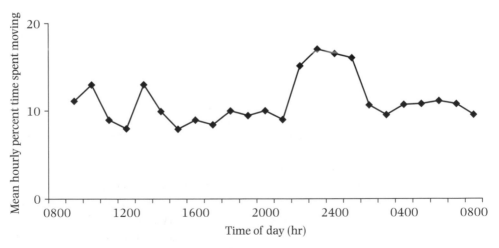

Figure 4.3 Fetal movement at 38–39 weeks, plotted as the average percent time spent moving in a 24-hour interval. Adapted from Patrick et al. (1982). Reprinted by permission of Harcourt Inc.

some breathing movements, and her heart rate tends to be irregular, often with large accelerations. Her eyes will move rapidly back and forth and probably even open and close from time to time. However, since the fetus's brain has matured in the last month, more inhibitory pathways have now developed, thus reducing the amount of movement the fetus performs. Consequently, the fetus will have longer periods when she is resting quietly in a deep sleep (Nijhuis, 1992). On the whole, the fetus's activity and rest periods alternate cyclically throughout the day. Already the length of one entire activity–rest cycle has lengthened from that seen 1 month ago, and now probably lasts about 80 to 100 minutes (Visser, 1992). However, superimposed on this cyclical rhythm are maternal physiological factors such as hormone levels, breathing, heart rate, and uterine activity (Mirmiran & Swaab, 1992). Variations in some or all of these factors are thought to influence the fetus's behavior over the course of the day. In general there is a peak in activity occurring when the mother is asleep, in the late evening, and a relative lull in activity in the early hours of the morning (Patrick, Campbell, Carmichael, Natale, & Richardson, 1982).

The Earliest Sensations

The emergence of the senses follows a set predetermined pattern of development that is similar in all mammals. It is fascinating that the sensory systems function even before they are anatomically complete. The first system to develop is touch. By about 8 weeks, if the area around the lips is touched the fetus will respond by moving. By 12 weeks the fetus will begin to make grasping movements when her fingers are touched. Initially the fetus moves her head and neck away from the source of touch, often with her mouth open; later in pregnancy, the fetus will move toward the "touch." This is the precursor of the **"rooting reflex"** which helps the baby to find the nipple for nursing. Similarly, a little later in development, if the palm of the fetus's hand is stroked then her fingers will close for a moment and the toes curl if the sole of the foot is touched (Hepper, 1992). Once the fetus starts to move around she will be touching the uterine wall, the umbilical cord, and also herself. The fetus will touch her own face more frequently than any other body part. So the fetus is provided with a wide breadth of physical sensations, which probably help to promote further development of the physical sensation of touch.

The Chemosensory System

Chemosensory development encompasses both the gustatory and olfactory senses, but it is difficult to say exactly what the fetus can smell and taste. Both flavors and smells from the mother's diet can pass into her bloodstream and then into both the amniotic fluid and fetal blood. There are three possible sites where "chemosensation" can occur during development: the nose, the mouth, and via the bloodstream itself (Schaal, Orgeur, & Rognon, 1995). The fetus swallows amniotic fluid regularly throughout the day. This fluid passes into the stomach where it will then be broken down further and sent to other organs, the brain, liver, and kidneys, before it is expelled from the bladder back into the amniotic fluid again. During the fourth month, the plugs of tissue that were previously blocking the nostrils have gone, and when the fetus "inhales," amniotic fluid also passes through the nose. The fetus actually inhales twice as much fluid as she swallows (Duenholter & Pritchard, 1976), so the sensory receptors within the nose are continuously being bathed in amniotic fluid. During the second half of pregnancy, the constitution of amniotic fluid becomes increasingly dependent on fetal urination. This may be particularly important for stimulation of the chemosensory system since it contains large amounts of ammonia-smelling urea.

Flavors and smells from the food consumed will also pass into the bloodstream after digestion. These will then pass via the placenta into the fetal circulation. Unlike the amniotic fluid, the smells and tastes within the blood have not been broken down or metabolized and are relatively undiluted and consequently more intense. The blood will flow in tiny capillaries through the fetal nose and mouth and therefore have ample opportunity to diffuse into the sensory apparatuses that detect smell and taste. It appears that nearly all babies, whether before or after birth, show a preference for sweet substances over bitter. If the amniotic fluid tastes sweet then the fetus will swallow more regularly than if it contains bitter substances (Hepper, 1992). Not surprisingly, after a meal and when glucose levels rise within the maternal bloodstream and the amniotic fluid, there is more breathing and swallowing. The amniotic fluid probably tastes sweeter as a result of the additional glucose. Swallowing by the fetus will also regulate the volume of the amniotic fluid.

While some of the fetus's ability to detect and prefer certain flavors to others may be genetically determined, other preferences may be learned *in utero*. Exposure to alcohol while in the womb has been shown to increase fetal swallowing and may cause preferences for alcohol later in life (Molina, Chotro, & Dominguez, 1995). It appears that preferences for smells may be more individually tailored for individual babies, depending on what flavors and smells they have been exposed to during life in the womb. Research with newborns has shown that babies can recognize the smell of their mother's breastmilk and it has been suggested that this arises through the early learning about their mother's diet that took place in the womb. This has been particularly supported by studies suggesting that if a mother dramatically changes her diet after her pregnancy, the infant may have a more difficult time learning to suckle (Hepper, 1988). (See Schaal et al., 1995, for a thorough review.)

The Vestibular System

As described above, the fetus does a lot of moving around *in utero*, constantly changing position within the warm amniotic fluid that cushions her from the outside world. Additionally, since the mother is moving about for much of the day, the fetus is also subjected to constant passive motion and will experience positional changes relative to gravity, depending on whether the mother is standing up, sitting, or lying down. This information is sensed by the **vestibular** apparatus consisting of three semi-circular canals, set at right angles to each other within the fetus's inner ear. These canals are fluid-filled and when the fetus moves (or is moved) the fluid within at least one of the canals will also move, stimulating tiny hairs within the canal lining. Depending on the direction and plane of movement, one semi-circular canal may be stimulated more than another. This information is then sent to the brain to be processed and information about motion and position extracted.

Although it is difficult to elicit responses to vestibular stimulation in babies *in utero* (Hepper, 1992), this does not mean that this system is not functioning. By 25 weeks, the fetus will show a righting reflex (Hooker, 1952), and it is possible that the vestibular system is in some way responsible for most babies lying head down prior to delivery. We do not know exactly how much information about position and motion the fetus is actually processing at this time. We do know that the system is actively being stimulated, and that this stimulation is very important for many aspects of normal fetal growth and development. Vestibular stimulation plays an important role in changing arousal states and this will become more apparent as time goes on. Initially, during the pregnancy, the fetus is often quiet when the mother is moving about a lot and causing a lot of vestibular stimulation. In contrast, when the mother is lying down at night, the fetus is receiving minimal vestibular stimulation and is often at her most active. Once the fetus is born, the parent will probably instinctively rock the baby when she is fussy or to put her to sleep. Again, the vestibular system is being stimulated and may play a role in eliciting changes in the arousal state of the child. The level of vestibular stimulation received by the fetus during the pregnancy is particularly high. The activity alone provides a level of stimulation to the vestibular system that will probably not be matched until the baby starts to walk independently (Hofer, 1981). Studies of **preterm** infants (who are deprived of the vestibular stimulation that would have been provided by their mother's movement) show that they have lags in neurobehavioral development that may in part be due to a lack of vestibular stimulation. Weight gain, visual responsiveness, and even later expressive language development have been shown to be improved if the incubator is gently rocked (Masi, 1979). Along the same lines, if preterm babies are put on waterbeds instead of mattresses, the rocking movement of the water may compensate for the vestibular stimulation that they missed out on *in utero* and may result in better sleep organization (Korner, Schneider, & Forrest, 1983).

The Visual System

Pregnancy is a time for structural formation of the basic components of the visual system, from the development of the eyes to the specialized areas in the brain that receive and process visual input. There is relatively little "visual stimulation" within the developing baby's world. It is dark within the womb, only the brightest of lights can filter through a naked abdomen, and this would provide a reddish glow. The eyelids are fused closed shortly after their formation, reducing the amount of light reaching the developing retina even further. Since premature infant experience with ambient light is implicated in subtle visual deficits, this dark environment may be necessary for the prenatal development of the visual system (Fielder & Moseley, 2000). In contrast, after birth, visual development can proceed normally only when the system is adequately stimulated.

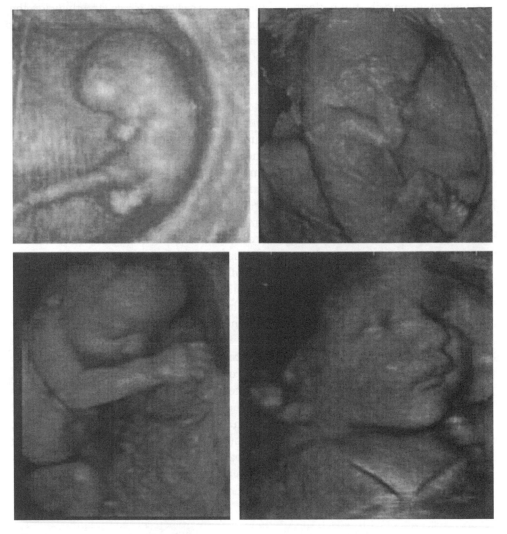

Plate 4.1 Noninvasive ultrasound pictures of fetal development at various stages of pregnancy, using 3D technology. Photo 1: Dr. Saied Tohamy; photos 2–4: Dr. Armin Breinl, Austria.

Development of the eyes

At about 5 weeks postconception, two balloon-like structures form on either side at the front of the brain. These are the future eyes. As they develop they become separated from the brain by a small stalk; this is where the nerve fibers will travel between the eye and brain. A few days later, the "balloons" infold to form a two-layered cup, and the retina develops from this cup. The mature retina is a complex neural structure made of many layers, whose function is to capture the light entering the eye and to convert it into electrical impulses or messages that can be transmitted to the brain. The cells that perform this task are the **rods and cones**, and they develop from the inner wall of the optic cup. The outer wall forms a pigment-containing layer that actually absorbs the light. This outer wall also goes on to develop the nutritive network of blood vessels needed by the rods and cones.

The lens of the eye begins to form at about 2 months of pregnancy. The eyelids and muscles that move the eyes are also beginning to form around this time. The circular ring of pigmented muscle, the iris, begins to develop. By three months the eyelids have fused together. The cornea, the clear, curved part of the eye, is forming different layers; the organization of the cells and fibers in these layers is crucial in providing a strong but transparent window to the eye. By 6 months, all the muscles that move the eyeball are in place. Eye movements usually begin between the sixteenth and twenty-third week of pregnancy, even though not all the muscles may be fully formed. The eyes will sometimes make slow rolling movements, or faster movements that may be smooth or jerky in nature. It is known that even premature babies, as immature as 26 weeks gestation, are able to distinguish light from dark and are soon able to make tracking eye movements to follow an attractive moving object.

DEVELOPMENT OF THE VISUAL PATHWAY

There is simultaneous development of the visual pathway connecting the light-sensitive cells in the eye (rods and cones) to the brain. In other words, it deals with the transmission and interpretation of the electrical impulses encoding the visual information that enters the eye. There is a series of relay stations that form between the eye and cerebral cortex, connecting cells from one level to the next. In humans, the lateral geniculate nucleus of the thalamus (a structure in the forebrain) has evolved to be one such relay station. By 9 weeks of pregnancy, the optic nerve has already penetrated the neural tube, there is a partial crossing over of the fibers of the optic nerve, i.e., some fibers from the right eye go to the right side of the brain, and others go to the left, and vice versa. This allows for information from both eyes to be integrated. This crossing is complete by 15 weeks of pregnancy. By the end of the first **trimester**, the nerve fibers interconnect with cells in the lateral geniculate nucleus of the thalamus, an area of the brain that is highly developed in primates. At about 5 months, the cells in this structure take on a very particular arrangement: six stripes appear. The cells within the stripes are highly specialized to deal with particular types of visual information. Cells in two of the stripes respond maximally to moving stimuli and gross form, whereas the cells in the other four stripes are concerned with the transmission of information about color and fine detail.

DEVELOPMENT OF THE VISUAL CORTEX

As the nerve fibers pass on from here they go to the visual cortex, an area at the back of the brain. The visual cortex is organized like a map of the two retinas. Each point on the retina represents a point in space within the field of vision, and because of the optics of the eye the image formed on the retina is upside down; similarly, an object on the left will form an image on the right of the retina. The visual cortex makes sense of this information, turning the image right way up. Since the optic nerves from each eye partially cross, the left side of the field of vision of each eye is represented on the right side of the brain, and vice versa. Area 17 is the part of the brain concerned with many aspects of basic visual function. The surrounding brain areas are involved with perceptual processes, that is, the interpretation of sensory information, and their development is less well known, but they are thought to begin formation somewhat later in the last trimester. The development of the cerebral cortex is characterized by the formation of layers of varying cell densities and by about 7 months, area 17 attains the definitive laminar structure seen in the adult.

At this time, the fetus's eyelids are no longer fused closed. The fetus will spend some time with her eyes open and will now be making blinking movements. Externally, the fetus's eyes will look fully formed. There are still some minor immaturities in the gross structures of the eyes, but the major source of immaturity in the fetus's visual system is within the neural structures of the eye, the retina, and the pathways to the brain. Nonetheless, if the fetus were born now, she would have some vision, even at this early age. Babies of this age can easily distinguish between light and dark (Taylor, Menzies, MacMillan, & Whyte, 1987) and have the ability to discriminate form to some extent (Dubowitz et al., 1983). Certainly by 30 weeks of age, the premature newborn is able to see patterns of fairly large size, providing that they are of sufficiently high contrast (e.g., black stripes on a white background) and fairly close to the baby's eyes (Grose & Harding, 1990). The fetus does have the basic "equipment" to be able to see, even though this ability is really not in use until birth and at this point in time the baby is relatively near-sighted. This is perfect for the task in hand, looking at the faces of the people who are holding her. The ability to focus on objects across the room will develop in the first months of life (see chapter 5).

The Auditory System

The development of the auditory system begins at about 6 weeks of pregnancy. At this time, two small, inward-facing bubbles appear on either side of the back of the brain. These become the inner ear and will later contain the auditory and balance organs. The middle ear tube has also begun to develop from the pharynx. At 7 weeks, the external part of the ear along with the canal leading into the ear and the eardrum develop from a groove between the mouth and the heart. At this stage, the external part of the ear looks rather like a "wrinkled mouth." By 8 weeks of pregnancy, the inner ear begins to develop the semi-circular canals that will eventually house the organs that are able to sense balance and position. A week later, the **cochlea** in the inner ear forms one coil, the first step in the formation of the spiral shell-like structures that will be the auditory organs. By 10 weeks, sensory cells are present in the semi-circular canals. The middle ear forms two soft structures that later become two of the three bones that conduct sound from the outer to the inner ear. The fetal ears will look like simple skin folds now.

By 14 weeks, the vestibular system begins to work. This system will be receiving high levels of stimulation at this time, and the baby is almost constantly moving about, not only because of her own constant activity but also in response to maternal movement. The cochlea has become more coiled and now contains sensory cells, the auditory nerve attaches to the cochlear duct. By 20 weeks the third bone of the ear is present and all three have begun to harden. This process is likely to improve the ability of the middle ear to conduct sound. At this time, the external ear is adult-shaped, but continues to grow in size until 9 years of age. Its function is to collect the sound from the external environment and channel it into the ear canal.

RESPONSES TO SOUNDS

It is at about the twenty-fourth week that the fetus begins to respond to sounds, though lower frequencies will be heard better than higher-pitched sounds (Abrams, Gerhardt, & Peters, 1995). One major immaturity can be seen within the sensors of the ear itself, i.e., the tiny hair cells within the cochlea, which vibrate when stimulated by sound and convert these vibrations into electrical messages that are then sent to the brain. Another immaturity is apparent within the nerve fibers that carry these messages. Consequently, the fetus's ability to hear different sounds is somewhat limited by these factors. However, almost all frequencies can be heard. The sounds that the fetus hears have to pass through various maternal tissues which effectively cut out the higher frequencies; consequently, those sounds entering the fetus's ears are predominantly low-frequency ones. However, even though the auditory environment of the fetus is largely limited to lower-frequency sounds, it is quite varied. These include the background noises of the mother's pulsing heartbeat, which changes constantly as both mother and fetus move and when maternal pulse and blood pressure change. Borborygmi are the gastrointestinal sounds associated with digestion, and these are part of the fetal sound experience. The mother's voice is by far the most frequently heard and loudest sound (Abrams et al., 1995). However, there is no unambiguous way of determining exactly what the fetus is hearing, since the mother is listening to sound traveling through air, whereas the fetus is listening to sound that has traveled through the amniotic fluid with no air spaces on either side of the eardrum. Furthermore, the rest of the auditory system is still immature, and so we do not know how well these sounds are converted into electrical signals by the sensors in the ear or what the fetus's brain makes of these messages. However, at this age, fetuses' hearts beat faster in response to most sounds.

Very loud sounds will result in a very fast heart rate. As the fetus gets older, her response will change based on the sound intensity, how deeply she is sleeping, and how familiar she is with the sounds (LeCanuet, 1996). The fetus will also respond to some sounds by moving her limbs, or sometimes by stopping her movement in the middle of a high-activity period. One study has shown that fetuses will actually startle and empty their bladders following the loudest of sounds (Zimmer et al., 1993). Changes in brain electrical activity during sound stimulation have been measured in prematurely born infants by 27 weeks gestational age. Sounds are thought to shape permanent changes in the auditory system which are probably required for normal brain development. Permanent changes are also reflected in newborn perceptual capacities and sound preferences as a newborn. Areas of the brain devoted to processing and remembering "multimodal" stimulation are probably also affected, since during some sound experiences several senses are activated at once. For example, when a mother speaks, her diaphragm moves, resulting in movement of the fetus, consequently those pathways that sense pressure, touch, and balance are also stimulated along with the auditory system.

 Transnatal Auditory Learning

Although there is much converging scientific evidence of fetal auditory learning carried forward into the newborn period, there are relatively few carefully controlled human studies on the topic of such **"transnatal" learning**. From the researcher's perspective, the paucity of published empirical studies in peer-reviewed journals that directly address transnatal learning is understandable. There are daunting methodological and practical hurdles to surmount in asking fetuses or newborn infants whether they have learned about specific sounds or smells.

Despite the relative paucity of research on learning during the several weeks prior to and following birth (the perinatal period), several studies of fetal and newborn habituation learning do exist. Habituation occurs when there is a reduction in fetal responding to a repeated, typically auditory, stimulus, and the decrement cannot be attributed to sensory or response system fatigue (Hepper, 1997a,b; Zelazo, Weiss, & Tarquinio, 1991). Demonstrations of habituation learning are especially convincing when, after a decrease in responding to a repeated stimulus, the fetus begins responding anew when a discriminably different stimulus is presented. Recovery of both motor (Shahidullah & Hepper, 1994) and cardiac (LeCanvet et al., 1994) responding to a change in auditory stimulation has been reported for late-term fetuses. Full-term neonates have revealed themselves to be adept learners and it is likely that much of this capacity was already present at the end of gestation prior to birth. Within the first days after birth, newborns demonstrate habituation learning. Habituation experiments with newborns typically take place over a period of minutes and demonstrate that infants retain stimulus characteristics long enough to compare them with a new exemplar.

If we accept that fetuses can learn about sounds that they hear *in utero*, then it becomes reasonable to ask whether there is any indication that newborns respond differentially to sounds that occurred during the prenatal period either naturally or through deliberate exposure. One candidate natural prenatal sound is the rhythm of a heartbeat. Salk (1962, 1973) reported that playing recordings of a heartbeat sound for groups of newborns in a hospital nursery resulted in greater weight gain and reduced crying time. Other researchers have also found that intrauterine sounds calm neonates (Murooka et al., 1976; Rosner & Doherty, 1979). Based partially upon this research, commercial products using heartbeat sounds have been devised for pacifying young infants. Other research has, however, called the soothing effect of heartbeat sounds into question. There have been failures to replicate (Detterman, 1978; Tulloch et al., 1964). There have also been many experiments with sounds other than heartbeats that show that a neonatal arousal response to sound depends upon many variables including broad characteristics of the stimulus, the infant's initial state of arousal, and the experimenter's choice of response (Detterman, 1978; Gerber, 1985). One study has demonstrated that heartbeat sounds acted as a reinforcer for the infants (DeCasper & Sigafoos, 1983). The experiment did not compare responding to heartbeat sounds with other rhythmic sounds, thus it is not clear whether it was the presumably familiar prenatal cardiovascular sounds or the characteristic of rhythmicity that was reinforcing for the newborns.

LEARNING ABOUT THE MOTHER'S VOICE

In addition to the cardiovascular sounds present on recordings made *in utero*, the maternal voice has been noted to be a prominent sound, more intense than other voices. It is, however, not more intelligible than other voices. All voices on the intrauterine recordings sound muffled, largely due to the attenuation of frequencies above 500 Hz resulting from the low-pass filtering properties of the intrauterine environment (Abrams et al., 1995). Several studies support the hypothesis that newborns prefer a low-pass filtered recording of the maternal voice compared to an unfiltered recording of her voice (Fifer & Moon, 1995; Spence & Freeman, 1996). This preference for the prenatal version of mother's voice strongly suggests that newborns can learn about sounds available in the womb and that early postnatal responding is influenced by this experience.

The salience of mother's voice to infants shortly after birth has been the focus of several experiments in which responding to the maternal voice has been compared to stranger female voices. In one study infants within 2 hours after birth reacted with more movement when mother was speaking compared with the strangers (Fifer & Moon, 1989). Another study, using recordings of mothers' and stranger females' voices (DeCasper & Fifer, 1980), employed the non-nutritive sucking preference procedure to compare responses by infants less than 3 days after birth to familiar and unfamiliar female voices. Infants activated the recordings of their own mothers' voices proportionately more frequently than the recordings of other mothers' voices. DeCasper and Fifer (1980) replicated this finding in the same study using a new group of neonates and a variant of the sucking procedure. The maternal voice preference was again replicated in a different non-nutritive sucking experiment with 2-day-olds (Querleu et al., 1984). In a recent intriguing study using event-related potentials, differential brain activity was recorded in newborns to mothers' versus strangers' voices (Deregnier, Nelson, Thomas, Wewerka, & Georgieff, 2000). Father's voice has received scant attention from researchers, and although newborns apparently discriminate between the paternal and a stranger male voice (DeCasper & Prescott, 1984; Ockleford et al., 1988), a preference has not been documented (DeCasper & Prescott, 1984).

In addition to demonstrating preferences for listening to particular voices, newborns have shown that they respond differentially to languages. Within the first 4 days after birth, infants discriminate the language that their mother speaks compared to a foreign language (Mehler et al., 1988), and 2-day-olds have demonstrated a preference for the maternal language compared to a foreign language (Moon, Cooper, & Fifer, 1993). The rhythmic structure of the two comparison languages appears to be important in neonates' ability to classify utterances (Nazzi et al., 1998). However, in the experiments with voices and languages described above, it is not possible to rule out the effect of postnatal experience. Remarkably, there is only one published experiment that is a direct test of prenatal learning about speech. DeCasper and Spence (1986) asked women to read a particular 3-minute speech passage out loud two times a day during the last 6 weeks of pregnancy. After these infants were born, 16 of them were participants in the non-nutritive sucking preference procedure, and their activation of recordings of the familiar or a novel speech passage was compared. Infants activated the tape recording of the prenatal story more frequently than the novel story. For a group of control infants who had not been previously exposed to the speech passages, there was no systematic preference. This is one experiment in which postnatal experience with the auditory stimulus can be ruled out as an explanation for newborn response to a prenatal event.

SUMMARY

Taken altogether, the studies of perinatal learning and the experiments on fetal and newborn responses to familiar prenatal sounds suggest: (1) fetal sensory experience shapes the developing brain; (2) prenatal experience with the maternal voice may provide a sensory and perceptual bridge into postnatal life; and (3) we still know very little about the extent, limits, and underlying mechanisms of transnatal learning.

Risks to Fetal Development

Perinatal complications can have their origins in parental preconception conditions, as well as emerge from gene–environment interactions throughout embryogenesis and gestation. Genetic factors are thought to account for roughly 10–15 percent of congenital defects, while environmental agents acting alone – such as alcohol, excess quantities of vitamin A, and radiation – are thought to cause another 10 percent of them. The rest of congenital anomalies are believed to be the result of multifactoral causation, that is, the result of genes and environment interacting together (Ashmead & Reed, 1997; Milunsky & Milunsky, 1998).

In chromosomal defects, whole **chromosomes** are missing or duplicated, or parts of them are missing or duplicated. Overall, chromosomal abnormalities are seen in 1/200 live births and in 50–70 percent of first-trimester miscarriages (Ashmead & Reed, 1997; Robinson, Linden, & Bender, 1998). Abnormal numbers of chromosomes are usually caused by an error in the separation of chromosomes into appropriate daughter cells during **meiotic division**. For reasons still only partially understood, there is a dramatic increase in the risk of chromosomal anomalies with advancing maternal age. For example, risk of Down's syndrome at age 20 is 1/2,000; at age 30, it is 1/1,000; by age 37, it is 1/200 (Davidson & Zeesman, 1994; Hsu, 1998).

Disorders can result from a single gene abnormality. The risk of an affected individual having a child with the disorder depends on their partner's status with respect to the genetic mutation, and, therefore, on how rare the disease is. Examples of **autosomal genetic disorders** are: sickle cell disease, cystic fibrosis, Tay-Sachs disease, Huntington's disease, and Marfan syndrome (Ashmead & Reed, 1997). Certain ethnic groups are at greater risk for specific genetic disorders than others. For example, in Ashkenazi Jews (Jews of Eastern European descent), 1 in 30 is a carrier of Tay-Sachs disease while approximately 8 in 100 African Americans from North America are carriers of the sickle cell gene (Davidson & Zeesman, 1994).

EFFECTS OF MATERNAL SUBSTANCE ABUSE

Heavy maternal alcohol consumption profoundly influences fetal and child development. For the children who survive, the effects include mild to severe physical anomalies and cognitive and behavioral impairments. However, other adverse fetal outcomes include increased risk for spontaneous abortion, stillbirth, premature placental separation, intrauterine growth restriction, and, some studies suggest, preterm birth – itself a risk factor for future health problems, poor development, and newborn mortality (Smigaj, 1997). Follow-up reports of behavior and cognitive development indicate that significant *in utero* exposure to alcohol is associated with attentional deficits, mental retardation, and poor academic performance.

Despite major efforts to warn pregnant women of the dangers cigarette smoking poses for their fetus, smoking is still one of the most preventable risk factors for an unsuccessful pregnancy outcome (American College of Obstetricians and Gynecologists, 1997). On average, babies born to smokers weigh 100–200 g less than those of non-smokers and have twice the risk for fetal growth restriction (Horta, Victora, Menezes, Halpern, & Barros, 1997; Walsh, 1994). Furthermore, independent of the risks for lower birthweight, smoking is associated with risk for prematurity and perinatal complications, such as premature detachment of the placenta (Andres, 1996; Kyrklund-Blomberg & Cnattingius, 1998). Cigarette smoking also is associated with a two- to threefold increase for sudden infant death syndrome (SIDS) (Golding, 1997). Finally, more subtle effects of fetal exposure to maternal smoke have been found during childhood. Behavioral problems and cognitive weaknesses, including problems with attention and visuoperceptual processing, have been associated with smoking during pregnancy (Fried & Watkinson, 2000; Fried, Watkinson, & Gary, 1992; Wakschlag et al., 1997). The strong effects that active smoking exerts on pregnancy outcomes have led researchers to investigate whether maternal exposure to environmental tobacco smoke (ETS) also has an influence on fetal development. New data indicate that even ETS poses risks for the fetus (Mainous & Hueston, 1994; Spitzer et al., 1990; Windham, Eaton, & Hopkins, 1999).

NUTRITION AND FETAL DEVELOPMENT

Specific nutritional requirements must be met for healthy fetal development. For example, adequate amounts of calcium are needed for fetal bone, muscle, and transmitter production; sufficient supplies of iron are necessary for fetal red blood cell and tissue production (Judge, 1997). Recently, the central importance of folic acid to fetal development has emerged. Research from epidemiological and animal studies indicates that independent of gross congenital anomalies, women's food intake and/or weight gain during pregnancy may subtly affect fetal development in ways that have implications for the child's future medical and mental health. For example, in several large samples, low birthweight has been linked to an increased risk for future cardiovascular disease (CVD), and for factors, such as high blood pressure, associated with CVD (Clark et al., 1998; Law et al., 1993; Moore, Cockington, Ryan, & Robinson, 1999; Rich-Edwards et al., 1997). To account for this association, researchers hypothesize that aspects of the fetus's cardiovascular functioning are "programmed" *in utero* by maternal nutritional and/or hormonal factors (Barker, 1995). New research also indicates that women's nutrition during pregnancy and baby's birthweight also might be markers for physiological processes that place the infant at risk for future breast cancer (Michels, Trichopoulos, Adami, Hsieh, & Lan, 1996; Morgan et al., 1999) and psychiatric illness (Susser, Brown, & Matte, 1999). Specifically, epidemiological studies suggest that higher birthweight is associated with an increased risk for breast cancer (Morgan, Damber, Tavelin, & Hogberg, 1999). Other studies based on the offspring of Dutch women pregnant during the Nazi food embargo ("the Dutch Hunger Winter") suggest that extreme undernutrition (fewer than 1,000 calories a day) during first and second trimesters (and thus occurring during rapid brain reorganization) is associated with those at risk of becoming schizophrenic or having antisocial personality disorder (Neugebauer, Hoek, & Susser, 1999; Susser et al., 1999). Although the mechanisms underlying these associations are not yet known, it is likely that future research will clarify the impact of variations in maternal nutrition and newborn weight on the child's physical and mental health.

Effects of maternal stress

Psychosocial stress during pregnancy has long been linked to negative birth outcomes such as low birthweight and prematurity as well as alterations in fetal neurobehavioral development (Istvan, 1986; Lobel, 1994; Lobel, Dunkel-Schetter, & Scrimshaw, 1992; Stott & Latchford, 1976). In a comprehensive examination of fetal **ontogeny**, DiPietro et al. assessed fetal variables in relation to maternal variables (DiPietro, Hodgson, Costigan, & Johnson, 1996). Fetuses of pregnant women who reported greater life stress had reduced parasympathetic and/or increased sympathetic activation as measured by reduced fetal heart rate variability (HRV) (DiPietro et al., 1996). Anxiety during pregnancy also has been linked to alterations in pregnant women's physiology and fetal behavior. The data indicate that over the course of gestation, maternal psychological variables such as stress and anxiety acting via alterations in maternal physiology may influence fetal neurobehavioral development (Monk et al., 2000).

 ## *Prenatal Development of Postnatal Functions: The Bridge to Infancy*

Most of the reflex behaviors that the baby will demonstrate after she is born, including breathing, rooting, sucking, and swallowing, are part of the fetal repertoire. Other reflexes that have less obvious functional significance for present-day humans include the toe-curling reflex, the finger-grasping reflex, and the startle reflex. These reflexes all disappear within the first year of life. Another reflexive behavior that has received a good deal of attention is the stepping reflex. If resistance is provided to her feet the fetus will make stepping movements placing one foot in front of the other. This reflex usually disappears in the first 2 months after birth. There is some argument as to whether this activity is a kicking motion (Thelen, 1986) or whether it is the precursor of early walking (Zelazo, 1983). It has also been suggested that this reflex may help in the birthing process itself (Kitzinger, 1990).

There are now several studies, though as yet unreplicated, suggesting more fundamental psychobiological continuities between fetal and infant development. For example, work from Kagan and colleagues suggested that low resting heart rate during the prenatal period predicts lower levels of crying and motoric responses to novelty at 4 months old (Snidman, Kagan, Riordan, & Shannon, 1995). Using sonographic visualization, another group of researchers found that fetuses, who move at certain rates during active sleep, move at the same relative rate at 2 and 4 weeks postpartum (Groome et al., 1999). Groome has also observed that the duration of quiet sleep epochs provides a stable measure of behavioral state development between the **prenatal** and **postnatal** periods (Groome et al., 1997). Other exploratory research suggests that a relatively greater number of weak body movements, as opposed to strong, full-body ones, were positively associated with the amount of crying during the first 3 months of life (St. James-Roberts and Menon-Johansson, 1999). The authors speculate that an inability to inhibit responsiveness is the common underlying characteristic linking increased fetal body movements and greater crying. In an extensive study of fetal to newborn continuities, indices of fetal neurobehavior accounted for as much as 60 percent of the variance of infant temperament (DiPietro et al., 1996). In general, higher fetal activity resulted in increased fussiness and inconsistent behavior while greater periodicity resulted in lower scores on these variables.

SUMMARY AND CONCLUSIONS

Behavioral continuity, or lack thereof, is often difficult to confirm, whether due to differences in (1) rapidly developing brain behavior infrastructure, (2) intra- and extrauterine constraints and supports for activity, or (3) amount and patterns of sensory stimulation, e.g., fluid versus air transmission of sound and chemosensory stimulation, and marked differences in visual and vestibular stimulation. Furthermore, at birth there are abrupt transformations in physiological requirements or motivation, e.g., hunger, temperature variation, and ventilatory needs. The triggers for and characteristics of **circadian** (daily) and ultradian (less than 24-hour) rhythms are clearly altered at birth, e.g., interfeed intervals and light–dark cycles versus maternal-generated patterns of physiological, physical, and hormonal activity. Technological advances have been made, e.g., 3D ultrasound imaging and improved detection of fetal heart and blood-flow patterns, that may serve as markers for continuities in attentional capacities, temperament, or risk status. An emerging technique may offer the potential to investigate sensory capacities prenatally. Magnetoencephalography, which has been used to record brain activity in the adult brain, is now being used to monitor fetal brain waves (Eswaran et al., 2002). However, other serious methodological hurdles remain, such as limited access to the maternal/fetal dyad and control over and accurate measurement of fetal versus infant sensory input. Though direct assessment of brain activity remains largely an unfulfilled promise, indirect reflections of CNS function, specifically patterns of heart-rate activity, are shedding light on fetal to newborn trajectories in brain development. Hopefully, continued improvements in technology and experimental methods will lead to new creative approaches to investigation of the fetal origins of human behavior and development.

DISCUSSION POINTS

1   Think about the similarities and differences existing between environments pre- and postbirth.
2   List the forms of sensory information that the fetus picks up and consider how this information may affect sensory development.
3   What different functions are served by fetal behaviors?
4   In the fetal period, is development of all sensory systems dependent on input to these systems?
5   Think about the auditory environment of the fetus and compare it to the auditory environment of the newborn.
6   List the different environmental factors that constitute risks to fetal development.
7   Think of reasons why some fetal behaviors disappear after birth while others are maintained.

SUGGESTIONS FOR FURTHER READING

LeCanuet, J. S. B. (1996). Fetal sensory competencies. *European Journal of Obstetrics and Gynecology and Reproductive Biology*, 68, 1–23.

LeCanuet, J., Fifer, W., Krasnegor, N., & Smotherman, W. (Eds.) (1995). *Fetal development: A psychobiological perspective*. Hillsdale, NJ: Erlbaum.

Nathanielsz, P. (1996). *Life before birth: The challenges of fetal development*. San Francisco: W. H. Freeman.

Nijhuis, J. (1992). *Fetal behavior: Developmental and perinatal aspects*. New York: Oxford University Press.

chapter 5

Perception, Knowledge, and Action

Gavin Bremner

KEY CONCEPTS

A NOT B ERROR
CLINICAL METHOD
COGNITION
COGNITIVE DEVELOPMENT
CONSTRUCTIVISM
CORE KNOWLEDGE
DISHABITUATION
EMPIRICISM
EXECUTIVE FUNCTIONING
FRONTAL CORTEX
HABITUATION

INFANT-DIRECTED SPEECH
 (MOTHERESE)
INNATE MECHANISM
INTONATION
NATIVISM
OBJECT PERMANENCE
OBJECT UNITY
PROTOTYPICAL FACE
REPRESENTATIONAL ABILITY
RESPONSE PERSEVERATION
RETINAL IMAGE SIZE

RETROACTIVE INTERFERENCE
SHAPE CONSTANCY
SIZE CONSTANCY
SUBITIZING
SUBJECTIVE CONTOUR
VIOLATION OF EXPECTATION
 TECHNIQUE
VISUAL ACCOMMODATION
VISUAL ACUITY
VISUAL PREFERENCE
 TECHNIQUE

OVERVIEW

This chapter reviews evidence bearing on fundamental questions about infants' ability to perceive and understand the physical and social world. Infancy researchers have devised a number of ingenious techniques that make it possible to discover a great deal about infants' perceptual and cognitive abilities, and these studies reveal that even very young infants are surprisingly advanced.

Although young infants are unable to resolve fine visual detail, even newborns have a remarkably well-developed ability to perceive the structure of the world, making visual discriminations between shapes and apparently perceiving the world as an arrangement of objects in three-dimensional space, much as adults do. However, the ability to fill in gaps in perception, such as when one object partly hides another, does not appear to be there at birth, but develops by around 4 months.

Young infants' perception of people is also highly advanced. From birth, they recognize facial configurations as special and learn to discriminate parents from strangers within days of birth. The fact that newborns imitate facial gestures adds to the evidence that infants are capable of processing faces. Similarly, auditory perception is well developed, and there is even evidence of auditory learning prior to birth.

The chapter then considers research on infants' cognitive development, where the focus is on understanding of the perceived world. From around the age of 4 months, infants appear to be aware of the permanence of objects and the rules which govern the movement of one object relative to another. Most of the evidence pointing to this is based on simple measures of looking time; infants look longer at events that violate some physical principle, and longer looking is interpreted as recognition by the infant that the event was impossible. However, tests based on more complex behaviors reveal less positive findings. For instance, 6-month-old infants fail to search for hidden objects, and older infants make characteristic search errors, which suggest that their understanding of the world is relatively limited.

The likely resolution of the conflicting data arising from these different methods of investigation is that young infants are aware of an objective world of permanent objects, but that they are unable to use this knowledge to guide their actions in that world. Seen this way, early cognitive development is more to do with constructing relationships between knowledge and action than with constructing knowledge itself.

Introduction

Questions about the perceptual and cognitive abilities of infants are of interest in their own right and are also particularly important because infancy is in many ways a starting point for later development. Although this statement needs some qualification in the sense that a great deal of development takes place prior to birth (see chapter 4), the moment of birth marks the infant's emergence into the world that he or she will inhabit for some 80 years. Although some continuities exist between the environment of the fetus and that of the newborn infant, there is a whole range of entirely new experiences. In particular, for the first time the visual sense is provided with patterned light stimuli that change and move both in themselves and in response to movements of the infant. A fundamental question concerns what the newborn makes of such stimuli. Are they just meaningless patterns of light, or can infants identify them as arising from the objects and people in their surrounding world, much as we do? Not surprisingly, a major focus of infancy research has been to do with these starting states, and the reader will see how evidence of this sort relates directly to questions arising in chapter 3 concerning the origins of knowledge, specifically the issue of **nativism** versus **empiricism**.

In addition to investigating infants' perceptual abilities, we can also ask what they understand of the events that they perceive. These questions lie in the domain of **cognitive development**. Traditionally, a key aspect of the distinction between perception and **cognition** was the concept of **mental representation**. When we view a world of objects, this is a matter of perception, whereas when we call to mind an environment that is not present, we are engaged in internal processes through which this environment is mentally represented. Although there is a lot to be said for this distinction (and the concept of representation will crop up again in this chapter), its application to infancy has not been so productive as once seemed likely. This is in large part because, prior to gaining the ability to reflect on absent environments, infants have to learn how to perceive and act appropriately in their here-and-now environment. In the pages that follow, I shall review evidence indicating that, right from birth, infants perceive the world in a sophisticated way, and that in the early months, they develop perceptual abilities that "fill in the gaps" in perception so that invisible parts of objects are perceived, and objects that are temporarily hidden are treated as continuing in existence. Additionally, there is now a very large body of evidence indicating that from about 3 months on, infants have a well-developed awareness of the physical properties of objects and relationships between objects. However, I shall also point to evidence indicating that these abilities are not initially used successfully to guide the infant's actions; though the motor abilities are present, in some important respects the links between knowledge and action do not seem to be in place, and some interesting errors in action result.

 ## Visual Perception from Birth to 4 Months

EARLY LIMITATIONS OF VISION: ARE THEY REALLY A PROBLEM?

We know that newborns' vision is significantly poorer than that of older individuals. **Visual acuity**, which is basically a measure of the fineness of detail that can be resolved, is probably around one-thirtieth the level of perfect adult acuity (Mohn & van Hof-van Duin, 1985). Additionally, young infants have poor control over focusing the eyes (**visual accommodation**), something that is necessary to the creation of a sharp retinal image of objects at different distances from the viewer. These limitations are short-lived, because both acuity and accommodation improve rapidly during the first 6 months. Nevertheless, you would be forgiven for concluding that the early limitations paint a pessimistic picture regarding visual perception of the world at birth and soon after. However, poor visual acuity and focusing only limit the fineness of detail that can be resolved: although much of the detail of the visual world may not be available to young infants, these limitations should not affect perception of the larger-scale structure of objects, and provided we present sufficiently large stimuli at an appropriate distance from the infant, it is perfectly possible to investigate just what young infants are capable of perceiving.

HOW CAN WE INVESTIGATE INFANT PERCEPTION?

Given that we know that there is potentially an ability to be detected, how can we go about measuring it? If we were working with adults, we could present different stimuli and ask participants whether or not they discriminated some particular variation between them. But we cannot ask infants these questions, so our approach has to be rather less direct. Around the beginning of the 1960s, some techniques were developed that opened up exciting possibilities.

The visual preference technique

The spontaneous **visual preference technique** simply involves presenting infants with two different stimuli and measuring whether they look consistently longer at one than the other. Such a looking-time difference is defined as a visual preference, and if one thinks about it, such a preference implies discrimination: without discrimination there would be no basis for the preference. Of course, one has to be sure that a looking preference is not simply a tendency to look in one direction. Thus, the two stimuli are presented over a series of trials in which their left–right locations are systematically varied.

Habituation techniques

If an infant is presented with the same stimulus over a series of presentations, the time spent looking at it declines. This phenomenon, the technical term for which is **habituation**, is often described as an early example of boredom, but that description runs the risk of diverting the reader from the important psychological implications of the phenomenon. If the infant looks for shorter periods over trials, this implies that progressively more of the stimulus has been committed to memory, thus if infants habituate they must have a form of visual memory. Additionally, we can use this phenomenon to investigate visual discrimination. If, after habituation to one stimulus (say a cross), we present a different stimulus (say a circle), we would predict that if infants can discriminate between the two they should recognize the new stimulus as novel and hence look longer at it. If, on the other hand, they cannot discriminate between the two stimuli, looking should remain as low as it was before the stimulus swap. A more sensitive variant on this technique involves habituation to one stimulus followed by paired presentation of familiar and novel stimuli, the measure in this case being the proportion of time spent looking at each of the two stimuli, the prediction being that if infants discriminate the two they should look longer at the novel stimulus.

SHAPE PERCEPTION IN NEWBORNS

As already indicated, despite the poor visual acuity of young infants, we can still investigate shape perception provided we present sufficiently large stimuli at an appropriate viewing distance. And it turns out that even newborns are capable of perceiving differences between simple shapes such as crosses, triangles, squares, and circles. Slater, Morison, and Rose (1983) habituated newborns to one of these four simple shapes and then tested their looking at the familiar (habituated) one when it was shown paired with a new shape. Infants looked longer at the stimulus that they had not been habituated to, indicating that they discriminated between them and treated as novel the stimulus to which they had not had prior exposure.

The components of shape

This was an exciting result, but it poses the problem of whether infants are discriminating between the forms as such or simply on the basis of the presence of a single feature in one stimulus (for instance, the pointed apex of the triangle) and its absence in the other. Thus, some of the subsequent work took a rather different approach, starting with the lowest-level components of a shape and working upwards. For instance, Slater, Morison, and Somers (1988) showed that newborns could discriminate between

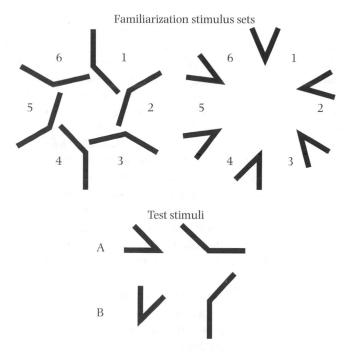

Figure 5.1 Figures used by Slater et al. (1991). During familiarization trials infants see either the set of obtuse or the set of acute angles, with stimulus orientation varied across presentation, so that the only constant feature is the angular relationship. They are then tested for a novelty preference between acute and obtuse figures. Reprinted by permission of Academic Press.

different line orientations. Going a step higher, Cohen and Younger (1984) investigated whether infants could discriminate between different angular relationships between lines. Their finding was that although 4-month-olds discriminated on this basis, 6-week-olds did not, discriminating instead on the basis of the orientation of the constituent lines. However, this is not the end of the story. Any figure consisting of a pair of intersecting lines contains both an angular relation and two lines in specific orientations, and it seems that during habituation young infants have a tendency to process on the basis of the simplest variable, in this case line orientation. The way around this problem is to habituate infants to a constant angular relationship but to vary the overall orientation of the figure so that the angle is the only constant during habituation. When Slater, Mattock, Brown, and Bremner (1991) did this, they found that newborns discriminated on the basis of angular relationship. This finding indicates that even newborn infants perceive simple shapes as a whole, and not just as a collection of parts.

NEWBORNS PERCEIVE A THREE-DIMENSIONAL WORLD

Knowledge that very young infants perceive at least the angular elements of patterns is of great interest. However, the infant's world is not totally inhabited with flat patterns; although adults typically surround infants with pictures, the world is com-posed of 3D objects arranged in 3D space. This presents a challenge for the perceptual system, because as objects move and reorient, the retinal image they produce changes in form and size. Despite these changes, the adult viewer perceives an object as having a constant shape and size. The principle of **size constancy** leads to an object being perceived as the same size however much its distance from the viewer changes. Sim-ilarly, the principle of **shape constancy** leads to perception of a constant form whatever angle the object is viewed from. The developmental question is whether such prin-ciples guide infant perception, or whether they are developed through experience. For some time, the general assumption was that these principles were not present at birth, but developed toward the end of the first year (Piaget, 1954). However, evidence for both shape constancy (Slater & Morison, 1985) and size constancy (Slater, Mattock, & Brown, 1990) has now been obtained with newborns. The technique used is similar to that in studies of shape perception. In the case of size constancy, infants are habituated to an object of constant size, with its distance (and hence the **retinal image size**) vary-ing over trials. Following this, newborns look longer at an object of different size than at the same object at a new distance (and hence with a new retinal image size). This happens even though the new object is placed at a distance that leads it to produce the same retinal image size as the old object at one of its habituation distances. In other words, infants respond to a change in true size but not to a change in retinal image size, an impressive ability by any account.

PERCEPTUAL DEVELOPMENT IN THE FIRST 6 MONTHS

So far we have seen that newborn visual perception, though not well tuned to detect fine detail, is in other respects much like adult perception. However, current evidence suggests that there are some important aspects of perception that emerge during the first few months of life.

Perception of object unity

If you look at the top half of figure 5.2, you will probably interpret what you see as a complete rod behind a box; the adult visual system "fills in" the invisible parts of the partly hidden rod. This is referred to as object unity, that is, perceiving a complete object despite the fact that parts of it cannot be seen. An important question is whether infants perceive object unity in this way. Kellman and Spelke (1983) tested this by habituating 4-month-olds to the display at the top of figure 5.2, a rod moving back and forth behind a box, and they then measured looking at the two displays at the bottom of the figure, the complete rod versus the parts which they had literally seen. The rationale was that if the infants had perceived the complete rod during habitu-ation, it would be familiar and so they would look more at the separate parts, whereas if they had perceived only the parts, they would look longer at the complete rod because it would be novel. Kellman and Spelke found that infants looked longer at the separate parts than at the complete rod, and they concluded that 4-month-olds perceive object unity in displays of this sort. It is important to note that there was

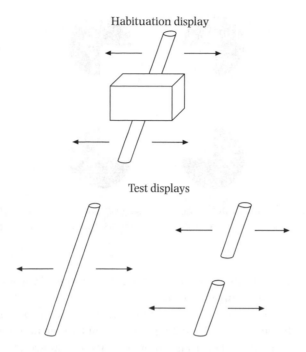

Figure 5.2 Displays presented by Kellman and Spelke (1983). Reprinted with permission of Academic Press.

no spontaneous preference for the rod parts over the whole, so there is no way to explain these results other than in terms of object unity perceived during habituation. Interestingly, the effect only occurs if the rod moves, and it seems likely that *common motion* is one principle infants use to perceive object unity – by "common motion" is meant the fact that the upper and lower portions of the rod moved at the same time and in the same direction.

Newborns' perception of these displays seems to be fundamentally different (Slater, Johnson, Brown, & Badenoch, 1996). Instead of looking longer at the rod parts after habituation, they look longer at the complete rod. Slater et al. (1990) concluded that, unlike 4-month-olds, newborns do not perceive object unity, instead being limited to perception of what is literally in view. Subsequent work (Johnson & Aslin, 1995) demonstrated that 2-month-olds showed the same result as 4-month-olds, though only if the occluding box was made quite narrow so that the amount of object invisible was relatively small. All this presents a picture of gradual emergence of object unity during the early months.

Perception of subjective contours

Another form of perceptual organization that involves filling in invisible parts can be seen in figure 5.3. You will probably see a white square partially occluding four black disks. However, there is no square there of course, only four disks with quadrants missing. The arrangement of the missing quadrants creates the illusion of a complete

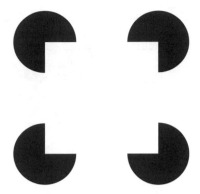

Figure 5.3 Subjective contours. The arrangement and orientation of missing segments from the circles create the percept of a complete square.

square, although there are no contours connecting these four "corners." For obvious reasons this is called a **subjective contour**.

Perception of subjective contours can be investigated in infants by habituating them to something like that in figure 5.3 and then measuring looking at a real square versus some other shape. The rationale is that if they perceive the subjective square, the real square presented on test trials should be familiar, and so they will look longer at the other test shape. And this is what was found, initially with 7-month-olds (Bertenthal, Campos, & Haith, 1980), and later with 3-month-olds (Ghim, 1990). So far, however, no such ability has been shown to exist at birth, so again it seems likely that this ability develops shortly after birth.

SUMMARY

The evidence reviewed in this section indicates that newborns and young infants are capable of perceiving objects and shapes and apply the perceptual constancies that are necessary for perception of an objective, three-dimensional world. Newborn abilities appear to be limited to the "here and now" of perception, but during the first 4 months infants develop the ability to fill in gaps in perception in order to perceive object unity and subjective contours.

 ## *Infants' Perception of People*

As well as being surrounded with inanimate objects, from birth infants are embedded in a social world, and important questions exist concerning their ability to perceive people. These questions are of interest in their own right but are also vital in relation to accounts of the infant's social and emotional development. For instance, if an infant is to form an emotional attachment to a specific person (see chapter 6), he or she must have some means of identifying the individual as a person and of discriminating

(a)   (b)   (c)

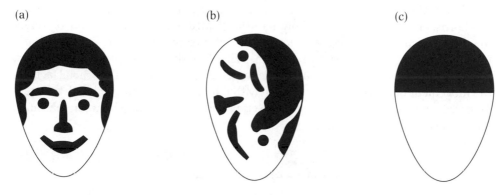

Figure 5.4 Face stimuli used by Fantz (1961): (a) facial arrangement, (b) jumbled facial features, (c) control stimulus with same overall brightness as the other two.

between that individual and others. One might expect such recognition and discrimination to be a simple matter, given how much interest infants take in people. However, people provide highly complex dynamic information to both the visual and auditory system, so it is by no means a foregone conclusion that young infants will be well equipped for person perception.

Face perception

Fantz (1961) carried out a classic study of face perception, in which he presented infants with the schematic stimuli shown in figure 5.4. One stimulus contained facial features in the correct configuration, another presented them in a jumbled array, and the third provided no specific features but the same overall amount of stimulus brightness. Even in the first month, infants showed a small but consistent spontaneous preference for the facial configuration, and Fantz concluded that even the youngest infants had the ability to perceive a facial configuration in this schematic stimulus. However, there were a number of criticisms of this early study. The main one that concerns us here is that the facial arrangement contained more information around the edge of the stimulus. This might not seem to matter, but there is evidence that young infants tend to scan around the periphery of complex stimuli. Given this tendency, they may have looked longer at the facial arrangement simply because there was more to look at around its edge.

Subsequent work applied better controls in the design of the stimuli, and revised the estimated age regarding the emergence of face perception to at least 4 months (Wilcox, 1969), though later, this was revised downwards again to 2 months (Maurer & Barrera, 1981). There is, however, always the chance that negative results obtained with younger infants are due to the fact that the technique used is not the most suitable for very young infants. And in parallel with this work was another study using a different technique with newborns. Instead of using the visual preference technique, Goren,

Sarty, and Wu (1975) moved schematic stimuli back and forth in the visual field of newborns, and found that they followed the facial arrangement further and for longer than a jumbled face. This different form of visual preference strongly suggests that a form of face perception is present at birth. Why does this technique appear to work better than the spontaneous visual preference technique? Probably the crucial factor is the movement of the stimuli. It seems likely that if infants are equipped with a system for perceiving faces, it will be tuned to detecting and discriminating between real faces, which of course are rarely static.

DISCRIMINATING BETWEEN FACES

The question of most relevance in relation to infants' social and emotional development is at what age infants are able to discriminate between faces, in particular between their parents' faces and those of others. The tendency has been to tackle this question by investigating infants' responses to real faces. Typically, infants are presented with a familiar and an unfamiliar face side by side, with a view to measuring any spontaneous visual preference. Although use of real faces has the advantage of realism, it carries with it a number of difficulties, as we shall see.

Several studies have obtained evidence for discrimination between mother's and a female stranger's face by young infants (Carpenter, 1974; Maurer & Salapatek, 1976) and even newborns with only a few hours' contact with their mother (Bushnell, 2001; Field, Cohen, Garcia, & Greenberg, 1984). In all cases, infants showed a visual preference for their mother's face.

However, this finding is hard to interpret without applying quite strict controls. For instance, infants are capable of identifying their mother by sense of smell, and this, rather than visual recognition, could have directed looking to their mother. Bushnell, Sai, and Mullin (1989) reduced the likelihood of this by providing a strong-smelling perfume to act as an olfactory mask. Another problem is that in most studies the mother presumably recognized her infant and so may have produced more dynamic facial expressions, something that could have attracted more looking without any implication that the infant identified his or her mother. However, Walton, Bower, and Bower (1992) effectively ruled out this possibility by presenting videotaped images of mother's and stranger's faces. Because these images were captured while both mother and stranger were looking at a camera (and one baby's "strange" mother was another baby's real mother!), it is clear that the infants' longer looking at mother than stranger was a genuine visual preference for her face.

It thus appears clear that, even within a day of birth, newborns are capable of discriminating between their mother's and a female stranger's face. What remains unclear, however, is the basis on which this discrimination is made. Although most investigators have gone to considerable lengths to match mothers and strangers on coloring, hair color, and style, it is still possible that discriminations are made on gross differences of this sort rather than on recognition of the mother's face as a whole. However, the evidence on face perception indicates that, even at birth, there is a distinct possibility that discrimination is based on configurational differences, that is, differences in the spacing of the eyes, the relationship between eyes and nose, etc.

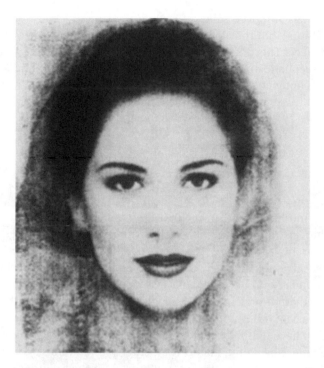

Plate 5.1 An averaged female face.

PREFERENCE FOR ATTRACTIVE FACES

One intriguing recent finding is that 2-month-old infants (Langlois, Ritter, Roggman, & Vaughn, 1991) and even newborns (Slater et al., 1998) will look longer at a face rated attractive by adults than they will at faces rated less attractive. We can begin to make sense of this finding by considering another finding; if one averages a set of faces to produce a **prototypical face**, adults rate the product more attractive than the individual instances. Possibly, then, attractiveness preferences have their origins in preferences for prototypes. It is fairly unlikely that infants have a concept of attractiveness, but they may possess an **innate** "face recognition system" that triggers attention to faces and which is maximally stimulated by a prototypical face.

IMITATION

The conventional view put forward many years ago by Piaget was that imitation was impossible until infants were capable of representing self and other, a capacity which was thought to develop late in infancy (Piaget, 1954). However, it now seems clear that even newborns are capable of imitating facial and manual gestures. Meltzoff and Moore (1977) were the first to report well-controlled studies of imitation in early infancy. It is tricky to carry out work of this sort. In order to provide a fair test of

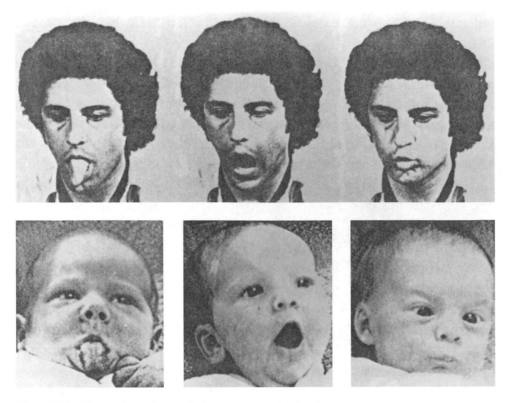

Plate 5.2 Examples of modeled gesture and infant's response
(Meltzoff & Moore, 1977).

the phenomenon, investigators must focus on gestures that the infant is capable of producing spontaneously, and so we are faced with the problem of establishing whether the infant is truly imitating or simply exercising a gesture that they produce frequently anyway. Thus, if one focused purely on tongue protrusion, apparent agreement between the modeled act and the infant's response might simply reflect the high spontaneous rate of tongue protrusion by young infants.

Meltzoff and Moore surmounted this problem by presenting different facial gestures (see plate 5.2) and asking raters who were blind to the gesture modeled to judge the gesture that infants were making. Working with data from infants within their first month, judges showed a significant tendency to identify the gesture made by the infant as matching the one the adult had been modeling. Later they found similar evidence with newborns (Meltzoff & Moore, 1983).

Although these claims were highly controversial at the time (and to some extent continue to be controversial, e.g., Anisfeld et al., 2001), the findings have now been replicated in many laboratories and neonatal imitation appears to be a real phenomenon. In addition to its relevance regarding infants' social awareness, the ability to imitate implies a great deal regarding infants' face perception. After all, in order to imitate a facial gesture, infants have to be able to perceive the internal parts of the face making the gesture, and be able to make matches to the corresponding parts of their own face.

VOICE PERCEPTION

Evidence presented in chapter 4 makes it clear that even prior to birth the fetus picks up auditory information. Kisilevsky, Muir, and Low (1992) found that from 26 weeks gestation onwards, fetal heart rate changed consistently in relation to auditory stimulation, and Hepper (1992) obtained evidence for fetal responsiveness to sounds at only 12 weeks gestation.

Research with young infants reveals some remarkable abilities to discriminate speech sounds. Newborns reveal the ability to discriminate between certain speech syllables (Moon, Bever, & Fifer, 1992; Moon & Fifer, 1990). Additionally, unlike adults, very young infants appear to discriminate speech distinctions that exist in other languages but not in their own (Eilers, Gavin, & Oller, 1982; Trehub, 1976), later narrowing their discriminative capabilities to distinctions contained in their own language (Eimas, Siqueland, Jusczyk, & Vigorito, 1971). These changes in infants' speech discrimination abilities are discussed in chapters 1 and 9.

Some investigators saw this as evidence for a language acquisition device; the newborn was receptive to all languages and later became focused on the one to which he or she was exposed. However, some of the magic was taken out of these findings when it was shown that other species, including chinchilla rabbits, made similar speech sound discriminations to very young infants! It seems likely, then, that human language evolved to suit the characteristics of the auditory system, characteristics that have much in common across species. However, the evidence for the progressive narrowing of discriminations to those existing in the language infants are exposed to does suggest the presence of an important speech-learning process.

VOICE AND SPEECH DISCRIMINATION

Just as in the case of facial discrimination, it turns out that newborn infants show an attentional preference for their mother's voice compared to that of a female stranger of similar age (DeCasper & Fifer, 1980). Because these infants were only 3 days old with only 12 hours' contact with their mother, we might assume that, as with face discrimination, we are dealing with a very rapid learning process. However, hearing is different from vision in the sense that there is scope for learning prior to birth. If the fetus is responsive to sounds, does she learn about sounds? This whole topic is treated in detail in chapter 4, but it is worth commenting on this here to complete the picture. It has been demonstrated that speech sounds, particularly those produced by the mother, are available in the uterine environment, and a fascinating study by DeCasper and Spence (1986) indicates that the unborn child learns about auditory information. In their study mothers were asked to read a prose passage repeatedly prior to the birth of their infant. Once the infants were born, they were exposed to this passage again and a novel one. They showed an attentional preference for the preexposed passage even though both were read by the mother, or even when both were read by another speaker. Nobody is claiming that these infants discriminated between these passages in terms of meaning. But the finding is exciting nevertheless, indicating that the fetus and newborn infant are capable of encoding speech in sufficient detail to extract differences in rhythm and/or **intonation** between the two passages, independent of the reader's tone of voice.

Preference for infant-directed speech

When parents speak to infants, they typically use a form of speech in which intonation patterns are exaggerated, that is, there is more rise and fall in the pitch of the voice than when addressing other adults. It has been shown that infants prefer to hear this speech over adult-directed speech (Fernald, 1982). This form of speech is often called *motherese*, and it is further discussed in chapters 7 and 9. However, the term motherese is a bit of a misnomer, because similar preferences emerge even when the speaker is male (Pegg, Werker, & McLeod, 1992). It seems likely that **infant-directed speech** not only attracts the infant's attention, but presents clearer examples of speech from which the infant is more capable of learning relationships between words, objects and actions.

SUMMARY

Current evidence indicates that the ability to perceive faces is present at birth, and that discrimination between mother's and stranger's faces develops within the first days after birth. Preferences for "attractive" faces appear at birth and are probably linked to infants' internal model of the prototypical face. The existence of neonatal imitation of facial gestures further reinforces the conclusion that newborns are capable of perceiving the internal detail and configuration of the human face. Voice and speech perception is also well developed in early infancy, and it is likely that voice discrimination actually develops prior to birth. Further development of voice perception is likely to be supported by parents' spontaneous production of infant-directed speech which contains exaggerated pitch contours that both attract infants' attention and are likely to support speech perception.

 Infants' Knowledge of the World

The conventional view is that cognitive processes involve mental representations of the world. This sets cognition apart from perception, because cognitive processes can act on representations of aspects of the world that are not available to the senses, whereas perception is limited to the "here and now." In recent years, the clarity of this distinction has been somewhat watered down. For instance, take Kellman and Spelke's "rod and box" study illustrated in figure 5.2. The fact that 4-month-olds appear to "fill in" the invisible parts of the object could be taken either as evidence of a high-level *perceptual* process, or of the ability to form a mental representation of the absent part (and hence a *cognitive* ability), and the choice of account is determined very much by the investigator's theoretical orientation. Nevertheless, there is a large body of work dating back since the early twentieth century that is aimed specifically at investigating infants' knowledge and representations of the world.

JEAN PIAGET AND THE DEVELOPMENT OF OBJECT PERMANENCE

Piaget's (1954) view was that infants were not born with knowledge of the world, but instead gradually constructed knowledge and the ability to represent reality mentally – this theoretical view is known as **constructivism**. Note that this view is not necessarily incompatible with the evidence cited earlier pointing to sophisticated perception of the world at birth, because Piaget was making his claims primarily about *knowledge* or understanding, rather than perception. A key aspect of Piaget's account related to the development of mental representation, specifically, the ability to maintain a representation of objects that are out of sight, leading to awareness of their permanence. According to him, prior to the age of 9 months, infants do not exhibit **object permanence**, and although this appears in simple form at 9 months, it does not develop fully until near the end of the second year of life.

Piaget reported a multitude of convincing observations to substantiate his claims, and although these were from his own three children as infants, the main phenomena have replicated readily in controlled laboratory investigations involving large numbers of infants. His principal examples involved infants' responses to an object being hidden. Prior to 9 months, he found that infants made no response when an object was hidden; even if they were very interested in it and thus highly motivated to retrieve it, their actions toward it ceased when it went out of sight. It was as though out of sight was out of mind, which is more or less Piaget's claim. Not being able to represent the hidden object, there was no way that the young infant could hold it in mind.

Search onset and the A not B error

In contrast, by 9 months the infant's reaction to disappearance had changed. Now, if an object was hidden, the 9-month-old would search for it successfully. To Piaget, this indicated the beginnings of the ability to represent the absent object. However, Piaget always went on to complicate the task, to test the extent of the infant's ability (note that this is the essence of the **clinical method**, which is described in more detail in chapters 1 and 2). He found that after having searched successfully at one location (A), infants failed to take account of its disappearance at a new location (B); even though its disappearance at the new location was perfectly obvious, infants continued to search at the old place. For obvious reasons this has become known as the **A not B error**. Piaget took this as evidence that their representation of the hidden object was not yet fully objective; they repeated an old action to "recreate" the object, as if their own actions, rather than objective knowledge of where it had gone, defined its existence.

Recent Work on Infant Cognition

Persuasive though Piaget's observations were, over the past 20 or 30 years a substantial body of work has emerged suggesting strongly that, well before Piaget would have recognized, infants have an awareness of object permanence and an advanced general understanding of the physical world. One of the limitations of Piaget's techniques was that in many cases he relied on measuring the infant's actions toward objects, such as reaching and manual search, and because we know that motor skill develops with age, investigators sought ways of investigating infant knowledge in ways that did not rely so heavily on complex actions.

THE VIOLATION OF EXPECTATION TECHNIQUE

The technique used in most recent studies of young infants' ability is called the **violation of expectation technique**, and is very much like the habituation–novelty technique described earlier. Infants are familiarized with an event sequence, and are then presented with two test trials that are variants on the original, one involving a possible event and the other involving an impossible event. Infants' looking at the two test events is measured, but in this case longer looking at one event does not just indicate discrimination between the events. In all these studies, if there is a looking-time difference, it is the impossible event that infants look at longer, and this is taken as evidence that they have detected the impossibility of the event sequence.

EVIDENCE OF OBJECT KNOWLEDGE: THE "DRAWBRIDGE STUDY" AND OTHERS

An example should make the technique clear. Baillargeon, Spelke, and Wasserman (1985) familiarized 5-month-old infants with a repeated event in which a flap (the drawbridge) rotated from flat on the table with its free edge near to the infant, through 180° so that it was again flat on the table with its free edge away from the infant, and then back through 180° to its starting point. Following these trials, infants were presented with two types of test trial (see figure 5.5). In both cases, a block was introduced in the path of the flap, such that it would impede its full rotation. In the *possible* test event, the flap rotated to hide the block and stopped at the point at which it would contact the block, and then rotated back to its starting point. In the *impossible* test event, the flap rotated 180°, appearing to move through and annihilate the block in the process. What is particularly neat about this study is that, in terms of surface familiarity, the impossible event is most similar to the familiarization event, and so if infants were processing at a simple level, we would expect them to look at the possible event because it is superficially more novel. However, what Baillargeon et al. (1985) actually found was that infants looked longer at the impossible event. Their conclusion is that 5-month-old infants have knowledge of object permanence (they know that the block continues to exist when hidden by the flap)

Habituation

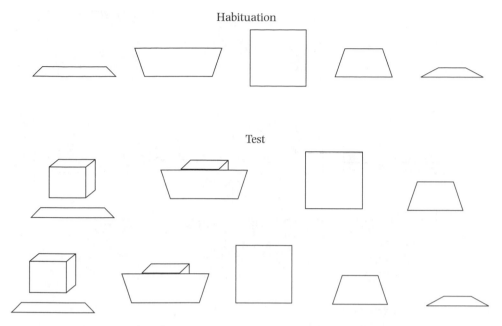

Test

Figure 5.5 Habituation and test displays used by Baillargeon, Spelke, and Wasserman (1985). Reprinted by permission of Elsevier Science.

and know about the conditions under which one object will impede the movement of another.

Another even more striking demonstration comes from the results of a study by Baillargeon (1986), illustrated in figure 5.6. Infants were familiarized with an event in which a truck ran down a track and passed behind a screen, reemerging at the other side. Prior to each trial, the screen was lifted, revealing the unobstructed track. Following familiarization, two test events were presented: (1) a possible event in which, prior to the truck's movement, the screen was lifted to reveal a block placed *behind* the track (and hence would not impede the movement of the truck), and an impossible event, in which the screen was lifted to reveal a block placed *on* the track. In both cases, the truck then rolled down the track as usual, reemerging from the screen as before. Baillargeon found that 6- and 8-month-olds looked longer at the impossible test event, a finding replicated by Baillargeon and DeVos (1991) with 4-month-olds. Again, the conclusion is that infants are capable of detecting the impossibility of the truck moving through the block. Given that the block is hidden when the truck event takes place, this requires knowledge of object permanence as well as knowledge of the solidity and impenetrability of objects.

It appears that even 2-month-olds have some ability of this sort. Spelke, Breinlinger, Macomber, and Jacobson (1992) familiarized infants to an event in which a ball rolled behind a screen, whereupon the screen was raised to reveal the ball resting against an end wall. On test trials, an obstruction was introduced behind the screen between the ball and the end wall, and the possible event involved the screen lifting to reveal the ball resting against the obstruction, whereas the impossible event involved it being

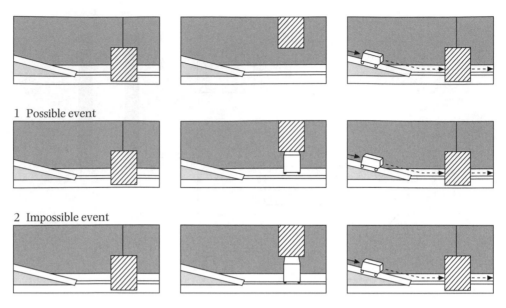

Figure 5.6 Displays presented by Baillargeon (1986). The habituation event is shown above the possible and impossible test events. © 1986, with permission from Elsevier Science.

revealed beyond the obstruction against the wall. These very young infants looked longer at the latter event, despite the fact that the ball rested where it had on familiarization trials. One simplification in this task was that the top of the obstruction was visible above the screen. Thus, it can be argued that success at this task does not require full object permanence since at least part of the obstruction could be seen throughout. Again, however, the conclusion is that these 2-month-olds realize that the ball cannot move through the obstruction.

Young infants reason about the number of objects in an event

Investigators such as Spelke and Baillargeon argue that infants possess **core knowledge** of the world, on the basis of which they reason about the events that they see. In the case of the studies outlined above, this leads them to conclude that certain events are impossible. It has also been claimed that young infants reason about the *number* of objects involved in an event. Spelke, Kestenbaum, Simons, and Wein (1995) familiarized 3- and 4-month-old infants to two types of moving object events (see figure 5.7). In both, two screens were present, and in one case – the continuous event – an object moved behind the first screen, reemerged from it, disappeared behind the second screen, and reemerged from it. In the other case – the discontinuous event – the middle segment of the object's trajectory was omitted; it disappeared behind the first screen and an identical object emerged after a delay from the second screen.

Infants were then presented with test displays in which the screens were absent and the movements either involved a single object moving the full distance, or two

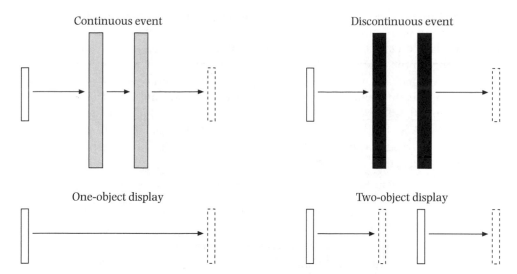

Figure 5.7 Displays presented by Spelke et al. (1995). Habituation displays (top half of figure) are either continuous or discontinuous, and test events involve either one or two objects. Reproduced with permission from *The British Journal of Psychology*, © The British Psychological Society.

objects, the first moving to the point where the first screen had been and stopping, and the second moving from where the second screen had been. Infants who had been familiarized with the *continuous* movement looked longer at the two-object test, and those that had been familiarized with the *discontinuous* event looked longer at the single-object movement. The conclusion was that infants reasoned that there was one object involved in the continuous event and two objects involved in the discontinuous event, and so on test trials they looked at the event involving the number of objects that differed from their expectation.

Wilcox and Baillargeon (1998) used a particularly ingenious technique to detect whether infants reason about numerosity on the basis of object features. They presented 7- to 9-month-olds with a moving object event in which an object disappeared behind a screen and a different object reemerged from the other side. In one event, the screen was wide enough to conceal both objects at once, whereas in another event, the screen was only just wider than one object. Wilcox and Baillargeon found that infants looked longer at the narrow-screen event, and their conclusion is that on the basis of the featural differences between objects, they reasoned that two were involved and that both could not be hidden behind the narrow screen.

YOUNG INFANTS DISCRIMINATE DIFFERENT NUMBERS OF ITEMS

Over 20 years ago, Starkey and Cooper (1980) habituated 4- to 7-month-old infants to patterns of a particular number of dots (either two or three) and then tested for **dishabituation** to the other number (three or two). They also included a large number condition in which there were either four or six dots. Infants dishabituated to number change in the small number but not in the large number condition. This suggested that infants are capable of discriminating between arrays in terms of numerosity, though only in the case of small numbers. Starkey and Cooper were of the view that numerical competence was based on **subitizing**, which can be defined as the ability to perceive directly a small number of items without counting or carrying out any calculation. This ability only applies to very small numbers, which fits the results they obtained. Starkey, Spelke, and Gelman (1990) replicated this effect using arrays of widely differing everyday objects, thus showing that the ability did not simply apply to arrays of identical dots.

YOUNG INFANTS CAN COUNT!

More recently, Wynn (1992, 1995) carried out a number of ingenious studies aimed at assessing not just whether infants could discriminate on the basis of number, but whether they had knowledge of addition and subtraction operations. Her task is indicated in figure 5.8. In the addition task, 4- and 5-month-old infants were presented with a single object, a screen was raised to hide it, whereupon a hand appeared with a second object and placed it behind the screen (the addition operation). The screen was then lowered for the test trial to reveal either one object (original array, but impossible given the addition of the second object) or two objects (novel array but correct given the addition). In the subtraction task, initially two objects were presented, and the hand removed one once they were screened. Thus in this case on the test trial the single-object outcome is correct and the two-object outcome is incorrect. Infants looked longer at the single object in the addition case and longer at the double object in the subtraction case. In other words, they looked longer at the unexpected event, as if registering that it was impossible.

Wynn concluded that young infants have an understanding of addition and sub-traction, but recognized that this could be a very approximate system in which any larger or smaller number would be accepted as the result of addition and subtraction, respectively. Thus, she conducted a further study in which 4-month-olds were exposed to the 1 + 1 addition task and on test trials were presented with either two or three objects. Infants looked longer at the three-object outcome, and Wynn concluded that their knowledge of addition was quite precise, to the extent that they expected exactly two objects, and not just more objects, to result from a 1 + 1 operation. This conclusion attributes a great deal of knowledge to young infants, and continues to be controversial – for instance, Wakeley, Rivera, and Langer (2000a) failed to replicate Wynn's finding that infants' numerical expectations are very precise.

SUMMARY

The evidence reported in this section provides compelling evidence that quite young infants understand object permanence and the rules that constrain the movement of one object relative to another, and also that they have some basic awareness of

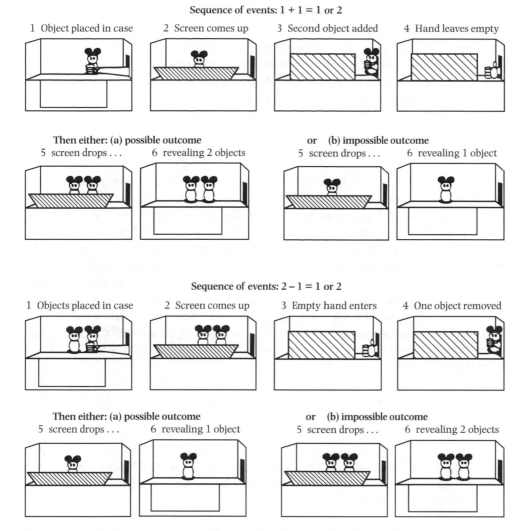

Figure 5.8 Event sequences presented by Wynn (1992): addition events above, subtraction events below. Reprinted with permission from *Nature*, copyright 1992 Macmillan Magazines Limited and Professor K. Wynn.

number and numerical operations, relating to small numbers. And there is much other evidence bearing on other aspects of awareness of the physical world that yields a similar picture of early competence. It should be noted, however, that these results have not gone unchallenged, and there is a growing tendency to ask whether the findings can be explained in terms of much lower-level perceptual and attentional processes (see, for example, Haith, 1998). It is beyond the scope of this chapter to go into these critical accounts in detail. But there is one question that should be tackled here, namely, how to reconcile these findings with the suggestion from Piaget's object search tasks that object permanence does not begin to emerge until 8 or 9 months.

Object Search Revisited

If infants of around 4 months understand that an object that is hidden continues to exist, why do they fail to search for hidden objects until they are 8 or 9 months old? And when they do start to search, why do they make search errors of various sorts that persist right through to around 18 months?

SEARCH FAILURE IS NOT DUE TO LACK OF MOTOR SKILL

An obvious possible reason for infants under 8 months failing to search for a hidden object is that they lack the motor skill of reaching. However, it seems clear that this is not the explanation. Bower and Wishart (1972) showed that infants who failed to retrieve an object from under an opaque upturned cup succeeded when the cup was transparent. In each case, the action required was identical, and success with the transparent case indicates that they at least have the necessary motor skill to dislodge the cup. It seems clear from this that it is the invisibility of the object that is a major factor preventing successful retrieval. However, it turns out that not just *any* form of invisibility leads to problems for this age group, since it has been shown that infants will reach out and grasp an object suspended in front of them after the lights have been turned off and the object is therefore invisible (Bower & Wishart, 1972; Hood & Willatts, 1986).

Here, out of sight does not seem to be out of mind, and Bower claims that infants have problems with cases where one object conceals another because they have difficulty perceiving or understanding the relationship between object and occluder. This view is partly in keeping with Piaget's account, because he claimed that it was through constructing the relationship between hidden object and occluder that infants began to represent the hidden object. The difference, however, is that Bower claimed that very young infants possess object permanence, *before* they understand relationships between objects and occluders.

SEEKING AN EXPLANATION OF THE A NOT B ERROR

Over the years, a great deal of research effort has gone into attempts to explain the A not B error. As indicated earlier, infants of about 9 months search successfully for an object hidden in one position (A), but when the object is hidden in a new position (B), they continue to search back in the old location (A).

Response perseveration?

Could the error simply arise because infants carry on with a response habit established during hiding trials at A? Thus, maybe when the object is hidden in a new place, they do not attend fully and repeat the old response, a phenomenon referred to as **response perseveration**. If this were all there was to it, we would expect them to correct their error on subsequent trials, realizing the need to attend more closely. However, although some infants correct themselves quickly, others will make a string of errors over many trials – that is, persisting in searching at the "A" location. Curiously, it turns out that infants make errors even if they have only *seen* the object hidden and revealed at the A location, and have not been given the opportunity to reach for it (Butterworth, 1974; Evans, 1973; Landers, 1971). Under these circumstances, they have executed no action to A, but on being allowed to search for the first time on B trials, they search at A! Thus it does not seem that response perseveration can easily explain the error.

Memory limitations?

It has frequently been pointed out that absent-minded adults often search for objects in customary places despite just having put them elsewhere. Adults do not have problems in representing hidden objects; in this case the problem is to do with memory of the past history of the object in question. Note, however, that these adult errors tend to occur when the individual is not fully attentive, and as Piaget pointed out, infants make these errors even when they are fully attentive. This, however, does not rule out a memory explanation, it being quite possible that infants have more profound memory limitations than adults. Harris (1973) showed that infants rarely made errors if they were allowed to search immediately for the hidden object at B, and this led him to suggest that the phenomenon was memory-based. It was not a matter of simply forgetting about the object entirely, because infants search accurately at A, and continue to search there on B trials. Instead, Harris suggested that **interference** occurred between memory of the object at the first location and memory of it at the new location, such that information about its prior location often predominated over the more recent information about its new location.

There is, however, a major problem for any memory account. Piaget (1954) noted that errors occurred even when the object was fully in view at the B location. Additionally, Butterworth (1977) and Harris (1974) both obtained errors when the object was placed under a transparent cover at B. Some suggested that these errors arose partly due to infants' difficulty understanding transparent covers. However, Bremner and Knowles (1984) obtained errors even when the object was fully visible and uncovered at A. In this study, provided there was a covered location at A, infants made errors at much the usual rate even though the object was in full view and fully accessible at B. It is difficult to see in what way memory for the new location of the object can enter into this form of the task. These errors with the object in view indicate just what a powerful phenomenon we are dealing with. Although making the object visible under a cup helped younger infants to begin to search, making the object visible in the B location does not help them to search accurately after successful search at A.

Frontal cortex immaturity

There is strong evidence that an area of the brain known as the **frontal cortex** is involved in planning and guidance of action, processes that are often referred to as **executive functions**. Diamond (1985, 1988) argues that immaturity of frontal cortex in early infancy leads to deficits in infants' ability to use certain types of information to guide action. Specifically, she argues that infants are unable to use their memory of the absent object to inhibit an old response (search at A) that is now inappropriate.

This account is a combination of the memory and response perseveration accounts presented above. In this respect, it is a significant advance on previous models in recognizing that it is probably a *combination* of factors that leads to error. However, the same problems that provide difficulty for single-factor accounts apply here as well. This model does not predict errors in searching at the "B" location after simply observing the object being hidden at A, and yet such errors occur, in circumstances under which there is no prior response to inhibit. Similarly, this model does not predict errors when the object is visible at B, because there is no memory load in this case, and yet such errors occur.

Converting knowledge to action

The answer to our dilemma may be that we need to identify a more general role of frontal cortex in using high-level information to guide action. The evidence presented earlier in this chapter strongly suggests that quite young infants have knowledge of object permanence and the rules governing object movement. However, research using object search tasks shows that they are unable to use this information to guide action. Thus, when faced with the A not B task, infants are aware of the continued presence of the object, but are simply unable to use this information to guide action (Bremner, 2001; Willatts, 1997). Thus, initial success at finding the object at A is based on trial-and-error manipulation of the cover at which it disappeared rather than on knowledge of the existence of the object, and they repeat this action whenever and wherever the object disappears, and even if the object is placed in view at the B location. Development of frontal cortex involves formation of links between object knowledge and action, leading to accurate search based on knowledge of the object's position rather than trial and error.

There is some evidence in keeping with this interpretation. Ahmed and Ruffman (1998) showed that infants who made A not B errors nevertheless showed evidence in a nonsearch A not B task of knowing where the object was on both A and B trials. If, after seeing the object hidden and retrieved from A, infants saw it hidden at B, they looked longer if it was then retrieved from A than if it was retrieved from B. Thus, they appear to know where the object is wherever it is hidden, and are capable of holding that location in memory for quite some time. But they are unable to use that information to guide their manual search.

Summary and Conclusions

Early knowledge

The evidence reviewed in the early parts of this chapter indicated that even at birth, infants are capable of discriminating patterns and shapes and perceiving an objective world. In addition, they have special perceptual abilities regarding human faces and voices, they learn to discriminate between people in the first few hours of life, and are capable of imitating facial gestures. These abilities appear to be limited to the "here and now" of perception, and it is a few months before infants show the ability to fill in the gaps in perception, for instance by perceiving the invisible part of an object in object unity tasks (figure 5.2) or perceiving subjective contours (figure 5.3). Additionally, evidence from ingenious *violation of expectation* studies reveals that around this time young infants show impressive awareness of the rules governing objects, including object permanence and the impenetrability of one object by another – they are budding physicists.

Early knowledge does not guide action

Set against this impressive array of early abilities, strong evidence remains indicating that, whatever form this early knowledge takes, it does not appear to guide action successfully. Even though they are capable of the necessary action, infants do not search for hidden objects until they are 8 or 9 months old, and even then they make characteristic search errors, in particular the A not B error. The best way at present of reconciling these conflicting bodies of evidence is to conclude that although young infants possess quite sophisticated knowledge of the world, either this knowledge is not sufficient to guide action or the necessary links between knowledge and action have not been developed.

Remodeling the Piagetian account

Recent evidence indicates that some aspects of Piaget's account of infancy require modification. Contrary to his view, it appears that young infants perceive an objective world and are at some level aware of object permanence and of the basic rules governing relationships between objects. Although the recent accounts identify further elaboration of knowledge throughout the first year of life, Piaget's view that the infant begins life without knowledge of the world now seems untenable. However, Piaget's evidence suggests a clear developmental sequence in infants' ability to act on the world. As we have seen, this is not simply a matter of motor development; 6-month-old infants are motorically capable of what is required to retrieve a hidden object and yet they do not search. Thus it may be concluded that the Piagetian account remains relatively intact if we shift the emphasis in one major way. Instead of conceptualizing infant development as primarily to do with constructing knowledge of the world, we should treat infants as possessing much of this knowledge from the start. But instead they are faced with the task of constructing links between this knowledge and action. It is here that the Piagetian concept of *construction through action on the world* is likely to remain very useful in reaching an understanding of development during the early months and years.

DISCUSSION POINTS

1 Considering the evidence, think of as many ways as you can in which newborns' perception of the world is (a) similar to and (b) different from that of adults.

2 Are you more convinced by claims about infants' knowledge of objects that are based on infants' manual action (for instance, object search) than claims based on longer looking at an event that violates a principle of reality?

3 Select a study using the violation of expectation technique and see if you can think of an alternative explanation of the results that does not assume high-level knowledge of the world on the part of the infant.

4 Think of what awareness of self and others infants must possess to explain their ability to imitate facial gestures.

5 Given evidence that fetuses can pick up sounds from their mother and the external environment, consider what sort of information infants might have already learned by the time they are born.

SUGGESTIONS FOR FURTHER READING

Bremner, J. G. (1994). *Infancy* (2nd ed.). Cambridge, MA, and Oxford: Blackwell.

Bremner, J. G., & Fogel, A. (Eds.) (2001). *Blackwell handbook of infant development*. Cambridge, MA, and Oxford: Blackwell.

Bremner, J. G., Slater, A., & Butterworth, G. (Eds.) (1997). *Infant development: Recent advances*. Hove: Psychology Press.

Messer, D., & Millar, S. (Eds.) (1998). *Exploring developmental psychology: From infancy to adolescence*. London: Arnold.

Muir, D., & Slater, A. (Eds.) (2000). *Infant development: Essential readings*. Cambridge, MA, & Oxford: Blackwell.

chapter 6

Emotional Development and Early Attachment Relationships

Elizabeth Meins

KEY CONCEPTS

AFFECT	INSECURE-RESISTANT	SECONDARY DRIVE
ATTACHMENT BEHAVIOR	MATERNAL DEPRIVATION	SECURELY ATTACHED
EGOCENTRISM	PEERS	SELF-CONCEPT
EMOTION	PRIMARY DRIVES	SOCIAL REFERENCING
EMOTION REGULATION	PSYCHOPATHOLOGY	STRANGER ANXIETY
INNATE MECHANISM	ROUGE TEST	VISUAL CLIFF
INSECURE-AVOIDANT		

OVERVIEW

Feelings of emotions accompany all our activities, and yet the topic of emotion is often neglected. Even from birth, infants display a wide range of emotional expressions, and it seems likely that emotional expression is innate. Most of the arguments about innateness concern simple emotions such as happiness, sadness, fear, and anger. However, it has been claimed that more complex emotions such as self-consciousness and jealousy can be detected in infancy.

There is also evidence that infants perceive facial expressions of emotions and that, even at birth, they show emotional resonance by expressing the same emotions in response. The ability to perceive the emotions of others makes it possible to learn a good deal about the world through seeing how adults respond to particular events. Known as social referencing, this allows infants to detect the emotional significance of a situation, such as the danger of a vertical drop. Emotional awareness is also seen in infant–parent interaction, with infants showing distress if parents stop responding as expected.

The emergence of language provides additional evidence regarding children's emotional world, because even very early utterances include emotion words such as "happy" and "scary." It has been claimed that the rich use of emotion words indicates a well-developed understanding of emotions early in development.

Research on emotional awareness in early school-age children includes work on children's ability to feel more than one emotion simultaneously. Presented with stories involving a conflict of emotions, 6-year-olds tend to deny the possibility of emotional conflict whereas 10-year-olds are much more likely to recognize that experience of two conflicting emotions is possible. Also, during this period, children show growing recognition that in certain situations another individual may feel a different emotion from them, and they also become better able to identify the causes of others' emotions.

The focus of the chapter then shifts to attachment relationships. Work in this area is rooted in Bowlby's theory that attachment is a primary drive to maintain proximity to the primary caregiver. The author reviews work stemming from Ainsworth's classification of attachment security, suggesting that different types of attachment are linked to later emotional development. Cross-cultural differences indicate that the predominant attachment type is not always secure attachment, a finding that suggests that parental style has a large part in determining the type of attachment that is formed.

It has been suggested that secure attachment in infancy is an advantage for the development of certain types of cognitive and emotional awareness during childhood, such as knowledge relating to the minds of others. Both attachment security and emotional development are likely to relate closely to parental sensitivity and parents' emotional characteristics, and there is fascinating evidence for intergenerational transfer of attachment patterns. The way in which parents represent their own childhood attachment experiences relates to the type of attachment their infant forms.

Introduction

In introductory texts on developmental psychology, a chapter on the development of the child's emotional engagement with and understanding of the world is commonly conspicuous by its absence. This oversight is curious, since emotional development would appear to underlie many other areas of developmental psychology, and has serious implications for how we conduct research on children. For example, the results of a study on the development of a cognitive ability such as problem-solving will only be valid if we can be confident that children's performance was not influenced by shyness, anxiety, or lack of interest or motivation. Consequently, it is important for all of us to be cognizant of the emotional context in which research is carried out, and the emotional maturity and engagement of each individual child.

The aim of this chapter is to provide an introductory overview of emotional development and early attachment relationships, and to consider research that has investigated links between these areas. The chapter reviews certain key theoretical positions and empirical findings, but since the individual literatures on emotional development and attachment are vast and complex, it is impossible to cover everything. Rather, I begin with a broad review of the literature on emotional development from birth to adolescence, and then focus on how researchers have investigated one particular kind of emotion: the child's feelings of attachment toward the caregiver. The final section describes the relatively new area of research on relations between adult and infant patterns of attachment and children's emotional development and **regulation**.

 ## *Are Expressions of Emotion Innate?*

Darwin (1872) argued that the ability to communicate **emotions** through a wide repertoire of facial expressions is **innate**. More recent researchers have attempted to investigate this claim in two ways: (1) by establishing whether different emotional facial expressions are universally understood; and (2) by observing whether newborn infants spontaneously produce recognizable facial expressions.

CROSS-CULTURAL EVIDENCE

There is good evidence for universality of human facial expressions of emotion. For example, Ekman and Friesen (1971) found remarkable cross-cultural similarity in adults' interpretations of facial expressions. They tested a group of Fore people from New Guinea, who had never had contact with westerners, on a task that required them to choose a photograph of the facial expression that matched the emotional context. The facial expressions in the photographs were posed by western adults and children, and yet the Fore could easily select the correct photographs for happiness, anger, disgust, and sadness, although they found surprised and fearful expressions somewhat difficult to distinguish. Similarly, Americans were equally skilled in correctly judging the emotional facial expressions of the Fore (Ekman, 1973). Cross-cultural work such as this demonstrates that human understanding of how emotions are conveyed through facial expressions is universal, but, as Harris (1989) pointed out, this does not necessarily mean that understanding emotional expressions is innate, since it is possible that all cultures learn about facial expressions merely by copying those of others in specific emotional contexts.

EXPRESSION OF EMOTION IN INFANCY

More convincing evidence of the innate quality of emotional expression is that, from birth, infants spontaneously display a wide repertoire of emotions through their facial expressions. Moreover, adults are skillful in accurately reading infants' expressions. For example, Izard, Huebner, Risser, McGinnes, and Dougherty (1980) reported that adults could accurately judge whether the facial expressions of 1- to 9-month-old infants arose because of a pleasant experience, such as interacting with their mothers, or a painful event, such as being given an injection. However, adults are less accurate in discriminating infants' negative facial expressions indicative of fear, anger, sadness, or disgust (Oster, Hegley, & Nagel, 1992). This appears not to be due to a lack of subtlety in the young infant's expression, but to the fact that the facial expressions arising from these different emotions are quite similar. Figure 6.1 shows diagrammatic depictions of some emotions. Try to label each expression. How confident are you in your discrimination of the negative emotional expressions? To find out if you are correct, see p. 163!

Figure 6.1 Exaggeratedly drawn facial expressions of emotion.

EMOTION AND SELF-AWARENESS

More controversially, some researchers have argued that, in the first year of life, infants' behavior betrays feelings of more complex emotions. Reddy (2000) argued that infants as young as 3 months display coyness and self-consciousness when confronted with their mirror images. Similarly, Draghi-Lorenz (1997) reported that infants between 2 and 11 months show jealousy if their mothers hold and coo over other infants. Such assertions are controversial since these emotions depend upon the infant being able to represent and recognize self, an ability that is assumed not to be acquired until much later (e.g., Lewis & Brooks-Gunn, 1979). While it seems reasonable to conclude that emotions such as pleasure, disgust, and fear are innate and the consequences of evolutionary adaptation, it is more difficult to make such claims about more complex emotions like jealousy, guilt, shame, and pride. These latter emotions clearly appear to involve a comparison between a representation of one's own ideal or goal and one's current behavior or state (see Barrett & Campos, 1987, for a further discussion of different classes of emotion). For example, in order to feel proud, one must recognize that one's goals have been achieved or surpassed, whereas shame arises from an admission that one's behavior has not come up to personal moral standards. Thus, in order to demonstrate these emotions, the infant must have a **self-concept**.

The development of one's self-concept is assessed using a classic paradigm called the **rouge test** (Amsterdam, 1972), whereby a dab of rouge is surreptitiously put on the child's nose before he or she is placed in front of a mirror. Children are said to have acquired a self-concept when they touch their own noses when confronted with their red-nosed mirror image. Using this technique, the evidence shows that children do not appear to develop an understanding of self until 15 months of age (Amsterdam, 1972; Lewis & Brooks-Gunn, 1979); before this age, children typically touch the red mark on the reflected mirror image. Some researchers are therefore skeptical about whether behaviors that appear to arise from self-consciousness or jealousy are true manifestations of such complex emotions. Others, however, may argue that the rouge test underestimates young infants' understanding of self, and are more willing to entertain the possibility that infants can feel and express such complex emotions at surprisingly young ages. Anecdotally, infants in the first year do seem capable of jealous behavior and of showing pride in their achievements. My 5-month-old daughter, for example, looks unmistakably proud when she pulls herself into a standing position! A task for the future is therefore to try to replicate these findings of early complex emotions and to establish reliable methods for their assessment.

 ## Infant Discrimination of Facial Expressions

Even if one accepts that infants can demonstrate complex emotions, this ability tells us very little about whether they can discriminate emotions in other people, and therefore whether they have any fundamental *understanding* of emotions. In order to address this question, researchers have employed the habituation–dishabituation technique (see chapter 5) to assess infants' discrimination of a variety of facial expressions. Barrera and Maurer (1981) reported that 3-month-olds could distinguish between photographs of people smiling and frowning, and Caron, Caron, and Myers (1982) found that 4- to 7-month-olds could distinguish between expressions of happiness and surprise. Even more astounding is Field, Woodson, Greenberg, and Cohen's (1982) finding that neonates could discriminate between happy, sad, and surprised expressions posed by a live model. However, although infants appear capable of quite impressive feats of sensory discrimination, this does not necessarily mean that they can understand that there is *meaning* in emotional facial expressions. In other words, such studies cannot tell us whether these infants can distinguish expressions *as* expressions. In order to begin to make such a claim, one needs to analyze how infants *respond* to different facial expressions.

Some results from Field et al.'s (1982) study suggest that these very young infants may be empathizing with the emotion they see being portrayed. In addition to investigating infants' responses to the emotional expressions, Field et al. had adult judges assess which emotional expression they thought the infant was viewing purely by watching the infant's response during the procedure. The adults could do this at levels above chance because the infants actually appeared to *imitate* the facial expression they were watching, and did not merely view the stimuli passively (see plate 6.1). By 6 months, infants can respond to expressions in more sophisticated and appropriate ways, crying and frowning at angry and sad faces (Kreutzer & Charlesworth, 1973). But once again, there are problems with making strong claims that this research demonstrates an understanding of emotion in young infants. Infants' responses to these emotional expressions were measured in a nonemotional context, where changes in facial cues were unrelated to events, and their responses may have been mere imitation. The infant's response therefore still does not indicate an understanding that expressions relate to emotional feelings. Because of these shortcomings, one can only be confident that infants understand the relation between people's feelings and their facial expressions if a study manipulates the emotional context, and not merely the visual cues present in emotional expressions.

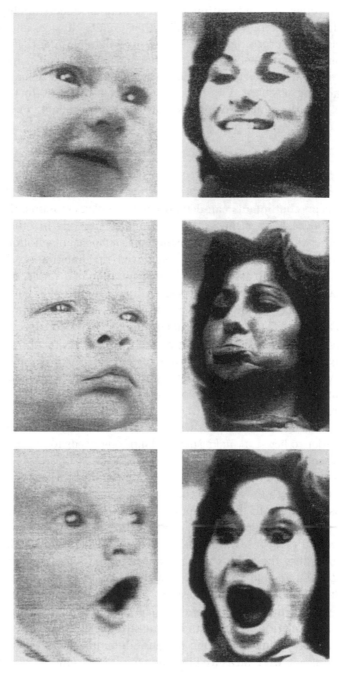

Plate 6.1 Modeled and matching expressions of adult and neonate (from Field et al., 1982). Copyright 1982 by the AAAS.

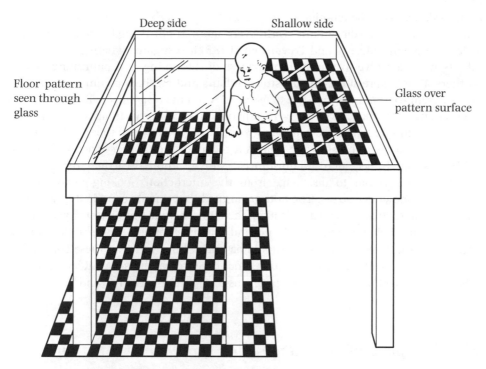

Figure 6.2 Gibson and Walk's (1960) visual cliff apparatus. Used by permission of *Scientific American*.

 ## *Emotional Discrimination in Context*

SOCIAL REFERENCING

The phenomenon of **social referencing**, whereby the infant looks to the caregiver in order to glean information on how he or she should act, provides an excellent way to assess infants' understanding of other people's emotional expressions. Sorce, Emde, Campos, and Klinnert (1985) investigated whether infants could utilize their caregivers' facial expressions to appraise a potentially dangerous situation. Using Gibson and Walk's (1960) **"visual cliff"** paradigm (see figure 6.2), mothers coaxed their 12-month-olds close to the "deep" side before posing a happy or fearful expression. Sorce et al. reported that none of the infants crossed over to the deep side if the mother posed a fearful expression; on the contrary, such facial expressions tended to result in infants retreating or showing distress. Conversely, when their mothers looked happy, three-quarters of the infants crossed to the deep side.

EXPECTATIONS ABOUT EMOTIONAL RESPONSES OF OTHERS

Studies such as those above suggest that infants are not only able to discriminate between facial expressions, but can modify their own emotional response and behavior in accordance with the emotion conveyed by the mother's facial expression. Indeed, some researchers credit infants with even more sophisticated understanding of facial expressions. Murray and Trevarthen (1985) investigated whether 2-month-old infants were sensitive to the appropriateness of the timing and patterning of their mothers' facial expressions. In this study, infants and mothers communicated via a video system so that it was possible to assess how infants responded when face-to-face interactions with their mothers were put out of synchrony. Infants' responses to interactions in real time were compared with those when the mother's behavior was made non-contingent by showing infants a replay of the mother's face from earlier in the session. Under such circumstances, Murray and Trevarthen reported that infants quickly began to disengage from the interaction, looking away, and in some cases, showing distress. The authors argued that infants can identify when the "rules" of interaction are violated, leading them to conclude that infants have *expectations* of what their mothers should do and which emotions they should show in response to their own behavior. It should be noted, however, that these conclusions should be treated with a degree of caution, since other researchers (e.g., Rochat, Neisser, & Marian, 1998) have encountered problems in replicating Murray and Trevarthen's results.

 ## *Beyond Infancy: Linguistic Expression of Emotion*

As in all areas of developmental psychology, the onset of language enables one to pinpoint more precisely the exact level of emotional understanding a child has reached. Children begin to talk about emotions at a surprisingly young age, and parents readily give anecdotal accounts of their children using *emotion words* in the second year of life. Bretherton, McNew, and Beeghly-Smith (1981) reported on a search of published diaries and accounts of children's acquisition of emotion words that showed some children begin to use emotion words as young as 18 months of age, with a rapid increase in children's vocabularies of emotion words during the third year of life. In a follow-up study, Bretherton and Beeghly (1982) found that 28-month-olds could use emotion words to explain and comment on their own and other people's current behavior:

> "I see tiger. That too scary."
> "You sad, Daddy?"

The children in this study even used emotion words in a decontextualized fashion to predict an emotional response in the future, and showed that they understood the causal relation between behavior and emotional response. Examples of such uses of emotion words included the following:

> "Daddy be mad?" (future)
> "Santa will be happy if I pee in the potty."
> "No watch the Hulk. I afraid" (several hours before the television program *The Incredible Hulk* was due to be shown).

UNDERSTANDING EMOTIONS

Bretherton and Beeghly (1982) made strong claims on the basis of their data, arguing that the use of emotion words implies that children really understand emotions. Consequently, they opposed the view that early social understanding consists exclusively of script knowledge (whereby children do not understand the emotions involved, but know the "script" for how to act in a given situation), which later becomes replaced by a true understanding of psychological functioning. Bretherton and Beeghly's account is persuasive, and the evidence does point to children having quite a sophisticated understanding of their own and other people's emotional lives well before they reach their third birthday. Clearly, though, everyday experience tells us that there are differences between the emotional responses of infants and young children and those of older children and adults. The question now is how such differences can be characterized. One way in which researchers have approached this question is to investigate children's understanding of emotions when people's feelings may not be clear-cut or easy to read from their facial expressions. This research on *emotional ambiguity* has focused on three major areas of more complex emotional understanding: (1) emotional conflicts; (2) hiding true emotions; and (3) differing emotional responses to the same event.

Emotional conflicts

Harris (1983) investigated whether 6- and 10-year-olds understood that it was possible to feel more than one emotion simultaneously. Children were told stories, each involving an emotional conflict, whereby the protagonist would be likely to feel two emotions at the same time. For example, one story was as follows:

> Late one night there is a bark outside the door. It's Lassie, your dog. She has been lost all day and she has come home, but she has cut her ear in a fight.

After each story, children were asked whether they would feel any of four emotions: happiness, fear, anger, sadness. For example, the above story was meant to elicit a mixture of happiness that Lassie has come back, tinged with sadness about her injury. The other stories detailed happy/angry conflicts (e.g., opening a present, but having it snatched away by a sibling) and happy/afraid conflicts (e.g., seeing a monster on TV after being allowed to stay up late). Harris found an age-related shift in children's ability to acknowledge the emotional conflict in the stories. Moreover, the design of the study allowed Harris to rule out a number of obvious explanations, unrelated to emotional understanding, for this shift. First, the poor performance of the 6-year-olds could not be explained in terms of their memory for the stories' events, since there were no differences between the younger and older children in their recall of the stories. Second, Harris also presented the children with the stories in a "separate" version (which was actually two substories) where the events were identical, but there was no emotional conflict. For example, the two substories for the "separate" version of the Lassie story were as follows:

> Late one night there is a bark outside your door. It's Lassie, your dog. She has been lost all day and she has come home.

> Late one night there is a bark outside the door. It's Lassie, your dog. She has cut her ear in a fight.

In the separate condition, there were no age-related differences in children's ability to predict the correct emotional response, showing that the results on the conflict stories were not due to the younger children's ignorance of which emotion is elicited by each separate component of the story. Rather, the age-related shift appeared to arise because the 6-year-olds were more likely to believe that emotional conflicts were impossible. This conclusion is borne out by their responses when they were explicitly asked whether one could feel happy and sad at the same time. Of the 6-year-olds, 79 percent asserted that this was not possible, compared with 33 percent of the 10-year-olds. The children's justifications for such a belief show that they typically maintained that emotional conflicts were logically impossible ("Because they're the opposite of each other; it's either good or it's bad") or behaviorally impossible ("Because you can't make your face go down and up"). One should note, however, that a substantial minority (a third) of 10-year-olds still denied that it was possible to feel two emotions simultaneously, showing that age cannot fully explain the observed increase in children's understanding of emotional conflicts.

Hiding emotions

Anyone with any experience of looking after young children will know that they are very bad at hiding their true feelings. Witness the child who broadcasts to the whole bus how ugly the woman opposite is, or tells Daddy how disgusting lunch is, or who fails to hide the fact that the birthday present really doesn't live up to expectations! It is therefore somewhat surprising to learn that children as young as 3 years show some ability to control their expression of mild negative emotions in a test situation (Cole, 1986), and by age 6, children are able to understand the difference between real and apparent emotions. For example, Harris, Donnelly, Guz, and Pitt-Watson (1986) compared the performance of 4-, 6-, and 10-year-olds in predicting how a story character would look and how he or she would really feel in a situation where it was appropriate to hide one's emotion. For example:

> Diana wants to go to her friend's party tonight but she has a tummy ache. She knows that if she tells her mum she has a tummy ache, her mum won't let her go. She tries to hide how she feels so that her mum will let her go.

Harris et al. found that all of the age groups were capable of recognizing that one can mask one's true feeling by posing a conflicting facial expression, although there was an age-related increase in how well children could justify and explain the distinction between real and apparent emotions. One should, however, bear in mind that the younger children's poorer performance when asked to justify their responses might be related to their comparatively less sophisticated understanding and use of language. Nevertheless, this study suggests that preschool children are capable of making quite remarkable judgments on whether a person's facial expression is always an accurate portrayal of their true feelings.

One reason why children may understand that true emotions can be hidden or attenuated before they grasp the concept of emotional conflict is that hiding one's emotions is more explicitly dealt with in children's general socialization. For example, in the scenarios given at the beginning of this section, it is highly likely that the reaction of adults or older children will help young children to learn that it is not always socially permissible or desirable to voice one's true negative feelings about a person's ugliness, standard of cuisine, or choice of gift. Indeed, there is evidence that, as early as the second year of life, children have begun to regulate their displays of emotion by, for example, tightly compressing their lips to control their feelings of anger (e.g., Malatesta, Culver, Tesman, & Shepard, 1989). One could argue that children's ability to control their feelings will be encouraged particularly for socially undesirable emotions, and there is evidence to support this position. For example, Morency and Krauss (1982) found that children are less able to deceive someone of their pleasant feelings compared with their unpleasant feelings. Interestingly, by as young as 5 years of age, children have even learnt that generally positive emotions, such as pride in one's achievements, can be seen to be socially undesirable showing off or gloating, and will therefore attempt to hide their pride (Reissland & Harris, 1991).

Differing emotional responses to the same event

Gnepp, McKee, and Domanic (1987) investigated whether children between 5 and 8 years recognized that it was possible for different people to feel different emotions about the same situation. Children were asked to predict the emotional responses of a same-sex character to emotionally equivocal and unequivocal situations (shown in table 6.1). The older children were found to be better at discriminating between equivocal and unequivocal situations, with the younger children rarely giving mixed positive/negative responses to the equivocal situations. By age 8, children had begun to realize that different children might react in different ways in the emotionally equivocal situations, such that one child might be terrified of dogs, while another child may love dogs. However, even the 8-year-olds only gave mixed responses to the equivocal situations about half of the time.

Table 6.1 The emotional situations used in Gnepp et al.'s (1987) study

Equivocal situations	Unequivocal situations
Child gets an egg sandwich for lunch	All the lights go off when child is playing alone
A butterfly lands on the child's arm	
Mum tells child to brush teeth	Child drops and breaks favorite toy
Child is approached by a small dog while playing	Parents give child a new toy
Child gets tomatoes with dinner	Child runs a race and loses
Mum asks child to do a job for her	Parents let child stay up late to watch TV
A cat sits down next to child on front porch	Best friend comes over and asks child to play
Parents ask child to sing a song for their friends	

EMOTIONAL JUDGMENT AND COGNITION

It is important to note that these findings do not seem to be caused by any broad cognitive limitations, since even the youngest children were capable of entertaining multiple possibilities when confronted with equivocal situations that did not involve emotions. For example, Gnepp et al. repeated their task using nonemotional stories, and children were asked to think of the color of a story character's choice of object in unequivocal (e.g., "Jim told me about the time he was coloring. He only had a blue crayon. Think about the color of the picture that Jim colored") and equivocal (e.g., "Sally told me about the time she was raking fall leaves. There were yellow leaves and red leaves. Sally took a leaf home with her. Think about the color of the leaf that she took home") situations. Even the youngest age group reported that they were thinking of two colors when the situations were equivocal. It may therefore be that children have specific problems in understanding different people's potential emotional reactions to any given situation. However, an alternative explanation may be the young child's **egocentrism** (first discussed by Piaget, see chapter 2) or inability to represent other people's perspectives on the world. Unfortunately, Gnepp et al.'s study did not analyze whether children who only gave one emotional response to the equivocal situations were acting egocentrically, and simply stating how *they themselves* would feel.

SUMMARY

In summary, it seems that although children quickly become skilled at reading people's emotions from their facial expressions and at talking about emotions, their understanding of the rich complexities of human emotion continues to develop throughout the primary school years. Indeed, one could argue that the ability to sympathize and empathize develops throughout the lifespan, leading to considerable individual differences in adults' emotional understanding.

 ## *Emotion in the Family*

Given that children tend to express their emotions most freely in the home environment, and the intuition that parents' ability to read and deal with their children's emotions is central to emotional development, it is surprising that remarkably little systematic investigation of children's understanding of intrafamilial emotions has been conducted. There are, however, some notable exceptions. Dunn and colleagues have investigated how families discuss emotion and whether differences in the emotional content of such discussion relate to children's understanding of emotion. Dunn, Brown, and Beardsall (1991) reported marked differences in the frequency with which both 3-year-olds and their mothers talked about emotions, with some families never mentioning emotions during the observational period. Moreover, this tendency to discuss people's feelings and the causes of such emotions was related to children's subsequent understanding of the emotional states of story characters (Dunn, Brown, Slomkowski,

Tesla, & Youngblade, 1991) and emotional conflicts (Brown & Dunn, 1996). While these authors point out that their data are correlational, and cannot therefore be used as proof of early discussion of emotion improving children's later understanding of emotion, they highlight clear consistencies in children's tendency to engage with human emotions. In more recent work, Dunn and colleagues (e.g., Hughes, Dunn, & White, 1998) reported that children who are rated as being "hard to manage" and who demonstrate behavior problems showed poorer emotional understanding than control group children. This suggests that emotional understanding may be related to children's ability to form harmonious close relationships with others.

UNDERSTANDING THE CAUSES OF EMOTION

Other research on emotion in the family has focused on children's understanding of the *causes* of people's feelings. Harter (1982, 1983a) reported that 83 percent of 4- to 11-year-olds cited themselves as the cause of parental anger, with 65 percent believing themselves to induce parental happiness, 49 percent parental sadness, and 41 percent parental fear. Citing themselves as the cause of their parents' emotions was more common in younger children, a finding that was replicated by Covell and Abramovitch (1987). This later study also extended Harter's findings by questioning 5- to 15-year-olds about the causes of their own emotions, as well as those of their mothers. Covell and Abramovitch found that the youngest group of children (aged 5 and 6 years) were more likely to reference *only* themselves as the cause of their mothers' anger and happiness. Across all ages, children were likely causally to attribute their own anger, rather than their happiness or sadness, to their families.

Clearly, these results have important implications for real life and how parents interact with their children on a day-to-day basis. In particular, the fact that young children appear to take sole responsibility for whether their mothers are happy or angry gives some cause for concern, especially if families are undergoing stress, for example during parental conflict or divorce. Some naturalistic studies have shown that children's distress in response to angry exchanges is more marked if they come from families where there has been serious family conflict (Cummings, Zahn-Waxler, & Radke-Yarrow, 1981, 1984). Unsurprisingly, overt parental conflict appears to be particularly detrimental, and is related to emotional and behavioral problems in the child (Jenkins & Smith, 1991). Experience of severe parental conflict may also exacerbate children's feelings of responsibility for their mother's emotional well-being. For example, Cummings, Pellegrini, and Notarius (1989) reported that children whose parents had a history of physical violence would actually intervene in a staged quarrel between their mother and another individual. Even though the children in this study were only between 2 and 5 years, they attempted to defend or comfort their mothers. These findings on the deleterious effects of parental conflict on children's emotional development, coupled with the ever-rising divorce rate, highlight the need for further investigations into why young children feel such a burden of emotional responsibility, and whether such misattributions of the causes of parental emotions may be one reason why periods of intense family emotion have a negative impact on children's understanding of emotion.

These relations between children's experience of emotional extremes and their general emotional development highlight the question of how more commonplace individual differences in children's social environment influence their emotional understanding. For example, there is considerable variation in emotional sophistication between children of the same age, with some showing precocious skill in reading and analyzing emotions while others are somewhat slower in grasping the fundamentals of emotional understanding. Similarly, some children will be more emotionally resilient than others. Why do such individual differences arise? One possible explanation is that individual differences in emotional development may relate to the type of attachment relationship the child forms to the primary caregiver (usually the mother) in infancy. Infant–caregiver attachment is the focus of the next part of this chapter.

 ## *Bowlby's Theory of Attachment*

ATTACHMENT AS AN INNATE DRIVE

The infant's expression of emotion and the caregiver's response to these emotions lie at the heart of John Bowlby's theory of attachment. Bowlby's theory was influenced by an eclectic range of disciplines, including Freudian psychoanalysis, ethology, and the biological sciences. Before Bowlby, the predominant view of infant–mother attachment was that it was a **"secondary drive"** or by-product of the infant associating the mother with providing for physiological needs, such as hunger. In contrast, Bowlby argued that attachment was an innate **primary drive** in the infant. Although the theory underwent several revisions over a period of many years, this argument remained fundamental. Thus, in the original theory (Bowlby, 1958), the focus was on how instinctual behaviors such as crying, clinging, and smiling served to elicit a reciprocal attachment response from the caregiver: "There matures in the early months of life of the human infant a complex and nicely balanced equipment of instinctual responses, the function of which is to ensure that he obtains parental care sufficient for his survival. To this end the equipment includes responses which promote his close proximity to a parent and . . . evoke parental activity" (Bowlby, 1958, p. 364). In contrast, in the 1969 version of his theory (the first volume of his trilogy *Attachment, Separation,* and *Loss*), Bowlby sought to highlight the dynamics of **attachment behavior**, with a move toward explaining the infant–mother tie in terms of a *goal-corrected system* which was triggered by environmental cues rather than innate instinctual behaviors. But regardless of whether attachment behavior is instinctual or goal-corrected, it results in the infant maintaining proximity to the caregiver.

Bowlby recognized that the establishment of an attachment relationship was not dependent purely upon the social and emotional interplay between infant and caregiver. Since attachment behavior is seen primarily when the infant is separated from the caregiver, it is clearly dependent upon the infant's level of cognitive development in terms of being able to represent an object that is not physically present (object permanence – see chapter 5). Bowlby based his argument on Piaget's (1954) contention that this level of object permanence is not acquired until the infant is approximately

8 months of age (although see chapter 5 for alternative accounts). Consequently, while infants are capable of recognizing familiar people before this age, they will not miss the attachment figure, and thus demonstrate attachment behavior, until they have reached the level of cognitive sophistication that allows them to represent absent objects and people.

THE PHASES OF ATTACHMENT

Bowlby therefore proposed that attachments develop in phases. Initially, infants are in the pre-attachment phase (0–2 months) and typically show little differentiation in their social responses to familiar and unfamiliar people. During the second phase (2–7 months), the foundations of attachment are being laid, with infants beginning to recognize their caregivers, although they do not yet show attachment behaviors upon separation. Clear-cut attachments are seen after 7 months, when infants protest at being separated from their caregivers and become wary of strangers (so-called **stranger anxiety**). The final phase of attachment (from around 2 years) is reached when the attachment relationship has evolved into a goal-corrected partnership between infant and caregiver. This phase is marked by the child's increased independence and recognition of the caregiver's needs and motives that sometimes make separation necessary.

Bowlby's theory was concerned mainly with the making and breaking of attachment ties, probably because his experiences of working as a child psychiatrist exposed him to the negative consequences for emotional development of severe **maternal deprivation**, such as long-term separation or being orphaned. Nowadays, however, researchers are generally less concerned with *whether* a child has formed an attachment, since a child who experiences any degree of continuity of care will become attached to the person who provides that care. Research interest now focuses on the quality or *security* of the attachment relationship. This shift in emphasis was due to the pioneering empirical work of Mary Ainsworth.

 ## *Ainsworth's Empirical Work*

Mary Ainsworth became interested in Bowlby's ideas on attachment after working with him in London during the 1950s. When she later went to live with the Ganda people in Uganda, she set about making systematic observations of infant–mother interactions in order to investigate Bowlby's goal-corrected attachment systems in operation. What was striking about these observations (Ainsworth, 1963, 1967) was the lack of uniformity in infants' attachment behavior, in terms of its frequency, strength, and degree of organization. Moreover, such differences were not specific to Gandan infants, since she replicated these findings in a sample of American children when she moved to Baltimore. Such variation in attachment behavior was not accounted for in Bowlby's theory, and this led Ainsworth to investigate the question of individual differences in attachment.

THE STRANGE SITUATION PROCEDURE

The richness of the data she had collected over a period of many years, and her experience of working with Bowlby, put Ainsworth in a unique position to develop attachment as an empirical field of research. Ainsworth's contribution meant that attachment issues became part of mainstream developmental psychology, rather than being confined to child psychiatry. She achieved this by investigating the development of attachments under normal family circumstances and by developing a quick and effective way of assessing attachment patterns in the developmental laboratory. Although this *strange situation procedure* (Ainsworth & Wittig, 1969) circumvented the need for researchers to conduct lengthy observations in the home, it was not developed purely for research convenience but because there are problems in trying to evaluate attachment behavior in the home environment. For example, if a child becomes extremely distressed upon the mother going into another room at home, this may indicate a *less* than optimal attachment, since if a child feels secure, such a separation should not result in severe distress. Ainsworth's extensive experience of observing infant–mother interactions enabled her to identify the situations that were most crucial in attachment terms, and therefore formed the basis of the strange situation procedure. (See Marvin's interview with Ainsworth [Ainsworth & Marvin, 1995] for a fascinating insight into how the strange situation evolved.)

DIFFERENT ATTACHMENT TYPES

The strange situation is typically conducted when the infant is between 1 and 2 years of age and assesses infants' responses to separations from, and subsequent reunions with, their mothers, and their reactions to an unfamiliar woman (the so-called "stranger"). In the testing room, there are two chairs (one for the mother and one for the stranger) and a range of toys with which the infant can play. As table 6.2 shows,

Table 6.2 The strange situation procedure

1 Mother and baby introduced into room.
2 Mother and baby alone, baby free to explore (3 minutes).
3 Female stranger enters, sits down, talks to mother, and then tries to engage the baby in play (3 minutes).
4 Mother leaves. Stranger and baby alone (up to 3 minutes*).
5 First reunion. Mother returns and stranger leaves unobtrusively. Mother settles baby if necessary, and tries to withdraw to her chair (3 minutes).
6 Mother leaves. Baby alone (up to 3 minutes*).
7 Stranger returns and tries to settle baby if necessary, and then withdraws to her chair (up to 3 minutes*).
8 Second reunion. Mother returns and stranger leaves unobtrusively. Mother settles baby if necessary, and tries to withdraw to her chair (3 minutes).

* If the mother feels that her child is becoming overly upset, these episodes may be terminated before the full 3 minutes have elapsed.

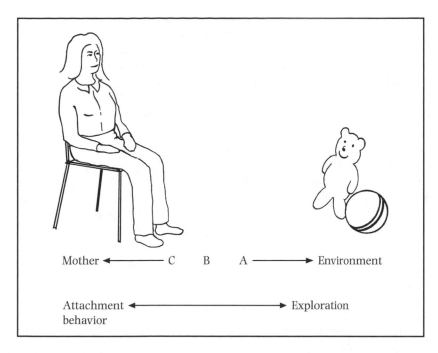

Mother ◄─────── C   B   A ──────► Environment

Attachment ◄──────────────► Exploration
behavior

Figure 6.3 Attachment as a balance of behavior directed toward mother and the environment. Adapted from Meins (1997).

the episodes are ordered so that the infant's attention should shift from exploration of the environment to attachment behavior toward the caregiver as the strange situation proceeds. Infants' responses during the two reunion episodes are most crucial, and form the basis for assessing an infant's security of attachment. The coding scheme for attachment security was developed by Ainsworth, Blehar, Waters, and Wall (1978) and describes infant behavior according to four indices: proximity-seeking, contact maintenance, resistance, and avoidance. Ainsworth et al.'s original coding scheme identified three major *categories of attachment*: **securely attached** infants (Type B); **insecure-avoidant** (Type A); and **insecure-resistant** (Type C). If one sees the dynamics of the attachment relationship as a balance between exploratory behavior directed toward the environment and attachment behavior directed toward the caregiver (see figure 6.3), securely attached infants have got the balance right. The caregiver's presence in the pre-separation episodes affords them the security to turn their attention to exploration and play, confident in the knowledge that the caregiver will be available for comfort or support should it be needed. However, the separation episodes trigger securely attached infants' attachment behavior, leading them to seek comfort, contact, proximity, or interaction with the caregiver when she returns. Securely attached infants may or may not become distressed by being separated from their caregivers, making infants' response to separation a relatively poor indicator of attachment security. But regardless of their response to separation, securely attached children are marked by their positive and quick response to the caregiver's return, shown by their readiness to greet, approach, and interact with the caregiver.

In contrast, the two patterns of insecure attachment have the balance of infant attachment tipped to either extreme. Insecure-avoidant infants show high levels of environment-directed behavior to the detriment of attachment behavior, whereas insecure-resistant infants are overly preoccupied with the caregiver to the detriment of exploration and play. Consequently, insecure-avoidant infants show little if any proximity-seeking, and even tend to avoid the caregiver, by averting gaze or turning or moving away, if she takes the initiative in making contact. Throughout the whole strange situation, insecure-avoidant infants appear indifferent toward the caregiver, and treat the stranger and caregiver in very similar ways; indeed, these infants may show less avoidance of the stranger than of the caregiver. Conversely, insecure-resistant infants are overinvolved with the caregiver, showing attachment behavior even during the pre-separation episodes, with little exploration or interest in the environment. These infants tend to become extremely distressed upon separation, but the overactivation of their attachment systems hampers their ability to be comforted by the caregiver upon reunion. This leads to angry and petulant behavior, with the infant resisting contact with and comfort from the caregiver, which in extreme cases manifests itself as tantrum behavior where the caregiver may be hit or kicked.

In addition to Ainsworth et al.'s (1978) original categories, Main and Solomon (1986, 1990) established a fourth category, Type D, for infants whose behavior appeared not to match that of any of the A, B, or C categories. These insecure-disorganized infants seem disoriented during the strange situation procedure, and show no clear strategy for coping with separations from and reunions with their caregivers. The insecure-disorganized infant may simultaneously demonstrate contradictory behaviors during the reunion episodes, such as proximity-seeking coupled with obvious avoidance, e.g., backing toward the caregiver or approaching with head sharply averted. These infants may also respond to reunion with fearful, stereotypical, or odd behaviors, such as rocking themselves, ear-pulling, or freezing.

Main and Hesse (1990) argued that these infants have been unable to establish an organized pattern of attachment because they have been frightened by the caregivers or have experienced their caregivers showing fearful and frightened behavior. This is supported by findings that have linked insecure-disorganized attachment to infant maltreatment or hostile caregiving (Carlson, Cicchetti, Barnett, & Braunwald, 1989; Lyons-Ruth, Repacholi, McLeod, & Silva, 1991), maternal depression (Radke-Yarrow et al., 1995), maternal histories of loss through separation, divorce, and death (Lyons-Ruth et al., 1991), and to caregivers experiencing unresolved mourning (Main & Hesse, 1990). Negative developmental outcomes have been linked to the insecure-disorganized pattern of attachment. For example, Carlson (1998) reported a long-term follow-up of disorganized infants that suggested that this pattern of attachment in infancy was related to child behavior problems at preschool age and with **psychopathology** in adolescence.

CULTURAL DIFFERENCES IN PREDOMINANT ATTACHMENT TYPE

In samples of British and American infants, the majority (around two-thirds) are securely attached, with approximately 20 percent of infants being classified as insecure-avoidant and around 10 percent falling into the insecure-resistant group.

Insecure-disorganized infants are rarely found in samples of infants recruited from the general community. There are, however, cultural differences in the proportion of children in the three major attachment categories. For example, Grossmann, Grossmann, Huber, and Wartner (1981) found that only 35 percent of their German sample were securely attached, with the majority of infants (52 percent) showing the insecure-avoidant pattern of attachment. Conversely, studies in Israel (Sagi, Lewkowicz, Shoham, Dvir, & Estes, 1985) and Japan (Miyake, Chen, & Campos, 1985; Takahashi, 1986) reported an overrepresentation of infants in the insecure-resistant category, and Miyake et al. (1985) found no insecure-avoidant infants in their sample.

It seems unlikely that certain nationalities are predisposed to be more likely to form insecure attachment relationships with their infants. Rather, these cultural differences suggest that parenting practices and attitudes play an important role in establishing attachment relationships. For example, in a later paper, Grossmann, Grossmann, Spangler, Suess, and Unzner (1985) explained the heightened numbers of insecure-avoidant infants in the original German sample in terms of German mothers' traditional enforcement of independence toward the end of the first year, which was typical of the mothers in their sample. This explanation was backed up by the fact that German mothers who do not impose such caregiving traditions are no more likely than American samples to form insecure-avoidant attachments with their infants. Similarly, differences in parenting practices may explain the high number of insecure-resistant infants in Japanese samples. It is commonplace for Japanese mothers to sleep with their infants and to be in constant bodily contact with them during the day, carrying them around in slings. Lack of close bodily contact, let alone the physical separation employed during the strange situation, is therefore highly unusual for Japanese infants. Consequently, the extreme distress the strange situation seems to cause these infants, and their inability to be quickly comforted upon their mothers' return, is likely to lead to insecure-resistant classification. Thus, in traditional Japanese culture, it would appear that the strange situation is not an appropriate and accurate measure of attachment security, since the procedure is too far removed from the infants' everyday experiences of caregiving. This interpretation is supported by Durrett, Otaki, and Richards's (1984) finding that Japanese career women who have approached caregiving in a way that is more in line with western practices are likely to show the typical American distribution of attachment patterns across the three categories.

If cultural differences in caregiving relate to security, are other individual differences in the family environment also related to attachment security? Given the focus of this chapter, of particular interest is the question of whether security-related differences exist in children's emotional development.

Attachment and Emotional Development

THE INTERNAL WORKING MODEL

The infant's earliest means of engaging with the world centers on conveying emotions: fear, discomfort, pain, contentment, happiness. Individual differences in caregivers' sensitivity to such emotional cues were the earliest reported predictors of attachment security. Ainsworth, Bell, and Stayton (1971, 1974) found that mothers who responded most sensitively to their infants' cues during the first year of life tended subsequently to have securely attached infants. The insecure-avoidant pattern of attachment was associated with mothers who tended to reject or ignore their infants' cues, and inconsistent patterns of mothering were related to insecure-resistant attachments. Attachment theory proposes that children use these early experiences with their caregivers to form *internal working models* (Bowlby, 1980) which incorporate representations of themselves, their caregivers, and their relationships with others. The child will then use these internal working models as templates for interacting with others. Consequently, because of the sensitive, loving support that securely attached children's caregivers have supplied, these children are self-confident and have a model of themselves as being worthy; they therefore expect others to behave in a sensitive and supportive fashion. Conversely, given the patterns of interaction typically experienced by avoidant and resistant infants, insecurely attached children expect people to be rejecting, or inconsistent and ambivalent when interacting with them. Given such links between early emotional responses and attachment security, it is surprising that so little research has been conducted on the relation between security and children's emotional development. However, researchers have reported some differences between secure and insecure group children.

ATTACHMENT AND EMOTIONAL REGULATION

Security-related differences have been identified in the way in which infants regulate their emotions. Insecure-avoidant infants have been found to mask their negative **affect** when interacting with their caregivers. For example, Spangler and Grossmann (1993) took physiological measures of infant distress during the strange situation procedure and compared these with infants' outward shows of upset and negative affect. The physiological measures showed that insecure-avoidant group infants were as distressed or more distressed than their secure group counterparts, despite the absence of overt behavioral distress observed in avoidant group infants. Spangler and Grossmann therefore concluded that insecure-avoidant infants mask or dampen their expression of negative emotions as a means of coping with the fact that caregivers are likely to reject their bids for contact and comfort (e.g., Isabella, 1993).

SECURE ATTACHMENT AND EMOTIONAL
UNDERSTANDING IN CHILDHOOD

In comparison with their insecurely attached peers, secure 5-year-olds have been found to demonstrate a better understanding of how people's beliefs and preferences affect their emotional reactions (Fonagy, Redfern, & Charman, 1997; Meins, Fernyhough, Russell, & Clark-Carter, 1998). Differences between secure and insecure children's memory for emotional events have also been reported. Belsky, Spritz, and Crnic (1996) found that securely attached 3-year-olds were more likely to remember the positive emotional events that they had witnessed in a puppet show, whereas insecurely attached children tended to remember the negative events. This suggests that insecurely attached children show a comparatively greater sensitivity to negative events, perhaps because they have had to deal with negative emotional exchanges more frequently than their securely attached **peers**. In contrast, Laible and Thompson (1998) reported that a secure attachment relationship was associated with children's understanding of negative, but not positive, emotions. Laible and Thompson argued that their findings may reflect security-related differences in the openness with which negative feelings are discussed by mother-child dyads. In secure dyads, sensitive issues such as negative emotional experiences will be openly discussed, whereas such topics may be problematic for insecure dyads, leading insecure children to put up defenses against confronting and dealing with negative emotions. In contrast, mothers of insecure-avoidant infants have been found to withdraw when their infants express negative emotions (Escher-Graeub & Grossmann, 1983). This withdrawal may teach insecure-avoidant children that negative emotions are inappropriate, and lead to the observed dampening of their outward expressions of negative affect (Cassidy, 1994). Conversely, mothers of insecure-resistant infants appear to heighten their infants' negative affect by failing to comfort them, thus prolonging their infants' feelings of distress (Ainsworth et al., 1978). These differences in how mothers deal with their infants' expressions of emotion bring to the fore the characteristics of the *caregiver* that might result in them engaging in interactions that may facilitate both a secure attachment relationship and a better understanding of emotions.

CAREGIVER CHARACTERISTICS RELATED TO ATTACHMENT AND EMOTIONAL DEVELOPMENT

One characteristic that may be important for both attachment and emotional development is the way in which a parent represents his or her own attachment experiences in childhood. Parents' representations of their early childhood experiences with attachment figures are assessed using the *Adult Attachment Interview* (*AAI*: George, Kaplan, & Main, 1985), a semi-structured interview in which adults are asked to describe their childhood relationships with mother and father, and to recall times when they were separated from their parents or felt upset or rejected. According to their responses during the AAI, adults are placed into one of four attachment categories: autonomous, dismissing, preoccupied, unresolved. Adults' attachment classifications are based not upon the nature of their actual childhood experiences, but on the way they represent these experiences, be they good or bad. Thus, autonomous adults are able to give coherent, well-balanced accounts of their attachment experiences, showing a clear valuing of close personal relationships. These adults may have experienced problems in childhood, or even had very difficult or abusive upbringings, but they can talk openly about negative experiences and seem to have managed to resolve any early difficulties and conflicts. In contrast to the open and balanced way in which autonomous adults talk about childhood experiences, adults in the remaining three categories have difficulties in talking about attachment relationships. Dismissing adults deny the importance of attachment experiences and insist they cannot recall childhood events and emotions, or provide idealized representations of their attachment relationships that they are unable to corroborate with real-life events. Conversely, preoccupied adults are unable to move on from their childhood experiences, and are still overinvolved with issues relating to their early attachment relationships. The final category is reserved for adults who have not been able to resolve feelings relating to the death of a loved one or to abuse they may have suffered.

These AAI classifications have been found to relate systematically to the security of the infant–parent attachment relationship. Autonomous parents are more likely to have securely attached infants, and parents in the three nonautonomous groups (dismissing, preoccupied, and unresolved) are more likely to form insecure attachment relationships with their infants. Specifically, dismissing parents tend to have insecure-avoidant attachment relationships with their infants, preoccupied parents are more likely to have insecure-resistant infants, and unresolved attachment status has been linked to insecure-disorganized attachment. This relation has been identified both for patterns of infant–mother attachment (e.g., Fonagy, Steele, & Steele, 1991; Levine, Tuber, Slade, & Ward, 1991) and for infant–father attachment (Steele, Steele, & Fonagy, 1996). Thus, the way in which a parent represents his or her childhood attachment experiences is related to the types of relationship formed with his or her own child.

These findings of *intergenerational transfer* of attachment patterns may help to explain the observed links between children's attachment security and mothers' responses to their infants' emotional expressions. Cassidy's (1994) view is that caregivers may enable their children to develop good emotional coping and regulation strategies by virtue of their willingness to acknowledge and respond to their children's emotions. She argued that the openness with which autonomous adults recognize and discuss the full spectrum of emotions will teach their children that emotions do not need to be suppressed and can be dealt with effectively. In contrast, mothers of insecure-avoidant infants fail to respond to their infants' negative emotions because their dismissing attachment style leads them to undervalue attachment relationships and to bias interactions in favor of positive emotional expressions. Cassidy explained the tendency of mothers of insecure-resistant infants to heighten their negative affect in terms of these mothers' preoccupation with attachment experiences. She maintained that these mothers need to emphasize the importance of the attachment relationship, and therefore adopt strategies that fail to help the child efficiently regulate negative emotion, thus prolonging the need for contact with the caregiver.

Thus, according to Cassidy's account, an autonomous AAI classification and sensitive parenting foster not only a secure attachment relationship, but the child's ability successfully to regulate their emotions. Cassidy's views are consistent with other theoretical positions, such as Stern's (1985) characterization of sensitive parenting in terms of *affect attunement*. Stern described the sensitive mother as someone who is attuned to all of her infant's emotions, accepting and sharing in their affective content. Insensitive mothers undermatch or overmatch their infants' emotional signals because of their own perceptual biases. However, although these theoretical perspectives on the relations between patterns of attachment, parents' acknowledgment of their infants' positive and negative emotions, and differences in infants' emotional regulation have intuitive appeal, little empirical work has been carried out to test these hypotheses.

Summary

In summary, questions focusing on the interrelations between attachment experiences, individual differences in caregiver characteristics and family interaction, and children's emotional development represent a rich area of untapped research. A priority for the future should be to address such questions to provide a clearer picture of how children acquire and develop their understanding of the building blocks of human emotional experience, and how parents and adults may help or hinder this process.

Figure 6.1, p. 144: the expressions are fear; anger; surprise; sadness; disgust; happiness; neutral.

SUMMARY AND CONCLUSIONS

EMOTIONAL COMPETENCE IN INFANCY

- Emotional facial expressions are understood cross-culturally, and neonates spontaneously produce recognizable facial expressions. These findings suggest that communicating emotions through facial expressions is innate.
- There is evidence that infants can discriminate between different facial expressions from birth.
- During the first year of life, infants begin to use other people's emotional responses to appraise how to act.

LATER EMOTIONAL COMPETENCE

- Children begin to talk about emotions during the second year of life, and by 28 months their linguistic expression of emotions is quite sophisticated.
- In comparison with their linguistic emotional expression, children's understanding of more complex emotional events does not develop until much later, with some 10-year-olds still having problems in acknowledging the existence of emotional conflicts.
- Differences in family interaction (e.g., parental conflict) impact negatively on children's understanding of emotion.

ATTACHMENT THEORY

- Bowlby's attachment theory proposed that all infants have an innate drive to form an attachment to the caregiver.
- Ainsworth highlighted different patterns of attachment, and introduced the concept of *security* of attachment, assessed using the strange situation procedure.
- Main and Solomon introduced a fourth attachment category (insecure-disorganized) that has been linked to parental psychopathology and poor psychological outcomes in the child.
- Cultural differences in security of attachment suggest that parenting practices and attitudes play an important role in the establishment of the attachment relationship.

ATTACHMENT AND EMOTIONAL DEVELOPMENT

- Caregivers' sensitivity to their infants' early emotional reactions relate to subsequent security of attachment.
- Children use their early experiences with their caregivers to form internal working models of their attachment relationships, which are utilized as templates for interacting with others throughout life.

- Parents' internal working models of attachment relationships are assessed using the Adult Attachment Interview, and there is considerable evidence for intergenerational transfer of attachment patterns.
- Security of attachment relates to early emotional regulation and to children's later understanding of emotions, but few studies have been conducted on the links between attachment patterns and emotional development.

DISCUSSION POINTS

1   What evidence would you need to be convinced that expressions of emotion are innate? Are there some emotions that cannot be innate?
2   We know that newborns mirror the emotional expressions of adults. How could we tell whether this is evidence for emotional understanding or simply imitation of the facial expression without any understanding?
3   Consider the different forms of evidence presented here for emotional awareness, and assess which are the stronger forms and which the weaker.
4   What abilities must children have to be able to identify that another's emotional reaction to a situation differs from theirs?
5   Bowlby argued that attachment behavior was aimed at maintaining proximity between infant and caregiver. Think of the different ways in which infants could achieve proximity and how they are liable to change with age.
6   Do you think that the evidence on cultural differences in predominant attachment type weakens the argument that secure attachment is important?
7   Consider the evidence indicating that attachment patterns are transmitted from one generation to the next. Does this seem plausible and, if so, are there ways in which the cycle might be broken?

SUGGESTIONS FOR FURTHER READING

Bowlby, J. (1969). *Attachment and loss. Vol. 1. Attachment.* London: Hogarth Press.

Bretherton, I. (1992). The origins of attachment theory: John Bowlby and Mary Ainsworth. *Developmental Psychology*, 28, 759–75.

Cassidy, J., & Shaver, P. R. (Eds.) (1999). *Handbook of attachment: Theory, research, and clinical applications.* New York and London: Guilford Press.

Fox, N. (Ed.) (1994). The development of emotion regulation: Biological and behavioral constraints. *Monographs of the Society for Research in Child Development*, 59 (2–3, Serial No. 240).

Harris, P. L. (1989). *Children and emotion.* Cambridge, MA, and Oxford: Blackwell.

Meins, E. (1997). *Security of attachment and the social development of cognition.* Hove: Psychology Press.

Solomon, J., & George, C. (1999). *Attachment disorganization.* New York: Guilford Press.

chapter 7

Social Interaction and the Beginnings of Communication

H. Rudolph Schaffer

KEY CONCEPTS

AUTISM	INNATE MECHANISM	THEORY OF MIND
EGOCENTRISM	OBJECT PERMANENCE	TURN-TAKING
EMOTION	SOCIAL REFERENCING	VISUAL PREFERENCE
EMOTION REGULATION	SOCIAL SIGNALING DEVICES	TECHNIQUE
INFANT-DIRECTED SPEECH (MOTHERESE)	STILL-FACE PROCEDURE	

OVERVIEW

Psychological development invariably takes place in the context of interacting with other people, and the author traces the development of these social interactions from birth and for the first 2 years. Learning about early interactions is not only a goal in its own right, but also helps us to gain insight into the development of such functions as language, attachment, cognitive achievements, and emotional regulation. The progressive changes occurring in infants' social behavior during the first 2 years are considered as falling in five developmental stages:

* The regularization of the infant's biological functions and their harmonizing with parental requirements.
* The regulation of mutual attention and responsiveness in face-to-face exchanges.
* Objects become incorporated into social interactions.
* The infant develops more flexible and symmetrical relationships.
* Verbal and other symbolic means help the infant to relate to others and to reflect on social exchanges.

As development proceeds, the initially helpless and utterly dependent newborn baby becomes a toddler who is able to act in cooperative, prosocial ways, and has developed sophisticated ways of communicating with people that make possible the reciprocal interchange of ideas and intentions.

Introduction

Psychological development invariably takes place in the context of interacting with other people. This is as true of the newborn baby as of the older child – in one sense more so because the baby is so utterly dependent on the attention and care of adults, and in another sense less so because early interactions are in certain respects one-sided affairs and not yet truly reciprocal in nature. At all ages, however, a child's psychological functions derive their meaning from the social context in which the child is reared, and the nature, content, and rate of development are all closely related to the kind of interpersonal experiences that the child encounters therein. Learning about early interactions is thus not only a goal in its own right, but also helps us to gain insight into the development of such functions as language, attachment, cognitive achievements, and **emotion regulation**.

Changes in Social Interactions in Early Development

Drastic changes occur in the nature of social interactions in the course of early development. Compare a newborn baby with a 2-year-old toddler. The former still treats all individuals as interchangeable, having little if any ability to recognize specific persons. As yet he or she cannot understand that other people are independent agents, with thoughts and feelings of their own. Communicating with others is dependent on primitive actions such as crying, which are not employed intentionally but which others need to interpret. From the second year on, on the other hand, a great range of sociocognitive abilities is in place: for example, the toddler not only knows his or her caregivers but has developed intense feelings of attachment towards them; has begun to view others as independent, intentional beings; is able, under certain conditions at least, to act in a cooperative, prosocial manner; and has developed sophisticated ways of communicating with people that makes possible the interchange of ideas and intentions. And yet even at the earliest age a child's interactions with his or her caregivers give the impression, more often than not, of being "well coordinated," "meshed," "smooth," i.e., from the beginning there is a certain order which characterizes most of a child's social encounters. How that order is brought about, how it changes with age, why occasionally it breaks down – these are questions which developmental psychologists have tried to answer, both to gain theoretical insight into the nature of childhood and to provide practical help to those caring for children.

Much effort has been devoted to describing the way in which social interactions manifest themselves in the early years, to analyzing the processes on which they depend, and to converting such intuitive impressions as "smoothness" into objective terms. In undertaking these cold-blooded scientific efforts it is easy, however, to overlook one essential point: interacting with others is often a highly emotional business that can be a source of intense pleasure or of great sorrow. It is there that children first learn to understand the nature of **emotions**, both their own and those of others, and to regulate and control these feelings and express them in ways regarded as socially desirable. To what extent these early learning experiences influence children's later

Table 7.1 Stages in parent–infant interaction

Stage	Starting age	Developmental task
1 Biological regulation	Birth	To regularize the infant's basic biological processes such as feeding and waking–sleeping states, and harmonize them with parental requirements.
2 Face-to-face exchanges	2 months	To regulate mutual attention and responsiveness in face-to-face situations.
3 Topic sharing	5 months	To incorporate objects into social interactions and ensure joint attention and action to them.
4 Reciprocity	8 months	To initiate actions directed at others, and develop more flexible and symmetrical relationships.
5 Symbolic representation	18 months	To develop verbal and other symbolic means of relating to others and reflect upon social exchanges.

emotional development remains largely a matter of conjecture; here we shall discuss them in their own right as they occur in the first 2 years or so rather than in terms of any possible implications they may have for later life.

A Developmental Framework

The basic question to which we need to find an answer is how the separate activities of two individuals, parent and child, become coordinated in such a way that they form a unitary entity – a feed, a game, a conversation, or any other joint activity that is dependent on the behavior of both participants. We shall examine what has been learned so far within the framework outlined in table 7.1. This presents a developmental scheme which traces the progressive changes occurring in infants' social behavior during the first 2 years of life and gives an outline of the tasks which infant and parent must jointly cope with at each developmental stage.

Initial Encounters

Let us consider one of the very first situations in which an infant comes upon another person: the feeding situation. For it to go "smoothly" and be "successful" feeding requires mutual adjustment of both child and adult, and this can be observed at two levels: a macro and a micro level.

MACRO-LEVEL ADJUSTMENTS

The former refers to the feeding schedule which infant and mother need to settle between them. On the one hand infants have certain internal periodicities which determine their hunger rhythms; on the other hand mothers have particular prefer-ences as to how their daily lives are arranged, and ideally mutual adjustment should take place between these two sets of requirements. Mothers must clearly learn to "read" their infants' requirements and adjust feeding times accordingly; however, even quite young infants already have the ability to adapt their rhythms to others' demands, as demonstrated in a classical study by Marquis (1941). This investigated the hourly changes in activity of two groups of infants during the first 10 days of life, one of which was fed regularly every 3 hours and the other every 4 hours. After just a few days each group showed a peak of restlessness just before its respective feeding time – something that became particularly obvious when the 3-hour group was shifted to a 4-hour schedule and so the infants had to wait an extra hour for the feed. The infants, that is, had learned to adjust to the particular contingencies with which their respective environments confronted them.

Micro-level adjustments

As to the micro level, let us consider what happens from moment to moment when a mother feeds her baby. An infant's sucking has been shown (e.g., by Wolff, 1968) to be a highly complex behavior pattern. For one thing, it is closely coordinated with such other aspects of feeding as breathing and swallowing, and for another it is organ-ized in temporal sequences which normally take the form of a *burst–pause* pattern: sucks, that is, tend to occur in series of bursts, with pauses interspersed between bursts. It is, in other words, a *high-frequency micro-rhythm* – an extremely intricate, innately organized response that turns out to be well adapted not only for the immediate busi-ness in hand of taking in food, but also for interacting with the person doing the feeding. This becomes apparent when the mother's behavior is investigated and related to what the infant is doing. As Kaye (1977) has shown, mothers tend to interact with their infants during a feed in precise synchrony with the burst–pause pattern of sucking. As illustrated in figure 7.1, during a sucking burst the mother is generally quiet and inactive; during pauses, on the other hand, she will jiggle, stroke, and talk to the infant, thereby setting up a **turn-taking** pattern in which first one and then the other partner is principal actor while the other is spectator. The mother thus fits in with the infant's natural sucking rhythm, accepts the opportunity to intervene offered by pauses between bouts of sucks, and in this way sets up a turn-taking pattern and introduces her infant to a way of interacting that is typical of many social situations which the child will encounter subsequently.

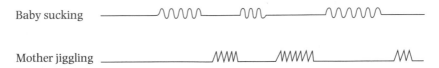

Figure 7.1 Baby's sucking bursts interspersed by mother's activity (from Schaffer, 1996). Reprinted with permission.

TWO CONDITIONS OF EARLY SOCIAL INTERACTIONS

Thus, early social interactions depend on two conditions, referring respectively to the characteristics that infants and mothers contribute:

- First, the *temporal organization of the infant's behavior*, seen here in the burst–pause pattern of sucking. Such an on–off arrangement lends itself well to social interaction because of the opportunities it offers for adults' intervention; it can thus be regarded as one aspect of infants' *social preadaptedness* in that the inborn nature of the infant's response organization facilitates the to-and-fro interchange with another person.
- Second, *the adult's sensitivity* to the signals that the infant provides. By the infant's means she can allow herself to be paced by the burst–pause pattern and respond to the onset of pauses as though they were a signal to her to play her complementary part in the exchange. Thus, by fitting in with the infant's behavioral organization, and treating the child's behavior as though it were already intentionally communicative, mothers provide their infants from a very early age with the chance of learning something about the format of social interaction generally, and so of acquiring in due course the skills necessary to act as a full partner.

Both adult and child, from the very beginning on, thus play their part in bringing about the coordination of their separate activities and weaving them into one interactive stream. How they do so will change with the child's age: initially, as we saw in the case of feeding, their dialogue is really a *pseudo-dialogue*, for as yet the infant cannot appreciate the communicative function of his or her behavior and it is therefore up to the mother to make their encounter into an interactive one. Only in the course of subsequent development, as a result of further social experience and cognitive maturity, will infants begin to learn about the rules which govern social interactions and thus become capable of playing a more equal role to that of the adult.

INDIVIDUAL DIFFERENCES

Let us note, however, that even at this early age there are already marked individual differences in the way adult–child pairs achieve coordination. For one thing, not all parents are equally sensitive to their infants' signals: those less so are likely to make the infant's task of learning about the social world a more difficult and prolonged one. And for another, not all infants are equally easy to be sensitive to: the behavior of some may be so disorganized as to be unpredictable, making caregivers' task to "read" their children an uncertain and difficult one. This applies, for example, to premature children (Eckerman & Oehler, 1992), who in the early months may show abnormally high or low thresholds to stimulation and have difficulty in paying and maintaining attention; similarly, some categories of mentally handicapped infants act in ways that adults may find lacking in clear communicative messages (Field, 1987; see also chapter 19). Under such circumstances the "smoothness" of interaction becomes a much harder objective for adult and child to achieve.

Face-to-Face Exchanges

In the earliest weeks of life infants' interactions with others are mainly concerned with the regulation of biological functions such as feeding and sleeping. Somewhere around 2 months, however, infants increasingly turn from the inner to the outer world; as a result of a sharp increase in visual efficiency they now become much more aware of and interested in their external environment, and especially so in other people. Social interactions consequently are primarily face-to-face affairs: parent and infant looking at each other, smiling at each other, having fun together. The regulation of mutual attention and responsiveness now becomes the main developmental theme.

By far the most attention-worthy aspect of the external environment at this stage is the human face. By using the **visual preference technique**, i.e., by simultaneously confronting an infant with two stimuli and measuring the amount of attention paid to each, Fantz (1961) was able to demonstrate that infants are equipped from the beginning with certain perceptual biases, as a result of which they are predisposed to attend to faces above all else. Initially, they may not possess the perceptual abilities to see faces *as* faces: as seen in figure 7.2, a 1-month-old infant scans only the external boundaries and neglects the rest. By 2 months, however, attention is also paid to internal features, for increasingly the infant is now able to take in information from a number of facial features and combine them into one perceptual object.

Despite these seeming limitations, there is clear evidence that infants are able to recognize specific individuals and differentiate, say, the mother's face from that of a stranger, within hours of birth (Bushnell, 2001; Slater & Quinn, 2001). Recognition of voices also appears at a very early age (DeCasper & Fifer, 1980; DeCasper, LeCanuet, Bunuel, Granier Deferre, & Maugeais, 1994) – one can find evidence for this ability already in newborns. As contact with the mother following birth would have been too limited to provide proper opportunities for familiarization, the possibility

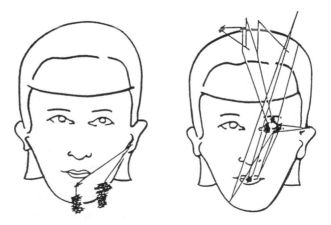

Figure 7.2 Visual scanning lines of a human face by a 1-month-old (left) and a 2-month-old infant (right). From A. Fogel & G. F. Melson, *Child development* (St. Paul, MN: West Publishing, 1988).

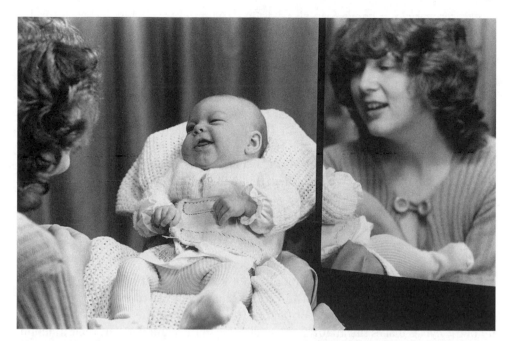

Plate 7.1 Studying mother–infant communication in a laboratory situation. From C. Trevarthen, "Descriptive analyses of infant communicative behavior." In H. R. Schaffer (Ed.), *Studies in mother–infant interaction* (London: Academic Press, 1977).

of *prenatal learning* must be taken seriously, for the auditory apparatus of the fetus is already fully functioning several weeks before birth (LeCanuet, 1998). It may well be, therefore, that exposure to the mother's voice while still in the womb could account for this very early ability to discriminate her speech from that of unfamiliar individuals.

What actually goes on when mother and infant are in a face-to-face situation – one where there is no "business" to transact such as feeding but where only gazing at each other and playfully vocalizing together take up all their interest? Studies of these encounters are useful in that they shed light on the way in which infants come to learn something about the rules that govern social intercourse, and especially so if the interactions are filmed and subjected to microanalytic techniques in order to reveal just how the considerable variety of signals – visual, vocal, bodily – which they exchange are integrated into coherent patterns of communicative significance to the other person (plate 7.1).

MUTUAL GAZING

Take mutual gazing – probably the most versatile of all interactive patterns, which can be the prelude to further interactions such as smiling, vocalizing, or bodily games but which, as every lover knows, can also exist in its own right as an intensely pleasurable and moving experience. Indeed, when one analyzes the mother's looking behavior one finds it to resemble very closely the way lovers act, in that she will gaze at her infant almost continuously as though totally absorbed, thereby constantly monitoring the child's actions and enabling her immediately to adjust the timing, nature, and intensity of her stimulation in the light of the infant's behavior. Thus, when the infant's attention is on her, the mother will do her best to provide "interesting" stimulation such as exaggerated facial displays or rhythmic and repetitive vocalizations; during the infant's looking away periods, on the other hand, she will respect the child's need for time out by keeping quiet but also watchful, ready to help the infant to resume the next cycle of activity. We have here another example of maternal sensitivity, in that the mother is constantly prepared for interaction but leaves it to the infant to determine when interaction actually takes place.

To-and-fro gaze-on/gaze-off cycles

Infants' gazing in face-to-face situations is not continuous but assumes a to-and-fro pattern, which has been ascribed to certain biologically based cycles of attention–nonattention (Lester, Hoffman, & Brazelton, 1985). However this may be, the regularity of the cycles makes the infant more predictable to the adult partner; their function, moreover, is to modulate the infant's arousal level and ensure that the excitement obtained from looking at another person can be kept within bounds by periodic time-out periods. Thus even quite young infants already have the capacity to control the social situation by deciding when to engage with the other person, and with increasing age infants become ever more sophisticated in their visual strategies for seeking or excluding stimulation. The rate of gaze-on/gaze-off cycles, for example, has been found to double in the first 6 months, indicating a growing ability to get rid of stimulation and yet readily return to it; at the same time, there is also an increase in the use of peripheral vision as a means of remaining in contact with the other person (Kaye & Fogel, 1980).

Vocal exchanges

In the vocal exchanges of mothers and infants, as in the feeding situation, turn-taking has been found to be a prominent feature. This is, of course, an essential aspect of adult conversations, for when information is exchanged it is necessary that one person talks while the other listens, and that their roles are then switched smoothly and without overlap. This usually takes place at a split-second level; it is therefore interesting to note that the same can already be observed in the vocal to-and-fro of mothers and infants, even though the latter are still at a preverbal level and are not in fact conveying any information as such in their vocalizations (Schaffer, 1984). Infant and adult, that is, alternate their contributions, rarely clashing and managing the exchange of speaker–listener roles with great precision. Yet, unlike the conversations of two adults, there is an asymmetry in the way in which the two partners take responsibility for managing the to-and-fro, for this is brought about primarily by the mother skillfully inserting her contributions in the pauses between the bursts of vocalizations produced by the infant. The mother, that is, allows herself to be paced by the infant; being highly attentive she can ensure that there is no clash, and in this way is able to provide the exchange with all the appearance of a conversation. As with feeding, we see again that the interaction is based, on the one hand, on the infant's spontaneous burst–pause patterns and, on the other hand, on the mother's sensitivity to this pattern. However, the experience of participating in such social formats provides the child with the opportunity of learning how to conduct them and, eventually, how to play an equal role in maintaining them.

INFANTS LEARN QUICKLY ABOUT INTERACTIONS!

That infants very quickly do learn about the nature of interactions is well illustrated by experiments in which the customary conduct of the adult partner is deliberately distorted. In the so-called **still-face procedure** mothers are asked not to respond to their infant as they normally do but to remain silent and expressionless (e.g., Muir & Nadel, 1998; Tronick, 1989). Infants as young as 2 or 3 months can already show signs of disturbance under such circumstances – gazing warily at the mother, alternately giving brief smiles and sobering, looking away for lengthening periods when their overtures are not reciprocated, and eventually withdrawing altogether or becoming overtly distressed. This may continue for a while even when the mother resumes her normal responsiveness. The infant, it seems, has acquired certain expectancies as to what transpires in a face-to-face situation, and is consequently disturbed when these expectancies are not met.

The exchange of emotional expressions

One of the more important experiences that infants are deprived of in the still-face situation is the exchange of emotional expressions. Among adults these are an essential part of any social interaction: the facial and vocal cues that one's partners provide can serve as an important guide to their feelings and thus constitute a most useful communicative device. The same normally applies in infant–mother exchanges: indeed, as videotaped sessions show, the facial displays mothers provide tend to be grossly exaggerated in comparison with their behavior with another adult (see plate 7.2) – as though quite unconsciously compensating for the limited information-processing capacity of young children and ensuring that the infant's attention remains on them as long as possible. The mother's face, as well as her voice, conveys messages about the mother's underlying emotional state and attitude – pleasure or displeasure, approval or disapproval, and so on – and before the onset of speech these cues are therefore a most important source of interpersonal information. As research has shown (Schwartz, Izard, & Ansal, 1985), by at least 5 months of age infants are able reliably to differentiate emotions such as anger, fear, and sadness, and what a mother does with her face and voice will thus from quite early on affect the way her baby responds to her.

Plate 7.2 A mother pulls an exaggerated face at her baby.

INFANTS SEND EMOTIONAL MESSAGES

Young infants are not only capable of receiving emotional messages; they can also from the very beginning send such messages. According to a great deal of evidence (Izard, 1994), every individual, irrespective of race or culture, is equipped from birth with a number of basic emotions, each of which is expressed in a distinct manner and associated with a specific feeling tone. Some are present from birth; others emerge later, at a time of the life cycle when they first become adaptive to the individual. There is still no general agreement as to the number and identity of these emotions; however, here it is worth singling out two that are clearly discernible from early on and have considerable communicative significance – *distress* and *joy*. The former gives rise to a distinctive facial expression involving such features as frowning and a turned-down mouth, and is linked to what is surely one of the most essential signaling devices infants bring into the world with them, namely, crying. As detailed analyses have shown (e.g., by Wolff, 1969), there are in fact three distinct types of cry, associated respectively with hunger, anger, and pain, each of which carries different information and which mothers soon become adept at recognizing. The emotion of joy, too, is linked to a particular response pattern (including the smile!). While present from birth, it is only from about 6 weeks of age that smiling appears primarily in response to other people, and by increasing the infant's attractiveness helps to ensure that they will attend to the child and take pleasure in his or her company.

SOCIAL SIGNALING

Smiling and crying are **social signaling devices** with which the infant is equipped from birth and which serve to ensure its survival. They are thus further examples of the fact that infants arrive in the world preadapted for social interaction and, by virtue of possessing **innate** communicative patterns of such efficacy, help to bond the child to his or her caregivers. Initially, however, these devices are of a somewhat primitive nature – evoked in an automatic, reflex-like manner by crude stimuli. In the first few weeks, for instance, the smile is elicited merely by eye-like dots and not the full human face; similarly, crying is a response to just a limited set of circumstances such as pain and hunger. Only subsequently will these devices evolve into much more complex, sophisticated communicative patterns – targeted at quite specific individuals, employed deliberately with certain aims in mind, and suppressed where not judged appropriate. Such improvement requires considerable cognitive learning and development; it also, however, requires a great deal of relevant experience with social partners: only if, for example, the child has learned that his or her cry is regularly responded to by a caring adult will he or she in due course become capable of employing this device as an intentional signal; and only if, in repeated face-to-face situations, the child has discovered the power of the smile will this response become part of his or her general social repertoire. One need only refer to descriptions of infants brought up under conditions of extreme deprivation, such as in institutions characterized by grossly deficient personal attention, to see how quickly responses like crying and smiling can become extinguished (e.g., Dennis, 1973).

 Incorporating Objects in Social Interactions

At around 5 months of age a notable change occurs in infants' orientation to the environment: they switch their main preoccupation from faces to objects. This is primarily because at that age infants discover the use of their hands and become proficient at grasping, handling, and manipulating things; as a result, a new world opens up for them. The parent's face has become familiar and is no longer as fascinating: according to one study (Kaye & Fogel, 1980), a drop in visual attention to the mother occurs from 70 percent of session time at 6 weeks of age to 33 percent at 26 weeks. Face-to-face interaction is no longer the sole vehicle of social exchange: increasingly, the infant's contacts with others is structured around objects. How to bring about such *three-party contacts* is the new task confronting parent and child.

The problem of limited attentional capacity

Initially at least, this is not easily accomplished. The problem is that infants' attentional capacity is limited: they can attend only to one thing at a time and do not flexibly move from one focus to another. The 6-month-old infant, that is, plays with the parent *or* with a ball, but cannot yet play ball *with* the parent. It is therefore up to the adult to convert an *infant–object* situation into an *infant–object–adult* situation: the adult, that is, needs to take the initiative in making the object a focus of *shared* attention and so convert it into a topic to which both partners can attend and around which the interaction of parent and child can take place. Such topic sharing is basic to every social interaction; its nature, however, varies according to age. Thus in the early months the topic to which the two participants address themselves arises from within the dyad itself: it is changes in facial expression or vocal sounds that form the focus around which the interaction takes place. Later on, when verbal proficiency makes conversation possible, the shared topic will be a symbolic one, conjured up by the words used by the two participants. Before then, however, it is the balls, rattles, buttons, spoons, and bits of paper that the child finds so intriguing that need to be incorporated in social exchanges as shared topics.

The development of shared attention

There are a number of devices which we all use in everyday life in order to share with another person an interest in some aspect of the environment. They include direction of gaze, gestures like pointing, object contact, and referential language. The last of these has probably received most attention: words can stand for things, and by introducing them into a conversation one person can convey to another their interest of the moment. In infancy, however, the other devices, being nonverbal in nature, form the primary vehicle for attention sharing, even though it is not until the end of the first year that infants begin to understand their communicative function.

The development of pointing

Take pointing – a particularly useful way of indicating to someone else what in the environment one is interested in at the moment, and what one wants the other person to be interested in too. Pointing-like movements, with the arm and appropriately named index finger extended, can already be observed in infants as young as 4 months, but at that age there are no indications that the infant uses them in any indicative, let alone communicative, sense (Blake, O'Rourke, & Borzellino, 1994). It is not till 10 or 12 months that pointing emerges as a gesture, elicited regularly by objects too far to reach or by books with attention-captivating pictures in them. Even then, however, the gesture is not yet used for communication: the infant points at the object but does not check whether the other person is following. Only in the second year will such *pointing-for-self* gradually be replaced by *pointing-for-others*:

the infant can now attend to both object and partner, integrate the two in one communicative act, and thus use the gesture in order to influence others (Schaffer, 1984). As to comprehending the meaning of another person's pointing, it is again not till the end of the first year that one can first find evidence for that. Up to about 9 months an infant will look at the extended finger but remain "stuck" there, with no apparent appreciation of the indicative significance of the gesture. After 9 months infants begin to follow the direction of the finger to the relevant object, but only under "easy" conditions, e.g., when finger and target are close together in the visual field, and it is not till the beginning of the second year that infants can locate most objects pointed out to them by another person and so share their topic of interest (Murphy & Messer, 1977).

Following another person's gaze direction

Following another person's gaze direction is the other most common means of topic sharing. Here too there are indications that it is not till the end of the first year that infants become capable of understanding the significance of such an action and begin to look where the other person is looking, though again this ability emerges first under "easy" conditions, when person and object are both readily accessible (Butterworth & Grover, 1988). Until then it is up to the adult to take the initiative for topic sharing by this means: mothers in particular tend closely to monitor their infant's focus of interest and, almost automatically, look where they are looking (Collis & Schaffer, 1975). What is significant about such topic sharing is that it is often only a start to further interaction: having established the infant's focus of interest, the mother may then point to it, name it, comment on it, and perhaps fetch it for the child to play with.

FROM ASYMMETRY TO SYMMETRY IN SOCIAL INTERACTIONS

Once again we see that initially social interactions are largely asymmetrical in nature: it is very much up to the adult to ensure that they are indeed of an interactive nature. Just as the mother needs to fill in the pauses between bursts of sucks or bouts of vocalizations in order to embed the infant's individual behavior in a *social* situation, so she must be prepared to follow the infant's gaze or early points and use these to construct a dialogue, based on the child's interests. And once again, a mother's sensitivity to her child's signals is crucial in terms of both timing and kind of response: thus, gazing can switch so rapidly that the adult can easily elaborate on an object no longer of interest to the infant, and talking about the object in incomprehensible adult terms will also do little to further the interaction or, for that matter, foster language acquisition. Where there is sensitive responsiveness, on the other hand, infants have the opportunity of finding out that their actions are of interest to the adult and that they can thereby elicit some sort of predictable reaction, thus encouraging them eventually to act *in order to* elicit such behavior. Once an infant has learned that it has a part to play in bringing about the to-and-fro of social exchanges, interaction tends to become a much more symmetric affair than hitherto.

TOWARD A "THEORY OF MIND"

The establishment of joint attention is significant because it represents the first real "meeting of minds" with another person. When infants follow someone else's focus of attention, and even more so when they actively attempt to direct it, they show that they are able to view other people as independent, intentional beings, with interests of their own that do not necessarily coincide with the infant's interests. It is for this reason that the emergence of joint attention in the second half of the first year can be viewed as the forerunner of the **theory of mind** skills that appear 2 or 3 years later (see chapter 10), and that its occurrence in infancy has been said to provide the foundation for all subsequent acts of communication and learning that involve some reference to the outside world (Carpenter, Nagell, & Tomasello, 1998).

From Interactions to Relationships

In the final third of the first year a positive blossoming of abilities takes place, in that a considerable range of capacities emerges during this period which together make the child's behavior vastly more flexible, coordinated, and purposive. Table 7.2 gives examples of these new achievements, and while these are largely based on the development of cognitive abilities, they do have considerable social implications.

THE DEVELOPMENT OF OBJECT (AND PERSON!) PERMANENCE

Let us examine one of these cognitive abilities, the development of **object permanence**. This refers to the ability to remain aware of an object even in its absence – something

Table 7.2   Examples of new capacities emerging around 8 months of age

Invokes adult help in performing a task with an object.
Obeys simple requests.
Imitates demonstrated actions of objects.
Points to objects and follows the pointing gesture of an adult.
Plays peekaboo, hiding own face for another to watch.
Holds cup to doll's mouth.
Opens and closes book, looking at mother after each move.
Follows adult's visual gaze.
Shakes head and says "no" in refusal.
Begins to use conventional labels for objects. Names persons and pets.
Demonstrates affection by hugging and kissing.
Plays at carrying out adult activities (mopping floor, driving car, etc.).
Shows toes when these are named by mother.
Plays "appropriately" with cup, spoon, and saucer.

which is absolutely fundamental to our conception of the world but which, as Piaget (1954) argued, the young infant does not possess. According to him, for the first 8 or 9 months infants behave on the basis of "out of sight, out of mind": for example, the moment an object is hidden they cease to show any orientation toward it and make no effort to look for it. Object permanence is one of the most fundamental achievements of infancy; it transforms the child's perception of the world and gives it a stability which it lacked before. This is perhaps most vividly seen in its social equivalent, *person permanence*: the realization that people do not stop to exist when no longer in the infant's presence but can be remembered, missed, and searched for in their absence. In the early months infants separated from their mothers will contentedly accept the attention of complete strangers – even though they recognize them to be strange; from the second half-year of life, however, they are able to cling to the image of the absent mother and will accordingly reject the unfamiliar substitute. What is more, the knowledge that people continue to exist when out of sight is clearly critical to the establishment of enduring relationships with them: the child must be able to count on the other person to be continuously accessible and not merely when they happen to be in the same environment. Thus, whereas previously infants' social *interactions*, taking place at particular times and places, made up their experience with other people, now it is enduring social *relationships* that constitute that experience and organize it to transcend time and place. Developmentally, this is a tremendous step forward. Attachments, for example, can now be formed to individuals who are not only familiar but who will form a focus around which the child's emotional life revolves (Schaffer, 1996).

LEARNING TO TAKE THE INITIATIVE

At the level of specific social interactions too there are changes as a result of the newly emerging abilities – changes such as a greater symmetry in the respective roles of adult and child. This is well seen in the games that mothers and infants play, such as give-and-take, peekaboo, and patacake (Gustafson, Green, & West, 1979). Such games involve oft-repeated, conventionalized routines requiring the participation of both partners according to certain set rules that usually include turn-taking, role exchange, and repetition of rounds, and which thus provide infants with the opportunity to acquire and display the social skills that they need for interacting with people in a wide range of situations. For example, in give-and-take games the infant's participation up to 8 months or so tends to be limited to "take": the mother offers the toy, the infant takes it, and the sequence ends there. After that age the infant comes to realize that there are further moves: first at the request of the mother, but then spontaneously, the infant hands the toy back, having come to appreciate that each action forms part of a wider sequence, i.e., the "game," and that the roles of giver and taker are both reciprocal and exchangeable. In addition, instead of always being dependent on the mother to start the game, infants may come to take the initiative by offering her the toy, thereby clearly indicating that they are no longer wholly dependent on others to structure their experience.

SOCIAL REFERENCING

The increasingly flexible and purposive behavior of infants can be seen in other situations too. Take the **social referencing** phenomenon: a young infant, confronted by a strange object, will stare fixedly at it for a brief while and then take some form of action – approach or withdrawal. From the age of 9 or 10 months, however, the infant will not merely look at the object but also at the mother – referring to her, that is, in order to check out her reaction and seek cues from her expression that will guide the child's appraisal of the situation (Klinnert, 1984). The infant shows thereby that he or she can now integrate information from multiple sources and, instead of reacting impulsively, is able to produce a much more purposive and complex plan of action. Or take the way in which infants become capable of making use of the mother in order to achieve some goal, such as getting access to or working a toy (Mosier & Rogoff, 1994). It is once again in the final third of the first year that this ability becomes notable – at a time, that is, when according to Piaget (1954) the child becomes capable of differentiating means from ends and understanding the connection between these two. As a result, instead of merely stretching out a hand for an out-of-reach toy, the infant is able to call for or gesture to the mother to fetch the toy, using her as the means for obtaining the desired end. Intentional initiation of interactions, understanding of their reciprocal nature, the consequently greater symmetry of all social exchanges and their organization into relationships are thus the developmental achievements which characterize infants' behavior with others as they approach the end of the first year.

Communicating By Means of Symbols

In the second year of life yet another drastic change takes place in the way in which children relate to other people, for increasingly from then on their interactions take a verbal form. The first words usually appear somewhere around one year of age, but just as pointing is initially employed for the self rather than for communicative purposes, so words are at first merely labels that children attach to people or objects for their own purposes rather than to convey some meaning to another person. Talking, as a *social* device, is mostly found from the middle of the second year on; it occurs because children become capable of understanding the symbolic use of words, e.g., that the sound *apple* can be used to stand for the real thing and that, moreover, other people share this system of representation.

FROM SENSORIMOTOR FUNCTIONING TO THE USE OF SYMBOLS

As Piaget (1950) pointed out, the progression from sensorimotor functioning to the use of symbols in the second year is one of the major transitions in cognitive development. It can be seen in various spheres of the child's activity: play, for example, is no longer a matter of mere manipulation of things for the sake of their feel or sound but becomes imaginative and make-believe in nature. The child, that is, realizes that a doll may be thought of as a baby or a piece of wood as a boat, and that one can talk on a toy telephone pretending there is someone listening. In the same way, words are discovered to be more than mere sounds; they can be used to represent things even in their absence, so that an apple can be asked for or talked about although none is to be seen. Language, as a rule-governed way of using verbal symbols, eventually becomes a powerful tool of thought; for our purposes, what matters is that it also, even in the early years of childhood, serves as a uniquely human interactive tool.

TALKING TO BABIES: IS "MOTHERESE" NECESSARY?

There is still much to be learned about the beginnings of language, and in particular about the role which social experience plays in the prelinguistic period (a detailed account of language development is given in chapter 9). It is noteworthy that, although infants do not comprehend language for most of the first year, adults still talk to them, even in the earliest weeks of life. Rheingold and Adams (1980) observed nurses in a maternity hospital while caring for newborn babies and found that virtually everything they did was accompanied by talk. What is more, 23 percent of their utterances were questions that the babies were obviously not expected to answer and 14 percent were in the form of commands, none of which the babies could possibly carry out! It is conceivable that being inundated by talk, day in, day out, primes infants in some way to acquire language once they are ready, and in popular childcare books parents are certainly urged constantly to involve their babies in conversation. Yet there are some interesting cultural variations which throw doubt on the notion that such early experience is a *necessary* precondition to language acquisition. For instance the Kaluli, a tribe living in an isolated part of Papua New Guinea, think of babies as "having no understanding" and therefore rarely address them verbally in any way. Nevertheless, despite this lack of verbal experience, Kaluli children become speakers of their language within the normal range of development (Schieffelin & Ochs, 1983). For that matter, once their children do begin to talk, Kaluli parents also do not use the particular style of **infant-directed speech** found among western adults – generally referred to as *motherese*, though it is by no means specific to mothers, or even to parents. Some of the features of motherese are listed in table 7.3; in sum, they make speech to young children simpler, briefer, more repetitive and more attention-worthy, the extent of such fine-tuning depending on the child's age and being carried out quite automatically and without prior planning. It is tempting to believe that such a style facilitates children's acquisition of language, and it is interesting to note that features of motherese such as simplifying, exaggeration, and slowing down are found even in mothers' manual signing to deaf children (Masataka, 1996). Yet not only the Kaluli but various other cultures (e.g., Pye, 1986) make no use of it, and the fact that this happens with no obvious disadvantage to their children makes it unlikely that it is quite the essential teaching device it was once thought to be.

Table 7.3 Some features of "motherese"

Phonological characteristics	Semantic characteristics
Clear enunciation	Limited range of vocabulary
Higher pitch	"Baby talk" words
Exaggerated intonation	Reference mainly to here and now
Slower speech	
Longer pauses	
Syntactic characteristics	**Pragmatic characteristics**
Short utterance length	More directives
Sentences well formed	More questions
Fewer subordinate clauses	More attention devices
	Repetition of child's utterances

THE DESIRE TO COMMUNICATE

Of one thing there can be no doubt: children have a powerful desire to communicate with others, and when prevented from doing so in conventional ways will find alternative means. This is clearly seen in deaf children: unable to communicate verbally, they are highly likely to develop their own nonverbal system of gestural signing, and do so apparently quite spontaneously without any indication of being influenced by teaching or imitation. As shown in a series of reports by Goldin-Meadow (e.g., Goldin-Meadow & Mylander, 1984; Goldin-Meadow, Mylander, & Butcher, 1995), such children, despite not being able to acquire spoken language naturally even with a hearing aid and despite not being exposed to a conventional sign language, will nevertheless construct for themselves a structured gestural system that enables them reasonably effectively to communicate to others their needs and wishes and thoughts. Prevented from following the conventional route to language learning, these children can nevertheless discover on their own other means of keeping in touch with people. What is more, the manual system they invent for themselves is in many respects comparable in content and structure to spoken language. Thus, the deaf children described by Goldin-Meadow first developed single gestures to denote specific objects or events – just as hearing children begin by using single words; they then proceeded to link together gestures into "sentences," and these gradually increased both in number and complexity. Though these gestural systems never became as complex and subtle as spoken language, they did provide a means of communication that was remarkably sophisticated for something that developed quite spontaneously.

SUMMARY: THE DEVELOPMENT OF EFFECTIVE COMMUNICATION

Effective communication, whether by verbal or by other means, involves a substantial range of skills, which are acquired only gradually in the course of the early years.

Consider children's ability to participate in a conversation (McTear, 1985). Initially, adult–child conversations tend to be asymmetrical in nature: the adult allows the child to set the topic, follows up that topic by commenting and enlarging on it in some way, and thereby ensures that continuity is maintained from one contribution to the other. Children's ability to pick up a topic introduced by the adult is at first limited: **egocentrically** they prefer to set their own agenda, and both topic and temporal contingencies between adult and child speech are thus largely the responsibility of the adult (Bloom, Margolis, Tinker, & Fujita, 1996). Yet very early on children become aware that adult communications require responses, and though mismatches may occur, children by the age of 2 already have a firm idea of the to-and-fro nature of a conversation, and will accordingly try to provide some sort of answer when a question is put to them. The rate and extent to which conversational skills develop depend largely on the parents' willingness to provide relevant experience: the more parents involve their children in conversations, and the more they facilitate the child's participation in them, the sooner the child will acquire the necessary skills. Thus parents need to time their own contribution to the conversation in such a way that they leave plenty of time for the child's reply; in some cases they may even need to go further by filling in for the child when the latter fails to respond, thereby at least keeping the conversation in being, albeit in a one-sided manner, and also incidentally modeling for the child what the answer ought to have been. By employing techniques such as these parents help children to become increasingly competent participants, and conversations thus become lengthier, more explicit, and more cohesive. Once again we see that, with increasing experience and maturity, the respective roles of adult and child gradually change toward a greater degree of symmetry.

SUMMARY AND CONCLUSIONS

In this chapter we have focused on the beginnings of social interactions – their emergence at the start of life and their characteristics during infancy. There is, of course, a lot more that must develop before the individual becomes a fully sophisticated social partner; however, the first steps are the vital ones and set the tone for all that follows.

WHEN DEVELOPMENT GOES WRONG

Just how important the first steps are can be seen by considering children who have, for one reason or another, failed to take them. One group of such children are those suffering from **autism**, in whom the most basic social abilities such as making eye contact with another person or establishing a focus of joint attention have failed properly to develop and in whom subsequent abilities like verbal communication or the understanding of others' mental states may then also not emerge (Sigman, 1998; autism is discussed in detail in chapter 19). While the cause of this disorder remains as yet unknown, it is almost certain that it is inherent in the child's basic make-up and thus present from birth. In other children, however, social development may be adversely affected by experiences following birth, as seen in institutionalized children reared under conditions of extreme interpersonal deprivation (Chisholm, 1998), where the lack of consistent, emotionally responsive caregiving results in children failing to develop whatever potential they have to become properly functioning members of society. It is clear that to reach that potential, a child must have both the required inborn capacities to relate to other people and be raised in a supportive environment that allows these capacities to develop.

The complexity of the task facing the child

From an adult's point of view, the mutual regulation that occurs when interacting with another person is such a natural, spontaneous function, carried out with split-second precision and generally without any conscious awareness, that it is not easy to appreciate just how complex an activity this really is. One benefit of studying its beginnings is to realize that we are dealing not just with one unitary ability, but rather with a whole range of different skills – skills such as orienting to the other person's face and voice, attending to all relevant communicative cues, integrating these cues into meaningful messages, timing one's own messages to fit in with those of the partner, employing particular gestures or words to convey particular meanings, sharing a focus of attention to some aspect of the environment with the other person, making allowance for other people's different orientation to the same situation, matching their emotional mood – and so forth. The various components must then be combined into organized wholes: part of the task the infant faces, that is, involves *intrapersonal* coordination, where each component skill becomes one constituent of the ability to relate to another person. However, the other part involves *interpersonal* coordination, namely, fitting one's behavior to that of the other. Intrapersonal coordination needs to go hand in hand with interpersonal coordination if the coming together of two individuals is to have a "successful" outcome. The accomplishment of such a capacity in the early years of childhood is a very impressive undertaking.

Discussion Points

1 Think about how early interactions change from being one-sided affairs to becoming truly reciprocal in nature.
2 How do face-to-face interactions between the infant and caregiver develop over the first 2 years from birth?
3 How do infants overcome their initial limited attentional capacities to engage in reciprocal social interactions?
4 What are the major changes in social interactions that appear from around 8 months?
5 Why is the development of object and person permanence important in social development?
6 Consider the ways in which the infant develops effective communications using language and other symbols.
7 What sorts of sophisticated means of communication enable the 2-year-old to exchange ideas and intentions with others?

SUGGESTIONS FOR FURTHER READING

Durkin, K. (1995). *Developmental social psychology*. Oxford: Blackwell.

Goldberg, S. (2000). *Attachment and development*. London: Arnold.

Schaffer, H. R. (1984). *The child's entry into a social world*. London: Academic Press.

Schaffer, H. R. (1996). *Social development*. Oxford: Blackwell.

part III

Childhood

CONTENTS

chapter 8

Cognitive Development

Michael Siegal

KEY CONCEPTS

ACCOMMODATION
APPEARANCE–REALITY
    DISTINCTION
ASSIMILATION
CLASS INCLUSION
CONCRETE OPERATIONS
    STAGE
CONSERVATION
DOMAIN-SPECIFIC
EGOCENTRISM

EQUILIBRIUM
FALSE POSITIVE
FOLK THEORIES OF
    DEVELOPMENT
HORIZONTAL DÉCALAGE
INFORMATION PROCESSING
INVARIANCE
ONE-TO-ONE CORRESPONDENCE
PERSPECTIVE-TAKING
PHENOMENISM

PRAGMATIC SYSTEM
PREOPERATIONAL STAGE
REALISM
SCHEMAS
SPATIAL COGNITION
SYNTHETIC MODELS
THEORY OF MIND
TRANSITIVE INFERENCE
ZONE OF PROXIMAL
    DEVELOPMENT

OVERVIEW

There are many changes that take place in children's thinking in early and middle childhood. In particular, children change from a magical belief in characters such as Santa Claus to an ability to reason logically about the physical, concrete world. The first person to give a detailed description and theoretical account of these developments was the Swiss psychologist Jean Piaget – "the giant of developmental psychology." In this chapter the author focuses on Piaget's theory with an account of major changes in thinking in several areas of development:

- The **appearance–reality distinction**: an awareness that things are not always what they appear to be.
- **Spatial cognition**: an understanding of the three-dimensional world and symbols, and that one thing (the symbol or model) can stand for another (the real thing).
- **Conservation**: an understanding that certain properties of objects (such as number or weight) remain unchanged despite superficial transformations in appearance.

- **Class inclusion**: the ability to coordinate and reason about parts and wholes simultaneously in recognizing relations between classes and subclasses.
- **Transitive inferences**: understanding the relation between two (or more) premises (e.g., A > B, B > C) that leads to an inference that follows and is logically necessary (A > C).
- **Perspective-taking**: the lessening of young children's egocentricity so that they become able to see things from others' points of view.

Piaget's account of these changes has received many challenges, and it is also clear that by varying the tasks children can appear to display competence at very early ages. The author describes the need to update and revise Piaget's cognitive developmental theory to take into account the impact of *culture*, *brain development*, and changes in children's *conversational awareness*.

Introduction

The Swiss psychologist Jean Piaget (1896–1980) has long been regarded as the "giant of developmental psychology" (Hunt, 1969). It is hard to exaggerate his importance in contemporary research. Some commentators have recently even gone so far as to endorse the statement that "assessing the impact of Piaget on developmental psychology is like assessing the impact of Shakespeare on English literature, or Aristotle on Philosophy – impossible" (e.g., Beilin, 1992, p. 191; Lourenço & Machado, 1996, p. 143). Such has been the prominence of Piaget's work that it has sparked a worldwide search for the authentic nature of the child's capacity for understanding.

Piaget's impact is reflected in several chapters of this book. A brief outline of his theory of intellectual development is given in chapter 2, his account of infant development is described in chapter 5, and his contribution to our understanding of changes in intelligence in adolescence is presented in chapter 15. In addition, his contribution to educational practice is discussed in chapter 17.

In this chapter our account of cognitive development in children focuses on Piaget's description and account of the major changes in children's thinking that occur around ages 6 to 7 years, and some of the cognitive prerequisites for these changes.

The Ability to Solve Logical Problems

Piaget sought to characterize children's cognitive development in terms of an increasing ability to solve logical problems. At the heart of his theory is his proposal that children younger than about 7 years display a form of **preoperational logic** in which they attend to states of objects and substances rather than transformations: what is meant by *states* and *transformations* is made clear in the later section on **conservation**. In this respect, children tend to focus on one dimension or viewpoint in problem-solving rather than integrating different dimensions or viewpoints together. Around 7 years of age a major transition in thinking occurs when children progress from a *preoperational* to a **concrete operations stage** of development. Here we review evidence relating to this transition, and focus on children's understanding of problems involving the use of logic such as *conservation*, **class inclusion**, **transitive inferences**, and **perspective-taking**. First, we will discuss two important developments in early childhood that are thought to be prerequisites for these later changes – the **appearance–reality distinction** and **spatial cognition**.

It will be seen that, despite the enduring enthusiasm for Piagetian orthodoxy, the theory – which must still be taken seriously – has some challengers. These have power-fully shaken the Piagetian paradigm for research in illustrating the need to update and revise his cognitive developmental theory to take into account the impact of *culture*, *brain development*, and changes in children's *conversational awareness*.

 ## Cognitive Abilities in 2- to 6-Year-Olds

THE APPEARANCE–REALITY DISTINCTION

One important ability that develops in early childhood, and is closely related to children's later understanding of conservation and perspective-taking, is the ability to discriminate between appearance and reality. This distinction is important at several levels of understanding. For instance, at a concrete level we need to know whether something that *looks* good to eat (appearance) actually *is* good to eat (reality), or whether an animal that looks friendly isn't going to bite! At a more abstract level we know that people can be very good at hiding their feelings and intentions – sometimes it is helpful if we can work out whether someone is telling us the truth or not! Children's ability to distinguish between real and apparent emotions is discussed in chapter 6 (p. 150), but here we focus on the distinction as it applies to physical objects.

John Flavell and his colleagues have arrived at the position that young children have little or no understanding of the distinction between appearance and reality (Flavell, 1993; Flavell, Green, & Flavell, 1986). For example, in one task children aged 3 years were shown milk in a glass with a red filter wrapped around it. The children were asked, "What color is the milk really and truly? Is it really and truly red or really and truly white? Now here is the second question. When you look at the milk with your eyes right now, does it look white or does it look red?" Fewer than half the children correctly identified the milk to *look red* but to *be white* really and truly.

Phenomenism versus realism

In another of Flavell's studies, an experimenter questioned 3-year-olds on a task in which an adult named "Ellie" was seen to put on a disguise as a bear. The children were asked, "When you look at her with your eyes right now, does she look like Ellie or does she look like a bear? Here is a different question. Who is over there really and truly? Is she really and truly Ellie, or is she really and truly a bear?" On this task, children's performance was no better than what would be expected by chance. Two types of errors were equally common. Children would either say that Ellie both looked like and truly was a bear, or she looked like and truly was Ellie. In this sense, they may give **phenomenism** answers and report the *appearance* of an object when asked about its real properties, or **realism** answers and report the *reality* of an object when asked about its appearance.

Task variations and the effects of language

Why do young children typically fail appearance–reality tasks? One possibility is that they may not even see that there is a contradiction to be addressed. Instead of recognizing that the purpose of the questions is to determine their knowledge of appearance and reality, they may believe that it is to evaluate the effectiveness of a disguise. Should they applaud the effectiveness of a disguise, they may give *phenomenism* answers and report on the appearance of an object when asked for reality. Alternatively, should they perceive the disguise to be ineffective, they may give *realism* answers to both questions.

Another possibility that has been suggested is that their lack of success may not reflect children's intrinsic inability to deal simultaneously with two representations in general, but rather their lack of knowledge about how to deal with the apparent contradiction between the two, or perhaps their misunderstanding of the experimenter's questions (Keil, 1989). Consistent with these explanations, Rice and her co-workers (1997) found that 3-year-olds were usually able to trick someone into thinking that a sponge that was shaped and colored to look like a rock was actually a rock (it was a dark gray, irregularly shaped sponge that looked like a piece of granite). In a nonverbal version of this "sponge–rock" task, Sapp, Lee, and Muir (2000) asked 3-year-olds to find an object that they could wipe the floor with, and one that looked like a rock – that is, although the instructions were verbal, the critical object (the sponge that looks like a rock) was not referred to by name. In this nonverbal version 90 percent of the children were able to select the rock-sponge when asked either of the questions, but in the standard verbal version only 30 percent of the children were correct.

Thus, 3-year-olds display a grasp of the distinction between appearance and reality in a variety of different settings. They may also succeed on related tasks where the purpose and relevance of the task is abundantly clear. For example, they overwhelmingly indicate that juice that is apparently good to drink has in reality been contaminated (Siegal & Share, 1990). Though the conditions under which 3-year-olds understand the distinction between appearance and reality are variable, by the age of 4 years children certainly do have some capacity to represent different perspectives and viewpoints. However, when asked even a simple appearance–reality question such as whether a piece of white paper placed behind a blue filter is "really and truly white," it is not until around age 6 or 7 that children will consistently give the correct answer.

Understanding spatial relations in 2-year-olds

In a series of influential studies, Judy DeLoache (1987, 1991, 2000) has shown that before the age of 3 years there is a sense in which children's ability to represent the locations of objects in space, and to understand symbolic objects, appears to change very rapidly and abruptly. In a first experiment, two groups of children, the first with a mean age of 2 years 7 months and the second with a mean age of 3 years 2 months, were shown a furnished room and its scale model located in an adjoining room. An experimenter explicitly described the correspondence between a large and a small toy, one that was to be hidden in the room, the other in the scale model, and the furniture that served as hiding places. All children were told that the larger toy was in the "same place" as the miniature toy that was concealed by the furniture of the scale model. The older, 3-year-old children could retrieve the object very well from the analogous location (the larger room), in contrast to few of the younger ones, who nonetheless were able to succeed when provided with a corresponding photograph.

According to DeLoache, children younger than 3 years may not be able to maintain a dual representation – that is, treating the scale model both as an object itself and also a representation, or symbol, of the larger room. They succeed using photographs as these do not provide symbolic information.

The credible shrinking room!

Under what other conditions might children as young as 2.5 years use their knowledge of a miniature model of a toy hidden in a room to infer the location of the actual toy? In a study carried out by DeLoache, Miller, and Rosengren (1997), a group of children with a mean age of 2 years 7 months was given a practice memory task in which they retrieved a large toy troll (21 cm high) called Terry that was hidden in a room. They then witnessed a shrinking event in which Terry was placed in front of a "machine that can shrink toys." When the machine was switched on, the child went away and heard sounds. Once the sounds stopped, the child returned to discover that Terry had shrunk to about a quarter of his original size. The procedure was reversed and the full-sized Terry appeared. Then the shrinking machine was aimed at the room where Terry originally had been hidden. The same shrinking and enlargement demonstrations ensued – a model replaced the room and then the room replaced the model. The child watched as the full-sized Terry was hidden in the original room. He or she waited in an adjoining area and heard the sounds of the shrinking machine again. Then the child was encouraged to find the troll that had been hidden in the miniature model – "Can you find Terry? Remember where we hid him. That's where we hid him."

In contrast, another group of 2.5-year-olds was given a symbolic task. They were shown the same two rooms – the large one and its smaller model – and also the large and small dolls called Terry. Then "Big Terry" was hidden in the large room while the child watched, and the child was told to find "Little Terry," who was hidden in "the same place" in the smaller room. The findings were very clear: the children who witnessed the shrinking event could succeed in finding the toy, but those who were given the symbolic task couldn't find "Little Terry" in the smaller room!

DeLoache and her colleagues contend that the shrinking event was nonsymbolic – for the credulous child who believes that the "shrinking machine" works, "the model simply *is* the room," so that there is no need for children to use a dual representation that is beyond their **information-processing** capacity. For the children given the symbolic version of the task, however, they must mentally represent both the symbols themselves (the small troll and the miniature room) and the objects they represent (the large troll and the full-size room), that is, they must have a dual representation.

Even so, children of this age might have succeeded in the nonsymbolic version of the task, not only because the shrinking event was nonsymbolic but also because it was so novel and attractive in captivating their attention. Whether or not they can succeed as well on a symbolic hiding task that is not accompanied with such exceptional drama is a matter for further investigation.

Summary

In our discussion of young children's understanding of the appearance–reality distinction and of the use of symbolic objects in spatial relations tasks, there are two main underlying themes. One is that preschool children often find it difficult to comprehend two representations, or dual relations, at the same time (e.g., that an object can be two things at once – it can *look like* a rock, but *really be* a sponge, or that a model can be a symbol and stand for the real thing). The other is that the way in which the task is presented to the children will often result in different answers to the experimenter's questions. This means that it can often be very difficult to know whether the children really possess the ability being tested or not. Children's ability to comprehend dual relations is important for their successful performance on the tests of logical reasoning that mark the transition to concrete operational thought, and it is these to which we now turn.

Conservation

For Piaget (1952, 1970), there is a watershed in child development that is exemplified by performance on his celebrated conservation experiments. The results of these studies remain one of the most influential demonstrations of preoperational logic in young children. According to Piaget's theory, young children under approximately 7 years are *nonconservers*. They lack an understanding of **invariance**, the concept that quantities remain the same despite perceptual changes if nothing is added or subtracted. Older children and adults know that an amount of liquid stays the same if it is poured from one container to another of a different shape, but young children seem to judge quantities that have been transformed in appearance by focusing on the *results* of such transformations in appearance (i.e., the end state) rather than taking into account the transformation itself. By contrast, older children correctly conserve, as they have attained a stage of *concrete operations*. They judge quantities by focusing on invariant properties irrespective of perceptual changes in appearance.

The different conservation problems

Piaget's conservation problems have been studied with tasks involving liquid, number, length, mass, weight, and volume, and these are illustrated in figure 8.1. In a conservation of liquid experiment, young children are first shown two identical glasses of water and they will all say that there is the same amount in each. Then the water from

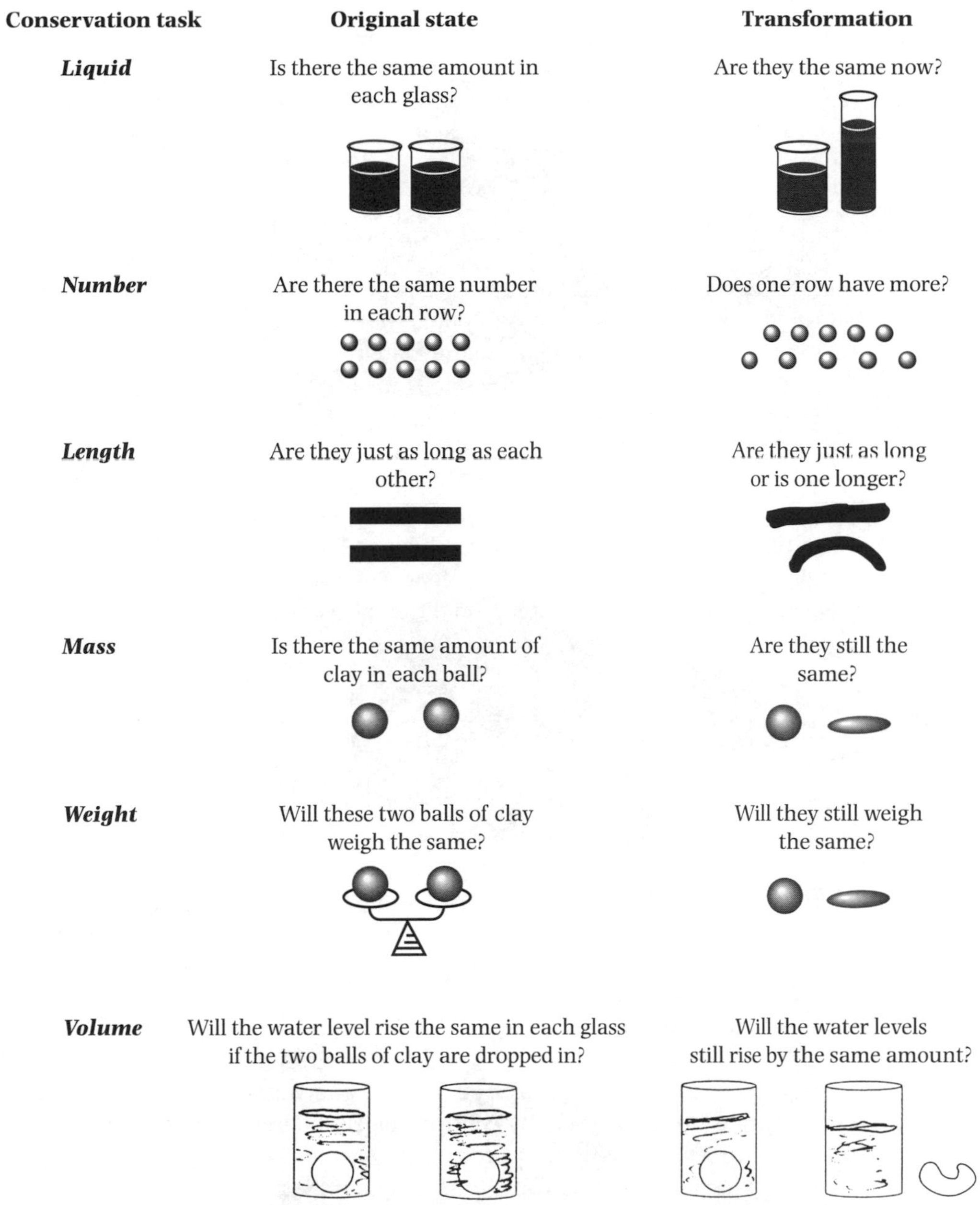

Conservation task	Original state	Transformation
Liquid	Is there the same amount in each glass?	Are they the same now?
Number	Are there the same number in each row?	Does one row have more?
Length	Are they just as long as each other?	Are they just as long or is one longer?
Mass	Is there the same amount of clay in each ball?	Are they still the same?
Weight	Will these two balls of clay weigh the same?	Will they still weigh the same?
Volume	Will the water level rise the same in each glass if the two balls of clay are dropped in?	Will the water levels still rise by the same amount?

Figure 8.1 Piaget's conservation tasks (from Piaget & Inhelder, 1956). Reprinted by permission of Psychology Press Limited, Hove, UK.

one of the glasses is poured into a third glass that is taller and narrower. Nonconserving children will now typically say that there is more in the taller, narrower glass than in the remaining original glass. They will justify their answer by saying "There's more water because it's higher." That is, they will focus on one aspect of the change – the

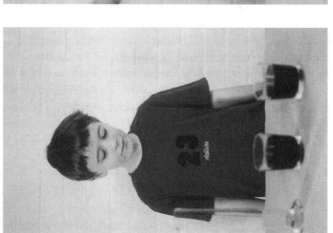

Plate 8.1 A conservation of liquid experiment. (a) A child is shown two identical glasses of water. (b) The water from one of the glasses is poured into a third glass that is taller and narrower. (c) The nonconserving child will now typically say that there is more in the taller, narrower glass than in the remaining original glass.

increase in height – and will ignore the other aspect – the decrease in width. They also seemingly ignore the pouring transformation and do not reason that "nothing has been added or taken away so the two amounts must be the same."

The different conservation tasks are typically passed at different ages: conservation of number, liquid, length, and mass typically appears around 6 to 7 years, conservation of mass/weight is mastered around 9 years, and volume around 11 or 12 years. This "gap" in the attainment of the different conservation problems, despite the fact that they all seem to require the same logical abilities, was termed by Piaget a **horizontal décalage**. The pattern of findings from experiments on conservation is certainly stunning. It has been replicated many times. If the tasks are carried out according to Piaget's original procedure, young children often answer incorrectly and do not conserve. However, a number of alternatives have been proposed to Piaget's interpretation that children possess a preoperational logic and lack the logical structures to conserve.

ALTERNATIVES TO PIAGET'S INTERPRETATION OF THE CONSERVATION PROBLEMS

Are nonconservers "perceptually seduced"?

One alternative interpretation is that children are liable to be "perceptually seduced" by the state that arises following a transformation. Thus their attention is so captured by the new state that they disregard the previous state and fail to attend to it when asked conservation questions (Bruner, 1966). To prevent this sort of seduction from occurring, children who would ordinarily not display evidence of conservation on Piaget's tasks can be asked to predict the outcome of a transformation without actually witnessing it occurring. Under these conditions, they are more likely to give what might be regarded as a truly correct answer, that is, they seem to conserve.

In a similar vein, Gelman (1982) attempted to illustrate the ability of even 3-year-olds to conserve number by directing their attention to toy turtles in rows placed in **one-to-one correspondence**. In her study, children were asked to count the number of items in one of the rows. The row was then covered and the children were asked, "How many are under my hands?" The question was repeated for the other row. When both rows were uncovered and one of the rows was transformed (and made either shorter or longer), the children now retained their initial correct answer that there was the same number in both rows. In this way, by having their attention very carefully directed to the number of turtles in the rows, the 3-year-olds appeared to discount the transformation. They were able to give a response consistent with an understanding of conservation and the invariance principle.

A frequent objection to these types of studies is that children do not *genuinely* conserve, and do not *really* understand that the same amount remains regardless of the transformation. Changes to Piaget's procedure might have yielded **false positive** results by simply signaling to children that it is acceptable to give an answer that turns out to be correct. In any event, beyond the issue of false positives, such experiments are vulnerable to the criticism that these amount to a weak test of children's conservation abilities. That is, if children really did understand the principle of invariance, they should be able to overcome the representation of the new state that follows a transformation without the need to ensure that they attend to the relevant attributes of the problem. The more stringent test, as embodied in Piaget's conservation tasks, requires children to display and explain in words the logic that quantities remain the same if nothing is added or taken away.

Conversational confusions: Do children understand the questions?

However, there is another major reservation to accepting Piaget's interpretation that children's answers on conservation tasks reveal a preoperational logic. It is that children may not recognize the underlying rationale behind the transformation carried out by an experimenter and might misunderstand the purpose and relevance of repeated questioning on conservation tasks. Instead, they may ponder why an experimenter would ask a question all over again after an answer has just been given. Rather than understanding that the experimenter's aim is to determine whether they understand the principle of invariance, they may think that the experimenter has rejected their first answer (for example, that the number of counters placed in one-to-one correspondence in two rows is the same). They may see a need to switch their response in order to please an adult questioner. This reinterpretation can be seen in terms of a problem of *a clash of conversational worlds* between children and adults. In this scenario, the well-meaning adult investigator misleads the child into giving a nonconserving response that does not reflect the depth of the child's cognitive development, and at the same time misleads the adult into believing that the child is at a preoperational stage (see figure 8.2).

The hypothesis that children's inability to conserve is due to a misunderstanding of the question has been addressed in several different ways. For example, McGarrigle and Donaldson (1974) provided a plausible context for asking conservation questions twice. They had a "naughty teddy" intervene and mess up one array of counters just after children, aged 4 to 6 years, had judged that the numbers of counters in two rows placed in one-to-one correspondence were the same. When naughty teddy "accidentally" carried out the transformation and the conservation question was asked again, children were significantly more likely to conserve. Thus, when the transformation was seemingly carried out accidentally, rather than deliberately, the children seemed able to conserve.

Similarly, in a conservation of liquid task, Light, Buckingham, and Robins (1979) gave a group of 5- and 6-year-olds two glasses that were the same size and containing the same amount of water. The children acknowledged that there was the same amount of water in each glass. Then the experimenter exclaimed that one of the glasses was chipped, poured the liquid into a new glass that was taller and narrower, and asked the children to indicate whether there was the same amount as before. As in McGarrigle and Donaldson's research, the children were now more likely to conserve.

In a series of related studies with 6-year-olds, Rose and Blank (1974) more directly tested the hypothesis that nonconservation is influenced by the language used in the experiment. Rose and Blank found that children gave significantly more conservation responses when only one question was asked *after* the rows had been transformed

Figure 8.2 An illustration of the possible context of nonconservation answers (Siegal, 1997, p. 26). The child is misled into giving a nonconserving response and the experimenter is misled into believing that the child is at the preoperational stage. Reprinted by permission of Psychology Press Limited, Hove, UK. Originally published in Piaget, J. (1967), *The Child's Conception of Space*, by Routledge, Kegan & Paul.

than in a standard two-question condition where the question is asked both before and after. They maintained that the standard repetition of the question (e.g., "Are there the same number in both rows or does one row have more?") misleads children into changing their answers and responding incorrectly. This is similar to the effect that occurs in adult conversations when repeated questioning produces response switching or, perhaps in some cases, annoyance at having to repeat the answer: for example, if you are asked "How are you?" and you reply "OK," and then you're asked "How are you?" again, would your answer be the same?!

In a further effort to determine whether children's failure on conservation problems is due to a deep limitation in understanding or to the nature of a methodology that can provoke children to respond inconsistently and incorrectly, Lorraine Waters, Simon Dinwiddy, and I designed a series of studies in which we aimed to explore children's appreciation of repeated questioning (Siegal, Waters, & Dinwiddy, 1988). Children aged 4 to 6 years were shown videotaped segments of puppets who either conserved or did not conserve on conservation of number and length tasks, either with or without repeated questioning. Indicating considerable certainty, children of all ages for the most part (at about a 75 percent rate) claimed that nonconservation responses following repeated questioning were due to a desire to please the adult questioner (an *external attribution*). By contrast, they claimed that conservation responses – whether the question was repeated or not – reflected a genuine conviction that these responses were correct (an *internal attribution*). Thus, children are highly sensitive to the perceived demands of an experimenter whose repeated questioning appears to set aside the ordinary rules for conversation, which are that such redundancy should be avoided in effective communication (Grice, 1975). In young children's performance on tests of recognition memory ability, response switching under repeated questioning may result in the appearance of suggestibility; it may serve to underestimate what children can and do remember (Bruck & Ceci, 1999; see also chapter 12).

DO WE UNDERSTAND THE CONSERVATION PROBLEMS?

To summarize, a variety of attentional and linguistic factors have been proposed to account for children's lack of success on conservation problems. On the one hand, regardless of the research that has been generated by alternative proposals to Piaget's theory, there always remain a substantial number of children under the age of approximately 7 years who are nonconservers. Moreover, Piagetians have claimed that the responses of many of the others who *do* show apparent conservation abilities reflect false positive results. In this respect, the influence of attentional and linguistic factors – to the extent that these do exist – seems in keeping with the uneven performance in children's success across conservation tasks during the transition from preoperational to concrete operational thinking – the *horizontal décalage* that we referred to earlier.

On the other hand, a majority of preschoolers who ordinarily would be deemed incapable of conservation do appear to understand the principle of invariance. They can evaluate nonconservation responses as incorrect, and attribute these responses to the effects of repeated questioning that apparently prompts respondents to switch their answers. Still, many children do not seem to be able to evaluate answers on conservation tasks

Figure 8.3 A class inclusion problem: are there more roses or more flowers? Preoperational children will typically claim that there are more roses.

accurately, let alone to use this skill themselves to succeed on standard conservation tasks. No one explanation has been shown to account fully for the transition from nonconservation to conservation abilities that occurs in middle childhood.

 ## *Class Inclusion*

According to Piaget (1970), the preoperational logic of young children is also well illustrated in their difficulties with class inclusion tasks that require knowledge of part–whole or "inclusion" relations. To illustrate, children may be shown bunches of flowers, many of them roses, and asked, "Are there more roses or more flowers?" (figure 8.3). Typically, children say that there are more roses. Equally typically, the first reaction that adults give when this task is described to them is that the question must contain a trick! Clearly, in this instance, the listener must be informed that the purpose and relevance of the task and the questions is to test whether he or she under-stands the logical relations between *superordinate* (flowers) and *subset* (roses) classes. Why anyone should care is likely to be beyond the comprehension of young children inexperienced in the ways of adult scientific thinking! Thus, it is hardly surprising that researchers have sought to explore the basis for wrong answers on class inclusion tasks in terms of language comprehension and **pragmatic understanding**.

THE EFFECTS OF CHANGING THE TASK

One way to promote successful responses is to change the nature of the task altogether by referring to the superordinate category in terms of collections such as a herd, pile, army, or forest rather than in class terms such as cows, blocks, soldiers, or trees. Thus, young children are more likely to give correct answers to questions referring to five white cows and two black ones such as "Who would have more, someone who owned the white cows or someone who owned the herd?" than questions such as "Who would have more, someone who owned the white cows or someone who owned the cows?" (Markman, 1981).

Linguistic misunderstandings?

However, lessening the task demands in this way does not directly address the fact that there are age differences in performance on Piaget's original class inclusion tasks. Chapman and McBride (1992) examined the possibility that young children's incorrect answers might reflect linguistic misunderstandings. In their study, Chapman and McBride gave 4- to 10-year-olds two versions of a class inclusion task involving seven toy horses, of which five were brown and two were white. For one version, the children were asked a class inclusion question of the type, "Are there more horses or more brown horses?" with all the horses placed standing. Although this form of question is standard in Piagetian class inclusion research, it seems odd, and is unlikely to be one that would fall within young children's frame of reference since it is of a type that they would never have encountered before. For the other version, the children were asked a question in which the linguistic cues to the frame of reference were saliently marked – the horses were all placed on their sides and the children were asked, "Are there more sleeping horses or more brown horses?" Chapman and McBride found that children performed well on a class inclusion task in which linguistic cues were made salient. They were more successful in answering this question than the standard one. However, most children could not effectively justify their answers. When the lack of justifications was taken into account, the difference in correct answers to the two forms of questions disappeared, apparently pointing to a preoperational level of competence.

Young children's conceptual difficulties

All the same, research on class inclusion demonstrates that correct answers do not flow spontaneously. It is often necessary to go to some extraordinary lengths to promote success. Again, there remain a substantial number of children who still answer incorrectly even under conditions in which the task demands are reduced. Embedding class inclusion questions in a sequence intended to clarify their meaning does not guarantee success, suggesting that there is a deep conceptual difficulty as well as a linguistic one. The issue of class inclusion is relevant to children's capacity to profit from instruction about number, as many aspects of arithmetic – ratios, decimals, fractions, and proportions – rely on the ability to conceptualize comparisons between parts and wholes.

 Transitive Inferences

Piaget and his colleagues also maintained that young children under about 7 years of age cannot reliably coordinate two separate pieces of information together in order to make a logical inference (Piaget, Inhelder, & Szeminska, 1960). Suppose young children are told that a yellow rod is taller than a blue rod, and that a blue rod is taller than a red rod, they cannot then reliably make the *transitive inference* that the yellow rod must be taller than the red rod. In abstract terms we can represent this problem as the two premises A > B and B > C, leading to the transitive inference that A > C.

In a seminal series of experiments, Bryant and Trabasso (1971) contended that children aged 4–6 years could succeed on this task should steps be taken to ensure that they remembered the premises. The standard version in Piagetian research involves three objects (A, B, C). However, Bryant and Trabasso noted that, in this version, A is described only as "tall," and C is described only as "short," whereas B is described as both "short" and "tall," since it is shorter than A, and taller than C. Thus, it would be possible for a child to give the correct answer to the A C question simply by remembering that A is tall and C is short. To surmount the difficulty that any success on training could simply be due to learning verbal labels for A and C (such as "tall" and "short"), children were trained to remember the lengths of variously colored rods representing five terms in descending order of size (for example, red, green, blue, yellow, pink). Thus in *red > (bigger than) green, green > blue, blue > yellow*, and *yellow > pink*, the green, blue, and yellow rods attract verbal labels of both "tall" and "short" so that children's performance on the critical *green > yellow* test comparison could not be attributed to their proficiency at learning a unique verbal label. Even the 4-year-olds in their experiment appeared to display clear evidence of an ability to do transitive inferences. According to Bryant and Trabasso (1971, p. 458), "very young children are able to make transitive inferences extremely effectively. They can combine separate quantity judgements very well and they can do so at a far younger age than has generally been assumed."

Yet, in this case, the issue of a false positive pattern of responses reappears. Children may answer the inferential test question correctly simply by learning to remember the *order* of the premises on which they are trained, without necessarily making a genuine inference – that is, they may remember that the green rod was mentioned before the yellow one, so say that it is bigger. To test this interpretation, Pears and Bryant (1990) gave groups of 4-year-olds a transitive inference task where the order of premises was varied, and found that the children succeeded at an above-chance level. However, again a sizable number of children gave incorrect answers.

This work seems to provide some support for the hypothesis that young children after all do possess inferential abilities. However, it can be argued that far from using *logical necessity* in drawing inferences from two (or more) premises, children may simply be relying on *spatial representation abilities* (i.e., having a mental image of the size of the objects). What is developing in children remains controversial. Is it the capacity to reason logically, or the ability to use spatial representations effectively? If the latter is the case, might children be giving what appear to be logical responses only incidentally? The further development of inferential abilities is discussed in chapter 15.

Perspective-Taking

Piaget claimed that **egocentrism** permeates young children's thinking and is a severe, general limitation on their knowledge of the world. The term *egocentrism* is used to refer to the child's difficulty in understanding things from another person's point of view (it does not mean that the child is *egotistical* or self-centered). Here is an example of a 3-year-old's egocentrism, described by a doting parent:

> Our 3-year-old son knows that, once he has gone to bed, he is not allowed downstairs again. But one evening he had forgotten to take his favorite book up with him. So he tiptoed downstairs, put his hands over his eyes, sneaked into the lounge where my husband and I were watching TV, grabbed his book and went back to bed, convinced we hadn't seen him!

Piaget contended that young children rely purely on their own perceptual point of view when judging the visual perspectives of others, and that they are not capable of understanding how another's viewpoint differs from their own. According to Piaget and Inhelder (1956, p. 209), children's understanding of the physical world is "at first completely egocentric."

Evidence for egocentrism in the case of children's ability to take the perspective of others and to share their visual perception comes from their performance on the "three mountains" task. This task consists of a model of three mountains presented at table height. When children sit in front of the model they see a small mountain on their right with a little house at the summit. Slightly behind this mountain, on the child's left, there is a taller mountain topped with a cross. The highest mountain is at the back, and is peaked with snow (see figure 8.4). The child walks around the table to become familiar with what the mountains look like from the different perspectives,

Figure 8.4 The three mountains task. The child walks around the display and is then asked to choose from photographs to show what the scene would look like from different perspectives. Before age 6 or 7, most children select the photograph showing the scene from their own point of view.

and then is asked to point to photographs to indicate what an observer would see from different perspectives on the model. Children under 7 years are confined to reproducing their own point of view, that is, they usually select a photograph showing what they see from their own vantage point: they fail to realize that different observers will enjoy different perspectives.

In a fresh approach to this perspective-taking task, Newcombe and Huttenlocher (1992) reasoned that children's difficulties on the Piagetian tasks come from their lack of knowledge or experience in selecting different perspectives from an array of pictures. That is, the children's inexperience and unfamiliarity with the task demands lead them to fail the task, even though they might genuinely have perspective-taking abilities. In their experiment young children were shown four toys on a table and a doll was then put in different locations around the table. The children were asked to say what would be viewed by the doll from each location with questions like "From where the doll is sitting now, can you tell me which toy is closest to the doll?" In this situation, where the task was simpler and made more sense to the children, even 3-year-olds responded correctly most of the time.

Overall, children's perspective-taking seems crucially dependent on task demands. Prompting active involvement in the solutions to such tasks, and having tasks that make more sense to the children, serves to enhance their performance (Lidster & Bremner, 1999). A reasonable conclusion is that young children are not egocentric all of the time, but their perspective-taking skills clearly improve during childhood. The very strong views of Piaget and Inhelder have generated an enduring surge of research on egocentrism and perspective-taking, and modern research is often conducted under the topic of **theory of mind**, which is discussed in detail in chapter 10.

What is the Cause of the Transition in Cognitive Development?

Children's performance on Piagetian tasks provides a description of the transition in their cognitive development that occurs between early and middle childhood. Compared to older children, those under approximately 7 years – and particularly under 5 years – often do not succeed on measures of the appearance–reality distinction, spatial cognition, conservation, class inclusion, transitive inferences, and perspective-taking. But the Piagetian approach does not provide a clear explanation that rules out all alternatives for why children undergo this transition. For Piaget, there is a process of **assimilation** and **accommodation** that results in the child's attainment of developmental stages. Thus children who are restricted to the use of preoperational logic interact with the environment using preexisting "**schemas**" or mental structures in their thinking that are egocentric in nature. They *assimilate* by attempting unsuccessfully to use these structures as strategies to solve tasks involving conservation, class inclusion, and transitive inferences. Eventually, children adapt to the environment. They recognize the existence of a conflict between their present strategies and the strategies required for solving the problem at hand. In relinquishing their egocentric orientation, they *accommodate* (change) the structure of their thinking in order to embrace a new strategy that enables successful problem-solving. Once this has been accomplished, the conflict is resolved and children arrive at a new **equilibrium** as demonstrated by their success on a range of cognitive tasks.

Captivating though Piaget's description of development is, an explanation couched in terms of processes of assimilation and accommodation is unsatisfying. It circumvents the crucial question of precisely *what* cultural and brain mechanisms are producing change. Based on research generated by Piaget's pioneering work, two things can be seen to be happening to children during the course of this transition: changes in their information-processing capacity, and changes in their linguistic and conversational abilities.

Information-processing changes

Information-processing approaches can be seen as akin to Piaget's stage analysis and, for that reason, are often called "neo-Piagetian." The work of investigators such as DeLoache et al. (1997), Andrews and Halford (1998), and Case (1985) suggests that cognitive development is explainable in terms of a computer metaphor in which generations of hardware have evolved to become more powerful in their capacity to process information. In this sense, children acquire more and more powerful abilities to represent and process information. In early childhood, children can only consider one perspective or relation at a time. By about the age of 7, their information-processing capacity has increased to the point where they become able to consider more than one relation simultaneously and can reliably make inferences by integrating two premises together. This increase in information-processing capacity enables the child to succeed at the Piagetian tasks we have described.

The development of specific brain structures

In keeping with the computer metaphor, an important step is to specify the physiological basis of increasing capacity. Quite recently, it has been shown that performance on Piagetian tasks may involve the functioning of specific brain structures. Studies carried out with brain-damaged adult patients have been used to determine what areas in the brain are necessary to succeed. For example, Waltz and his colleagues (1999) have proposed that processing more than one relation requires the prefrontal cortex to be intact. Patients who have suffered damage in this area, unlike patients whose damage is restricted to the anterior temporal lobe, have a great deal of difficulty on transitive inference tasks that involve the integration of two relations. On this basis, it may be proposed that development in the prefrontal cortex is associated with development in children's successful performance on Piagetian tasks.

Conversational awareness

However, explanations set out as changes in information-processing capacity cannot be considered separately from changes that are occurring between the ages of 4 to 7 years in children's ability to understand how language is used. These changes can be rather deceptive to adults in that children, on the face of it, would seem to be highly fluent grammar-abiding conversationalists by the time they reach the age of 3 years. Yet, paradoxically, children may not yet have the conversational experience and awareness to understand the purpose and relevance of questions in specialized, instructional, or experimental settings. As Chomsky (1975, pp. 89–140) has maintained, knowledge of grammar is distinct and separate from other cognitive systems, such as *pragmatic competence* (understanding the *intentions* expressed in utterances; see chapter 9), with which it interacts. Thus, children's knowledge of grammar may develop in advance of their competence in using pragmatic knowledge in interpreting the purpose and relevance of language in communication. Several investigators have suggested that children's difficulties on Piagetian tasks are often due to difficulties in interpreting meaning in language, particularly in following the narratives of storytellers.

Evidence for this proposal comes from other studies of brain-damaged patients. It is well established that patients who have suffered damage to the right hemisphere of the brain have difficulty in understanding the implications of conversations. They are impaired in drawing the inferences that are required in understanding jokes, lies, and the gist of stories that require perspective-taking abilities in conversation (Molloy, Brownell, & Gardner, 1990). These findings are compatible with other developmental evidence. Children who are impaired in their conversational understanding – especially those with autism or Asperger's syndrome (marked by a milder form of autism-like symptoms associated with normal verbal intelligence but a deficit in pragmatic understanding) – often have suffered right-hemisphere damage (Ellis & Gunter, 1999; Ozonoff & Miller, 1996). In this regard, coherence in the electrical activity of the right hemisphere of the brain has been found to increase at 4–5 years of age in normal children (Thatcher, 1992). Although it may be an anatomical coincidence, such growth concurs with children's successful performance on Piagetian tasks.

Using new techniques of brain imaging, future research promises to reveal much more about the neural basis of cognition in children (Nelson & Bloom, 1997). Nevertheless, caution about the specific role of brain processes in cognitive development is necessary since such processes are themselves dependent on the culture and environment. This point is well illustrated by research with the deaf. For example, brain activation in response to language comprehension tasks is dependent on the time at which the deaf have been exposed to sign language (Neville et al., 1997). Moreover, as Hunt (1969) long ago pointed out in his consideration of children's performance on Piaget's tasks, the environment must be critically important because, if it made no difference, deaf children would mature in the same way as their hearing counterparts. This is patently not the case since lack of linguistic access acts as a barrier to certain aspects of cognitive development (Marschark, 1993).

Cultural influences on cognitive development

We have seen that children appear to demonstrate more success on Piagetian tasks if these are modified. If placed in settings where the task demands are reduced and the questions and problem to be addressed are made clear in terms of their previous experience, children are more likely to succeed. But the culture does expect children to invent solutions to problems that they have never directly encountered before. Piaget (1977) intentionally designed his tasks to reflect the importance of this issue and, on "standard" versions of his tasks, the gap between the performance of children aged 3–4 years and those aged 7 years and above is typically very large. In this respect, a strong case can be made that learning from culture requires sharing the perspectives of others and the ability to select and focus on the appropriate solution to a problem (Tomasello, Kruger, & Ratner, 1993). Under cultural influences at home and school and through the media, children with increasing age may undergo a "social transformation of mind" that reflects the bridge between what they can achieve spontaneously by themselves, and what they can achieve from exposure to cultural influences (the **zone of proximal development**, Vygotsky, 1978; see chapters 2 and 17). They may come to be more flexible in their search for appropriate problem-solving strategies (Siegler, 1995), and gain accessibility to an explicit awareness of how the self and symbols are to be represented (Karmiloff-Smith, 1992b; Rozin, 1976).

The role of culture can be characterized as "**domain-specific**" in that it operates unevenly and in different ways in the acquisition of knowledge across various subject matters. Certain abilities appear to develop spontaneously, or seem to need very little cultural reinforcement, such as the edible–inedible distinction as a measure of the knowledge of the distinction between appearance and reality. In the case of spatial cognition, the ability to make sense of photographs (and even charts and graphs) seems to develop spontaneously and does not require specific training (Gattis, 2001).

How culture interacts with the child's own perspective

Knowledge acquisition in many domains may be better characterized as an amalgam of what is spontaneously provided through the child's own perspective and that provided by the culture. To this extent, some have proposed that children's cognitive development can often be well explained in terms of a transition from **synthetic models** to mature, culturally received mental models. Vosniadou (1994) provides an illustration from studies of children's knowledge of the shape of the earth. By this account, children's initial mental models of the earth's shape are derived from a *naive theory* that lends consistency to their beliefs and misconceptions (see chapter 1 for an account of naive, or **folk theories** of human development, and chapter 15 for adolescents' naive theories of physics). Such theories are generated by constraints that can be seen as "entrenched presuppositions" which are resistant to change as these are constantly confirmed by everyday experience. By this account, children's early models of the earth's shape appear to be constrained by two presuppositions: (1) the earth is a flat plane (the "flatness" constraint) and (2) unsupported objects "fall down" on an up-down gradient (the "support" constraint). Thus even though children may be told that the earth is round, these constraints serve to organize their thinking. They may resort to synthetic models that reflect a coherence of beliefs and assumptions about the earth's shape that are wrong, or only partly adjusted to the cultural norm. For example, children under 7 years may believe that people live on the flat surface of an earth on top of a platform that takes the shape of a hemisphere.

Yet it is by no means certain that synthetic models are inevitable with respect to all groups of children regardless of culture and circumstance (Schoultz, Säljö, & Wyndhamn, 2001). According to Harris (2000), children: (1) are not necessarily aiming at a more objective conception of reality; (2) do not rely primarily on empirical feedback in constructing a model of reality; and (3) frequently rely on verbally expressed "collective representations" of the mental and physical world transmitted by authority in the culture in which they live. For example, Australian children mostly seem to avoid such synthetic models in their geographic and astronomical concepts; even Australian preschoolers often express the beliefs that the world is shaped as a sphere and that one cannot fall off the edge (Siegal, Butterworth, & Newcombe, 2002). These beliefs are ones that reflect strong cultural influences stemming from a unique set of conditions: Australia's distinctive remote position in the southern hemisphere and Australians' close ties with people in the northern hemisphere.

A belief in magic!

If children do have coexisting or synthetic models in their cognitive development, these may often be seen as approved by the culture rather than as unintended by-products of it. Encouraged by cultural conventions to engage in the practice of magical fantasies such as a belief in Santa Claus, children often strive to reveal charming violations of logical necessity such as those examined in Piaget's tasks. Most 3–7-year-olds are able to distinguish between the causality of physical events that are possible – i.e., that conform to normal physical laws – and those that are "magical" – i.e., impossible without some form of special magic. Their credulity in wishing to accept "magical" outcomes can be deemed rational in the absence of evidence that invalidates the existence of supernatural creatures (Johnson & Harris, 1994).

Take conservation as an example of such coexisting understanding. Why would children ever think of the need to check whether a quantity was the same or not after a transformation unless they were asked to in the first place? In this case, the "magic" inherent in the perceptual transformation induced by an experimenter, and the experimenter's questions, may prompt children to dispense with the logical necessity stipulated by the principle of invariance and to assume that the quantity really has changed. Until asked to investigate, they may operate as if the invariance principle applies. But if the experimenter is granted the ability to summon up a special form of magic, they may assume that the impossible has indeed taken place and offer a nonconservation response.

Summary and Conclusions

The elegance of Piaget's (1970) theory of cognitive development can be seen in the manner in which he set out with precision what we should expect in cognitive development, and the sheer brilliance of the tasks that he conceived in order to test his predictions. He demonstrated that it was possible to carry out clever experiments with young children, and generations of subsequent researchers have been able to replicate his findings. With respect to cognitive developments in childhood, we have focused on young children's understanding of the appearance–reality distinction, and symbolic understanding in the use of scale models and spatial cognition. The abilities that enable children to solve these tasks, particularly an understanding of dual representations and a growing understanding of language use, are important prerequisites for the major transition in children's thinking around 6–7 years that were first described in detail by Piaget – in particular, children's developing understanding of conservation, class inclusion, transitive inferences, and perspective-taking.

We have seen that there are alternative approaches to those offered by Piaget for the age-related changes that he described. These approaches serve fundamentally to elucidate or even challenge the theory. Research in cognitive development may be entering into a time of changing paradigms that attend more deeply to explanatory issues. We are becoming aware of the significance of cultural demands, brain processes, and children's developing conversational awareness in explaining the nature of cognitive development. Nevertheless, it is clear that Piaget's intriguing observations opened up many fruitful lines of enquiry and that while many of his interpretations have by and large been modified or superseded, he set the agenda for a vast body of productive research in the twentieth and twenty-first centuries.

DISCUSSION POINTS

1 Think about the changes that take place in children's thinking around the ages of 3 to 6 years. How might these developments help children solve Piaget's concrete operational tasks?
2 Is it reasonable to claim that young children understand the experimenter's questions in tests of their cognitive understanding and development?
3 What evidence suggests that young children are egocentric?
4 Can children make transitive inferences?
5 Think about the roles of culture and brain development in cognitive development.
6 Do we understand what causes the major developments in children's thinking that occur around ages 6 to 7 years?
7 Think about Piaget's conservation problems. Why do you think young children fail them, and what develops to enable the older child to succeed at these tasks?

SUGGESTIONS FOR FURTHER READING

Carey, S., & Gelman, R. (Eds.) (1991). *The epigenesis of mind: Essays on biology and cognition.* Hillsdale, NJ: Erlbaum.

Chapman, M. (1988). *Constructive evolution: Origins and development of Piaget's thought.* Cambridge: Cambridge University Press.

Cole, M. (1996). *Cultural psychology: A once and future discipline.* Cambridge, MA: Harvard University Press.

Lee, K. (Ed.) (2000). *Cognitive development: The essential readings.* Cambridge, MA, and Oxford: Blackwell.

chapter 9

The Development of Language

Stan A. Kuczaj and Heather M. Hill

KEY CONCEPTS

BABBLING	INTONATION	PROTOCONVERSATIONS
CANONICAL	MATURATION	PROTODECLARATIVE
COMPREHENSION	MODULATED BABBLING	PROTO-IMPERATIVE
D-STRUCTURE	NATIVISM	REFLEXIVE VOCALIZATIONS
EMPIRICISM	OVEREXTENSION	SEMANTIC SYSTEM
GENERALIZATIONS	OVERGENERALIZATION	SPEECH STREAM
HABITUATION	OVERREGULARIZATION	S-STRUCTURE
INFANT-DIRECTED SPEECH	PEER	SYNTAX
(MOTHERESE)	PHONEME	TURN-TAKING
INNATE MECHANISM	PRAGMATIC SYSTEM	UNDEREXTENSION

OVERVIEW

The authors begin by asking what is human language. It is many things: a means of communication, a symbolic system, a rule-governed grammatical system, and it is productive in that we all can produce and comprehend sentences that have never previously been produced or heard. Language acquisition is discussed under four main headings.

- The abilities that enable us to communicate effectively comprise the pragmatic system, which involves a variety of cognitive and social skills.
- The development of the phonological system is described, from speech and word perception in infancy, to the production of speech sounds, and the child's developing ability to articulate and pronounce words and speech.
- The development of the syntactic system gives an account of how children learn the grammatical structures and rules which allow us to produce and comprehend grammatical sentences.

- The acquisition of word meaning – the semantic aspect of language development – is discussed in the next section.

Language acquisition does not proceed in isolation from other aspects of development, and the authors discuss the relationship and interaction between language and cognitive development. The concluding section gives a brief account of some of the different theoretical views that attempt to explain language development.

Introduction

The apparent ease with which young children acquire their first language masks the inherent difficulty of the task. During the course of language acquisition, children must learn to perceive and produce particular types of sounds, associate thousands of words with the appropriate meanings, combine words to produce sentences, and discover the rules that govern the manner in which speakers of a language communicate with one another. Clearly, children learning language must sort through and make sense of an impressive amount of information.

In this chapter, we will consider the general characteristics of language acquisition and possible explanations for these characteristics. Evident in explanations of many biological and psychological phenomena, the debate between **nativists** and **empiricists** continues to be quite lively in the area of language development. Theoretical accounts of language acquisition are shaped by assumptions about the nature of human language. For example, if a theorist believes that human language is the result of learned associations of words (such as "the" and "boy"), then his or her account of language acquisition will focus on how children learn such associations. However, a theorist who believes that human language depends on knowledge of abstract grammatical classes (such as *noun* and *verb*) will attempt to explain language acquisition in terms of such classes. Given the importance of assumptions about the nature of human language for theories of language acquisition, we will first consider the characteristics of human language.

What is Human Language?

A COMMUNICATION SYSTEM

Human language is primarily a communication system, a means for speakers of a language to communicate with one another. The ability to communicate is not unique to the human species. Communication systems have been found in species as diverse as bees, lions, and dolphins. However, none of the communication systems of other species has been found to possess all of the characteristics found in human communication (Hauser, 1996; Kuczaj & Kirkpatrick, 1993). Human language is the most complex, diverse, and efficient means of communication known to any species on earth. This is because human language is a symbolic, rule-governed system that is

Plate 9.1 The ability to communicate is not unique to the human species. Kittiwakes (*Rissa tridactyla*) greet each other when one returns to the cliff nesting site with cries of "kit-i-waak" and entwining of their necks. The longer the returning bird has been absent from the nest, the longer this greeting ceremony.

both abstract and productive, characteristics that enable its speakers to produce and comprehend a wide range of utterances.

A SYMBOLIC SYSTEM

Language is a symbolic system because words and parts of words (e.g., the English past tense suffix "-ed") represent meaning. The meaningful units of a language are symbols because they refer to things other than themselves. These symbols are conventional because speakers of a language use the same words to express the same meanings. For example, speakers of English use the word "bird" to refer to the wide variety of creatures that comprise avians. The conventional nature of language symbols makes communication possible. If everyone chose their own symbols, communication would be difficult, if not impossible. At the same time, however, language symbols are *arbitrary* because there is no necessary relation between sounds and meanings. Consider the word "bird" again. It is not necessary for this sound pattern to refer to the particular class of animals that it does. Speakers of English could just as easily refer to what we now call "birds" as "girts" or "mantels." The arbitrary nature of language symbols is readily apparent when we consider different human languages. Different languages use different sound combinations to refer to the same meaning. The English "bird" is *vogel* in German, *ptaszek* in Polish, and *oiseau* in French.

A RULE-GOVERNED SYSTEM

Language is a rule-governed system, meaning that each human language is constrained by a set of rules that reflects the regularities of the language. For example, in English, words such as "the" and "a" must precede the noun to which they refer: "the dolphin ate a fish" is a correct English sentence, but "dolphin the ate fish a" is not. The rule system of a language is abstract because it goes beyond the simple association of individual words and instead involves the manipulation of abstract classes of words. Thus, rather than saying that "the" must precede "dolphin," we may state that *articles* (the abstract class of words containing words such as "the" and "a") precede *nouns* (the abstract class of words containing words such as "dolphin" and "fish"). The abstract classes and the rules that manipulate them make possible the most important characteristic of human language, its productivity.

LANGUAGE IS PRODUCTIVE

Human language is productive in the sense that a finite number of linguistic units (sounds, words, and the abstract classes that contain these units) and a finite number of rules are capable of yielding an infinite number of grammatical utterances. Even though no speaker of any human language will produce all of the sentences that their language makes possible, the capacity to do so means that speakers of human language are not limited to reproducing sentences that they have heard, but may instead produce and comprehend novel utterances. As a result, humans can communicate a wide variety of information. We are capable of communicating facts, opinions, and emotions, regardless of whether they occurred in the past, are occurring in the present, or will occur in the future. Language also makes it possible to discuss fantasies and hypothetical situations and events. The potential productivity of language and the richness of the human mind combine to make possible the communication of a very broad array of topics. This capability for communicative diversity makes human language unique among all known communicative systems. The abilities that enable us to communicate effectively are discussed next.

The Development of the Pragmatic System

The abilities that enable us to communicate effectively and appropriately in a social context comprise the **pragmatic system**, which involves a variety of cognitive and social skills. For example, the abilities involved in **turn-taking**, initiating new topics and conversations, sustaining a dialogue, and repairing a faulty communication are all important aspects of the pragmatic system (Pan & Snow, 1999).

TURN-TAKING

Conversations take place when participants take turns responding to each other's queries or statements. Simply defined, turn-taking requires individuals to alternate between the roles of listener and speaker during the course of a conversation. Effective turn-taking requires that the listener recognize that a response is necessary, and realize when it is appropriate to make a response. Therefore, minimizing the number of unnecessary interruptions is an important aspect of turn-taking since interruptions disrupt the flow and cohesiveness of a conversation.

Mother–infant interactions

Turn-taking behavior makes its first appearance in the earliest interactions between mothers and infants. For example, nursing sometimes involves an early nonverbal type of turn-taking (Kaye, 1977; see also chapter 7). During nursing, infants pause between bursts of sucking. During these pauses, mothers sometimes jiggle the nipple or nudge the infant in order to stimulate the sucking response. Of course, young infants do not realize that they are taking turns when they rest after a sucking burst. Nonetheless, this form of interaction may set the stage for the development of other forms of turn-taking.

Turn-taking is also involved in other forms of mother–infant interactions. Mothers often talk to their infants while playing games such as peekaboo and give-and-take. During such games, mothers tend to vocalize when their infants are not vocalizing or after their infants have finished vocalizing. These patterns of interactions have been called **protoconversations** (Bateson, 1975), and may be important precursors to the turn-taking observed in early conversations. In early protoconversations, adults bear the burden of turn-taking. They must maintain the interaction by interpreting their infants' sounds and responding appropriately. However, sometime between 8 and 12 months, infants begin to take a more active role in turn-taking (Reddy, 1999). These later protoconversations are *dyadic* interactions since they involve only the child and the adult. These dyadic interactions evolve into *triadic* interactions which involve the infant, an adult, and an object. Triadic interactions are often **proto-imperatives** and **protodeclaratives** (Messinger & Fogel, 1998). A proto-imperative occurs when an infant points to an object and then alternates her gaze between the object and the adult until she obtains the desired object. A protodeclarative occurs when an infant uses pointing or looking to direct the adult's attention to an object.

Imitation

Turn-taking is also involved in infants' imitation of others (Masur & Rodemaker, 1999; Nelson, 1996). Children frequently use imitation in their conversations with other children or adults (e.g., Keenan, 1974; Kuczaj, 1982a). Imitation allows children to take a turn by repeating all or part of what the speaker has just said. The average 2-year-old takes only one to two turns per conversation (Brinton & Fujiki, 1984). In contrast, 3- to 5-year-old children are able to engage in conversations that contain as many as 12 turns (e.g., Garvey & Hogan, 1973). Imitation may be a means by which children learn to increase the number of turns that they take in a conversation.

INITIATING INTERACTIONS

Infants must also learn to initiate interactions. Infants' first attempts to initiate interactions with an adult often focus on directing the adult's attention either to the infant, or to an object. These first attempts are typically nonverbal. Instead of vocalizing, infants as young as 8 months will point or reach toward an object in which they are interested (Masur, 1983; Werner & Kaplan, 1963). Although pointing seems to be a universal characteristic of human cultures (Butterworth, 1995; Call & Tomasello, 1994), infants point to objects before they understand that others may point out objects to them (Butterworth & Grover, 1990; Desrochers, Morissette, & Ricard, 1995). As children learn to respond to the points of others, they also learn to direct better the attention of others. Thus, sometime between 12 and 18 months of age, infants learn to coordinate gestures, looks, and vocalizations in order to communicate their intents and wants to others (Franco & Butterworth, 1996; Tomasello, 1995). As children acquire language, their attempts to initiate interactions become more verbal and less gestural (Foster, 1986).

Children younger than 2 years tend to talk about things that exist in the here and now. They are most likely to refer to familiar and visible objects or people. As their language skills increase, children come to discuss a much broader range of topics, including imaginary, possible, and hypothetical events (Kuczaj & Daly, 1979; Morford & Goldin-Meadow, 1997; O'Neill & Atance, 2000).

MAINTAINING CONVERSATIONS

Appropriate turn-taking is an important aspect of conversation maintenance. Young children are likely to interrupt others, and so disrupt the conversational flow. Older children are more likely to wait until the other speaker has finished before attempting to gain their intended listener's attention (e.g., McLaughlin, 1998).

Children must also learn to add relevant information to the dialogue as well as learn when it is their turn to speak. Young children are likely to use their turns to refer to something completely different from the topic at hand, making sustained conversation difficult. This is true even if children are asked questions. Children under the age of 2 years typically answer only a third of the questions posed to them (Pan & Snow, 1999). By 3 years of age, children answer more than 50 percent of the questions they are asked (Olson-Fulero & Conforti, 1983). Although parents may sometimes find this difficult to believe, children are more likely to *respond* to questions than they are to *ask* questions. As a result, most of their conversations with adults involve children being asked lots of questions (Hoff-Ginsberg, 1990).

By now, it should be clear that adults contribute a great deal to the structure and maintenance of conversations with young children. As one might expect, young children's conversations with their **peers** tend to be problematic. When children "converse" with one another, topics are rarely consistently maintained (Blank & Franklin, 1980). Instead, young children's conversations with peers contain high proportions of imitations, repetitions, and sound play (Garvey, 1975; Keenan & Klein, 1975). However, if the conversation concerns a topic that is familiar to both children, even young children are able to sustain meaningful conversations (Nelson & Gruendel, 1979).

REPAIRING FAULTY CONVERSATIONS

In order to communicate effectively, children must learn when and how to repair conversations as miscommunications occur. In order to repair a miscommunication, one must both realize that a miscommunication has occurred and understand how to correct the problem. Sometimes all that is necessary is to repeat the original statement. Other times one must revise the original message in order for it to be understood.

Children as young as 1 year sometimes appear to recognize the failure of their nonverbal communicative attempts. For example, if infants do not receive the object they want, they may continue to point to the object until they are given it (Golinkoff, 1983). In such a case, the infant seems to be trying to repair the communicative failure by repeating the pointing. Of course, it is possible that the infant neither perceives the miscommunication nor is trying to repair it, but is instead simply producing a behavior that has resulted in desired objects being provided in the infant's past experience. Regardless of the communicative intent of these early "repairs," young children do learn to use repetition to correct faulty communications. As they get older, children add revisions and substitutions to their increasing repertoire of strategies for repairing and maintaining conversations (Brinton, Fujiki, Loeb, & Winkler, 1986; Furrow & Lewis, 1987; Gallagher, 1977; Golinkoff, 1986; Tomasello, Farrar, & Dines, 1984). For example, a child might revise a request by adding an additional word in order to clarify exactly what was being requested (e.g., "I want the *big* box"). Similarly, a child might substitute a phrase to improve communication (e.g., "The *thing* eats baby chicks" might become "the *fox* eats baby chicks").

Adults play an important role in the development of this aspect of the pragmatic system. Adults often request children to repeat utterances or to clarify the portion of the conversation that they did not understand (e.g., Gallagher, 1981). These forms of interactions help children learn that utterances can be misunderstood, why particular utterances are not understood, and how to correct a miscommunication.

By the age of 3 years, children have learned to request clarification of messages that they do not understand. These early requests for clarifications are characterized by single-word questions such as "Huh?" or repetitions of portions of the adults' utterances (Gallagher, 1981; Ninio & Snow, 1996). As children become more proficient users of their language, they learn to question more clearly specific aspects of others' messages.

Children have learned many of the aspects of the pragmatic system before their fifth birthday, which is why 3- and 4-year-old children are able to participate in the many delightful conversations that characterize the preschool years. Pragmatic skills are based on the acquisition of other aspects of their mother tongue, including the phonological system, the syntactic system, and the semantic system. We consider the acquisition of each of these systems in turn.

The Development of the Phonological System

Phonology is the aspect of language that is concerned with *the perception and production of sounds that are used in language.* In order for effective communication to occur, children must learn which sounds are important in the language that they hear.

SPEECH PERCEPTION

Speech segmentation

Deciphering the sounds of the language that they hear should be a formidable problem for infants. Like all of us, they are exposed to an undifferentiated series of speech sounds known as a **speech stream** (Jusczyk, 1997). Children must separate the speech stream into individual sounds and sound combinations in order to learn the relevant sounds of their language. Consider the following example, written without any word boundaries (from Slobin, 1979):

wheredidyougowithgrandpa

Because it is in English, this uninterrupted string is relatively easy to separate into its component words. Now try the following example:

dedenlenereyegittinsen

This is the Turkish equivalent of the first example. Unless you are a Turkish speaker, knowing the meaning does not help to segment the string of sounds. Turkish speakers recognize that the example consists of the following components:

dede n le ne re ye git t in sen

Despite the inherent difficulty of the task, infants do learn to divide the speech stream into meaningful units. Their attempts to do so may be facilitated by the nature of the speech that adults direct to infants. When compared to speech directed to adults, speech directed to infants has a higher pitch, more exaggerated pitch contours, a larger pitch range, and is more rhythmic (Trainor, Austin, & Desjardins, 2000): this is often called **infant-directed speech** or *motherese.* By the age of 7 months, infants are able to recognize familiar words in an uninterrupted speech stream (Jusczyk & Aslin, 1995). Thus, the capacity to segment the speech stream into words is present in infants at this age. By 7 months, they are also able to remember the words that they have segmented (Houston, Jusczyk, & Tager, 1997). Young infants seem to use a variety of cues to determine when words begin and end in the speech stream, including strongly stressed syllables to indicate the onset of new words (Goodsit, Morgan, & Kuhl, 1993; Jusczyk, Cutler, & Redanz, 1993). The task of segmenting the speech stream may also be facilitated by infants' preference for listening to human speech rather than to other sounds in their environment (Butterfield & Siperstein, 1974; Gibson and Spelke, 1983).

Categorical perception of speech sounds

Human speech uses sound categories that are called **phonemes**. A phoneme is a set of sounds that are not physically identical to one another, but which speakers of a language treat as equivalent sounds. Human languages differ in terms of the number and types of phonemes that they employ. For example, both the [k] sound in "key" and the [k] sound in "ski" are members of the same phoneme in English. This means that the two [k] sounds are perceived as the same sound by English speakers despite the fact that the [k] sound in "key" is aspirated (it concludes with a short puff of breath) and the [k] sound in "ski" is unaspirated (it does not conclude with a short puff of breath). In contrast, the two [k] sounds are members of different phonemes in Chinese. As a result, speakers of Chinese can readily discriminate the two sounds. Thus, speakers of English and speakers of Chinese differ in terms of their ability to discriminate the two sounds.

Infants discriminate between phonemes

In a pioneering study, Eimas, Siqueland, Jusczyk, and Vigorito (1971) used **habituation** to test 1-month-old infants' ability to discriminate the syllables /ba/ and /pa/. The habituation technique involved the presentation of a stimulus (e.g., /ba/) until the infant ceased to pay attention to it. At this point, another stimulus (e.g., /pa/) was presented to the infant. If the infant paid attention to the new stimulus, then Eimas et al. assumed that the infant could distinguish between the new stimulus and the old stimulus.

Using this paradigm, Eimas et al. found that the infants could discriminate the phonemes /ba/ and /pa/. Remember that the sounds that constitute each phoneme represent a range of possible sounds. Thus, there is a set of physically distinct sounds that comprise the phoneme /ba/. There could be, for example, variations in the way a particular speaker produces the sound from one utterance to the next, or the sound as spoken by different speakers. Nonetheless, adult speakers of English find it very difficult to discriminate one /ba/ sound from another, even though they have no difficulty discriminating a /ba/ sound from a /pa/ sound. In other words, adults can readily distinguish sounds that are from *different* categories (e.g., /ba/ versus /pa/), but find it difficult to discriminate sounds from the *same* category (e.g., two different /ba/ sounds). Similarly, the 1-month-old infants studied by Eimas et al. could not discriminate one /ba/ sound from another, although they could distinguish a /ba/ sound from a /pa/ sound.

The ability of infants to discriminate phonemes has considerable implications (Eimas, 1985; Jusczyk, 1997). First, the fact that infants can discriminate sounds from different phonemes but cannot distinguish sounds from the same phoneme class suggests that even young infants engage in the *categorical perception* of speech sounds.

Categorical perception is the process that allows us to distinguish sounds between categories (different phonemes) yet at the same time makes it difficult to distinguish sounds within a category (a particular phoneme such as /ba/). Second, the young age at which infants are able to discriminate phonemes suggests that categorical perception may be an **innate mechanism** for interpreting sounds. This mechanism may rest on general auditory processing skills rather than on skills specific to human speech (Jusczyk, Pisoni, Reed, Fernald, & Myers, 1983). In other words, infants may be predisposed to categorize sounds, which then may influence their perception of speech sounds. This possibility gains support from cross-species research in which nonhuman species such as chinchillas and macaque monkeys have demonstrated categorical perception of human speech sounds (Kuhl & Miller, 1975; Kuhl & Padden, 1982, 1983). If categorical perception of speech sounds depended on an innate knowledge of human phonemes, one would not expect species such as chinchillas and macaque monkeys to process human speech sounds categorically.

Becoming a native listener

The human ability to discriminate between phonemes diminishes with age. At 6 months of age, infants are able to discriminate a wide range of phonemes, including those that adult speakers of the infant's native language cannot discriminate. Nonetheless, the discriminative capabilities of the 6-month-old infant are influenced by experience, specifically, the language that they hear (Kuhl, 1992). The effects of experience become more pronounced with increasing age, so that by 12 months of age, infants remain able to discriminate the phonemes of the language they are learning, but are unlikely to discriminate the phonemes of other languages (Werker, 1989).

It seems, then, that children's acquisition of the phonemes of their native language depends on both the *innate predisposition* for categorical perception of sounds and *experience* with sounds used as phonemes in their native language(s). Children who are

Plate 9.2 Children become "native listeners" by learning which sounds are important in the language they hear. Children who hear Chinese learn the Chinese set of phonemes, whereas children who hear English acquire the English set.

exposed to English hear sounds used as English phonemes, and learn this set of phonemes. Children who hear Chinese are exposed to sounds that function as Chinese phonemes, and so acquire the Chinese set of phonemes. Basically, children who hear sounds used as particular phonemes retain the ability to discriminate these phonemes. Experience with phonemes is not necessary for categorical perception *per se*, but experience is necessary for the infant to learn which categories are most relevant to the language being learned. In Werker's terms, the infant gradually becomes a "native listener."

SPEECH PRODUCTION

The ability to *produce* speech sounds lags behind the ability to *perceive* the same sounds. The sounds that infants can perceive at an early age are not reliably produced for months or even years. This developmental lag reflects the difficulty of learning to control the vocal cords, mouth, tongue, and lips, all of which are involved in the intentional production of speech sounds. Perhaps because of the **maturation** that is required for sound production, all children pass through the same phases of vocal production (Oller, 1980; Stark, 1980), as discussed below.

Reflexive vocalizations (birth–2 months)

The first sounds produced by infants are **reflexive vocalizations**, including cries, coughs, burps, and sneezes. During the first month of life, infants produce more than one type of cry, raising the possibility that different infant cries might mean different things. If parents are asked to discriminate their young infant's cry types, they are unable to do so if the cries are tape-recorded and played back to them in the absence of external context (Muller, Hollien, & Murry, 1974). Even if infants are attempting to communicate with their cries, parents are more likely to respond to external context (e.g., a wet diaper/nappy) than to the type of cry itself.

Cooing and laughing (2–4 months)

During this period, infants begin to laugh and to combine sounds with one another. For example, the *coo* sound emerges toward the end of the second month of life. This sound combines the [u] sound with other sounds, and is often produced while the infant is in what appears to be a happy state. The parent–infant interactions following infant cooing are usually pleasant in nature. Parents may coo back at their child, who may in turn coo back at the parent, and so on. The reciprocal cooing between infant and parent may help the infant to learn that communication involves taking turns.

Babbling and vocal play (4–6 months)

Play with sounds (**babbling**) is the main characteristic of this period. As they gain control over their vocal cords, lips, tongue, and mouth, infants begin to produce a wide range of sounds and sound combinations.

Canonical babbling (6–10 months)

Infants begin to produce sound combinations that *sound* like words (hence the term **canonical**). However, there is no evidence that infants actually attach *meaning* to these sound combinations. During this period, infants continue their experimentation and play with sounds. The most common form of multisyllabic utterance during this period is the reduplicated babble, in which syllables are repeated (e.g., "mamama").

Jespersen (1922) suggested that infants produce virtually all human speech sounds during the babbling period, but it is now known that this is not true (Locke, 1983). Nonetheless, babbling is a universal phenomenon that seems to be genetically determined. Infants tend to babble during the same age period and to produce a similar range of sounds during early babbling. Many deaf children babble, as do hearing infants of deaf parents (Lenneberg, Rebelsky, & Nichols, 1965; Stoel-Gammon & Otomo, 1986). These results demonstrate that neither hearing human speech nor having others respond to infant vocalizations are necessary for early babbling to occur. However, babbling is rare in deaf infants older than 7 months, suggesting that hearing speech sounds plays an important role in the continuation of babbling past its early stages (Oller & Eilers, 1988). In addition, some form of interaction seems to be important for maintaining the infant's efforts to produce language sounds. Infants in institutions that provide little infant–adult interaction do not produce many vocalizations, and may not even cry (Bowlby, 1952; Spitz, 1965).

Modulated babbling (10 months on)

This is the final period of babbling and language play. This period is characterized by a variety of sound combinations, stress and **intonation** patterns, and overlaps with the beginning of meaningful speech. While early babbling and vocal play may help infants to learn purposely to produce the sounds that are relevant for their language, **modulated babbling** may play an important role in the acquisition of the intonation patterns that are important for the infant's native language (Boysson-Bardies, de Sagart, & Durand, 1984). For example, infants learning English must learn that different intonation patterns signal statements and questions. The statement "The boy likes to dance with girls" ends with a flat intonation pattern. In contrast, the question "Does the boy like to dance with girls?" ends with a rising intonation pattern. Modulated babbling may help infants learn to produce these different intonations. Regardless of the actual functions that babbling plays, it is clear that infants enjoy playing with speech sounds and intonation patterns, and that this play is a cornerstone for subsequent language development (Kuczaj, 1999a).

THE DEVELOPMENT OF ARTICULATION

As they learn the phonological system of their language, children must learn to pronounce words correctly. Children are more likely to use words that they can pronounce (Ferguson, 1989; Ingram, 1986; Macken & Ferguson, 1983). This suggests that they are aware of the differences between their incorrect pronunciations and the correct ones (Berko & Brown, 1960; Kuczaj, 1983; Smith, 1973). For example, one 3-year-old child consistently deleted the [s] sound from the beginnings of words when it was followed by a consonant sound. Thus, "I smell a skunk" was produced as "I mell a kunk." However, the child recognized that his form was the immature form, as illustrated in the following comment that the child made when asked to choose between one of his words ("neeze") and the correct word ("sneeze"): "You talk like him. You say *neeze* (*sneeze*). I can't say *neeze* like you do. I say *neeze*. I'll say *neeze* like you when I get big" (Kuczaj, 1983, p. 72).

As children learn to produce correct pronunciations, they may produce phonological distinctions that adults cannot perceive. Kornfield (1971) found that the "gwass" for "glass" and the "gwass" for "grass" produced by 2-year-old children were in fact slightly different sounds, even though adults equated the two "gwasses." Children consistently produced one "gwass" for "grass" and another "gwass" for "glass," suggesting that they were beginning to produce the two different sounds that would eventually yield "grass" and "glass." However, it is not known if children can perceive the differences between the two pronunciations of "gwass" if they are produced by another child.

The above examples suggest that children are aware that their incorrect pronunciations differ from those of adults, and that at least some children's pronunciations that are viewed as equivalent by adults may be functionally distinct for children. However, we do not know if children are aware of *how* their pronunciations differ from those of adults. Nor do we know the manner in which children's and adults' representations of pronunciations are related.

To sum up, the capacity to produce sounds and sound combinations reflects a combination of hereditary and environmental factors. The apparent universality of children's early sounds and babbling suggests that maturation plays an important role in these developments. However, children must hear adult sounds in order to determine the sounds and sound distinctions that are relevant for the language they are learning. Although it has proven difficult to demonstrate the relation of early sounds to later sounds, it seems likely that the entire course of sound production is important in that it enables children to practice and improve their articulatory skills (Vihman, 1996).

 ## The Development of the Syntactic System

Syntax deals with the manner in which words and parts of words are related to one another to produce grammatical sentences. Sentences are not created in a haphazard fashion. Instead, the production of sentences is governed by grammatical structures and rules. Chomsky (1957, 1982) suggested that the syntactic structure of every human language is the result of an interrelated set of elements. At one level is the **s-structure** (or surface structure), which roughly corresponds to the spoken sentence. At another level is the **d-structure** (or deep structure), which is a more abstract representation of a sentence. In order to understand the significance of the distinction between s-structure and d-structure, consider the following three sentences: "The shooting of the hunters was awful," "Mary is easy to please," and "Mary is eager to please." The first sentence is ambiguous. It could mean that the hunters were terrible marksmen. Or it could mean that someone shot the hunters. The important point about this example is that one s-structure can have more than one meaning. The intended meaning is determined by the d-structure, which specifies that the hunters were either the ones doing the shooting or the ones being shot. The second and third sentences share similar s-structures: noun-verb-adjective-infinitive verb. However, the meaning of the two sentences is quite different. Mary is the subject of the verb "to please" in "Mary is eager to please," but in "Mary is easy to please" the subject of "to please" is whoever or whatever pleases Mary. Once again, the meaning of the s-structure is determined by the d-structure. For the past 30 years, the study of syntactic development has revolved around debates about the role of d-structures and s-structures.

THE ONE-WORD PERIOD

Children's acquisition of syntax follows a relatively predictable pattern during the first 2 years of life. Sometime between 10 and 18 months of age, children begin to produce single-word utterances. More than 70 years ago, DeLaguna (1927) suggested that the utterances of children in the one-word period are based on more complete thoughts than can be represented by a single word. According to DeLaguna, the single-word utterances that children produce actually represent simple complete sentences. In other words, although children in the one-word period are limited to producing single-word utterances, they are capable of conceiving of and comprehending more complete sentences. Thus, the child who says "doggie" while pointing at his pet might mean "there's my doggie," whereas the child who points to a toy dog that is on top of a shelf and says "doggie" might mean "I want the toy doggie." In such a scenario, the s-structure "doggie" has different d-structures.

What's in a word?

Most adults do interpret children's single-word utterances as if they mean more than the literal single word. However, Brown (1973) and Bloom (1973) both pointed out the dangers of such "rich interpretation." The basic problem is deciding exactly how much more a child means to produce than the single word contained in the s-structure. A child who says "hot" while looking at a lit stove might mean "that is hot," "the stove we heat our food on is hot right now," or even "if someone touches that hot stove, they will receive a bad burn." While few of us would be willing to grant the young child the knowledge required to produce the second or third d-structure, the available information does not provide sufficient cues to determine exactly what a child means when a single-word utterance is produced. Thus, assumptions about what children mean in the one-word period must be made with great caution (Barrett, 1986). As a result, the implication of the one-word period for syntactic development is unclear.

Despite the inherent ambiguity of children's one-word utterances, what is clear is that children do *comprehend* more than they can produce. Golinkoff and Hirsh-Pasek (1995) presented 17-month-old infants with two videos, each of which portrayed two different scenes. For example, one video might show a dog licking a cat and the other video might show a cat licking a dog. While the videos were playing, the infants heard one of two sentences ("the dog is licking the cat" or "the cat is licking the dog"). The infants looked longer at the video that corresponded to the sentence that they heard, suggesting that infants who can produce only a single word at a time nonetheless understand at least some aspects of word order.

THE TWO-WORD PERIOD

The next major period of syntactic development is the two-word period. Between 18 and 24 months of age, most children begin to produce two words at a time. These words are not chosen randomly. Instead, children consistently use the words that convey the most meaning (e.g., nouns, verbs, and adjectives), and omit other sorts of words such as "in," "and," "the," and "of" and word endings such as the past tense "-ed" and the plural "-s." Thus, children are likely to produce utterances such as "mommy go" and "kick ball." Children's language environment increases the likelihood that they first learn and use high-meaning words. Such words are more likely to be stressed in adult speech, and so are perceptually salient compared to other words (Brown, 1973; Gleitman & Wanner, 1982; Miller & Ervin, 1964). It seems, then, that children are most likely to use words that are highly salient in their environment, which turn out to be nouns, verbs, and adjectives.

Word order

Children's knowledge of language and their use of this knowledge are limited during the two-word period. For example, many children do not consistently use word order to mark semantic relations in the two-word period (Maratsos, 1983). Children learning English might say "doggie lick" or "lick doggie," regardless of whether the dog is licking or being licked. Children's use of consistent word order seems to reflect limited knowledge rather than general rules. For English, the most general way to relate an agent and an action is to place the agent before the action, as in "doggie lick" when the dog is the one doing the licking. Young children are most likely to use the correct "agent + action" word order in a limited sense. For example, children may use the "agent + action" word order only when the agent is animate. Thus, they would be more likely to say "doggie bark" than "balloon pop" or "hat fall" since "doggie" is an animate noun and "balloon" and "hat" are not.

The manner in which speech in the two-word period is related to later syntactic development is a matter of considerable debate (Maratsos, 1999). Some (e.g., Bloom, 1990; Pinker, 1987) have argued that children learn syntax by learning to associate concepts such as *agency* (the thing producing an action) and *action* (what something does) with syntactic categories such as subject (e.g., "the boy") and verb (e.g., "draws"). Others believe that children in this period lack certain aspects of d-structure, although there is little agreement about exactly what aspects of d-structure are missing (Hyams, 1989; Ingram, 1992; Radford, 1990). So, although it is clear that children in the two-word period are progressing toward a more mature understanding of syntax, it is not clear exactly how much they know.

LATER SYNTACTIC DEVELOPMENT

Children's syntactic knowledge increases dramatically following the two-word period, resulting in rapidly improving language skills. For example, one of the children studied by the first author was producing two-word utterances such as "me happy" at 24 months of age. This same child produced the following sentence about 1 year later: "I don't want to go to sleep and dream the dream I dreamed last night." The difference between this child's language competence at 24 months and at 36 months of age is striking. This type of grammatical development is typical, as evidenced by the following two speech samples (obtained from one child at two different ages). In the first sample, the child is 24 months old.

Speech sample 1

Adult: It is hot.
Child: Hot. This hot. This hot this time.
Child: Mommy, help me. This hot.
Adult: Do you want a cinnamon one?
Child: Yes.
Adult: Okay.
Child: Cinnamon on them.
Adult: Cinnamon's already on them.
Child: Ow! Hot! This burn my hand.
Adult: You better be careful.
Child: Mommy, put butter on mine.
Adult: You want butter?
Child: Yes. Right there. Right there, mommy. Ow! I burn my hand. I burn my hand.

The following is another conversation involving the same child at 36 months of age:

Speech sample 2

Child: Mom fixed this for me and I don't like it.
Adult: You don't like bacon?
Child: No. Abe's gonna eat rest of it.
Adult: What?
Child: A coupon. Look. For McDonald's.
Adult: What kind of sandwich would you like?
Child: I like a mayonnaise sandwich.
Adult: Okay.
Child: (laughs). That is bad. Mom will come home and not like it.
Adult: What?
Child: This mess. I want a sandwich. Where is my sandwich? I don't want meat. I want not meat. Not peanut butter. Not cheese. Only mayonnaise.
Adult: Okay.
Child: And you will put it here. Okay? Put it right here so I can eat it.
Adult: Okay. I will after it's made.
Child: What kind you gonna make me? I don't want cheese. Only mayonnaise.

There are a number of differences in the speech produced by this child at 24 months and at 36 months of age. The child's utterances are longer and more complex in the second speech sample than in the first speech sample. For example, the child uses a verb ending (the past tense "-ed"), a "be" form ("is"), a modal auxiliary ("will"), and conjunctions ("and," "so"). None of these forms was present in the first speech sample.

As is evident in our example, children learn to use a variety of linguistic forms and structures relatively quickly in the months following the two-word period. The speed with which children learn a vast amount of their language has perplexed scholars of language acquisition for some time.

THE SIGNIFICANCE OF OVERREGULARIZATION ERRORS AND CREATIVE OVERGENERALIZATIONS

All languages have rules that govern the use of grammatical forms. As children learn syntax, they produce a variety of "errors" that demonstrate that they are learning these rules. **Overregularization** errors occur when children apply a rule to an exception to the rule. For example, a child learning English might say "thinked" rather than "thought" because the child is using the regular past tense rule (attach "-ed" to the end of the verb) rather than the correct exception to the rule ("thought"). Children who produce these sorts of errors are making reasonable and understandable mistakes. They are acting as if the rules they are learning do not have exceptions (languages contain exceptions to their rules because languages have evolved over long periods of time). Significantly, children who produce overregularization errors are using forms that they have not heard. This suggests that they are using the rules of the language they are learning in order to produce *novel* words. Hence, children are already using language in a productive fashion. The extent to which children generalize the rules that they are learning depends at least in part on the ease with which children can relate the bits of information that they glean from the language that they hear (Kuczaj & Borys, 1988).

Plurals

In English, singular nouns are made plural by adding the suffix "-s," as in "cats" and "dogs." These nouns are called regular nouns. Other nouns have plural forms that are exceptions to this rule, and are called irregular forms. Examples of irregular plural forms include "men" and "mice." Soon after children begin to produce correct regular plural forms such as "dogs," they also begin to produce overregularized forms such as "foots" and "mans" (Brown, 1973). These errors demonstrate that children have acquired a regular plural rule, but have not learned all the exceptions to the rule. Interestingly, children are unlikely to attach the plural suffix to *mass nouns* such as "water" and "air" (McNamara, 1982). Thus, children overregularize the plural to irregular *count* nouns (which refer to objects that can be counted) like "foot" and "man," but not to mass nouns like "water" and "air" (which cannot be counted). This finding suggests that young children can distinguish nouns that refer to countable objects from nouns that refer to entities that cannot be counted.

Past tense

In English, the suffix "-ed" is used to express past tense, as in "called" and "showed." English also has many irregular past tense forms, such as "ran" and "hit." As they learn the past tense, children often overregularize their use of "-ed," producing forms such as "runned" and "hitted" (Brown, 1973; Kuczaj, 1977; Maratsos, 2000). In fact, they produce such errors for many years. This is not surprising given that English has many irregular past tense forms and the fact that children must learn every exception to this regular rule.

Creative overgeneralizations

The progressive "-ing" form is the first suffix to be acquired by young children learning English (Brown, 1973). There are no irregular progressive forms in English, and so no opportunities for overregularization errors. Nonetheless, children's use of the progressive does go beyond simply repeating what they have heard. Children (and adults) occasionally create new verbs by treating a noun as if it were a verb. Children also use the progressive with some of these novel forms, as in "why is it weathering?" (referring to rain and thunder) and "I'm ballereening" (dancing like a ballerina) (Kuczaj, 1978). Both overregularization errors and creative **overgeneralizations** demonstrate that children do not simply reproduce forms that they have heard others use. Instead, they create new forms ("runned," "ballereening") based on the regularities in the language that they hear.

Plate 9.3 "I'm ballereening." Children do not simply reproduce forms that they have heard others use. Instead, they overgeneralize, creating new forms (e.g., "ballereening") based on the regularities in the language they hear.

How can syntactic development be explained?

Innate knowledge?

The speed with which children acquire syntax, and the creativity that they exhibit at an early age, must be explained by any theory that attempts to explain syntactic development. One of the most famous explanations focused on the notion that children are born with innate knowledge of language (Chomsky, 1972, 1987). Chomsky's arguments for innate knowledge rested on the following points: (1) Language requires the ability to relate d-structures to s-structures. (2) The environment only provides children with information about s-structures. Since knowledge of d-structures is not available in the environment, such knowledge must be innate. (3) The sentences that children hear are complex and often ungrammatical. (4) Children receive little feedback about the grammatical correctness of their utterances. (5) Children acquire their first language relatively quickly and easily.

Do parents correct their child's language?

As we have seen, children do learn their first language relatively quickly and easily. Chomsky's claim that parents pay little attention to their young children's syntax is also true. Parents are unlikely to correct their children's ungrammatical utterances (Brown & Hanlon, 1970; Hirsh-Pasek, Treiman, & Schneiderman, 1984). In fact, parents may actually reinforce ungrammatical utterances. For example, a mother responded to her child's statement "No dinosaur no go here" with "That's right. We don't put dinosaurs there." To complicate matters further, parents sometimes correct grammatical sentences because the *meaning* of the sentence is incorrect, even though the *syntax* is perfect. For example, a child's grammatical statement that "And Walt Disney comes on Tuesday" was corrected by the mother, who responded "No. He does not."

Even when parents make a conscious effort to correct their child's ungrammatical constructions, they often encounter a resistant child. Braine (1971) reported the following interchange between himself and his daughter:

Daughter: Want other one spoon, daddy.
Father: You mean you want *the other spoon*.
Daughter: Yes, I want other one spoon, please, daddy.
Father: Can you say "the other spoon"?
Daughter: Other . . . one . . . spoon.
Father: Say . . . "other."
Daughter: Other.
Father: Spoon.
Daughter: Spoon.
Father: Other spoon.
Daughter: Other spoon. Now give me other one spoon.

To the extent that parents' role in their children's syntactic development is limited to reinforcing their children's grammatical utterances and correcting children's ungrammatical utterances, Chomsky's claim that parents do not play significant roles

Plate 9.4 "I want other one spoon, please, daddy." Photograph © Heather Vickers.

in their children's syntactic development is supported by the data. However, even though young children produce utterances and constructions that they have not heard before (as evidenced by overregularization errors and creative overgeneralizations), they do in fact learn the language that they have heard their parents speak. Although overregularization errors and creative overgeneralizations demonstrate that imitation cannot be the primary method by which children learn syntax, children do imitate some of the speech that they hear (Kuczaj, 1982a; Ochs & Schieffelin, 1984). The parents' role in providing language models is an important one.

The language input to the child

Parents do a much better job of providing children with good examples of grammatical sentences than Chomsky supposed. Newport, Gleitman, and Gleitman (1975) found that mothers produced ungrammatical sentences *less than one-tenth of 1 percent* of the time that they spoke to their young children. Parents usually speak to young children in short grammatical sentences (a characteristic of infant-directed speech: Farwell, 1975; Gleason & Weintraub, 1978), as do adults who have never had children. In fact, even 4-year-old children simplify the speech they direct to children younger than themselves (Shatz & Gelman, 1973).

Despite the fact that children hear a much more simplified version of language than do most adults, Chomsky still believes that innate knowledge of language is necessary for language acquisition. The reason is that no matter how simple the language input to the child is, it consists of s-structures. For Chomsky, d-structures must be innate, since spoken language can provide no direct information about this aspect of language. In his view, the role of experience is to provide information about s-structures. This information will be combined with the child's innate knowledge of language to yield the particular grammatical rules for the language the child is learning. A similar view has been offered by Pinker (1989), who proposed that children are born with knowledge of the categories of verb and noun. According to Pinker, children use the information from s-structure to sort out the precise manner in which their language uses nouns and verbs to express meaning in sentences.

The notion that children are born with knowledge of d-structures and possible types of grammatical categories is very controversial (Bloom, 1991; Tomasello, 1992). Although it seems clear that children are born with a very strong *predisposition* to learn a language, this does not necessarily mean that children are born with *innate knowledge* of language (see Maratsos, 1999). Perhaps the innate predisposition consists of a set of mechanisms that help children to sort out the information that they hear. For example, recall the earlier discussion of categorical perception of phonemes. We are born with the ability to perceive phonemes, but we are not born with knowledge of particular phonemes or a general understanding of what phonemes are.

 ## The Acquisition of Word Meaning

Word meaning acquisition is a **comprehension**-based process. In order to learn a word, children must hear it being used. As children acquire their first words, they learn that words are meaningful sounds that can be used to represent something else (Bever, 1970; Dromi, 1999; Kuczaj, 1975, 1999b; Reddy, 1999). This process may begin in early infancy. Tincoff and Jusczyk (1999) presented 6-month-old infants with side-by-side videos of their parents. The infants looked longer at the video of the mother if the word "mommy" was heard, but looked longer at the video containing the father if the word "daddy" was heard. This pattern did not occur if a strange man and woman were substituted for the mother and father. These results suggest that young infants are learning the meanings of at least some words in their environment.

Before their fourth birthday, children will learn to use words to represent and refer to real, possible, and imaginary aspects of their world (Kuczaj & Daly, 1979; O'Neill & Atance, 2000). Thus, the toddler who uses the word "ball" only while holding a baseball becomes a 3-year-old who can use words to express complex thoughts such as "if that dinosaur eats it, there won't be any more" (Kuczaj & Daly, 1979).

GUESSING A WORD'S MEANING

The child's interpretation and memory of the situation in which the word was first encountered determines the child's initial guess about the word's meaning. The manner in which a child interprets a recently discovered word depends on the child's existing semantic system, his knowledge of the world, and the level of his cognitive skills (Kuczaj, 1975, 1982b, 1999b; Masur, 1995).

If a word that the child has just heard refers to an object, the child's attention might be drawn to the object while the word is being spoken, as when a parent points to a cow while saying "there's a nice cow." In such a case, the child must first understand that the parent intends to communicate something about the object to which the parent is pointing. If the child does comprehend the parent's intention, she is likely to guess that the word has something to do with the cow. Initially, children build their vocabulary by focusing on one-to-one correspondences between words and things. But concentrating on one-to-one correspondences does not make the child's task much easier. Consider a situation in which a child is shown a man riding an elephant and told to "look at the elephant." Prior to this, the child has neither heard the word "elephant" nor seen an elephant. The possible meanings of "elephant" in this situation are numerous. The child might guess that elephant means "man riding elephant," "long nose," "big ears," "big feet," "animal under a man," and so on. As noted by Quine (1960) and Goodman (1983), there are many possible interpretations for every situation.

Given the number of possible interpretations that children might make about a word's meaning, it is not surprising that some of their initial guesses about the meanings of object words are incorrect. Children sometimes believe that a word refers to many more objects than it actually does. For example, the child might use the word "bird" to refer to birds, airplanes, hot air balloons, falling leaves, and kites. The child who extends the meaning of a word too broadly is making an **overextension** error. The opposite extreme occurs when children extend the meaning of a word to too few instances, as when a child restricts his use of a word like "duck" to situations in which the child is playing with a toy duck while in the bath. Using a word too narrowly is called an **underextension** error.

THE COMPLEXITY OF THE TASK

Although children do make mistakes when attaching meaning to words, they make relatively few mistakes given the complexity of the task. In addition to the fact that words occur in situations that may be interpreted in numerous ways, many things may be referred to with a variety of words and linguistic forms. For example, the same creature might be called "Susie," "Mom," "honey," "sister," "daughter," "friend," "doctor," etc., depending on the speaker and the context. To complicate matters further, some categories are part of larger categories. For example, a person might be a Caucasian (a race included in the larger category *people*). A person is also a *mammal* (a category that includes people), an *animal* (a category that includes mammals), and a *terrestrial* (a category that includes animals). In addition, many words have more than one meaning. Hence, there is ample opportunity for children to be confused. Despite the complexity of the task, children somehow construct a vocabulary of approximately 14,000 words by the time they are 6 years old (Carey, 1978; Smith, 1926; Templin, 1957).

As the child gains additional experience with a word and its uses, she must compare recently acquired information with that she has already stored in her semantic system. This process will eventually allow the child to determine the correct meaning of the word. Regardless of the type of word being acquired, the basic processes of word meaning acquisition are the same. The child encounters the word in a situation. This information is interpreted in terms of the existing semantic system, the result being an initial guess about the meaning of the novel word. As a result of subsequent experiences and interpretations, this initial guess will be modified until the child has determined the correct meaning of the word. Building a semantic system requires the child to process vast amounts of information within a context in which words can mean virtually anything and are related to one another in myriad ways (Clark, 1993; Kuczaj, 1982b).

IS CHILDREN'S ACQUISITION OF WORD MEANING CONSTRAINED?

The complexity of the word learning task has led some researchers to suggest that children acquire words and meanings as quickly as they do because their choices are constrained. The notion of constraints on semantic development assumes that children neither consider all of the information available to them nor are overwhelmed by possible interpretations. Instead, both the types of information to be considered and the possible interpretations of this information are constrained by innate factors.

A number of constraints have been suggested to influence word meaning development (Clark, 1993; Golinkoff, Hirsh-Pasek, Mervis, Frawley, & Parillo, 1995; Golinkoff, Shuff-Bailey, Olguin, & Ruan, 1995; Markman, 1990; Soja, Carey, & Spelke, 1991). The following are offered as examples:

- **Whole object constraint**: Assumes that children believe that words refer to whole objects rather than to parts of objects. Thus, the child who hears an adult say "elephant" while pointing to an elephant assumes that the adult is referring to the entire elephant rather than to some part of the elephant.
- **Mutual exclusivity constraint**: Assumes that children believe that there is a one-to-one correspondence between words and meanings. Thus, if a child knows that certain creatures are called "dogs," she will not use "dog" to refer to other types of objects or creatures. She will also assume that the things she calls "dog" can have no other name.

Although the notion of constraints seems to simplify the task the child faces in constructing a semantic system, there is little support for the notion that constraints are involved in word meaning acquisition (Gathercole & Min, 1997; Kuczaj, 1990, 1999b; Nelson, 1988). None of the hypothesized constraints has been shown to be an absolute predisposition (Behrend, 1995; Bloom, 1994; Bloom & Kelemen, 1995; Golinkoff et al., 1995; Merriman, Marazita, & Jarvis, 1995). In addition, many of the proposed constraints would actually make word meaning acquisition *more* difficult. For example, if the whole object constraint actually constrained children's acquisition of word meaning, why and how do they acquire so many words that refer to parts of objects? Similarly, if children are constrained to believe that word meanings are mutually exclusive, how do they ever learn that an "elephant" is also a "pachyderm," a "mammal," and an "animal"?

THE IMPORTANCE OF SEMANTIC RELATIONS

Children construct a **semantic system** rather than a list of independent words because words are related to one another rather than existing in isolation. The development of the semantic system is facilitated by children's acquisition of semantic relations.

We have already noted that children must learn that objects can be referred to by more than one word (a fact which even young children can learn: Mervis, Golinkoff, & Bertrand, 1994). The child must also determine how words relate to one another. Some words are opposites ("hot"–"cold"), others form semantic dimensions ("hot," "warm," "cool," and "cold"), and still others are structured in terms of subordinate–superordinate relations. For example, the word "dog" is subordinate to the word "mammal," which in turn is subordinate to the word "animal."

Semantic dimensions

As children learn the words contained in semantic sets such as "hot," "warm," "cool," "cold" or "always," "usually," "sometimes," "seldom," and "never," words that express the far ends of the dimension ("hot"–"cold," "always"–"never") are learned before words that fall between the two extremes (Kuczaj, 1975, 1982b). The end points of semantic dimensions seem to be more salient to young children than are points between the two extremes. The salience of end points may be one reason that polar opposites are important aspects of the semantic system (Lyons, 1977).

As children discover the semantic relations that are necessary to structure their semantic system, they are better able to organize their growing vocabulary (Kuczaj, 1982b, 1999b). In addition, learning semantic relations helps children become aware of gaps in their vocabulary (Clark, 1993). For example, the child who knows that people have hair and that dogs have fur may wonder what one calls the stuff that covers a bird's body.

The Interaction of Language and Cognitive Development

Before children begin to acquire words, they have formed concepts of the world. Children's first words are most likely to be those that express these early concepts because children search for ways to communicate what they know (Bowerman, 1981; Clark, 1973; Mervis, 1987). However, even the early development of the semantic system results in changes in children's concepts. As children construct their semantic system, they are building a rich and complex means to represent their world mentally. Hearing a novel word causes children to search for the meaning of the word, which often results in new concepts being learned (Balaban & Waxman, 1997; Kuczaj, Borys, & Jones, 1989; Waxman, 1999; Waxman & Markow, 1995).

Kuczaj (1982b) suggested that children use two strategies when faced with gaps in their semantic and/or conceptual system. These strategies reflect the interrelationship of language and cognitive development.

- **Strategy 1: Acquiring a new word.** When acquiring a new word, search known concepts in case the word denotes a previously acquired concept. If no existing concept seems appropriate, attempt to construct a new one.
- **Strategy 2: Acquiring a new concept.** When acquiring a new concept, attempt to attach a known word to it. If no word seems appropriate, look for one.

In the process of building a semantic system, children acquire a world view that is shaped at least in part by the language they hear (Gellatly, 1995; Gopnik & Choi, 1995; Kuczaj, 1975, 1982b; Kuczaj et al., 1989; Nelson, 1996; Rotterman & Gentner, 1998). The development of the semantic system influences conceptual development by virtue of the manner in which language dissects and organizes the world (Gopnik & Meltzoff, 1997; Kuczaj, 1999b).

SUMMARY AND CONCLUSIONS

The complexity of the task facing the language learning child has produced a variety of types of theoretical views that attempt to explain language development. Barrett (1999) categorized these views in terms of four general theoretical stances.

(1) One stance is characterized by advocates of the notion that at least some aspects of language development are dependent on *innate capacities and knowledge* that are specific to language (e.g., Chomsky, 1986; Pinker, 1989; Richie & Bhatia, 1999). The most extreme nativist position proposes that both information-processing skills specific to the acquisition of language and knowledge about certain aspects of language are passed from generation to generation via the genes. According to this view, knowledge of d-structures is not learned but innate.

(2) A second theoretical stance also assumes that aspects of language development are strongly influenced by *innate information-processing predispositions*, but does not assume that children are born with innate knowledge of language (Kuczaj, 1982c; Tomasello & Brooks, 1999). For example, children are born with the ability to discriminate phonemes but must learn which phonemes are important in the language they are acquiring.

The remaining two theoretical stances offer empiricist views and emphasize the importance of experience in language acquisition.

(3) One of these stances assumes that children acquire language-specific concepts and representations because of their *experiences with language* rather than because the concepts and representations are innately specified (Karmiloff-Smith, 1992a). For example, in this view, children must learn that nouns are used to refer to objects, and so acquire the notion of noun from this sort of learning.

(4) The remaining stance also emphasizes the role of experience, but assumes that children acquire aspects of language because of *more general abilities* that play a role in cognitive development *per se* (Barrett, 1986). This theoretical position assumes that language development occurs in much the same way that other aspects of cognitive development do, and so minimizes the notion that language development is a unique aspect of children's development.

As we have seen, the particular stance taken by a theorist depends on the aspect of language development with which he or she is concerned and his or her beliefs about the nature of language and its development. A true explanation of language development will require a combination of innate and environmental factors, and so researchers need to look beyond their "favorite" theories and consider all possible explanations. As this occurs more and more frequently, we will move that much closer to understanding the incredible feats that characterize language development.

DISCUSSION POINTS

1 What are the major characteristics of human language? Think about the ways in which language is a communication system, a symbolic system, a rule-governed system, and is productive.

2 What are the pragmatic abilities that enable children to communicate effectively, and how do they develop?

3 How does the phonological system develop, and why is it important to distinguish between the perception and production of speech?

4 What are the differences between the one-word and two-word stages of speech acquisition? Do one-word utterances stand for (or mean) a whole sentence?

5 What sort of attempts have been made to explain semantic development?

6 How do children learn the meaning of words?

7 How does language development interact with cognitive development?

SUGGESTIONS FOR FURTHER READING

Barrett, M. (Ed.) (1999). *The development of language*. Hove: Psychology Press.

Hoff-Ginsberg, E. (1997). *Language development*. Pacific Grove, CA: Brooks/Cole.

Holzman, M. (1997). *The language of children*. Cambridge, MA, and Oxford: Blackwell.

Karmiloff, K., & Karmiloff-Smith, A. (2001). *Pathways to language: From fetus to adolescent*. Cambridge, MA: Harvard University Press.

Tomasello, M., & Bates, E. (2001). *Language development: The essential readings*. Cambridge, MA, and Oxford: Blackwell.

chapter 10

Acquiring a Theory of Mind

Peter Mitchell

KEY CONCEPTS

AUTISM
CHRONOLOGICAL AGE (CA)
COGNITIVE DEVELOPMENT
CONCEPTUAL SHIFT
CROSS-CULTURAL STUDY
DECEPTIVE BOX TASK
DOWN'S SYNDROME
EGOCENTRIC
FALSE BELIEF

HUNTER-GATHERER TRIBE
INSTINCT
INTUITIVE PSYCHOLOGY
INTELLIGENCE QUOTIENT
 (IQ)
MATURATIONAL UNFOLDING
MENTAL AGE (MA)
METACOGNITION
PERFORMANCE LIMITATIONS

POSTING VERSION OF THE
 DECEPTIVE BOX TEST
REPRESENTATIONAL ABILITY
STAGE-LIKE CHANGES IN
 DEVELOPMENT
STATE CHANGE TEST
THEORY OF MIND
UNEXPECTED TRANSFER TEST
WING'S TRIAD OF IMPAIRMENTS

OVERVIEW

The term theory of mind has been used to describe our everyday understanding of our own and others' minds. An understanding that others may hold beliefs that may be wrong (i.e., false beliefs) is seen as critical to an understanding of others' minds, and researchers have devised tests of false belief for assessing the development in children's understanding of the mind. These tests include the following:

• The unexpected transfer test of false belief.
• The deceptive box task.
• The state change test, and variations on this and other tests.
• The posting version of the deceptive box test.

Many children below about 4 years of age fail these tests, while older children pass. On the strength of these findings, some theorists have concluded that children negotiate a radical conceptual shift in their thinking around 4 years. The author suggests that a more plausible account is that children undergo a *gradual* change that allows them to disengage from a focus on current reality. Indeed, even adults have been found to fail certain types of false belief tasks!

Introduction

One of the most striking human qualities surrounds our ability to interact with others. We exchange ideas, learn from each other, coordinate efforts, and influence one another. It is true that other creatures can do some of these things too. But the way in which humans do it is probably unique: unlike in other creatures, it is substantially achieved as an intellectual feat. In nonhumans, social behavior might have a great deal to do with **instinct**, in which case it would not be quite so insightful or creative. People experience a meeting of minds, and that feeling could be a special human privilege.

EARLY ATTUNEMENT TO OTHERS' MINDS

The ability to connect with other minds is present very early in development. Parents sense that their newborn has a unique set of feelings, desires, needs, pleasures, and temperamental characteristics. Before long, the relationship is cemented when the baby shows a range of social responses to the parents. In infancy and early childhood, the toddler ventures into the social realm of peers and has a repertoire of skills which allow play and cooperation, especially in the sphere of fantasy. They will show awareness of others' desires, motives, and beliefs, and will appear to anticipate others' reactions and behavior. In brief, they spontaneously and easily seem to become attuned to other minds. This impressive beginning lays the foundations for the growth of a sophisticated **intuitive psychology**. In extreme cases, people can sometimes seem unnervingly telepathic in figuring out your thoughts.

There is a sense, then, in which we are able to read each others' minds – not through extrasensory perception (ESP), but thanks to a special aptitude for working out what other people think. We are effective at inferring that a person needs to have the necessary informational access if they are to know something. For example, you would not know that United won the cup, or that the Atlanta Braves won the World Series, unless you watched the game, someone told you, or you read about it. Indeed, if someone told you that Munich had won the cup, or the New York Yankees the World Series, you would probably believe them and thereby harbor a **false belief**. The fact that you can be ignorant or misinformed is not particularly noteworthy. It is much more important with respect to the theme of this chapter that other people are capable of diagnosing that you are ignorant or holding a false belief. In other words, people have an aptitude for figuring out what you think.

FOCUSING ON FALSE BELIEFS: THE UNEXPECTED TRANSFER TEST

Why concentrate on ignorance and false belief? Why not concentrate on being amply informed? There are two reasons, one posed by the challenge of trying to find out whether a person is attuned to other minds, and the other concerned with the special value of understanding about others' *false* beliefs. We shall tackle each in turn.

If we ask a child to make judgments about another person's true beliefs, she would respond correctly even if she did not know anything about other minds. Imagine that we told her a story about Maxi, a little boy who stored a bar of chocolate safely in the cupboard, so that he can eat it when he returns from play. If we ask her where Maxi thinks the chocolate is or where he will look for it, she will correctly say "cupboard." But perhaps she is merely answering according to where she herself would look for the chocolate. Children usually answer questions in some fashion, even when not furnished with all the necessary information; so long as they are at ease, it is rare for them to remain mute. Asking about a person's true belief thus offers no opportunity to differentiate between a child who understands about the mind and one who does not. Both children would answer in the same way, even though one is actually reporting where she herself knows the chocolate is.

A test of false belief is very different (see figure 10.1, which shows the **unexpected transfer test** of false belief). Imagine that after Maxi went out to play, his mother

Scene 1: Maxi puts his chocolate in the cupboard

Scene 2: Later, Mom moves it to the fridge

Figure 10.1 The unexpected transfer test of false belief, featuring Maxi, his bar of chocolate, and his mother.

moved the chocolate from the cupboard to the fridge. Because this happens in Maxi's absence, and quite unexpectedly, he has unwittingly come to hold a false belief. By default, he would assume that the chocolate remained in the cupboard, where he left it. A competent observing child would predict that Maxi will look in the cupboard on his return; she would say that Maxi will search in the place he last saw his chocolate. In contrast, a child who did not understand about minds would probably judge that Maxi will look in the place she herself knew the chocolate was located – the fridge. Hence, a test of false belief is methodologically useful because it helps us to differentiate between those who do and do not understand that minds hold beliefs.

Another reason for focusing on false beliefs is because it is particularly important for children to be attuned to false as opposed to true beliefs. If we can accurately diagnose when a person holds a false belief, then we can take steps to help them gain a true understanding. On the other hand, if we wanted to manipulate another person, we could misinform them to instill a false belief.

 ## When Do Children Begin to Understand that People Hold Beliefs?

Piaget characterized children below about 7 years of age as **egocentric**, so he would not have expected younger children to have any grasp of other people's mental states (see chapter 8 for a description and evaluation of Piaget's account of the transition in children's thinking that occurs around 7 years of age). In Piaget's studies, children below age 7 wrongly judged that another person at a different vantage point had the same perspective as themselves. They also neglected to take account of a person's intention when apportioning blame or reward for an act. Moreover, their verbal communication was very poorly adapted to the informational needs of their listeners. With that background, Piaget would have been amazed at Wimmer and Perner's (1983) seminal discovery that from about 4 or 5 years, children put aside their own knowledge in making correct attributions of other people's false beliefs. These researchers presented children with the story about Maxi and his bar of chocolate. The results, along with those from a host of replication studies (see Mitchell, 1997, for a summary), suggest there is a sharp increase in the number of children who answer correctly around the age of 4 years. Because the developmental trend was so striking, Wimmer and Perner concluded that children negotiate a radical **conceptual shift** around the time of their fourth birthday, which equips them with a **representational** theory of mind that allows them to acknowledge false belief. These children judged that Maxi would look for his chocolate in the place he last saw it – the cupboard. Younger children, in contrast, judged that he would look in the place they themselves knew it was located. In effect, when asked about Maxi's belief, they reported their own.

 ## Do Children Acquire a Theory of Mind?

Undoubtedly, children rapidly develop in their understanding of the mind at about 4 years of age. What form does this understanding take? Does it have the properties of a naive theory? In other words, do children acquire rules and principles from which they can explain and predict behavior, just as a physicist has principles for explaining and predicting the motion of objects? That would be one way to do it. Another would be to use the power of your imagination to simulate a person's mind (Harris, 1991). In effect, you could say to yourself that "if I went out and Mom moved the chocolate in my absence, I would think it was still in the cupboard." Just as an aviator uses a wind tunnel to simulate real conditions as a test for his or her prototype aircraft, so we might present a kind of thought experiment to our own mind to find out what we would think if we were in a particular situation. We could then treat the outcome of the mental simulation as telling us what another person would think in a certain situation.

THE DECEPTIVE BOX TEST

According to Gopnik (1993), understanding other minds by a process of simulation is implausible. She argues that being able to find out what someone else thinks by working out what you yourself would think in that situation depends on having reflective access to your own states of mind: this reflective access – effectively, thinking about how you are feeling or thinking – is often called **metacognition**. Gopnik and Astington (1988) found that children below about 4 years of age have just as much difficulty reporting their own states of belief as they have assessing another person's. In their study, children were shown a Smarties tube (Smarties are small sweets, usually sold in a small cardboard tube) and asked to guess what was inside. After children replied "Smarties," the experimenter opened the lid to reveal unexpectedly that there was only a pencil. The experimenter replaced the lid with the pencil still inside and asked, "When you first saw this tube, before we opened it, what did you think was inside?" Many children below about 4 years reported their current belief and said "pencil." In contrast, many older than 4 years correctly recalled that they had thought there were Smarties in the tube. Gopnik and Astington also presented an unexpected transfer test based on Maxi and his bar of chocolate. The children who reported their current belief in this **deceptive box task** (pencil) tended to be the same who wrongly predicted that Maxi would look for his chocolate in its current location (the fridge). In contrast, the children who correctly recalled their prior false belief (Smarties) tended to be the same ones who judged correctly that Maxi would look for his chocolate in the place he last saw it (the cupboard).

It seems that the children who were unable to acknowledge another person's false belief were not even attuned to their own prior beliefs. Gopnik (1993) argued that whether or not children could imagine what they would think in a different situation was not the issue. If children do not know their own mind, then they cannot use insights into their own mind as a basis for working out what another person thinks. Accordingly, their difficulty in understanding the mind seems to lie at a more fundamental level. Gopnik speculated that perhaps children had not yet acquired the principles of belief that would allow them to explain and predict other people's behavior. She suggests that children have to acquire a naive *theory* of the mind, a theory that gives them access to their own states of belief as well as other people's. Once children

Plate 10.1 The deceptive box test of false belief. The Smarties tube unexpectedly contains a pencil.

have acquired this theory, they have a basis for making judgments about people's beliefs.

Is There a Developmental Stage?

Some argue that there is a developmental stage in the sense that children move onto a radically different level of understanding at about 4 years of age once they acquire the principles for explaining and predicting other people's behavior (e.g., Gopnik, 1993; Perner, 1991). This fits neatly with the notion that competent children's understanding of the mind has the properties of a theory: some of the theoretical leaps in natural science are sudden. For example, the important parts of Einstein's theory of relativity are radically different from the theories and understanding that existed before. His contribution to theoretical physics was not of an incremental nature. Theoretical revolutions are a hallmark of scientific development, so it would be fitting if the child's understanding of the mind were acquired in a kind of intellectual revolution. The apparently sudden emergence of children's correct judgments of false belief is consistent with such a possibility. (Chapters 1 and 2 discuss the differences between **stage-like** [qualitative] versus gradual [quantitative] changes in development.)

THE CASE FOR GRADUAL CHANGE

However, perhaps we should not be so hasty in ruling out the possibility of gradual development in acquiring an understanding of the mind. I shall now summarize evidence which suggests that children younger than 4 years might be capable of acknowledging false belief and also that sometimes older individuals, including adults, have difficulty. Success will thus be seen to depend not on the underlying competence of the child, but on the demands placed on his or her performance by the particular task in question. This evidence stands in stark opposition to the view that an understanding of the mind is acquired in a singular conceptual revolution occurring around the time of the fourth birthday.

DO CHILDREN SUDDENLY BEGIN GIVING CORRECT JUDGMENTS OF FALSE BELIEF?

When performing on a test of false belief (as with many of Piaget's tests of **cognitive development**), you can answer either correctly or incorrectly. The test is incapable of detecting degrees of performance that fall somewhere in between. For this reason, even if development were gradual, the test of false belief would nonetheless make it appear as if development were discontinuous. The probability of a child answering correctly might increase gradually between 3 and 5 years of age. Despite that, if we simply take a snapshot of his or her performance in a single or small number of tests, we could easily be fooled into thinking that the child has not yet acquired the concept of mind. If development is gradual, we would expect there to be many instances where a child passes one test of false belief but fails another. What do the data tell us?

Even the data reported by Gopnik and Astington (1988) suggest that children are variable in their performance at about 4 years of age. Although children who passed one test of false belief tended also to pass another, there were very many instances of children passing one but failing the other. Moreover, giving a correct judgment in a test of false belief does not guarantee future success. Mayes, Klin, Tercyak, Cicchetti, and Cohen (1996; but see Hughes et al., 2000) report that children's performance changed over a period of two or three weeks. In many cases, those who gave a wrong answer in the first session went on to give a correct judgment in the second. Notably, however, several children who *succeeded* in the first session *failed* in the second. It is very difficult to square this finding with the claim that children undergo a radical conceptual shift that equips them to answer correctly. Instead, it seems that whether or not children answer correctly can be described in terms of an age-related probability. What factors might determine whether children answer correctly?

UNDERSTANDING THE QUESTION ASKED

An obvious contender is the wording of the question. As we saw in chapter 8, it has often been claimed that young children may not understand exactly what it is that experimenters mean when they question them. With respect to a theory of mind, Lewis and Osborne (1990) suggested that whilst children aged 3 and 4 years have much the same understanding about minds, they might differ drastically in how they interpret questions. In particular, the younger children might not be clear on the point in time that the question refers to. They might think that the experimenter is asking,

"What did you think was inside *after* we had opened the lid and showed you the pencil?" Lewis and Osborne offered the necessary clarification by explicitly asking children what they "thought was inside before we opened the lid?" In this condition, significantly more children aged 3 gave a correct judgment compared with those asked a vague question of the kind used in previous research. Errors were not eradicated, but the modified question gave children a better chance of answering correctly.

Similarly, Siegal and Beattie (1991) modified Wimmer and Perner's (1983) question from the temporally ambiguous "Where will Maxi look . . . ?" to "Where will Maxi look . . . *first of all*?" As in Lewis and Osborne (1990), children had a better chance of answering the question correctly with the new wording. Both Lewis and Osborne, and Siegal and Beattie, concluded that children's errors stemmed from difficulty comprehending the question rather than a deep-seated conceptual deficit.

The state change test

Although misunderstanding the question seems to account for some of the errors children make, a study by Wimmer and Hartl (1991) suggests it is not the only important factor. They devised a new test they called the **state change test**, which is similar to a deceptive box test, and is shown in figure 10.2. The child sees a Smarties tube and guesses that it contains Smarties when prompted to do so. The experimenter opens the tube to reveal that it does indeed contain Smarties, but as the child

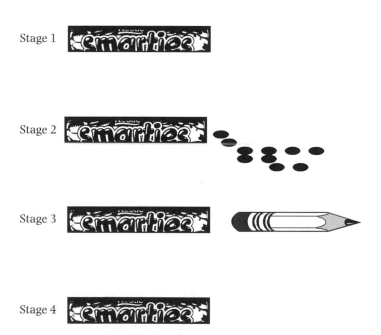

Figure 10.2 The state change test of true belief. The Smarties tube initially contains Smarties, but these are replaced with a pencil as the child watches.

watches, the experimenter empties the tube and replaces the Smarties with a pencil. The experimenter closes the lid and then asks the standard question, "When you first saw the box, before we opened it, what did you think was inside?" In a sample of children aged 3 and 4 years, over 80 percent gave a correct judgment of "Smarties." In sharp contrast, only about 40 percent of the same sample gave a correct judgment in a deceptive box task (see plate 10.1), in which the tube contained a pencil from the beginning. In short, replacing Smarties with pencils as the child watched had a massive impact in helping him or her to answer correctly. Why?

One thing we know for sure is that it had nothing to do with the wording of the question. After all, the question was worded exactly the same in the deceptive box and the state change tests. Indeed, we might have predicted that children would give an incorrect answer in both tasks on the grounds that both contained the same vague question. Children's success in state change suggests that their problem does not lie entirely with the wording of the question. What enabled them to give a correct answer in state change?

Wimmer and Hartl (1991) offered an ingenious explanation, though further research has since proved this wrong also, as we shall see later. They quite plausibly suggested that any child who did not have a concept of the mind necessarily would not understand words that related to this concept – words like *think*. As we already know, failure to comprehend words seldom renders children mute. So how would they answer the question about what they used to think was inside the Smarties tube? According to Wimmer and Hartl, the simplest explanation is that children answer as if the word *think* had not been included in the question. Hence, "What did you think was inside?" would be interpreted as "What was inside?" The correct answer to the latter question is "Smarties" in the state change and "pencil" in the deceptive box, which is precisely how most younger children did answer. The authors suggested that when children acquire the concept of minds at about age 4, they are then equipped to acquire the adult meaning of the word *think* and thereby successfully acknowledge false belief. Wimmer and Hartl accept that young children have a linguistic problem, but insist that this is merely a symptom of a deeper conceptual deficit. To understand development, our focus should therefore be on the conceptual rather than linguistic or conversational.

HYBRID OF DECEPTIVE BOX AND STATE CHANGE TESTS

Despite the elegance of Wimmer and Hartl's (1991) argument, subsequent research has proved it wrong (Saltmarsh, Mitchell, & Robinson, 1995), although they have had a lasting impact in suggesting that children have much more than a superficial linguistic or conversational problem. Proving Wimmer and Hartl wrong is of great importance in that it raises the possibility that children younger than 4 years of age do after all understand something about minds holding beliefs. The damaging evidence for Wimmer and Hartl followed the creation of a *hybrid test* based on the deceptive box and state change tests: this is shown in figure 10.3. The Smarties tube was opened to reveal an atypical item (toothbrush), which was exchanged for a second atypical item (pencil) as the child watched. As in the state change test, items

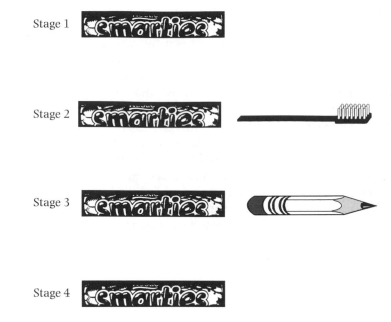

Stage 1

Stage 2

Stage 3

Stage 4

Figure 10.3 Hybrid of deceptive box and state change tests.

were swapped in front of the child, but as in the deceptive box test, the Smarties tube never contained Smarties. When asked, "When you first saw the box, what was inside?" nearly all answered correctly by reporting the first content (toothbrush), but when asked, "When you first saw the box, what did you think was inside?" most reported the current content (pencil). Hence, children who were unable to give a correct judgment of their own false belief (presumably, they originally thought the box contained Smarties) were drawn to the current content and were not answering the question as if they had been asked "What was inside?" This very clear finding unequivocally refutes Wimmer and Hartl, who would have predicted that children aged about 3 years would have given the same answer, irrespective of whether the question did or did not contain the word *think*. Maybe those authors were correct to argue that children's difficulty cannot be explained purely as a misinterpretation of the question, for the reasons already stated, but they are not correct in saying that a deep-seated conceptual deficit causes them to ignore the word *think*.

We are left trying to explain why young children easily give a correct judgment in Wimmer and Hartl's (1991) state change task. Perhaps it is not preposterous after all to suggest that children answer correctly for the correct reason. Perhaps they do understand both the word and the concept *think*, and a feature of the state change helps them to tune in to that concept. A conspicuous feature of the task is that children's initial belief that the tube contains Smarties is proved correct according to the physical evidence before their eyes on opening the tube. If a belief were supported with hard evidence, as in the state change test, perhaps it would be easier to acknowledge. In that case, can children be helped to acknowledge a *false belief* by endorsing that belief with a counterpart in reality?

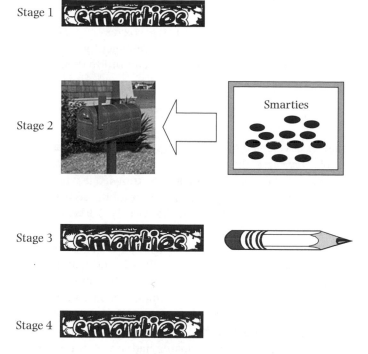

Figure 10.4 The posting version of the deceptive box task.

THE POSTING VERSION OF THE DECEPTIVE BOX TEST

A task schematized in figure 10.4 yielded evidence which suggests that children can indeed be helped to acknowledge false belief so long as that belief has a tangible counterpart in reality. Children were asked to post a picture of what they thought a Smarties tube contained when it was first introduced to them: the **posting version of the deceptive box test** (Mitchell & Lacohee, 1991). Children dutifully selected a picture of Smarties and placed it in a postbox where it remained out of sight until the end of the procedure. The experimenter revealed the pencil in the tube and then closed the lid with the pencil still inside. Finally, the experimenter asked, "When you posted your picture, what did you think was inside?" Under this condition, many more children correctly acknowledged their prior false belief (Smarties) compared with children who participated in a standard deceptive box procedure.

Did children in the posting task give correct judgments for the wrong reason (i.e., they might have thought they were being asked what was in the picture they posted, which of course was a picture of Smarties)? This seems unlikely when considering the results of a control condition, in which children posted a picture of their favorite cartoon character (e.g., Mickey Mouse) instead of Smarties. Apart from this, the procedure and the question were exactly the same. If the children in the Smarties-posting condition answered "Smarties" because they wrongly thought they were being asked about the picture in the postbox, then a tell-tale sign from the children in the cartoon-posting condition – the control group – would be to answer "Mickey Mouse," but none did so.

The results of the posting version of the deceptive box task suggest that children below age 4 might possess the concept of belief but have difficulty using it. What changes with age, seemingly, is the ease with which they can utilize their understanding.

Adults' Difficulty with False Beliefs

If the explanation for developmental change lies with **performance factors** rather than changing levels of *competence*, then sometimes we could expect to see older children – even adults – systematically reporting their own knowledge when trying to diagnose another person's beliefs. Surprisingly, evidence that adults sometimes have difficulty acknowledging false belief has been around for nearly 30 years, but the full significance of the findings has only been recognized recently. The evidence is a phenomenon known as "hindsight bias." In a classic study, Fischhoff (1975) told adult participants about a historical battle between British and Gurkha armies that took place a couple of centuries ago. The participants heard about various factors that might advantage one or another army. For example, the British were well disciplined, well organized, had excellent equipment and good logistics. On the other hand, the Gurkhas knew the terrain intimately, had numerical superiority, and were renowned for their bravery and courage. The participants had to weigh up the advantages that favored each army and then make a judgment on who they thought would have the best chance of winning. Incidentally, the participants were also told of the actual "outcome" but were instructed to put that information out of their minds when arriving at a judgment. Despite the instruction, it became apparent that the participants were being influenced by what they were led to believe was the true outcome. Those told that the British actually won tended to judge on balance that they thought the British had the best chance. Those told that the Gurkhas actually won tended to judge that the Gurkhas had the best chance.

Although Fischhoff (1975) called this striking phenomenon *hindsight*, it was actually something more general. Indeed, it seems to qualify as an instance of a difficulty in acknowledging false belief. This became apparent in another part of Fischhoff's study in which the adult participants had to judge not who *they* thought would win, but what another group of people would think who were told everything except the actual outcome. Participants advised that the British actually won judged that the other group would favor the British, while participants advised that the Gurkhas actually won judged that the other people would favor the Gurkhas.

CONFUSING ONE'S OWN AND OTHERS' KNOWLEDGE

A more recent study supports this interpretation of Fischhoff's findings (Mitchell, Robinson, Isaacs, & Nye, 1996). Participants watched a video about a couple of protagonists, Kevin and Rebecca, set in their kitchen, which is schematized in figure 10.5.

Figure 10.5 The story about Kevin and Rebecca, devised to reveal adults' difficulties with false belief.

There was a conspicuous jug on the shelf and Kevin noticed that it contained orange juice. Later that day, Kevin and Rebecca were together in their kitchen making lunch, when Kevin volunteered to prepare something to drink. Rebecca then announced that there is milk in the jug. At this point Kevin was the victim of conflicting information. He had previously seen juice in the jug but was told subsequently that it contained milk. The observing participants were invited to judge what Kevin now thought was inside the jug. Obviously, there is no way of determining the right answer. Although we might suppose that people believe what they see in preference to what they are told, this was a special circumstance. Rebecca's utterance was the most recent information, so it is possible that although the jug used to contain juice, it now contains milk.

Half the participants heard only the information just presented, while the rest were told additionally that Rebecca had poured out the juice and replaced it with milk. Effectively, half were told that Rebecca's utterance was true. However, it was made very clear to the participants that this was privileged information, available only to them and not to Kevin the protagonist. Despite that edict, participants simply could not help but be influenced by their knowledge of the true content of the jug. Nearly all those told that there was really milk in the jug judged that he would believe the jug contained milk. In contrast, those given no additional information usually judged that Kevin would believe the jug contained juice, in accordance with what he had seen. In other words, their judgment of the believability of Rebecca's utterance was massively influenced by whether *they* knew it was true. It seems the participants were inclined to report what they assumed to be the actual current content of the jug when asked about Kevin's belief. In this respect, they bear a remarkable resemblance to children aged 3 years!

It is a striking paradox that under some circumstances, adults have difficulty making unbiased judgments of belief, while children aged 3 years in other contexts succeed in acknowledging belief. This possibility suggests that it is wrong to think that young children categorically lack a concept of belief while adults possess it.

Factors that Influence Development

NATURE VERSUS NURTURE

When making judgments about beliefs, we need to resist the lure of current reality as we know it. Although the ability to do this is not all or nothing, it seems easier for older than younger participants. Is age the only factor that determines success? If it were, then it would be a fair bet that development is an inevitable and predetermined **maturational unfolding**. Another possibility, though, is that development is greatly influenced by social experience. How can we decide between these two possibilities? If social experience were an important influence, then we would expect to find different rates of development depending on the particular milieu the child inhabited. The environment varies between families within a given society, and also between the cultures of different societies. Perhaps we should begin by asking whether the developmental trend seen in western societies occurs in nonindustrialized cultures. To address the question, Avis and Harris (1991) trekked out to the rainforest of the Cameroon and visited a traditional **hunter-gatherer tribe**. Participants were recruited from the tribe and cajoled into enacting a version of the unexpected transfer test. An older boy from the tribe volunteered to act as a confederate and cooked some mango in a pot as requested. While the fruit was cooking, he left the hut to have a chat with friends. In his absence, the observing child participant was assisted to empty the mango from the pot and put it in a jar. Subsequently, the older boy returned to eat the mango and at this point the observing young child was asked to predict where the older boy would look for it. Older members of the sample predicted that he would look in the place he last saw his mango (the pot), while younger children predicted that he would look in the place they themselves knew it was hidden, namely, the jar. In other words, the younger children failed to acknowledge false belief. What was the specific age-trend? There were no accurate records of the date of birth of the participants, so their parents were asked to make their best estimate. The findings were approximately consistent with those reported in studies involving children from western cultures. Children aged around 3 years tended to report current reality, while those aged around 5 years successfully acknowledged another person's false belief.

DO HUMANS POSSESS A SPECIAL MODULE THAT IS DEDICATED TO UNDERSTANDING MINDS?

If an understanding of the mind were uniform across humans and unique to them, this would be consistent with having evolved a brain module dedicated specially to the task. To explore uniqueness in understanding the mind, it would be valuable to study our most closely related cousins in the animal kingdom – the apes. Although apes sometimes seem to strategically behave in a way that would deceive another individual (Whiten & Byrne, 1988) and seem to distinguish between a person who is furnished with knowledge and someone who is ignorant (Povinelli, 1993), their performance is very much inferior to a human child aged about 4 years. Therefore, it might be reasonable to explain the far superior performance of humans by suggesting that they are equipped with a brain module that is dedicated to the task of understanding minds.

Accordingly, Fodor (1992) proposed that we are born with a module for understanding minds and that such a module is active from the very beginning of life. The module supposedly undergoes refinement at about the age of 4 years which allows children to pass a standard test of false belief. However, Fodor suggests that the module is demonstrably active at a younger age in tasks that have a different form from the standard test of false belief, although supporting evidence for his specific predictions is somewhat scant.

Perhaps the most compelling case for modularity in understanding the mind is made by Leslie and Thaiss (1992). They borrowed a procedure called *the false photo test* developed by Zaitchik (1990). The test is modeled on Wimmer and Perner's (1983) unexpected transfer test, except that children are not asked about Maxi's outdated belief; instead, they are asked about the outdated image in a photograph. In Scene 1, a doll sat on a box and the participant took a photo. Then, in Scene 2, the doll moved to the mat. Finally, participants were asked to anticipate which of the scenes would emerge in the developing photo.

Leslie and Thaiss (1992) presented the false photo test, and also a standard false belief test to normally developing children and to children with autism. The normally developing children aged about 3 years tended to fail both tests, while older children tended to pass both. In sharp contrast, all individuals with autism passed the false photo test but a large majority failed the false belief test (see the section on autism further on in this chapter). Leslie and Thaiss concluded that children with autism lack the brain module needed for making judgments about beliefs, which is the reason why they specifically failed on the test of false belief. They suggested that normally developing young children, in contrast, possess the relevant module but are yet to acquire the general processing skills to give a correct judgment in any task that has the form of a test of false belief. In other words, the reason they fail a test of false belief is not because it has mind-related content, but because the form of the problem makes demands on processing that are beyond a typical 3-year-old.

Another study converges with Leslie and Thaiss (1992) in suggesting that children have difficulty with the form of the task, even if it does not have mind-related content (Riggs, Peterson, Robinson, & Mitchell, 1998). Children were presented with an un-expected transfer task concerning Maxi and his chocolate, and in a novel condition they were asked a counterfactual question: "If Mom had not baked a cake, where would the chocolate be now?" Children who failed to reason counter to fact (they pointed to the current location of the chocolate) were nearly always the same children who failed to acknowledge Maxi's false belief. Conversely, children who succeeded in reasoning counter to fact were nearly always the same who succeeded in acknowledg-ing Maxi's false belief. So long as children could acknowledge a counterfactual state, they had no difficulty in attributing this to another person as that person's false belief.

At the very least, the evidence suggests that whether or not children succeed in acknowledging false belief depends on more than the activity of a special brain module dedicated to the task. In the studies by Riggs et al. (1998) and Leslie and Thaiss (1992), children's difficulty in acknowledging false belief seems best explained by the general processing demands posed by the task. However, children with autism might have a more fundamental difficulty with false belief, due to an impaired mind-related module, which could explain their failure with the task. In that case, children with autism and young children with typical development might fail tests of false belief for different reasons.

The role of the family: Siblings

Although the basis of an understanding of the mind might be a special human ability that owes a great deal to our genetic inheritance, there is still scope for environmental influences to play a major part in development. Perhaps we should focus on the char-acteristics of families to see how these correlate with precocity in acknowledging false belief. A variable of particular interest is the size of the family, and especially how many siblings the child has. There are some reasons for thinking that having lots of siblings would be an advantage, but other reasons for thinking it would be an impedi-ment. A child with many siblings would encounter the potentially beneficial experi-ence of other points of view. Perhaps siblings typically assert their point of view in a somewhat unyielding manner. Obviously, this might be a socially uncomfortable or even annoying experience, but it could have cognitively beneficial spin-offs in terms of becoming attuned to other minds.

As mentioned, though, there are different reasons for supposing that having lots of siblings could be seen as a disadvantage. Perhaps children become attuned to other minds not through the experience of a clash of perspectives with siblings but by being informally tutored about the mind by wiser individuals, especially the parents. Per-haps children gain most benefit from having psychological states explained to them.

For example, "John isn't going out to play because he can't find his ball. He thought he put it in the garage but it isn't there." In a family with lots of children, the potentially beneficial adult input would have to be divided, with the consequence that each child would not be receiving the optimum level of tutoring about the mind. A parallel can be drawn with the development of children's general intellectual abilities. Zajonc (1983) reported that the number of siblings correlates with the child's **IQ score**, as does birth order. The singleton tends to have a higher IQ than the child with several siblings; the child who is first born tends to have a higher IQ than the second born, who in turn has a higher IQ than the third born, and so on. Note that these birth-order IQ differences are very small, so if you have several younger brothers and sisters don't assume you're the brightest! Zajonc suggested that intellectual development depends partly on beneficial parental input which becomes diluted as the family grows, and this is measurable as an adverse effect on the IQ scores of the later-born children.

Perner, Ruffman, and Leekam (1994) collected the relevant evidence and found that children aged 3 years who had siblings were more likely to pass a test of false belief than those of the same age but without siblings. Moreover, those with several siblings stood a better chance of giving a correct judgment than those with just one or two siblings. A study, by Jenkins and Astington (1996), clarified things a little further. The apparently beneficial effect of having siblings was confined to those with older siblings. Children who only had younger siblings were no better in acknowledging false belief than those with none at all, while those with older siblings did show the kind of advantage reported by Perner et al.

Just because having siblings correlates with success in acknowledging false belief, this need not imply that the experience of interacting with siblings promotes an understanding of the mind. Perhaps the presence of siblings coincides with another as yet unspecified variable, and perhaps it is this that is crucial to development. Lewis, Freeman, Kyriakidou, and Maridaki-Kassotaki (1996) investigated such a possibility in a **cross-cultural study** that included Greek families. They recorded a wide range of variables concerning family structure, in addition to the number of siblings a child had. Lewis et al. confirmed that children with siblings were at an advantage in acknowledging false belief compared to those without. They also established that the advantage was stronger among those with older siblings than those with younger ones. The most important discovery, though, was that another social factor was even more strongly related with children's success in acknowledging false belief. Large families with many children also tended to be extended rather than nuclear. Consequently, there were numerous opportunities for adults to interact with the children, and indeed this was the best predictor of whether or not a child would succeed in acknowledging false belief. These findings give a hint to the effect that children are helped to acknowledge false belief if adults informally and perhaps even unwittingly offer tutoring on the characteristics of the mind.

The role of the family: Adults

Valuable as they are, the findings from Lewis et al. (1996) do not tell us exactly what features of adult input are beneficial. Much of the relevant information can be found in a study by Dunn, Brown, Slomkowski, Tesla, and Youngblade (1991). They observed individual differences in how mothers interacted with their toddlers aged 33 months. Some provided a narrative on the actions of people or on the characters in pretend scenarios that was embroidered with abundant references to psychological motives. For example, they might comment that Jane is looking in her toy box for her teddy because she thinks it is there and that she did not see her older brother put it behind the settee. Other mothers would give commentary on Jane's behavior but without making reference to what Jane might be thinking. Hence, children of these parents did not hear much in the way of psychological explanations of human behavior. Six months later, Dunn et al. tested the children for their ability to acknowledge false beliefs. The children who were *successful* tended to have parents who, 6 months previously, had been observed to give explanations of behavior with reference to psychological states. The children who were *unsuccessful* tended to have parents who had seldom referred to psychological states.

In sum, the findings reported by Lewis et al. (1996) suggest that the correlation between having siblings and successfully acknowledging false belief could be coincidental to variations in adult input. The study by Dunn et al. effectively identifies the aspects of adult input which are likely to be especially beneficial. It raises the possibility that toddlers gain a great deal from verbal explanations in psychological terms of why people behave as they do.

THE CHARACTERISTICS OF THE CHILD

Because the social environment appears to influence development in the ability to acknowledge beliefs, it does not follow that the intrinsic characteristics of the child are unimportant. The characteristics of the environment and the characteristics of the child probably interact in complex ways with respect to the influence they have on development. Indeed, the characteristics of the child are likely to shape the way people respond to him or her, which in turn will impact upon the extent to which social input is beneficial. Offering explanations to a child who has a fractious temperament might present a much greater challenge than offering explanations to one who has a calmer disposition. Notably, one characteristic within the child stands out above all others: **autism**. As we shall see in the next section, having autism is devastating in that it constrains insights into minds.

 ## *Autism*

General aspects of autism are covered elsewhere in this book (see especially chapter 19, which discusses several possible causes of the disorder). In the current chapter the aim is to examine the possibility that individuals with autism are lacking in an understanding of the mind. Wing and Gould (1979) characterized autism as a triad of impairments (**Wing's triad of impairments**): imagination, social behavior, and communication.

Lack of imagination

The lack of imagination is manifest in many ways, but notably as an impairment in the capacity to engage in pretend play. Leslie (1987) suggested that the kind of mental processing required for pretense is the same that is needed to understand states of belief. He suggests that the kind of disengagement from current reality that you need in order to acknowledge a false belief is precisely the same kind of disengagement you exhibit when indulging in pretend play. A person who did not have the ability to disengage from reality in pretense probably would not be able to disengage from reality in order to acknowledge a false belief. The finding that individuals with autism are impaired in pretense is in itself a striking clue to the possibility that they might be unable to attune to other minds.

Socialization and communication deficits

Impairments in socialization and communication also point to an underlying deficiency in understanding other minds. Without an understanding of the mind, an individual would perpetually be in danger of misjudging social situations, of acting in an inappropriate way, and of saying inappropriate things. Social skill depends on being able to diagnose other people's sensitivities, attitudes, and knowledge. A person who was oblivious to such things might appear bad-mannered, boorish, and inconsiderate. This could be described as an impairment in social behavior and communication. Hence, a difficulty in understanding the mind could present itself in the triad of impairments identified by Wing and Gould (1979), and these impairments are typically seen as defining of autism. In short, autism could be a manifestation of an impaired understanding of the mind.

Causes of autism

There is a distinct possibility that at least one of the causes of autism has a genetic origin (Happé, 1994a). Other causes could arise from accidental injury or virus infection. These various factors could lead to an abnormality in the brain that forms the physiological seat of autism. It is conceivable that certain benign environments could go some way to counteract these effects, but it is also conceivable that the environmental effects would be somewhat limited. In this case, the mental constitution of the child would impose a ceiling on the value of the normally beneficial environmental influences.

Failure to understand the mind

There are sound reasons, then, for thinking that autism is essentially a lack of understanding about the mind. What does the evidence tell us? Baron-Cohen, Leslie, and Frith (1985) sought an answer by presenting an unexpected transfer test of false belief to a group of 20 participants with autism, and found that 15 judged wrongly by reporting their own knowledge of the whereabouts of the item. Obviously, this result would only be noteworthy if the participants had a **mental age** above 4 years. We already know that individuals with a **chronological age** (and, by implication, a mental age) below 4 years tend to fail standard tests of false belief, so to find the same in young children with autism would be no surprise. Baron-Cohen et al. were thus careful to test their participants for mental age and discovered that even some members of the sample in their teens who had a verbal mental age well above 4 years failed to acknowledge false belief.

Still, we should question whether the failure to acknowledge false belief is due to the autism or due to the associated learning difficulties. Apart from presenting the triad of impairments, many individuals with autism are also afflicted with learning difficulties and this alone could account for their difficulty acknowledging false belief. Baron-Cohen et al. (1985) figured that if learning difficulties alone were sufficient, then children with **Down's syndrome (DS)** would also have problems. Accordingly, they tested individuals with Down's syndrome who had a very similarly impaired intellectual profile to the autistic sample. In contrast to those with autism, however, most children with Down's syndrome passed the test of false belief. The difficulty in acknowledging false belief therefore seemed to arise from autism rather than any associated learning difficulties. Some studies have required the participant to listen to a story and then answer questions at the end, while some have involved them directly, as in the deceptive box task (Perner, Frith, Leslie, & Leekam, 1989). The findings are largely consistent, suggesting that autistic difficulty in acknowledging false belief is not confined to any particular version of the standard test.

We are left with the impression that autism might essentially be a failure to understand the mind, which is measurable as failure to acknowledge false belief. However, what of the minority of individuals with autism who give a correct judgment of false belief? Is it possible that their success is a fluke or that they have been wrongly diagnosed? It seems to be no fluke, since some autistic individuals who pass a test of false belief do so reliably and repeatedly. Neither are there grounds for thinking they are all wrongly diagnosed. Baron-Cohen (1989) suspected that they might still have a subtle impairment that could be revealed by a more sophisticated test of understanding the mind. Instead of testing participants for their understanding of what a person thinks about an aspect of reality, he tested understanding of what a person thinks *another* person thinks about an aspect of reality. Instead of asking where John thinks *his* chocolate is, Baron-Cohen asked where John thinks *Mary* thinks the chocolate is. Individuals with autism who passed a simple test of false belief failed this more complex test. As before, their poor performance was not commensurate with their relatively high verbal mental age. However, Bowler (1992) found that members of a sample of high-functioning adults with autism reliably passed this sophisticated test of belief. Despite that, these individuals still presented the defining features of autism. Their ability to process simple and complex beliefs did not relieve them of the symptoms of autism. Consequently, it is invalid to argue that autism is the product of a failure to understand the mind as defined by an inability to acknowledge beliefs. Nonetheless, individuals with autism are likely to be developmentally delayed. Verbal mental age is a good predictor of whether or not a person with autism will succeed in acknowledging false belief, but it seems that verbal mental age has to be substantially higher in autism than in typically or "normally" developing children (Happé, 1995). Whereas a verbal mental age of around 4 years is common for the onset of success in a standard test of false belief in typical development, it seems a verbal mental age of 7 years is more common in autistic development.

SUMMARY AND CONCLUSIONS

Researchers have devised tests of false belief for assessing the development in children's understanding of the mind. Many children below about 4 years of age fail these tests, while older children pass. It is possible that children undergo a gradual change that allows them to disengage from a focus on current reality. Modified tests that direct children away from current reality reveal early competence. On the other hand, even adults might never be fully rid of the allure of current reality and under special circumstances they too are shown systematically to report their *own* belief when trying to diagnose *another person's* belief.

The development in children's ability to acknowledge beliefs can be influenced by factors associated with the social environment, particularly characteristics of the parent's style of interaction with the child. However, the intrinsic characteristics of the child are also relevant and in extreme cases, as in autism, it seems that development is destined to be aberrant. Even so, there is no reason to think that individuals with autism are impervious to a beneficial environment. Those with autism undergo developmental change, even if not quite so rapid as in typical development.

DISCUSSION POINTS

1   Why is it important for people to have a theory of mind?
2   Why is an understanding of false belief seen as important in testing children's theory of mind?
3   When do children begin to understand that people hold beliefs?
4   Think about the different tasks used to test children's theory of mind. Which of these, if any, seems to be the best?
5   What sorts of social and cognitive factors affect the development of a theory of mind?
6   Is there a radical (qualitative) conceptual shift in children's thinking around 4 years of age, or is there a gradual (quantitative) change?
7   What evidence suggests that adults sometimes have difficulty with theory of mind tasks?

SUGGESTIONS FOR FURTHER READING

Astington, J. W. (1994). *The child's discovery of the mind.* London: Fontana.
Happé, F. (1994). *Autism.* London: University College Press.
Mitchell, P. (1997). *Introduction to theory of mind: Children, autism and apes.* London: Arnold.
Mitchell, P., & Riggs, K. (2000). *Children's reasoning and the mind.* Hove: Psychology Press.

chapter 11

Reading and Mathematics

Peter Bryant

KEY CONCEPTS

ABSTRACTION PRINCIPLE
ALPHABETIC SCRIPT
CARDINALITY
CONDITIONAL SPELLING
  RULES
CONSERVATION
CULTURAL TOOLS
DERIVATIONAL CONSTANCY
GENITIVE
HABITUATION
INNATE MECHANISM
INTRASYLLABIC UNITS

LAST-NUMBER-COUNTED
  PRINCIPLE
LETTER–SOUND ASSOCIATIONS
MORA
MORPHEME
ONE-TO-ONE CORRESPONDENCE
ONE-TO-ONE PRINCIPLE
ONSET
ORDER IRRELEVANCE PRINCIPLE
ORDINALITY
ORTHOGRAPHY
OVERGENERALIZATION

PHONEME
PHONOLOGICAL SKILLS
PROCEDURAL SKILLS
PSEUDO-WORD
RHYME
RIME
STABLE ORDER PRINCIPLE
SYLLABARY
SYLLABLE
TRANSITIVE INFERENCE
UNIVERSAL COUNTING
  PRINCIPLES

OVERVIEW

Reading ability and mathematical skills are key aspects of children's development that deservedly attract a great deal of research interest. This chapter provides an up-to-date account of research on the development of both of these skills.

Reading and writing systems differ between cultures and thus we can consider children's development of these systems as the acquisition of cultural tools. The author indicates the difficulties that children encounter in learning alphabetic languages. One problem is in breaking down words into their basic units and recognizing the relationship between these units and the sounds of language, and there is clear evidence that such awareness is a key aspect of learning to read. An important means of learning new words is recognition of words that rhyme; this recognition helps children to work out how new words should sound. Another aspect of reading that presents difficulty is learning conditional spelling rules. Children often overgeneralize learned spelling patterns beyond their occurrence in adult language. The conclusion of the chapter is that both instruction and the child's own organizational efforts make important contributions to overcoming these problems.

The chapter then shifts its focus to children's awareness of the principles underlying number and counting. Some investigators claim that babies as young as 4 months old have a basic knowledge of number and of addition and subtraction operations. These claims are, however, controversial, and some investigators believe that the evidence does not demand explanation in terms of an understanding of number as such. Despite this, some investigators conclude that numerical knowledge is innate and that the errors shown by young children are procedural rather than conceptual.

Number is a cultural tool in the sense that different number systems exist in different cultures, and the chapter reviews cross-cultural comparisons of competence with different number systems. However, all number systems possess an underlying logic, and understanding of this logic is crucial to numerical competence. There is evidence that part of children's difficulty with number can be traced to deficits in their logical capacity. As such, this is evidence against the notion that children's difficulty with number is purely procedural.

The general conclusion is that although formal instruction is important for learning to read and count, the child's own active constructions are enormously important. The implication is that children learn best when they are allowed to do so actively in their own way.

Introduction

Reading and mathematics lie at the heart of almost everything that children do at school, but in other respects these two subjects may seem to have little in common. Mathematics is a strict logical system; reading and spelling rules are capricious and heterogeneous. Mathematics employs abstract symbols; reading and spelling are about words with meaning. Yet, the two forms of learning actually pose the same basic problem for psychologists. The problem is how much of children's learning must depend on instruction, and how much children learn for themselves without formal help from others.

Vygotsky's argument (Vygotsky, 1962, 1978; Vygotsky & Luria, 1993) about **cultural tools** has convinced most developmental psychologists that instruction must play a part in children's intellectual development. Vygotsky's starting point was his claim that humankind's intellectual power is enhanced by the inventions of previous generations. Abacuses, slide rules, calculators, and now computers help us to calculate, produce models, make predictions, and understand the world more fully than we could have without these inventions, which Vygotsky called cultural tools.

These tools, Vygotsky argued, always involved some intellectual barrier that humankind took a long time to surmount. How, then, can we expect children to reinvent or even to understand these inventions for themselves? They haven't the time or the ability to reinvent the inventions. Their intellectual inheritance has to be passed on to them.

Many psychologists, however, and in particular Piaget (2001), maintain that children construct much of their knowledge for themselves. The distinction between

Vygotsky and Piaget is important, but one has to tread carefully here. The difference between these two titanic figures was not so much in their views, for they had many views in common, but in emphasis. Both rejected the idea that children acquire new knowledge just by being told something. Both made the point that other people play an important role in promoting children's knowledge. Vygotsky, however, stressed the transmission of knowledge from one person to another, while Piaget concentrated on the children's own constructions. Piaget, who was much more concerned with children's logical abilities, did not share Vygotsky's interest in the use and the power of human inventions. He argued, for example, that no one can understand standardized measures without an adequate grasp of the logic of measuring (Piaget, Inhelder, & Szeminska, 1960). You use rulers to compare quantities which cannot be compared directly, and you will not understand how these indirect comparisons work unless you can also make the logical inference that A = C when A = B, and B = C. This is a compelling argument, but it does not follow from this that learning about standardized units is a trivial matter, as Piaget was inclined to imply.

The issue here is of great significance in the study of children's intellectual development. No one disputes the fact that books and number systems and maps help us to acquire knowledge, but they may do more than that. They may also transform the way that we think, learn, and remember. Thus the discussion of cultural tools and children's own constructions provides an interesting set of questions. The first concerns the role of children's own informal experiences. The second is about the need for instruction. A last question is about the effects of learning these basic skills on children's cognitive processes.

Reading and Writing

One characteristic of cultural tools is that they can vary from culture to culture. Writing systems, or **orthographies**, as we shall call them, vary greatly. In some, like English, individual letters for the most part represent **phonemes**, which are the smallest unit of sound that can affect the meaning of a word. Such scripts are called **alphabetic**. There are several different alphabetic scripts, and there are radical differences among orthographies that use exactly the same script. Finnish and English, for example, are both written in Roman letters, but the relationship between sounds and letters in the two orthographies is different. This relationship is more regular in Finnish than in English. Each letter always represents the same sound in Finnish, but not in English, where, for example, the letter "i" represents one sound in "pin" and quite another in "pint." In Finnish there is even a straightforward relationship between the length of a sound and the number of letters representing it. The rule is one letter for a short vowel or consonant and two letters for a long one. This is not the rule in English.

There are many viable scripts that are not alphabets. In Chinese each character signals a **morpheme** (a unit of meaning). Most characters are complex structures, in which a part (the phonetic component) indicates something about the sound of the morpheme and another part (the radical component) something about the morpheme's meaning. The Japanese use two kinds of script. One, called "kanji," is based on the Chinese orthography. "Kana," the other kind of script, is a **syllabary**: every kana character represents a **mora**, which is the term for the rather simple Japanese **syllables**. To make matters even more complicated, there are two different kana scripts.

All these scripts have stood the test of time and there is a good reason for their resilience. Many of their characteristics fit well with the language that they represent. There are, for example, few syllables in Japanese and so one does not need many characters for an effective syllabary for that language. In English, in contrast, there are thousands of different syllables, and far more than one could expect children to learn and remember. The English language needed the alphabetic solution, the Japanese language did not.

THE DIFFICULTY OF ALPHABETIC LANGUAGE

The alphabetic solution is neat, but it comes at a price. The *solution* is to represent speech at the level of phonemes. This is a good and economic idea, because no language has many phonemes in it and thus one does not need many letters to represent them. In English, it is true, we do have a few more phonemes than we have alphabetic letters, but we have found ways round that problem. The alphabet is an effective way of representing English speech.

The *price* of the alphabetic solution is a psychological one. Phonemes, at first, pose an enormous problem to young children. It is hard initially for children even to realize that letters represent phonemes. Ferreiro and Teberosky (1983) showed this in some ingenious research that they did with young Argentine children at the time when these children first realized that alphabetic letters indicate the sounds in words. In one of their tasks, the experimenter showed the children a word and read it out to them, and then pointed to individual letters in the word, asking the children what sound each letter represented. Those children who had only recently learned that written script works by representing sounds tended to answer in syllables, not in phonemes.

The problem that children have with phonemes is deep-seated. It is not solved just by learning the alphabet, which most children do soon after they go to school. They still have to learn how individual words can be broken down into phonemes and assembled from them, and there is a large amount of evidence that this is at first a barrier for them.

This evidence comes from work on children's explicit awareness of phonemes. Bruce (1964) asked young schoolchildren what a word like "sand" would sound like without the "s." The children thus had to imagine a new word by removing a phoneme from the old one. Bruce found that none of the 5-year-old children succeeded with any of the 30 words that they were given. The 6-year-olds were not much better. The idea that words consist of a sequence of phonemes does not come easily to young children.

This initial difficulty with phonemes has been confirmed time and again. A team from the famous Haskins laboratory (Liberman, Shankweiler, Fischer, & Carter, 1974; Liberman, Shankweiler, & Liberman, 1989) introduced the "tapping" task in which 4-, 5-, and 6-year-old children had to learn either to tap the number of phonemes (2 taps for "up," 3 for "cat") or the number of syllables (2 taps for "donkey," 3 for "elephant") in words read out to them. The youngest children, who had not yet learned to read, made hardly any progress at all in the phoneme task, but did quite well in the syllable task. The older children, too, fared better in the syllable than in the phoneme task, although their performance in the phoneme task was superior to that of the younger children.

Learning to read and phonemic awareness

The least surprising result here and in Bruce's study was that children get better with phonemes as they grow older. One expects children to become more effective at practically everything with the years. But there is an alternative to this "developmental" explanation, which is that the improvement has nothing to do with age and much to do with instruction. The older children could have become aware of words as sequences of phonemes because of being taught about alphabetic letters.

One of the reasons why it took humankind so long to produce the alphabet in the first place may have been the difficulty of isolating the phoneme as a usable phonological unit. The inventors of the first alphabetic scripts took an impressive but difficult intellectual step when they recognized and harnessed phonemes in their new writing systems (Olson, 1994, 1996), and it would be quite unrealistic to expect generations of children to take this step on their own. They need instruction, and one of the effects of this instruction may be to make them aware of the phonological basis of the alphabet – the phoneme.

If awareness of phonemes is the product of learning to read, illiterate adults should be as young children at detecting and isolating phonemes. In the 1970s there was a crash literacy program in Portugal to eradicate the alarming amount of illiteracy that existed then in rural communities. This allowed Morais and his colleagues (Morais, Bertelson, Cary, & Alegria, 1986; Morais, Cary, Alegria, & Bertelson, 1980) to compare two groups of adults who were similar in every way, except that the people in one group had recently been through a literacy course and now could read, while those in the other had not taken a course and were still illiterate. Morais and his colleagues gave both groups two tasks. One was a deletion task like Bruce's. In the other, they had to add a sound to the beginning of the word: they were asked, for example, what "urso" would sound like if it began with "p." In some of these deletion and addition problems the experimenters used real words like "purso" (purse) and "urso" (bear), and in others made-up, nonexistent words (**pseudo-words**). The illiterate group was at a severe disadvantage in all of the tasks and particularly with pseudo-words. Their relative failure suggests that the experience of learning to read an alphabetic script does make people aware of phonemes.

In that case, literate people who read and write a nonalphabetic script should also be at some disadvantage in the phoneme tasks that we have been discussing. A study by Mann (1986) of American and Japanese 7-year-old children supports this view. (Remember that the Japanese have a phonological script, but that this is based on syllables, not on phonemes.) She gave them versions of the deletion and the tapping tasks. In some trials the children had to deal with (i.e., had to tap out or delete) phonemes, and in others with syllables.

Mann found little difference between Japanese and American children with syllables, but the American children were better than the Japanese with phonemes. The reason for Americans' relative success with phonemes was probably due to their experience of using the alphabet.

SUMMARY

The connection between children's experience of learning to read and their growing awareness of phonemes suggests that they need this form of awareness to become successful readers. Ample evidence supports this suggestion (Bjaalid, Holen, & Lundberg, 1996; Demont & Gombert, 1996; Ehri, 1995; Lundberg, Olofsson, & Wall, 1980; Stanovich, Siegel, & Gottardo, 1997; Vellutino & Scanlon, 1987; Wagner & Torgeson, 1987). There are hundreds of studies of the relation between children's performance in phoneme tasks and their success in learning to read. As far as I know, all these studies have produced thumpingly strong positive relations: the more children have learned about phonemes, the better they read and write, at the time when the phoneme measures are taken and later on too. This discovery is one of the most important achievements of modern psychology. It concludes the first part of the story that I am telling about children's reading.

 ## *Rhymes and Rimes*

Although the alphabetic script is based on the phoneme, some research suggests that children's awareness of other **phonological** units, besides the phoneme, plays a part in learning to read. Between the syllable and the phoneme lies a set of phonological units which linguists call **intrasyllabic**. These are usually smaller in size than the syllable and larger than the phoneme.

The most obvious, and probably the most important, are the units that linguists call **onset** and **rime**. The onset is the consonant (if there is one) or cluster of consonants at the beginning of a syllable. The rime is the syllable's vowel sound plus any consonant that follows. Thus "c" is the onset and "at" the rime in "cat," and "st" is the onset and "ick" the rime in "stick." Monosyllabic words **rhyme** with each other when they share a rime: "cat" and "hat" rhyme because they have a rime in common, and so do "six" and "picks."

EARLY AWARENESS OF RIMES PREDICTS READING SUCCESS

Most children are aware of rimes from an early age and often actively and spontaneously create and play with rhymes (Chukovsky, 1963; Dowker, 1989). We ourselves (Bryant, MacLean, & Bradley, 1990) have shown that 3-year-old children can solve rhyme oddity problems (i.e., can tell us which word in "cat," "hat," and "pin" does not contain a sound that the other two have) reasonably well, but not perfectly.

Some time ago we ran two longitudinal studies (Bradley & Bryant, 1983; Bryant, Maclean, Bradley, & Crossland, 1990), which showed that children's scores in rhyme oddity tasks, given to them before they went to school, predicted their success in reading over the next few years and also their ability to detect phonemes. These two relationships held even after we had controlled for the effects of differences in the children's IQ and their social background. Other studies have also shown a good relationship between children's sensitivity to rhyme and their success in reading.

Of these two relationships, the second one, between rhyme and phoneme awareness, is the more straightforward. It suggests that children's awareness of phonemes is not just the product of reading instruction (the cultural tool argument), but also stems from their earlier experiences with other easier phonological units, like onset and rime.

The other relationship, between rhyme and reading, has been confirmed many times (Baker, Fernandez-Fein, Scher, & Williams, 1998; Bowey, Cain, & Ryan, 1992; Chaney, 1992; Cronin & Carver, 1998; Ellis & Large, 1987; Greaney, Tunmer, & Chapman, 1997; Hansen & Bowey, 1994; Naslund & Schneider, 1996; Stahl & Murray, 1994; Walton, 1995). The reason for this relationship may seem less obvious, but it is at least as compelling, at any rate as far as English is concerned. English script is notoriously capricious at the level of the relationships between single letters and phonemes, but the relationship between sequences of letters and sequences of phonemes is a great deal more reliable. The letter sequence "ight," for example, always represents the same sound, as in "light," "sight," "might," and "fight," even though the individual letters in the sequence, like "i" and "g," represent different sounds in different words. This letter sequence represents the rime of the syllables that it appears in, and there is good statistical evidence that the relations between letter sequences and sounds are stronger in sequences that represent rimes than in other sequences (Kessler & Treiman, 1997; Treiman, Mullenix, Bijel-Babic, & Richmond-Welty, 1995).

Using onsets and rhymes to learn letter sequences

The possibility that children take advantage of rhyme to learn letter sequences that represent rimes is supported by Goswami's research (Goswami, 1986) on children's inferences about spelling. She argued that a child who is sensitive to rhyme and who has just learned, for example, what the word "beak" means, should now be able to work out what an unknown written word, like "peak," signifies. The child would see that the written word "peak" ends with the same letter sequence as "beak" and infer that it has the same rime, on the basis of knowing that rhyming words often end with the same spelling sequence.

Her way of testing this kind of inference was:

1   to show children a set of words, most of which were at the time too hard for them to read, in order to establish how well, or rather how badly, each child read these words. One such set contained the words "beak," "peak," "lake," and "rain";
2   to select one word, which she called the *cue word*, from the set and to teach the children what it meant. With the set that I have already given the cue word was "beak";

3   to show the children the rest of the words in the set again and ask them to read these words, in order to find out whether they could use their new knowledge of the cue word to work out the meaning of any of the other words. Of these remaining words, "peak" shared a rime with the cue word which was spelled in the same way in both words, "lake" did have three letters in common with the cue word but they were in a different sequence and did not represent a common sound, while "rain" was a control word.

If children make inferences on the basis of rimes and common letter sequences, they should be able to read the word "peak" in the post-test rather well, even when it had completely defeated them in the pretest.

In her first experiment Goswami (1986) found a distinct improvement in children's success in reading words that rhyme with the cue word, and a greater improvement than in reading the other test words in the set. In later experiments she showed that this improvement was stronger when the test words shared a rime with the cue word than when they shared other sequences: there is more transfer from "beak" to "peak," which rhyme, than from "beak" to "bean," which do not. She also found a good relationship between children's ability to detect rhyme in the rhyme oddity task and their success in making inferences in her inference task (Goswami & Mead, 1992). This is impressive support for the case that children also learn about the links between sequences of letters and sequences of phonemes, and that the most important of these phoneme sequences are the intrasyllabic units, onset and rime. Associations between single letters and phonemes, and between sequences of letters and intrasyllabic units, both play a part.

The claim that onsets and rimes as well as phonemes play an important role in learning to read has its critics. For example, Muter, Hulme, Snowling, and Taylor (1998) reported that two phoneme tasks, which they gave to young children in a longitudinal study, predicted reading much better than two rhyme tasks did. But the methods that they used to test awareness of phonemes were different from their methods for testing sensitivity to rhyme. Bryant and Cavendish (2001) established that when awareness of rhyme and of phonemes is tested in the same way, rhyme and phoneme scores both predict reading well. For the moment, the rhyme hypothesis seems secure.

SUMMARY

We started with the possibility that learning to read is simply a matter of skills imparted to children by their teachers – skills that enable children to master a cultural tool that depends on ways of analyzing words that do not come naturally to them. We end with the conclusion that this idea is correct in part, but that there is more than this to children's use of phonology. Children also take advantage of phonological units that come much more easily to them. Rhyme is a natural part of children's lives long before they go to school, and yet they use this informal knowledge when learning to read. It even helps them come to grips with that stubbornly difficult intellectual hurdle, the phoneme.

Conditional Spelling Rules

There is a great deal more to the English script and to many other alphabetic scripts than **letter–sound associations**. Many phonologically based spelling patterns are based on quite sophisticated, **conditional rules**. The final "e" that lengthens and changes the quality of the preceding vowel ("hop" as opposed to "hope") is an example, and so is the doubling of the final consonant that ensures the shortening of the preceding vowel ("hopping" as opposed to "hoping"). These particular rules are well known and actively taught. Other conditional rules are not taught and any knowledge that experienced readers have of them is probably quite implicit. When, for example, the /k/ sound ends a syllable and is immediately preceded by a vowel, it is spelled as "ck" if the vowel is short ("brick," "luck") and as "k" or "ke" if the vowel is long ("steak," "hike"). Few people are explicitly aware of this rule, but many obey it.

CHILDREN'S AWARENESS OF CONDITIONAL SPELLING RULES

We know that children pay little or no attention to these conditional rules at first. Instead they stick to letter–sound associations in a most literal manner. Read (1986), a distinguished American linguist, gave us the first systematic demonstration of children's initial concentration on letter–sound associations. For example, he reported a caption that an American child wrote under a picture, "Fes sowemeg ed wodr," which meant "Fish swimming in water." Every word is spelled wrongly here, but "sowemeg" and "wodr" capture the phonetic sequence of the spoken words remarkably well. Americans tend to convert the /t/ into a /d/ sound when it falls between two vowels and the boy's spelling represented this more accurately than conventional spelling does.

INVENTED SPELLING, THE FINAL "E" RULE, AND THE "C" RULE

Read's work on what he called "invented spelling" was revolutionary because it demonstrated that inexperienced children use their knowledge of letter–sound relationships in original and ingenious ways. He also showed certain stubborn weaknesses in these spellings. One was a frequent confusion between letter-names and letter-sounds. Read argued that a child who spells "car" as "cr" does so because the name of the letter "r" corresponds to the rime of the word "car." This is an entirely understandable confusion. However, it is hard sometimes, particularly where vowels are concerned, to be sure whether children are confusing letter-names and letter-sounds or are making some other kind of error. A child who writes "hope" as "hop" may do so because the name of the letter "o" is the same as the sound of the vowel in that word (and this is what Read and others maintain). Another explanation is that the child knows that "o" is actually the right spelling for the vowel sound, but has not yet realized that he or she must also put an "e" at the end of the word to represent this vowel sound.

This final "e" rule is quite difficult for young children, despite the intensive instruction that they are given about it at school. It usually takes several years for them to learn the rule when writing real words. The most striking work on this was done by Marsh and his colleagues (Marsh & Desberg, 1983; Marsh, Friedman, Welch, & Desberg, 1980). They tested children's grasp of the final "e" rule by giving them pseudo-words to read and to write. This is a good move: children who read the word "rope" correctly may do so by rote learning of this word, but if they also read "rofe" in the right way they must be doing so on the basis of a rule about the effect of the final, silent, "e." Marsh found that most children only pass the pseudo-word test by around the age of 10 years.

Marsh and his team also looked at a conditional rule about the use of the letters "c" and "k" and the sounds /s/ and /k/. The letter "c" at the start of a syllable represents the sound /k/ when it is followed by the vowels "a," "o," and "u" and by any consonant ("cat," "cod," "cup," "clod"), but "s" when it is followed by "i," "e," or "y" ("city," "center," "cycle"). The study showed this rule to be harder than the rule about the final "e." Many adults had no knowledge of it, even though it seems no harder than the rule about the final "e." The difference is almost certainly in the degree of teaching that children are given about these two rules. The final "e" is well known and in most English-speaking schools children are taught it repeatedly after a year or so instruction in reading. The "c" rule does not feature nearly as prominently in teaching manuals, and some children are probably never taught it at all.

We confirmed Marsh's conclusion that children do have some initial difficulty with the final "e" rule. In England they are first taught this rule at the end of their first year. Claire Davis and I asked over 100 children who were in their second, third, or fourth year at school to read and to write both real words and pseudo-words with long and short vowel sounds. The long-vowel words that they had to read all ended in the silent "e." The younger children made a large number of mistakes, particularly with the pseudo-words. The fact that they did better with the real words suggests that they learn the spelling of many of these words by rote before they learn the underlying rule about the presence and absence of the final "e."

The study also showed that in the pseudo-word spelling task some children used the final "e" as often with short vowels as they did with long vowels. The age of these particular children makes it probable that they were at an intermediate stage between not using and using the final "e" rule. Their indiscriminate use of the final "e" suggests that they had realized that some words end in a silent "e" and some do not, but that they had not yet grasped the rule for this ending. If that is so, some or all children may need to go through a phase of actively using the silent "e" in order to learn the conditional rule about its use. We shall return to this idea – *that children have to adopt and use a spelling pattern before they understand its underlying rule* – later.

Read's data threw up another important negative result. Consider the characteristic invented spellings of "kild" for "killed," "kist" for "kissed," "halpt" for "helped," "watid" for "waited," and "wotid" for "wanted." These follow the now familiar pattern of children using letter–sound correspondences in a literal way at first, but there is more to say about these mistakes. The children were ignoring a spelling rule based on morphemic structure. Spoken regular past verbs in English end in three different sounds, /d/ or /t/ or /id/, but this ending is always spelled as "ed." This rule is a powerful reminder that many orthographies, including English, are not phonemic scripts: they are *morphophonemic*, which means that the spelling rules are based not just on phonemes but also on morphemes and the way that they are spelled.

MORPHEMES: THE UNITS OF MEANING

Morphemes are units of meaning. The past verb "packed," for example, has two morphemes, the stem "pack" and the /t/ sound at the end which tells you that it is about a past action. "Unpacked" is a three-morpheme word. Adding "un" changes the word's meaning, which means that "un" is a third morpheme. These added-on morphemes, "un" and "ed," are called *affixes*, and they come in two kinds. Inflectional morphemes, like the "ed" past verb ending or the plural "s" ending, tell you about the grammatical status of the word. Derivational morphemes like "un-" or "-ness" change the meaning of the word.

MORPHEME-BASED SPELLING RULES

Once one understands the significance of morphemes, English spelling loses much of its capriciousness. Morphemic rules explain why the same rimes in "list" and "kissed" are spelled differently. "List" is a one-morpheme word. "Kissed" contains two morphemes, and the conventional spelling for the second morpheme – the past tense morpheme – is "ed." The plural ending, too, plays an important role in English spelling. The singular–plural distinction is why we spell "box" and "socks" differently: "box" is a one-morpheme word and "socks" a two-morpheme word which therefore has to have "s" – the plural inflection – at the end of it. The plural–possessive distinction is another morphemic rule. "The boy's drink" and "The boys drink" sound the same, but the apostrophe in the first phrase, and its absence in the second, tell us that "boy's/boys" is **genitive** (possessive) in the first case and plural in the second.

The spelling of derived words – words with a derivational affix – also often goes beyond letter–sound associations. "Health" is derived from the word "heal," and this relationship is captured in the spelling of the derived word because its stem preserves the spelling of "heal," even though the vowel sound in the two words is different. This phenomenon, known as **derivational constancy**, is frequent (e.g., "sign–signify," "muscle–muscular," "telegraph–telegraphy"), and therefore important in English.

Spelling rules based on morphemes are important in other scripts too – even in scripts that are regarded as highly regular. Modern Greek is so regular that if you know the letter–sound rules you can read any word in the language and know exactly how it is pronounced. However, there are more letters for vowels than there are vowels in Greek, which means that there are alternative spellings, which Greek children must learn, for each vowel sound. This learning often depends on morphemes. All Greek nouns, adjectives, and verbs end in inflectional morphemes, which have distinctive spellings and are often single vowels. The /i/ ending, for example, can indicate that the word is masculine plural, feminine singular, neuter singular, or a third person singular verb in the present tense, and this one sound is spelled quite differently in each of these four cases. Thus Greek children need to learn about morphemes as well as about letter–sound associations.

Morphemes are important in learning to spell French words as well. One example is the spelling of plurals, which the French represent in writing but not in speech. When they write the phrase "les grandes maisons," they put the plural "s" inflection at the end of the adjective and noun, but when they say these words they do not pronounce these plural inflections. Thus the plural adjective and the noun sound no different from the singular version of these words. The same is true of French verbs. The French write the "nt" ending to indicate the third person plural, but they do not pronounce this plural inflection. So the third person singular "aime" and plural "aiment" sound the same but are spelled differently. French children, therefore, have to be aware of the morphemic structure of adjectives, nouns, and verbs in order to be able to spell them properly. They certainly cannot rely just on letter–sound associations.

CHILDREN'S ERRORS IN SPELLING MORPHEMES

Children make errors with the conventional spelling of morphemes long after they have acquired a good working knowledge of letter–sound associations. We showed (Nunes, Bryant, & Bindman, 1997) that many English children as old as 10 years still ignore the "ed" ending for regular past verbs and spell the endings of these verbs phonetically ("killd," "kist"). We also found that children make many mistakes over the right ending for words ending in /ks/ ("box" or "bocks") (Bryant, 2001), and we (Bryant, 2001; Bryant, Devine, Ledward, & Nunes, 1997) have established, to no one's surprise, that children often put apostrophes in wrong places and fail to put them in the right places.

One reason for these difficulties could be that children are not at first aware of the morphemic structure of the words that they are trying to write. There is some support for this idea. Nunes et al. (1997) tested children's awareness of morphemes by giving them pairs of related words such as "writer–wrote" and then the first word of another pair, "teacher." The children had to produce the word that had the same relation to "teacher" as "wrote" had to "writer." Their scores in these morpheme tasks were strongly related to their success in spelling the endings of regular past verbs over a year later. Young children may fail to use the conventional spellings for morphemes because they simply do not understand the morphemic structure of the words that they are trying to spell. A child who does not realize, for example, that the word "kissed" consists of two parts – the root "kiss" and the /t/ sound at the end which signifies that this is a past verb – probably will not learn that this and other past verbs are spelled with an "ed" at the end.

There is another possible reason for their difficulties. We have evidence that children must go through a sequence of steps to learn morphemic spelling rules. Our longitudinal work on the "ed" spelling showed that the youngest children ignore the conventional "ed" ending completely and that many of the older ones used it correctly all the time. But in between these two states, we found another pattern. Children, who were just beginning to use the "ed" ending with appropriate words like "kissed" also applied this spelling to inappropriate words. They often spelled irregular past verbs with an "ed" ending. They wrote "slept" as "sleped," for example, and "heard" as "heared." More surprising was that they used the ending with other parts of speech: they sometimes wrote "next" as "necsed" and "ground" as "grouned."

There are parallels for this striking pattern in other languages. In Greek, children start by spelling different inflections that have the same sound in one way only (Bryant, Nunes, & Aidinis, 1999). Although there are four different affixes with the /i/ sound, all spelled differently, young children typically apply one spelling (usually a single letter) to all of them. Later they adopt two or three spellings for this sound, but then put these new spellings on inappropriate as well as appropriate words. Although they are now better at spelling words which take the spellings that they have just adopted, they actually become worse with words that they used to spell correctly, because the new spellings are quite inappropriate for these particular words.

OVERGENERALIZATION OF LEARNED SPELLING PATTERNS

The pattern of children's spelling getting worse with some words at the same time as it gets better with others is a surprisingly wide one. The apostrophe is a striking case (Bryant, 2001; Bryant et al., 1997). We gave children of 8, 9, and 15 years sentences containing a word ending in /s/. In half the cases this word was a singular possessive noun, and in the other half a nominative or an accusative plural. The first kind of words needed an apostrophe and the second did not. Our question was whether the children would put apostrophes into possessive words and leave them out of plurals.

The youngest children hardly ever used the apostrophe, which meant that they spelled the plural endings nearly perfectly and the possessive endings wrongly for most of the time. The older children used the apostrophe more frequently and so their spelling of the possessive improved, but they used it with plural endings as well and this meant that their spelling of the plural word endings got worse.

A final example comes from the way that French children learn to spell the unsounded plural affixes. At first (Fayol, Thenevin, Jarousse, & Totereau, 1999; Totereau, Thenevin, & Fayol, 1997) they leave them out altogether, but soon, as a result of intensive instruction, they learn about the "s" ending for plural nouns and adjectives. However, at the same time as they begin to use this ending with plural nouns, they also begin to put "s" at the ends of plural verbs as well, which is quite wrong. Eventually, however, they learn about the "nt" ending for plural verbs, but then they behave in a way that is closely similar to the behavior of English children as they learn about the "ed" ending and the apostrophe. While their spelling of plural verb endings gets better, their spelling of plural noun endings actually declines, because they begin to put "nt" or "ent" endings on plural nouns, e.g., "les merlent chantent" instead of "les merles chantent."

These fascinating **overgeneralizations** of newly learned spelling patterns may be an essential part of learning. This may be the underlying three-step sequence:

1   Children start by spelling a particular sound like the /t/ ending in one way only ("kist," "list").

2   Then they learn another way of spelling this ending ("ed"), and at first begin to use it without understanding when it is right to do so, and thus occasionally write "list," for example, as "lised."
3   Then, as a result of the feedback that they get when they use this new spelling, they learn the rule for its use.

The important point in this sequence is that children have to use the new spelling first before they can understand its underlying rule. They use it first and learn about it later.

Summary

At the beginning of this chapter we asked about the relative importance of instruction and of the child's own contribution to learning how to read and to do mathematics. We have shown how instruction is indeed an essential part of the process of learning letter–sound associations. These associations involve a phonological unit, called the phoneme, which young children, and any other uninstructed human, find difficult to detect and isolate. So, children need instruction about phonemes and this instruction has important cognitive effects.

Children have to learn rules as well as associations, and here their own contribution is quite striking. Instruction may be necessary, but the most interesting outcome of research on learning morphemic spelling rules is its conclusion that children have to try out new spellings in order to learn about them. This has been shown many times now in research on children's learning of morphemic rules. It may also be true of learning conditional phonological spelling rules.

Plate 11.1   Reading ability and mathematical skills are key aspects of children's development. How much of children's learning depends on instruction, and how much do children learn for themselves? Photograph © Heather Vickers.

Number and Counting

With number, as with reading, it is wise to consider what children need to learn before discussing how they manage to learn it. When children learn about number they have to come to terms with a mixture of universal, logical principles and of human inventions that vary quite considerably from place to place.

THE LOGICAL PRINCIPLES OF NUMBER AND COUNTING

The logical principles are the essential ingredients of number. Unless a system conforms to these principles, it cannot be called a number system. One is **cardinality**: any set of items with a particular number is equal in quantity to any other set with the same number of items in it. This may sound banal at first, but it is not. Cardinality is what makes the recognition of number more sophisticated and interesting than the recognition of particular patterns. To understand the cardinal properties of number, we must go beyond perceptual information. Two sets of objects have the same number despite looking completely different (four cars arranged in a square, four garages in a line), and a set of items stays numerically the same despite changes in its perceptual appearance (a group of children now in an orderly queue, later running around in a school playground).

A second principle is **ordinality**. Numbers come in an ordered scale of magnitude: 2 is more than 1 and 3 more than 2, and as a logical consequence 3 is more than 1. Thus the understanding of ordinality is a matter not just of knowing that numbers come in a certain order of magnitude, but also of being able to understand and make what are called **transitive inferences** (A > B, B > C: ∴ A > C).

These are essential characteristics of number. When we count, we use number words that are pure inventions but, whatever these words are, we must obey certain **universal counting principles**. Unless we do so we are not really counting. Five such principles were set out by Gelman and Gallistel (1978).

The first three were "how to count" principles. These include the **one-to-one principle**, which is that one must count all the objects in a set once and once only: each one must be given just one number tag. Another principle is the **stable order principle**: one must produce the number words, when counting, in a set order, and in the same set order each time. You must be making a mistake if you count 1–2–3 on one occasion and 3–1–2 on another. The third is that the last number counted represents the value of the set. Gelman and Gallistel misleadingly called this the cardinal principle, but it would be better to call it the **last-number-counted** principle.

The remaining two principles were the **abstraction principle** and the **order irrelevance principle**. The first of these states that the number in a set is quite independent of any of the qualities of the members in that set: the rules for counting a heterogeneous set of objects are the same as for counting a homogeneous one. The order irrelevance principle is that the order in which members of a set are counted makes no difference, and anyone who counts a set, for example, from left to right will come to the same answer as someone else who counts it from right to left.

DIFFERENT COUNTING SYSTEMS

All counting systems must obey these principles. Nevertheless, these systems vary across languages and across cultures (Saxe, 1981). The most obvious variation is in the words for numbers. Some languages lay linguistic traps, others do not.

In English, for example, words like "eleven" and "thirteen" are opaque: these words do not reveal the fact that they stand for 10 + 1 and 10 + 3. "Quatre-vingt-dix," the French word for 90, is not much better, and German children have to solve the problem that numbers between 20 and 99 start with the smaller denomination when spoken, but with the larger denomination when written.

Counting systems vary in another way too. We are so used to the decimal system that we tend to think of it as inevitable, but it is not. In the past, various cultures have used other base systems: the Mayans used a base 20 system for centuries, and so did the British, until quite recently, for their currency (20 shillings to a pound). There are even-number systems that have no base system at all. One is the system developed by the Oksapmin in Papua New Guinea (Saxe, 1981), whose number words are names of body parts. Their counting starts with the word for the right thumb, which also means "1," and continues up the arm over the head (the word for the left eye is also the word for "16") and down eventually to the right hand. The base system of counting is undoubtedly an invention and it is a tool of great significance, because it makes numerical calculations much easier for human beings.

The universal principles of number and of counting systems add up to a formidable list of logical requirements that children must follow to be able to make the simplest numerical calculations. When we put these together with the sophistication of the invented base systems and the vagaries of the language used in counting, we can see that there are many difficulties on the way to learning about number. Some psychologists, however, have suggested that children have the help of a remarkable resource during this learning – an **innate** understanding of number. The evidence for this claim comes mostly from work with infants.

INFANTS' KNOWLEDGE OF NUMBER

The idea that humans are born with the ability to reason mathematically is now taken extremely seriously (Butterworth, 1999; Dehaene, 1997; Gelman & Gallistel, 1978; Gelman & Meck, 1983; Gelman, Meck, & Merkin, 1986).

Gelman used two kinds of evidence to support this hypothesis. The first was research on babies that was done by herself and her colleague Starkey, who used the technique of **habituation** in his experiments (Starkey & Cooper, 1980; Starkey, Spelke, & Gelman, 1990). Habituation experiments are based on the fact that babies show more interest in novel than in familiar objects (see chapter 5).

Starkey and Cooper (1980) set up an experiment to see if 4-month-old babies can discriminate numbers. There were two phases in their experiment. In the first they showed the babies, over series of trials, a certain number of dots. In each trial the baby saw the same number of dots, but the perceptual arrangement of the dots (bunched up or spread out) varied from trial to trial. Some children were shown "small" numbers – either two or three dots – and others "large" – either four or six dots. During this first phase the babies' attention to the number displays usually declined. The aim of the second phase was to find out if a change in the number of dots would restore their interest. All the babies were shown a new number of dots in this phase.

When the numbers of dots were small, the babies looked at the displays with the new number of dots for a relatively long time and thus seemed to recognize a change in their number. Starkey and Cooper claimed, therefore, that infants do distinguish small numbers.

Many other studies have repeated and refined this result (e.g., Strauss & Curtis, 1981). Antell and Keating (1983) found that even neonates reacted in the same way, and van Loosbroek and Smitsman (1990) reported the same pattern in a study in which the objects in the displays moved all the time while the babies saw them.

However, the meaning of these results has been seriously questioned. The question is whether the experiments are about number. One research group (Clearfield & Mix, 1999; Mix, Levine, & Huttenlocher, 1997; Mix, Levine, & Huttenlocher, 2001) argues that infants made discriminations entirely on the basis of continuous quantity in these experiments. They claim that the infants in these habituation studies were aware with the small-number displays of the total size taken up by the items in the display, but not of the number of items (the judgment about total size was not possible for infants with the large-number displays, according to this hypothesis, because of their greater complexity). None of the studies had included any control against the possibility that children were making a judgment about total size.

Clearfield and Mix (1999) produced evidence for this alternative hypothesis. They compared the effects of:

1   varying the amount of material, while holding the number constant;
2   varying the number of items, while holding the total amount of material constant.

In the first case the change did provoke increased interest in the babies who saw it. But in the second case the babies showed no sign of revived interest in the second phase. The result supports the idea that the babies in Starkey's research might not have been attending to number. The issue of innate number discrimination is still open to debate.

Infants' knowledge of addition and subtraction: Wynn's work

However, another set of experiments provided support for the idea of innate mathematical structures. Wynn (1992, 1998, 2000) looked at the understanding of adding and subtracting in babies as young as 6 months old. She did this by enacting additions and subtractions in front of the baby, so that sometimes these led to the correct and at other times to the incorrect result. She argued that if babies can do the additions and subtractions, they should be surprised by incorrect outcomes and should look longer at them. In her first study she enacted addition (1 + 1) by:

1   putting a Mickey Mouse on a platform in front of the child;
2   raising a screen in front of this toy so that the child could not see it;
3   placing another Mickey Mouse behind the screen;
4   lowering the screen so that the child could see how many toys there now were on the platform.

The right outcome was two toys on the platform. On half the trials two toys were indeed there, but on the other half, by trickery, only one toy was left, and the child therefore saw an incorrect outcome.

Wynn carried out her subtraction (2 − 1) in the same way:

1   she began by showing the child two toys on the platform;
2   she raised the screen to block the child's view of these toys;
3   she then put her hand behind the screen and removed one of the two toys;
4   finally, she lowered the screen, revealing one toy on some trials (the correct outcome), and two (the incorrect outcome) on others.

On some subtraction trials the children were presented with the correct outcome (one toy there), and on others with an incorrect one (two toys on the platform).

The results were positive. The infants did look longer at the wrong outcomes. Wynn recognized, however, that these results could be explained in another way. In the first experiment the incorrect outcome was always the same as the starting point in each of the problems (1 in the addition and 2 in the subtraction problems). The babies may have expected a change – any change – from the original state as a result of the addition or subtraction, and may simply have been surprised to see everything unchanged.

So, Wynn carried out a second study with 1 + 1 addition. Her procedure was exactly as before, except that the incorrect outcome, this time, was 3. Thus both the correct and the incorrect outcomes were different from the starting point. Wynn found that the infants still showed more interest in the new incorrect outcome (1 + 1 = 3) than in the correct one. She concluded that the babies must therefore have been able to work out the 1 + 1 addition.

CRITICISMS OF WYNN'S WORK

These experiments have been criticized and are still controversial. One relatively small criticism is that Wynn did not include subtraction in her second experiment. She did not, for example, give infants trials in which 3 − 1 led to the incorrect outcome of 1, and thus both outcomes were different from the initial state. So one cannot be sure that infants of this age have a genuine understanding of subtraction (Bryant, 1992).

Another criticism, made by Wakeley, Rivera, and Langer (2000a, 2000b), is that in the crucial second experiment the infants could have attended more to the $1 + 1 = 3$ than to the $1 + 1 = 2$ outcome merely because they were more interested in larger numbers, or because it takes them more time to process three objects than two objects. Again the crucial test would be to introduce the $3 - 1 = 1$ outcome. In this case the incorrect outcome $3 - 1 = 1$ is less numerous than the correct outcome of $3 - 1 = 2$. So a preference here for the incorrect outcome would go against the idea that children are just responding on the basis of numerosity.

Wakeley et al. carried out an experiment that repeated all four conditions of Wynn's first study and introduced the $3 - 1 = 1$ and $3 - 1 = 2$ sequences. They found no significant difference in the amount of attention that the infants paid to the $3 - 1 = 1$ and the $3 - 1 = 2$ outcomes. Worse still, when the experimenters repeated Wynn's original tasks, their results were different from hers. The babies did not look longer at the incorrect than at the correct outcomes.

Thus the research on addition/subtraction, like the habituation research, provides us with no convincing consistent evidence for innate mathematical knowledge. We must turn now to work with a different age group.

Principles before skills

Gelman supported Starkey's conclusion about innate understanding of number because she herself thinks that the understanding of her five counting principles is a basic, built-in part of our cognitive system. She acknowledges that children make mistakes when they count, but argues that this is a matter of **procedural skills**, which are never perfect. According to Gelman, however, knowledge of the principles is innate.

Her own work was mainly with preschool children. In a classic study, Gelman and Gallistel recorded how well children aged between 2 and 5 years count sets of objects. They gave the children sets that varied in number from 2 to 19, asked them to count each set, and recorded whether the children always produced number words in the same order and always counted each object once, and also whether they seemed to recognize that the last number counted signified the number of the set.

The main result was a large effect of set size. The children respected the counting principles with small number sets more than with large ones. Gelman and Gallistel's explanation was that children possess a knowledge of the principles long before they can put them into effect consistently. They called this the *principles-before-skills* hypothesis. They argued that children's mistakes with the larger sets are due to difficulties in applying the right procedures in increasingly difficult circumstances. For example, young children lose their way in one-to-one counting with large sets because of forgetting which items they have already counted.

Gelman and her colleagues (Gelman & Meck, 1983; Gelman et al., 1986) tested this hypothesis by asking preschool children to make judgments about a puppet which they saw counting. Sometimes the puppet counted correctly, but at other times it failed to respect the one-to-one principle or the last-number-counted principle. The experimenters wanted to see whether the children could spot these violations. The results of these puppet studies supported Gelman's claim that young children do have some understanding of the "how to count" principles, as these were set out in her model.

These studies do show some understanding in young children of the process of counting, but they sidestep some of the basic requirements for the understanding of number. Gelman's model and her empirical work leave out cardinal number, which is about relations between sets, because her research concentrates entirely on counting single sets. It also leaves out ordinal number, for there is nothing in the research about children's understanding of the increasing magnitude of numbers.

Thus the claim for innate understanding of number is unimpressive. Research on number discrimination in babies may not be about number, and research on principles before skills leaves out some essential principles. We need to examine the alternative idea, which is that children acquire an understanding of number gradually and as a result of much experience.

Number as a Cultural Tool

The difficulty of establishing any hard evidence for the innate hypothesis makes it seem more likely that we spend a lot of our childhood acquiring mathematical knowledge and skills. But how do children acquire mathematics? One possible answer is that they learn mathematics by being taught about it. With cultural tools we can be sure that some instruction is needed. As we have seen, children cannot be left to reinvent these tools for themselves.

THE DECIMAL SYSTEM

The decimal system is an obvious example of a cultural tool. Like other cultural tools, it does not come easily to young children (Fuson, 1988). One task that shows this is the shop task, described in Nunes and Bryant (1996). The children are given money and are charged for items that they want to buy in a shop set up by the experimenters. In some trials they need to pay in one denomination only – just in pence or just in 10p coins. In other trials they must mix denominations by combining 10p coins and pence to reach a sum such as 24. These mixed trials are a good test of children's understanding of the base 10 system, because the whole point of the system is the combination of units with tens, tens with hundreds, and so on. The mixed trials in our shop task were by far the hardest for the 5- and 6-year-old children, who usually go wrong by treating these trials as single-denomination problems. They start counting out the 1p coins as pence, but then continue by counting the 10p coins as units too.

Cross-cultural differences in difficulty of the decimal system

One explanation for English-speaking children's difficulty with the decimal system is a cultural one, and therefore absolutely consistent with the cultural tool approach.

The teen and decade words are more opaque in European languages than in Asian languages. The Chinese, Japanese, and Koreans do not have words like "eleven," "twelve," "thirteen," "twenty," and "thirty": they say the equivalent of "ten-one," "ten-two," "ten-three," "two-ten," and "three-ten." Children from these Asian countries are also better at counting and at constructing numbers than European and American children. Miller and Stigler (1987; see also Miller, Smith, Zhu, & Zhang, 1995) asked 4-, 5-, and 6-year-old American and Taiwanese children to count up to just over 100, and also to count sets of objects that were arranged either in a straight row or higgledy-piggledy. The Taiwanese children did better than the Americans in the free counting. The Americans tended to make mistakes when they got to the teen numbers, while the Taiwanese coasted serenely through these particular numbers with hardly an error. When the children counted sets of concrete objects, the Americans and Taiwanese were similar in some ways, but different in others. Both groups of children made more mistakes with the randomly arranged objects than with the objects in a row, mainly because it was harder for them with the random arrangements to remember which objects they had already counted. With both arrangements, the Americans too were just as good as the Taiwanese when it came to applying the one-to-one principle – counting each object once and only once. However, the Americans made many more mistakes that took the form of producing the wrong next number: they were much more likely than the Taiwanese to get the number sequence wrong.

We find the same Asian superiority when children construct numbers. Miura and several colleagues devised a task in which children are given quantities of bricks that are either in units or joined together in groups of ten, and are asked to produce a certain number of bricks – 21, 34, 53. The question here is whether the children will laboriously count out units to reach the desired number, or whether they will take the quicker and more efficient option of combining tens and units. Children from Asian countries adopted the sophisticated way of combining tens and units much more often than children from European countries did (Miura, Kim, Chang, & Okamoto, 1988; Miura et al., 1994).

The most plausible explanation for this European/Asian difference is the linguistic one. However, we must be cautious. We cannot yet rule out the possibility that some other cultural differences, such as differences between East and West in teaching practices or in parental motivation, may have been responsible for the effect, as Towse and Saxton (1997) pointed out.

 ## Logic in the Understanding of Number

No one disputes the importance of logical reasoning in mathematics. The only argument is over the question of whether children initially lack the necessary logical power and have to acquire it along the way. Piaget (1952, 1953; Piaget & Inhelder, 1974) claimed that children are at first held back by their lack of logic, and do have to acquire logical abilities in order to understand mathematics.

His view of young children's grasp of number was the direct opposite of the hypothesis of an innate number sense. He claimed that young children may know number words quite well, and yet do not actually understand what they are doing when they count. They do not at first understand what the number sequence means, because they have no idea of cardinality and ordinality.

LOGIC AND CARDINALITY

I will concentrate on cardinality here, because Piaget's work on this is more closely related to number than his work on ordinality is. Piaget's work on **conservation**, and particularly the work that he did together with his colleague Greco, was directly concerned with children's use and understanding of number words.

Greco (1962) gave 4- to 8-year-old children three versions of the conservation of number task. One of these was the traditional conservation task: the children saw two identical-looking sets, judged correctly that the two sets were equal in number, then saw the appearance of one of the sets being altered, and were asked once again to compare the quantity of the two sets (see chapter 8). The second task was the same, except that after the transformation the children had to count one of the sets and were then asked to infer the number of the second set. In the third task the children were required to count both sets after the transformation and then were asked whether they were equal in quantity.

Most of the children younger than 6 years failed all three tasks. Thus in the third task these children counted both sets in the final part of the task, arrived at the same number, and yet still said that the more spread-out of the two sets had more objects in it than the other one did. They judged that one set with "eight" objects in it was more numerous than another set, also with "eight" objects, and that meant, according to Piaget and to Greco, that they really could not know what the word "eight" means.

A second important result was that slightly older children tended to get the first task (the traditional conservation problem) wrong, and yet were right in the second task in which they counted one set and then were asked to infer the number of objects in the second set. These children therefore judged that spreading out a set of objects alters its quantity (their mistaken judgment in the traditional task) but not its number, in the sense of the number one would reach if one were to count the set.

YOUNG CHILDREN DO NOT REALIZE THAT
SAME NUMBER = SAME QUANTITY

Piaget and Greco explained these results by making a distinction between "quantité" and "quotité." "Quotité" is the understanding of the children who realize that two sets of objects have the same number, in the sense that counting each one leads to the same number word, and yet may think that there are more objects in the more spread-out set. They realized that the number words (quotité) stayed the same despite the perceptual transformation of one of the sets, and yet did not realize that the actual number (quantité) was also unaffected by this irrelevant, perceptual change.

The Greco experiment was about comparisons between sets. Other studies of such comparisons lead to much the same conclusion. Michie (1984), Saxe (1979), and Frye, Braisby, Lowe, Maroudas, and Nicholls (1989) in separate studies asked children who could count to compare two sets of objects quantitatively. All reported a reluctance in these children to count in order to compare.

This failure to see that number can be used as a comparative measure was also demonstrated in a study by Sophian (1988). She showed 3- and 4-year-old children a puppet who counted two sets of objects. The children had to judge whether the puppet counted in the right way. In some trials the puppet had to compare the two sets and in other trials to find out how many objects there were in the two sets altogether. In the first condition the right thing to do was to count the two sets separately, while in the second it was to count them together. Sometimes the puppet did the right thing, and sometimes not.

The younger children were completely at sea in this experiment. They did badly when the puppet was asked to compare two different sets. They did not seem to know that one must count two sets separately in order to compare them. They cannot have understood the cardinal properties of the numbers that they knew so well. Their performance fits the Piagetian picture of quotité without quantité.

The importance of one-to-one correspondence

One way of making a number comparison is to use **one-to-one correspondence**. If two sets are in correspondence, in the sense that each object has its own counterpart in the other set, then the two sets are equal in number. One of the main pieces of evidence that Piaget cited for children's difficulties with cardinality was the difficulties that they have with one-to-one correspondence.

Piaget (1953; Piaget & Inhelder, 1974) showed children a row of objects and asked them to lay out another row with the same number. The younger children did not pair off (or count) the items and usually equated the rows in terms of their length rather than their number. Piaget and Inhelder (1966), and also Cowan and Daniels (1989), showed that children fail to use one-to-one correspondence to compare the number of items in two straight rows of counters laid side by side, even when every counter in each set is explicitly linked by a straight line to an equivalent counter in the other. Even this blatant cue has little effect on children's use of one-to-one correspondence.

Piaget concluded that young children have no understanding at all of one-to-one correspondence, but one must be cautious about this negative view, because there are grounds for thinking that children use one-to-one correspondence easily and effectively in another context. This context is sharing, which is something that children often do. Three studies (Desforges & Desforges, 1980; Frydman & Bryant, 1988; Miller, 1984) have shown that children as young as 4 years share things competently between two or more recipients, usually on a repetitive "one for A, one for B" basis. This sharing seems to be a temporal form of one-to-one correspondence.

Frydman and Bryant (1988) also looked at children's ability to relate number words to sharing. We asked some 4-year-old children to share out some "sweets" (unifix bricks) between two recipients. When they had done this, we counted out aloud the number of sweets given to one recipient, and then asked the child how many sweets had been given to the other. Most children were unable to infer that the second recipient would have the same number as the first.

It seems that young children do grasp one-to-one correspondence and cardinality when sharing, but do not apply this understanding to number words. This is an example of quantité without quotité. The children had a good grasp of the mathematical principle, but did not apply it to number words.

CONCLUSIONS ABOUT THE BEGINNINGS OF THE UNDERSTANDING OF NUMBER

The evidence for effective innate structures that are especially tuned to numerical principles is not strong. The research on infants is unreliable. The mistakes that preschool children make in simple number tasks cannot be dismissed as mere procedural errors. Tasks in which these children have to compare quantities show serious gaps in young children's understanding of basic number principles. Young children do not at first realize that counting is a way of measuring the relative quantities of two different sets, and they are happy to maintain that two sets with the same number are nevertheless different in quantity. Even when they know that two sets are equal in quantity and they also know the number of items in one set, they often fail to infer the number of items in the uncounted set. They plainly have a lot to learn.

SUMMARY AND CONCLUSIONS

The question of how much children contribute to their own learning and how much they depend on instruction in reading and in mathematics was the starting point for this chapter. My answer, at the chapter's end, is that children's own constructions are hugely important in both subjects. These constructions affect children's progress in two ways.

First, there are the strong effects of children's own informal experiences and actions in circumstances which have nothing to do with school or formal learning but which eventually make a formidable impact on their school learning. Rhyming with its effects on reading, and sharing with its effects on the understanding of cardinal number, are two examples here.

The importance of informal learning should not blind us to the need for formal instruction. Cultural tools, such as the decimal system and the use of alphabetic letters to represent phonemes, have to be taught. Here too children's constructions play a significant part. They must use and misuse the new tools before they understand the underlying rules for their use. This is the second way that children's constructions affect their learning at school.

These two effects fit well with a central theme in the theories of many developmental psychologists, including Piaget and Vygotsky. This is that children learn best when they learn actively and on their own terms. We should respect that.

DISCUSSION POINTS

1 Think about the relative contribution of instruction and the child's own constructions in the development of reading.
2 Why is it that rhyme is so important in learning to read?
3 Think of ways in which cross-cultural studies of reading development can enhance our understanding of the reading process.
4 Think about the major challenges presented to a child learning to read an alphabetic script.
5 Consider the evidence for and against the proposition that infants have innate knowledge of number.
6 Think about the evidence suggesting that children must acquire certain logical abilities before they can understand number.
7 What can we learn from cross-cultural studies of the development of numerical knowledge?

SUGGESTIONS FOR FURTHER READING

Butterworth, B. (1999). *The mathematical brain*. London: Macmillan.

Dehaene, S. (1997). *The number sense*. London: Penguin.

Frydman, O., & Bryant, P. E. (1988). Sharing and the understanding of number equivalence by young children. *Cognitive Development*, 3, 323–39.

Goswami, U., & Bryant, P. (1990). *Phonological skills and learning to read*. London: Erlbaum.

Nunes, T., & Bryant, P. (1996). *Children doing mathematics*. Oxford: Blackwell.

Read, C. (1986). *Children's creative spelling*. London: Routledge & Kegan Paul.

chapter 12

Memory Development and Eyewitness Testimony

Stephen J. Ceci, Stanka A. Fitneva, and Livia L. Gilstrap

KEY CONCEPTS

AFFECT
CHILDHOOD AMNESIA
CLUSTER EFFECT
COGNITIVE DEVELOPMENT
COGNITIVE PROCESSES
CORRELATIONAL STUDY
DEMAND CHARACTERISTICS
ECOLOGICAL VALIDITY
ELABORATION
ENCODING
EPISODIC MEMORY

EXPLICIT MEMORY
EXTRAVERSION
IMPLICIT MEMORY
INFORMATION PROCESSING
INTROVERSION
LONG-TERM MEMORY
METAMEMORY
MNEMONIC STRATEGY
ORGANIZATION
PAIRED-ASSOCIATE TASK
PERSONALITY TRAIT

RECALL
RECOGNITION
REHEARSAL
RETRIEVAL
RETROACTIVE INTERFERENCE
SCRIPT
SEMANTIC MEMORY
SHORT-TERM MEMORY
SUGGESTIBILITY
THEORY OF MIND
TOP-DOWN STRUCTURES

OVERVIEW

Memory, the retention of experience, is a ubiquitous cognitive process, and is essential for our functioning and development. There are three stages of the memory system. The first stage is called encoding. This stage determines how the events we witness are stored in memory, and how detailed is their representation. In the second, storage, phase, encoded events enter short-term memory and may then enter into long-term memory. The final step in remembering involves the retrieval of stored information.

The authors discuss in detail three factors which change during development, and which influence the encoding, storage, and retrieval of information.

- The first factor is children's existing knowledge.
- The second is awareness and application of mnemonic strategies that facilitate remembering.

- The third is metamemory, which refers to understanding the properties of memory and what strategy is needed in a given situation. Metamemory skills are extremely important to students engaged in the active learning of information.

How accurate is children's testimony when they are asked to be witnesses? A key notion here is suggestibility, or the child's tendency to change his or her memories and beliefs in response to interrogation. The authors discuss the many factors that can lead both to false testimony and to accurate reports of past events.

Introduction

THE BRONX CASE

In 1997 the *New York Times* reported that a group of boys who attended Bronx Public School 44 were arrested for assaulting two young girls during recess. The four boys, aged between 8 and 9, were charged with juvenile delinquency (Ojito, 1997).

According to the statements taken from six aides and a parent volunteer – all of whom were said to be supervising the recess – a little girl approached a teacher's aide and told him that her friend had been pushed and shoved by the boys and that one of them had rubbed his body against her friend's body. A female aide interviewed the two girls. During this interview the alleged victim kept silent. "Each and every time she was asked a question, her friend would speak up for her," the aide wrote in her report (Ojito, 1997). When the girls returned to their classroom, the friend repeated the story to her teacher. The principal called the boys in for questioning. They denied having rubbed their bodies against any of the girls.

Up to this point, neither of the girls nor any of the boys had mentioned a boy pulling his pants down and putting his penis into a girl's mouth. However, later that night, the girl in question told her 18-year-old sister that a boy had rubbed his genitals against her mouth. The girl's mother took her to the hospital and called the police. While the police investigation was going on, the principal wrote a letter to all the parents of children at the school assuring them that "I made a complete investigation by listening and speaking to our students. I have determined that no inappropriate behavior took place at any time." Whose story was right?

HOW RELIABLE ARE CHILDREN'S REPORTS?

Cases such as this one occur with all too great frequency. Courts and law enforcement professionals are faced with the daunting task of sorting out what actually occurred. And when physical evidence is scarce, as is often the case in sexual offense investigations, they have to rely on the reports of alleged victims, perpetrators, and eye-witnesses to reconstruct the event. Thus, it becomes critical to evaluate the factors that might have influenced or influence the reliability of those reports. The critical issues are whether the witnesses have any reason to distort the truth and whether their memories of the events are complete and reliable. In particular, the alleged victim's report in the Bronx case can be evaluated if we could answer the following questions: What kept her from saying anything about the sexual assault at school? How did the circumstances at home prompt her report of sexual assault to her sister? What influence could her friend's assertions have had on her own memory for the event? What influence could the repeated questioning by aides and teachers have had on the accuracy of her statement?

Increasingly, officials dealing with cases involving child witnesses have turned to experts in the field of memory development for help in evaluating the reliability of the children's reports. Research in memory development addresses the questions of how everyday events are initially experienced, how they are represented in our brains, and how they are later retrieved. In this chapter we shall review some fundamental influences on children's memory development. The pressure to respond to the public need of establishing the credibility of child witnesses has moved the field to exploring a variety of factors that might influence children's reports. The key notion in this broader research is **suggestibility**, or the child's tendency to change his or her memories and beliefs in response to interrogation (Ceci & Bruck, 1993). Suggestibility is perceived as a dangerous characteristic of children since it allows memories to become tainted, and inaccurate testimony to be given in court. In the third part of the chapter we shall survey the findings generated by this research agenda.

 ## *The Development of Memory*

We often become aware of memory when it fails us; when we just cannot retrieve a detail of an event although there is no doubt that we know it, or when the name of an actor starring in a particular movie is on the "tip of the tongue." Memory, the retention of experience, is a ubiquitous **cognitive process**. In English and other languages, "remembering" is synonymous with learning, reporting past experiences, and planning future actions. We involve memory intentionally in our activities, e.g., studying facts for a final exam, but most of the time memory works without our awareness. We retain memories of life events without thinking that later we will be questioned about them: we do not attend to our walks through the park, intimate moments with a partner, or trips abroad thinking about how we will later describe them to our friends. Still, our conversations are replete with references to such past experiences.

Children's experiences are as rich as ours but if you have ever observed a young child, you know that they do not talk about the past. They readily remember and recite nursery rhymes but their narratives focus on their immediate experiences. The transition to reports of past events is a major accomplishment since it allows children to share experiences with their community and become integrated with it. But, if you have talked with young children, you will have observed that their memories are missing essential (for us) details and that they are somewhat fragmented and disorganized. Sometimes it is difficult to tell what really happened from what the child fantasizes. From this chaotic state in early childhood, memory becomes a system that produces coherent and reliable accounts of events in early adulthood.

Recognition and recall

Researchers have developed a variety of methods to study remembering. Two common tests of memory are **recognition** and **recall**. After a person has been presented with study items or an event has occurred, he might be asked to identify the items he had been exposed to from a list of novel items and items that were present during the event. This test format measures *recognition* memory. Alternatively, the individual might be asked to retrieve details of the experienced event in an open format (e.g., "Tell me what happened on the playground yesterday"). This is a test of *recall* memory. As you can imagine, it is much more difficult to recall events than merely to recognize them. Just try recalling the names of all classmates from a previous school; you may recall 75 percent of them if you are exceptionally skilled. However, if you were presented with a list of all past classmates as well as some names of nonclassmates, you would have little trouble correctly recognizing the names of the actual classmates at close to 100 percent accuracy. Recognition is easier because of the absence of *retrieval demands* – the task provides all of the retrieval cues needed by presenting the actual names (or shopping list items, etc.).

Recognition and recall measure **explicit memory**, i.e., experience that is accessible to consciousness and can be reported verbally. However, on some occasions, our thoughts and actions are influenced by events that we cannot consciously remember. In these cases we say that we have **implicit memories** of these events (Schacter, 1987). Such memories require other types of measurement, e.g., observations of changes in behaviors like searching. Since we are interested in children's ability to recount verbally past events, most of the studies we report use recognition and recall procedures to assess memory.

The cognitive process that recall and recognition procedures assess is complex and sometimes effortful. The likelihood that we can recall an event from our past depends on the skill with which we execute a set of tasks, initially during the event in question, then later at the time of its retrieval. Psychologists who study human memory usually model the execution of these tasks as a flow of information from one stage of the memory system to another. The three main stages of the system are *encoding*, *storage*, and *retrieval*.

 ## *The Memory Process*

Encoding

The first phase of the memory system is called **encoding**. This stage determines how the event we witness is stored in memory, and how detailed is its representation. There is selectivity in what gets encoded into the storage system, and not everything we experience actually gets stored. In part, this selectivity in encoding reflects the limited attentional resources of the human organism; we cannot attend to everything at one time, and as a result we generally attend only to certain aspects of an event, and ignore other aspects. As an example, a beginning driver may invest her entire attentional capacity to keeping her car in the center of the lane. She may have no attentional capacity left over to attend to peripheral information such as what songs were played on the radio or what signs were posted on the road. Thus, not everything that is "out there" gets attended to.

Unattended event features are of two types: those that were experienced but attention was not focused on them, and those that were simply inaccessible to the senses of the particular individual. The former are encoded in memory but are not accessible for verbal reports; the latter are not encoded. In addition to limited attentional capacity, there are a number of other factors that can potentially influence what enters the memory system. These include the expectations about the events, the duration and repetition of the original event, and the stress level at the time of its encoding.

STORAGE

In the second phase of the memory system, encoded events enter **short-term** and **long-term memory** stores. Information stays for only a few seconds in short-term memory, and not all memories survive the short-term memory's limited storage capacity. Those that do survive enter into long-term memory storage. The passage of time, the number of times that the event has been reexperienced (or mentally rehearsed), and the number and types of intervening experiences, which also become encoded and stored, can have a strong impact on the strength and organization of the stored information. The strength of memories varies as a function of how long they have been stored (usually shorter delays result in better recall) and as a function of the number of times that the original event has been recalled (repetition strengthens the memory for the features of the event that have been recalled). The composition of a memory during the storage phase can also change due to expectancies, even ones created after the event. Previous visits of granny create expectations about what events are going to occur during her current visit and how they are going to unfold, e.g., if she has previously cooked savory meals we would expect that the meal she is cooking at the moment would be also tasty. However, having a savory meal prepared by granny also creates expectations, namely that on previous visits she has prepared similarly tasty meals.

New expectancies generate pressure on old memories to be consistent with them. Long after we can no longer retrieve a memory, we use our expectations to reconstruct what was its likely content. Finally, intervening experiences may at times serve to solidify the initial memory (when they are congruent with the initial event), and at other times they may compete with and interfere with the stored memory (when they are inconsistent with the original event). Thus, all these factors influence memory decay and the accuracy of recollections.

RETRIEVAL

The final step in remembering involves the **retrieval** of stored information. Retrieval is seldom perfect. In fact, there are times when the contents of the memory system are simply not accessible, even though in principle they are available. A variety of cognitive as well as social factors influence the retrievability of stored information, e.g., motivation to retrieve old memories, the willingness to cooperate with the examiner, and the comprehension of what is important to recall. Some of these factors at times enhance recall, whereas at other times the same factors may decrease the accuracy of the recall. For example, memory retrieval is strongly influenced by context. The retrieval of a memory may be facilitated when the conditions prevalent at the time of retrieval parallel those that existed at the time of the original encoding. One of the best examples of this principle is provided by a study by Godden and Baddeley (1975). In this study, deep-sea divers were asked to learn lists of words either on the beach or while they were beneath the sea, and then asked to retrieve the words either on the beach or underwater. The divers retrieved the words encoded on the beach better when they were on the beach, and the words encoded underwater were recalled better when the divers were back underwater.

An extension of this finding is that when an interviewer provides cues that may reinstate the encoding context, accuracy of recall improves. Various types of cues can be given. Some involve reminding the subject about parts of the actual event, whereas others induce emotional or cognitive states that match those present at the time of encoding. Although these techniques may facilitate the recall of stored experience, they may also induce false recall if the cues suggest an event that was never experienced or call up an event different from the target one.

So at every stage of remembering – encoding, storage, and retrieval – there are ways in which we can lose information about past experience. To start, not everything "out there" that impinges on our senses actually gets encoded (because our attention is limited). Furthermore, of that portion that does get encoded, not all survives a lengthy storage period. And finally, of that subset of features that get encoded and stored, not all are retrievable. Losing information about past experiences, i.e., forgetting, is often supplemented with *false recall*. False recall is the phenomenon of a person retrieving event features that subjectively are veridical parts of his memory for the event, but objectively these features were not part of the event and/or of the person's original experience.

Adults have access to a variety of techniques, knowledge, and insights to minimize information loss at each stage of remembering. People start learning such techniques very early in childhood and continue mastering them through adulthood. Preventing false recall, however, to the extent that this is possible, depends on the awareness of this phenomenon and the determination to prevent it rather than on learning some specific techniques.

SEMANTIC AND EPISODIC MEMORY

The encoding–storage–retrieval process applies to different kinds of remembering: from the acquisition of skills and factual knowledge, to the learning of a foreign language, and learning the spatial layout of a novel location. Among these different kinds of remembering, an important distinction is drawn between **semantic** and **episodic memory** (Tulving, 1983). *Semantic memory* is defined as the long-term storage of all of our world knowledge, including concepts, algorithms, definitions of words and the relations between them. The semantic memory for "market," for example, includes the knowledge that that is a place for buying and selling goods.

In contrast, *episodic memory* is conceptualized as memory of specific events, including their temporal and spatial contexts. Thus the episodic memory for "market" would represent the trips to the market on Saturday and where you can find the best honey. As you will notice, most examples in this chapter are from research on episodic memory. This is because of the applicability of this research to the discussion of children's eyewitness testimony. In court, children are questioned about events of their lives rather than their conceptual knowledge. However, semantic memory researchers have arrived at similar conclusions about the problems of memory development discussed here.

 ## *Three Factors that Influence the Development of Memory: Knowledge, Strategies, and Metamemory*

We have briefly pointed out factors that influence each of the three stages of memory: encoding, storage, and retrieval. Next we discuss in more detail three of these factors and how they influence the development of memory. The first factor is existing knowledge. The second factor is awareness and application of **mnemonic strategies** that facilitate remembering. The third factor is **metamemory**, which refers to understanding the properties of memory and what strategy is needed in a given situation. For instance, metamemory allows us to have insights into how our memories work, such as knowing when we have memorized a list, and what actions we need to take to maintain that list in memory.

KNOWLEDGE DEVELOPMENT

To a large extent, the ability to encode, store, and retrieve information directly depends on the knowledge that one possesses. Knowledge is the material that influences how we experience the flow of events and what we pay attention to. At the same time, it is the material that our experiences modify. Children differ from adults in the number of facts they have stored in their memories, in their understanding of the structure of events, and in their expectancies about the way the world works. Occasionally, children may have knowledge advantages in certain areas (for example, when they possess greater knowledge about cartoon characters than adults do). But, generally, knowledge increases as a function of age. In this section we will discuss the role of content knowledge on remembering.

Event representations, or scripts

The most productive construct used to explain how knowledge influences memory is that of a **script** (Schank & Abelson, 1977). Scripts are generalized event representations. They are abstracted from the occurrences of similar events and, as conceptual structures, represent with varying specificity different types of events. Scripts specify the

Plate 12.1   Going to a restaurant is typically a scripted event, with the order and structure of the components being clearly known (e.g., the entrée comes before the dessert). Photograph © Getty Images/ PhotoDisc.

structure of events by having "slots" for the participants in the events and links between these slots. The links represent causal and temporal relations between the participants. For example, a script for "Going to a Restaurant" has slots for the restaurant goers, the maître d'hôtel, the waitress, the menu, the table setting, and the different courses. The links between these slots denote the components of a "Going to a Restaurant" event. These include the maître d'hôtel taking a party to its table, the use of a menu to make a selection, eating the entrée that was ordered, followed by dessert, and then paying the bill. The links are indexed so that the order of the components is specified and eating the dessert follows eating the entrée. The number of scripts a person possesses and the elaboration of these scripts can stand for his or her total amount of knowledge.

We assume that every experience leaves a specific memory trace and contributes to our knowledge by influencing the structure of the script representing that type of event. The parts of the script that are present in the new experience are strengthened, and those that are absent are weakened. The features observed for the first time might lead to the addition of new slots or links to the script. Reporting a memory is different from reporting a fact. While the latter directly represents scripted knowledge, the former targets the retrieval of a specific representation, i.e., a specific instantiation of a scripted event.

Words and scripts

In order for scripted knowledge to influence the encoding, storage, and retrieval of an experience, that experience needs to be connected to the script. One way in which a particular life experience is identified as an instantiation of a script is through words. When you hear or think "restaurant" you probably activate the script "Going to a Restaurant." Evidence for the hypothesis that language is involved in the organization and the recall of experience comes from a curious memory phenomenon, known as **childhood amnesia** (sometimes referred to as **infantile amnesia**). Childhood amnesia refers to the relative dearth of memories for events from the first 3 years of life compared to the amount of memories from other periods in life. One of the most salient characteristics of children younger than 3 years of age is that they have no or very impoverished linguistic skills. Around the age of 2 and a half, children go through a "vocabulary spurt," i.e., a very quick growth of the size of their vocabulary. This point in language development is strongly associated with the dates of people's first memories. This suggests that language development can be one of the explanations of childhood amnesia and, therefore, that language can be a factor in remembering. Verbal labeling, even when it is implicit, probably helps get experience organized into meaningful chunks. Subsequently, the words associated with the event can be used to call up the memory of it.

Top-down structures

Scripts influence how we experience events and retrieve specific memories. First, they influence what we attend to. Selective attention helps us to move faster from identifying an event to behaving adequately in it but might lead to overlooking novel features of the event. Second, they have an interpretative function influencing the perception of ambiguous features and adding typical information where no information is available. In other words, scripts are **top-down structures**: they lead to the automatic generation of expectations about the causal structure of an event and what or who fills the slots in the script.

The top-down nature of scripts is evident in that the default slot fillers can fill in missing information or substitute ambiguous ones both at the time an event is experienced and encoded, and later at the time of its retrieval. For example, when asked to recall a faded event, we may use our knowledge about what "typically" happens to fill gaps in our memory. We may start a description of a dinner at a restaurant by saying that we were taken to our table by the maître d'hôtel, even though we have no clear memory of how we entered the restaurant. Because being taken to a table is usually the first thing that happens at a restaurant, there is a high probability that the description we provide of our evening is correct. We may also "disambiguate" information in favor of the script-provided expectations. In some restaurants it is impossible to distinguish the maître d'hôtel from the waiters, and some restaurants don't have one. In these cases, we might decide that the person who takes us to our table is the maître d'hôtel although there is no clear evidence for that. Again, given that most frequently it is the maître d'hôtel who takes a party to its table, we are probably going to be right.

Congruity and mismatch

When an event conforms to, or is highly congruent with, our script-based knowledge, then it is likely to be retrieved and, moreover, retrieved accurately. When there is a mismatch between what is expected and what is actually experienced, it is not uncommon for this mismatch to be resolved by the expectation intruding into the experience record and preventing accurate retrieval. In the restaurant example above, we might have in fact chosen our table ourselves and a waitress might have taken our party to a table. Scripts can be potent reminders of features of events, but they also can lead to erroneous filling in of missing or expected features and activities.

But the relationship between script-based knowledge and retrieval of memory of specific events is not linear. If an event is highly incongruent with our script-based knowledge, it is also likely to be retrieved – presumably because of its bizarreness. Imagine, for example, that you interact with a red-haired individual. Presumably, your script of interacting with people provides you with an expectation that the people you meet have brown hair, the most typical hair color in European nations. This expectation might lead you to not encoding the hair color of your new acquaintance (as atypical information, it is useless in predicting the features of other people you will meet), to encode it wrongly (as a result of script interference), to forget it easily (because it does not repeat), and to not retrieving it successfully (due to forgetting and script interference). But you might also form a long-lasting impression of the hair color of your new acquaintance because of its deviation from the typical.

Memory is constructive

The idea that script-generated expectations influence memory is consistent with current theories emphasizing that memory does not resemble a tape recorder or camera – devices that store and retrieve information veridically. These theories propose instead that the memory system is an integral part of the larger cognitive and social mechanisms underlying social interaction. There is abundant evidence to support this *constructive view of memory*. An example of this principle is provided by a study of preschool children's recall of a fire drill at their day-care center (Pillemer, Picariello, & Pruett, 1994). Very young preschoolers, but not older ones, erroneously recollected some of the events because of their lack of understanding of the causal structure of the event. For instance, younger children recollected that they left the building and *then* heard the fire alarm. Older children did not make this error, presumably because they understood the procedures of a fire drill. Children's memory for events that transpired during a doctor's visit is also related to their knowledge of the types of activities that usually occur in a doctor's office (e.g., Greenhoot, Ornstein, Gordon, & Baker-Ward, 1999), and their memory for chess positions is highly related to their knowledge of chess (Chi, 1978).

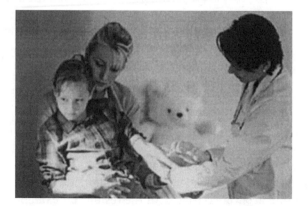

Plate 12.2 In order to study the reliability of children's accounts of stressful events, researchers investigate normally occurring events, such as immunizations, that are often naturally stressful. Photograph © Getty Images/PhotoDisc.

The relationship between age, scripted knowledge, and recall

The relationship between age, scripted knowledge, and recall is quite complex. Scripts develop with age but even very young children possess scripts for familiar events, and these scripts influence the way the children reconstruct past events (Flannagan & Hess, 1991; Hudson & Nelson, 1986). Once children of different ages have acquired a script, preschoolers may be more vulnerable to the negative effects of script-based knowledge than elementary school-aged children (Hudson & Nelson, 1986). Some work suggests that preschoolers' vulnerability to scripted information reflects their difficulty distinguishing "special" events from "scripted" events (Farrar & Goodman, 1992); younger children are more likely to incorporate one-time special events into their scripts. It seems that with age, children become better able to tag unexpected events and to note that they are special.

In sum, the theoretical construct "script," representing knowledge structure, helps explain why what a person "remembers" does not always correspond to his or her actual experience. Memory, like dreams, is highly *constructive*: it elaborates, deletes, and shapes its contents. These transformations occur at the encoding, storage, and

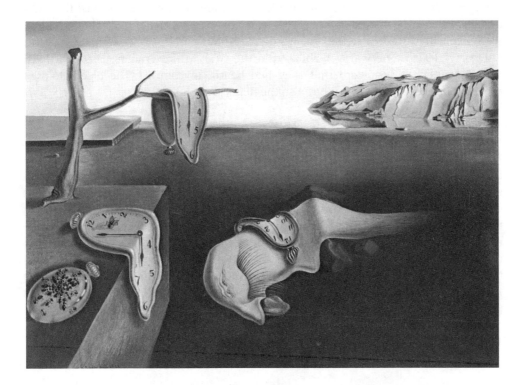

Plate 12.3 Like dreams, fantasies, imagination, and Surrealist art, memory is not a copy of reality but an eclectic compilation of bits and pieces of different realities. (Salvador Dali, *Persistence of Memory*. Digital Image © 2002 The Museum of Modern Art, New York/ Scala, Florence. © Salvador Dali, Gala-Salvador Dali Foundation, DACS, London 2003.)

retrieval stages of the memory process. As a result, what gets retrieved is rarely a direct representation of the original event.

Strategy development

All of us have applied effort to remember poems, telephone numbers, and dates when important events took place. A strategy is a "routine or procedure deliberately employed to achieve some end" (Wellman, 1988, p. 5). Strategies that facilitate remembering are called *mnemonics*. We are going to review three of the most popular mnemonics: *rehearsal*, *organization*, and *elaboration*.

Rehearsal

Rehearsal is the repetition of the items to be remembered, as in repeating a telephone number so as not to forget it before dialing it. In an early investigation of children's use of strategies, Flavell, Beach, and Chinsky (1966) documented that children would repeat to themselves the items they had to remember. Although this strategy appears early in children's repertoire of mnemonic devices and its use is very robust throughout life, rehearsal patterns change with age. This was demonstrated when children were explicitly asked to repeat the words they have to remember (Ornstein, Naus, & Liberty, 1975). The younger children in the study (third graders, 8–9-year-olds) repeated only the last word that they had heard. In contrast, the older children repeated not only the last item but also the items preceding it.

Organization

Organization refers to the classification of the items to be remembered into meaningful groups or categories. The study of the organization strategy has been motivated by the **cluster effect** in recall tests: subjects consistently retrieve objects that can be grouped together according to some principle (Bower, 1970). This finding motivated the hypothesis that imposing a structure on the set of stimuli to be remembered can guide later performance on memory tests. In tests of organization, children are usually given time to group the items they have to remember in any way that might be helpful and then tested on their memory for the items. Such tests show that children do not use the organization strategy consistently until the age of 8 years (Best & Ornstein, 1986). However, preschoolers *can* organize items on the basis of semantic meaning: they comply with explicit instructions to do so (Corsale & Ornstein, 1980).

Elaboration

Finally, **elaboration** refers to the action of making visual or verbal connections between the items to be remembered or between these items and salient objects in one's memory. Elaboration is a strategy that works well for the **paired-associate task**. In this task children have to remember pairs of unrelated items. In the recall test they are given one of the items as a cue and have to retrieve the other one. Using elaboration, children create a representation in which the items to be remembered are meaningfully connected. For example, if the child has to remember the pair "fish–fork," she might imagine eating fish with a fork. Beuhring and Kee (1987) found out that 96 percent of the increase in performance on the paired-associate task between 5th (10–11-year-olds) and 12th (17–18-year-olds) graders is explained by the increased use of the elaboration strategy. The spontaneous use of this strategy does not appear until adolescence (Pressley & Levin, 1977).

Other mnemonic devices

In addition to rehearsal, organization, and elaboration there are a number of other mnemonics that can improve memory. For example, external cues (e.g., notes on the calendar, tying a thread on a finger) are extensively used to help recall. Even preschoolers know to leave a mark on the place a toy is hidden when told they would have to retrieve it later (Yussen, 1974). Ten-year-olds know to check the clock regularly when they are baking cupcakes and have to remember to turn off the oven (Ceci & Bronfenbrenner, 1985). Although very young children spontaneously perform actions that facilitate remembering, it is not clear when they start using these procedures deliberately for remembering (Wellman, 1988). Flavell (Flavell et al., 1966) has in fact suggested that children have a *production deficit*, implying that children do not apply the mnemonics when they are necessary.

Utilization deficiency

Another feature of the development of strategy use is that the initial use of a strategy might not accrue any benefit for its user. On the contrary, it might even decrease the efficiency of remembering. This leads to a U-shaped effect of the use of a strategy on actual memory – after initially decreasing the efficiency of memory, the use of a strategy eventually leads to performance better than the original.

This effect has been called *utilization deficiency* and is documented by Miller and Bjorklund (e.g, Bjorklund, Coyle, & Gaultney, 1992; Miller & Seier, 1994). Miller and her colleagues have identified this deficiency in *selective* memory tasks. In these tasks children have to remember a subset of the items present. Thus the appropriate strategy is to attend only to the subset of items they have to remember. Exploring the application of this simple strategy, DeMarie-Dreblow and Miller (1988) instructed the children either to remember 6 out of 12 items hidden behind doors or to remember all the items. The youngest children in this study aged 7 showed worse recall when asked to apply their attention selectively.

Knowing when to use a strategy

Research shows that the major reason for the utilization deficiency is the effort required to produce the strategy and the limited resources of younger children. In the previously cited study, DeMarie-Dreblow and Miller (1988) enhanced children's memory capacity by allowing children to concentrate on memorization while the experimenter opened the doors behind which the items were hidden. (In the previous condition the child herself opened the doors.) Other causes of the utilization deficiency are limited knowledge, inadequate metamemory (to be discussed in the next section), and failure to inhibit another strategy or to integrate the strategy with other mnemonic activities (Miller & Seier, 1994).

In general, the utilization of a strategy does not necessarily improve performance. The child needs to be able to tie a bow or a knot since an untied thread on a finger can easily slip off. She also needs to recognize that tying a thread on one's finger can remind her to call up a friend but will not help with the memorization of a poem. Thus, not only the procedure defining a strategy needs to be mastered, but also the identification of circumstances of its appropriate use. The discovery and mastery of strategies continues through life. Later, individual patterns of strategy use are strongly influenced by two factors. First, we become more knowledgeable about our memory. We come to realize that we are good at remembering some things, e.g., numbers and dates, and bad at others, e.g., faces. Second, work environments often require specific memory skills, e.g., good memory for numbers in accounting and good memory for faces in the service sector. These factors allow us to approach strategy use in a very deliberative way. Mastering a strategy can make up for discrepancies between our memory skills and the memory skills required by our life situations.

METAMEMORY DEVELOPMENT

Cognitive capacities (e.g., attention, working memory span) are limited and oftentimes remembering is an effortful process. Thus effort allocation in remembering needs to be regulated. We need to be able to recognize the type of effort different situations require, and to distinguish the situations in which applying effort will help us accomplish the memory task at hand from the situations in which the memory tasks are just too hard to be accomplished. Metamemory is the mechanism regulating effort allocation in the memory process. The better the regulatory mechanism, the more efficient memory should be. This reasoning leads to the hypothesis that remembering should improve with the development of metamemory, and has motivated its close examination by developmental psychologists.

Metamemory has two components (Flavell & Wellman, 1977). The first one is *awareness of how memory works*, e.g., awareness of what is easier or more difficult to remember and the circumstances that facilitate encoding and recall. The second component is *memory monitoring* or knowledge about the appropriate use of mnemonics.

Awareness of how memory works

Researchers working on the first question concentrate on how much overlap there is between the scientific findings about how memory works (e.g., the benefit of strategy use, the role of time delay in recall, etc.) and children's intuitive understanding of memory processes. For example, Kreutzer, Leonard, and Flavell (1975) explored children's understanding of 14 properties of memory ranging from the strategies facilitating remembering to **retroactive interference** (i.e., the phenomenon that sub-sequent information can impair recall of the target information). For example, they asked children what they would do in order to remember to take their skates to school the next day, and how they would go about finding a lost jacket. The participants in Kreutzer et al.'s study were students from kindergarten (5–6-year-olds) to fifth grade (10–11-year-olds). Generally, not until second grade (7–8 years) did children show adequate performance on the tasks. Consequently, their understanding of how memory works develops quite late in childhood.

Memory monitoring

Researchers working on the second question concentrate on studying how children learn to use strategies, and how they respond to instruction in the use of strategies. They look at whether children benefit from parents and teachers explicitly telling them how to approach a memory problem. For example, Rogoff and Gardner (1984) documented how mothers teach their daughters to organize kitchen items and the positive consequences of this interaction on locating the items afterwards. The adults first provided examples of strategies to do the task and engaged the children in the process. Then, they monitored and provided feedback on their children's performance. In experimental situations, researchers also look at whether children benefit from feed-back on the appropriate use of a strategy by measuring the application of the strategy to a novel problem (e.g., Ringel & Springer, 1980).

The results from these studies suggest that metamemory skills are trainable rather late in childhood. For example, the children in Ringel and Springer's (1980) study were taught the organization strategy and then the positive results of its application were pointed out to them. While the third graders (8–9-year-olds) applied the strategy to a new set of to-be-remembered items, the first graders (6–7-year-olds) did not. A limitation of metamemory enhancement approaches is that naturalistic observations show that parents and teachers rarely provide children with metamemory informa-tion (Baker, 1994).

The development of metamemory

The development of metamemory might depend on the child's exposure to memory tasks. Facing the challenges of remembering, children may gain insights into the prop-erties of memory, spontaneously identify successful strategies, come to understand the benefit of applying strategies, and acquire knowledge about selecting the successful strategy in a new situation. However, we lack data to substantiate such a process. Another mechanism proposed to explain the development of metamemory is Vygotsky's theory of **cognitive development** (see chapters 2 and 17), which emphasizes the role of social context in cognitive growth (Vygotsky, 1962). In terms of this theory, the development of metamemory is a result of the socialization process. Children acquire their understanding of memory through the guidance of adults who point to them the requirements of the task at hand and to the relevant strategy. Thus, Vygotsky's theory provides motivation for training and intervention studies.

The relationship between metamemory and memory

Although it makes sense to hypothesize that metamemory influences remembering, notably through the application of mnemonic strategies, the empirical data on the connection between metamemory and memory have been mixed. Sorting through them, Schneider (1985) concluded that children's knowledge of memory is weakly related to their actual memory performance. However, children's memory monitoring abilities are strongly related to their memory performance. Verbal metamemory assessments usually do not correlate with memory performance, but concurrent ones, such as effort and time allocation, do (e.g., Brown & Smiley, 1978). Since the majority of the studies looking at the relation between memory and metamemory are **correlational**, we cannot be sure whether memory improvement leads to the development of metamemory skills or whether the acquisition of these skills spurs memory development. While metamemory is unquestionably important for memory performance, we should not forget that the two form part of a symbiotic system.

OTHER FACTORS INFLUENCING MEMORY DEVELOPMENT

So far we have discussed how children's growing knowledge, mnemonics repertoire, and metamemory influence their remembering. These are the most prominent factors in the development of memory, but not the only ones. (For example, general intelligence level has been also proven to affect how well one remembers; Bjorklund & Schneider, 1996.) The relative importance of each factor is yet to be determined. There are many interesting questions about memory that we did not address, either because of lack of space or because there is no research on them. To start, why do some people in general have better memories than others? How is memory performance in early childhood related to memory performance in adulthood? How is early childhood experience with strategy and metamemory training related to memory performance later in life? These questions reveal how fascinating thinking about memory is. Memory development is also discussed in chapter 15 with specific emphasis on memory changes during adolescence. We now turn to the question of how memory development and other factors influence the accuracy of children's testimony.

 Children's Eyewitness Testimony

As our opening vignette illustrated, children are often involved in criminal investigations. More and more often they are asked to testify when these cases reach the courts. Their testimony influences the verdicts delivered by judges and juries and thus can influence the lives of many people. Given the important consequences of children's presence in the courts, we need to ask how competent as a witness a child can be. The judicial systems of most countries require that every witness be able to distinguish between a truth and a lie and be able to retain and report information. The concern about children giving testimony is that their reports might be inaccurate for lack of either one of these abilities.

SUGGESTIBILITY

Suggestibility is children's proneness to give false reports of their experiences. Children's reports can be false because they can intentionally (or unintentionally) distort the truth about an event that they remember. The intentional distortion of truth is *lying* and the unintentional distortion *compliance*. Both behaviors aim to manipulate external forces: please people, avoid punishment, and decrease pressure. Children's reports can be false also due to vulnerabilities of their developing memory systems or because they don't understand the questions. If the child does not remember the event she is questioned about, her false report may be simply a fantasy or irrelevant information.

More precisely, we will use "suggestibility" to refer to the degree to which the encoding, storage, retrieval, and reporting of events can be influenced by a range of cognitive and *social* factors (Ceci & Bruck, 1993). Cognitive factors are those related to properties of memory, and social factors those related to properties of the situation that elicits the report. This definition of suggestibility accords with both the legal and everyday uses of the term. It connotes that subtle suggestions, expectations, stereotypes, and leading questions can unconsciously alter memories, as well as that explicit bribes, threats, and other forms of social inducement can lead to the conscious alteration of reports without affecting the underlying memory.

ECOLOGICAL VALIDITY

Suggestibility research, as an outgrowth of memory development research, capitalizes on the argument for **ecological validity**. The ecological validity argument dovetails with a larger argument having to do with the general relevance of laboratory research to behavior that takes place *outside* the laboratory. Bronfenbrenner (1979) has described the typical laboratory study of children as "the strange behavior of children in strange situations with strange adults for the briefest period of time" (p. 17). Narrowly, the ecological validity argument is that aspects of the context can systematically differentiate behavior. If researchers obtain results in one setting or context, there is no guarantee that these results will generalize to a different context. Indeed, there is a venerable history in psychological research demonstrating context effects: people reason more effectively in one context than in another, despite the fact that the two reasoning tasks are isomorphic (for review, see Ceci, 1996). As we mentioned, Godden and Baddeley (1975) demonstrated that word lists learned by divers while underwater were retrieved better when they were tested underwater than when tested on the beach!

Since the 1980s the ecological validity argument has motivated two research programs, both of which insist on looking at central events in children's lives that are analogous to crimes children are asked to testify about. These events usually involve potentially emotional experiences, e.g., touching, and/or misinformation about such experiences. The debate between the two research programs is on whether a child's testimony containing incriminating information is reliable or not.

The first program maintains that children's reports of abuse or neglect are *not* amenable to manipulation and genuinely reflect real events. Some, like Goodman, Rudy, Bottoms, and Aman (1990), have argued that this may be the case because of an evolutionary mechanism built in to protect children from life-threatening risks, thus giving privileged encoding to life-threatening events. Others have argued that abuse events are simply a lot more salient and hence memorable to children.

The second research program maintains that suggestibility is an ecologically valid concept in the sense of it being pervasive (Ceci, 1991). These researchers emphasize that in every suggestibility study there are children who come to give false reports about their experiences even about such central events in their lives like bodily touching (Bruck, Ceci, Francoeur, & Renick, 1995).

INFLUENCES ON CHILDREN'S REPORTS

The prevailing format of suggestibility experiments allows us to study a number of influences on children's reports. In a typical study, the participants are first exposed to an event, e.g., a visitor comes to the playground, or the children watch a sequence of slides. Next, they are exposed to false information about the event in which they have participated or which they have observed (e.g., that the man they had seen at the playground had a beard, when in fact he did not). Finally, they are questioned about their memories of the event. Their responses indicate suggestibility if the questions contain suggested erroneous details.

Using this procedure a researcher can study how new information alters an underlying memory by varying the number of times the misinformation is presented (i.e., the strength of the suggestion). Or, he might manipulate the relation between the child and the interviewer to examine the place of compliance and lying in producing false reports. The straightforwardness and flexibility of the procedure have contributed to making suggestibility a prolific area of research. Indeed, the majority of studies we report have employed this design.

Suggestions can be given in a variety of ways. *Leading questions* make the child accept the suggestion as part of the communication process since the focus of these questions is elsewhere. For example, children can be asked, "What color was the visitor's beard?," a question which presupposes that the man had a beard! In order to answer the question (with a beard color), the child has to imagine and thus implicitly accept that the man had a beard. Another way of presenting a suggestion is by directly providing the child with false information which she then integrates into her memory of the event. This technique relies on the effect of scripted knowledge on the interpretation of new information. Yet another example is when children are asked to imagine the situation they will have to report on with additional details (imagery induction). This can create "memories" for events that have not actually occurred. In misinforming a subject, researchers can also claim that the misinformation is an opinion shared by others, e.g., to create peer pressure, and to evoke important goals of the subject (e.g., being moral or cool).

The relationship between suggestibility and memory development

Since suggestibility research is an offshoot of memory development research, we could expect children's suggestibility to be influenced by the factors defining memory development. Many studies have taken basic findings about the development of memory and extrapolated their validity to forensic contexts. A couple of examples of the effect of memory strength and knowledge on the truthfulness of children's reports should suffice.

Strength of memory and suggestibility

A considerable amount of research has been done on the effect of memory strength on suggestibility. The reasoning is that it should be easier to implant a false suggestion if information about an event was weakly encoded or has degraded than if the memory about the event was strongly encoded and is well preserved in storage. A straightforward way to manipulate the strength of a memory is through repetition of the event to be remembered, and a number of studies on suggestibility have explored the effect of repeating erroneous information on children's reports. While some researchers have provided support for the proposal that there is a link between suggestibility and memory strength in children (Pezdek & Roe, 1995; Warren, Hulse-Trotter, & Tubbs, 1991), others have argued that there is no consistent relationship between a memory's strength and children's susceptibility to suggestion (Howe, 1991; Zaragoza, 1991). However, what might be important in suggestibility is the strength of the memory for the original event relative to the strength of the memory for the new, suggested information.

Scripts can produce false reports

Suggestibility researchers have also extensively studied the role of scripts in inducing false reports. As we previously noted, scripts are top-down structures: they lead to the automatic generation of expectations about the causal structure of an event and what or who fills the slots in the script. Leichtman and Ceci (1995) manipulated the role of scripts on the truthfulness of children's reports by giving some of the children participating in their study information that triggered the script for a clumsy person. A friend of the children (the experimenter) told them about her friend, the clumsy Sam Stone.

Eventually, Sam Stone came into the classroom, listened to a story with the children, walked around, and waved goodbye. In a few weeks, the children were asked about Sam Stone's actions in the classroom. Consistent with the interpretative effect of activated scripts, children in the study used the "clumsy character" script to attribute to Sam Stone behaviors that were not actually observed but fitted his "clumsy" personality, e.g., ripping a book or soiling a teddy bear. This study, among many others, corroborates the thesis that expectations influence what is remembered and how it is remembered, and that they can lead to false reports.

Scripted knowledge can cause age changes in suggestibility

We also pointed out that due to more extensive scripted knowledge, older children's memories might come to be *less* reliable than the memories of younger children. When younger children's scripted knowledge is insufficient or poorer than that of older children, older children might be expected to make more false reports of features that were not witnessed but that are part of their scripts for the witnessed events.

Suggestibility researchers have documented this idea as well. For example, Lindberg (1991) showed third (8–9-year-olds) and sixth (11–12-year-olds) graders and college students (over 18) a movie of students taking a test. This included scenes in which some students asked others the time. To half the subjects in each age group he erroneously told that the film they were viewing depicted cheaters. Then he asked the subjects to estimate the number of cheaters they saw in the movie. As expected, the misled third graders identified significantly more cheaters in the movie than the college students. However, the subjects were also asked whether a student asking another student for the time was a cheater. In this situation, the misled sixth graders and college students identified the student as a cheater more often than the misled 8–9-year-old third graders. One can explain this reversal in the effect of misinformation by assuming that younger children's scripts for cheating did not contain the scenario of asking for the time as a pretext for cheating. Their limited "cheating" script made them less prone than older children to the erroneous suggestion. In contrast, the older subjects' scripts could allow for a scenario where the student asking for the time looks into the other student's test book. Thus the absence of knowledge might actually benefit younger children's recall.

These examples show how suggestibility research has built upon and expanded research on children's memory. Suggestibility studies address issues of memory strength and knowledge representation but are set in contexts for which children's reports may be indeed solicited – e.g., someone's clumsiness and cheating – and their truthfulness matters. Naturally, the studies we cited barely give a hint about the diversity of the research emphasizing memory factors as driving forces behind the suggestibility effect.

SOCIAL FACTORS LEADING TO FALSE REPORTS

Children's greater susceptibility to suggestion, when compared with adults', can be viewed as a direct outgrowth of their relatively weaker ability to accurately encode, store, retrieve, and monitor different types of information. But since the turn of the twentieth century, researchers have also emphasized the importance of social factors in accounting for suggestibility effects. Based on what we know about the social development of children, it seems clear that social factors should play a large role in the creation of false reports.

Understanding the language used by the questioner

The social aspect of suggestibility is defined by the interaction between the child and another person. To understand the dynamics of this interaction, we need to ask first of

Plate 12.4 As this painting shows, asking children to testify in court is not a recent invention. (William Frederick Yeames, *"And When Did You Last See Your Father?"* 1878. The Board of Trustees of the National Museums and Galleries on Merseyside.)

all whether there is understanding between the speakers. Since children's reports are usually prompted verbally and the child uses language to report her memories, it is crucial that the child understands the vocabulary used by the interrogator and that she possesses the language skills necessary to express herself unambiguously and in a way that does not allow misunderstandings to arise (Brennan & Brennan, 1988; Snyder, Nathanson, & Saywitz, 1993; Walker & Warren, 1997). One leading British researcher into children's testimony tells this story of a criminal trial he attended: "To one 6-year-old the prosecuting lawyer said 'I put it to you that a response like that in a court of law such as this is inappropriate. Do you agree?' This was a lawyer examining a 6-year-old witness, supposedly for his own side of the case!!" (Ray Bull, personal communication).

In one study (Goodman & Aman, 1990), some 3-year-old children inaccurately reported that a male experimenter had touched their "private parts." In response to the question, "Did he touch your private parts?," they answered "yes" even though the experimenter had not. Upon further examination, the experimenters noted that the children simply did not know the meaning of the phrase "private parts." As Goodman and her colleagues note, if this term had been used inappropriately in an actual case, a misleading conclusion, eventually leading to a potential false allegation, could have occurred (Goodman, Batterman-Faunce, & Kennedy, 1992). Thus, the level of linguistic comprehension and production skills influences children's tendency to produce false reports. Children's answers to questions that they have incorrectly understood, in addition to adults' misunderstanding of their limited productions, may be incorporated into future interrogations, further increasing the likelihood of tainted reports.

Social pressure on the child

Even when children's command of the language is adequate, several other constraints in child–adult interactions might lead to children's false reports. First, both children and adults approach a conversation with certain assumptions, e.g., about the topic of conversation, but these assumptions are often incompatible. For example, most children assume that if an adult asks a question, then a "good" child should provide a response. Conversely, the adult assumes that if the child does not know the answer she will tell the interviewer "I don't know" rather than guess (which increases the likelihood of an inaccurate response). Although such misunderstandings appear even in adult–adult conversations, they are much more common in adult–child interactions.

Second, children can be and often are motivated to please the experimenter, end the interview, and avoid some sort of punishment. Children generally see adult interviewers as omniscient and truthful and rarely question their statements or actions. Therefore, they may comply with the adult norms or what they perceive to be the adult's wishes, thus inadvertently producing false statements.

Finally, children may also lie in order to achieve a goal that is under the adult's control, e.g., get a prize or avoid reprimand. Furthermore, when children are part of an investigative interview, regardless of the coercive nature or unpleasantness of the interview, they are required to participate until the adult decides to terminate. Children are seldom allowed to end an interaction by saying, "I am not talking about this any more" or "I want my attorney present." Children might and do express their discomfort and wishes to interrupt an unpleasant conversation with an adult, but these are rarely taken seriously and respected. Thus, when interacting with adults, and especially in the context of an investigative interview, children are under a lot of pressure and do not have at their disposal techniques that have the potential to ward off suggestive and coercive questioning methods.

A straightforward demonstration of the imbalance in adult–child interactions was obtained by Ceci, Ross, and Toglia (1987), who conducted an experiment in which the misleading information was presented to the children either by another child or by an adult. It was found that the children who were misled by an adult were much more likely to incorporate the misleading information into their reports of the story they had heard than the children misled by another child. These results suggest that the authority of the speaker influences the veracity of children's reports.

Do children lie and deceive?

But can children consciously distort the truth with the deliberate goal of deceiving their interviewers? This is a particularly thorny question because of the moral implications of lying. Historically, it was felt that young children were incapable of lying because this act required a level of cognitive sophistication beyond the capability of the young child (e.g., Piaget, 1926). Since the time of Piaget, much progress has been made in understanding the development and definitional features of lying (see Flanagan, 1992). With advances in our understanding of young children's cognitive sophistication, there is now evidence that even very young children sometimes do lie, with full appreciation of the differing perspectives of their listeners (Ceci, Leichtman, & Putnick, 1992; McGough, 1994).

The most recent research on lying has attempted to approximate real-life crime contexts by weaving **affect** and *motive* into studies of recollection, and by using highly familiar contexts such as observing loved ones break toys, or being kissed while in the bathtub. For example, Ceci, DeSimone, Putnick, Lee, and Toglia (1990) investigated children's responses to five motivations to lie or tell the truth: (1) avoiding punishment, (2) sustaining a game, (3) keeping a promise (e.g., to protect a loved one), (4) achieving personal gains (e.g., rewards, being accepted in a group), and (5) avoiding embarrassment. Generally, these studies demonstrate that, like adults, preschoolers are sensitive to the **demand characteristics** of a situation, and therefore succumb to a wide range of motives to lie or withhold information.

The motivation to deceive

Different motivations do not produce comparable levels of lying, though. The motivation to mislead provided by strangers, for example, is weaker than the motivation provided by familiar people. In one study, taking place in the school library, an adult experimenter pretended to find a watch left behind by the teacher (Ceci et al., 1990). After showing the watch to the child, the experimenter told the child that they were going to play a game of hiding the watch from the teacher. The child was told the game was a secret and was instructed not to talk to anybody about it. Later, the returning teacher asked the child who had taken her watch. Only 10 percent of the preschoolers lied to sustain this game (see also Tate & Warren-Leubecker, 1990).

However, when a well-known adult coaches a child to tell a lie, the motivational salience of the experimental procedure is higher. Using such a procedure, Tate, Warren, and Hess (1992) got 35 percent of 2- to 8-year-olds to lie to sustain a secret game. It appears that the degree to which children will lie to sustain a game is context-dependent, and that the use of stronger coaching will result in higher rates of deception.

The conclusion is that young children will sometimes consciously distort their reports of what they witnessed, and they will do so more in response to some motives (e.g., fear of reprisal and avoidance of embarrassment) than to others (to sustain a game, gain rewards). Subjects of all ages will lie when the motives are right for them. Children may be no better and no different than adults in this regard! Thus, the argument that children are incapable of lying should be discarded, as should the insinuation that they are hopeless liars.

The interaction of cognitive and social mechanisms

Some researchers have attempted to determine the relative importance of social and cognitive factors in accounting for suggestibility effects (e.g., Ceci et al., 1987). The results of these studies are inconsistent, and the issue as to the ascendance of one factor over the other remains unresolved. Still, the most feasible position on what causes false reports rests on the *interaction* of cognitive and social factors.

This interaction can have several forms. One possibility is that the degree to which social factors play a role in producing a false report has a cognitive basis. When memories are weak (or when there is no memory at all for the original event), children may be more compliant and willing to accept suggestions because there is no competing memory to challenge the suggestion. On the other hand, when memories are strong the child is less likely to incorporate misleading suggestions into memory. Another possibility is that social factors underpin the effectiveness of cognitive mechanisms in producing a false report. For example, a child may attend more to suggestions from an authority figure (a social factor), thus insuring greater encoding (a cognitive factor).

Finally, the child's false report may initially be the result of some social factor, but over time the report may become a part of the child's actual memory. Consider again the study in which the experimenters created an expectation in preschool children to meet a clumsy person (Leichtman & Ceci, 1995). Children later used the script for clumsy behavior to reconstruct what Sam Stone might have done, telling the interviewer, "Maybe Sam did it," or "It could have been Sam." Upon repeated postevent questioning, however, these children often became more and more convinced that the accidents implicating Sam's clumsiness had actually occurred, as opposed to "might have occurred."

In the legal arena, in response to strongly suggestive – even pressurized – interviews, children may initially realize that they are providing the interviewer with an erroneous account in order to please him (a social factor), but after repeated retellings to different interviewers, the erroneous account may become so deeply embedded as to be indistinguishable from an actual memory (a cognitive factor). Leichtman and Ceci (1995) documented just such a development in children's reports. The children who participated in their study became highly resistant to debriefing: they rejected the researcher's challenge that their reports were incorrect.

Another question that requires attention is whether there are age-related differences in the interaction of cognitive and social factors. Specifically, do younger children differ from older children and adults in terms of how quickly false reports, which may have been initially motivated by social factors, come to be believed? Clearly, much more research is needed to gain a comprehensive understanding of the conditions in which memories change.

IS SUGGESTIBILITY A PERSONALITY TRAIT?

Personality traits such as **extraversion/introversion**, *agreeableness*, and *emotional stability* are stable characteristics of individuals. Some traits persist with age, others are typical of a person's behavior during a certain period of time, but all are exhibited in a wide variety of circumstances. Is suggestibility a trait? Research data overwhelmingly show that younger children are more suggestible than older children and adults

(Ceci & Bruck, 1993). A fairly large literature indicates that a variety of memory skills do improve with age (e.g., see reviews by Kail, 1989; Schneider & Pressley, 1997) and that younger children tend to lose information from storage more rapidly than older children do (e.g., Brainerd, Kingma, & Howe, 1985). These age-related differences suggest that younger children might form weaker memories in general and be more suggestible across the board.

Are suggestible children always suggestible?

If suggestibility is a personality trait, then a person would exhibit this behavior in a variety of situations. For example, we might expect that a suggestible child's memory is easily influenced for events that personally concern the child as well as events that the child has only observed. We might also expect that the child is as easily influenced by peers and strangers as by relatives. Unfortunately, most of the work that compares children's suggestibility in different situations does not allow us to address the question of whether suggestibility is a personality trait, because different children participate in the different conditions of the experiment. For example, some children would be misled by another child and some by an adult (e.g., Ceci et al., 1987). In order to assess the claim that suggestibility is a trait, we need to measure the proneness of the *same* children to produce false reports across several different situations.

Some recent work supports the hypothesis that suggestibility is a trait of individuals. Scullin and Warren (1999) presented 3- to 6-year-old children with three situations: a painting event, reading a story, and watching a video. The day after each event the children were interviewed about it. The researchers found that children who were suggestible about the painting event were also suggestible about the video event, and that children who were suggestible about the video event were also suggestible about the reading event. Only the correlation between the painting and the reading events was not significant. These findings suggest that suggestibility might be a trait of individuals rather than a characteristic of particular situations.

Is suggestibility situation-dependent?

It is possible of course that suggestibility is a property of situations rather than individuals. It is easy to locate in the literature studies claiming that even young children are quite resistant to suggestion about traumatic, abuse-related events (e.g., Goodman & Clarke-Stewart, 1991; Saywitz, Goodman, Nicholas, & Moan, 1991). Some researchers claim that age differences in suggestibility are evident principally with nonparticipating children (i.e., bystanders as opposed to children who were the recipients of some action), and principally on nonsexual questions (Rudy & Goodman, 1991).

But a careful reading of the scientific literature shows that memories for all types of events are susceptible to alteration as a result of suggestive techniques and there are reliable age differences in suggestibility even for events that are stressful, painful, and potentially sexual, including ones where the child is a participant. The safest conclusion is probably that situations differ in degree and not in kind with regard to producing suggestibility effects. Suggestibility effects have been found for all types of events, but perhaps they are somewhat harder to get when the event is salient, persistent, and well understood by the child.

How well can we measure suggestibility?

Although the question about the existence of a suggestibility trait is far from settled, we are nearer to creating an instrument to measure an individual child's suggestibility. Scullin and Ceci (2001) developed a scale that is highly correlated with children's suggestibility in other situations. After viewing a brief videotape of a children's birthday party, the children are asked a series of questions, some of which contain misleading information. Children are then told that they have made mistakes on some of the questions and the series of questions is repeated. Two components of suggestibility are assessed by the Scullin and Ceci scale: children's tendency to incorporate the misleading information into their answers to the questions (known as "yield"), and their tendency to shift answers, particularly ones that were originally correct, when the interviewer tells the child that he or she made a mistake on some (known as "shift").

Scullin and Ceci (2001) reported that, surprisingly, 3-year-olds actually changed their answers *less* in response to negative feedback ("You missed some answers, so let's go over the questions again") than did older children. Shifting one's response when told "you've missed some questions" may require an ability to hold the two conflicting mental representations in their minds simultaneously in order to distinguish between what they originally said and what they think the interviewer wants them to say (Welch-Ross, Diecidue, & Miller, 1997). In other words, they need to be aware of both their memory and the interviewer's belief. To infer an interviewer's belief entails a so-called **theory of mind** that allows a child to "mindread" another (a detailed account of the development of a theory of mind is given in chapter 10). Such a theory of mind develops most rapidly between the ages of 3 and 5, and consequently may contribute to the increase in suggestibility found among the older children in Scullin and Ceci's study.

In contrast, the tendency for children to "yield" (i.e., to incorporate the misleading information into their original answers) appears to remain relatively stable over the age span covered in this study.

Summary and Conclusions

In this chapter we mapped our understanding of how memory works and illustrated the practical importance of this knowledge by focusing on the problem of the reliability of children's eyewitness testimony. We discussed the role of knowledge, strategies, and metamemory in the improvement of children's ability to retain and report information. We also surveyed the causes of children's false testimonies. We did not focus on the biological underpinnings of memory, though a thorough treatment of memory would also require discussion of its biological basis. However, doing so would have taken us beyond the constraints of this chapter. In this section we would like to highlight what in our view are the three most important forces that will define memory development research in the next decade.

ECOLOGICAL VALIDITY

First, we think that the notion of "ecological validity" will continue to shape memory research. No single study captures the panoply of factors involved in an actual forensic case. (No study is designed to do this, either.) The goal of scientific research is to accumulate to the point where it provides the "best light to go by when making decisions." Not perfect light, but better light than other ways of knowing provide. Each new study is designed to fill in a missing piece in the literature, not to mimic a forensic case. Judges, juries, and law enforcement officials need to weigh and sift this evidence to decide how relevant it is for any particular case. In sum, the concern for ecological validity will continue to motivate the expansion of naturalistic and laboratory studies so that they combine to cover all relevant factors that can be expected to influence children's suggestibility in the everyday world.

INDIVIDUAL DIFFERENCES IN SUGGESTIBILITY

Second, we think that the issue of individual differences in suggestibility will also continue to inspire research. The stakes in this research are high because of the need to develop an instrument that can measure the trustworthiness of eyewitnesses' reports. As our review showed, researchers have recently discovered a greater consistency for suggestibility than might be expected if it was completely situationally determined, because the same children who are the most suggestible in one situation appear to be the most suggestible in others, too (Scullin & Ceci, 2001; Scullin & Warren, 1999). This newer research does not imply that situational variables are unimportant, but rather that both situational and individual (trait) variables need to be considered. Much more research is needed to determine the relative contributions of individual and situational factors in producing false reports.

ALTERNATIVE MODELS OF MEMORY

Finally, we think that researchers will try to explore alternative models of memory (e.g., Glenberg, 1997). The current encoding–storage–retrieval model of memory follows the **information-processing** tradition in psychology where cognitive processes are modeled in terms of inputs and outputs. This approach, however, ignores the functional significance of memory. What does memory bring to our lives? How did the evolution of memory change the lives of the organisms on earth? These alternative approaches would allow us to move beyond studying memorization and the accuracy of memory. The questions they focus on are instead how memories form within the context of action, how they influence our behavior, and how their change reflects the requirements of the environment on our behavior. These new questions are already enriching our field both theoretically and methodologically.

DISCUSSION POINTS

1   Think about the distinction between recognition and recall. Can you explain why people often (rightly!) complain, "I can't remember names, but I never forget a face"?
2   What sort of items go into short-term memory, and which are likely to enter long-term memory?
3   Think about the difference between semantic and episodic memory.
4   Three factors that influence the development of memory are knowledge, strategies, and metamemory. What are the main characteristics of these different factors?
5   How do scripts, or scripted knowledge, influence the encoding, storage, and retrieval of an experience?
6   How competent as a witness can a child be, and what age changes are there in the accuracy of children's recall and testimony?
7   Why is suggestibility such an important factor in affecting the accuracy of children's testimony?

SUGGESTIONS FOR FURTHER READING

Bruck, M., & Ceci, S. J. (1999). The suggestibility of children's memory. *Annual Review of Psychology*, 50, 419–39.

Bull, R. (Ed.) (2001). *Children and the law: The essential readings*. Cambridge, MA, and Oxford: Blackwell.

Ceci, S. J., & Bruck, M. (1999). *Jeopardy in the courtroom: A scientific analysis of children's testimony*. Washington, DC: APA Books.

Cowan, N. (Ed.) (1997). *Memory development*. Hove: Psychology Press.

Schneider, W., & Pressley, M. (1997). *Memory development between two and twenty* (2nd ed.). Mahwah, NJ: Erlbaum.

chapter 13

Play and Peer Relations

Peter K. Smith

KEY CONCEPTS

ASSOCIATIVE ACTIVITY	PARALLEL ACTIVITY	SELF-SOCIALIZATION
COGNITIVE DEVELOPMENT	PEER	SEX-ROLE STEREOTYPES
CONTROL GROUP	PLAY HIERARCHY	SOCIAL LEARNING THEORY
COOPERATIVE ACTIVITY	PRETEND PLAY	SOCIODRAMATIC PLAY
CORRELATIONAL STUDY	PSYCHOPATHOLOGY	SOCIOMETRIC STATUS
DOMINANCE	RACIAL PREJUDICE	SOCIOMETRY
ETHNIC IDENTITY	ROUGH-AND-TUMBLE PLAY	STANDARDIZATION
GENDER IDENTITY	SCAFFOLDING	THEORY OF MIND
LONGITUDINAL DESIGN		

OVERVIEW

We all know that children play, but it has proved surprisingly hard to define play and to identify its functions. This chapter begins by distinguishing different types of play in early childhood: sensorimotor play, language play, and pretend play. Much play is social and soon takes place largely with peers and siblings. Thus, the approach taken here is to treat play in the context of peer relationships.

Interest in peers can be seen even before the toddler is 2 years old, and interaction with peers grows from that point on. Brothers and sisters are also important partners in social interaction and play, particularly if the age gap is small, and there is evidence that interaction with siblings can have important effects on cognitive development.

Once children are 2 or 3 years old, many of them go to nursery school or playgroup. During this period social participation increases, as children develop a degree of independence from parents and interact more with peers. The chapter reviews evidence on the different forms of play observed during this period and discusses the possible functions of these activities. There is evidence that sociodramatic play enhances language and cognition, and particularly children's knowledge of the minds of others. The functions of physical play are less clear, but may relate to development of muscle strength and establishment of the child's position in a dominance hierarchy.

The focus of the chapter then shifts to social relationships in the peer group, with particular emphasis on the reason for social rejection and its consequences. Children rejected by peers are often aggressive and may lack appropriate social skills. Closely related to this topic is friendship. Friendships are different from other peer relationships, involving more intense, intimate relationships, more cooperation and conflict resolution. It is widely argued that having friends helps to guard against loneliness, but providing conclusive evidence for the importance of friendship is surprisingly hard.

The chapter then considers sex differences in play and social behavior, reviewing the different factors – biological, social, and cognitive – that lead to establishment of these differences. This leads finally to the consideration of ethnicity, with an assessment of evidence regarding children's tendency to maintain segregation between racial and ethnic groups in their play activities. Such segregation and recognition of differences between groups can easily develop into prejudice, although multiracial curricula in the school years can do much to counteract this.

Introduction

In this chapter we will look at the development of play in childhood, and the role of play in social relationships, including friendship. We will discuss peer relations – social relationships with same-age children, usually classmates in school. This will mainly focus on friendship – what friendship is, and whether it is important in development. Other aspects of social relationships are discussed in chapter 14 (especially moral development) and chapter 18 (aggression and bullying).

The Beginnings of Play

The term "play" refers to behavior which is enjoyable, done for its own sake, but which does not have any obvious, immediate purpose. Examples of early play would be:

- an infant repeatedly dropping an object, even when handed it back;
- an infant banging objects together to make a noise;
- an infant babbling and cooing to herself, while lying in a cot;
- an infant laying a teddy down "in bed."

The first two of these would be sensorimotor play; the third, language play, the fourth, pretend play.

SENSORIMOTOR PLAY

Sensorimotor play refers to play with objects, making use of their properties (falling, making noises) to produce pleasurable effects – pleasurable for the infant, that is! The kinds of "secondary circular reactions" described by Piaget (see chapter 8) as part of his sensorimotor period appear to be playful in this way. This simple play with objects appears in the second half of the first year, but play with language and pretend play do not emerge until well into the second year, as sensorimotor development is completed.

PRETEND PLAY

Psychologists have made a lot of the study of **pretend play** – sometimes called *make-believe play* or, by Piaget, **symbolic play**. In pretend play, a child makes a nonliteral use of an object or action – that is, it does not mean what it usually means. Piaget (1951) was one of the first psychologists to describe the beginnings of pretend play in detail, by recording the behavior of his children. He noted that at the age of 15 months, his daughter Jacqueline put her head down on a cloth, sucked her thumb, blinked her eyes – and laughed. He interpreted this as Jacqueline pretending to go to sleep; indeed, she did similar actions with her toy animals a month or so later. Characteristically, young children do pretend actions first with themselves, then with a doll or teddy – a process called "decentration."

A lot of early studies of pretend play were carried out by watching a child when he or she was put with some objects in a laboratory play room. This had the advantage of a **standardized** procedure, but was rather unnatural. Basically, these were observations of solitary play. Such studies were put in perspective by Haight and Miller (1993). These investigators made videofilms of nine children playing at home; they started when the children were 12 months and continued until they were 48 months, a **longitudinal** study. While a minority of the pretend play they observed was solitary,

Plate 13.1 In pretend play, children may act out real-life situations, e.g., putting teddy to bed, or make believe that one object (e.g., a brick) is another (e.g., a car). Photograph © Heather Vickers.

the surprising finding they obtained was that about 75 percent of pretend play was social – first with mothers or parents, later with friends (peers).

Howes and Matheson (1992) have described stages in the development of social pretense. It appears that the mother (or older partner, perhaps a sibling) has a **scaffolding** role – supporting the play a lot at first, by for example suggesting and demonstrating actions. For instance, the mother might "give teddy a bath" and then hand teddy to the infant. Thus a lot of early pretend play by the child is largely imitative; it tends to follow well-established "scripts" or storylines, such as "feeding the baby," or "nursing the patient." In addition, realistic props, such as miniature cups, help to sustain pretend play. However, as children get to 3 or 4 years, they are less reliant on older partners and realistic props. They take a more active role in initiating pretend play; they adapt less realistic objects (a block could be a cup, for example), or even just imagine the object completely; and they show an awareness of play conventions and competently negotiate roles within play sequences.

Early Peer Relationships

In the first few years, parents and adults are very important in a child's life. They provide care and protection, and act as models for language use and for many kinds of behavior. A few adults, usually including parents, act as attachment figures, providing security for the infant. However, by the time the child is about 2 years old, **peers** – other children of about the same age – are becoming increasing sources of interest. Even at this age, children seem to be especially interested in peers. In a study of 12–18-month-old infants, two mother–infant pairs who had not previously met shared a playroom together. The infants touched their mothers frequently (remaining in proximity to them, as we would expect from attachment theory – see chapter 6), but *looked* most at the peer, who clearly interested them (Lewis, Young, Brooks, & Michalson, 1975).

Another study was made of French infants at 11 months and at 23 months (Tremblay-Leveau & Nadel, 1996). They put two toddlers together with a familiar experimenter in a play room. The researchers used this triadic situation to see how an infant would react to being left out when the adult interacted with the other infant. Some social interaction did occur just between the toddlers; but a toddler made much more effort to interact with the other toddler if the latter was playing with the experimenter! At 11 months this made the first toddler five times more likely to try to get into interaction; and at 23 months, the toddler was eight times more likely to do so.

Observations of under-2s in toddler groups – where mothers bring their infants to play together – show that the interactions between under-2s are brief, infrequent, and often consist of just looking at another child and perhaps smiling, or showing a toy, or making a noise (Mueller & Brenner, 1977). Infants at this age have not yet learnt many skills of social interaction. They can interact with adults, who support the interaction by responding appropriately and at the right time; but – as we discussed for social pretend play earlier – it takes a while for two infants to learn how to do this. There is some evidence that early peer experience in toddler groups or day nurseries can assist this development; in addition, infants who are securely attached to their mothers are more confident about exploring both objects and peers, and making new social relationships (Bretherton & Waters, 1985; Turner, 1991).

Are Siblings Important?

Parents are much older than their infants. J. Harris (1998) argues that adults are more or less a "different species" as far as infants are concerned! Peers are children of the same age – generally, within perhaps a year of one's own age. However, it is interesting to consider the impact of siblings (brothers and sisters). Not everyone has siblings, but the majority do. Usually, siblings differ in age by a few years. Although not exactly peers, they are often close enough in age, and similar enough in interests and developmental stages, to be an important social partner for the young child.

An older sibling may be ambivalent about a younger sibling, in a way in which a parent usually is not. Especially for the firstborn child in the family, the new brother or sister displaces them from being the center of attention in their parent's eyes. Although an older sibling can show great tolerance for younger ones, and act as an important model for more competent behavior (such as pretend play), studies in many societies agree that they can also show hostility and ambivalence (Eibl-Eibesfeldt, 1989).

In the UK, Dunn and Kendrick (1982) carried out a detailed study of sibling relationships. They made observations in the homes of 40 firstborn children living with both parents. At first visit, a new sibling was due in a month or so, and the first child was usually nearing his or her second birthday. After the birth of the sibling they made further visits, when the second child was about 1 month old, and again at 8 months and at 14 months. They found that many firstborns showed some signs of jealousy after the arrival of the new sibling. Much of this jealousy and ambivalence was directed toward parents, less as overt hostility to the infant, but some showed ambivalence or hostility, as the following extract of conversation shows:

Mother: I don't know what we're going to do, do you? [Baby is crying]
Child: Smack him.
Mother: He's too little to smack.
Child: Smack him.

Most of the firstborn children also showed a lot of interest and affection toward their new sibling. Dunn and Kendrick (1982) felt that the sibling relationship was one in which a range of powerful emotions may be aroused – envy, but love as well.

SIBLING RELATIONSHIPS AND THE DEVELOPMENT OF SOCIAL UNDERSTANDING

The subtitle of Dunn and Kendrick's (1982) book is "love, envy, and understanding." They argue that because the sibling relationship is both close and emotionally power-ful, it may be an optimal situation in which to learn understanding. Siblings seem to be learning how to frustrate, tease, placate, comfort, or get their own way with their brother or sister. Dunn and Kendrick (1982) relate one incident in which Callum (14 months old) repeatedly reaches for and manipulates some magnetic letters that his 3-year-old sister Laura is playing with on a tray. Laura repeatedly says "no" gently. Callum continues trying to reach the letters. Finally, Laura picks up the tray with the letters and takes it to a high table that Callum cannot reach. Callum is furious and starts to cry. He turns and goes straight to the sofa where Laura's comfort objects, a rag doll and a pacifier, are lying. He takes the doll and holds it tight, looking at Laura. Laura now gets very upset, starts crying, and runs to take the doll. Callum seems to have calculated how to annoy Laura so as to get his own back on her.

This behavior suggests an ability to take account of the likely mental state of another at a surprisingly early age, since **theory of mind** abilities are usually thought of as appearing at age 4 (see chapter 10). In this incident, the younger sibling wished to have a negative effect on his older sister; but the following incident shows empathic behavior, with an intention to help the sibling by alleviating distress. Fifteen-month-old Len has previously learnt that he can make his parents laugh by pulling up his T-shirt, sticking out his tummy, and walking in an odd way. When his older brother fell off the climbing frame and cried vigorously, Len watched solemnly and then approached him with the funny walk, calling out to his brother.

Observations such as these suggest a powerful role for siblings in social and **cognitive development**. However, children can learn social-cognitive skills with adults and peers as well as with siblings. There has been a large body of research on only children, including much research in China, where, because of the one-child policy, many children are only children. The consensus of evidence appears to be that only children do well on achievement and intelligence scores, and show no deficits in sociability or adjustment (Falbo & Polit, 1986). Probably, there are many ways of achieving social skills and competence; for a lot of children, siblings are a help here, but for those without siblings, other routes are available.

The Growth of Social Participation

At 2 or 3 years of age, many children start going to a nursery school or playgroup. They have begun to develop some independence from adults and are ready to interact with peers through play and other activities. From 2 to 4 years there is a great increase in what is called *social participation* – the extent to which children play interactively and cooperatively with others. This was first documented by Parten (1932) in her doctoral dissertation at the University of Minnesota – a classic study and one of the first generation of systematic studies of young children's social behavior. Parten observed 2- to 4-year-olds in nursery classes; she described how they might be unoccupied, an onlooker on others' activities, or, if engaged in an activity, they could be solitary, in **parallel activity** with others or in **associative** or **cooperative activity** with others. These categories of social participation are defined in table 13.1. Parallel activity may be a strategy used by children to get involved in group play. Parten found that the first four categories declined with age, whereas associative and cooperative activity, the only ones involving substantial interaction with peers, increased with age.

Table 13.1 Parten's categories of social participation

Category	Description
Unoccupied	Child is not engaged in any activity.
Onlooker	Child is just watching others, not joining in.
Solitary	Child plays alone, away from others.
Parallel	Child plays near other(s) with the same materials, but does not interact much – for example, playing independently at the same sandpit.
Associative	Child interacts with other(s) at an activity, doing similar things – for example, each adding building blocks to the same tower.
Cooperative	Child interacts with other(s) in complementary ways – for example, one child gets blocks and hands them to another child, who builds the tower.

If you watch preschool children, you will usually see just two or three children playing together. However, the size of groups of children playing together does tend to increase in older preschoolers and in the early school years. A study of more than 400 Israeli children aged 5–6 years in outdoor free play found a lot of group activity, with parallel activity becoming infrequent, while the size of groups in which children played increased (Hertz-Lazarowitz, Feitelson, Zahavi, & Hartup, 1981). By the middle school years, boys especially are playing in large groups as team games like football become popular. At early adolescence the nature of children's groups alters, with large same-sex cliques or gangs becoming common, changing again in later adolescence as heterosexual relationships become more important.

Social play

A lot of the time that preschool children are together they spend playing. Piaget (1951) described three main (though overlapping) stages in play – sensorimotor play with objects in infancy; symbolic play (fantasy or pretend play) from around 15 months to 6 years; and games with rules from around 6 years onwards; he linked these play stages to his stages of cognitive development (see chapter 8). Later, developing Piaget's ideas, Smilansky (1968) postulated four stages in the development of play, shown in table 13.2. Smilansky's main contribution was to add a stage of constructive play with objects – play that was more focused and mature than the sensorimotor play of infancy, but which was not pretend. Smilansky also popularized the idea of the importance of **sociodramatic play**; this is pretend play involving social role-playing in an extended story sequence, for example playing doctors and nurses and patients, or spacemen and aliens, or parents and children.

Rubin, Watson, and Jambor (1978) felt it would be useful to combine Parten's scheme of social participation (table 13.1) with Smilansky's scheme of play (table 13.2) to create a **play hierarchy**. This nested categorization means that you can watch a preschool child and categorize his or her play according to both social and cognitive dimensions, for example, solitary practice play or associative dramatic play. Categories

Plate 13.2 Playing doctors and patients is an example of sociodramatic play – pretend play that involves social role-playing in an extended story sequence. Photograph © Heather Vickers.

Table 13.2 Smilansky's four-sequence developmental model of play

Label	Description
Functional	Simple body movements or actions with objects, e.g., banging bricks.
Constructive	Making things with objects, e.g., building a tower with bricks.
Dramatic	Acting out roles in a pretend game, e.g., pretending to be a doctor.
Games with rules	Playing in a game with publicly accepted rules, e.g., football, hopscotch.

higher up either scale were argued to be more mature. This is useful for coding children's activities, but the nested hierarchy has two limitations. First, it implies a developmental progression that is not universally accepted; some solitary play can be quite mature, for example; and constructive play seems to coexist with dramatic play rather than precede it. Second, it omits important kinds of play, particularly physical activity play, **rough-and-tumble play** (friendly play-fighting with a partner), and language play.

Physical activity play

Although much play is with objects – especially play seen in laboratory play rooms with little space and many toys – in fact quite a lot of play involves gross physical activity, often without objects. In a review of what they argued was a neglected aspect of play, Pellegrini and Smith (1998) suggested there were three developmental phases in physical activity play. First were *rhythmical stereotypes*, bodily movements characteristic of babies such as kicking legs and waving arms. Then, during the preschool years, there is a lot of *exercise play* – running around, jumping, climbing – whole-body movements which may be done alone or with others. Overlapping with and succeeding this is *rough-and-tumble play*, most common in the middle school years.

Rough-and-tumble play

Rough-and-tumble play, or play-fighting, involves wrestling, grappling, kicking, tumbling and rolling on the ground, and chasing. These are activities which look like real fighting; in fact, they sometimes are mistaken by teachers and playtime supervisors, who may intervene to break up a "fight" only to be told, "we were only playing, Miss!" Rough-and-tumble play is common in the preschool years and especially in middle childhood. Observations in school playgrounds show that it takes up about 10 percent of playground time (Humphreys & Smith, 1987) – though this does depend on factors such as how soft or hard the play surface is! Children enjoy play-fighting, especially boys. It is characterized by laughter, self-handicapping (a stronger child does not necessarily "win"), restraint (not hitting or kicking hard or even making contact at all), and reversals (taking it in turns to be on top).

Sometimes playground supervisors clamp down on play-fighting because they think it often leads to real fighting. This appears to be a misconception, perhaps based on the behavior of a small number of children. Both interviews with children and observations in playgrounds show that, most of the time, rough-and-tumble play does not lead to real fighting (Schaefer & Smith, 1996). Although the great majority of rough-and-tumble is really playful, occasionally things can go wrong and a fight develops or someone gets hurt. This could happen for two main reasons: one would be lack of social skills – a play signal such as a playful punch is misinterpreted; the other would be deliberate manipulation or cheating – one child deliberately abuses the play expectations of the other to inflict hurt while "on top." The likelihood of this happening seems more common in sociometrically rejected children (Pellegrini, 1994; we examine peer rejection later in this chapter); indeed, this behavior could contribute to their dislike by classmates.

Functions of Play

Is play important in development? This has turned out to be a controversial question that has yet to be resolved. Most of the relevant research has been on play with objects – what Smilansky would call constructive play and dramatic play. In fact, most research effort has been put into possible functions of sociodramatic play. In her book on this topic, Smilansky (1968) had argued that sociodramatic play was essential for normal development, and that if a child is deficient in it, intervention should be carried out in the preschool to encourage and enhance such play.

EFFECTS OF PLAY ON LANGUAGE AND COGNITION

Smilansky had observed that immigrant children in Israeli preschools did not show much sociodramatic play, and were also behind in language and cognitive skills. Subsequently, other studies in the United States and elsewhere documented similar findings for children from disadvantaged backgrounds. This may be because these parents did not encourage or "scaffold" pretend play at home, and provided an unstimulating environment for their children. Of course, it might be that an unstimulating environment leads to both poor play skills and poor linguistic and cognitive skills. Nevertheless, Smilansky and others hypothesized that sociodramatic play in itself contributed to development (or, in the strong version of the argument, was essential for it), because of the rich practice in language skills, social negotiation, and object transformation that such play entailed.

As a result, a number of intervention studies were carried out to test the hypothesis. These could be done because Smilansky, and many other investigators, found that it is quite possible to get children to do more and better sociodramatic play by having preschool teachers and staff model such play, encourage it, take children on visits (e.g., to hospitals, zoos), and provide suitable props and equipment. This was called play tutoring; it led to studies following the broad design shown in table 13.3. Differences between pre- and post-test performance on various developmental tasks were compared for children who received some kind of play tutoring and those who did not; the latter, the **control group**, was to allow for effects of age and general preschool experience. If the play-tutored children improved more, this was felt to be strong evidence that sociodramatic play really was important.

For quite some time through the 1970s and 1980s, a number of studies of this kind got positive results. Indeed, it seemed that almost whatever tests the researchers used, play-tutored children improved more! This seemed too good to be true. Subsequently, some investigators argued that these earlier results were confounded by two main problems. First, the design in table 13.3 is flawed. Generally the play-tutored children got extra intervention from adults – more verbal and educational stimulation than the control group. Second, most studies did not use "blind" testing, so that the testers knew which condition the child was in and might have been subconsciously influenced by this. When further experiments were run to control for these two mistakes, the benefits of play tutoring were not found (Christie & Johnson, 1985; Smith, 1988). It seemed that the general adult stimulation was important, rather than specifically the pretend play.

Table 13.3 Design of play-tutoring studies

Play-tutored group	*Control group*
Pretests carried out on social, cognitive, linguistic skills.	
Children receive extra tutoring: support and encouragement in social pretend play.	Children follow the normal curriculum with no special emphasis on social pretend play.
Post-tests carried out on social, cognitive, linguistic skills.	

PLAY AND THEORY OF MIND

More recently, it has been argued that pretend play is important for development of theory of mind skills (see chapter 10). Pretend play and theory of mind do both get going properly at around 4 years of age, and pretend play does seem to exercise a child's understanding of a play partner's understanding – of the play convention, agreement on pretense, etc. Also, children who score highly on theory of mind tasks tend to be good at pretend play (Taylor & Carlson, 1997). However, positive correlations might be due to a third variable, such as intelligence; and the link to theory of mind remains disputed (Lillard, 1993). Well-designed experimental studies might give more informative evidence (for an example, see Key Study 1 at the end of this chapter).

FUNCTIONS OF PHYSICAL PLAY

Less attention has been paid to physical activity play. Pellegrini and Smith (1998) discuss the evidence that physical activity play is useful for developing muscle strength and stamina. Particularly controversial is the role of rough-and-tumble play. It is not yet clear what function this play may have, but it appears similar to the kinds of play-fighting seen in many species of mammals – kittens and puppies, for example. Most likely, it helps develop physical strength for skills such as fighting, and especially as children approach adolescence, it may help children realize their own strength and that of others and establish their position in a **dominance** hierarchy. Dominance refers to being able to take precedence over another child, or beat them in a fight or conflict, or gain competitive access to resources. A dominance hierarchy refers to children's recognition of an ordering with respect to dominance. Dominance relationships appear to become more important in adolescence, especially in boys' peer groups, and boys may use play-fighting to test out others and try to improve their own status without actually fighting (Pellegrini & Smith, 1998).

Social Status and Sociometry: The Measurement of Social Relationships in the Peer Group

We saw earlier how the work of Parten and others described social participation in preschool children. By the time they are in school, children mix with large peer groups, and social relationships are an important part of their life. Some children are popular, others are disliked by peers generally. Rather separately from popularity, some children have close friends, others are lonely. How can we find out about these patterns of relationships?

This can be done by observation. For example Clark, Wyon, and Richards (1969) observed nursery school children to record who was playing with whom, and constructed *sociograms* (an example is shown in figure 13.1). The large concentric circles show the number of play partners a child has. Each symbol represents a child, with circles being girls, triangles boys. The number of lines joining two children

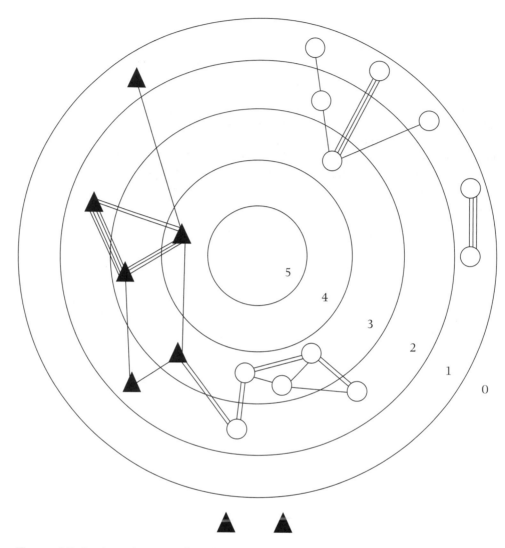

Figure 13.1 A sociogram of a class of preschool children: circles represent girls, triangles boys (from Clark et al., 1969). Reprinted with permission.

represents the percentage of observations on which they were seen playing together. In the class shown here, there is one rather popular boy with four friends, central to a loose association of all the boys, except for two who are "isolates" with no clear partners. There are three groups of girls, one of five girls loosely linked to the boys, another group of five, and a pair. This diagram allows one to see the social structure in a group of children at a glance.

The general technique here is called **sociometry**. Although observations can be used to get sociometric data, for reasons of time and also to get more information, interviews are often used. For example, each child might be asked, "Who are your best friends?" or "Who are the three classmates you like most?" This *nomination* data can also be plotted on a sociogram. If Susan chooses Elisabeth as a best friend, but Elisabeth does not choose Susan, this can be indicated by an arrow from Susan to Elisabeth; if the choice is reciprocated, the arrow would point both ways on the sociogram.

It is also possible to ask children, "Who are the three classmates you like least?" There may be ethical objections to this, as such questions might bring about increased negative behavior to unliked peers, but so far this has not been found (Hayvren & Hymel, 1984). The combined procedure – asking children for names of both liked-most and liked-least classmates – was used by Coie, Dodge, and Coppotelli (1983) in a seminal article, which defined what are called *sociometric status types*. These researchers found that they needed a two-dimensional rather than a one-dimensional model of social relationships. The older, one-dimensional model was from lonely to popular – for example, children high or low on Parten's social participation scale. A two-dimensional model was needed, Coie et al. argued, because they found that the children who got a lot of "liked most" nominations from classmates were not necessarily the opposite of those who got a lot of "liked least" nominations; some pupils got a lot of both kinds, and some got few of either kind. So, they devised a five-category model, of popular, controversial, rejected, neglected, or average children, according to whether they are high or low on positive and on negative nominations (see figure 13.2).

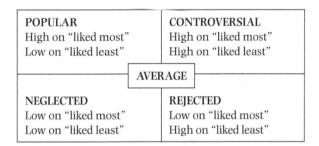

Figure 13.2 Sociometric status categories (based on Coie, Dodge, & Coppotelli, 1983).

CONSEQUENCES OF SOCIOMETRIC STATUS

Does it matter which sociometric status group a child is in? A number of studies suggest possible problems with being in rejected status. In young children, poor social skills in joining play may lead to peer rejection. Dodge, Schlundt, Shocken, and Delugach (1983) looked at how 5-year-olds attempted to get into ongoing play between two other children. Children who were of popular status waited and watched, and then got to join in by making group-oriented statements; neglected children tended to stay at the waiting and watching stage, while rejected children tended to try disruptive actions such as interrupting the play. In an observational study of 8- to 9-year-olds in US playgrounds, Ladd (1983) found that rejected children spent less time in co-operative play and social conversation than did average or popular children, and more time arguing and fighting; they played in smaller groups, and with younger or with less popular companions. And at 11 to 13 years, a study by Wentzel and Asher (1995) found that rejected children often did poorly at school work; interestingly, neglected children were quite well motivated and liked by teachers.

REASONS FOR PEER REJECTION

Aggression and disruptive behavior

Children can be disliked and peer-rejected for different reasons, but the most common reason seems to be because of being aggressive and disruptive (as in the study by Pellegrini referred to earlier, in which rejected children often "cheated" in play-fighting). In a large study in the Netherlands of 5- to 7-year-old boys, nearly half the rejected children were categorized as "aggressive-rejected," being impulsive, dishonest, and noncooperative. The next largest category was "rejected-submissive," children who were shy but not particularly aggressive (Cillessen, van IJzendoorn, van Lieshout, & Hartup, 1992). In the Wentzel and Asher study, it was only the aggressive-rejected children who had problematic academic profiles.

This picture of rejected children may become more complicated by adolescence. Studies with adolescents suggest that aggressive pupils may associate together in anti-social cliques or gangs, which reject academic values. Such pupils may be disliked by many, but are liked or popular within their own group (Cairns, Cairns, Neckerman, Gest, & Gariépy, 1988; and see chapter 16).

Lack of social skills

Children who are rejected in the middle school years may be in need of help – probably more than those who simply keep a low profile and are ignored or neglected. The findings above suggest that rejected children are lacking in some social skills. Dodge, Pettit, McClaskey, and Brown (1986) suggested that the social skills of peer inter-action can be envisaged as an exchange model, with five steps. Suppose child A is interacting with child B. The five steps for child A are:

1 encode the incoming information – perceive what child B is doing;
2 interpret this information;
3 search for appropriate responses;
4 evaluate these responses and select the best;
5 enact that response.

Child B engages in a similar process with respect to child A.

Given this model, it might be possible to find out if rejected children lack skills at certain stages in the process. There is some evidence for this. For example, aggressive children have been found to misinterpret others' behavior (stage 2) and to readily select aggressive responses (stage 4). Evidence relating to the model is reviewed by Crick and Dodge (1994).

However, not all behavior labeled as maladjusted may be due to lack of social skills. Some rejected children may be simply reacting to exclusion by the popular cliques and would not necessarily be rejected or lacking in social skills in other situations outside the classroom. Also, some aggressive children may be quite skilled at manipulating others. A study of English children aged 7 to 11 years by Sutton, Smith, and Swettenham (1999) found that children nominated by others as ringleader bullies (chapter 18) actually scored particularly highly on theory of mind tasks (chapter 10); although these children did lack empathy, they were skilled at knowing how to hurt others with little risk of retaliation or detection by adults. At times, good social skills can be put to antisocial ends.

Following the model that rejected (and, perhaps, neglected) children lack social skills, attempts have been made by psychologists to help improve social skills by training children: for example, by providing training in sharing, negotiating, joining in, and being assertive but nonaggressive. Some of these methods have had some success; see Malik and Furman (1993) for a review.

Friendship

A related research area to that of sociometric status is friendship. However, it is not quite the same; sociometric status refers to the general degree of being liked or disliked in the peer group, whereas friendship refers to some close association between two (or more) children. We tend to conceive of friendship as implying closeness and trust – psychological characteristics. For a preschool child, it is something more straightforward – if you ask, "what is a friend?," he or she is likely to reply, "someone who plays with you." Bigelow and La Gaipa (1980) studied understanding of friendship in 6- to 14-year-old children in Canada and Scotland. They found three stages in expectations of friendship. From 6 to 8 years, friendship was seen as based on common activities, living nearby, having similar expectations. From 9 to 10 years, shared values, rules, and sanctions became more important. From 11–12 years, a conception of friendship based on understanding and self-disclosure, as well as shared interests, emerged – similar to how adults usually describe friendship. These and other studies suggest a shift from physical to more psychological ideas of friendship during the middle school years, with intimacy and commitment becoming important in adolescence.

Not surprisingly, friends tend to be similar in many respects. A study carried out in the Netherlands, with pupils aged 9 to 13 years, found that children were more similar to friends than to nonfriends on a range of characteristics – such as being cooperative, or shy, or starting fights, being helpful or sociable. This was true whether the characteristics were rated by the child him- or herself, or by classmates (Haselager, Hartup, van Lieshout, & Riksen-Walraven, 1998).

Most children have friends, and usually one or a few best friends. A question that has intrigued psychologists for some time is whether having a friend or friends is important for some aspects of healthy development and well-being. An American psychotherapist, Harry Stack Sullivan, had argued back in the 1950s that having at least one best friend or "chum" was very important for preadolescent children, and that without this a child would feel lonely, lack feelings of competence or self-worth, and be more at risk of later maladjustment and poor mental health (Sullivan, 1953). We will look at some of the relevant evidence for this.

WHAT IS SPECIAL ABOUT FRIENDS?

Part of the answer to the issue of what is important about friendship is to see how relations and activities with friends actually differ from those with nonfriends. Newcomb and Bagwell (1995) reviewed a large number of studies and concluded that interactions between friends showed four features compared to interactions between nonfriends:

1   More intense social activity; friends play together more.
2   More reciprocity and intimacy in interactions.
3   Although there may be conflicts with friends, as with nonfriends, there is more frequent conflict resolution between friends.
4   More effective task performance; in joint or cooperative tasks, friends help each other better and criticize each other more constructively.

An example of this kind of research comes from a study of 8-year-old Italian children (Fonzi, Schneider, Tani, & Tomada, 1997). Friendship pairs were compared with pairs of nonfriends in two structured tasks designed to simulate real-life situations of

Figure 13.3 A car-racing task (from Fonzi et al., 1997, figure 1, p. 499). Reprinted by permission of the Society for Research in Child Development.

potential conflict, for example where equipment had to be shared, or turns had to be taken (one task is shown in figure 13.3). Friends were more effective about this in a number of ways: they made more proposals than nonfriends, spent more time negotiating sharing arrangements, and were more able to make compromises. Those friendship pairs that were stable through the school year also showed more sensitivity in negotiations.

WHY IS IT IMPORTANT TO HAVE FRIENDS?

Hartup (1996) suggests that there are three important factors to consider:

1   having friends;
2   having high-status friends;
3   having good-quality friendships.

It may be that, while having a good friend may protect against loneliness, the other factors are also influential. For example, research on children who are victims of school bullying suggests that they may be low on all three of the above, but especially that if they have friends, these friends may also be low status (maybe victims too) and the friendships are of low quality, lacking trust and reciprocity; the result is that these friends either cannot or do not give much help when one is in trouble (for example, being bullied); see Smith, Shu, and Madsen (2000), and chapter 18.

While it seems likely that having friends is important for a child's development, it is difficult to prove this. Parker and Asher (1987) reviewed a large number of relevant studies which had data on peer relationships and friendships in childhood, and three main kinds of later outcome: dropping out of school early; being involved in juvenile and adult crime; and adult **psychopathology** (mental health ratings, or needing psychiatric help of any kind). They found a consistent link between low peer acceptance (or having few friends) and dropping out of school early; and between aggressiveness at school and juvenile/adult crime. The data on effects of shyness/withdrawal and on predictors of adult psychopathology were less consistent, with any links unproven at present. Being **correlational**, these studies do not prove a causal effect, but they certainly suggest it. Key Study 2 at the end of this chapter details research (subsequent to the Parker & Asher review) which supports the long-term importance of school friendships. No one study can be conclusive here, but many researchers believe that having good friends is a causal factor of importance, and that children lacking friends need help of some kind to remedy this.

Sex Differences in Play

Boys and girls obviously differ substantially in play and social behavior, especially in the school years (Archer & Lloyd, 1986; Golombok & Fivush, 1994). This starts at preschool if not before. Observations of 2- to 4-year-olds have found that boys tend to prefer playing with transportation toys, blocks, and activities involving gross motor activity such as throwing or kicking balls, or rough-and-tumbling; girls tend to prefer dolls, and dressing-up or domestic play. Many activities, however, do not show a sex preference at this age.

Even in nursery school, children tend to select same-sex partners for play (see figure 13.1 for example), and by the time children are getting into team games at about 6 or 7 years, sex segregation in the playground is much greater. Boys tend to prefer outdoor play and, later, team games, whereas girls prefer indoor, more sedentary activities, and often play in pairs. Boys more frequently engage in both play-fighting and in actual aggressive behavior. Girls tend to be more empathic, and remain more oriented toward adults (parents and teacher) longer into childhood. In a study of 10–11-year-old children in American playgrounds, Lever (1978) found that boys more often played in larger mixed-age groups, while girls were more often in smaller groups of same-age pairs. Boys liked playing competitive team games that were more complex in their rules and role structure, and which seemed to emphasize "political" skills of cooperation, competition, and leadership in their social relations. Girls put more emphasis on intimacy and exclusiveness in their friendships.

Maccoby (1998) has summarized these sorts of sex differences into three main phenomena:

1 *Segregation*: a strong tendency for children to play with others of their own sex from 3 years onwards.
2 *Differentiation*: different styles of interaction in boys' and girls' groups.
3 *Asymmetry*: boys' groups are both more cohesive and more exclusionary than girls' groups.

Explanations of sex differences

Biological factors

It seems almost certain that sex hormones have some effect on behavior (Collaer & Hines, 1995). In normal fetal development male sex hormones predispose boys to become more physically active and interested in rough-and-tumble play. This is strongly suggested both by animal studies and also by evidence from human children who are exposed accidentally to unusual concentrations of sex hormones. It is also consistent with evidence that such sex differences appear early in life, and in most human societies.

Social learning

However, biological factors do not in themselves explain the process of **sex-role identification** and the variations in sex roles in different societies. Bandura (1969) argued that children are molded into sex roles by the behavior of adults, especially parents and teachers. This **social learning theory** approach postulates that parents and others reward or reinforce sex-appropriate behavior in children; for example, they may encourage nurturant behavior in girls, and discourage it in boys. Children may also observe the behavior of same-sex models and imitate them; for example, boys might observe and imitate the behavior of male figures in movies and television in their playful and aggressive behavior.

Barry, Bacon, and Child (1957) made a survey of the anthropological literature on childrearing in 110, mostly nonliterate, societies. In more than 80 percent of societies, girls more than boys were encouraged to be nurturant, whereas boys more than girls were subject to training for self-reliance and achievement. In many societies responsibility and obedience were also encouraged in girls more than boys. Pressure for sex-typing is especially strong in societies where male strength is important for hunting or herding; it is less strong in societies with small family groups where sharing of tasks is inevitable.

Cognitive-developmental interpretations

While reinforcement does seem to have some effect, a number of studies suggest that it is not the whole story (Fagot, 1985). For example, in nursery schools teachers generally reinforce quiet, "feminine" behaviors, and do not reinforce rough-and-tumble play. But this does not stop boys doing rough-and-tumble! In fact, boys seem to be influenced by other boys, and girls by other girls. The cognitive-developmental approach in this area argues that the child's growing sense of **gender identity** – the awareness that one is a boy, or a girl – is crucial. Children attend to and imitate same-sex models, and follow sex-appropriate activities, because they realize that this is what a child of their own sex usually does. Maccoby and Jacklin (1974) called this **self-socialization** since it does not depend directly on external reinforcement.

A study by Martin, Fabes, Evans, and Wyman (1999) illustrates this approach. They questioned and observed children aged 3 to 6 years of age in the United States. All children held gender-typed beliefs about what behaviors and play partners were appropriate for each sex, and these beliefs became stronger with age. They believed that other children would be more likely to approve of their behavior when they played with same-sex peers, and this belief too became stronger with age. Children themselves preferred to play with same-sex peers; and, those who held stronger beliefs about gender-appropriate behavior also showed the most sex-segregated play preferences. Although both biology and adult reinforcement have influences on sex differences, it does seem as though the direct influence of the peer group is a very powerful one (Maccoby, 1998).

Ethnicity

Besides differing by gender, people differ in terms of their racial or ethnic group; both are often obvious from physical characteristics such as hair and skin color and facial appearance. Besides country of origin, other important dimensions of difference are language (e.g., English Canadian and French Canadian) and religion (e.g., Muslim Indian and Hindu Indian). By 4 or 5 years children make basic discriminations, for example between black and white, and during the next few years more difficult ones, such as Anglo and Hispanic. By around 8 or 9 years, children understand that **ethnic identity** remains constant despite changes in age or superficial attributes such as clothing.

Children seem to show some segregation by race as well as by gender, for example in playground friendships. In a study in the United States by Finkelstein and Haskins (1983), 5-year-old black and white children showed marked segregation by race, which increased during a year in kindergarten. In older children too, segregation by race is noticeable (Boulton & Smith, 1993). However, segregation by race seems to be less marked than segregation by sex in the middle school period. It is also not so evident amongst boys as girls, perhaps because boys play in larger groups than girls; when playing football, for example, ethnic group may be ignored in order to fill up a team with the requisite number of good players.

Preference is not the same as prejudice, which implies a negative evaluation of another person on the basis of some general attribute (for example sex, race, or disability). **Racial prejudice** means a negative evaluation of someone as a consequence of his or her being in a certain racial or ethnic group. Prejudice can be measured by asking children to put photos of other children from different ethnic groups along a scale of liking (Aboud, 1988), or to assign positive adjectives such as "works hard" and "truthful," or negative adjectives such as "stupid" or "dirty," to all, some, one, or none of the photos representing different ethnic groups (Davey, 1983). These studies suggest that prejudice increases from 4 to 7 years, mainly at the expense of minority ethnic groups. During middle childhood, white children tend to remain prejudiced against black or minority group children, while the latter show a more mixed pattern but often become more positive to their own group.

Aboud (1988) argued that from 4 to 7 years, children perceive other ethnic groups as dissimilar to themselves, and because of this tend to have negative evaluations of them. From 8 years onward, children become able to think more flexibly about ethnic differences, and in terms of individuals rather than groups, so that their earlier prejudice can be modified. Schools have been a focus for work to reduce racial prejudice in children. A multiracial curriculum approach which emphasizes the diversity of racial and cultural beliefs and practices and gives them equal evaluation may help in this process. Procedures such as *Cooperative Group Work* (Cowie, Smith, Boulton, & Laver, 1994) bring together children of different race (and sex) in common activities, and may help to reduce ethnic preference and prejudice in the classroom.

SUMMARY AND CONCLUSIONS

Although early important influences on the social development of the child are parents or caregivers, as the child enters school and progresses to middle childhood the influence of peers becomes very important. Much play is social, and sociodramatic play and rough-and-tumble play occupy much time in the kindergarten and early school years, moving into play with rules by middle childhood. Social participation and friendships with peers, and sociometric status in the peer group, probably are very influential for the course of later development. Children pay great attention to age-mates and are influenced by them in terms of appropriate behavior, sex segregation, and choice of activities. In fact, J. Harris (1995, 1998) has argued that once children go to school, by far the dominant influence on behavior is the peer group rather than the parents; she believes that by then, the direct influence of parents is largely limited to genetic factors passed on, such as temperament.

Many researchers believe that the family continues to exert an influence, for example through patterns of attachment, management practices of parents (including a direct influence on the out-of-school peer network), and the effects of siblings. The older child, too, is increasingly aware of, and influenced by, the expectations of society for someone of their age, gender, ethnicity, and social background, as mediated by peers and by socializing influences such as schools and the mass media. By adolescence, the separation from parents is becoming more complete, and the young person is moving toward a mature sense of identity and social being.

DISCUSSION POINTS

1 What factors assist the development of pretend play?
2 Does play have an important or essential role in development?
3 How can we measure friendship?
4 How would you design a study to ascertain whether the quality of childhood friendships is important in later life?
5 What is meant by sociometric status, and why might it be important to measure it?

SUGGESTIONS FOR FURTHER READING

Aboud, F. E. (1988). *Children and prejudice.* Oxford: Blackwell.

Blatchford, P. (1998). *Social life in school.* London: Falmer Press.

Bukowski, W. M., Newcomb, A. F., & Hartup, W. W. (Eds.) (1996). *The company they keep: Friendship in childhood and adolescence.* Cambridge & New York: Cambridge University Press.

Dunn, J. (1988). *The beginnings of social understanding.* Oxford: Blackwell.

Hellendoorn, J., van der Kooij, R., & Sutton-Smith, B. (Eds.) (1994). *Play and intervention.* Albany: SUNY Press.

Maccoby, E. E. (1998). *The two sexes: Growing up apart, coming together.* Cambridge, MA: Harvard University Press.

Pellegrini, A. D., & Blatchford, P. (2000). *The child at school: Interactions with peers and teachers.* London: Arnold.

Power, T. (2000). *Play and exploration in children and animals.* Mahwah, NJ: Erlbaum.

Schneider, B. H. (2000). *Friends and enemies: Peer relations in childhood.* London: Arnold.

Slee, P. T., & Rigby, K. (Eds.) (1998). *Children's peer relations.* London: Routledge.

Singer, D., & Singer, J. (1991). *The house of make-believe.* Cambridge, MA: Harvard University Press.

KEY STUDY 1
Constructing understandings through play in the early years
by Sue Dockett
International Journal of Early Years Education, 6 (1998), 105–16

This intervention study examined the issue of whether pretend play may facilitate theory of mind skills. It was carried out in Australia, at a preschool in Sydney, over one term. There were 33 children aged around 4 years, of whom 15 attended in the mornings and 18 in the afternoons. The design was a standard pretest/post-test format with an intervention. During the first three weeks of pretest, each child was observed to record the quality of their play – particularly, the amount and complexity of shared pretend play. Also, each child was given a range of theory of mind assessments appropriate for this age.

The four-week intervention was carried out with the morning group, taking pizzas as a theme that could involve both boys and girls. There was a visit to a pizza restaurant where the chef demonstrated how pizzas were made, followed by designing a pizza area in the preschool and centering a lot of play and activities around this. Teachers took opportunities to extend such play. Meanwhile, the afternoon group acted as a control, following the normal curriculum. In the final three weeks of post-test, the observations of play were repeated, and the theory of mind assessments were given both immediately after the intervention stopped (immediate post-test), and again three weeks later (delayed post-test).

Using the statistical test known as *analysis of variance*, changes in the intervention group and the control group were compared, taking account of the child's sex. It was found that the amount and complexity of shared pretend had – as intended – increased in the intervention group, but not in the control group. During post-test (when the pizza activities had stopped), the intervention group children did more make-believe with objects, actions, and situations, and talked more about pretend activities.

Although the control group showed some slight increases in the theory of mind tasks, these were small and not statistically significant. By contrast, the intervention group children showed substantial and significant increases on these tasks, including tests of false belief, representational change, and the appearance–reality distinction. These increases were maintained from the immediate post-test to the delayed post-test. Dockett argued that the social negotiations and verbal communications in the shared pretense had helped develop the theory of mind skills of the intervention group children (at an age, around 4 years, when these first-order theory of mind skills are on the threshold of being acquired).

The experimental design is a powerful one for trying to establish causal relations, making this study perhaps the best evidence for a link from pretend play to theory of mind. However, the sample is small and the two groups were not closely matched, so replication is important. In addition, the testing was not done blind to condition (whether the child was intervention or control); there is a possibility of unconscious experimenter bias in such situations, and ideally testing is done with the tester unaware of which condition a child has experienced.

KEY STUDY 2
Preadolescent friendship and peer rejection as predictors of adult adjustment
by Catherine L. Bagwell, Andrew F. Newcomb, and William M. Bukowski
Child Development, 69 (1998), 140–53

This study was carried out in the midwest United States. Some 12–13 years previously, the researchers had made a study of fifth grade (10-year-old) students in school. Now, they contacted some of these students again as young adults (aged 23 years). The aim of the study was to see if friendships and peer rejection at school were related to adjustment in adult life. This is therefore a longitudinal, follow-up study.

At school, 334 students had taken part, being assessed twice over a one-month interval. They were each asked to name their three best friends, and the three classmates they liked least, of the same sex. The combination of scores could be used to calculate peer rejection. Subsequently, the researchers formed two contrasting subgroups based on these data. The *friended* subgroup had a stable, mutual best friend at this time. Stable meant they chose the same best friend (as one of three) at both assessments; and mutual meant that this choice was reciprocated (the friend also chose the first child) at both time points. Fifty-eight children fitted these strict criteria. The *chumless* subgroup did not receive any reciprocated friendship choice (out of three) at either assessment point. Fifty-five children fitted these criteria. From these subgroups the researchers contacted and interviewed 30 from each as young adults (15 males, 15 females in each subgroup).

At the follow-up, the young adults were given questionnaires to assess life status, self-esteem, psychopathological symptoms, and quality of adult friendships. The researchers were interested in whether the two groups differed on these outcome measures. They were also interested in whether the extent of peer rejection could explain any correlations, or whether it was the presence/absence of a stable reciprocal friend that was a more powerful predictor; for this purpose, they used regression analyses.

The main findings were as follows. First, peer rejection appeared the most important for predicting poorer life status, such as job aspiration and performance, or extent of social activities, although friendship did predict relations with family members. By contrast, it was friendship rather than peer rejection that predicted self-esteem as an adult. Both lack of friendship and peer rejection appeared to be predictors of psychopathological symptoms. Neither predicted quality of adult friendships in this sample.

The results suggest that both absence of a close friend in preadolescence and the experience of peer rejection have negative consequences for later well-being, but with each being stronger predictors of different aspects of later life. The researchers acknowledge that causal links cannot be proved by this correlational design, even given its longitudinal nature. It is possible that some other personality factor or underlying difficulty leads to both the friendship/peer difficulties and the later outcomes. However, as more research on effects of friendship accumulates, the causal hypothesis looks an increasingly plausible one.

chapter 14

Prosocial Tendencies, Antisocial Behavior, and Moral Development

Daniel Hart, Debra Burock, Bonita London, and Robert Atkins

KEY CONCEPTS

AFFECT
ANTISOCIAL BEHAVIOR
ATTENTION DEFICIT
   DISORDER
ATTRIBUTIONS
AUTONOMOUS STAGE OF
   MORAL REASONING
BEHAVIOR GENETICS
COGNITIVE FUNCTIONING
CONTINUITY IN SOCIAL
   DEVELOPMENT
DISTRIBUTIVE JUSTICE
EMOTION

EMOTION REGULATION
EXTRAVERSION
GENETIC PREDISPOSITION
HETERONOMOUS STAGE OF MORAL
   REASONING
HUMAN RIGHTS AND SOCIAL
   WELFARE MORALITY
INSTRUMENTAL MORALITY
INTERPERSONAL NORMATIVE
   MORALITY
IQ TEST
MORAL DILEMMAS
MORAL JUDGMENT STAGES

NEUROPSYCHOLOGICAL
   DEFICITS
PARENTAL STYLE
PEER
PERSONALITY TRAIT
PROSOCIAL BEHAVIOR
PUNISHMENT AND
   OBEDIENCE ORIENTATION
SOCIAL COGNITION
SOCIAL SYSTEM
   MORALITY
STANDARD DEVIATION
STANDARDIZED TEST

OVERVIEW

Without prosocial social interactions, no society or social group could survive. Similarly, no group could sustain itself over time if its members' social interactions with each other are principally aggressive and antisocial. In this chapter the authors begin with a description of behavior, thought, and emotion in early childhood, and end with an overview of prosocial and antisocial actions in adolescence. A major concern is theories and findings on moral reasoning and judgment. Some of the main themes and topics are the following:

- Discussion of the many influences that account for continuity and change in social and antisocial behavior, including biology, social interactions, relationships, and culture.
- Piaget's two stages of moral reasoning – the heteronomous and autonomous stages.

- Kohlberg's five stages of moral reasoning and claims about these stages.
- Factors that cause changes in moral judgment reasoning and that influence social development.

The development of prosocial and antisocial behaviors is a complex process, influenced by a range of factors which include personality, emotions, social relationships, social context, the ability to make moral judgments, and culture.

Introduction

Social life changes dramatically in the transition from infancy to childhood. As we have seen in chapter 7, for infants the social world is largely limited to interactions with parents and family members. This is so for obvious reasons. For example, the ability to communicate with others depends heavily on language skills, which are only in their nascent stages in infancy. The channels of communication that allow sophisticated, reciprocal exchanges between infants and caregivers – gestures, facial expressions, incompletely articulated words – require mutual experience in order to be decoded. The utterance "dah" from the mouth of a 14-month-old we have observed is correctly understood by his parents to mean "dog," but has little meaning to other adults. Not only do infants have difficulty in communicating with those outside their families, they are limited by immature motor skills from exploring new social contexts. Infants cannot walk around their neighborhoods to make new friends, for instance.

Children, on the other hand, live in social worlds that are diverse and complicated. The ability to speak enables each child to communicate with every child and adult in the community. Children play with each other, seek friends out in their neighborhoods, participate in social institutions such as schools, churches, teams, and community groups, look at billboards, listen to music, and watch television. The incredible range of social activities, relationships, and institutions in which the child is engaged requires, and produces, forms of thought, **emotion**, and behavior rarely seen in infancy.

The contrasts between infancy and childhood do not mean that at 18 months of age infants magically acquire capabilities that make them children. There is no single social skill, piece of knowledge, or type of interaction that divides the social world of infants and children, as every aspect of childhood has sophisticated precursors in infancy. However, the differences in social worlds noted earlier make some developmental tasks more apparent in childhood than in infancy. In this chapter, we use the development of **prosocial** and **antisocial** behavior as a lens to reveal some of the most significant transformations to occur in social development over the course of childhood. Using prosocial and antisocial behavior to focus our review means that other facets of social development are given short shrift. We do not give full attention to the development of friendships, the formation of political views, or transformations in relationships with parents – issues that are discussed elsewhere in this volume (see chapters 13, 15, and 16).

In this chapter we look closely at the development of morality, aggression, altruism, and similar qualities that have been at the heart of the most important considerations of childhood in western history. In the pages that follow, we shall describe the development of prosocial and antisocial behavior, focusing primarily on development as it typically occurs in western societies. Our account will begin with a description of behavior, thought, and emotion in very young children, and end with an overview of prosocial and antisocial action in late childhood and the transition into adolescence: the story of social development in adolescence is taken up in chapter 16. Important studies are described in some detail so that readers can judge for themselves the current state of research. We shall conclude with a discussion of how relationships and culture influence the course of development.

What Do Prosocial and Antisocial Mean?

Social interactions serve a variety of goals. Many social interactions seem intended to benefit others with no apparent instrumental benefit to the self: children are protected, the ill are cared for, donations to charities are made, help is offered to strangers, and so on. Without prosocial social interactions, no society or social group could survive. Similarly, no group can sustain itself over time if its members' social interactions with each other are principally aggressive and antisocial. Because prosocial and antisocial behavior are both complex and key to every society's survival, understanding the nature of socially appropriate behavior and the means necessary to foster its emergence are core issues for political philosophers, educators, government officials, and parents, as well as for those interested in child development.

It is easier to pronounce that prosocial and antisocial behaviors are essential for social organization than it is to characterize precisely what these terms mean. The definitional task is made particularly difficult by the fact that behaviors considered prosocial or antisocial in one culture might be viewed quite differently in another. Even within a culture it can be difficult to determine whether a specific behavior is genuinely prosocial. In the United States and the United Kingdom, for example, it was customary for many years for males to open doors for females. Whether this tradition promotes social organization – by reducing uncertainty about who should proceed first toward a door – or poisons egalitarian interaction by reinforcing stereotypes that women have significant physical limitations is not immediately discernible from an observation of the act. Indeed, as this example illustrates, a full understanding of prosocial behavior requires some knowledge of what an actor thinks and feels as the behavior is executed. To open a door with the intention of reinforcing a status hierarchy that places males above females is an act that is inconsistent with the notion of prosocial behavior. The centrality of intention and emotion in determining our interpretation of an act is also illustrated by the actions of mechanical and electronic devices. The actions of these devices are frequently helpful to us (computers "remind" the authors about meetings, for example), but, lacking the requisite characteristics of appropriate emotion and intention, these devices are not viewed as prosocial actors.

For these reasons, our definitions of *prosocial* and *antisocial* integrate *intentions*. Prosocial refers to behavior that is intended to promote the welfare of specific others or social groups, when this behavior has no instrumental benefits (or some cost) for the actor (for a similar definition of prosocial behavior, see Eisenberg & Fabes, 1998). Antisocial connotes actions that harm specific individuals or social groups, either when such harm is intended or when the harm is foreseen but judged irrelevant (for a related definition, see Loeber, 1985). The kinds of thoughts and emotions that define our topics of prosocial and antisocial action can occur outside of awareness (see Bargh & Chartrand, 1999, for a discussion of the automaticity of behavior). In other words, while children and adolescents often do engage in extended introspection or conversation about what is good, moral, kind, mean, cruel, hurtful, etc., much of their action in daily life occurs without conscious reflection on what should be done or how a situation makes one feel.

Continuity and Transformation

Thought and emotion not only serve to define prosocial and antisocial behavior, they are constructs that are used to explain why social development is characterized by both *continuity* and *transformation* (change). **Continuity** refers to the remarkable consistency in some facets of behavior across childhood and adolescence. For example, the tendency for children to be aggressive shows considerable continuity: the child who fights with other children a lot is likely to be the adolescent who is judged by **peers** to be aggressive. In fact, aggression shows greater continuity across childhood and adolescence than any other facet of social development (see Loeber & Stouthamer-Loeber, 1998, for a discussion of the continuity of aggression). In the sections that follow, we shall describe research demonstrating that the continuity of behavior across development is in part a consequence of characteristic patterns of emotion, **emotion regulation**, and cognition that are relatively stable over time.

Explanations for *transformation*, or qualitative change, in social behavior across childhood also must rely on cognition and emotion. As most adults know, there is something profoundly different about reasoning with a 5-year-old about keeping a promise than discussing the same topic with a teenager. Adolescents think and feel differently than young children about the social world, and these differences are reflected in prosocial and antisocial behavior.

Are Prosocial and Antisocial Poles on the Same Dimension?

To this point, we have discussed prosocial and antisocial behavior together, as if these two categories constitute the opposite poles of a single dimension. A dimensional perspective implies that an act can be placed on a continuum from "bad" antisocial behavior to "good" prosocial behavior. Placing antisocial and prosocial behavior on the same dimension implies that the same process gives rise to both. For example, one might hypothesize that the personality trait of *sympathy* determines where on the continuum a child will be found; a child high in sympathy is presumed to act prosocially while a child low in sympathy should act antisocially. In fact, as we shall see, this perspective is largely correct. Research findings do suggest that the factors that lead to prosocial behavior are also associated in the opposite way with antisocial behavior.

Plate 14.1 Aggression shows greater continuity across childhood and adolescence than any other facet of social development. Photograph © Heather Vickers.

Plate 14.2 Young children's social worlds include relationships with peers, and they display many prosocial behaviors such as comforting a friend in distress. Photograph © Heather Vickers.

However, not all antisocial behavior and prosocial behavior can be explained using the same processes. Later in the chapter, we shall describe research demonstrating that children and adolescents who are extremely antisocial are best understood in terms of processes with little relevance for understanding dedicated, committed, moral behavior. In other words, our view is that explaining why persons are at the extremes of the dimension requires consideration of psychological processes that are specific to each pole.

 ## *The Development of Prosocial and Antisocial Behavior and Thought: Early Childhood*

In contrast to infants, young children have the language and motor skills necessary to engage peers, older children, and adults in sustained social interaction. Three-year-olds talk, fight, play with their peers; they help one another and engage in long periods of synchronized interaction with adults; they think about what's wrong and what's fair; they experience sympathy and anger. The substantial differences in capacity between infants and young children to sustain social interaction mean that infants and young children experience different social worlds. Infants interact principally with their parents and family members. While young children obviously continue to have relationships with their parents, their social worlds begin to include relationships with peers, older children, teachers, and other adults. These relationships are contexts to learn about and to exhibit prosocial and antisocial action. Noteworthy as well is that in contrast to infants, young children are in direct contact with sources of cultural information. Many young children attend schools where information about culturally relevant prosocial and antisocial behavior is transmitted. In some western countries, children also receive messages about cultural expectations concerning prosocial and antisocial behavior from television. In the United States, apart from attending school, watching television occupies more of children's time than any other activity (Committee on Communications, 1995), and there is no question but that television presents messages about antisocial and prosocial behavior. In short, by the age of 3, children are capable of behavior that we have labeled prosocial and antisocial, and have had ample opportunity to learn about it in social and cultural context.

Personality traits and social behavior

Not only are prosocial and antisocial behaviors evident in early childhood, so are prosocial and antisocial *tendencies* in children, and it is from this latter point that we begin our exploration of social behavior in childhood. Observers can easily identify characteristic patterns of behavior in children 2 to 3 years of age. In other words, children clearly have **personality traits**. Personality traits are relatively stable dispositions to act in particular ways. It is certainly possible to distinguish among 3-year-olds by reference to personality traits: some are shy and others are outgoing; some are emotional, while others are calm; some are impulsive, while others are controlled. As children develop stable patterns of behavior, it is also possible to identify children who are characteristically antisocial and prosocial. Crick, Casas, and Mosher (1997) examined aggression, one form of antisocial behavior, in 3- and 4-year-old children in a preschool. Teachers were asked to rate children on items that tapped overt aggression (e.g., "kicks or hits others"), aggression in relation with others (e.g., "tries to get others to dislike others"), prosocial behavior (e.g., "is kind to others"), and depression (e.g., "looks sad"). Students in the preschool named three other students who "they liked to play with the most" (p. 582) and three students "they liked to play with the least."

Several findings from this study are of interest for our goals in this chapter. First, children who were judged to be high in overt and relational aggression were low in prosocial behavior. This is consistent with the dimensional perspective on prosocial and antisocial behavior, according to which being high in one characteristic necessarily means being low on the other. Second, children judged to be especially aggressive by the teachers were prone to rejection by their peers ("play with the least"). This finding demonstrates that individual differences in antisocial behavior are apparent to adults and to children by age 3; teachers and peers were selecting the *same* children in their identifications of those with difficulties in adjustment. Third, Crick et al. (1997) found that children who were judged to be high in negative emotions – high in depression – were more likely to be high in aggression than those low in negative emotions. This suggests that emotions, and emotion regulation, are important factors in understanding antisocial behavior.

Individual differences in antisocial and prosocial behavior

What leads to individual differences in antisocial and prosocial behavior? Is today's prosocial 3-year-old likely to be prosocial in school? No simple answer can be offered for these important questions. However, we do know that the emergence of stable personality traits in early childhood reflects the interaction of **genetic predispositions** with early experiences. While predispositions to personality traits in the form of temperamental variations (for example, precursors to shyness can be identified in the first year of life) and social experience are present in infants, it appears necessary for these to become integrated over the first several years of life in order for observers to recognize personality traits.

What implications does the emergence of personality traits have for the development of prosocial and antisocial behavior? As we shall discuss below, one very active line of investigation focuses on the organizing effects of early personality on both poles of the dimension.

Personality traits and antisocial behavior

There is a long history of research on antisocial behavior in childhood, and a related interest in childhood antecedents of adolescent delinquent behavior and adult criminality (see, for example, Glueck, 1982). We shall not review the history of this work, but instead will review some of the recent work on this topic.

The Dunedin study

One particularly informative study (Caspi, Henry, McGee, Moffitt, & Silva, 1995) has followed a group of children in Dunedin, New Zealand. A very valuable feature of this study is its sample. First, the sample of children studied is large, approximately 800 children, which makes it possible to detect relationships that might not be apparent in small samples. Second, the sample includes almost every child born in a single year in Dunedin, which means that the sample is not biased (toward wealthy families, for example). Because the sample is not biased, the results of the study of the individuals in the sample are more likely to generalize to other populations.

Caspi and his colleagues began measuring personality when the children in the sample were 3 years of age. An examiner rated each child on 22 personality items, such as emotional lability ("extreme instability of emotional responses," Caspi et al., 1995, p. 58), impulsivity ("explosive, uncontrolled behavior"), self-reliance ("overt confidence"), and passivity ("placid, sluggish"), after observing the child responding to a series of cognitive tests. The 22 personality items were condensed into three scales, representing three traits: *lack of control*, *approach*, and *sluggishness*. The lack of control trait incorporates the items for emotional lability, negative emotions, and restlessness; broadly, it reflects problems in emotion regulation; approach is constituted of items suggesting **extraversion**; and sluggishness is reflected in items focusing on passivity.

Years later, when the children were adolescents, their parents provided ratings of them on scales tapping antisocial, delinquent behavior such as bullying peers, teasing peers in order to hurt them, and so on. When correlations were calculated among the age 3 personality measures and the ratings of delinquency at age 12, the results suggested that children who exhibited a lack of control in early childhood were more likely than other children to exhibit antisocial behavior in adolescence. This suggests that antisocial behavior is connected to personality. Particularly relevant is that it is the personality trait most directly relevant to emotion – lack of control – that is associated with later antisocial behavior. That is, young children who had difficulty regulating emotion, and who were prone to experiencing negative emotions, were susceptible to the development of antisocial behavior.

As exciting as this finding is, it is extremely important to understand that early personality does not determine by itself whether antisocial behavior will occur later in childhood and adolescence. There is a great deal of development that occurs between early and late childhood, and the changes that occur may shift children off – and in some cases onto – the path to antisocial behavior.

PERSONALITY TRAITS AND PROSOCIAL BEHAVIOR

Personality traits and emotion regulation are important for prosocial behavior as well as for antisocial behavior. Some evidence for this claim can be adduced from investigations of the sample of children from New Zealand just discussed. Newman, Caspi, Moffitt, and Silva (1997) grouped the 3-year-olds into five groups according to their temperament scores on the three personality dimensions described earlier – *lack of control*, *approach*, and *sluggishness*. One of the five groups was composed of children who were impulsive and tended to have negative emotions; children in this group were labeled undercontrolled (the nature of the other groups is not important for our discussion here).

Eighteen years later, the participants nominated peers who rated the participants for a variety of characteristics, with a subset of these characteristics constituting a scale tapping prosocial tendencies (e.g., items included "reliable," "trustworthy").

Newman and her colleagues found that children who belonged to the undercontrolled group as 3-year-olds, in comparison to those in the other groups, were judged to be less prosocial at 21 years of age. This pattern suggests that positive emotions, self-control, and effective emotion regulation in childhood form part of the foundation on which adult prosocial tendencies are built.

Extreme antisocial behavior, and breaks in the continuum

The two reports of research on the Dunedin study considered above suggest that antisocial and prosocial behavior are poles of a single dimension, and can be understood to have roots in a single process, emotion regulation. One final study conducted with the Dunedin sample suggests that an account of consistently antisocial behavior requires constructs that are *not* part of the process that gives rise to prosocial behavior. Moffitt, Caspi, Dickson, Silva, and Stanton (1996) identified boys in the sample who were consistently highly antisocial from age 5 to age 18 (this pattern is so rare among girls that it was impossible to identify a group to study even in the large Dunedin sample). These were children who were rated as much higher (1+ **standard deviation**) than average on scales tapping aggression and delinquency at the majority of seven measurement points (5, 7, 9, 11, 13, 15, and 18 years of age). Only 32 (7 percent) of the boys in the sample were consistently high in antisocial behavior across childhood and adolescence; chronic antisocial behavior across childhood and adolescence is therefore very atypical. A second group of antisocial adolescents was formed of boys who were rated as much higher than average on the measures of adolescent delinquency, but who were not especially high on measures of antisocial behavior in childhood. There were 108 boys from the sample (24 percent) in this group. Moffitt and her colleagues compared the two groups on the measures of age 3 temperament described in previous paragraphs. The results indicated that the boys who were consistently high in antisocial behavior across childhood and adolescence had very difficult temperaments as 3-year-olds, while those who were only antisocial in adolescence (and not in childhood) had not been noticeably different from other children in terms of age 3 temperament.

Neuropsychological deficits in extremely antisocial children

Not only were the children who were consistently antisocial extremely irritable as 3-year-olds, they showed evidence of **neuropsychological deficits** when tested with a battery of tests at age 13. These tests tapped areas of **cognitive functioning** that are affected by brain injury. For example, some of the tests tapped verbal functioning (e.g., a vocabulary test), while others assessed mental flexibility (e.g., the Wisconsin Card Sort Test). Moffitt, Lynam, and Silva (1994) found that the consistently antisocial boys had scores that suggested neuropsychological problems. This finding is consistent with research with other samples, which has found considerable evidence that extreme antisocial behavior in childhood and adolescence is associated with **attention deficit disorder** (Hinshaw, Lahey, & Hart, 1993). Together these studies suggest that at least *some* extreme antisocial behavior may have roots in neurological deficits and extreme temperamental irritability.

Note that these constructs do not have polar opposites that can be used (sensibly) to characterize consistently prosocial individuals. It would not make sense to suggest that genuinely moral people are characterized by an absence of neurological deficits – because such a description would accurately characterize almost everyone! In this sense, then, extremely antisocial children and adolescents may best be considered as a separate category with unique features.

SUMMARY

Our account so far has focused on personality traits, particularly those related to emotion regulation, as they are related to prosocial and antisocial behavior over the course of childhood and adolescence. The results of the studies that have been reviewed suggest the following: (1) there is continuity in prosocial and antisocial behavior, with continuity in aggressive behavior particularly high, though change in all facets occurs; (2) antisocial behavior seems related to difficulties in regulating emotion, impulsivity, and high levels of negative **affect**; and (3) a small percentage of boys who are consistently antisocial may have extremely difficult temperaments and neurological deficits. What is missing in the account is a consideration of cognitive factors in antisocial and prosocial behavior, and it is to these that we turn in the next section. Conveniently, much of the research on cognitive factors has focused on older children and adolescents, and consequently our discussion moves on from toddlers to middle childhood.

The Development of Prosocial and Antisocial Behavior and Thought: Middle Childhood

MORAL REASONING AND JUDGMENT

Every discussion of the development of prosocial and antisocial behavior must cover the work of Piaget (1932) and Kohlberg (1984), because they founded the developmental investigation of moral thinking. Piaget was the first to study in a systematic way the moral judgments of children. To elicit moral judgment from children, Piaget presented them with hypothetical **moral dilemmas** and then asked children to make judgments. For example, children were told about two boys, one of whom breaks 15 teacups accidentally as he opens a door, and the other who breaks a single cup while sneaking into a cupboard to obtain forbidden sweets. Children were then asked to judge which of the two boys was "naughtier." Piaget found that younger children tended to judge the first child's action more harshly than the second child's, while older children showed the reverse.

PIAGET'S TWO STAGES OF MORAL REASONING

From responses to dilemmas like this one and to queries concerning the rules of the games that they played, Piaget concluded that younger children's moral judgment was governed by unilateral respect for adults and adults' rules, with little understanding of reciprocity or the intentions of others. Piaget called this the **heteronomous stage** since children judge that moral rules (and rules in general) are fixed and rigid and laid down by others ("hetero"), especially by persons in authority such as parents, and have to be obeyed. Consequently, young children judge that the greater damage in the teacup dilemmas constitutes a larger moral violation, because the intentions of the children will not be salient to the adults who observe the damage.

With experience, and Piaget believed as a result of interaction with peers, children develop a morality of cooperation and social exchange. This means that children come to understand that intentions matter, that roles can be reversed, and that moral conflicts must be resolved through discussion and compromise with peers. This latter form of reasoning Piaget termed the **autonomous stage** of moral reasoning since it comes from within, developing out of children's ability to put themselves in the position of others. Obligations, rights, and rules are no longer felt to be one-way or unilateral, but reciprocal. This stage becomes more common in late childhood, somewhere around age 10.

Kohlberg's research on moral judgment

Piaget's pioneering work was the starting point for Kohlberg's research on moral judgment, and it is Kohlberg's research that provides a backdrop for many of the recent investigations of moral judgment. Like Piaget, Kohlberg used moral dilemmas to elicit moral reasoning. The most famous of Kohlberg's dilemmas is about "Heinz":

> In Europe, a woman was near death from a very bad disease, a special kind of cancer. There was one drug that the doctors thought might save her. It was a form of radium that a druggist in the same town had recently discovered. The drug was expensive to make, but the druggist was charging ten times what the drug cost him to make. He paid $200 for the radium and charged $2,000 for a small dose of the drug. The sick woman's husband, Heinz, went to everyone he knew to borrow the money, but he could get together only about $1,000, which was half of what it cost. He told the druggist that his wife was dying and asked him to sell it cheaper or let him pay later. But the druggist said, "No, I discovered the drug and I'm going to make money from it." Heinz got desperate and broke into the man's store to steal the drug for his wife. (Kohlberg, 1981, p. 12).

Kohlberg's five stages of moral reasoning

Children, adolescents, and adults were asked to judge whether Heinz's action was moral, and to justify their judgments. Kohlberg and his colleagues (Colby, Kohlberg, Gibbs, & Lieberman, 1994) identified five **stages**, or patterns, of judgment revealed in reflections about the dilemmas (a sixth stage, not clearly evident in the research but theoretically relevant, was also proposed – this stage was later dropped from the scheme and will not be discussed here).

Stage 1: Punishment and obedience orientation

At the first of these stages, **punishment and obedience orientation** (which is very similar to Piaget's *heteronomous stage*), children believe that "right" and "wrong" are determined by powerful adult figures; to act morally, then, is to follow the rules laid down by authorities ("Heinz was wrong because the police arrest people who steal"). Little consideration is given to the intentions or desires of individuals other than the self when making moral judgments.

Stage 2: Instrumental morality

At the second stage, **instrumental morality**, children become aware that others have intentions and desires, but this awareness influences moral judgment only when others' desires affect the pursuit of one's instrumental goals. Heinz might be judged to have acted morally if "his wife helped him a lot around the house or at work."

Stage 3: Interpersonal normative morality

Interpersonal normative morality (sometimes called the "Good boy/good girl orientation") is characterized by an emergent concern for the perspectives of others toward the self. In contrast to stage 2 in which the desires and intentions of others mattered only as they conflicted or advanced instrumental goals, at stage 3 individuals are concerned with how the self is evaluated by these others. Individuals at stage 3 seek to be viewed as "good" and feel guilt when it is likely that others would condemn their behavior. In Heinz's case, if he "wants to be a good, loving husband," then he should steal the drug.

Stage 4: Social system morality

The appreciation of perspectives of others first evident at stage 3 is expanded at the next stage, **social system morality** (sometimes called "law and order orientation"). Individuals at stage 4 understand that all members of a society have intentions and pursue goals. Accompanying this realization is the understanding that rules and laws are necessary so that the pursuit of goals does not lead to anarchy. Moral judgment, then, focuses on the congruence of an individual's actions with the rules and laws necessary to preserve social harmony; Heinz might be judged in the wrong because "if everyone stole property from others, then there would be no property rights, and society would disintegrate."

Stage 5: Human rights and social welfare morality

Finally, at stage 5, **human rights and social welfare morality** (or the *social contract orientation*), individuals make use of ethical principles to guide moral judgments. For example, the rightness of an action might depend upon whether the action is consistent with the rules that individuals would accept for an ideal world. Heinz might be obligated to steal "because in an ideal world, everyone would believe that the right to life supersedes the right to property."

Claims about the stages of moral judgment

Kohlberg made a number of claims about the stages of moral judgment, and these claims have been scrutinized by philosophers, educators, and psychologists (for a particularly thoughtful review, see Lapsley, 1996). We shall review a few of the claims and the associated debate.

Age and stage

Kohlberg claimed that development across childhood and adolescence is characterized by sequential passage through the stages. Research indicates that stages 1 and 2 are most characteristic of children, with stage 3 emerging among adolescents. Stage 4 increases in salience across adolescence, and stage 5 appears in adulthood, although even then it remains fairly rare. Generally, longitudinal research (e.g., Colby et al., 1994) indicates that individuals move up a single stage at a time (i.e., move from stage 1 to stage 2, not from stage 1 to stage 3) and that regression over time is rare (individuals who are characterized as being at stage 3 are unlikely to use stage 2 reasoning when tested years later). The evidence is compelling for development from lower stages to higher stages over the course of childhood and adolescence in western cultures, and consequently there is little debate about this claim.

Moral judgment and action

One very common criticism of Kohlberg and Piaget is that the sorts of justifications offered for moral dilemmas are not associated with action. Most people can recall instances in which they acted in ways they knew were morally inappropriate, and it is this awareness that gives considerable credence to claims that the reflective judgment tapped by questions concerning hypothetical dilemmas has little influence on conduct. The relation of judgment to action is extremely complex and poorly understood; however, there is sufficient research to conclude that moral stage *is* related to behavior in moral contexts, although this relation is weak (Lapsley, 1996). In short, those who reason at higher stages are more likely to act prosocially than those who reason at lower stages.

The loose connection between moral judgment and action means that it is impossible to predict accurately a person's behavior in a specific situation from his or her moral stage. This is not altogether surprising: a person's behavior in any one situation is determined by many psychological factors (emotions, perceptions, memories, as well as judgments) and by contextual factors (which persons are present and the actor's relationships with those persons, home versus the workplace, and so on). For these reasons behavior is said to be multiply determined, and no single factor – such as moral stage – can be expected to direct behavior. Moreover, as Blasi (1980) pointed out, moral stages represent ways of thinking about moral issues, not specific behavioral tendencies. Two persons at the same moral stage may reach different decisions about action. For example, at stage 3, one person might conclude, "Heinz should steal the drug if he wants to be a good loving husband," while another person at stage 3 might assert that "Heinz shouldn't steal the drug because people in his neighborhood will think that he's untrustworthy."

Moreover, persons at different stages can choose the *same* action, but for *different* reasons. While the individual at stage 3 wants to preserve the self's reputation by stealing for his wife, the individual at stage 5 might be doing so as the result of a belief in a hierarchy of rights. For these reasons, the multiply determined nature of behavior and the complicated connection of moral stage to action, predictions from moral stage to moral behavior are tenuous.

Comprehensiveness of moral stages

In much of Kohlberg's writing (e.g., 1981, 1984) there is an assumption that the stages of logical cognition outlined by Piaget (see chapters 2, 5, 8, and 15 for a detailed account of Piaget's theory of cognitive development) are sufficient for an account of the development of intelligence, and that the moral stages suffice for a broad understanding of **social cognition**. In other words, one can understand social interactions, moral emotions (guilt, shame), attitudes, and so on as deriving in one way or another from the five stages of moral judgment. However, much of the research of the past two decades has demonstrated that the stages outlined by Kohlberg do not provide a comprehensive depiction of social-cognitive development.

Distributive justice

One line of investigation has demonstrated that young children's understanding of moral regulation is much more sophisticated than what is allowed by stage 1 in Kohlberg's theory. Damon (1977) was one of the first to demonstrate that young children, at Kohlberg's stage 1, reasoned in thoughtful ways about sharing in peer contexts. Damon suggested that he was able to detect moral sophistication overlooked by Kohlberg and Piaget by questioning children about familiar issues involving peers.

A typical task used by Damon is referred to as **distributive justice** and goes something like this. Imagine that there is a school that desperately needs funds to purchase essential writing materials – pens and notebooks. The teachers organize an Open Day and Fair at which there will be entertainments and stalls in order to raise the money. The art teacher asks her class to paint pictures so that these can be sold. The Open Day arrives and it is a great success, and more money is raised than is needed. The art teacher is then given some money to give to her class. The problem then becomes, how does she distribute the money to the children? A little thought reveals that there are three ways in which the money can be distributed, each of them having some merit. These are: *equality* – each child in the class is given the same amount of money; *need* – the poorer children are given more; *merit* – those children who worked hardest and whose paintings sold best are given more. Even 4-year-olds recognize the importance of sharing, and by 8 years children can appreciate and discuss all three ways of sharing the money.

Children have considerable experience sharing food and toys with their friends, and this experience is translated into implicit principles. In sharp contrast, young children have little experience with the kinds of issues posed by Kohlberg, like theft from stores and the importance of human life, and consequently their reasoning on these issues is rather muddled. Research by Damon and many others has demonstrated convincingly that young children judge moral issues, weigh moral claims, and make moral judgments (Damon, 1999); there is much more to young children's moral understanding than was thought three decades ago.

Distinguishing between moral and nonmoral domains

Research over the last two decades (for a review, see Turiel, 1998) also has demonstrated that children and adolescents make sharp distinctions between moral and nonmoral domains, and consequently moral stages are unlikely to be used in reasoning about all social issues. For example, even young children (age 4 and older) use *moral arguments* ("nobody should") about actions that inflict harm (e.g., hitting another child) and *social conventional reasoning* ("it's easier for everyone") for actions that are arbitrary rules (e.g., family members bringing their dinner plates to the sink to be washed). Researchers have also argued that even within the moral domain there are types of judgments (e.g., about helping others [see Eisenberg & Fabes, 1998, for a review]; concerning obligations to the natural world [Kahn, 1999]) that are not well addressed by Kohlberg's scheme.

Attributions and antisocial behavior

Finally, there is now a great deal of research indicating that one form of antisocial behavior, aggression, is best understood in terms of the **attributions** children make rather than moral stages. Aggressive children are much more likely than nonaggressive children to attribute hostile intent to ambiguous situations (Coie & Dodge, 1998), especially when the aggressive child is emotionally aroused (Dodge & Somberg, 1987). A child who employs hostile attribution biases is more likely to perceive a threat of physical or emotional harm whether the circumstances are hostile or, in fact, clearly benign. The tendency to attribute hostile intentions to others is stable, and predicts future aggressive behavior (Dodge, Pettit, Bates, & Valente, 1995). Furthermore, aggressive children when forced to make moral evaluations consider aggressive responses to be more acceptable (Deluty, 1983) and "friendly" (Crick & Ladd, 1990) than do nonaggressive children. Children who are aggressive often do not view themselves as deviant or immoral, but rather assume that they are adhering to an acceptable societal standard of behavior.

Universality

Finally, one of Kohlberg's boldest claims (1981) was that the moral stages that he used to characterize moral judgment development in the United States could also be used to understand moral judgment in all other cultures. Supporters of Kohlberg's theory (e.g., Snarey, 1994) have reviewed studies from a variety of cultures that used Kohlberg's measures, and conclude that there is considerable evidence that stages 1, 2, 3, and 4 can be found in cultures radically different from the United States; there is less evidence for the presence of stage 5 in nonwestern cultures, however.

While such reviews support claims that responses to Kohlberg's measures are similar across many cultures, the reviews do not lead to the conclusion that persons from different cultures reason in exactly the same way about moral issues. As we noted earlier, evidence has accumulated demonstrating that there is considerably more to social and moral reasoning than what is represented by Kohlberg's stages; it is in these other areas that the search for cross-cultural *variability* has had considerable success. Shweder and his colleagues (Shweder, Much, Mahapatra, & Park, 1997), for instance, have demonstrated that adolescents and adults in India make frequent reference to notions of the divine in their moral justifications, in contrast to the emphasis on justice so characteristic of the justifications of westerners.

Academic achievement and personality

In western cultures, moral judgment sophistication, as reflected by Kohlberg's and similar measures, is associated with academic achievement, whether this is measured by grades in school or by **standardized tests** (e.g., **IQ tests**). Given that Kohlberg's measure draws on some of the same skills necessary for academic success – comprehension of stories, verbal facility – this is an eminently reasonable association.

Particularly interesting is recent research that indicates that moral judgment is associated with *personality*. Earlier in the chapter, we reported that children who are able to regulate their emotions were less likely to become involved in antisocial behavior. Hart and his colleagues (Hart, Hofmann, Edelstein, & Keller, 1997) found that children of this type passed through the stages of moral judgment development at a faster rate than other children. Their interpretation was that children who could regulate their emotions were better able to listen carefully to the moral arguments made by others, and consequently to benefit from the insights that others have about the adequacy of moral claims. In contrast, children who had difficulty regulating their emotions presumably became too anxious or too angry in discussions about moral conflicts to benefit from others' insights and suggestions.

SUMMARY

There is both continuity and transformation in development across childhood. Young children who have difficulty regulating emotions are likely to retain this trait through adolescence. The consequences of poor emotion regulation are likely to be increased aggression, a tendency to attribute hostile intentions to others, and slow moral judgment development. There are dramatic changes in children's understanding of moral obligations. With age, children evidence increasingly sophisticated understanding of rights and responsibilities to others. Sophisticated moral reasoning is predictive of higher levels of prosocial action, and a lower likelihood of behaving in an antisocial fashion.

Social Influences on Prosocial and Antisocial Development

Our review so far has focused on the psychological features within children that are the foundation for prosocial tendencies, antisocial behavior, and moral development. These features – personality traits, emotion regulation, moral reasoning, and so on – are profoundly shaped by social influences. In the sections that follow, we review the effects of social relationships and culture on the constituents of prosocial and antisocial development.

Development Within Relationships: Parents and Peers

Parents

Psychologists have often noted that children bear remarkable psychological similarities to their siblings and parents. For example, impulsive children tend to have brothers and sisters who behave likewise, and students who excel have parents who earned high grades. There are many exceptions to this general finding, of course, and no child is a duplicate of any other. Nonetheless, for most psychological characteristics, on average, children resemble their siblings and parents more than randomly selected nonfamily members.

Most typically, the similarity of children to their families has been interpreted to mean that through their social interactions, parents shape children in their own image. Parents who behave aggressively toward each other and their children, for example, are thought to be setting examples that children then imitate. An enormous body of research has accumulated over the past 50 years characterizing the **parenting behaviors** that may lead children to resemble their families.

In recent years, however, many researchers, particularly those who advocate a **behavioral-genetic** approach to the study of development, have argued for a different interpretation of the resemblance of children to their families. These researchers point out that parents share genes with their children, and that many (if not most) psychological characteristics are influenced by genes (Turkheimer, 2000; see also chapter 3). In fact, behavioral geneticists have argued that the resemblance of children to their parents is more attributable to genes than it is to parents' systematic behavior toward children (Turkheimer, 2000).

For our purposes in this chapter, the findings of behavioral genetics are cautionary. Until research is done on the influence of parents on adopted, biologically unrelated children – in which case parents do not share genes with their children – then it is impossible to be certain that parenting patterns, not genes, influence prosocial and antisocial development. Our interpretations of this research must therefore be appropriately tentative.

Parents and personality

There is a clear relation between emotion regulation in parents and their children. Eisenberg, Fabes, Schaller, Carlo, and Miller (1991) measured sympathy and negative emotions in children, and measured sympathy in the parents. The results indicated that sympathetic parents had children who were sympathetic. Kochanska (1991) studied a group of children between the ages of 2 and 10 years of age. At age 10, the children were asked to respond to stories like those used by Kohlberg. Moral sophistication at age 10 was related to both emotional regulation and parenting at age 2. Children prone to anxiety at 2 years of age, and whose parents reasoned with them, were higher in sophistication at age 10 than children high in anxiety whose parents behaved autocratically (see chapter 16). Interestingly, parental behavior at age 2 seemed little related to moral sophistication at age 10 for the fearless children. Together these two studies suggest that parents who reason with and behave sympathetically toward their children are fostering the development of a prosocial personality. Kochanska's research suggests that children's personalities may affect how much influence parents have on children, although there is a need for future research to replicate this finding.

If democratic, warm, reasoning parenting (see chapter 16) is associated with an increased capacity for prosocial behavior, then it comes as no surprise that autocratic, cold, harsh, inconsistent parenting is predictive of antisocial tendencies (Coie & Dodge, 1998). Parental physical abuse is particularly detrimental, as it interferes with the development of emotion regulation and sympathy, which in turn are internal resources that allow children to avoid aggression and antisocial behavior (Coie & Dodge, 1998).

Parents and moral judgment

Families are traditionally assumed to influence moral development, and a number of studies have examined the influence of parents on moral judgment development. There is some research that indicates that the rate of moral judgment development is increased by warm supportive relationships with parents (e.g., Hart, 1988a, b) and by family discussions that are supportive of children's comments (Walker & Taylor, 1991). Generally, then, studies of the influence of parents on moral judgment development are consistent with those assessing parents' roles on prosocial personality. Parents who are sympathetic, warm, and supportive of their children tend to have children who are able to regulate emotion effectively, sympathize with others, and judge moral issues with sophistication.

PEERS

Peers and antisocial behavior

Peers are powerful influences on the development of antisocial behavior. Friends often draw children into delinquent activity, and children involved in antisocial activity are likely to choose like-minded peers. A child's network of peers is therefore a powerful context for initiation into, and the consolidation of, antisocial behavior (Coie & Dodge, 1998).

Children's social relationships are influential in other ways as well. Particularly interesting are the consequences of *peer rejection* (see chapter 13). Rejected children are those who are both influential (high impact) and disliked (identified by peers as undesirable interaction partners). Unsurprisingly, children who are very aggressive are often rejected by their peers, although there are exceptions to this generalization (in fact, in some peer networks, for example within delinquent peer groups, it is possible to be both aggressive and popular). More important, however, are a host of findings that suggest that peer rejection *increases* aggressive behavior (Coie & Dodge, 1998). Apparently, the experience of rejection leads children to expect hostility in others, which has the effect of priming children to behave aggressively in peer contexts.

Peers and moral judgment

Surprisingly, little is known about the influence of peers on prosocial development (Eisenberg & Fabes, 1998). We do know that entry into voluntary community service (e.g., working in a shelter for homeless adults) is more common among older children and adolescents with peers engaged in similar activities than it is among those whose friends are not (Youniss & Yates, 1997). Whether this finding applies to younger children and is representative of other forms of prosocial action is not known, however.

Far more work has focused on peer influences on moral judgment development. There is a general consensus that moral judgment development is the result of individuals reflecting on moral claims, observing the behavior of significant others, and negotiating with others when moral conflicts arise. Individuals formulate rules for moral conduct, apply these rules, and then revise them when the rules prove unsatisfactory to the self or to others. Piaget and Kohlberg – whose work was reviewed earlier in the chapter – argued that these processes are more likely to occur in peer relationships. This is because adult unilateral authority often dominates adult–child relationships, thus precluding discussion about moral decisions, while the equality of peer relationships allows for mutual negotiation for the resolution of moral problems.

Research findings are consistent with this theoretical position. For example, Walker, Hennig, and Krettenauer (2000) examined the relation of discussions about moral issues among peers to subsequent moral judgment development. Walker and his colleagues found that children who attempted to understand fully their friends' perspectives experienced the most rapid moral judgment development. This finding suggests that effective peer collaboration facilitates development, a pattern consistent with the theories of Piaget and Kohlberg.

 Culture and Development

CULTURAL VARIABILITY

Cultural context is profoundly important for understanding prosocial and antisocial behavior. For example, adolescents in the United States are about twice as likely to experience a violent death than are youth in European countries (National Center for Educational Statistics, 1991). There is no evidence to indicate that American and European youth differ in important ways in personality or moral judgment, and consequently the dramatically different rates of violent death are not attributable to differences in personality. Nor would it be accurate to characterize this difference in violent death rates as an indication that European cultures are more prosocial than the United States, because on some indices of prosocial behavior, such as volunteering for charitable causes, the United States is much higher (Greeley, 1997) than European countries. There is also considerable variation of the same sort within countries: in the United States, for example, homicide – an extreme antisocial behavior – is much more common among adolescents living in poor urban areas than among those in affluent suburban neighborhoods (Federal Interagency Forum on Child and Family Statistics, 1999).

Cultural norms and social context are also essential for understanding the complicated developmental trajectories of prosocial and antisocial behavior across childhood and adolescence. We have described the developments in personality and moral judgment that enable children to better regulate their emotions and consider moral claims. One might conclude from these trends that prosocial behavior ought to increase regularly across childhood and adolescence, and generally this is so (Eisenberg & Fabes, 1998). This is not uniformly the case, however, and a consideration of one exception to the expected trend is illustrative.

Stanger, Achenbach, and Verhulst (1997) had a large sample of Dutch mothers rate their children and adolescents on measures of *aggression* (attacking others, screaming, temper tantrums) and *delinquency* (lying, swearing, vandalism). Aggression consistently declined between ages 4 and 17, a trend consistent with the growth of personality and moral judgment over this age range. Interestingly, however, while the development of delinquency decreased from ages 4 to 10, it increased from age 10 to 17. The increase in delinquent behavior is likely due to a number of social factors: the influence of peers, the freedom granted by many western cultures to adolescents from parental and adult supervision, and so on.

MEDIA AND DEVELOPMENT

One form of cultural influence on development that has received considerable attention is television. Television is pervasive in the lives of many children. For example, children in the United States are estimated to watch an average of 3 hours a day (Committee on Public Communications, 2001), with children in Canada watching almost as much (Statistics Canada, 2001). Given our themes in this chapter – prosocial and antisocial development – it is reasonable to ask how moral life is portrayed in television programming.

American television presents a wide range of extremely violent, aggressive activity. For example, one analysis found that 66 percent of programs targeted toward American children contained violence (Federman, 1998). Because violence permeates television in the United States, a great deal of research has examined the association between television watching and childhood aggression. The evidence is clear: children

Plate 14.3 In the United States and other western countries, watching television occupies more of children's time than any other activity, apart from attending school. There is no question but that television presents messages about antisocial and prosocial behavior. Photograph © Heather Vickers.

Plate 14.4 Children's interactions with others are contexts to learn about and to exhibit prosocial actions. Photograph © Getty Images/ Digital Vision.

who watch a lot of television tend to be more aggressive than children who watch little. It appears to have this effect for several reasons (Coie & Dodge, 1998). First, violent TV models aggressive actions that children imitate. Second, televised violence desensitizes children to the dangers of aggression, because much of the violence depicted on television appears to have no harmful effects to innocent parties. Finally, televised violence heightens children's fears that the world is dangerous. Some researchers estimate that television is responsible for 10–20 percent of the aggression observed in the United States (Comstock & Strasburger, 1993).

If television can make children aggressive, can it promote prosocial behavior as well? Indeed, watching television with a prosocial theme increases altruistic behavior, cooperation, and compliance with adult rules, an effect particularly evident in young children (Mares, 1996). We can conclude from the findings on aggression and prosocial behavior that television is an important influence on children's development. The messages that societies present through the mass media – television, for example – are received by children and integrated into their thoughts and their actions. As web-based content aimed at children becomes increasingly common and supplements television, it is reasonable to assume that development will be shaped by media to an extent greater than what is observed today.

CULTURE AND IDENTITY

While the transition from childhood to adolescence brings with it an increase in some forms of antisocial behavior, as noted above, it is also a transition during which at least some adolescents construct moral identities. Moral identities refer to commitments to prosocial action that are consistent with the self's goals and qualities (Hart, Atkins, & Ford, 1998). There are 12- and 13-year-olds who are deeply involved in prosocial activities such as working in food banks, working with younger children, organizing scout troops, and so on (Hart & Fegley, 1995). Interviews with these young adolescents suggest that their commitments reflect the integration of social relationships, personality characteristics, contacts with social institutions, and moral beliefs (Hart & Yates, 1997). This kind of integration is similar to that found among adult moral exemplars (Colby & Damon, 1995). The fusion of moral judgment, personality, and social experience typical of young adolescents committed to moral action does not seem to characterize adolescents who are frequently antisocial. In this sense, then, the formation of a moral identity in some at the transition of childhood to adolescence is a consequence of a process that cannot be used to explain antisocial behavior. At the extremes, antisocial and prosocial tendencies seem to have different roots: the former in emotion regulation difficulties and frequently in neurological deficits, and for the latter in the formation of an identity that integrates personality, moral commitments, and social opportunities.

Summary and Conclusions

The development of prosocial and antisocial behavior is a complex process, influenced by personality, emotions, judgment, social relationships, and culture. We have focused on two threads of the process, personality and judgment, and have described their development. Prosocial and antisocial development is shaped by social interactions and culture. While a great deal has been learned from 50 years of research, the most fascinating questions remain: To what extent can families foster prosocial behavior in their children? How can the media be utilized to help children develop into productive citizens? Can the interactions among genes, biology, parenting, and culture be understood in sufficient detail to permit effective intervention? Answers to these and other important questions await the efforts of future researchers.

Discussion Points

1 Why is it that without prosocial social interactions, no society or social group could survive?
2 Consider the factors that cause continuity and change in social behaviors.
3 What causes extreme antisocial behavior?
4 What are the essential differences between Piaget's two stages of moral reasoning?
5 What are the essential features of Kohlberg's five stages of moral reasoning, and has research supported his claims about these stages?
6 Consider the ways in which culture and social context influence prosocial and antisocial behavior.

SUGGESTIONS FOR FURTHER READING

Bornstein, M. H., Davidson, L., Keyes, C. M., Moore, K., & Smith, C. (2001). *Well-being: Positive development across the life course.* Hillsdale, NJ: Erlbaum.

Craig, W. (2000). *Childhood social development: The essential readings.* Cambridge, MA, and Oxford: Blackwell.

Eisenberg, N. (Ed.) (1998). *Handbook of child psychology* (5th ed.). *Vol. 3. Social, emotional, and personality development.* New York: Wiley.

Nucci, L. (1999). *Education in the moral domain.* New York: Cambridge University Press.

part IV

Adolescence

Contents

chapter 15

Cognitive Development

Kang Lee and Alejo Freire

KEY CONCEPTS

AMBIGUOUS FIGURES
ANALOGICAL REASONING
CLUSTER EFFECT
COGNITIVE DEVELOPMENT
COGNITIVE PROCESSES
COMBINATORY THOUGHT
CONCRETE OPERATIONS
  STAGE
CONFIGURATIONAL
  PROCESSING
CONSERVATION
CORRELATION COEFFICIENT
CRYSTALLIZED INTELLIGENCE
DEDUCTIVE REASONING
DOMAIN-GENERAL
DOMAIN-SPECIFIC

ELABORATION
ENCODING SWITCH HYPOTHESIS
FEATURAL PROCESSING
FLUID INTELLIGENCE
FORMAL OPERATIONS STAGE
HYPOTHETICO-DEDUCTIVE
  REASONING
INDUCTIVE REASONING
INFORMATION PROCESSING
INTELLIGENCE QUOTIENT (IQ)
INTELLIGENCE TESTS
INTUITIVE SCIENTISTS
LONG-TERM MEMORY
METACOGNITION
MORAL JUDGMENT STAGES

NEO-CORTEX
ORGANIZATION
PERCENTILE
PROPOSITIONAL THOUGHT
REHEARSAL
REVERSIBILITY
SECOND-ORDER ANALOGY
SELECTIVE ATTENTION
SHORT-TERM MEMORY
SPEED OF PROCESSING
STANDARD DEVIATION
STANDARDIZED SCORE
SYLLOGISM
TRANSITIVITY TASK
WORKING MEMORY

OVERVIEW

Decades of research indicate that important and sometimes fundamental changes in thinking occur during adolescence, and that adolescents become capable of sophisticated thinking. There are three interrelated components to thinking: the process by which adolescents perform basic and higher-level intellectual functions, the structure in which their thoughts are organized, and the content of their thinking. The authors discuss these topics by focusing on several aspects and theories of cognitive development:

- memory development
- the development of intelligence
- reasoning skills
- formal operational thinking
- alternatives to Piaget's theory of adolescent reasoning

What has become clear is that adolescent thinking is qualitatively different from the thinking of young children. However, adolescents are still apprentices in thinking. They are yet to learn some sophisticated ways of thinking such as conducting truly scientific investigations and carrying out abstract logical reasoning. Nevertheless, the thinking skills acquired during adolescence lay the foundation for taking on the more complex and diverse problems of adulthood.

Introduction

This chapter is about thinking in adolescence. Now, if one were to believe what is often presented in the popular media, it might seem adolescents do not do much thinking at all. Consider how adolescents are typically portrayed in movies, television, and newspapers. At worst they are depicted as violent, heavily involved with drugs, promiscuous, and in general a menace to society. Even what is often considered normal is not very flattering: it is common to characterize young people as overly self-conscious, egotistic, and in a constant state of emotional turmoil. They are obsessed with whether their appearance looks "cool" to others but are not concerned with their academic work. They hate school but love to party. They are impulsive and lack self-control. Neither view gives adolescents much credit for sophisticated thinking. But decades of research indicate that important and sometimes fundamental changes in thinking are occurring during this time.

In this chapter, we will use the word "thinking" in a very broad sense. It includes not only such higher-level intellectual functions as logical reasoning and problem-solving, but also some basic-level intellectual functions such as perception, attention, and memory (Siegler, 1993). As well, readers need to keep in mind that when we mention "adolescent thinking," the term refers to three interrelated aspects of thinking: the *process* by which adolescents perform basic and higher-level intellectual functions, the *structure* in which adolescents' thoughts are organized, and the *content* of adolescents' thinking. For example, to understand adolescents' ability in problem-solving, one needs to know how they attack a problem from the beginning to its final solution (the process of thinking), how adolescents' problem-solving is related to their other cognitive abilities (the structure of thinking), and what information is specifically used during problem-solving (the content of thinking). This chapter will touch upon these issues with a focus on two main questions: (1) Do adolescents have a unique way of thinking? and (2) What are the major characteristics of adolescents' thinking?

Perception and Attention

Perception

One area in which development is evident in adolescence is perception. As you have already read in chapter 5, perception is one of the cognitive abilities that develop earliest in life: even newborns are very sensitive to environmental stimulation. By the end of toddlerhood, children's vision, hearing, and senses of smell, taste, and touch are all quite well developed. What aspects of perception, then, continue to develop throughout childhood and into adolescence? Perhaps the broadest generalization to be made is that children's perception becomes increasingly flexible. Some examples will serve to illustrate what we mean by this statement. Consider the illustrations in figure 15.1(a). These are called **ambiguous figures** because more than one object can be perceived in each drawing. However, in a study with 4- to 11-year-olds, Elkind and Scott (1962) found that the younger children usually reported only seeing one element in the illustrations rather than two. Often, only when an adult made the distinction between the two very explicit did they indicate seeing both components. The older children in the study could readily perceive the figures in more than one way and alternate between them. This suggests that increased flexibility of thought in adolescence allows alternations between the different perspectives to be easily accomplished. In contrast, the relatively rigid perception of younger children makes it more difficult for them to see the figures in multiple ways. A related demonstration of increasing flexibility of perception is obtained when considering the composite figures shown in figure 15.1(b). Each illustration depicts an object composed of several other common objects. Similar to what is found in the case of ambiguous figures, young children tend to identify the component objects without perceiving the image gestalt, while adolescents can identify both components and wholes (Elkind, Koegler, & Go, 1964). In cases where young children do perceive the whole as well as the components, they typically require a much longer inspection time to do so than what is required by older children.

Selective attention

Development is also evident in the adolescent's superior ability to allocate attentional resources. The ability for **selective attention** has been assessed using a central–incidental learning task. A set of cards, each showing two objects belonging to different categories, is used. For example, a set might consist of cards that each depict one animal and one tool. The experimenter shows all the cards and gives the instruction to remember only one category of objects (the animals, for example). In such a task, children are required to focus attention on the animals while selectively ignoring the tools appearing in the pictures. Later, however, they are asked to recall both the animals and tools. It is reasoned that children high in selective attention should be able to devote more of their attentional resources to the central task than the incidental task. More specifically, a child with high selective attention should show high retention for

(a)

(b)

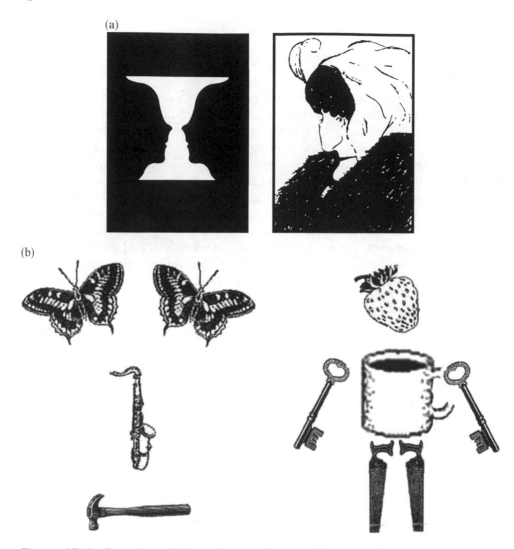

Figure 15.1 Examples of (a) ambiguous figures; (b) composite objects.

items in the *central* category (e.g., animals), but comparatively low memory of items in the *incidental* class (e.g., tools). In contrast, children with low selective attention may remember items in either category at a similar rate. What research has shown (e.g., Hagen, 1967) is that adolescents are more likely than younger children to remember a significantly higher number of items from the central class than the incidental class; in contrast, young children are more likely than adolescents to remember a comparable number of items from the two categories. There is also support for the interpretation that these differing patterns of results are due to differences in selective attention: whereas memory for central and incidental objects is positively correlated in young children, there is a negative correlation of these factors among adolescents (e.g., Miller & Weiss, 1981).

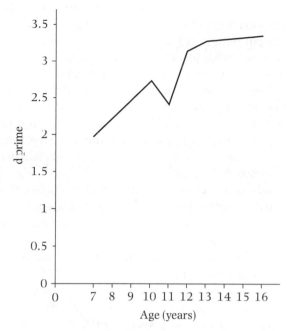

Figure 15.2 Development of face recognition (adapted from Flin, 1985); d prime is an index of recognition. Reproduced with permission from *The British Journal of Psychology*, © The British Psychological Society.

Memory

MEMORY FOR FACES

By early adulthood memory can be quite remarkable. An extreme example of this fact comes from a study by Bahrick, Bahrick, and Wittlinger (1975). In this study, individuals recognized former high school classmates from yearbook photographs with 90 percent accuracy, as long as 35 years after graduation and independently of class size. This incredible feat is a result of a rapid development in face-processing abilities during childhood and adolescence, with adult-level recognition reached by about 16 years of age (figure 15.2).

Whether there is a qualitative change in face processing between childhood and adolescence has been a focus of intense study. One proposal is a so-called **encoding switch hypothesis**. This hypothesis claims that different information about faces is represented in memory by children at different ages. On this account, young children rely on information about faces that is not as "good" for remembering them as is the information used by older children and adults. Carey and Diamond (1977) suggest that children prior to the age of 10 years primarily use information about individual features (e.g., eyes, nose, and mouth) in recognizing faces, whereas older children and adults use information about configuration, the spatial layout of face features. Face processing emphasizing features is referred to as **featural processing**, whereas that emphasizing configurations is called *configural* or **configurational processing**. There is some evidence consistent with Carey and Diamond's proposal: they found that children prior to age 10 years made identifications largely on the basis of paraphernalia items such as a hat or glasses. That is, shown an individual wearing a hat, and then later shown the same individual without a hat and a different person with the same hat, young children were more likely to say that the individual with the hat was the one they had seen previously. Carey and Diamond suggested that younger children's failure in recognizing the right person was because they encoded nonessential, featural information for determining face identity, while adolescents succeeded because they encoded the critical, configural information.

Figure 15.2 also indicates another interesting finding. Notice that there is a drop in performance on face recognition tasks occurring at about age 11 years. While this "dip" has not been found in every study carried out with children at these ages, it is reliable enough that several researchers have attempted to account for its occurrence. One intriguing proposal for which there is some support is that the dip coincides with hormonal changes associated with puberty. For example, Diamond, Carey, and Back (1983) compared performance of girls aged 8 to 16 years in a face recognition task. They found that regardless of age, girls undergoing puberty performed more poorly than did either prepubescent or postpubescent girls. The issue of a temporary dip in face recognition as well as that of the encoding switch hypothesis remain controversial, and await further research and clarification (for an excellent review of this literature, see Chung & Thomson, 1995).

Faces are just one type of stimulus for which adolescents show incredible memory skills. What about memory development more generally? Evidence indicates that development takes place in almost every aspect of memory. The three that will be highlighted here are short-term memory, long-term memory, and strategy use. Note that these topics are considered in detail in chapter 12, which gives an overview of memory development through childhood.

SHORT-TERM MEMORY

As the name suggests, **short-term memory** refers to memory that is only required for a short amount of time and that is necessary to carry out the current task (indeed, short-term memory is also referred to as **working memory**). Experimentally, the capacity of short-term memory has been investigated using memory span tasks: a series of items is presented at a rate of 1 per second – for example, letters, words, or digits – and the task is to repeat them in the same order as they were presented. A number of such studies have shown that short-term memory increases steadily throughout childhood and into adolescence (figure 15.3). The figure shows the number of items of various types that can be remembered by children 2 to 12 years of age. For example, whereas a 5-year-old can remember between 3 and 4 of each class of item, a 12-year-old can remember an average of about 7 digits, and between 4 and 5 letters or words.

There are a number of possible explanations for the developmental improvement in short-term memory. One possibility is simply that as children grow, the capacity of short-term memory increases as a result of neurological changes. But it remains an

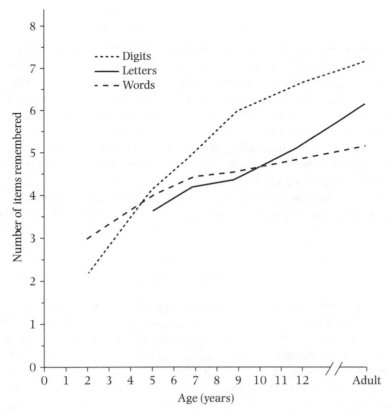

Figure 15.3 Development of short-term memory (adapted from Schneider & Pressley, 1997). Reprinted by permission of Lawrence Erlbaum Associates Inc., Professor W. Schneider and Professor G. M. Pressley.

open question whether this is indeed the case (Miller, 1956). The reason why this conclusion cannot be straightforwardly drawn becomes clear in considering figure 15.3. As can be seen, the number of items remembered at a given age is in part determined by the nature of the items. So, for example, it is in general easier to remember a list of digits than a list of words. This should not be the case if what is changing in short-term memory is its capacity *per se*. Instead, this may reflect children's greater familiarity with numbers than with words. Or it may reflect practice, in that while sometimes we are required to keep a short sequence of random numbers in short-term memory (for example, in calculating an arithmetic problem or dialing a phone number), it is rarer to have to remember a random string of words. Whatever the case, it is similarly possible that the developmental changes apparent in short-term memory studies reflect older children's greater familiarity and experience with words and numbers as a result of additional years of schooling. In other words, while it is possible that the capacity of short-term memory is greater in adolescence than at earlier times, it is also possible that advances are a result of increases in general knowledge about the to-be-remembered materials. These possible explanations are discussed in more detail in chapter 12.

Lᴏɴɢ-ᴛᴇʀᴍ ᴍᴇᴍᴏʀʏ

Long-term memory is more permanent than short-term memory, and includes such things as representations of people one has met and events one has experienced. It also includes knowledge acquired through schooling, such as times tables and the location of different countries on a map. And, even though one is not really aware of the fact, long-term memory is what allows you to drive a car with little effort or why you do not have to think consciously about how to move your arms and legs once you have learned to swim. For all intents and purposes, there are no limits on the capacity of long-term memory. This seems to be true even for young children, who may have quite detailed recollections of childhood friends or visits to grandma and grandpa's house. While its absolute capacity does not appear to change much, it is however not the case that the long-term memories of young children and adolescents are equivalent.

Speed of processing

One major type of development in long-term memory is in **speed of processing**, with older children generally able to retrieve information from long-term memory more rapidly than can young children. One demonstration of this comes from a famous study by Keating and Bobbitt (1978). Keating and Bobbitt asked 9-, 13-, and 17-year-olds to sort two sets of index cards, each with two letters stenciled on it, as quickly as possible. The set used in the *physical-sorting* condition was sorted into cards with letters that were identical (e.g., AA, aa, BB, or bb) and cards that differed in physical appearance (e.g., Aa, bA, Ba, or Bb). In contrast, in the *name-sorting* condition similar stimuli were used as those in the physical-sorting condition. However, children were asked to sort cards into those with the same name (e.g., AA, aa, BB, or bb) and those with a different name (e.g., Ab, bA, Ba, ba). Keating and Bobbitt reasoned that the name-sorting task should take longer because it required that the names of letters be retrieved from long-term memory, whereas the physical-sorting task was basically a perceptual task. Their other important assumption was that because in all other respects the two tasks were comparable, differences in the amount of time taken to complete the two tasks reflected the amount of time taken to retrieve letter-names from long-term memory. As expected, they found that at all ages the name-sorting task took longer to complete than the physical-sorting task. In addition, the differences in time taken were greatest for the 9-year-olds, next largest for the 13-year-olds, and smallest for the 17-year-olds, consistent with the notion that speed of retrieving information from long-term memory improves throughout these years.

Mᴇᴍᴏʀʏ ꜱᴛʀᴀᴛᴇɢɪᴇꜱ

Developmental differences between adolescents and younger children are also evident in the types of strategies used in order to remember information. This reflects adolescents' increased knowledge about ways to enhance their memory. Asked to remember the number sequence 3–6–5–2–5–1–1, a young child might use a **rehearsal** strategy, in which the sequence is repeated over and over. An older child might realize that the first three numbers are the same as the number of days in the year, that the fourth and fifth numbers are the same as the amount of cents in a quarter, and that the last two numbers are the same as the uniform number of a favorite athlete. Now there are only three things to remember rather than seven. Although both instances show evidence of providing a deliberate aid to memory, the latter strategy is more effective. It is an example of an **elaboration** strategy, whereby information to be remembered is transformed in some way that makes it more meaningful and therefore easier to remember.

A different kind of elaboration is an **organization** strategy. It is seen in older children's increased tendency to organize or *cluster* groups of items in memory when they are to be remembered: this is called the **cluster effect**. Presented with a list of items that includes subsets of different categories, for example animals, colors, and types of furniture, adolescents will more frequently use the information about categories to recall more items: when asked to recall as many items as they can from the list, they may begin with one category and name the items they remember from that category, then name items from the second category, and so on (Schneider, 1985). By actively imposing an organization on material to be remembered, older children and adolescents become skilled at remembering seemingly chaotic and disorganized information.

A number of general findings about the development of strategy use have emerged in the literature. As the above examples indicate, more sophisticated strategy use for remembering information increases throughout childhood. It also seems to be the case that effective use of strategies to increase memory may especially proliferate in adolescence (e.g., Rohwer & Bean, 1973). Finally, it is important to point out that even when young children use elaboration strategies, they will generally do so in only a limited way. That is, older children are much more likely to apply strategies more flexibly and broadly to aid memory in a wider range of tasks (Carr, Kurtz, Schneider, Turner, & Borkowski, 1989).

Intelligence

Although psychologists have not reached a consensus about how to define intelligence, it is generally agreed that intelligence, or general intellectual ability, is the underlying potential for individuals to understand the world around them and to function successfully in it. Measures of adolescent intelligence are often obtained by using **intelligence tests**. One commonly used test is Wechsler's Intelligence Scale for Children (WISC; Wechsler, 1991). This test, now in its third edition, is suitable for use with children between 6 and 16 years of age. It has a *verbal scale* and a *performance scale*, which are purportedly tapping into different aspects of a child's intelligence (e.g., left and right hemispheric functioning, respectively). The verbal scale has six subscales that assess children's verbal intelligence on different dimensions,

Table 15.1 Items on the Wechsler Intelligence Scale for Children

Verbal scale	Performance scale
1 *General information*: A sample of questions that most children have been exposed to (e.g., Where does the sun rise? How many weeks are there in a year?).	1 *Picture completion*: Children are asked to point out which part is missing in a picture (e.g., a cat without whiskers).
2 *Comprehension*: Children are required to explain why certain practices are desirable or what course of action is preferred under certain circumstances (e.g., Why does one need a driver's license to drive a car? What is the thing to do if you lose a friend's book?).	2 *Picture arrangement*: Children are asked to arrange a series of pictures that are in a wrong order (e.g., pictures depicting a child going to school, and returning home, and getting up) back to the correct sequence.
3 *Arithmetic*: A series of mental arithmetic problems ranging from easy ones (e.g., How much does it cost to buy 2 kilograms of bananas when it costs $.65 per kilogram?) to hard ones that most of us dreaded when we were in high school (e.g., Mr. Davis drives at 50 km per hour and Mrs. Davis drives at 100 km per hour but leaves half an hour later. After how many minutes or hours will Mrs. Davis catch up with Mr. Davis?).	3 *Block design*: Children are required to arrange a number of blocks to form a pattern within a certain period of time.
4 *Similarities*: Children are asked to point out the similarities between pairs of words (e.g., In what way are "food" and "book" alike?).	4 *Object assembly*: The child must assemble jigsawlike parts of a common object (e.g., a sailboat).
5 *Vocabulary*: Children are required to explain a series of increasingly difficult words (e.g., "carpet," "psychosis").	5 *Coding*: Children are asked to translate, as fast as possible, symbols to numbers based on a code given to them (e.g., @ = 1, * = 2, etc.).
6 *Digit span*: A series of numbers of increasing length is presented orally and children are asked to repeat the numbers in the same or reversed order.	6 *Mazes*: The child must trace the correct route from a starting point to an exit on a series of mazes.
	7 *Symbol search*: Children must indicate whether a pair of symbols is present in a row of symbols.

and the performance scale has seven subscales that tap into children's nonverbal intelligence (see table 15.1 for details). Adolescents' raw scores on these subscales are very informative and can tell us how adolescents' general intellectual abilities develop with age.

(a)

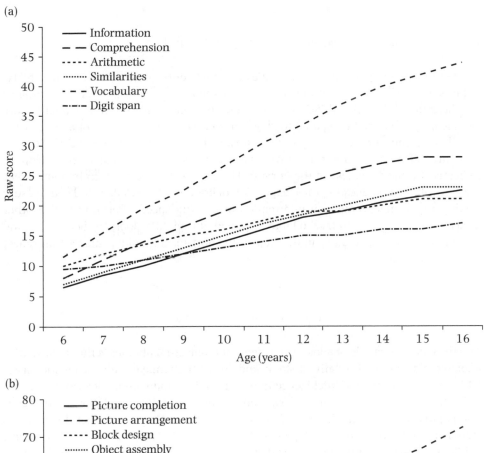

(b)

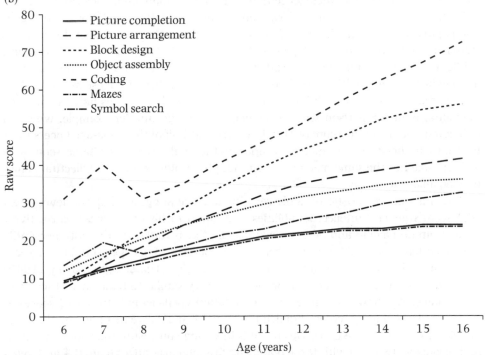

Figure 15.4 Age trend of raw scores in (a) the WISC verbal scale; (b) the WISC performance scale (adapted from Wechsler, 1991). Reprinted by permission of Harcourt Inc.

Rapid development

There are three important characteristics of adolescents' general intellectual ability. Figures 15.4(a) and 15.4(b) illustrate two of them. First, adolescents' performance on the subscales of the WISC suggests that their general intellectual abilities are significantly advanced compared to children younger than 10 years of age. As well, the abilities continue to develop rapidly during the entire adolescent period. Second, there are differences in the speed at which adolescents' intellectual abilities develop (as indicated by the steepness of the curves). Development is very sharp in some areas (e.g., vocabulary, suggesting rapid expansion of linguistic knowledge, and coding, suggesting rapid improvement in information-processing speed). Performance in other areas, however, seems to level off after a period of rapid development between 6 and 10 years of age (e.g., digit span that taps into short-term memory; mazes that reflect speed of learning).

Stability of development

The third characteristic of adolescents' general intellectual abilities is that a particular adolescent's IQ score is relatively stable and does not change greatly as age increases: IQ is the abbreviation of **intelligence quotient**, and an individual's IQ score gives an indication of how he or she performs on intelligence tests in relation to the general population. This stability of IQ scores across age does not contradict the previous statement about the rapid development of general intellectual abilities in adolescence. While an adolescent may develop rather significantly on a number of dimensions of intelligence, his or her IQ scores do not increase. This is because IQ scores are calculated based on age norms. That is, an individual's IQ only indicates how "smart" the individual is in comparison with his or her own age group. For example, when an individual obtains an IQ score of 100, it means that half of the same-aged peers have IQ scores higher than the individual and another half lower. The same score at a different age has the same meaning, even though absolute general intellectual ability may be different.

This third characteristic of adolescent intelligence suggests that the level of an adolescent's general intellectual abilities in relation to his or her peers is relatively stable from one age to another. For example, if Mike is ranked in the 90th **percentile** (i.e., his intellectual abilities are higher than 90 percent of his age group) at 11 years of age, he will continue to rank at similar percentiles at later ages. Bayley (1949) reported that the IQ scores of 18-year-olds were very similar to their own IQ scores in adolescence. As shown in figure 15.5, **correlation coefficients** between IQ scores at 18 years of age and IQ scores obtained between 11 and 17 years of age by the same individuals are all above 0.70. This result is in strong contrast to the poor correlation of IQ scores at 18 years with those obtained at much earlier ages (e.g., 0.4 at 3 years and 0.6 at 6 years; see figure 15.5). One possibility is that children's general intellectual abilities are more unstable at younger ages than in later years. Fagan and Singer's (1983) findings seem to support this idea: when they reviewed a number of studies that measured children's IQ at 1 year and again at ages 3 through 6 years,

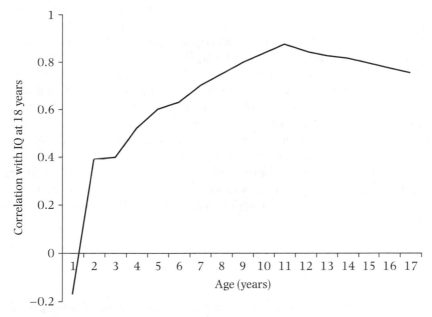

Figure 15.5 Correlation between IQ scores at 18 years of age and those at earlier ages (adapted from Bayley, 1949). Reprinted with permission of the Helen Dwight Reid Educational Foundation. Published by Heldoef Publications, 1319 Eighteenth St., NW, Washington, DC 20036-1802. Copyright © 1949.

the average correlation was only 0.14. There are other explanations for the high discrepancies in IQ scores in early childhood, but limitations of space do not permit us to go into further details. Interested readers should consult Slater, Carrick, Bell, and Roberts (1999) for an in-depth discussion about the controversy in the literature.

FLUID AND CRYSTALLIZED INTELLIGENCE

Several researchers have suggested that the developmental pattern of adolescents' general intellectual abilities may be more complex than figure 15.5 suggests. For example, Horn (1970) suggests that the developmental pattern of an individual's general intellectual ability depends on what type of intelligence is being measured. Based on earlier work (Horn & Cattell, 1967), Horn and his associates (Horn, Donaldson, & Engstrom, 1981) assessed two types of intelligence, *fluid* and *crystallized*. **Fluid intelligence** is defined as a person's ability to think and reason abstractly as measured by culture-free reasoning tasks, such as those measuring the ability to see relations among objects or patterns in a series of items (e.g., what letter comes next in this series: ADGJMP?). **Crystallized intelligence** is the store of information, skills, and strategies acquired through education and prior experience. Many tasks used in the WISC verbal scale are examples of such tasks.

Horn pointed out that typical intelligence tests fail to differentiate between the two types of intelligence, and as a result, IQ scores appear to be stable over time during and after adolescence. However, when fluid and crystallized intelligence were tested separately in more than a dozen studies conducted in Horn's laboratory between 1966 and 1982, a different pattern of results emerged: beginning in late adolescence fluid intelligence undergoes sharp decline, while crystallized intelligence increases rapidly. Horn (1978) suggested that this pattern of development might be related to changes in the nervous system. Specifically, he proposed that the decline of fluid intelligence is associated with the deterioration of the part of the brain governing alertness and attention, the onset of which begins as early as adolescence. In contrast, crystallized intelligence is associated with information processing in the **neo-cortex**. As age increases, the neural connections that represent various information become more elaborated and more easily activated, which accounts for the increase in crystallized intelligence. According to Horn's theory, adolescence appears to be the critical developmental period that marks both the dawn of crystallized intelligence and the dusk of fluid intelligence.

INTERGENERATIONAL IQ GAINS: WE'RE BRIGHTER NOW!

However, there is no need to feel depressed about the demise of adolescents' fluid intelligence. What is lost is apparently compensated for by an almost equal improvement in crystallized intelligence (Horn, 1970). In addition, James Flynn (1984, 1998), after analyzing archival IQ data from as early as the 1930s, discovered that young American children and adolescents made IQ score gains at the average rate of 3 IQ points per decade since 1932. What this means is that if we use the 1940s criteria to calculate the IQ scores of today's adolescents, those with an IQ score of 127 today would have had a score of 145 in 1939. In other words, a moderately smart young person in the year 2000 would have been considered a genius 60 years ago! Such substantial IQ gains are not limited to American children and adolescents. Slightly smaller gains have been observed with American adults (1.7 points per decade). Also, data from 14 countries (Flynn, 1987) reveal that within a single generation (30 years), IQ gains in children, adolescents, and adults vary from 5 points to 25 points. Moreover, the biggest gains are from mental tests designed to measure fluid intelligence. After reviewing reports since his first discovery of generational IQ gains in the 1980s, Flynn (1998) concluded that this so-called Flynn effect is a real, universal, and ongoing effect. It is clear that genetic factors cannot account for the massive change in IQ scores on such a small time scale. The effect must be due to certain environmental factors. However, exactly what environmental factors are responsible for the effect is still hotly debated. It is obviously beyond the scope of this chapter and interested readers are referred to Flynn (1998).

Reasoning

Although "reasoning" is not easily defined, it can be thought of approximately as the set of mental processes by which we draw conclusions on the basis of information known to us. For example, suppose you dislike getting wet in the rain. And suppose you know it is raining. Because both bits of information are known to you, you may reason that it is worthwhile to look for an umbrella before you go outside. As this example illustrates, reasoning is something we carry out on a frequent basis, often unaware of the fact we are doing so. But as anyone who has taken a course in formal logic knows, reasoning is rarely as clear or straightforward as in the above example. There are also many qualitatively different classes of reasoning. In this section we discuss three types of reasoning – *deductive*, *inductive*, and *analogical*.

DEDUCTIVE AND INDUCTIVE REASONING

Much of the reasoning done by humans can be classified as either *deductive* or *inductive*. **Deductive reasoning** is the "process of deriving inferences that make explicit what is implicit in the information available to us" (Small, 1990), while **inductive reasoning** is the use of specific examples to draw a general conclusion. One way to characterize the difference between them is that deductive reasoning involves drawing of specific conclusions from general premises. In contrast, inductive reasoning draws a general conclusion from specific premises. A couple of examples will help to clarify this distinction.

Deductive reasoning is often illustrated in the form of a **syllogism**. A syllogism is composed of two statements (called *premises*) and a conclusion that follows from the premises. Suppose the first premise is "all cows can fly," the second premise is "Bertha is a cow," and the conclusion is "Bertha can fly." This is deductive reasoning. The next example illustrates a typical form of inductive reasoning. Suppose we are told "Bertha the cow can fly," "Mabel the cow can fly," and "Trudy the cow can also fly," and Bertha, Mabel, and Trudy are the only cows living on Old MacDonald's farm. It logically follows that "all cows on Old MacDonald's farm can fly."

Universal and particular quantifiers

Developmentally, Piaget held that true deductive and inductive reasoning could not be carried out until the stage of **formal operations** (see below), at which time adolescents could reason reliably, that is, in agreement with rules of logic. Subsequent research has indicated otherwise in a couple of respects. While it is true that reasoning improves with age, it is not the case that adolescents reason reliably. Nor do adults, for that matter. A study by Erickson (1978) serves to illustrate this point. First, we point out that premises and the conclusion in a syllogism can each have a "universal quantifier" or a "particular quantifier." The word "all" is typically used as a universal quantifier and "some" as a particular quantifier. In addition, premises and conclusion can be stated in affirmative or negative form. The difference between universal and particular quantifiers is the difference between the statements "all birds can fly" and "some birds can fly." The distinction between an affirmative and negative form is the difference between the statements "all people are good" and "all people are not good."

What is important to point out for the present purposes is that it is generally easier to reason about *universal* premises than about *particulars*. In his study, Erickson had college students judge the validity of conclusions drawn from four types of abstract syllogisms, all with universal premises. He presented each type of problem in combination with four possible conclusions (i.e., universal-affirmative, universal-negative, particular-affirmative, particular-negative). For example, he could have had the following universal premises and four conclusions:

Premise 1:	All A are B.	(universal premise)
Premise 2:	All B are C.	(universal premise)
Conclusion 1:	All A are C.	(universal-affirmative conclusion)
Conclusion 2:	All A are not C.	(universal-negative conclusion)
Conclusion 3:	Some A are C.	(particular-affirmative conclusion)
Conclusion 4:	Some A are not C.	(particular-negative conclusion)

The above example is in fact quite straightforward, but other combinations of premises and conclusion are not. Reflecting this point, Erickson found that performance varied considerably depending on the form of the premises and conclusion. Consider the following example premises and two possible conclusions:

Premise 1 (P1):	All C are B.
Premise 2 (P2):	All B are A.
Conclusion 1 (C1):	All A are C.
Conclusion 2 (C2):	Some A are C.

In this case C1 is not valid and C2 is valid. However, subjects in Erickson's study tended to judge incorrectly both that C1 was valid (87 percent) and C2 not valid (95 percent).

Deductive reasoning

Thus even as adults we often have difficulty distinguishing valid from invalid conclusions in cases of deductive reasoning. Nevertheless, it would be wrong to conclude that there is no development of deductive reasoning in childhood and adolescence. One reason the participants in Erickson's study performed as poorly as they did was because all premises and conclusions were stated in abstract form. This becomes clear if we substitute "all basketball players are tall" and "all tall people are shy" for P1 and P2, respectively; the corresponding conclusions are "all shy people are basketball players" (C1) and "some shy people are basketball players" (C2). From P1 and P2 it follows that all basketball players are shy. Clearly this does not mean that all shy people are basketball players, as C1 states. But if all basketball players are shy, then it is also true that some shy people are basketball players, as C2 states.

The example above serves to illustrate what research has repeatedly shown: that for people of all ages deductive reasoning is facilitated by including concrete content rather than abstract symbols. Developmentally, what is important to note is that while even preschoolers show some evidence of deductive reasoning in cases where material is very familiar to them (Hawkins, Pea, Glick, & Scribner, 1984), the reliance on content over logical form becomes increasingly diminished as childhood progresses into adolescence (e.g., Overton, Ward, Noveck, Black, & O'Brien, 1987).

Although few studies have examined the development of inductive reasoning in childhood and adolescence, an informative study is one by Galotti, Komatsu, and Voelz (1997). Galotti et al., in two experiments, assessed deductive and inductive reasoning in kindergartners and second to sixth graders (in the age range 7 to 11 years). They looked at understanding of syllogisms like: "All shakdees have three eyes. Myro is a shakdee. Does Myro have three eyes?" (deductive version); and "Myro is a shakdee. Myro has three eyes. Do all shakdees have three eyes?" (inductive version). They asked children to state whether the conclusion was true. Importantly, they also asked them to rate their confidence in their responses, as well as to provide explanations for their answers. Galotti et al. found that beginning in the second grade (around 7 years of age), and clearly by the fourth grade (9 years), there was evidence that deductive reasoning problems were easier than inductive problems, in that they were answered more quickly and confidence ratings were higher than for the inductive reasoning problems. What this result suggests is that by the end of elementary school certain aspects of deductive and inductive reasoning are understood in an abstract sense; that is, it is increasingly understood that what is important is the logical form of the problem and not the content. This interpretation is supported by systematic changes in the types of explanations children provided for their responses: kindergarten children typically provided explanations that did not make reference to the logical form of the premises (for example, by attempting to relate the conclusion to their real-world knowledge and responding on that basis), with the form of the premises mentioned progressively more at higher grades.

ANALOGICAL REASONING

Another type of reasoning is reasoning by analogy. **Analogical reasoning** requires abstraction of a relationship between two elements, and mapping of the relationship onto two other elements with a similar relationship. Although there are different types of analogies, one common type is often expressed in the general form "A:B::C:D." This shorthand is read as "A is to B as C is to D," and states that the relationship of A to B is in some way equivalent or similar to the relationship of C to D. A very straightforward example is woman: man::girl: boy. Here, the relationships involved are related to genders and different parts of the lifespan. An analogy that is more abstract is food:body::book:mind.

In practice, even quite simple analogies like the first example above are typically beyond the grasp of very young children. By age 9 or 10 such simple analogies are understood; however, analogical reasoning undergoes rapid development after this time. Specifically, researchers have identified at least three qualitatively distinct stages in analogical reasoning between approximately the ages of 9 and 18 (Sternberg & Rifkin, 1979; see Case, 1985). As mentioned, by age 9 or 10 years analogies with familiar elements and very clear relations among elements can be solved. By about 12 years of age relations among elements that are not obvious can be considered, but this is possible primarily in the case that the elements themselves are concrete rather than abstract entities, as in the second analogy above. By about 13 or 14 years of age, analogies wherein both the entities comprising the analogy and the relationship between the entities are abstract can be understood (e.g., task:completion::problem:solution). Even more complex analogies, referred to as **second-order analogies**, are not solved reliably until about 16 or 17 years of age. An example of a second-order analogy is (Bert and Ernie):friendship::(Romeo and Juliet)::love (example from Case, 1985). Note that understanding the analogy requires that the relationships of *Sesame Street*'s Bert and Ernie, and Shakespeare's Romeo and Juliet, be derived: only then does the analogy reduce to "friends are to friendship as lovers are to love." In general, then, the progression is from a very concrete understanding of analogies limited to very familiar content to a much more flexible and abstract understanding.

Moral reasoning

The ability to make sophisticated moral judgments increases over the course of childhood and adolescence, especially in western cultures. Facets of the increase in moral judgment sophistication are captured by Kohlberg's **moral judgment stages** and these, together with an account of the several factors that influence moral judgment development, are discussed in chapter 14.

Formal Operational Thinking

The term *formal operational thinking* is used by Piaget to refer to the unique way of thinking in adolescence. Piaget theorized that the final stage of cognitive development is that of formal operations, by the end of which adolescents reach the highest level of thinking humanly possible.

According to Piaget, adolescent thinking is in some ways similar to that of children in the **concrete operations stage** (chapter 8). Adolescents, like concrete operational children, think rationally and logically. Both are able to use mental operations to represent and manipulate ideas. They can use logical rules to infer new information based on given information, without actually observing the new information. For example, in a **transitivity task**, concrete and formal operational children can use the transitional logic (if a > b and b > c, then a > c) to draw a conclusion about who is the tallest after being told that Mary is taller than John and John is taller than Mike. They do not have to know Mary, John, and Mike, nor do they have to line up Mary against John and Mike to confirm who is actually the tallest. One of the major features of mental operations is **reversibility**. Due to this feature, school-aged children and adolescents can carry out many of their daily activities internally. They can mentally alter realities back and forth without actually changing them. For example, imagine that you pick up one of your parents' favorite vases, drop it, and see it shatter. Now reverse the sequence to return the vase back to its original form. You can do this effortlessly and repeatedly, to your heart's content. Now, break the vase for real and try to put it back together. On second thoughts, maybe that would be a bad idea!

Abstract thought

Despite some similarities, Piaget believed that adolescents are fundamentally differ-ent thinkers than concrete operational children. First, they think abstractly and use operations that are extracted from a number of concrete operations (i.e., operation of operations). Therefore, these operations are abstract, general, and content-free (hence the term "formal"). An analogy for the difference between concrete and formal opera-tions is that between simple arithmetic calculations (1 + 2 = 3) and an algebraic equation (X + Y = Z). It is for this reason that concrete operational children pass num-ber, length, liquid, mass, and volume **conservation** tasks at different ages, while adoles-cents can do them all: the concrete operational child needs a specific operation for each task, while the adolescent applies one rule to all conservation tasks. Piaget called this characteristic of adolescent thinking **interpropositional thinking**, contrasted with the "*intra*propositional thinking" of concrete operational children. Adolescents' ability to think abstractly and globally perhaps leads to their struggles with big philosophical questions such as "What is the meaning of life?" and "Does God exist?"

Realms of possibility

Second, Piaget theorized that concrete and formal operational children conceptualize the relationship between reality and possibility differently. Concrete operational chil-dren are "earthbound, concrete, and practical-minded" thinkers (Flavell, Miller, & Miller, 1993, p. 139). In contrast, adolescents treat reality as only one of many possibilities. Their minds can move freely in and out of many different realms of possibility. They apply logical thinking to the possible (what might exist), not just to the real (what does exist). For example, it would be very difficult for a concrete operational child to solve the following problems:

1   If ants are bigger than dogs and dogs are bigger than elephants, which animals are the biggest?
2   All goldfish are green. Wanda is a goldfish. What color is Wanda?

Adolescents, in contrast, normally can answer these questions without any difficulty. The ability to think about what might be possible explains why for many people an interest in science fiction emerges in the teenage years.

The adolescent as an apprentice scientist

Third, according to Piaget, adolescents are apprentice scientists who can come up with theories in an attempt to explain certain phenomena, generate hypotheses based on these theories, and systematically devise tests to confirm or refute these hypo-theses. In other words, adolescents can carry out **hypothetico-deductive reasoning**. Unlike formal operational thinkers, concrete operational children tend to have a single theory about how a phenomenon in question operates. Although they do generate hypotheses to test their theories, only confirmatory evidence is accepted while counter-evidence is ignored. For example, in a study by Karmiloff-Smith and Inhelder (1975), both of whom were Piaget's research associates, children were presented with long wooden blocks that weighed differently at each end. Sometimes the weight differential was visible (an extra piece of wood was glued to one end), while other times it was not visible (a metal piece was inserted into one end). They were asked to balance the blocks on another piece of wood. Many concrete operational children hypothesized that the blocks would balance in their geometric middle. Children with this hypothesis repeatedly tried to balance the blocks without success. They attributed their failure not to a faulty hypothesis but to some anomalies in their procedure of testing. When they were asked to balance the blocks with eyes closed, they succeeded in the task by using touch. However, once they opened their eyes, they refused to acknowledge their correct solution and stubbornly refused to abandon their hypothesis. In contrast, adolescents tended to be more flexible about their hypotheses; they would readily give up a hypothesis if the counterevidence was strong.

Scientific problems

According to Piaget, adolescents' unique way of thinking is manifested in how they solve complex problems. In their book, *The Growth of Logical Thinking from Childhood to Adolescence* (1958), Inhelder and Piaget documented their innovative experiments with adolescents on more than a dozen scientific projects, to illustrate various character-istics of formal operational thought. Here we focus on two tasks only to illustrate the empirical evidence on which Piaget's theory of formal operational thought was based.

The balance scale problem

This problem was used by Piaget to illustrate how children develop the ability to think systematically about multiple dimensions. Children are shown a simple balance scale, with equally spaced pegs along each side. A number of same-sized weights can be placed on the pegs. The children's task is to predict whether or not the balance scale will balance when varying numbers of weights are placed at different distances from the fulcrum (see figure 15.6). The correct solution to this problem is to obtain the force torque of each side (i.e., weight × distance). When the force torque on one side is greater than on the other, the balance scale will tilt down on the side with greater weight. If the force torque on either side is equivalent the scale will balance. Piaget believed that, in order to succeed in such a task, children must be able to think using

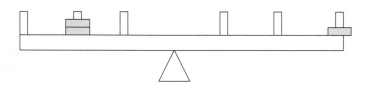

Figure 15.6 The balance scale task.

combinatory thought, that is, taking more than one factor into consideration (weight and distance). Single-minded thinking will lead to failure in some trials (e.g., only considering weight leads to the false prediction that the scale in figure 15.6 will fall on the *left* side; only considering distance, in contrast, leads to the incorrect prediction that the scale will fall on the *right* side). Piaget found that only adolescents can consider both weight and distance and succeed in predicting the behavior of the balance scale under various conditions.

The pendulum problem

To illustrate how children develop the ability to carry out hypothetico-deductive reasoning, Inhelder and Piaget presented children with the pendulum problem. This problem involves a wooden stand, various lengths of string, and several weights. The experimenter demonstrates how strings with different lengths and weights may produce different speeds of swinging when the weight is released at different heights. The children's task is to discover the law governing the pendulum's swinging speed. The correct response is that the length of the pendulum determines the speed; the shorter the string, the faster the pendulum swings. Inhelder and Piaget found that concrete operational children normally tried a few combinations of weights, lengths, and heights but in a random, unsystematic manner. In contrast, adolescents, especially older ones, proposed multiple hypotheses based on their observations. They isolated factors that could affect the pendulum speed, and tested the impact of each factor systematically. They first varied each factor alone while keeping other factors constant, then proceeded to test the effect of two or three factor combinations. From their observations of experiments with different factorial designs, they drew the conclusion that the speed of the pendulum varied only as a function of its length.

Controversies About Piaget's Theory and Research Regarding Formal Operational Thought

DO ALL ADOLESCENTS REACH THIS STAGE?

Piaget's theory and research on formal operational thinking has led to a considerable number of follow-up studies and heated theoretical debates about exactly how adolescents think. Later studies using exactly the same tasks developed by Inhelder and Piaget often failed to replicate their findings (e.g., Commons, Miller, & Kuhn, 1982; Epstein, 1979). In general, adolescents did not perform as well as documented by Inhelder and Piaget. For example, Epstein (1979) found that only 32 percent of 15-year-olds and 34 percent of 18-year-olds showed evidence of using formal operations. Piaget seemed to have overestimated adolescents' formal operational thinking.

Recall that Piaget suggested that the formal operational stage is the final level of cognitive development, by the end of which adolescents reach the highest level of logical thinking. Apparently, this conclusion is also flawed. For example, Keating (1980) and Capon and Kuhn (1979) found that only one-third of adolescents and adults passed formal operational tasks. Researchers now agree that formal operational think-ing continues to develop well into adulthood and many adults may never reach this level of thinking.

Piaget contended that formal operational thinking is a pervasive form of think-ing that emerges around 11 years of age and influences adolescents' performance in varying task domains. Follow-up studies showed that this claim is also inaccurate. Adolescents' ability to use formal operations appears to develop gradually. In early adolescence, formal operations are not fully developed, nor are they used consistently in different task domains. In late adolescence and adulthood, some, but not all, indi-viduals become capable of consistently and skillfully using formal operational thought to solve problems (e.g., Kuhn, Langer, Kohlberg, & Haan, 1977).

THE ROLE OF EXPERIENCE

Piaget further claimed that formal operational thought is constructed by an adoles-cent him- or herself, and educational and cultural experiences play little role in its development. Many studies have disputed this conclusion. With the use of both limited (giving hints; e.g., Stone & Day, 1978) and extended training procedures (e.g., Case, 1974), researchers found that training was effective with children in late middle childhood and adolescents who did not show formal operational thinking in the pretest. Individuals' knowledge and expertise has also been shown to affect how effect-ively they use formal operations. One study (De Lisi & Staudt, 1980) showed that university students' performance in formal operational tasks depended on their major subject: those majoring in physics did well in the Piagetian tasks, while political science students had better performance in tasks that required political reasoning. In addition, cultural experience also plays an important role in the development of formal opera-tional thinking. A study conducted in Hong Kong and the United States (Douglas & Wong, 1977) found that Chinese adolescents responded in the Piagetian tasks at less advanced levels than their American counterparts; Chinese males performed better than Chinese females, perhaps due to the Chinese culture's differential socialization processes for males and females. Cross-cultural studies also have revealed that adol-escents and adults in cultures where scientific thinking is not emphasized tend to perform poorly in the standard Piagetian tasks (Dasen & Heron, 1981). This does not mean that they do not think in a complex manner. In fact, in situations that are adaptively meaningful to them, their cognitive ability is very sophisticated (e.g., Micronesians' ability to ride canoes in high seas without the aid of navigational instru-ments; Hutchins, 1993).

CROSS-GENERATIONAL GAINS

A recent study (Flieller, 1999) further confirms the impact of environmental factors on cognitive development. Flieller (1999) compared data on five Piagetian tasks (Longeot, 1966) from 10- to 15-year-olds from two different generations (early 1970s versus mid-1990s). The five tasks were (1) weight and volume conservation tasks,

(2) the pendulum problem, (3) a permutation task that requires children to identify how many ways different colored tokens can be lined up, (4) a probability task in which children have to estimate the odds of obtaining certain types of tokens drawn from a container, and (5) a mechanical curve task in which children have to draw curves produced by a pencil that is fastened to a rotating cylinder. These tasks are all adapted from those used by Inhelder and Piaget (1958) and are thought to test adolescents' formal operational thinking.

Flieller (1999) found that at equal age, today's adolescents exhibited a higher level of cognitive development than the adolescents of 20 or 30 years ago. For example, for the samples taken in 1972 and 1993, the cross-generational gain in the overall score is about 5 points (**standardized score** with a mean of 100 and a **standard deviation** of 15). What this means is that an adolescent who was ranked average in 1993 (i.e., a score of 100) in terms of formal operational thought would have been ranked above average, with a score of 105, about 30 years ago. Flieller also observed that the amount of gain varied across tasks. Gains were greatest for combinatory thought (the permutation task) and quite large for the pendulum, probability, and mechanical curve tasks, but equivocal for the conservation tasks. A strong correlation was also found between the participants' IQ scores and their scores on these cognitive tasks. This suggests that the acceleration of cognitive development is related to the cross-generational gains in IQ scores; both are perhaps due to similar improvements in environmental factors over the last 30 years.

Beyond Piaget's Theory

Despite the fact that empirical evidence fails to confirm the major predictions of Piaget's theory regarding adolescents' thinking, Piaget's contribution to research on adolescent cognitive development is undeniable. His theoretical and empirical work has inspired many researchers to work in the area and to ask the same questions that Piaget asked almost a half-century ago: How do adolescents think? Are adolescents fundamentally different thinkers? What are the characteristics of adolescent thought?

THE INFORMATION-PROCESSING APPROACH
TO ADOLESCENT THINKING

One post-Piagetian approach to adolescent thinking is the **information-processing** approach. This approach uses the computer as a metaphor to describe **cognitive processes**. Information-processing theorists believe that adolescents' thinking is, in a nutshell, a process of obtaining information from the environment, storing information in the short-term and long-term memory systems, and using various rules and strategies to manipulate information. The goal of such a system is to derive new information and to guide actions.

To illustrate this approach, let us look at a study conducted by Siegler (1976). Siegler used the same balance scale task used by Inhelder and Piaget (1958) to test whether and how 5-, 9-, 13-, and 17-year-olds could solve this problem. However, he took an entirely different approach in analyzing children's thinking processes. He believed that thinking is rule-based and children use specific rules for solving specific problems in a specific domain. Using a so-called task analysis method, Siegler identified several rules that children could possibly use to solve this problem. Rule I is to consider only the weights on each side. Rule II is to consider solely the weight factor, except in the case that the weights are equal, in which case distance is considered. Rule III is to consider weights and distances simultaneously; however, when the two factors conflict (i.e., one side has more weight and the other side has more distance), the child simply resorts to guessing. Rule IV is the most advanced rule, based on the force torque on each side.

Siegler presented children with different combinations of weights and distances on the balance scale. He reported that children used increasingly more complex rules as their age increased. Nearly all 5-year-olds used Rule I, most 9-year-olds used Rule II, and many 13- and 17-year-olds used Rule III. Inconsistent with Piaget's conclusion, few adolescents actually used Rule IV. Siegler used a flow chart to illustrate how children adopting a particular rule solve the balance beam tasks (see figure 15.7).

Siegler (1981) has applied the same methodology to a number of additional Piagetian tasks and successfully obtained results consistent with the information-processing approach. Based on his results and those of others (e.g., Klahr & Robinson, 1981), Siegler (1981) concluded that children and adolescents may not think using general-purpose, or **domain-general**, formal operations that can be applied to problems across various domains. Rather, he claims their thinking is rule-based, and that these rules are **domain-specific**. That is, specific rules are only applicable to specific tasks in a specific domain. In different domains children's and adolescents' expertise may be different. Hence, they may use rules of different levels on different tasks.

ADOLESCENTS AS INTUITIVE SCIENTISTS

Another line of research on adolescents' thinking does not use the "children process information like a computer" metaphor. Rather, children and adolescents are viewed as **intuitive scientists** (Karmiloff-Smith, 1992a; Kuhn, 1989). The fundamental assumptions of this approach are that children and adolescents are capable of both constructing theories to explain how the world operates in a law-like manner and conducting "experiments" to confirm them. At this point, these notions do not depart significantly from those of Piaget. What makes this approach different from Piaget's theory is the assumption that cognitive development is domain-specific: there is no overarching principle that a child of a particular age can use to solve *all* problems, and different domains call for different theories and different methods. Along this line of thinking, an adolescent may be an expert in solving problems in one domain (e.g., mathematics) but not in another (e.g., physics), and may never reach a sophisticated level of thinking in certain domains.

Unlike the information-processing approach, the children-as-intuitive-scientists approach views children as naive theorists, not as rule users. Thinking is not a rule-governed behavior. Rather, it is a process guided by children's intuitive theoretical understanding of the world. As intuitive scientists, children divide problems they

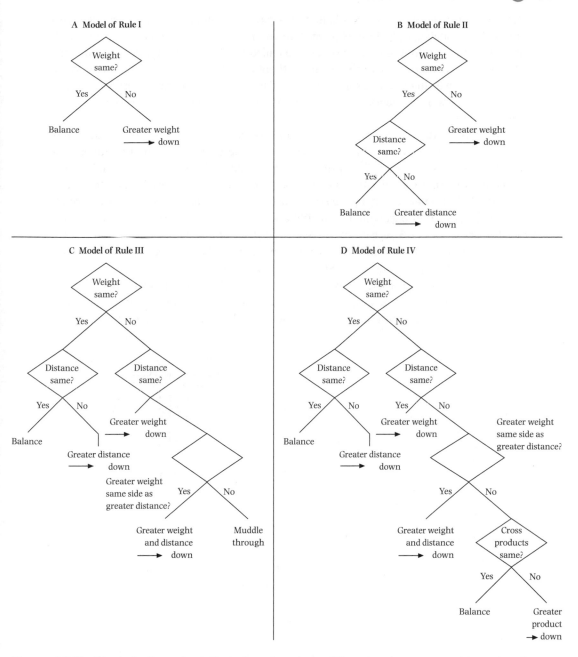

Figure 15.7 Siegler's flow chart that describes how different rules are used to solve the balance scale task. From R. S. Siegler, "Information processing approaches to cognitive development." In W. Kessen (Ed.), *Handbook of child psychology*, Vol. 1 (New York: Wiley, 1983), p. 160. Reprinted by permission of Robert S. Siegler.

encounter into different ontological domains (physical, biological, and psychological). For each ontological domain they formulate an intuitive theory that consists of loosely organized assumptions. When children are called upon to explain a certain phenomenon in a particular domain, the intuitive theory for that domain is activated. While children's naive theories are sometimes consistent with scientific theories, on many other occasions their theories are not supported by scientific evidence. Hence, errors are common.

For example, McCloskey and his colleagues conducted a series of studies to document the extent to which young children, adolescents, and university students understand the physical laws of motion. They presented participants with simple tasks that involved predicting the trajectory of a moving ball. For example, in one study (Kaiser, McCloskey, & Proffitt, 1986), participants were shown a curved tube (figure 15.8(a)) and asked to predict the path that a moving ball would take after it exits the tube. Only 44 percent of 12-year-olds and 65 percent of university students made correct predictions (figure 15.8(a): the solid straight line). Many participants mistakenly thought the ball would travel in a curved path (figure 15.8(a): the dotted line).

In a similar study (Kaiser, Proffitt, & McCloskey, 1985), preschoolers, first and second graders, third and fourth graders, fifth and sixth graders, and university students were asked to predict how a moving ball would fall after rolling over the edge of a

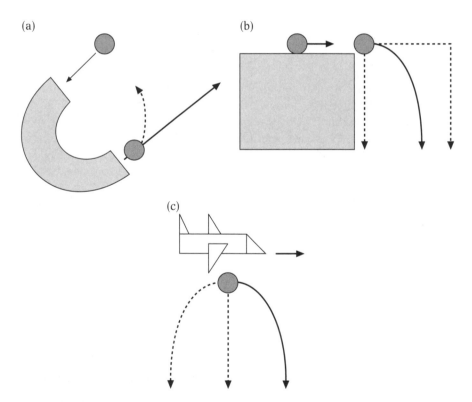

Figure 15.8 (a) The C-curve task used by Kaiser et al. (1986).
(b) and (c) Two tasks used by Kaiser et al. (1985). Reprinted by permission of the Psychonomic Society.

table. Most adolescents (79 percent) and all university students made correct predictions (i.e., the ball will continue to move forward as it falls, see figure 15.8(b)), while most preschoolers and first and second graders and half of the fifth and sixth graders predicted erroneously that the ball would fall straight down. However, when participants were presented with a new situation in which the ball fell off a moving model train, most children, regardless of age, made incorrect predictions. They either thought that the ball would fall behind the dropping point or straight down (the correct response is that the ball travels the same path as the ball falling off the edge of a table; figure 15.8(c): the solid line). Even 35 percent of the university students made similar mistakes. Interestingly, when children and adults were shown the actual falling event after they made erroneous predictions, they were surprised by the outcomes but refused to admit that they had made a mistake. Rather, they explained the discrepancy away by suggesting, for example, that the experimenter released the ball later than the experimenter had indicated or that the ball was pushed just before falling. This result indicates that it is the erroneous theory of motion, not the lack of direct evidence, that led children and adolescents to make incorrect predictions. Overall, the studies by McCloskey and his associates suggest that many adolescents and some adults still hold at least a partially erroneous theory of motion. They are apparently not ready to relinquish a theory even in the face of counterevidence.

Three common flaws in children's and adolescents' use of theories

Adolescents' reluctance to abandon an intuitive theory has also been found in areas other than physical motion (e.g., balance: Karmiloff-Smith & Inhelder, 1975; medicine: Kuhn, Amsel, & O'Loughlin, 1988; car mechanics: Schauble, 1991). Kuhn (1989), after reviewing a series of studies, identified three common flaws in children's and adolescents' use of theories. First, they tend to fail to separate theory and evidence. They seem to have difficulty in understanding that a theory needs to be confirmed or refuted by evidence. They find it even harder to understand the kind of evidence that is needed to refute a theory. Very often they carry out experiments in search of evidence that *supports* their theory rather than evidence that can *test* their theory. It should be noted, however, that the failure in differentiating theory from evidence mainly occurs with older children and adolescents when they already have a favored theory and when several possible explanations exist for a phenomenon in question (Flavell et al., 1993).

The second flaw of children's and adolescents' use of intuitive theory is that they tend to select evidence consistent with their theory instead of modifying or abandoning a theory in the face of mounting counterevidence. When encountering counterevidence, children and adolescents often ignore it or explain it away. Sometimes, they even manufacture evidence to support their theory. Overall, it seems that children and adolescents are often so attached to their theory that their eyes are blinded by it. In this regard, scientists often do not fare any better; they can be equally nonobjective about a beloved theory in the face of counterevidence (Kuhn, 1989). The third flaw of children and adolescents (and some adults) is that they need a plausible alternative theory in order to accept counterevidence to their existing theory. In other words, having a theory seems to be more important than having empirical evidence. They seem to believe and live by a motto proclaimed by Karmiloff-Smith and Inhelder (1975): "If you want to get ahead, get a theory" (or, as is often claimed of academics, "Professors need theories like dogs need fleas"!).

General characteristics of adolescent thinking

Despite theoretical debates and evidential discrepancies in the literature, and despite some weaknesses in adolescent thinking, many researchers agree that adolescent thinking is more sophisticated than that of younger children, as well as being fundamentally different. As Keating (1990) pointed out, "across a wide range of content areas, from logical and mathematical topics, to moral reasoning, to interpersonal understanding, to social and political issues, to the nature of knowledge itself, there is substantial consistency in the ways in which adolescents, compared to children, respond to problems posed to them" (p. 64).

Keating (1980) summarized five major characteristics associated with the development of thinking in adolescence:

1. In contrast to childhood thinking that focuses on the here and now, adolescent thinking emphasizes the world of possibility.
2. In adolescence the ability to carry out systematic hypothesis testing and scientific reasoning emerges.
3. Adolescents can think about the future by planning ahead.
4. They are also capable of introspecting about their own thought processes, that is, they can think about their thinking (or **metacognition**).
5. The content of adolescent thinking is expanded to include social, moral, and political issues, not only issues concerning the external world but also personal issues.

Summary and Conclusions

This chapter has been about thinking in adolescence. A large body of research has indicated that adolescent thinking is qualitatively different than the thinking of young children. This is true of the complex thinking involved in reasoning, for example, or in what we normally think of as "intelligence." It is also true, however, in areas you may not normally consider as part of "thinking," for example perception and attention. Compared to the perceptions and attention of younger children, perception and attention in adolescence are more flexible. Increased flexibility is also evident in the advanced ways adolescents use strategies to enhance their memory, relative to what young children are capable of. Reasoning and problem-solving can be carried out at a less concrete level than in younger years, ideas captured in Piaget's notions of formal operational thinking. Of course, adolescents are still apprentices in thinking. They are yet to learn some more sophisticated ways of thinking such as conducting truly scientific investigation and carrying out abstract logical reasoning. Nevertheless, the thinking skills acquired during adolescence lay the foundation for taking on the more complex and diverse problems of adulthood.

DISCUSSION POINTS

1 What is the difference between the process, structure, and content of adolescents' thoughts?
2 What aspects of perception and attention continue to develop throughout childhood and into adolescence?
3 In what ways do memory abilities improve during adolescence?
4 How does intelligence develop during adolescence?
5 What are the major features of formal operational thinking?
6 Think about the criticisms of Piaget's theory of adolescent thinking. How adequate are alternative approaches?
7 What are the major characteristics of adolescents' thinking? Do they have a unique way of thinking?

SUGGESTIONS FOR FURTHER READING

Adams, G. (2000). *Adolescent development: The essential readings.* Cambridge, MA, and Oxford: Blackwell.

Eysenck, M. W. (2001). *Principles of cognitive psychology.* Hove: Psychology Press.

Lee, K. (Ed.) (2000). *Cognitive development: The essential readings.* Cambridge, MA, and Oxford: Blackwell.

Parkin, A. J. (2000). *Essential cognitive psychology.* Hove: Psychology Press.

chapter 16

Social Development

Tanya Bergevin, William M. Bukowski, and Richard Miners

KEY CONCEPTS

AUTHORITARIAN PARENTING	EMOTION REGULATION	ONTOGENY
AUTHORITATIVE PARENTING	EPIGENETIC PRINCIPLE	PARENTAL STYLE
AUTONOMY	FIELD THEORY	PEERS
COGNITION	ID	PHYLOGENY
COGNITIVE DEVELOPMENT	INDULGENT PARENTING	PRIMARY DRIVES
CROSS-CULTURAL STUDY	LIBIDINAL FORCES	PSYCHOSEXUAL STAGES
DEFENSE MECHANISMS	LIFE SPACE	RECAPITULATION
EGO	MORATORIUM	SELF-CONCEPT
EMOTION	NEGLECTFUL PARENTING	ZEITGEIST

OVERVIEW

Recognizing the multifaceted nature of adolescence, this chapter approaches the topic by reviewing the contrasting accounts of five major figures in the field, along with the research that has followed in their wake.

According to G. Stanley Hall, adolescence is a time of storm and stress, a form of second birth through which individuals make a transition from the primitive ways of childhood to the refined values of adulthood. Fascinating though this picture may be, the authors point out that adolescence is not typically as stormy and stressful as he portrays it.

The claim of Kurt Lewin's field theory is that interactional forces existing between individual and environment can predict individual behavior, and Lewin suggests that adolescent problems can be understood as conflicts between competing forces. Such conflicts arise during adolescence in particular because individuals are in transition between child and adult group membership.

Anna Freud takes a psychoanalytic approach to adolescence, claiming that the upheavals of adolescence result from the growing challenge to the ego presented by developing sexuality. The prediction is that the onset of puberty should see an increase in "moody" behavior. It turns out that there is little evidence for this. However, boys' relationships with parents suffer during puberty. The strongest evidence concerns timing of puberty: early puberty in girls and late puberty in boys is associated with problems and conflict.

Peter Blos saw adolescence as part of a series of psychosexual stages during which personality development was completed. According to this account, a key factor in adolescence concerns the balance between the growing need for independence and the maintenance of parental bonds. The authors show how parental style has much to do with the success of this transition.

The work of Harry Stack Sullivan focuses particularly on peer relationships. Sullivan argues that behavior can only be understood as the result of interaction processes between self and others, claiming that psychological growth is driven by the need to satisfy interpersonal needs. In adolescence the need is for romantic relationships and friendships with peers.

Erik Erikson sees adolescence as a transition to adult identity during which the individual goes through a period in which he or she does not have a stable sense of identity. Consequently, he or she may adhere to a wide range of beliefs and ideologies. Thus according to Erikson, a major focus in adolescence is development toward a stable identity and self-concept.

In reviewing these accounts and the evidence that stems from them, the authors provide a convincing case for the need to consider many different factors in explaining developmental processes during adolescence.

Introduction

Social and personality development in adolescence is multifaceted and dynamic. It involves several highly interrelated forms of development that encompass a broad range of behaviors, feelings, thoughts, and health-related consequences. Compared to the school-age period, the social domains in which adolescents participate are more numerous, more complex, more challenging, and potentially more exciting and dangerous. In these domains, adolescents think, feel, act, and interact with others in ways that are new to them. It can be a period of intense interest, excitement, achievement, and happiness. It can be a time of confusion, anxiety, sadness, and disruption. For many youths, adolescence represents a time of accomplishments, health, and well-being; for others it is a time of insurmountable challenges that lead to an unsatisfying, troubled, and frustrating adulthood.

Key Characteristics of Development

What are the major characteristics of social and personality development in adolescence? Social development in adolescence has three central features. They are *growth*, *differentiation*, and *synthesis*. By *growth* we mean that adolescents develop new skills and concepts, experience new **emotions**, and begin to function in a larger number of social and personal domains. They display a wider repertoire of behaviors and experience a significant broadening of their social worlds. Certainly, some of the most pronounced forms of growth in adolescence are the quantitative and qualitative physical changes that result from puberty. Of the transformations that occur during adolescence, many are characterized by *differentiation*. That is, one's range of activities, behaviors, skills, ideas, social contacts, and emotions becomes broader, or more different, during adolescence than in childhood. Moreover, the differences, or variability, between individuals become larger as individual adolescents set off on their own developmental trajectories. As the range of an adolescent's behavior, thoughts, and experiences becomes larger and more complex, the adolescent is confronted with the challenge of bringing this diversity together. That is, adolescents need to *synthesize* this "newness" into a comprehensible and coherent approach to the world. Adolescents who can bring these new experiences and challenges together are likely to be on a trajectory toward a healthy and rewarding adulthood, whereas failing to do so may add to the challenges of becoming an adult.

Just as there are central features to adolescent development, there are also central goals or challenges that adolescents need to address. By the time they are ready to enter adulthood, adolescents should (1) be *autonomous* and **emotionally regulated**; (2) have a *sense of their identity*; and (3) be *able to form close relationships* with both same- and other-sex **peers**. These developments occur within five types of domains. They are the *social environment*, *puberty*, the *family*, the *peer group*, and the *self*. Separate sections of this chapter are devoted to each of these domains. Within each section, we use the intellectual biographies of the pioneering theorists to introduce the important issues of adolescent development. Their ideas provide the conceptual groundwork for our discussion of current research on adolescent social development.

 ## *Relations Between Social and Cognitive Development*

Before we begin this discussion it should be stated that one cannot understand social development in adolescence without understanding parallels in **cognitive development** during this time. It comes as little surprise that many of the ways in which adolescents come to think about themselves and others, about the way they behave, and about the emotions they experience can be traced to changes in **cognition**. It is likely also that experiences with parents and peers can challenge adolescents to think in new ways. Certainly, one cannot think about social and cognitive development as independent of each other.

We begin our discussion of social development in adolescence by considering an idea that has formed the foundation for the study of adolescence, proposed first by G. Stanley Hall. It is the idea that adolescence represents a period of storm and stress. We explain this idea and then evaluate it according to the data that are currently available. Following this we discuss the changes in the social domains in which adolescents function. To begin this discussion, we present the ideas of Kurt Lewin. We then discuss the question of how puberty affects the behavior and emotions of adolescents. This section is introduced with a discussion of the ideas of Anna Freud. Next, we focus on adolescent development within the family. The ideas of Peter Blos serve as the point of departure for this discussion. We next consider the peer system during adolescence, using the ideas of Harry Stack Sullivan as the foundation for this discussion. The last domain we consider is the self. Here we rely heavily on the ideas of Erik Erikson and his concept of identity.

 ## G. Stanley Hall: Adolescence as Storm and Stress

If any idea has dominated the study of adolescent development, it is G. Stanley Hall's pronouncement that adolescence is a time of storm and stress. According to this theory, human development is sequenced according to an evolutionary timeline. That is, each individual retraces the historical record of his or her species development (**phylogeny**) in his or her own growth (**ontogeny**) (Grinder, 1969, p. 357). Hence, according to Hall, ontogeny **recapitulates** phylogeny. Based on the notion that human development runs through the successive stages through which the human species has passed (Averill, 1982), Hall argued that normal human development follows a progression from animal-like dispositions to "civilized" higher-order functioning described as the "attainment of a superior mode or social existence or way of life" (White, 1992, p. 31). Believed to be mediated by biology, Hall argued that recapitulation occurs by virtue of the fact that more primitive areas of the brain mature before the ones that appeared more recently in our evolutionary past (White, 1992).

ADOLESCENCE AS A SECOND BIRTH

Hall depicts adolescence as the developmental period in which evolutionary momentum begins to subside – in which recapitulatory instincts, so important during childhood, begin to give way for new acquired characters to develop. It is in this capacity that adolescence is perceived as a second "birth," a second point of initiation and socialization in which individuals struggle to shed their primitive ways. He portrayed adolescence as a turbulent time of transition between what is coarse and what is refined – a struggle between behavioral patterns of opposing poles. In the words of White (1992, p. 31), Hall viewed adolescence as "a time of oscillation and oppositions between inertness and excitement, pleasure and pain, self-confidence and humility, selfishness and altruism, society and solitude." Given the proper educational influences and environment, it is during this crucial period that ontogeny can begin to surpass phylogeny and, as a result, the personality and intellect of the adolescent begin to blossom. The role of educators becomes to stimulate, nurture, guide, and prevent the arrest of social intellectual growth (Grinder, 1969); in brief, to foster adolescents' increased preparedness for selflessness, sacrifice, religion, and the appreciation of nature and science.

CRITICISM OF HALL'S ACCOUNT

Hall's notion that storm and stress are the central features of adolescence was at one time largely accepted as truth. More recently, however, empirical scrutiny of this concept has questioned its validity. This research, summarized by Arnett (1999), shows that although adults typically perceive adolescence as a time of upheaval and disorder, the actual occurrence of storm and stress in adolescence has been largely exaggerated. Together, studies of family relations and changes in emotion over time have failed to provide much support for the argument that adolescence is a universally difficult and disruptive period of the lifespan. As Arnett shows, however, although adolescence is not a universally stressful period, the evidence indicates that storm and stress are more likely during adolescence than at other times of the lifespan. Nevertheless, these characteristics are not necessarily characteristic of all adolescents. Whereas adolescence can be stressful for some youths, it is not so for all of them. Most of the discussion in this chapter will be oriented toward this modified storm and stress view of adolescence.

 ## *The Adolescent Social Environment: Kurt Lewin*

Before considering further ideas about adolescent development and the empirical evidence related to these concepts, it may be useful to ask, "What do adolescents do?" A conceptual basis to this question can be found in the work of Kurt Lewin. Inspired by the Gestalt school of thought, Lewin was a German social scientist who rejected the common *Zeitgeist* that psychological phenomena such as needs, hopes, and fears were beyond experimental reach. He challenged traditional thinking and methodologies by manipulating the intangible and doing what all contemporary psychologists aspire to do – to understand and predict "molar behavior patterns from information about the person (needs, motives) and about the situation (its opportunities, goal objects)" (Kelley, 1991, p. 211).

FIELD THEORY

Lewin's ideas were expressed as a coherent set of concepts known as **field theory**. Field theory, undoubtedly Lewin's most famous contribution, rests on the assumption that behavior (B) is a function (F) of an interaction between a person (P) and that person's environment (E), thus, expressed mathematically, $B = F (P,E)$. Stated somewhat differently, behavior can be predicted by the interactional forces between the individual and his or her environment. The Lewinian environment, or field, "is a perceptual or psychological environment" that has certain structural and dynamic properties (M. A. Lewin, 1998, p. 105). The structure of the environment is made up of regions that correspond roughly to physical areas and objects (the home), social entities (family, religious affiliations), and even concepts like abstract art and morality. Regions are defined by boundaries that may separate them sharply, for example, "religious affiliation may have nothing to do with abstract art" (M. A. Lewin, 1998, p. 106). On the other hand, boundaries may overlap – religious affiliation and morality may be deeply interdependent. Regions within the field have attracting or repelling properties, respectively known as positive or negative valences. It is these valences that orient and propel an individual into movement within the field. A person's movement toward or away from a valenced region is called *locomotion*. Lewinian theory suggests that conflicts arise when (1) different goals compete for the individual's locomotion, and (2) when goals carry both positive and negative valences. For example, being offered a highly desired job (positive valence) that involves long-term separation from loved ones (negative valence) may foster feelings of conflict within the individual.

The concept of life space

The person, like the environment, is also divided into regions that are separated by more or less permeable boundaries which correspond to the individual's characteristics, needs, and perceptions of the environment (M. A. Lewin, 1998). The number of regions within the person speak to the complexity of the individual and the "permeability of boundaries reflect the degree to which the different regions communicate with one another" (M. A. Lewin, 1998, p. 107). The activation of a region (i.e., when a person tries to solve a problem) puts that region under tension. This tension can alter the boundaries, paths, valences, and goals of the particular region. Thus, the make-up of the person and environment are ever-changing, creating the dynamic **life space**. One's life space, expressed as B = F (life space), represents the dynamic interchange between person and environment (M. A. Lewin, 1998). In sum, the person and the environment represent inseparable constructs, which together constitute the life space.

The development of life space

As a person matures, he or she becomes increasingly differentiated: "regions become more numerous and the boundaries between them become less permeable" (M. A. Lewin, 1998, p. 108). During adolescence, change is characterized by increased locomotion from one region to another. Increased locomotion promotes, and is promoted by, the widening of the life space (new geographic and social regions), and the entry into new situations that are "cognitively unstructured" (K. Lewin, 1939; rpt. 1953, p. 41). More specifically, adolescents find themselves in a social position between that of the child and that of the adult, which, according to the author, can be paralleled to that of a marginal member of an underprivileged minority group. This transient shift in group belongingness, or locomotion within the field, is what alters and shapes the adolescent's behavior. Because the move is toward an unknown region, behavioral uncertainty likely ensues. The adolescent may experience emotional instability and sensitivity. Moreover, he or she may be prone to unbalances in behavior, "to either boisterousness or shyness, exhibiting too much tension, and a frequent shift between extremes of contradictory behavior" (p. 40).

Besides locomotion toward cognitively unstructured regions, Lewin also describes how once familial regions also change during adolescence. For example, body change (i.e., puberty) and new physical experiences are also highlighted as "a baffling change of a central region of the established life space" (Lewin, 1939; rpt. 1953, p. 41). These factors are also pivotal in predicting adolescent behavior. Based on these changes in the life space (through locomotion, and changes that occur in once familial central regions), Lewin predicts that adolescents are susceptible to specific behavioral patterns.

Because they are uncertain in which group they belong, and because of the instability of their position, they experience conflict due to competing goals which relate to attitudes, values, ideologies, and styles of living. These conflicts in turn give rise to emotional tension (i.e., as exhibited by shyness, sensitivity, and aggression). Moreover, the adolescent is expected to display a "readiness to take extreme attitudes and actions and to shift his/her position radically" (Lewin, 1939; rpt. 1953, p. 41). Finally, field theory predicts that the "adolescent profile" should appear in anyone (adolescent or otherwise) who is experiencing some of the transitional phenomena noted above. In brief, the degree of any particular type of behavior should depend upon the degree of recognition and awareness of the nature of the field, and upon the strength of the conflicting forces within the field.

WHAT DO ADOLESCENTS DO?

Currently, an empirically derived answer to this question is limited as virtually all available studies have been conducted with largely western cultures. Certainly, many activities occupy adolescents' time. Some of these activities are mandatory or necessary in nature, others are leisurely or recreational. Although the distinction between necessary and leisure activities is somewhat arbitrary, it is typically based on the degree of voluntariness (i.e., freedom to engage or not to engage) associated with each type of activity (Flammer, Alsaker, & Noack, 1999). Leisure activities, characterized by more degrees of freedom relative to necessary activities (i.e., work), have been further subdivided into categories of "relaxed leisure," which includes free-time activities such as reading and watching television, and "transitional leisure," which includes sports, artwork, and hobbies considered more demanding and challenging (Kleiber, Larson, & Csikszentmihalyi, 1986). Still, based on reports from American high school students, "leisure" activities are construed as those associated with pleasure and passivity, whereas "recreational" activities are those associated with pleasure and active pursuits (Mobility, 1989). For simplicity's sake, leisure activities will be construed as the activities pursued during one's leisure time. Leisure time, in turn, is the time left when all commitments and duties are accomplished (Flammer et al., 1999).

Time allocation patterns

Building from the premise that within a 24-hour period investment in any one activity takes time away from any other, Bruno (1996) suggests that individuals' time-investment patterns are organized according to personal lifestyle goals which determine how time is spent. Time allocation patterns, thus, may provide insight into individuals' value systems and life goals. In adolescence, time allocation strategies may reflect social-cognitive development, and highlight the context in which developmental tasks are achieved. For example, it is proposed that leisure activities provide adolescents with the opportunity to develop **autonomy** and strengthen their sense of self (Gibbons, Lynn, & Stiles, 1997; Gordon & Caltabiano, 1996). Moreover, by alleviating boredom and increasing adolescents' feelings of well-being, socially accepted leisure activities may operate as deterrents to antisocial activities such as drug use and delinquency (Iso-Ahola & Crowley, 1991). As such, what adolescents do with their time, especially their free time, may have important developmental consequences (Bruno, 1996).

Gender differences in time allocation

Using time allocation surveys, Bruno (1996) studied adolescent time usage by dividing a 24-hour span into four categories: (1) outer-directed time: the time allocated to achieving external goals such as career/academic pursuits, financial or status-related gains; (2) other-people-directed time: the time allocated to enhance popularity with others and to develop close relationships; (3) inner-directed time: time allocated to self-development via hobbies, sports, creative expressions, and special interests; and (4) nondirected time: passive or "relaxation-"driven time allocated for entertainment purposes (e.g., television). Results reveal that American adolescent boys spend most of their time in outer-directed activities (35 percent), followed by other-directed (27 percent), inner-directed (23 percent), and finally in nondirected activities (14 percent). Although the net ranking of time allocation practices was similar for girls, the distribution of time varied as a function of gender. In other words, although girls spent most of their time pursuing outer-directed activities (36 percent), followed by other-directed (32 percent), inner-directed (20 percent), and nondirected activities (9 percent), they showed a preference for other-directed activities and less inclination toward nondirected activities relative to boys. Thus, girls allocate more time for social relationships compared to boys, whereas boys invest more time in passive entertainment relative to girls. Interestingly, time allocation patterns also varied for adolescents deemed at risk for negative outcomes (e.g., dropping out of school). At-risk adolescents showed the least preference for outer-directed (achievement) activities, and the greatest preferences for other-directed (social) and nondirected activities (passive entertainment).

Cross-cultural comparisons of time allocation

More recently, international studies were conducted to gauge the specific activities pursued by adolescents. For example, Alsaker and Flammer (1999) studied how much time adolescents from 13 different cultures allocated to necessary activities such as sleeping, body care, eating, traveling to school, school attendance, homework, chores, and shopping (a daily errand in many European countries). Results revealed that necessary activities take up an average of 18.90 hours per day, with French adolescents reporting the most time allocated to necessary activities and the Norwegians the least. Using the same sample of participants, Flammer et al. (1999) studied the allocation of free time according to seven leisure activities: playing music, leisure reading, sports activities, watching television, hanging around with friends, dating, or working for extra money (an activity considered non-necessary in the present context). Results showed an average of 4.42 leisure hours a day, with Norwegian adolescents reporting the most time invested in leisure, and the French the least. Watching television was the most popular leisure activity in all countries investigated, with Bulgarians watching the most and the French watching the least.

Factors influencing use of free time

Many factors can influence how adolescents spend their free time, such as (1) age, (2) gender, (3) race, (4) geographic, and (5) individual characteristics. As adolescents grow, it is clear that their interests change. For example, older adolescents spend more time with their friends and more time pursuing romantic relationships than do younger adolescents. As for gender differences, research suggests that males and females who adhere to traditional gender roles differ in their leisure preferences during adolescence (Colley, Griffiths, Hugh, Landers, & Jaggli, 1996). For example, whereas females report participating in noncompetitive sports (e.g., swimming), social activities (e.g., going to parties, to dance clubs), and home-based activities (e.g., watching television), males report greater participation in more competitive sports (e.g., soccer, rugby) and computer-based activities. Similarly, Gibbons et al. (1997) investigated gender differences in adolescents from Cyprus, India, the Netherlands, and the United States. According to the authors, boys participated in more group-oriented activities and, with the exception of Cyprus, participated in more sports. Peer groups shape the leisure activities in which their members take part. Based on a Canadian sample of adolescents, research reveals that girls' peers influence their leisure choices more strongly than do boys (Shaw, Caldwell, & Kleiber, 1996). In brief, it seems that girls feel more pressure to orient their activities to be in synchrony with their friends.

Evidence also suggests that different racial and ethnic groups, namely black and white youth, come to value different leisure activities (Philipp, 1998). Black teens are more likely to value activities such as basketball, going to the mall, and dancing relative to white teens. White adolescents, on the other hand, are more likely to value activities like soccer, horseback riding, and going on camping trips than are black teens. However, important group similarities also emerged in this study. For example, black and white youth valued watching television, reading for pleasure, visiting museums, and playing a musical instrument to similar degrees. Interestingly, black adolescents showed fewer gender differences than whites on the examined leisure activities (Philipp, 1998).

In addition to variables of age, gender, and race, geographic location can also shape the types of leisure activities pursued by adolescents. Drawing from an Australian sample, teens from rural areas have been found to engage in more sports and passive forms of leisure (e.g., watching television) than urban-dwelling adolescents (Gordon & Caltabiano, 1996). On the other hand, adolescents in urban centers were more likely to engage in more social forms of leisure such as going out to movie theaters and nightclubs. Perhaps because they have fewer resources at their disposition, rural youth report more leisure boredom than do those living in urban centers. This is important because leisure boredom has been associated with substance use (Gordon & Caltabiano, 1996) and delinquency (Iso-Ahola & Crowley, 1991). It has been suggested that unless leisure is optimally arousing it is experienced as boredom (Iso-Ahola, 1980), and that this boredom, paired with other factors like low self-esteem, heightens adolescents' risk for negative outcomes.

Now that we have seen how adolescents spend their time, we will shift our attention to the central question: What are the major events of adolescent development? As we noted above, we will use the biographies of major theorists as a means of explaining the hallmark ideas about adolescence. Following these discussions we will consider the empirical evidence taken from scientific studies of these theoretical positions. Our discussion begins with the ideas of Anna Freud, Sigmund Freud's youngest child, and Peter Blos. They propose that the central event of adolescence is puberty and that various developmental changes in personality and family relations result from pubertal maturation.

Puberty and Psychological Development: The Work of Anna Freud

Anna, the youngest of Martha and Sigmund Freud's six children, was born in Vienna on December 3, 1895, the same year that her father's *Studies on Hysteria* marked the beginning of the history of psychoanalysis. Sharing her birth year with psycho-analysis, Anna grew up to perceive it as a "sibling" that sparked her interest in under-standing the human mind, its socialization, and its development. Anna, together with her close friend Dorothy Burlingham, acted upon her belief that an appropriate mix of education and psychoanalysis "promised to create happier children, and thus, a happier world," a perspective that formed the basis of their close professional and personal relationship over the course of their lifetime (Henrik Peters, 1985). In 1927, the two women launched a small school which adhered to analytic principles. Its wide curriculum, designed to foster children's imagination, was implemented with help from Peter Blos and Erik Erikson, both of whom would later become leading analysts in postwar America. Anna's observation of children in her capacity as teacher, analyst, and mentor was meticulously recorded during these years. These observations would later serve as the foundation for her most celebrated work, *The Ego and the Mechanisms of Defence*, published in 1936.

THE EGO, DEFENSE MECHANISMS, AND LIBIDINAL FORCES

Anna Freud's interest in psychoanalysis revolved around the processes of the **ego**, which is the part of the psyche concerned with "directing action, coping with the external world and integrating competing urges within the self" (Stevens, 1983, p. 1). According to her, understanding **mechanisms of defense** – designed to protect the ego from noxious thoughts and feelings associated with the **primary drives** – not only provides insight into basic human motivation, but also allows the analyst to assess varying degrees of psychological adjustment. By investigating how individuals guard themselves against their primary instincts, ego maturity and ego integrity can be assessed, allowing the analyst to better understand normative and pathological occurrences. According to Anna Freud, synchronizing the biological with the social environmental represents the analyst's true challenge. As reported by Mayes and Cohen (1996), Anna Freud adhered to the notion that biology, through socialization, be-comes psychology, and it is on this level of psychology that appropriate interventions can restore healthy development. Anna Freud felt it ironic that psychoanalysts, who attribute much importance to the development of sexuality in shaping personality, would to a large extent neglect to discuss adolescence, the period of burgeoning genital sexuality (Henrik Peters, 1985). She described adolescence, or more specifically puberty, as a time of severe psychological upheaval. Using analogies of war and battle, she characterized the onset of puberty as a time of libidinal "invasion." As **libidinal forces** surge, instinctual pulls become stronger and the integrity of the ego is threatened. It is this disharmony between developmental lines which can make adolescence a time of opposition and paradox.

These developmental challenges of adolescence may lead to a temporary breakdown in ego controls. As a result, the adolescent may become more crude, less "sophisticated," as well as more primitively aggressive and narcissistic (Kaplan, 1996). According to Anna Freud, these features are an expression of issues surrounding the Oedipal conflict that were not entirely resolved. For this reason, adolescents may find themselves turning away from parents to focus on new "love objects" to cherish and admire, such as celebrities who become elevated to hero status. Interestingly, Anna Freud pointed out that these heroes are often at an intermediate age between that of the individual and that of his or her parents (Sayers, 1997).

Clearly, for Anna Freud, adolescence is characterized as a period of ego struggle as a result of the challenges presented by new energies that emerge during puberty, a period where the ego must grow, develop, and adapt to meet the increasing demands of drive regulation. In other words, adolescence is a time when the ego must mature and become more sophisticated at defending itself. Anna Freud contended that the most common defenses during adolescence are asceticism (the severe denial of anything **id**), intellectualization, and identification.

The role of pubertal development

If Anna Freud is right, then we should notice drastic changes in personality and behavior at the time of puberty. So far, the empirical literature has failed to provide much support for this hypothesis. In regard to emotional states, although it may be the case that adolescents are more moody than are children or adults (Csikszentmihalyi & Larson, 1984), mood fluctuations appear to be only modestly related to pubertal changes. How do we know this? We know this from studies that have tracked mood in adolescents on a daily basis and have examined whether mood changes more at the time of pubertal changes than at other times. In a review of this literature, Buchanan, Eccles, and Becker (1992) concluded that there may be some increases in variability in mood or in behavior during the earliest stages of puberty. Otherwise, however, there is little evidence to support the view that puberty *per se* is related to emotional or behavioral changes.

Another area of research, however, has shown an association between puberty and adolescents' interactions with their parents. Steinberg (1981a, 1981b) followed a group of boys over a period of one year during early adolescence. He kept track of their pubertal development and observed their interactions with their parents. He reported that as these adolescent boys reached the midpoint or height of their pubertal changes, they showed less warmth and more conflict in their interaction with their mothers, while patterns of family interaction became more rigid. These patterns became less pronounced as these boys moved toward the end of puberty.

These findings were replicated in a second study by Steinberg (1987). Using reports from adolescents and their parents, Steinberg found that pubertal maturation was associated with increased emotional distance between adolescents and their parents, and with increased conflict with their mothers. Other studies have shown equally unsupportive findings. Ruble and Brooks-Gunn (1982), for example, reported that menarche was rarely associated with any sort of upheaval for adolescent girls.

Nevertheless, there is much evidence that the timing of puberty, rather than puberty itself, is associated with behavioral changes in adolescence. In general, empirical studies have shown that early puberty in girls and late puberty in boys is associated with problematic indices during adolescence. For example, Savin-Williams and Small (1986) showed that according to parent reports, early puberty in girls led to greater conflict with mothers and fathers, and that there was more stress in the parent–child relationship when puberty was early in girls and late in boys. These findings confirmed earlier reports (Jones, 1957, 1965) that early-maturing boys were more socially poised, more popular, and more likely to be looked up to by their peers, whereas late-maturing boys were seen as unpopular, childish, and more likely to feel incompetent and inadequate. In this same study, early-maturing girls, relative to late-maturing girls, were observed to be lacking in poise and a sense of competence and were more likely to be withdrawn and reserved. Late-maturing girls were seen as being socially skilled, emotionally competent, and well liked. It should be pointed out also that more recent findings have shown that early-maturing girls, relative to girls of their age who mature on time, are at greater risk for psychiatric disturbances (Hayward, Killen, Kraemer, & Taylor, 2000). Clearly, the timing of puberty matters, but it appears to matter differently for boys and for girls.

These differences between boys and girls may reflect the fact that puberty typically happens earlier for girls than for boys. Therefore, girls who enter puberty early relative to other girls are typically far ahead of virtually all boys. Likewise, boys who enter puberty late are far behind most boys and behind almost all girls. These two sets of adolescents, early-maturing girls and late-maturing boys, are those who are clearly most out of step with their peers. These findings point to the necessity of understanding a biological form of development within a social context. Indeed, the effects of puberty appear to depend on when puberty happens.

Clearly, more evidence is needed for us to conduct a full evaluation of the validity of Anna Freud's ideas about puberty and psychological development. The current data, however, certainly fail to reveal any general upheaval related to puberty *per se*. Although research related directly to Anna Freud's ideas is very limited, there exists much more support for related lines of thinking, namely, those proposed by another psychoanalytic theorist, Peter Blos. His ideas are explained in the next section.

 ## *The Family and Adolescence: The Work of Peter Blos*

Peter Blos was a psychoanalytically oriented psychiatrist who was particularly interested in adolescence. Blos believed that human development occurred as a result of transitions through sequentially ordered **psychosexual stages** (see chapter 2). More specifically, he supported the notion that healthy development depended on the successful completion of the psychological tasks associated with each psychosexual stage. Unlike Freud, however, Blos did not believe that personality formation was primarily achieved by early childhood. Instead, he contended that later stages of development, namely, the stages associated with adolescence, played a critical role in mediating adult personality formation. Blos defined adolescence as "the sum total of accommodations to the condition of puberty" (Blos, 1972, p. 56). He conceptualized adolescence not as a unitary developmental stage but as a series of stages "defined in terms of drive and ego positions, as well as in terms of phase-specific conflicts and their resolutions" (Blos, 1972, p. 55).

INDEPENDENCE VERSUS MAINTAINING PARENTAL BONDS

During early adolescence individuals experience a basic struggle between reconciling a desire to break free of parental bonds while still wishing to maintain a certain dependency on parents. It is this essential conflict that leads to so many contradictions in adolescence, such as the observation that adolescent development and "progression" seem to detour via a series of regressions (Blos, 1972). Early adolescence, according to Blos, is characterized by the reactivation of infantile (i.e., more primitive) desires and ego skills. For example, a boy's successful negotiation of the latency stage (see chapter 2), in which the ego is distanced from the id, resulting in increased self-awareness and emotional control, seems to "fall into shambles at the onset of puberty" (Blos, 1972, p. 58). The young adolescent male tends to manifest "oral greed, smuttiness, oblivion to unkemptness and uncleanliness, motoric restlessness, and experimentation in every direction" (p. 58). Blos contended that boys' regressions are more obvious, concrete, and action oriented than girls', whose regressive tendencies assert themselves more peripherally and secretly (p. 59). Perhaps Blos implied that whereas boys exhibit their regression within public forums, girls' regressions manifest themselves within the private realm of their relationships.

According to Blos, in order to proceed into the stage of adolescence proper, young adolescents or preadolescents need to undergo a second individuation process much like the individuation that took place from mother in early childhood. This second individuation, according to Blos, represents the major developmental challenge during early adolescence. If successfully accomplished, the Oedipal conflict should once again dominate in terms of drive progression, and, concomitantly, push the ego forward in terms of higher levels of differentiation. Stated differently, the process of the second individuation is thought to promote character formation and "lend enduring and irreversible structures to the adolescent personality" (Blos, 1972, p. 62).

According to Blos, maladjustment occurs when the phase-specific developmental tasks are not completed, or are sidestepped altogether. Thus, accomplishing the psychological tasks central at one stage of development is crucial for successfully negotiating those associated with subsequent stages. As such, Blos warns against hastening normal developmental periods. Although preadolescents may be undergoing pubertal changes at increasingly younger ages (Blos, 1972), biology should not be followed blindly. The postpubescent 13-year-old remains psychologically a preadolescent, not an adult. Blos recommended environmental changes that would prolong the developmental stages associated with childhood and adolescence, and went so far as to claim that this would enhance not only psychological health, but the capacity for complex cognitive functions (Blos, 1972).

ACQUISITION OF AUTONOMY

The question of how adolescents achieve a sense of *autonomy* from their parents has been examined in several studies. An important point of these studies is that the process of achieving autonomy in adolescence is not a process of separating but is instead one of reorganizing or transforming relationships within the family. Indeed, as Steinberg (1990) has shown, most families that include an adolescent get along quite well. In this respect, although the research on adolescent family relations shows that families do go through some changes during adolescence, it would be difficult to describe these changes as a form of separation. Steinberg and Silverberg (1986), in a study of early adolescence, showed that from 10 to 14 years of age, adolescents showed three important changes related to autonomy. First, they felt a greater sense of individuation. This means that as they grow older, they become more aware of who they are and are more likely to take responsibility for their own behaviors. Second, with age, young people begin to deidealize their parents. That is, they recognize that their parents could have flaws like other human beings. Third, older adolescents were less likely to feel dependent on their parents. It is important to recognize, though, that this is not simply a process of separation. As Ryan and Lynch (1989) showed, adolescents who are emotionally autonomous but who are distant from their parents show lower levels of psychological adjustment than do adolescents who are autonomous but have close relations with their parents.

THE EFFECTS OF PARENTAL STYLE

Adolescents' ability to become autonomous appears to be related to the kind of family environment that was present in their homes. Of the many ways to characterize parents' behavior toward their children, Diana Baumrind's (1978) theoretical framework has been among the most useful. According to her work, there are two critical dimensions of parents' behavior toward their children: *parental responsiveness* and *parental demandingness* (Maccoby & Martin, 1983). Parental responsiveness refers to the extent to which parents respond to the needs of the child in a supportive and accepting manner. Parental demandingness points to the degree to which parents expect mature, responsible behavior from their adolescents. Furthermore, the degree to which parents are responsive and demanding varies from one family to the next. Some parents are very demanding of their children, yet offer little in the way of responsiveness and warmth. In other families, parents may be unresponsive and rejecting, and expect very little of their children.

Different parenting styles

As a result of parental responsiveness and parental demandingness being largely independent dimensions of parenting, it is possible to look at combinations of these dimensions. Because parents' levels of both responsiveness and demandingness may be characterized as either high or low, four possible combinations of these two dimensions are possible. These particular combinations, labeled **parenting styles** by Baumrind (1978), are known as *authoritative, authoritarian, indulgent,* and *neglectful.*

Authoritative parents are high on responsiveness and demandingness. They value both expressive and instrumental attributes (e.g., autonomous self-will and discipline conformity), yet they assume the ultimate responsibility for their children's behavior. They are cognizant of their own rights and also recognize their children's interests and idiosyncratic ways. Further, these parents set clear standards of behavior for their children which take into account the child's developing capabilities and needs. They guide their children's activities firmly and consistently and require them to participate in family functioning by helping out with household chores. When dealing with matters of discipline, authoritative parents engage their children in dialogue in a rational, issue-oriented manner. Moreover, these parents are considered warm and responsive to the needs of their children. They are affectively responsive by being loving, committed, and supportive, and cognitively responsive in the sense that they provide a stimulating and challenging home environment.

Authoritarian parents are high on demandingness and low on responsiveness. They value obedience as a virtue and favor punitive, forceful means (e.g., the coercive use of power) to curb the self-will of their offspring. They attempt to shape, control, and evaluate the behavior and attitudes of the child in accordance with a set of absolute standards of conduct. Authoritarian parents attempt to inculcate conventional values such as work, respect for authority, and the preservation of order and traditional structure. Because these parents believe that their children should accept their rules and expectations without question, they do not encourage verbal give-and-take on discipline-related issues. They do not foster their children's autonomy, but rather try to restrict independent behavior.

Indulgent (permissive) parents are high on responsiveness but low on demandingness. They interact with their children in a more benign and passive manner and avoid the use of power when dealing with matters of discipline. They view themselves as resources available to their children, which the children may or may not choose to use. Indulgent parents are likely to view discipline as an infringement upon the freedom of their offspring, which may impinge upon their healthy development. Consequently, these parents attempt to behave in a nonpunitive, accepting, and affirmative manner toward their children's impulses, desires, and actions. In summary, they make few maturity demands on the children's behavior and allow them a high degree of autonomy.

Neglectful (indifferent) parents are low on responsiveness and demandingness. They try to minimize the amount of time and energy required to raise their children. They know little about their children's lives, interact little with them, and do not include them in making decisions that affect the family. Whereas parents of the other types show concern for their children and espouse a set of beliefs oriented toward their healthy development, neglectful parents' concerns are primarily parent-centered. That is, they structure their home lives around their own needs and interests.

What makes the categorizations proposed by Baumrind (1978) important? First, parenting style has been found to be associated with a number of markers of psychosocial development. One of the more prominent of these markers is social competence. Children from authoritative homes have been found to be more socially competent than their peers raised in authoritarian, indulgent, or neglectful environments (Baumrind, 1978). In addition to their more developed social skills, children from authoritative households are more self-reliant, more self-controlled, more responsible, more creative, more intellectually curious, more adaptive, and more successful in school. In contrast, children from authoritarian households are less socially skilled, less self-assured, less curious, more dependent, and more passive. Children from indulgent homes are less mature, less responsible, more easily influenced by their peers, and less able to take on leadership roles. Those from neglectful homes are often impulsive and more likely to be involved in delinquent behaviors such as precocious experimentation with sex, alcohol, and drugs (Baumrind, 1967; Fuligni & Eccles, 1993; Lamborn, Mounts, Steinberg, & Dornbusch, 1991; Steinberg, Lamborn, Darling, Mounts, & Dornbusch, 1994). And while exceptions to these widely applicable patterns do exist, the majority of studies indicate that authoritative parenting is strongly linked with healthy adolescent development for a wide range of ethnicities and socioeconomic backgrounds (Maccoby & Martin, 1983; Lamborn et al., 1991).

WHY DOES AUTHORITATIVE PARENTING WORK SO WELL?

In an effort to understand why authoritative parenting leads to more healthy development and adaptation among adolescents, researchers have attempted to tease apart the main elements of this parenting style (Steinberg, 1990). Consensus among the majority of researchers indicates that there are three main elements: *warmth*, *structure*, and *autonomy support*. The first of these is related to the responsiveness dimension, whereas the latter two are related to demandingness. Warmth is the degree of affection and acceptance that exists in the parent–child relationship; it has been found to be associated with overall competence. Structure refers to the extent to which rules and expectations for the adolescent's behavior exist, and is associated with the presence of fewer behavioral problems. Autonomy support denotes the degree to which parents encourage the individuality and independence of the adolescent and is associated with fewer symptoms of psychological distress such as depression or anxiety (Barber, Olsen, & Shagle, 1994; Steinberg, 1990).

Why is it that authoritative parenting is so strongly associated with healthy adolescent development? First, authoritative parents provide an appropriate balance between restrictiveness and autonomy. This balance encompasses both standards and limits for the adolescent's behavior, which are needed by developing individuals, and the flexibility necessary to allow the adolescent opportunities to develop self-reliance. Second, authoritative parents are more likely to nurture the intellectual development of their children by engaging them in a verbal give-and-take about rules, expectations, and decisions. These discussions help to foster the development of social competence and enhance the adolescent's understanding of social systems and social relationships. Moreover, discussions of this type have also been argued to lead to the development of reasoning abilities, empathy, and more advanced moral judgment (Baumrind, 1978). Third, due to the combination of warmth and control used by authoritative parents, adolescents are more likely to identify with their parents. According to Steinberg (1996), "one of the strongest predictors of identification between children and their parents is warmth in the parent–child relationship" (p. 164). Moreover, evidence suggests that we are more likely to imitate those who treat us with warmth and affection (Hill, 1980).

The observation that the family environment is related to adolescent adjustment should not be interpreted to indicate that other forms of relationship are not important. As we show in the next section, peers also play a critical role in shaping individuals' psychological development.

Peer Relations: The Ideas of Harry Stack Sullivan

Sullivan believed that human beings, both the healthy and not so healthy, are much more similar than they are different. Highly attuned to the influence of social interactions, experiences, and social inequities in shaping human behavior, Sullivan suggested that it was *interpersonal* processes (i.e., the exchange processes that happen between individuals), and not Freud's *intrapsychic* processes (i.e., the processes that happen within the individual), that guide development and shape behavior. In other words, Sullivan proposed that behavior cannot be understood in a vacuum, but instead must be understood as the end result of a series of interaction processes between the self and others. Thus, according to the interpersonal perspective, the interpersonal "other" plays a central role in mapping the psychological development of individuals.

Interpersonal needs stimulate psychological growth

Sullivan's most important contribution to developmental theory lies in the notion that it is the motivation to fulfill *interpersonal needs* that stimulates psychological growth. According to Sullivan, development is organized around sequentially ordered interpersonal needs which emerge at specific times of development. For each emerging interpersonal need, there exists a key social relationship designed to satisfy the need. Therefore, Sullivan contended that the reduction of needs through age-appropriate social relationships is what guides healthy psychological development. Conversely, inadequate or deleterious relationships translate into ineffective need fulfillment, and subsequent negative outcomes (i.e., psychological maladjustment).

Developmental stages, divided into epochs, span the period from infancy into adulthood. Sullivan named these epochs as infancy (0–2 years), childhood (2–6 years), the juvenile epoch (6–9 years), preadolescence (9–12 years), early adolescence, late adolescence, and adulthood (the age demarcations of these latter stages are not clear). Each epoch is characterized by an emerging interpersonal need, like the need for tenderness during infancy, companionship during childhood, acceptance during the juvenile epoch, friendship intimacy during preadolescence, romantic intimacy during early and late adolescence, and the integration of a love relationship during late adolescence and adulthood. Each sequentially ordered interpersonal need may be satisfied by specific social relationships. For example, the infant's interpersonal need for tenderness is designed to be met by parents or primary caregivers, whereas the need for acceptance is met principally through the peer group.

SUBPERIODS OF ADOLESCENCE

Sullivan did not reduce adolescence to a singular, homogeneous period of development. Instead, he differentiated between pre-, early, and late adolescence. During preadolescence, individuals experience a need for intimacy from peers. For the first time in their developmental histories, preadolescents seek close, reciprocal, mutually validating relationships with others of similar status. It is the relationship of friendship with a same-sex peer, or what Sullivan called the "chumship," which is designed to satisfy emerging needs for intimacy.

During early adolescence, the onset of puberty and genital sexuality promotes the "psychologically strong interest" in members of the other sex (Barton Evans, 1996). It is at this stage that individuals must "resolve a complex interplay between the dynamics of lust, security, and intimacy" (Barton Evans, 1996, p. 73). Because these needs are often difficult to negotiate simultaneously, early adolescence is construed by Sullivan as a tense, often turbulent period of human development. The core relationship associated with satisfying emerging interest in genital sexuality, the need for personal security (freedom from anxiety), and the continuing need for intimacy is that of the *romantic relationship*. Although needs of isophilic intimacy (with same-sex others) may continue to be fulfilled by friends, a shift toward heterophilic intimacy (with members of the other sex) is typical during early adolescence.

This shift away from a primary affiliation with same-sex peers toward affiliation with other-sex peers represents a main challenge of adolescent development. It is not that prior needs have diminished; they haven't. But now a new set of needs requires a transformation in peer experiences. During late adolescence, individuals continue to experience needs for intimacy, security, and lust, but in a more integrative and age-appropriate fashion. During this stage, and into adulthood, the task is to integrate these various needs into a love relationship, that is, with another person who becomes as important to one as oneself. It is truly the component of intimacy-seeking which sets the stage for adolescence and shapes much of life's later stages. According to Sullivan (1953, p. 34), intimacy, throughout adolescence and adulthood, is "not the primary business of life, but is, perhaps, the principal source of satisfaction in life."

RESEARCH SUPPORTING SULLIVAN'S ACCOUNT

Although not all of the ideas proposed by Sullivan have been examined thoroughly, support for many of his ideas has been found in empirical studies. One noticeable feature of adolescent peer relations that is consistent with the views of Sullivan is an increase in levels of intimacy in friendship. Interviews and self-reports have shown that adolescents see more intimacy in their friendships than do younger children (Furman & Buhrmester, 1985; Sharabany, Gershoni, & Hofman, 1981; Youniss & Smollar, 1985). The importance of friendship for adolescents is also clear. Adolescents with friends report much higher levels of well-being than is shown by adolescents without friends (Newcomb & Bagwell, 1996). In fact, there is evidence that the effect of having a friend may help adolescent boys and girls overcome the problems that would derive from nonoptimal family environments. Specifically, Gauze, Bukowski, Aquan-Assee, and Sippola (1996) reported that early adolescents from either chaotic or poorly structured families who had a friend showed the same level of self-perceived adjustment as shown by early adolescents from family environments more likely to promote well-being.

THE ROLE OF THE PEER GROUP

In addition to changes in friendship in adolescence, the structure of the peer group changes. In early adolescence youngsters often form small groups of peers organized around particular themes or activities. These "cliques" replace the broader peer group as the adolescent's primary peer environment. It is within a clique that most teenagers will have most of their relations with friends. Cliques are often part of larger social structures known simply as crowds. Crowds are defined by the attitudes or activities their members share. Common crowd labels among American high school students might include some of the following: jocks, brains, loners, druggies, and populars. Crowds often restrict adolescents' social contacts. Crowd labels may force adolescents to associate with particular types of peers, thus limiting their access to other peers who might fall outside their group. In this way, crowd membership is a salient feature of adolescent social life that can either improve or restrict an adolescent's development.

ROMANTIC RELATIONSHIPS

Typically, romantic relationships do not come to mind when one thinks about peer relationships, but romantic relationships are typically relationships between peers. Although still in its infancy, developmental research on romantic relations is beginning to blossom, in large part due to recent attempts to strengthen relevant theoretical frameworks. Of particular interest have been the theoretical insights provided by Furman and Wehner (1994, 1997), which stipulate that individuals' conscious and unconscious cognitive representations (i.e., views) of romantic relationships are shaped by experiences across different *types* of close relationships. Unlike earlier perspectives that have uniquely highlighted the role of parent–child relations in influencing subsequent adult love relationships (Hazan & Shaver, 1987), Furman and Wehner have underscored the importance of both parent–child and peer relations as integral socialization agents in adolescent romantic development. Lessons extracted from experiences with both parents and peers are carried forward to influence how romantic relations are approached, negotiated, and experienced in adolescence.

According to Furman and Wehner (1994, 1997), romantic relationships involve the activation of four distinct behavioral systems, namely, the attachment, caregiving, affiliation, and sexual systems. It has been suggested that complete integration of all four behavioral systems, in which romantic partners become key figures in fulfilling attachment, caregiving, affiliation, and sexual needs, does not typically occur until the development of long-term, stable romantic relationships which usually emerge during late adolescence and early adulthood (Hazan & Zeifman, 1994). In early and middle adolescence, the sexual and affiliative systems are more salient, and thus are expected to play a greater role than the attachment and caregiving systems in shaping views about romantic relationships. Because the affiliative and sexual-behavioral systems are honed primarily within the peer system, age-mates have been shown to exercise a greater influence on romantic views than do parents in early and middle adolescence (Furman & Wehner, 1994). Moreover, evidence suggests that whereas parent–child relations are not strongly related to romantic views in middle adolescence, they become increasingly central to romantic views during late adolescence (Furman & Wehner, 1997).

Brown's model of romantic development

As adolescents' views of romance are subject to important transformations across time, so are the specific functions of, and motives for, romantic relationships. Not unlike Furman and Wehner's (1994) behavioral systems conceptualization of romantic development, Brown (1999) has discussed romantic functions from a developmental-contextual perspective, that is, uncleaved from the larger social arena in which they are embedded. From this perspective, romantic development is construed as an integral facet of identity formation, a growth process that is inextricable from the social contexts in which it is rooted. Brown's sequential model of romantic development reflects four distinct phases, namely, (1) the initiation phase, (2) the status phase, (3) the affection phase, and (4) the bonding phase. This model provides a frame for understanding the changing motives, developmental functions, and psychosocial transformations that characterize romantic growth across adolescence.

At the onset of adolescence, libidinal awakenings advance the relevance of romantic relations. During the *initiation phase*, young adolescents need to negotiate burgeoning sexual needs within the context of larger identity needs, such as those associated with fitting in and being accepted by peers (Brown, 1990, 1999; Erikson, 1963). Used primarily as a means of broadening one's **self-concept**, romance in adolescence first emerges as an identity issue, that is, as a vehicle of self-expansion and self-exploration, not necessarily as a relational issue (Brown, 1999). With time, however, the focus on the self widens to include the self in relation to others. During the *status phase*, young adolescents become acutely aware that romance is very much a "public affair" that provides feedback on one's image and reputation among peers (Brown, 1999, p. 308). In brief, romantic activity can become a tool in reputation management, a means by which one's social standing can be manipulated.

Research has shown that status and prestige variables are among the top three most frequently cited reasons for dating among younger adolescents, but are not among the top five reasons given by college-aged adolescents (Roscoe, Diana, & Brooks, 1987).

The power of peers in regulating romantic behavior is at its pinnacle during the status phase. Peers influence whom one "can and cannot" date, as well as how one should and should not behave. Social scripts, as well as social sanctions for failure to adhere to these scripts, are transmitted within the peer domain. Concordantly, research has provided clear support for the influence of peers on adolescents' attitudes and beliefs about sex and dating, as well as on actual sexual behavior.

As adolescents grow, they experience deepening needs for intimacy as expressed through increased desire for closeness, sharing, and support. During the *affection phase*, attention is shifted away from the context in which the relationship exists and onto the relationship itself (Brown, 1999). Although not divorced from the larger peer group, romance during this developmental period, like identity, becomes a personal and relational affair. Adolescents seek new relational depths and substance from their romantic relationships. In general, middle adolescence represents a time when individuals learn how to negotiate true romantic intimacy. As one would expect from adolescents in the affection phase, 15-year-olds most often cite companionship and intimacy as the most important benefits of dating (Feiring, 1996).

Lastly, the need to look beyond the current moment to make plans for the future is characteristic of the *bonding phase*. During this developmental period, individuals are expected to maintain the relational depths typical of the affection phase while "replacing some of the emotionality associated with earlier periods with increased levels of pragmatism" (Brown, 1999, p. 321). Issues related to commitment, and potentially life-long commitment, are hallmarks of the bonding phase. How confident are partners about building a future together? How willing are partners to embrace or endure each other's strengths and shortcomings? In brief, the bonding phase represents a time of important, sometimes sobering, decision making. Concordantly, relational characteristics such as shared interests and shared goals for the future are the most frequently cited reasons for dating among older adolescents (Roscoe et al., 1987).

Connolly and Goldberg's model of romantic development

In a similar vein, Connolly and Goldberg (1999) have also staged romantic growth using the descriptors of (1) infatuation, (2) affiliation, (3) intimacy, and (4) commitment in order to illustrate the motivational underpinnings of romantic relations across adolescence. The infatuation phase sparks the interest in romantic relationships which typically becomes manifest during the affiliation stage of development. During that latter stage, mixed-sex peer groups emerge and romantic relations are usually negotiated within the confines of the group. Because individuals develop primarily within sex-segregated peer groups, mixed-sex groups provide heterosexual adolescents a forum to enhance confidence and communication skills with members of the other sex. As needs for intimacy grow, the importance of the mixed-sex peer group as a social context declines, and the emergence of dyadic romantic relationships is observed (Connolly & Goldberg, 1999; Dunphy, 1963). Finally, in joining previous motives of infatuation, affiliation, and intimacy in motivating and defining romantic relationships, commitment leads to the conscious decision to maintain the relationship over the long term via some form of socially recognized partnership (Connolly & Goldberg, 1999).

Clearly the effects of peer relations can be either positive or negative. A central theme of the study of peer relations in adolescence is the idea that peer relations affect adolescents' views of themselves. This notion that adolescence is a time when youngsters develop a view of themselves is not seen only in theory related to peer relations. In fact, it is the central theme in the approach to adolescence developed by Erik Erikson.

Erik Erikson and the Development of Identity in Adolescence

Erik Homberger (later known as Erik Erikson) was born in Frankfurt, Germany, in 1902. He was raised by his mother, who was Jewish and of Danish descent, and his stepfather, a Jewish pediatrician whose last name Erik bore. Erikson's biological father, who was of Danish descent, left his mother before Erik was born. Growing up, Erikson felt that his physical appearance impeded him from being fully accepted as a Jew; he was tall, blond, and blue-eyed. Yet, at the same time, he was not raised to think of himself as Danish. He later recounted that these early feelings of alienation contributed greatly to his later interests in "identity" and identity development (Cloninger, 1993). Heavily influenced by classical psychoanalysis, Erikson, like Freud, believed that all living things grow according to a design plan or "blueprint" of psychological development. This belief, formally called the **epigenetic principle**, stems from the notion that the "parts" of an organism develop in a sequential order, each part having its own specific "time of ascendancy," until the "functioning whole" is complete (Erikson, 1959, p. 52). Much like physical development in the womb, Erikson believed that the ego, defined earlier as the part of personality concerned with "directing action, coping with the external world and integrating competing urges within the self" (Stevens, 1983, p. 1), also developed according to the epigenetic principle. In other words, for a whole healthy ego to develop, it is thought that several parts, called ego strengths, need to develop in a sequentially ordered fashion. Thus, like Freud, Erikson proposed a stage model of personality development in which each stage is characterized by a specific psychological task, or conflict that must be resolved, in order for an individual to successfully proceed to the next level (Pumpian-Mindlin, 1966).

ADOLESCENCE AS TRANSITION TO ADULTHOOD

According to the author, adolescence is a time of transition toward adult roles, where the individual ceases to "fit" nicely into any particular social role. It is during this time that the individual "struggles against a sense of identity confusion to attain a sense of identity" (Cloninger, 1993, p. 129). Simply put, it is a time where individuals ask, "Who am I?" The psychosocial stage of identity versus identity diffusion (i.e., confusion) represents a time of personal and interpersonal experimentation in which individuals strive to find their own sense of individuality and of self. The adolescent challenge, then, is to reach a sense of ego continuity and sense of self-awareness

Plate 16.1 Young adolescents identify with different values, beliefs, and ideologies during the period of moratorium. One consequence of this identity crisis may be the development of a negative identity based on undesirable roles in society. Photograph © Getty Images/ Digital Vision.

vis-à-vis this continuity. In other words, resolving the identity crisis, meaning that the adolescent's identity emerges as more intact (or formed) than diffuse, leads to the development of the ego strength of *fidelity* to both one's identity and sense of self.

Until a stable identity is achieved, it is not uncommon for young adolescents to identify with a string of different values, beliefs, and ideologies. This period of search, in which a consistent, stable sense of identity has not yet been achieved, is called a period of **moratorium** and is considered a normal, healthy part of psychosocial development. However, if, after a period of moratorium, a coherent identity cannot be achieved and "no one identity prevails at the core" of the individual, identity diffusion ensues (Cloninger, 1993). Another unhealthy consequence of the identity crisis is the development of a negative identity; that is, one based on undesirable roles in society (i.e., juvenile delinquent). Society provides clear images of such negative identities, making them attractive alternatives for adolescents who feel that positively valued identities are unattainable (Cloninger, 1993, p. 130).

Identity formation and self-concept

Research on identity in adolescence can be found in two different domains, one concerned with the process of identity formation itself, and the other concerned with the development of the self-concept. Research on identity formation has largely confirmed that identity changes during adolescence, especially in the older years of adolescence. For example, in one study, most 15–18-year-olds were either in a state of diffusion or moratorium, with very few students showing any indication of identity achievement

(Montemayor, Brown, & Adams, 1985). Nevertheless, the exact conditions that promote identity development are still unknown.

Research on the development of the self-concept has shown that in adolescence the self changes in both content and structure (Harter, 1983b). Whereas children's sense of themselves is typically defined by observable characteristics, adolescents think about and reflect upon their own thoughts, desires, and motives. They increasingly emphasize internal characteristics, such as beliefs, values, and psychological traits and characteristics, as the basis of self-definition. As a result, in adolescence the self becomes a richer and more pluralistic concept. One of the challenges of the self in adolescence is with identifying the ways that one is unique and how one is similar to others. Maintaining a sense of individuality while trying to fit into the group is an important task for adolescents. Emphasizing differences can lead to loneliness and alienation, while emphasizing similarities may impede the development of autonomy.

As adolescents become aware of their own inner world of thoughts and feelings, they become more aware that others also possess such an inner world. As a consequence, adolescents can have a heightened awareness of the ultimate isolation of one's inner world from the inner worlds of others. It is during this time that adolescents become increasingly focused on the uniqueness of the self from other (Elkind, 1967). For this reason, adolescents may initially view separation from others as a fundamental condition of human experience and, as a result, they may feel alone in their efforts to develop a new sense of self during adolescence.

In sum, achieving a clear and coherent identity, or sense of self, may represent one of the most central developmental tasks of adolescence.

SUMMARY AND CONCLUSIONS

Adolescent social development is a collection of interrelated changes and challenges. Adolescence refers to the changes in their bodies, in their thoughts and emotions, in their family experiences, in their relations with peers, and in their conceptions of self. Although it is far from the truth to say that adolescence is necessarily a time of storm and stress, it is the case that adolescence is a time of transition and challenge. The interrelated changes of adolescence happen in several domains at once. Just as adolescents are moving through puberty, they are also functioning in a broader set of environments that challenge them in new ways. These challenges are exaggerated not only by their "newness," but also by the transitions going on with their families. Adolescents face the task of changing their relations with their parents; this is not a process of separation but is instead a process of achieving autonomy and an interdependent identity. They also must contend with changes in their relations with peers. The peer group takes on a new structure, organized around thematically based cliques and crowds, and new forms of relationships, such as romantic attachments, emerge.

As adolescents become autonomous, form new relations with parents and friends, acquire new forms of competence, and develop new concepts of self, they become ready to confront the challenges of being an adult. Although adolescence may be a time of challenge, and perhaps even some anxiety, one should not forget that adolescence can be a time of much fun and excitement.

DISCUSSION POINTS

1   Taking account of the evidence presented here and referring to your everyday experience, consider whether adolescence is necessarily a period of storm and stress.
2   What do you think are the relative contributions of biological and social factors to the nature of adolescence?
3   To what extent is adolescence a product of the cultural environment?
4   Is it possible to provide evidence to support psychoanalytic interpretations of adolescence? If it is, what sorts of evidence would you be looking for?
5   What factors determine the development of autonomy in adolescence?
6   Thinking about the evidence presented here and arising from everyday experience, how important are peer relationships in adolescent development?
7   Discuss the factors that contribute to the development of romantic relationships in adolescence.
8   How much are the experiences and feelings of adolescence to do with development of a self-concept?

SUGGESTIONS FOR FURTHER READING

Arnett, J. J. (1999). Adolescent storm and stress, reconsidered. *American Psychologist*, 54 (5), 317–26.

Grotevant, H. D. (1998). Adolescent development in family contexts. In W. Damon & N. Eisenberg (Eds.), *The handbook of child psychology* (5th ed., Vol. 3, pp. 1097–1149). New York: Wiley.

Crocket, L., & Silbereisen, R. (ed.) (2000). *Negotiating adolescence in times of social change.* Cambridge: Cambridge University Press.

part V

Practical Issues

CONTENTS

chapter 17

Educational Implications

Alyson Davis

KEY CONCEPTS

ATTAINMENT TARGETS	EGOCENTRISM	NORM REFERENCING
CLASS INCLUSION	EXPERIMENTAL GROUP	PARADIGM
COGNITIVE CONFLICT	HEAD START	PEDAGOGY
COGNITIVE DEVELOPMENT	INTELLIGENCE QUOTIENT	PEER
COLLABORATIVE LEARNING	(IQ)	PERSPECTIVE-TAKING
CONSERVATION	INTERMENTAL ABILITY	PREOPERATIONAL STAGE
CONTROL GROUP	INTRAMENTAL ABILITY	SCAFFOLDING
CURRICULUM	KEY STAGES	SOCIOCOGNITIVE CONFLICT
DISCOVERY LEARNING	META-ANALYSIS	ZONE OF PROXIMAL DEVELOPMENT
EGOCENTRIC	NATIONAL CURRICULUM	

OVERVIEW

In addition to providing evidence and testing theories on how children develop, it is generally expected that developmental psychology will have things to say about applied issues concerning children. A prime example is the contribution of developmental psychology to educational practice. In this chapter, the author outlines the different images of the child created by two major developmental theorists: Jean Piaget and Lev Semenovich Vygotsky.

Piaget depicts the child as constructing his or her own understanding of the world through spontaneous activity on the physical world. He also identifies a role for social interaction with peers in the construction of knowledge, but argues that interaction with parents and teachers has little value, because the difference in intellectual levels and status is too great for children to benefit from these experiences. Thus, Piaget's major contribution to education was the concept of discovery learning. The chapter reviews evidence on the effects of peer interaction, showing that the presence of peers can have lasting effects on task performance, even when the peers are no longer present. However, it is not yet clear how their presence affects development. One would imagine that it is discussion of the problem that is crucial, but it turns out that simply the presence of an uninvolved peer enhances performance.

By contrast, Vygotsky's theory identifies a clear role for adults and teachers, seeing development as *drawn forward* through both informal and formal education. A popular term developing from this view is that of scaffolding: the adult provides vital support and structure for the child's learning. Evidence is reviewed pointing to the ways in which parents and teachers support children's development, and identifying the characteristics of effective spontaneous teaching by parents.

The chapter concludes with the view that although educational practice is some way from achieving aims such as the fuller involvement of parents in the educational process, there are grounds for optimism for the future, given the wealth of psychological knowledge about effective development and learning.

Introduction

Most developmental psychologists agree that the task of developmental psychology is twofold: first, to provide a good description of the developmental changes that take place from infancy into adulthood, and second, to offer sensible theoretical explanations of what causes these changes to take place. If we suppose that we are some way toward achieving this, then we ought to be in a position to make a substantial contribution to educational provision and practice. At the broadest level, knowing children's competencies and weaknesses at certain ages should let us have something to say about what we might expect children to be able to achieve or find difficult within a formal educational setting. Similarly, if we have powerful theories to explain why children's competencies change over time, it should also be possible to comment on the best ways of introducing children to a **curriculum**. In other words, we could define what constitutes "good" teaching and effective learning.

The above is of course just a characterization of a possible, rather optimistic model of the relationship between developmental psychology and education. One simple example will serve to show that our ability to apply psychology to practice is not just a function of the health of our research base. In the UK, a recent article in the *Psychologist* contained a table of teacher-training institutions at postgraduate level that had replied to a questionnaire stating that they would accept psychology graduates on their courses. The table was produced in response to the fact that many psychology undergraduates found their applications for primary teacher training being rejected on the very grounds that they were psychologists. It is difficult for psychologists to influence educational practice if they cannot get the teaching experience necessary for qualifying to practice as professional educational psychologists.

The reason why psychologists are not the most favored applicants for teacher-training places is because psychology is not one of the specified **National Curriculum** subjects. However, this situation cannot simply be attributed to a one-off political paradox. Two decades ago, long before the introduction of the National Curriculum, psychology graduates were similarly discriminated against, only then on the grounds that psychology was equated with sociology! The example serves to make the point that any account of how psychology might contribute to education is necessarily constrained by other factors such as educational policy, broader politics, and available resources. Despite these difficulties, it can be argued that developmental psychology has a great deal to offer to the field of educational practice. It is important to note, however, that the relationship between psychology and education is not necessarily best characterized as prescriptive. In other words, it is not the case that psychology should tell educators the "best" way of educating children. Instead it can be far more productive to see the relationship as bidirectional or transactional. This might be at a theoretical level, where both psychological and educational models inform each other, or at a policy level. For example, it is now common for research fund providers to invite psychologists to tender for research funding aimed at addressing a particular educational policy issue, such as the impact of information technology on learning.

In this chapter I aim to give a selective account of a few key areas in mainstream developmental psychology which have already impacted on, or have the potential to impact on, the education of children. In particular, I shall address research that can contribute to the question of facilitating children's learning, and shall consider what we know about the nature of development and learning that allows us to contribute to the debate on how to promote learning and how best to teach. Toward the end of the chapter, I shall examine some of the issues imposed by the fact that since 1988 there has been a compulsory National Curriculum in the UK to explore the implications for the future relationship between psychology and education in the context of the British system. The latter differs quite markedly from the American education system, which benefits from a broad research base of evaluating different types of educational practice.

Child-Centered Psychology and Education

If you were to visit a class of 5-year-olds during a typical day, you would find a very "child-friendly" environment – child-sized tables and chairs arranged in groups, walls covered in the children's work at child's eye level, a sandpit and water tray, and perhaps even a play house or shop. The children would typically be working in pairs or small groups using concrete materials such as building blocks to solve problems set them by the teacher, while others might be playing on their own building models, or engaging in pretend play with other children. The teacher might be working with a small group of children or with an individual child, and would rarely address the whole class except to control noise levels or make an announcement relating to events such as lunchtime. What you would be very unlikely to find is a room full of children sitting in silence at rows of desks, while the teacher stands at the front of the class writing instructions on a blackboard for children to copy meticulously into their workbooks.

These two **pedagogical** scenarios are familiar to most of us, and we can ask why the first has remained dominant in the UK primary education system for the last 30 to 40 years. The 1960s witnessed a huge shift from so-called "chalk and talk" pedagogy toward a "child-centered" one. This child-centeredness is encapsulated in the influential government-commissioned Plowden Report (1967), which argued that "at the heart of the educational process lies the child." Plowden was not simply arguing that children should be the beneficiaries of the educational process but was making the case that in order for us to maximize educational experience, it is essential to understand the nature of development and learning itself: "knowledge of the manner in which children develop is of prime importance both in avoiding educationally harmful practices and in introducing effective new ones." Such child-centered approaches had many advocates in educational philosophers such as Froebel, and were therefore readily welcomed by primary teachers. However, child-centeredness and Plowden's recommendations may well have been enforced and remained influential precisely because they map so closely ideas from **cognitive developmental** theory, particularly Piagetian theory. Piaget's account of development could, as I have argued elsewhere (Davis 1991), be used by those involved in early education as a formalization of many of the assumptions underlying child-centered education.

PIAGET'S IMAGE OF THE CHILD

One central tenet of Piagetian theory is the characterization of children being active in the construction of their own development through interaction with the largely physical environment. Such direct activity is essential not only in infancy during sensorimotor development but remains important during later stages as well. Paradoxically, Piaget wrote very little on the educational implications of his work, but where he did the emphasis was on the teacher's role in providing the best physical environment within which children could overcome their **egocentrism** and gain a decentered perspective on principles such as number conservation and transitivity. In educational practice, such so-called **discovery learning** became widespread. Supported by a theory such as Piaget's, playing in the sandpit or water tray is not simply playing for fun but is an activity that can result in learning and may even promote development itself. This aspect of Piaget's work can thus be argued to have been influential on the way that educators promoted learning, but the influence also extended to the curriculum itself – what it is that children should be learning about. Given that much of Piaget's work centered on aspects of physical causality, it is not surprising that the greatest impact was on the science and mathematics curricula. Some mathematics schemes popular in primary education even went as far as advocating that math should be taught by presenting children with Piagetian tests such as **class inclusion** and **conservation** (e.g., Copeland, 1979; Williams & Shuard, 1986; see also chapter 8). Even today, an understanding of number conservation remains a criterion for an **attainment target** in the UK National Curriculum for mathematics.

 ## Social Interaction, Learning, and Development

So far I have discussed in fairly general terms how psychological theory might be mapped onto educational practice. We now turn to a more empirically led investigation and consider experimental evidence from developmental psychology that has direct relevance on how we promote learning and introduce effective teaching. The area I have selected is the role of social interaction on cognitive development, specifically, **peer** interaction and adult–child interaction. This provides an ideal springboard for our present purposes, for two main reasons. First, the developmental literature on the effects of social interaction contains a lively theoretical debate on why interaction effects emerge in the first place. Within this debate, arguments remain as to the relative merits of cognitive theory and social constructionist theories based on the work of Vygotsky in explaining why it is that social interaction appears to exert such a powerful influence on learning. Second, although not always separated in the developmental literature, there are important educational reasons for understanding whether effective learning outcomes for children can best be achieved in individual interaction with an adult (teacher), or whether interaction with peers in groups can be similarly or more beneficial.

THE EFFECTS OF PEER INTERACTION

Earlier in this chapter it was argued that Piaget's interest in interaction was predominantly in the importance of interaction with the physical rather than interpersonal environment. This is definitely the case in relation to his later writing, but in his earlier work (e.g., Piaget, 1926, 1932) Piaget outlined a case for the importance of social interaction not only as a means to encourage learning, but also as a direct cause of development itself. The primary intellectual deficit of the **preoperational** child, according to Piaget, is the child's inability to decenter or take account of alternative perspectives on the world to their own. However, Piaget argued that this egocentrism could be overcome via a particular type of interaction – interaction with peers. Interaction with adults, be they parents or teachers, was considered to be of little value since the gap, both intellectual and in terms of status, between adult and child is simply too great. Peers, on the other hand, provide the ideal potential source of **sociocognitive conflict** necessary for development to take place. Two preoperational children may each hold opposing **egocentric** views on a situation which results in **cognitive conflict** within the child, which Piaget considered would be resolved. According to Piaget, such cases of conflict are crucial because it is through resolution of conflict that cognitive development occurs. More recently, Bryant (1990) has pointed out the fatal flaw in Piaget's position, namely that while conflict resolution may well take place, there is no logical reason why it should be in the direction of developmental advance. Nevertheless, Piaget's claims about cognitive conflict have inspired some important empirical work about the potential impact of peer interaction on development.

Working in pairs can promote perspective-taking

The initial experimental work was carried out by Willem Doise and colleagues in Geneva in the 1970s and early 1980s (Doise & Mugny, 1984). The experiments hinged on two fundamental tests of preoperational thinking, the **perspective-taking** task and the conservation task. The perspective-taking task was based on the classic "three mountains task" originally designed by Piaget and Inhelder (1956), in which children are presented with a three-dimensional display of three mountains with distinguishing features on each (see chapter 8, figure 8.4). The child's task is either to select a picture or to reconstruct the array to show how the mountains would appear from an alternative perspective. Young children find the three mountains task exceptionally difficult and a common response of children of around 5 years is to select the picture depicting their own view of the scene. This was taken by Piaget and Inhelder as good evidence for egocentrism in the preoperational child (see chapter 8 for a fuller description of Piaget's theory).

Doise and Mugny (1984) modified the materials to include buildings and features of a village rather than three mountains. The important modification to the task was the change in design to allow a test of peer interaction on perspective-taking ability. Doise and Mugny introduced a three-stage design that has become a common **paradigm** in the work on peer interaction effects. In stage one, all the children (aged 5–7 years) are tested on the task to assess their individual performance. At the second stage, the children are divided into two groups – **experimental** and **control**. The children acting as controls are again tested on their individual performance. In contrast, the experimental group are divided into pairs and their performance as a pair is assessed. In the third and final stage, children are tested on their individual performance as they had been at stage one. This pretest, test, post-test design allows two questions to be addressed. First, does the performance of the children working in pairs at stage two exceed that of those working alone? Second, are there any pretest to post-test gains measurable for the experimental group relative to the controls? In other words, a critical test of this design is whether children's individual performance on the stage three post-test is influenced by whether or not they worked alone or in pairs at the second experimental stage.

The results from this experiment showed that for the weakest children, namely, those who were totally egocentric at pretest, working in pairs at the test stage did indeed result in improvements on their individual post-test performance. The effect was strongest when these children were paired with other children who showed evidence of perspective-taking but whose performance was not at ceiling. Pairings of two children, both of whom were highly egocentric, did not in this instance show dramatic improvement in individual post-test performance. This said, other studies (e.g., Glachan & Light, 1982), and Doise and Mugny themselves, have found good evidence that the pairing of two weaker children can have a dramatic positive impact on the children's later individual performance compared to children who are never given the opportunity to work in a pair. These positive gains cannot be explained simply by proposing that more developmentally advanced children teach those children who are less advanced. Instead, as we shall see in the following sections, there are a number of possible reasons why peer interaction improves performance.

Peer effects in conservation

These so-called peer facilitation effects are by no means confined to perspective-taking tasks. Perret-Clermont (1980) reports similar findings using the standard conservation of liquid paradigm. Typically, preoperational nonconserving children will report a change in quantity when liquid is poured from one container to a container of a different shape. In contrast, conserving children will claim that the amount of liquid remains the same and justify their responses. In her work, Perret-Clermont was interested in the effects of allowing nonconserving and conserving children to work alongside each other in a conservation setting. Again, the same three-stage pretest, test, post-test design was used as in the work by Doise and Mugny (1984), with the experimental group comprising two conserving children and one nonconserving child whose task it was to share juice equally amongst the three of them, each of whom had differently shaped beakers. In this situation it is argued that sociocognitive conflict arises from the contradictions in the children's beliefs about the conservation of liquid. Again, the results indicated that the nonconserving children were benefiting from interaction, in so far as they did significantly better on individual post-test than children who had not experienced interaction.

Peer effects are persistent

In both the perspective-taking and conservation studies outlined above, the time delay between the children's interaction sessions and individual post-test was around a week to 10 days. This makes the results even more dramatic because it appears that not only can a relatively short exposure to paired interaction improve children's performance when subsequently working on their own, but these effects are relatively long-lasting. Furthermore, the results can be explained in terms of sociocognitive conflict. Taken as they stand, these results are a potential goldmine for extracting educational implications. Teachers frequently ask children to work in pairs or small groups, both for pragmatic reasons and because they can see the potential for children learning from each other when working on a task. The Genevan studies outlined above go beyond providing empirical justification for group work in the classroom since they suggest that such group activity has long-lasting effects which are measurable at the individual level. Given that the British educational system from infant school to university assesses understanding and knowledge at an individual level, these findings would be powerful indeed in their educational implications. However, first we must establish that these effects are not confined to these very young children on these very specific sorts of tasks.

Peer effects in older children: Computer-based tasks

Much of the experimental work on the effects of peer interaction on children's learning in middle childhood has centered on computer-based tasks. Initially this was for pragmatic reasons rather than because computers were thought to afford any special qualities for promoting interaction.

For example, Glachan and Light (1982) found that 7- to 9-year-olds benefited from interacting with another child when working on the classic Tower of Hanoi problem-solving task. The task involves reconstructing a tower of three seriated blocks in as few moves as possible without moving more than one block at a time or placing a larger block on top of a smaller one. However, their results also suggested that such benefits

Plate 17.1 Computer-based tasks are used in research to examine the effects of peer interaction on children's learning in middle childhood. Photograph © Getty Images/PhotoDisc.

may only manifest themselves when children literally cooperate by physically moving the materials together following verbal decision making over the appropriate next step. In order to follow this up, Light and colleagues devised a computer-based version of the task which allowed tight control over the children's decision making and actions, while at the same time allowing the children's responses to be recorded directly into the computer. Computer-based tasks also lend themselves to the three-step pretest, test, post-test design used earlier by the neo-Piagetians working in Geneva.

During the 1980s and early 1990s a body of evidence emerged which looked very promising indeed in terms of the possible positive effects of paired learning. For example, Blaye, Light, Joiner, and Sheldon (1991) presented junior school children with a computer-based complex adventure game that involved a good deal of planning. The experimental design, as before, involved children working initially individually, then either alone or in pairs at the test stage before being post-tested individually. The results showed that those children who worked in pairs fared better on their individual post-test than those children who did not have the opportunity for collaboration at the test phase. Furthermore, this type of evidence seemed to suggest that peer interaction not only improved how quickly children arrived at the correct solution, but also positively affected the kinds of strategies these children used. Taken together, this evidence coupled with that from workers such as Doise and Mugny could be summarized as follows. Positive peer interaction effects are not restricted to very young children working on Piagetian-based tasks. Instead, they have also been found on more complex problem-solving tasks in children as old as 11–12 years. Furthermore, the process by which these effects come about could fairly readily be attributable to a cognitive explanation such as sociocognitive conflict.

This constitutes an ideal base for approving group work in schools. Teachers rely out of necessity on children working together in small groups, since class sizes prevent one-to-one teaching, but also institute such work patterns for constructive reasons. It is widely believed by primary school teachers that children working together produce social benefits as children learn the social skills for effective cooperation. Therefore, the psychological evidence which suggests that group work may have a significant intellectual outcome should lend further support to this type of educational practice. Although there is clear evidence for the benefits of peer interaction, it has also become apparent that important qualifications must be applied to conclusions arising from computer-based, peer-assisted learning. First, marked gender differences began to emerge in those studies using computers as the basis for interaction. Second, some studies produced evidence to suggest that interaction effects may not be as specific as was initially thought. However, trying to resolve these problems with cognitive explanations of peer interaction has given rise to some important theoretical shifts which have had an enormous impact on the way that interaction effects are currently being investigated.

Gender effects in computer-based tasks

With hindsight, it was perhaps not surprising that gender should become an issue in interaction studies. In his work on children's attitudes to computers carried out in the early 1980s at the point where computers were becoming a feature of home life as well as school life, Hughes (1986) found a bias in favor of boys in terms of their access to and confidence about computers. The massive increase in the number of computers at both home and school since then has done little to alleviate this inequality. Culley (1993) found that boys are more positive about computers, are more likely to use them, and moreover use them for more diverse purposes than girls. Furthermore, studies of children working with the programming language LOGO revealed gender differences again in favor of boys (Hughes, 1986). Interestingly, these differences seem to arise not because girls are less able at computer-based tasks or less spatially adept but because of differences in interactive style between boys and girls, with boys tending to dominate when children are working in mixed-gender pairs (Light, 1997).

This type of gender inequality presents a serious educational challenge because girls enter school already disadvantaged in terms of their preschool access to computers, and this can then be compounded by differences in interactive styles and other, more subtle factors, such as the nature of software (Barberie & Light, 1992; Crook, 1994). Littleton, Light, Joiner, Messer, and Barnes (1995) found that minor modifications to the software had a dramatic impact on gender differences. For example, whereas their standard adventure game paradigm involving pirates capturing treasure resulted in superior performance in boys, replacing pirates with "honey bears" resulted in no gender differences. Interestingly, this change in software reduced the gender inequality by improving the performance of girls without reducing that of boys. This is an important finding because selecting appropriate software is a relatively straightforward means by which at least some of the disadvantage experienced by girls can be rectified. Interventions aimed at differences in interactive style are more likely to pose a greater research challenge. Nevertheless, the picture does not seem to be that gloomy. In an overview on **collaborative learning**, Underwood and Underwood (1999) reported that when girls are paired with each other, they perform at a level equal to if not better than boys. Mixed pairs appear to fail because in this situation girls are less likely to discuss ideas and contribute to the planning often required to solve complex reasoning tasks (Barberie & Light, 1992; Underwood & Underwood, 1999). These gender differences affecting productive learning will need to remain a central research question because it appears that they are not specific to childhood but have been found in experiments looking at interaction and learning in undergraduate students (Howe & Tolmie, 1999).

Peer interaction or peer presence?

Much of the research outlined above has assumed that the benefits of peer collaboration arise either directly or indirectly as a result of the interaction between children working on a given task. However, it is becoming clear that we are going to have to broaden our theoretical base to take into account some emerging paradoxical findings. Light, Littleton, Messer, and Joiner (1994) found that peer interaction itself is not necessary to improve children's performance on their standard computer adventure game task. Instead, they found that the mere presence of another child working on another computer in the same room resulted in a similar level of cognitive benefit to children working in pairs. Clearly, then, there are important affective and motivational factors operating on the effectiveness of learning. In considering this finding, Light claims that we should consider integrating models from social psychology into our traditional cognitive theories of learning. For example, he draws on Monteil's (1992) work on social comparison effects on secondary school-aged children. Monteil (1992) gave students feedback about their academic performance which either matched their actual performance or induced an expectation that their performance had been better or worse than it actually was relative to their peers. Subsequently, these students were presented with a learning situation either in the absence or in the presence of their peers. The results show a complex interaction. Learning outcomes were most positive in individual learning contexts when there was a mismatch between academic ability and "induced" academic ability from feedback. In other words, children performed better on their own when they had been given misleading feedback about their actual performance. In contrast, where the academic feedback matched actual academic performance, learning outcomes were more positive in the presence of peers. Monteil argued that social comparison with peers plays a key role in children's social construction of themselves and others which determines their concentration on the relevant task demands and, as a result, affects learning outcomes.

From a research point of view, findings such as this "peer presence" effect found by Light et al. (1994) are important for several reasons. First, they provide a clear example of how a simple research paradigm such as the three-step peer interaction design can be so thoroughly researched that the findings push us to broaden our theoretical horizons. In this case, a cognitive account of learning had become so well specified that it led to an integration with models from social psychology. Second, and perhaps more importantly for our present purposes, they show how experimental paradigm-based research can, with enough research effort, yield fruitful implications for educational practice. Yet I suspect that very few teachers would be surprised to hear that research findings show that learning involves a complex interaction between cognition, gender, and affective factors. On the contrary, many teachers might well argue that they already knew that! However, research plays a key role in that it serves to specify precisely how these separate factors operate and interact in specific situations.

Taken together, this review of some key evidence on the effects of peer interaction on learning must lead us to conclude positively with regard to future prospects for educational practice. Overall, the findings suggest that children can learn effectively from collaboration with their peers. Despite the fact that the studies vary in terms of the scale of these benefits, I know of no studies suggesting that peer collaboration is damaging from the point of view of learning! Even the findings regarding gender differences give rise to fairly clear indications as to how inequalities may arise and how they might be reduced. The fact that individual learning can also be enhanced without direct interaction but simply by having peers present in the same room paves the way for future research to enlighten classroom organization and curriculum delivery.

 ## Adult Interaction: What is Effective Teaching?

VYGOTSKY'S THEORY

An essential aspect of how developmental psychology might contribute educationally relevant implications is to go beyond providing evidence demonstrating where learning may be enhanced (such as through peer interaction) by having something to say about the process of teaching and learning itself. Paradoxically, research which has been predominantly inspired by Piagetian theory is unlikely to do this because, as has been argued earlier, Piaget simply was not interested in this question. Nevertheless, there are alternative, highly influential theories of child development which have at their core the question of the nature of learning and the role of direct teaching in promoting learning. The key theorist here is the Russian psychologist Lev Semenovich Vygotsky. In contrast to Piaget, who focused on mental activity at the individual level, Vygotsky's account prioritizes the social nature of learning. According to Vygotsky, knowledge exists between individuals before it can exist within an individual:

> Any function in the child's cultural development appears twice, or on two planes. First it appears on the social plane and then on the psychological plane. First it appears between people as an interpsychological category and then within the child as an intrapsychological category. This is equally true with regard to voluntary attention, logical memory, the formation of concepts and the development of volition. (Vygotsky, 1981, p. 163)

By emphasizing the social nature of development, Vygotsky's theory is not only a theory of learning, it also offers a theory of teaching, since language is the prime medium for sharing knowledge in formal contexts such as schools and informally in the home. Adults control the child's representation of the world from birth onwards and the presence of more knowledgeable others is a crucial condition for the development of higher mental functions. Over the last 20 years, Vygotsky's work has been highly influential on researchers as a framework for studying the importance of adult–child interaction on development. Two concepts in particular have attracted attention, namely, the *zone of proximal development* (ZPD) and *scaffolding*.

The zone of proximal development and scaffolding

The **zone of proximal development** (ZPD) is "the distance between the actual developmental level as determined by independent problem solving and the level of potential development as determined through problem solving under adult guidance or in collaboration with more able peers" (Vygotsky, 1978, p. 86; see figure 17.1). This definition carries with it two important implications. First, the concept of the ZPD characterizes learning through guidance or assistance as a normal but important part of development because the child's **intermental ability** ultimately becomes **intramental ability** by appropriate interaction. Second, it supposes that learning can be made more effective through the most appropriate form of teaching. The essential question is whether adults can or do pitch their interventions at the appropriate level when interacting with children so as to make effective teachers. I shall describe some of the research evidence relating to this question, but first let us consider a concept related to the ZPD – **scaffolding**. Scaffolding is a metaphor originally used by Jerome Bruner and colleagues (Bruner, 1983; Wood, Bruner, & Ross, 1976). It is the means by which adults structure and simplify the environment to facilitate children's learning. Scaffolding may occur in a variety of contexts, for example by pointing out the next piece in a jigsaw puzzle or offering the child a sock rolled down to make it easier to put on.

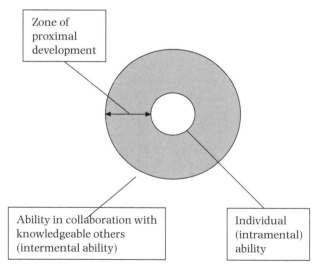

Figure 17.1 Vygotsky's zone of proximal development (ZPD). The inner circle indicates the limit of a child's ability working on his or her own. The outer circle indicates the child's ability working in collaboration with a knowledgeable other. The area between the two is the ZPD.

Are adults effective natural teachers?

As can be seen, the concepts of the ZPD and scaffolding are closely related since if we observe an adult providing appropriate scaffolding, then this implies that he or she has appropriately assessed the ZPD. But do adults know the best ways of structuring the child's world and the most appropriate time and course of intervention? In other words, do adults make effective teachers? I shall now consider some of the relevant empirical evidence that addresses this question. A key researcher in this area is David Wood (Wood, 1986; Wood & Middleton, 1975; Wood, Wood, & Middleton, 1978). I have selected his work since it represents a clear attempt to actually measure what goes on in adult–child interaction and specify what constitutes effective and ineffective teaching and learning. Furthermore, much like the research on peer interaction, Wood's work on adult–child interaction has also been highly paradigm-specific.

The task was intentionally devised so that the 4-year-old children being tested could not solve it without help from their mothers. It involved the construction of a pyramid comprising 21 wooden blocks of different shapes and sizes that could be joined together with pegs if correctly oriented. The mothers were shown in advance how to construct the pyramid one layer at a time, using blocks of decreasing size, and were told to teach their children how to make it so that the child would be able to reconstruct it for him- or herself. The results from this experiment allowed Wood and Middleton to identify five categories of the mothers' behavior to account for how they teach their children this particular task. One notable feature of these categories is that they are hierarchically organized in terms of the degree of control the mother takes of the situation. The first category identified was "General Verbal Prompts" such as "Now you make something." Here the mother suggests action on the child's part but does not specify what to do. The level 2 category that emerged was termed "Specific Verbal Instructions" and included remarks of the type "Get four big blocks." These comments identify relevant features of the task to be taken into account in the next move. The third-level category, "Indicates Materials," referred to mothers who helped their child by literally pointing out which block was needed next. Level 4 behavior referred to where the mother literally prepared the block for assembly by correctly orienting the block so that the hole faced the peg; if the mother actually demonstrated by attaching the block herself, this was described as level 5.

Wood's two rules of effective teaching

As can be seen, level 1 interventions involve a very low level of maternal control, whereas by level 5 the mothers have taken total control. On the basis of evidence taken from a series of studies, Wood (1986) was able to conclude that children were more likely to succeed on the task if their mothers followed what he terms the "two rules" of teaching: "the first dictates that any failure by a child to bring off an action after a given level of help should be met by an immediate increase in the level of control" (Wood, 1986). Thus, for example, if the child does not respond appropriately to a general verbal prompt, the mother needs to use a specific prompt.

The second of Wood's rules of teaching is that when a child is successful, then the adult needs to decrease the level of control. Teaching in line with these two rules is termed "contingent" and those mothers who showed contingent behavior were those whose children were subsequently more able to complete the task alone. In other words, effective teaching can lead to effective learning. Wood's emphasis on contingency is closely linked to the concept of ZPD since contingent behavior on the adult's part implies successful assessment of the ZPD.

Other researchers who also work within a neo-Vygotskian framework have been critical of the concept of contingency. For example, Hoogsteder, Maier, and Elbers (1996) argue that Wood's approach minimizes the child's role in the interaction and assumes the adult takes control in a piecemeal fashion. Hoogsteder et al. (1996) propose that adult–child interactions are far more dynamic, with the child having a key role to play in his or her own learning. Thus even in a highly controlled setting such as Wood has used, the way in which the child might influence the mother's behavior should not be underestimated.

IMPLICATIONS FOR EDUCATIONAL PRACTICE AND ASSESSMENT

In the United States there is already empirical evidence to support the efficacy of peer interaction and Vygotskian principles being put into educational practice. Work by Robert Slavin using a method known as Student Teams Achievement Divisions (STAD) has shown how cooperative learning can work. Children working within the STAD technique are allocated to work in small groups. Each group intentionally comprises children of varying ability, gender, and ethnic backgrounds. The teacher introduces a topic to the group and the group's task is to discuss the problem and query each other until members of the group as a whole agree that they understand the topic. Research shows that children operating within STAD show greater achievement than control children taught using more conventional methods (Slavin, 1990). The peer interaction involved is an important component of the success of these methods.

Another example of how Vygotsky's ideas have been put into practice is the development of "reciprocal teaching" (Palincsar & Brown, 1984, 1989). This technique has been particularly successful on students who, while competent at reading, have difficulty with comprehending text. The teacher's role is to introduce strategies that improve comprehension such as how to précis a passage of text, asking relevant questions, and making predictions about the storyline. Although the teacher models these strategies, the children are required to take on increasing responsibility for the teaching role. One key aspect of reciprocal teaching to have emerged from research aimed at measuring its success is the importance of the teacher offering the right level of support relative to a student's current level of understanding (Palincsar & Brown, 1984). This is a very similar effect to that found in Wood's work described earlier in relation to contingency and mother–child interactions.

Both STAD and reciprocal teaching provide very convincing evidence that psychological principles can be used to good educational effect. However, how feasible is it that these principles will influence educational practice across the whole curriculum and the way that children's learning is assessed? Mercer and Fisher (1998) argue that one reason why research on actual classroom activity may not embrace concepts such as the ZPD is a practical one. The ZPD is highly specific not only to particular children, but also to particular situations. Therefore, the demands on teachers who plan activities for groups or whole classes would simply be too great. In recognition of these constraints, Mercer and Fisher argue that we should radically revise the way we think about research and classroom practice away from our traditional focus on individual learning toward how groups of learners may advance.

Interestingly, this conclusion is similar to those put forward by Littleton and Light (1999) in their review of children interacting with computers. It is certainly the case that those researchers taking a Vygotskian perspective present a much more serious challenge to educational practice than those who take a more traditional neo-Piagetian cognitive view. My own view is that while children's learning environments may radically change as a result of developmental theorizing and research, other aspects of educational practice will not change in the foreseeable future. In relation to the assessment of children's learning, I suspect that we are a long way off from seeing major changes in the way that children are assessed in the manner being asked for by Mercer and Fisher. While collaborative learning may well increase and become more structured in classrooms, the assessment of pupils at the individual level will, in my opinion, remain with us for some time to come. There are two grounds for risking this prediction. First, much of the support for assessment that is not at the individual level is still at a theoretical level. We simply do not, as yet, have the tools available to know how we might go about assessing children in groups or classes which would fulfill the usual demands for reliability and validity. In order to do this, we will have to put in a good deal of empirical effort. The second reason for supposing that radical change is unlikely is more beyond the control of psychological researchers, and that is the political forces involved in educational policy. The last 15 years have already witnessed radical educational reform in the UK with the introduction of the National Curriculum. This reform is very much rooted in the principle of the assessment of individual learning, and it is to a discussion of this reform that we now turn.

Psychology, Schools, and Educational Reform

The question of the relationship between the content of a school curriculum and the nature of children's learning is key in all developed countries. The tension between curriculum and learning processes is often most apparent when the issue of assessment arises. One clear example of this comes from the United States, when in 1988 the state of Georgia instituted a required test that had to be passed before children could move from kindergarten to first grade. Despite the fact that this is now common practice across America, the move resulted in public outcry regarding the purpose of assessment and its relationship to learning (Woolfolk, 1998). Furthermore, the debate extended to the thorny issue of whether there should be national standards and a national test, and if so, what such standards and tests should be. In the UK the past 20 years have brought about an almost complete U-turn in educational practice, with the emphasis shifting from child-centered education to curriculum-centered education.

In the UK in 1967 the Plowden Report, entitled *Children and their primary schools*, stated that "at the heart of the educational process lies the child." In the mid-1980s the then secretary of state for education, Kenneth Baker, remarked that "at the heart of the educational process lies the curriculum." Such a radical shift must have an impact on how psychological research might and does influence educational practice.

The UK Education Reform Act of 1988 introduced a compulsory National Curriculum for all children between 5 and 16 years. It defined "foundation" subjects that would have to be taught, namely, English, mathematics, science, technology, history, geography, art, music, and physical education. Of these, English, mathematics, and science are considered "core" subjects demanding the majority of curriculum time and effort. Importantly, the National Curriculum specified *attainment targets*, or descriptions of the knowledge that children should have acquired as they work their way through the education system. It is these attainment targets at **key stages** that provide the benchmark for assessment of children's performance at ages 7, 11, 14, and 16.

THE MOVE TO CRITERION REFERENCING

Two crucial aspects of the assessment procedures introduced by the National Curriculum are relevant here. First, they represented the first compulsory assessment of children as young as 7 after only 2 or 3 years of formal schooling, and second, the method of testing was intentionally different from standard forms of testing. Most scholastic tests are **norm referenced**; that is, they provide a measure of a given child's performance only relative to other children. However, the tests introduced with the National Curriculum are *criterion referenced* in that they give a measure of the child's performance relative to a specified criterion, in this case a given attainment target in a core curriculum subject. Criterion-referenced testing brings with it both advantages and disadvantages. From a statistical point of view, measuring reliability is problematic with this form of testing since one simply does not have scores in the same way that norm-referenced tests generate, but new models are being developed that can overcome this (e.g., Schagen & Hutchinson, 1994). The main advantage of criterion-referenced testing is that it gives a description of what the child actually knows in a given area rather than an indication of whether the child is performing better or worse than other children. This formative nature of testing, at least in principle, indicates to teachers where their efforts need to be concentrated. Indeed, one of the principal aims of the National Curriculum was that testing children using criterion-referenced "standard assessment tasks" (SATs) would result in a significant increase in educational standards. Since the year 2000 saw the first cohort of children to have experienced the National Curriculum throughout their school career, this issue of its effect on standards will become an empirical question for crucial research.

INCREASING PARENTAL INVOLVEMENT

A further aim of the National Curriculum proposed by the government on its introduction was that it would alter the relationship between schools and parents by keeping parents better informed and getting them more involved with their children's education. The relationship between home and school has been well researched from a psychological and sociological perspective. Studies carried out before the implementation of the National Curriculum showed that home and school provide strikingly different contexts for development. Three major projects (Tizard, Blatchford, Burke, Farquhar, & Plewis, 1988; Tizard & Hughes, 1984; Tizard, Mortimore, & Burchell, 1981) concluded that most parents, irrespective of social class and race, were providing diverse and rich learning environments for their children preschool and were enthusiastic about becoming involved in their children's education once they started formal schooling. However, the evidence also suggested that despite the fact that parental involvement in school-based activities such as reading and writing predicted children's performance on entering school, this relationship did not hold after several years of education (Tizard et al., 1988). In other words, those children who were given the most help at home did no better after 3 years' schooling than those who received little help. The question is, then, whether this complicated relationship between parents and schools has been improved or even impeded by the implementation of the National Curriculum.

One study by Hughes, Wikeley, and Nash (1994) looked at parents whose children entered infant school when the National Curriculum had been introduced and who were assessed at the end of Year 2 (aged 7 years) by National Curriculum SATs. Unfortunately, the findings did not present strong evidence for positive changes in the relationship between home and school. Many parents reported that they did not know enough about the education their children were receiving and despite their desire to know, they knew little about the National Curriculum and were disappointed with what they learned from their children's SATs. So the situation of home and school operating as two independent worlds seems not to have been changed by the National Curriculum, despite this being one of its major goals. Why might this be the case? One possibility argued by Hughes (1996) is that although parents are better informed by being given full school reports and annual statements from the board of governors, they are not necessarily more involved with school policy and practice. Hughes found that although roughly half the parents in one study reported that they wanted to become more involved in supporting their children with their SATs and other school activity, this enthusiasm was not noticed by teachers (Hughes, 1996). In fact, not only were the teachers unaware of these parents' concerns, but they also viewed parental involvement with skepticism. The teachers considered that altering their own practice to accommodate the views of parents posed some kind of threat to their professionalism. Paradoxically, this finding mirrors the general findings from research carried out before the National Curriculum was introduced, and as such Hughes concludes that radical change is necessary if home and school are not to remain as two independent worlds. The need to understand how schools can build on preschool experience and capitalize on the potential contribution of parents during schooling is not a trivial one.

It may well prove to be the case that this rather negative view of parental involvement is somewhat premature, since there is a critical analogy with research carried out in the United States. Although the United States does not have a National Curriculum in the sense that the UK does, it does have experience of evaluating the impact of parental involvement on children's educational achievement. During the 1960s many so-called "compensatory education" programs such as **Project Head Start** were developed, aimed at providing educationally disadvantaged children with the skills necessary to succeed at school. Many of these programs offered educationally at-risk children an enriched educational experience in school and at home by involving parents with the program directly. Although initial evaluations of such programs did not look very promising, more detailed later assessments of these schemes produced positive results. For example, in a **meta-analysis** of 11 education programs, Lazar and Darlington (1982) found important differences between children from compensatory education programs and control groups.

Measures such as **intelligence quotient (IQ)** did not show remarkable differences between the two groups of children. However, those children benefiting from compensatory programs were less likely to be assigned to special education than control children and, more importantly, had mothers who had higher educational aspirations for their children. A further finding was that these educational programs had a positive impact on the children's social competence. This latter finding strikes me as crucial. This chapter has focused largely on the cognitive potential of using the knowledge of developmental psychology to inform educational practice. Yet there is every reason to suppose that any benefits on social development are equally as important. This point is well taken in the United States and is clearly relevant to future research in the UK on the effects of the National Curriculum.

SUMMARY AND CONCLUSIONS

In this chapter I have reviewed some of the theories and evidence from developmental psychology and highlighted a few key areas that I believe to be of direct relevance to those involved in children's education. In conclusion, we must ask whether developmental psychology as a discipline is sufficiently healthy to remain optimistic about possible future changes in educational practice and policy. I think there are three reasons why a reasonable degree of optimism is justified. First, there are no indications that developmental psychologists are losing interest in fundamental questions about the nature of learning and the factors that influence learning. There is lively theoretical debate coupled with solid empirical effort. The ever-increasing interest in more socially based models of development such as Vygotsky's can only be a good thing for the potential of our discipline to inform educational practice. It forces us to recognize the importance of children's learning both in and out of school and to accept that learning, like teaching, is rarely a solitary individual activity but involves interaction with adults and peers alike.

The second reason to remain optimistic is that there is a growing body of developmental research tackling specific curriculum areas such as reading and mathematics (see chapter 11). This research is already having a direct impact on the way that the curriculum is presented to children and will continue to do so. The third and final reason is slightly paradoxical. Although the National Curriculum was introduced for political rather than sound psychological reasons, it is beginning to spark new lines of research. As funds become available to measure the effects of the National Curriculum, this in turn will increasingly focus our attention on the way that learning is assessed. Hopefully this will force developmental psychology to come up with radical ways of measuring what constitutes effective learning. Despite the fact that it will require an enormous amount of empirical effort, I believe there is a strong enough theoretical base to support this goal.

DISCUSSION POINTS

1 Compare the implications of Piaget's and Vygotsky's theories for educational practice.
2 List and consider the factors that might lead to peer presence effects on children's performance.
3 How might gender differences on computer tasks be minimized?
4 Why is the zone of proximal development difficult to assess?
5 Can developmental psychology contribute more to designing a school curriculum than curriculum implementation?
6 How might the positive effects of peer interaction be encouraged in the classroom?
7 Think of the ways in which understanding of children's development and learning could or should influence educational practice.

SUGGESTIONS FOR FURTHER READING

Bernstein, B., & Brannen, J. (1996). *Children, research and policy.* London: Taylor & Francis.

Faulkner, D., Littleton, K., & Woodhead, M. (1998). *Learning relationships in the classroom.* London: Routledge.

Littleton, K., & Light, P. (1999). *Learning with computers: Analysing productive interaction.* London: Routledge.

chapter 18

Social Problems in School

Dan Olweus

KEY CONCEPTS

AGE-COHORT DESIGN	CORRELATION COEFFICIENT	PASSIVE OR SUBMISSIVE VICTIM
BASELINE GROUP	DIFFUSION OF RESPONSIBILITY	PEER
BULLYING	DOSAGE-RESPONSE RELATIONSHIP	PROJECTIVE TECHNIQUES
CONDUCT DISORDER	INTERVENTION GROUP	PROVOCATIVE VICTIM

OVERVIEW

Bullying is one of the biggest social problems affecting children in our schools, and at sadly regular intervals we read of another suicide by a victim of persistent bullying. The study of bullying is therefore of considerable importance, in the hope that by understanding it we can reduce its prevalence and its effects on the victims. In this chapter, the author gives an account of important information about bullying:

- basic facts about bully/victim problems, including prevalence, boy/girl differences, and common myths about bullying;
- characteristics of the typical bully;

This chapter is in large measure based on my 1994 article "Bullying at school: Basic facts and effects of a school-based intervention program," *Journal of Child Psychology and Psychiatry*, 35, 1171–90, with permission from the Association for Child Psychology and Psychiatry.

The research reported in this chapter was supported by grants from the William T. Grant Foundation, the Norwegian Research Council for Social Research (NAVF), the Swedish Delegation for Social Research (DSF), and, in earlier phases, from the Norwegian Ministry of Education. This support is gratefully acknowledged.

- characteristics of the typical victim;
- how aggressive reaction patterns develop.

The author makes the reasonable case that it is a fundamental human right for a child to feel safe in school and to be spared the oppression and repeated, intentional humiliation implied in bullying. He describes the characteristics of his school-based intervention program, which increases awareness of the bully/victim problem, develops clear rules against bullying, and provides support and protection for the victims. This program, which can be described as a "whole-school policy approach to bullying," has been highly successful in reducing the incidence of bullying in England, the United States, Germany, Norway, and Sweden.

Introduction

Bullying among schoolchildren is certainly a very old phenomenon. The fact that some children are frequently and systematically harassed and attacked by other children has been described in literary works, and many adults have personal experience of it from their own schooldays. Though many are acquainted with the bully/victim problem, it was not until fairly recently – in the early 1970s – that the phenomenon was made the object of more systematic research (Olweus, 1973a, 1978). For a number of years, these efforts were largely confined to Scandinavia. In the 1980s and early 1990s, however, bullying among schoolchildren has attracted attention also in many other countries such as Japan, the UK, the Netherlands, Australia, New Zealand, Ireland, Belgium, France, Italy, Greece, Spain, Portugal, Switzerland, Canada, and the United States among others (e.g., Smith et al., 1999). There are now clear indications of an increasing societal as well as research interest in bully/victim problems in many parts of the world.

The first part of this chapter gives an overview of research findings on bully/victim problems among schoolchildren. The presentation does not aspire to be exhaustive, in particular since several of the early Scandinavian studies were of a very preliminary nature, with small sample sizes and no clear definition of what is meant by bullying. In addition, they were often conducted by undergraduate students with little supervision from more experienced researchers. The main research findings discussed, therefore, are from the following four studies: a longitudinal project initiated in the early 1970s and comprising some 900 boys from Greater Stockholm, Sweden (Olweus, 1973a, 1978), and three large-scale studies conducted in connection with a nationwide campaign against bully/victim problems in Norwegian elementary and secondary/ junior high schools (grades 1–9, ages 7–14 years), launched in 1983 (e.g., Olweus, 1991, 1993b). See table 18.1 for an overview of the projects. Many of the findings to be reported have been replicated in several different samples and with different methods.

Although most of the generalizations and conclusions drawn in the chapter are derived from this research (e.g., Olweus, 1973a, 1978, 1979, 1980, 1984, 1991, 1992a, 1993a, 1993b; Olweus & Alsaker, 1991), I will give reference to other sources, where appropriate. In this context, it should be mentioned that an excellent overview

Table 18.1 Overview of studies

	Nationwide study in Norway (1983)	Large-scale study in Sweden (1983/4)	Intensive study in Bergen, Norway (1983–5)	Study in Greater Stockholm, Sweden (1970–)
Units of study	715 schools, grades 2–9 (130,000 boys and girls)	60 schools, grades 3–9 (17,000 boys and girls)	Four cohorts of 2,500 boys and girls in grades 4–7 (1983) 300–400 teachers 1,000 parents	Three cohorts of boys (900 boys in all), originally in grades 6–8 (1973)
Number of measurement occasions	One	One	Several	Several
Measures include	• Questionnaire on bully/victim problems (aggregated to grade and school level) • Data on recruitment area of the school: population density, socioeconomic conditions, percent immigrants • School size, average class size • Composition of staff	• Questionnaire on bully/victim problems • School size, average class size	• Self-reports on bully/victim problems, aggression, antisocial behavior, anxiety, self-esteem, attachment to parents and peers, etc., grades, some peer ratings • Teacher data on characteristics of class, group climate, staff relations, etc.	• Self-reports and reports by mothers on a number of dimensions, peer ratings, teacher nominations • Official records on criminal offenses, drug abuse for subgroups: interviews on early childrearing, hormonal data, psychophysiological data

of the research area is given by Farrington (1993). There are also other, more practically oriented overviews, for example by Besag (1989), Elliott (1991), Smith and Thompson (1991), and an extensive annotated bibliography of literature and resources (Skinner, 1992). Note also that chapter 14 gives an account of the development of both antisocial and prosocial development.

The second part of the chapter reports on the positive effects of an intervention program against bullying that I developed and evaluated over a two-year period in 42 schools in Bergen, Norway, in connection with the nationwide campaign. The content of the program, and the principles on which it is based, are also briefly described.

What is Bullying?

I define *bullying* or *victimization* in the following general way: *A student is being bullied or victimized when he or she is exposed, repeatedly and over time, to negative actions on the part of one or more other students.* It is a negative action when someone intentionally inflicts, or attempts to inflict, injury or discomfort upon another – basically what is implied in the definition of aggressive behavior (Olweus, 1973b). Negative actions can be carried out by physical contact, by words, or in other ways, such as making faces or obscene gestures, and intentional exclusion from a group.

In order to use the term bullying, there should also be an *imbalance in strength* (an *asymmetric power relationship*): the student who is exposed to the negative actions has difficulty in defending him- or herself and is somewhat helpless against the student or students who harass.

Bullying can be carried out by a single individual – the bully – or by a group. The target of bullying can also be a single individual – the victim – or a group. In the context of school bullying, the target has usually been a single student. Data from the Bergen study indicate that, in the majority of cases, the victim is harassed by a group of two or three students. A considerable proportion of the victims, some 35–40 percent, report, however, that they are mainly bullied by one student (Olweus, 1988).

In this definition, the phenomenon of bullying is thus characterized by the following three criteria: (1) it is aggressive behavior or intentional "harmdoing" (2) which is carried out "repeatedly and over time" (3) in an interpersonal relationship characterized by an imbalance of power. One might add that the bullying behavior often occurs without apparent provocation. This definition makes it clear that bullying can be considered a form of abuse, and I sometimes use the term *peer abuse* as a label of the phenomenon. What sets it apart from other forms of abuse such as child abuse and wife abuse is the context in which it occurs and the relationship characteristics of the interacting parties.

It is useful to distinguish between **direct bullying**/*victimization* – with relatively open attacks on the victim – and **indirect bullying**/*victimization* in the form of social isolation and intentional exclusion from a group.

In the present chapter the expressions *bullying, victimization* and *bully/victim problems* are used synonymously.

Basic Facts About Bully/Victim Problems

Prevalence

On the basis of a survey of more than 130,000 Norwegian students with the Olweus Bully/Victim Questionnaire (Olweus, 1990, 1993b, 1996), one can estimate that some 15 percent of the students in elementary and secondary/junior high schools (grades 1–9, roughly corresponding to ages 7 through 16) in Norway were involved in bully/victim problems with some regularity – either as bullies or victims (Olweus, 1985, 1987, 1991, 1993b). This figure corresponded to 84,000 students (autumn 1983). Approximately 9 percent, or 52,000 students, were victims, and 41,000, or 7 percent, bullied other students regularly. Some 9,000 students were both victim *and* bully (1.6 percent of the total of 568,000 students, or 17 percent of the victims). A total of some 5 percent of the students were involved in more serious bullying problems (as bullies or victims or bully/victim), occurring "about once a week" or more frequently.

Analyses of parallel teacher nominations in approximately 90 classes (Olweus, 1987) suggest that these results do not give an exaggerated picture of the prevalence of bully/victim problems (see Note 1, p. 453). Indeed, as both the student and the teacher questionnaires refer only to part of the autumn term, there is little doubt that the figures underestimate the number of students who are involved in such problems during a whole year.

It is apparent, then, that bullying is a considerable problem in Norwegian schools and affects a very large number of students. Data from other countries (in large measure collected with the Bully/Victim Questionnaire) such as Sweden (Olweus, 1992b), Finland (Lagerspetz, Björkqvist, Berts & King, 1982), England (Smith, 1991; Whitney & Smith, 1993), United States (Perry, Kusel, & Perry, 1988), Canada (Ziegler & Rosenstein-Manner, 1991), the Netherlands (Haeselager & van Lieshout, 1992; Junger, 1990), Japan (Hirano, 1992), Ireland (O'Moore & Brendan, 1989), Spain (Ruiz, 1992), and Australia (Rigby & Slee, 1991) indicate that this problem certainly exists also outside Norway and with similar or even higher prevalence rates.

Bully/victim problems in different grades

As seen in figure 18.1, the percentage of students who reported being bullied decreased with higher grades. It was the younger and weaker students who were most exposed. With regard to the ways in which the bullying was carried out, there was a clear trend toward less use of physical means (physical violence) in the higher grades. In the Bergen study, it was also found that a considerable part of the bullying was carried out by older students. This was particularly marked in the lower grades: more than 50 percent of the bullied children in the lowest grades (2 and 3, corresponding to ages 8 and 9 in this survey) reported that they were bullied by older students.

It is natural to invoke the latter finding at least as a partial explanation of the form of the curves in figure 18.1. The younger the students are, the more potential bullies

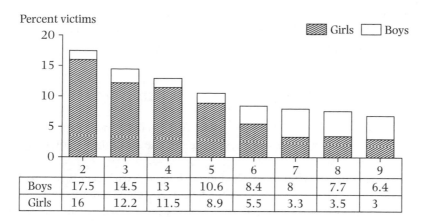

Figure 18.1 Percentage of students in different grades who reported being bullied (being exposed to direct bullying) (*n* for boys = 42,390; *n* for girls = 40,940).

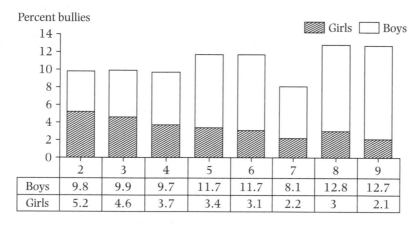

Figure 18.2 Percentage of students in different grades who reported having bullied other students (*n* for boys = 42,324; *n* for girls = 40,877).

they have above them; accordingly, an inverse relationship between percentage of victims and grade level seems reasonable. It may also be the case that the form of the curves reflects the possibility that a certain proportion of the victims are able gradually to develop strategies for escaping bullying as they grow older. In a similar vein, it can be argued that a certain proportion of the students may become less vulnerable with increasing age and, accordingly, will report being less bullied. All of these explanations (and perhaps additional ones) may be partly correct, and more detailed analyses of the factors affecting the shape of the curves are to be undertaken.

As regards the tendency to bully other students, depicted in figure 18.2, the changes with grades are not so clear and systematic as in figure 18.1. The relatively marked drop in the curves for grade 7 (around age 13), in particular for boys, may partly reflect the fact that these students were the youngest ones in their schools and accordingly did not have "access to suitable victims" in lower grades to the same extent. (The majority of Norwegian students make a transfer from primary schools to separate secondary/junior high schools with the start of grade 7, age 13 years.)

Bullying among boys and girls

As is evident from figure 18.1, there is a trend for boys to be more exposed to bullying than girls. This tendency is particularly marked in the secondary/junior high school grades.

These results concern what was called *direct bullying*, with relatively open attacks on the victim. It is natural to ask whether girls were more often exposed to *indirect bullying* in the form of social isolation and intentional exclusion from the peer group. Analyses of the questionnaire data confirm that girls were more exposed to indirect and more subtle forms of bullying than to bullying with open attacks. At the same time, however, the percentage of boys who were bullied in this indirect way was approximately the same as that for girls. In addition, a somewhat larger percentage of boys was exposed to direct bullying, as mentioned above. (Moreover, there was a fairly strong association between being a victim of direct and of indirect bullying.)

An additional result from the Bergen study is relevant in this context. Here it was found that *boys carried out a large part of the bullying to which girls were subjected*. More than 60 percent of bullied girls (in grades 5–7, aged 10–12 years) reported being bullied mainly by boys. An additional 15–20 percent said they were bullied by both boys and girls. The great majority of boys, on the other hand – more than 80 percent – were bullied chiefly by boys.

Figure 18.2 shows the percentage of students who had taken part in bullying other students with some regularity. It is evident here that a considerably larger percentage of boys than girls had participated in bullying. In secondary/junior high school, more than four times as many boys as girls reported having bullied other students.

It should also be reported that bullying by physical means was more common among boys. In contrast, girls often used more subtle and indirect ways of harassment such as slandering, spreading of rumors, and manipulation of friendship relationships (e.g., depriving a girl of her "best friend"). Nonetheless, harassment with nonphysical means (words, gestures etc.) was the most common form of bullying also among boys.

In summary, *boys were more often victims and in particular perpetrators of direct bullying*. This conclusion is in good agreement with what can be expected from research on sex differences in aggressive behavior (Ekblad & Olweus, 1986; Maccoby & Jacklin, 1974, 1980). It is well documented that relations among boys are by and large harder, tougher, and more aggressive than among girls (Maccoby, 1986). These differences certainly have both biological and social/environmental roots.

The results presented here should by no means be construed as implying that we do not need to pay attention to bullying problems among girls. As a matter of course, such problems must be acknowledged and counteracted, whether girls are the victims of bullying or they themselves perpetrate such behavior.

The pattern of results found in the Norwegian data has been replicated in all essentials in the corresponding analyses with Swedish students (Olweus, 1992b) and with students in the Sheffield area of Great Britain (though the levels of problems were somewhat higher for these students; see Whitney & Smith, 1993; Smith & Shu, 2000). For a number of other research findings on bullying, concerning, for example, teacher and parent awareness of the problems, bullying on the way to and from school, and levels of problems in "big-city" versus small-town schools, see Olweus (1993b) and Eslea and Smith (2000).

THREE COMMON "MYTHS" ABOUT BULLYING

Bullying is a consequence of large class and school sizes

A common view holds that bully/victim problems are a consequence of large classes and/or schools: the larger the class or the school, the higher the level of bully/victim problems. Closer analysis of this hypothesis, making use of the Norwegian survey data from more than 700 schools and several thousand classes (with great variations in size), gave clear-cut results: there were no positive associations between level of bully/victim problems (the percentage of bullied and/or bullying students) and school or class size. Thus, the size of the class or school appears to be of negligible importance for the relative frequency or level of bully/victim problems (Olweus, 1993b).

It is nevertheless a fact that the *absolute number* of bullied and bullying students is greater on average in big schools and in big classes. One might therefore think that it would be somewhat easier to *do* something with the problems in a small school or a small class. Analyses of data from the Bergen study conducted so far, however, do not support this assumption either. It may be added that international research on the "effects" of class and school size agrees in suggesting that, in general, these factors are of no great significance, at least within the ranges of size variation typically found (e.g., Rutter, 1983).

Bullying is a consequence of competition and striving for grades

In the general debate in Scandinavia (and probably elsewhere), it has been commonly maintained that bullying is a consequence of competition and striving for grades in school. More specifically, it has been argued that the aggressive behavior of the bullies toward their environment can be explained as a reaction to failures and frustrations in school. Such ideas are in fact central elements in many criminological theories. A detailed analysis of data on 444 boys in the Swedish study (Olweus, 1983), who were followed from grade 6 to grade 9 (from ages 13 to 16), gave no support at all to these ideas. Though there was a moderate association (a **correlation coefficient** of around 0.30) between poor grades in school and aggressive behavior both in grade 6 (13 years) and in grade 9 (16 years), there was nothing in the results to suggest that the behavior of the aggressive boys was a *consequence* of poor grades and failure in school. A similar finding, but more specifically concerned with delinquent behavior, has been reported by a Canadian research group (Tremblay et al., 1992).

Victims "stand out from the crowd"

Third, a widely held view explains victimization as caused by "external deviations," i.e., characteristics of the victims that cause them to "stand out." It is argued that students who are fat, red-haired, wear glasses, or speak with an unusual dialect etc. are particularly likely to become victims of bullying. Again, this hypothesis received no support from empirical data. In two samples of boys, victims of bullying were by and large found to be no more externally deviant (with regard to 14 external characteristics assessed by means of teacher ratings) than a control group of boys who were not exposed to bullying (Olweus, 1973a, 1978). It was concluded that external deviations play a much smaller role in the origin of bully/victim problems than generally assumed (see also Junger, 1990). In spite of the lack of empirical support for this hypothesis, it seems still to enjoy considerable popularity. Some probable reasons why this is so have been advanced, and the interested reader is referred to this discussion (Olweus, 1978, 1993b).

Summary

All of these hypotheses have thus failed to receive support from empirical data. Accordingly, one must look for other factors to find the (partial) origins of these problems. The research evidence collected so far and presented in the next few pages clearly suggests that personality characteristics/typical reaction patterns, in combination with physical weakness or strength in the case of boys, are quite important for the development of these problems in *individual students* (making them more likely to become victims or bullies). At the same time, environmental factors such as the teachers' attitudes, routines, and behavior play a major role in determining the extent to which the problems will manifest themselves in *a larger unit* such as a classroom or a school.

WHAT CHARACTERIZES THE TYPICAL VICTIMS?

A relatively clear picture of both the typical victims and the typical bullies has emerged from research (e.g., Björkqvist, Ekman & Lagerspetz, 1982; Boulton & Smith, 1994; Farrington, 1993; Lagerspetz et al., 1982; Olweus, 1973a, 1978, 1981, 1984; O'Moore, 2000; Perry et al., 1988). By and large, this picture seems to apply to both boys and girls, although it must be emphasized that less research has so far been done on bullying among girls.

The passive or submissive victim

The typical victims are more anxious and insecure than students in general. Further, they are often cautious, sensitive, and quiet. When attacked by other students, they commonly react by crying (at least in the lower grades) and withdrawal. Also, victims suffer from low self-esteem, they have a negative view of themselves and their situation. They often look upon themselves as failures and feel stupid, ashamed, and unattractive.

The victims are lonely and abandoned at school. As a rule, they do not have a single good friend in their class. They are not aggressive or teasing in their behavior, however, and, accordingly, one cannot explain the bullying as a consequence of the victims themselves being provocative to their peers (see below). These children often have a negative attitude toward violence and use of violent means. If they are boys, they are likely to be physically weaker than boys in general (Olweus, 1978).

I have labeled this type of victim the **passive or submissive victim**, as opposed to the far less common type described below. In summary, it seems that the behavior and attitude of the passive/submissive victims *signal to others that they are insecure and worthless individuals who will not retaliate if they are attacked or insulted.* A slightly different way of describing the passive/submissive victims is to say that they are characterized by an *anxious or submissive reaction pattern combined* (in the case of boys) *with physical weakness.*

In-depth interviews with parents of victimized boys indicate that these boys were characterized by a certain cautiousness and sensitivity from an early age (Olweus, 1993a, n.p.). Boys with such characteristics (perhaps combined with physical weakness) are likely to have had difficulty in asserting themselves in the peer group and may have been somewhat disliked by their age-mates. There are thus good reasons to believe that these characteristics contributed to making them victims of bullying (see also Schwartz, Dodge, & Coie, 1993). At the same time, it is obvious that the repeated harassment by peers must have considerably increased their anxiety, insecurity, and generally negative evaluation of themselves.

Some of our data also indicate that the victimized boys had closer contact and more positive relationships with their parents, in particular with their mothers, than boys in general. This close relationship is sometimes perceived by teachers as overprotection

Plate 18.1 The victims of bullying are often lonely and abandoned at school. Photograph © Getty Images/Digital Vision.

on the part of the mothers (Olweus, 1978, 1993a). It is reasonable to assume that such tendencies toward overprotection are both a cause and a consequence of the bullying.

The provocative victim

As mentioned earlier, there is also another, clearly smaller, group of victims, the **provocative victims**, who are characterized by a combination of both anxious and aggressive reaction patterns. These students often have problems with concentration, and behave in ways that may cause irritation and tension around them. Some of these students can be characterized as hyperactive. It is not uncommon that their behavior provokes many students in the class, thus resulting in negative reactions from a large part of or even the entire class. The dynamics of bully/victim problems in a class with provocative victims differ in part from problems in a class with passive victims (Olweus, 1978).

A follow-up study of two groups of boys (Olweus, 1993a) who had or had not been victimized by their peers in school (from grades 6 through 9) shows that the former victims had "normalized" in many ways as young adults, at age 23. This was seen as an indication that the boys, after having left school, had considerably greater freedom to choose their own social and physical environments. In two respects, however, the former victims had fared much worse than their nonvictimized peers: they were more likely to be depressed and had poorer (global) self-esteem. The pattern of findings clearly suggested that this was a consequence of the earlier persistent victimization which thus had left its scars on their minds.

WHAT CHARACTERIZES THE TYPICAL BULLIES?

A distinctive characteristic of the typical bullies is their aggression toward peers – this is implied in the definition of a bully. But bullies are often aggressive toward adults as well, both teachers and parents. Generally, bullies have a more positive attitude toward violence than students in general. Further, they are often characterized by impulsivity and a strong need to dominate others. They have little empathy with victims of bullying. If they are boys, they are likely to be physically stronger than boys in general, and the victims in particular (Olweus, 1978).

Are bullies anxious and insecure?

A commonly held view among psychologists and psychiatrists is that individuals with an aggressive and tough behavior pattern are actually anxious and insecure "under the surface." The assumption that the bullies have an underlying insecurity has been tested in several of my own studies, also using "indirect" methods such as measuring the level of stress hormones (adrenaline and noradrenaline), and the use of **projective techniques**. There was nothing in the results to support the common view; rather, they pointed in the opposite direction: the bullies had unusually little anxiety and insecurity, or were roughly average on such dimensions (Olweus, 1981,

1984, 1986; see also Pulkkinen & Tremblay, 1992). They did not suffer from poor self-esteem.

These conclusions apply to the bullies as a group (as compared with groups of control boys and victims). The results do not imply that there cannot be individual bullies who are both aggressive and anxious.

It should also be emphasized that there are students who participate in bullying but who do not usually take the initiative – these may be labeled *passive bullies*, *followers*, or *henchmen*. A group of passive bullies is likely to be fairly mixed and may also contain insecure and anxious students (Olweus, 1973a, 1978).

Are bullies unpopular?

Several studies have found bullies to be of average or slightly below-average popularity (Björkqvist et al., 1982; Lagerspetz et al., 1982; Olweus, 1973a, 1978; Pulkkinen & Tremblay, 1992). Bullies are often surrounded by a small group of two to three peers who support them and who seem to like them (Cairns, Cairns, Neckerman, Gest, & Gariépy, 1988). The popularity of the bullies decreases, however, in the higher grades and is considerably less than average in grade 9 (around age 16). Nevertheless, the bullies do not seem to reach the low level of popularity that characterizes the victims.

In summary, the typical bullies can be described as having an *aggressive reaction pattern* combined (in the case of boys) with physical strength.

It should be noted that not all highly aggressive children or youth can be classified as bullies. In an as yet unpublished study of one of the Swedish cohorts, the boys belonging to the upper 15–20 percent of the distribution of peer ratings of aggressive behavior ("Start Fights" and "Verbal Hurt" in grades 6–9 – ages 12–15 years – see Olweus, 1980) were examined as to whether they had been identified as bullies by their teachers (Olweus, 1978). Depending upon the cut-off point chosen, between 40 and 60 percent of the boys rated as "highly aggressive" were nominated as bullies by their teachers. Exploratory comparisons between the teacher-nominated bullies and the aggressive nonbullies suggested interesting differences. Because of their preliminary nature, they will not be reported on here, but they clearly indicate the need for more detailed analyses of possible differences between students who are identified as bullies and other aggressive youngsters.

Motives underlying bullying

As regards the possible psychological sources underlying bullying behavior, the pattern of empirical findings suggests at least three partly interrelated motives. First, the bullies have a strong need for *power and dominance* (of a negative kind); they seem to enjoy being "in control" and subduing others. Second, considering the family conditions under which many of them have been reared (see below), it is natural to assume that they have developed a certain degree of *hostility toward the environment*; such feelings and impulses may make them derive satisfaction from inflicting injury and suffering upon other individuals. Finally, there is an *instrumental component* to their behavior. The bullies often coerce their victims to provide them with money, cigarettes, beer, and other things of value (see also Patterson, Littman, & Bricker, 1967).

In addition, it is obvious that aggressive behavior is in many situations rewarded in the form of prestige (e.g., Bandura, 1973).

Bullies are generally antisocial

Bullying can also be viewed as a component of a more generally antisocial and rule-breaking (**conduct-disordered**) behavior pattern. From this perspective, it is natural to predict that youngsters who are aggressive and bully others run a clearly increased risk of later engaging in other problem behaviors such as criminality and alcohol abuse. A number of studies confirm this general prediction (e.g., Loeber & Dishion, 1983; Magnusson, Stattin, & Dunér, 1983).

The Swedish follow-up studies have also found strong support for this view. Approximately 60 percent of boys who were characterized as bullies in grades 6–9 – aged 12–16 years – (on the basis of a combination of teacher nominations and peer ratings) had been convicted of at least one officially registered crime by the age of 24. Even more dramatically, as much as 35–40 percent of the former bullies had three or more convictions by this age, while this was true of only 10 percent of the control boys (those who were neither bullies nor victims in grades 6–9). Thus, as young adults, the former school bullies had a fourfold increase in the level of relatively serious, recidivist criminality as documented in official crime records (Olweus, 1993b).

It may be mentioned that the former victims had an average or somewhat below-average level of criminality in young adulthood.

DEVELOPMENT OF AN AGGRESSIVE REACTION PATTERN

In light of the characterization of the bullies as having an aggressive reaction pattern – that is, they display aggressive behavior in many situations – it becomes important to examine the question: What kind of rearing and other conditions during childhood are conducive to the development of an aggressive reaction pattern? Very briefly, the following four factors have been found to be particularly important (based chiefly on research with boys; for details, see Olweus, 1980; see also Loeber & Stouthamer-Loeber, 1986):

1   The basic emotional attitude of the primary caregiver(s) toward the child during early years (usually the mother). A negative emotional attitude, characterized by lack of warmth and involvement, increases the risk that the child will later become aggressive and hostile toward others.
2   Permissiveness for aggressive behavior by the child. If the primary caregiver is generally permissive and "tolerant" without setting clear limits on aggressive behavior toward peers, siblings, and adults, the child's aggression level is likely to increase.
3   Use of power-assertive childrearing methods such as physical punishment and violent emotional outbursts. Children of parents who make frequent use of these methods are likely to become more aggressive than the average child – "violence begets violence." (See chapter 1, p. 6, for a reiteration of this theme.)

We can summarize these results by stating that *too little love and care and too much "freedom" in childhood are conditions that contribute strongly to the development of an aggressive reaction pattern.*

4   Finally, the temperament of the child. A child with an active and hot-headed temperament is more likely to develop into an aggressive youngster than a child with a quieter temperament. The effect of this factor is less powerful than the effects of the first two conditions.

The factors listed above can be assumed to be important for both younger and somewhat older children. For adolescents, it is also of great significance whether the parents supervise the children's activities outside the school (Patterson, 1986; Patterson & Stouthamer-Loeber, 1984) and check on what they are doing and with whom.

It should also be pointed out that the aggression levels of the boys participating in the analyses above (Olweus, 1980) were *not* related to the socioeconomic conditions of their families, measured in several different ways. Similarly, there were no (or only very weak) relations between the four childhood factors discussed and the socioeconomic conditions of the family (Olweus, 1981).

SOME GROUP MECHANISMS

When several students jointly engage in the bullying of another student, certain group mechanisms are likely to be at work. Several such mechanisms have been discussed in detail in Olweus (1973a, 1978). Because of space limitations, they are merely listed here: (1) social "contagion"; (2) weakening of the control or inhibitions against aggressive tendencies; (3) **diffusion of responsibility**; and (4) gradual cognitive changes in the perceptions of bullying and of the victim.

A QUESTION OF FUNDAMENTAL HUMAN RIGHTS

The victims of bullying form a large group of students who are to a great extent neglected by the school. We know that many of these youngsters are the targets of harassment for long periods of time, often for many years (Olweus, 1977, 1978). It does not require much imagination to understand what it is to go through the school years in a state of more or less permanent anxiety and insecurity and with poor self-esteem. It is not surprising that the victims' devaluation of themselves sometimes becomes so overwhelming that they see suicide as the only possible solution.

Bully/victim problems in school really concern some of our basic values and principles. In my view, *it is a fundamental human right for a child to feel safe in school and to be spared the oppression and repeated intentional humiliation implied in bullying.* No student should be afraid of going to school for fear of being harassed or degraded, and no parent should need to worry about such things happening to his or her child!

Even though an intervention program against bully/victim problems in school is particularly important in order to reduce the suffering of the victims, it is also highly desirable to counteract these problems for the sake of the aggressive students. As reported above, school bullies are much more likely than other students to follow an antisocial path in later life. Accordingly, it is essential to try to redirect their activities into more socially acceptable channels.

The Effects of a School-Based Intervention Program

Against this background, it is now appropriate briefly to describe the effects of the intervention program that I developed and evaluated in connection with the campaign against bully/victim problems in Norwegian schools. The major goals of the program were to reduce as much as possible existing bully/victim problems and to prevent the development of new problems. For more details about the program and its evaluation, the reader is referred to *Bullying at School: What We Know and What We Can Do* (Olweus, 1993b) and to other sources (e.g., Olweus, 1991, 1992a; Olweus & Alsaker, 1991; Olweus & Limber, 1999).

PARTICIPANTS AND DESIGN

Evaluation of the effects of the intervention program was based on data from approximately 2,500 students originally belonging to 112 grade 4–7 classes in 42 primary and secondary/junior high schools in Bergen (modal ages at Time 1 were 11, 12, 13, and 14 years, respectively). Each of the four grade/age cohorts consisted of 600–700 participants with a roughly equal distribution of boys and girls. The first time of data collection (Time 1) was in late May 1983, approximately 4 months before introduction of the intervention program. New measurements were taken in May 1984 (Time 2) and May 1985 (Time 3). The design employed is usually called a *selection-cohorts* or **age-cohort design**.

MAIN RESULTS

The characteristics and principles underlying the intervention program are described in the next section. First, we will give a summary of the main findings, which are as follows:

- There were marked reductions in the levels of bully/victim problems (for both direct and indirect bullying, and for bullying others) for the periods studied, 8 and 20 months of intervention, respectively. By and large, reductions were obtained for both boys and girls and across all cohorts compared.
- Similar reductions were obtained for the aggregated peer-rating variables "Number of students being bullied in the class" and "Number of students in the

class bullying other students." There was thus consensual agreement in the classes that bully/victim problems had decreased considerably during the periods studied.

- In terms of percentages of students reporting being bullied or bullying others "now and then" or more frequently, the reductions amounted to approximately 50 percent or more in most comparisons.
- There was no displacement of bullying from the school to the way to and from school. There were reductions or no changes as regards bully/victim problems on the way to and from school.
- There was also a clear reduction in general antisocial behavior such as vandalism, fighting, pilfering, drunkenness, and truancy (see Olweus, 1989, and Bendixen & Olweus, 1999, for details about the construction of the Bergen Questionnaire on Antisocial Behavior).
- In addition, we could register marked improvement as regards various aspects of the "social climate" of the class: improved order and discipline, more positive social relationships, and a more positive attitude to schoolwork and the school.
- At the same time, there was an increase in student satisfaction with school life, as reflected in "liking recess time."
- For several of the variables, the effects of the intervention program were more marked after two years than after one year.
- The intervention program not only affected already existing victimization problems; it also reduced the number (and percentage) of *new* victims (Olweus, 1992a). The program had thus both primary and secondary prevention effects (Cowen, 1984).

In the majority of comparisons for which reductions were reported above, the differences between **baseline** and **intervention groups** were significant/highly significant and of considerable magnitude.

Overview of the findings

A detailed analysis of the quality of the data and the possibility of alternative interpretations of the findings led to the following general statements (Olweus, 1991): it is very difficult to explain the results obtained as a consequence of (1) underreporting by the students; (2) gradual changes in the students' attitudes to bully/victim problems; (3) repeated measurement; and (4) concomitant changes in other factors, including general time trends (Olweus, 1994). All in all, it was concluded that *the changes in bully/victim problems and related behavior patterns were likely to be mainly a consequence of the intervention program and not of some other "irrelevant" factor.* It was also noted that self-reports, which were implicated in most of the analyses conducted so far, are probably the best data source for the purposes of this study. At the same time, largely parallel results were obtained for the peer-rating variables mentioned above and for teacher ratings of bully/victim problems at the class level; in the latter case, however, the effects were somewhat weaker.

In addition, a clear **dosage-response relationship** (a correlation of 0.51, with a sample size of 80) has been established in preliminary analyses at the class level (which is the natural unit of analysis in this case): those classes that showed larger reductions in bully/victim problems had implemented three presumably essential components of the intervention program (including establishment of class rules against bullying and use of regular class meetings) to a greater extent than those with smaller changes (additional information on these analyses can be found in Olweus & Alsaker, 1991). This finding provides corroborating evidence for the hypothesis that the changes observed were due to the intervention program.

Brief comments

The reported effects of the intervention program must be considered quite positive, in particular since many previous attempts to systematically reduce aggressive and antisocial behavior in preadolescents/adolescents have been relatively unsuccessful (e.g., Dumas, 1989; Gottfredson, 1987; Kazdin, 1987). The importance of the results is also accentuated by the fact that there has been a highly disturbing increase in the prevalence of violence and other antisocial behavior in most industrialized societies in the last decades. In the Scandinavian countries, for instance, various forms of registered criminality have typically increased by 400–600 percent since the 1950s or 1960s.

As mentioned in the first part of the chapter, we can estimate that approximately 80,000 students in Norwegian schools were involved in bully/victim problems (in 1983). On the basis of the reported results, the following conclusion can be drawn: *If all primary and secondary/junior high schools in Norway used the intervention program the way it was used in Bergen, the number of students involved in bully/victim problems would be reduced by 40,000 or more in a relatively short period of time.* Effective use of the intervention program would also have a number of additional positive effects, as indicated by the previously reported findings.

KEY PRINCIPLES OF THE INTERVENTION PROGRAM

The intervention program is built around a limited set of key principles derived chiefly from research on the development and modification of the problem behaviors concerned, in particular aggressive behavior. It is considered important to try to create a school (and, ideally, also home) environment characterized by (1) warmth, positive interest, and involvement from adults, on the one hand, and (2) firm limits to unacceptable behavior, on the other. Third, in cases of violations of limits and rules, *nonhostile, nonphysical* sanctions should be consistently applied (in chapter 1, the ineffectiveness of punishment as a way of controlling negative and promoting prosocial behavior was discussed). Implied in the latter two principles is also a certain degree of monitoring and surveillance of the students' activities in and out of school (cf. Patterson, 1982, 1986). Finally, adults are supposed to act as authorities at least in some respects. In a sense, the intervention program is based on an *authoritative* adult–child interaction, or childrearing, model (cf. e.g., Baumrind, 1967; see also chapter 16) applied to the school setting.

Table 18.2   Overview of Olweus's Core Program

General prerequisites
+ + Awareness and involvement on the part of adults

Measures at the school level
+ + Questionnaire survey
+ + School conference day
+ + Effective supervision during recess and lunchtime
+ Formation of coordinating group

Measures at the class level
+ + Class rules against bullying
+ + Regular class meetings with students
+ Meetings with parents

Measures at the individual level
+ + Serious talks with bullies and victims
+ + Serious talks with parents of involved students
+ Teacher and parent use of imagination

+ + core component; + highly desirable component

MEASURES USED AT THE SCHOOL, CLASS, AND INDIVIDUAL LEVELS

The principles listed above were translated into a number of specific measures to be used at the *school*, *class*, and *individual* levels. It is considered important to work on all of these levels, if possible. Space limitations prevent a description of the various measures, but such an account can be found in Olweus (1993b, 1999a). (See Note 2, p. 454.) Table 18.2 lists a set of core components that are considered, on the basis of statistical analyses and our experience with the program, to be particularly important in any implementation of the program.

With regard to implementation and execution, the program is mainly based on utilization of the existing social environment: teachers and other school personnel, students, and parents. Non-mental-health professionals thus play a major role in the desired "restructuring of the social environment." "Experts" such as school psychologists, school counselors, and social workers also serve important functions such as planning and coordinating, counseling teachers and parents (groups), and handling more serious cases.

ADDITIONAL CHARACTERISTICS

Further understanding of the program can be gained from a brief description of the following four major subgoals.

To increase awareness of the bully/victim problem and advance knowledge about it

This includes dispelling some of the myths about bullying and its causes. Use of the Bully/Victim Questionnaire for an anonymous survey is an important step in obtaining more specific knowledge about the frequency and nature of the problems in the particular school.

To achieve active involvement on the part of teachers and parents

Active involvement implies among other things that the adults must recognize that it is their responsibility to control to a certain degree what goes on among the children and youngsters at school. One way of doing this is to provide adequate supervision during recess time. Further, teachers are encouraged to intervene in possible bullying situations and give an *absolutely clear message* to the students: *bullying is not accepted in our class/school.* Teachers are also strongly advised to initiate serious talks with victims and bullies, and their parents, if a bully/victim problem has been identified in the class. Again, the basic message should be: *we don't tolerate bullying in our class/school and will see to it that it comes to an end.* Such an intervention on the part of the school must be regularly followed up and closely supervised, otherwise the situation may easily become worse for the victim than before the intervention.

To develop clear rules against bullying

Such as the following: "We will not bully other students"; "We will try to help students who are bullied"; "We will make it a point to include students who become easily left out." Such a set of rules can also serve as a basis for class discussions about what is meant by bullying behavior in concrete situations and what kind of sanctions should be used for students who break the rules. The behavior of the students in the class should be regularly related to these rules in class meetings ("social hour"). It is important that the teacher make consistent use of sanctions (some form of nonhostile, nonphysical punishment) in cases of rule violations, but also give generous praise when the rules have been followed.

To provide support and protection for the victims

If followed, class rules against bullying certainly support children who tend to be victimized. In addition, the teacher may enlist the help of "neutral" or well-adjusted students to alleviate the situation of the victims in various ways. Also, teachers are encouraged to use their imagination to help victimized students to assert themselves in the class, to make them valuable in the eyes of their classmates. Parents of victims are exhorted to help their children develop new peer contacts and to teach them in detail how to make new acquaintances and to maintain a friendship relation.

A WHOLE-SCHOOL POLICY APPROACH TO BULLYING

It should be emphasized that this core program in many ways represents what is usually called "a whole-school policy approach to bullying" in the English literature (e.g., Pepler, Craig, & O'Connell, 1999; Smith, 2001; Smith & Sharp, 1994, Smith & Shu, 2000). It consists of a set of routines, rules, and strategies of communication and action for dealing with existing and future bullying problems in the school. Possible reasons for the effectiveness of the program have been discussed in some detail in Olweus (1992a). They include a change in the "opportunity" and "reward structures" for bullying behavior (resulting in fewer opportunities and rewards for bullying behavior). It should also be emphasized that bully/victim problems are an excellent entry point for dealing with a variety of problems that plague today's schools, such as discipline problems, vandalism, and other antisocial or delinquent behavior.

After publication of the original paper on which this chapter is based, the present intervention program (with or without slight modifications) has been used in a number of schools in various countries. Positive effects have been documented in scientific evaluations of the program in England (Smith & Sharp, 1994), the United States (Olweus & Limber, 1999), Germany (Hanewinkel & Knaack, 1997), and in a large-scale project in Norway (Olweus, 1999b). For summary descriptions of these evaluations, see Olweus and Limber (1999).

It may be added that the intervention program has been evaluated by more than 1,000 Norwegian and Swedish teachers (Manger & Olweus, 1985). In short, their reactions have generally been quite favorable, indicating, among other things, that teachers see the proposed principles and measures as useful and realistic.

SUMMARY AND CONCLUSIONS

As is hopefully shown in this chapter, there is now available a good deal of reliable, research-based knowledge about bully/victim problems in school. At the same time, it must be recognized that the empirical base on which robust conclusions can be built is still somewhat limited in terms of methodology, contextual and cultural variation, and other important parameters (but see, e.g., Olweus, 1999c, 1999d; Smith et al., 1999). This is particularly true with regard to efforts to counteract and intervene systematically against the problems. In the years to come, a number of issues in the area of bully/victim problems will have to be dealt with in greater detail, with more methodological diversity, and under more varied contextual and cultural conditions. Because the phenomenon of bullying seems to be genuinely interesting to many developmental, educational, and child psychiatric researchers, and it has many important practical and societal implications, I feel confident that the next decades will see continuing solid research along these lines.

NOTES

1 With regard to the validity of self-reports on variables related to bully/victim problems, it may be mentioned that in my early Swedish studies (Olweus, 1978), composites of 3–5

self-report items on being bullied or bullying and attacking others, respectively, correlated in the 0.40–0.60 range (Pearson correlations) with reliable peer ratings on related dimensions (Olweus, 1977). Similarly, Perry, Kusel, and Perry (1988) reported a correlation of 0.42 between a self-report scale of three victimization items and a reliable measure of peer nominations of victimization in elementary schoolchildren. In the intervention study described in this chapter, we also found class-aggregated student rating estimates of the number of students in the class who were bullied or bullied others during the reference period to be highly correlated with class-aggregated estimates derived from the students' own reports of being bullied or bullying others: correlations were in the 0.60–0.70 range (see Olweus, 1991, for details).

2   The updated intervention program consists of the book *Bullying at School* (Olweus, 1993b), the revised Olweus Bully/Victim Questionnaire (Olweus, 1996), with accompanying PC program for processing the data, *Olweus' Core Program Against Bullying and Antisocial Behavior: A Teacher Handbook* (Olweus, 1999a), and a 20-minute Norwegian video cassette showing scenes from the everyday lives of two bullied children (with English subtitles) or the US video *Bullying* (1996), which is based on the original Norwegian video. The Bully/Victim Questionnaire, the PC program, and the teacher handbook can be ordered from Dan Olweus, Research Center for Health Promotion (HEMIL), Christies gate 13, N-5015 Bergen, Norway (e-mail address: Olweus@psych.uib.no). For a more detailed description of the program and for additional information, see Olweus and Limber (1999) and www.colorado.edu/cspv/blueprints.

DISCUSSION POINTS

1   Think about the negative consequences of bullying. Why are the effects on the victims so awful that at times they can lead to suicide attempts?
2   Think about the characteristics of the typical bully. When do their antisocial behaviors begin, and what rewards do you think they get from harassing and attacking their victims?
3   What do you think characterizes the typical victim of bullies? Do they stand out from the crowd, are they excessively timid, and are there personality characteristics that distinguish them from their peers?
4   Do you think it is reasonable to claim that it is a fundamental human right not to be bullied, whether in school, the workplace, or other context?
5   Think about the characteristics of a "whole-school" approach to developing an anti-bullying intervention scheme. What must such a scheme include in order to be successful?

SUGGESTIONS FOR FURTHER READING

Craig, W. (Ed.) (2000). *Childhood social development: The essential readings.* Cambridge, MA, and Oxford: Blackwell.

Skinner, A. (1992). *Bullying: An annotated bibliography of literature and resources.* Leicester: Youth Work Press.

Smith, P. K., Morita, Y., Junger-Tas, J., Olweus, D., Catalano, R., & Slee, P. (Eds.) (1999). *The nature of school bullying: A cross-national perspective.* London: Routledge.

Smith, P. K., & Thompson, D. (Eds.) (1991). *Practical approaches to bullying.* London: David Fulton.

chapter 19

Disorders of Development

Vicky Lewis

KEY CONCEPTS

AMNIOCENTESIS
ATTACHMENT BEHAVIOR
AUTISM
BLINDISMS
CENTRAL COHERENCE
CHROMOSOMES
CHRONOLOGICAL AGE
COGNITIVE DEVELOPMENT
COMPREHENSION
CRITICAL PERIOD
DEVELOPMENTAL DELAY
DEVELOPMENTAL
  MILESTONES
DEVELOPMENTAL
  QUOTIENT
DOWN'S SYNDROME
ECHOLALIA
EMBEDDED SHAPES

EXECUTIVE FUNCTIONING
EXPRESSIVE LANGUAGE
FALSE BELIEF
INTELLIGENCE QUOTIENT
  (IQ)
INTELLIGENCE TESTS
ISLETS OF ABILITY
LEXICAL SKILLS
LONGITUDINAL DESIGN
MENTAL AGE
MOTOR MILESTONES
OBJECT PERMANENCE
PHONOLOGICAL SKILLS
PRAGMATIC SYSTEM
PRAGMATICS
PRETEND PLAY
PROFOUND VISUAL
  IMPAIRMENT

PROSODY
REPRESENTATIONAL ABILITY
SAVANT SKILLS
SECONDARY
  INTERSUBJECTIVITY
SEMANTIC SYSTEM
SENSITIVE PERIOD
SENSORIMOTOR STAGE
SEVERE VISUAL
  IMPAIRMENT
SYNTACTIC SKILLS
SYNTAX
THEORY OF MIND
TURN-TAKING
VISUAL ILLUSION
WING'S TRIAD OF
  IMPAIRMENTS
WORKING MEMORY

OVERVIEW

The study of children with disabilities is important for two main reasons. First, an understanding of their development can often throw light on our understanding of the processes underlying the development of the typically developing child. Second, it can lead to an understanding and implementation of effective therapies and interventions. There are many different kinds of developmental disorders and disabilities, affecting almost every aspect of development. In this chapter the author discusses three areas of disability in detail.

- Children with profound visual impairments, defined as an inability to see anything more than shades of light and dark.
- Children with autism, who display a set of clinical behaviors characterized by impairments in social behavior and communication, and a restricted repertoire of activities and interests.
- Children with Down's syndrome, who are the largest group of individuals with learning difficulties.

The study of children with profound visual impairment helps to illuminate the role of vision in development, and indicates that there are alternative routes to development that do not require vision. Study of children with autism demonstrates that having an understanding of minds is probably a critical ability for typical development. Study of children with Down's syndrome indicates that their development may be different from that of typically developing children, rather than just delayed, and suggests that a range of different processes may underlie development.

Introduction

Many of the chapters in this book focus exclusively on studies of children who are following a typical pattern of development. Similarly, most of the theories that have been described have been based on the results of studies of typically developing children. However, a number of chapters have mentioned how particular disabilities affect certain aspects of psychological development. This is because the development of children with disabilities can often throw light on our understanding of the processes underlying development.

There are a number of different ways in which the study of children with disabilities can contribute to our understanding of development. For example, studies of typically developing children may suggest that a particular sense or experience is necessary for a certain development. The study of children whose senses or experiences are limited in particular ways can provide a means of testing these ideas. Further, as well as providing "tests" of our understanding of how development comes about, the study of children with disabilities can also lead to new and different ways of understanding development. Studies of typically developing children may suggest that certain **developmental milestones** are achieved through a particular "route" or pathway. However, if this route is not available to children because of their disability and yet they still develop the behavior, this indicates that they must be developing the behavior via a different process. Of course, this process may also be available to the typically developing child, although not apparently evident when we examine their development.

The study of children with disabilities can also contribute to our understanding of the relationship between different developments. For example, children with certain disabilities may have particular difficulties in one area of development. Study of how this difficulty impacts on other aspects of their development can help elucidate the nature of the relationship between different areas of development. This may be particularly helpful when study of typically developing children has led to suggestions that certain behaviors are prerequisites for the development of other behaviors, in other words, when some causal relationship between behaviors is suggested. If children with certain disabilities do not, or cannot, exhibit the first behavior, but do develop the second behavior, this indicates that the two behaviors are not necessarily causally related.

The study of children with disabilities can also contribute to the question of whether or not there are **critical** or **sensitive periods** for certain developments. Thus, if children with a disability develop a particular behavior at a much later age than typically developing children, this would negate any suggestion that there might be a critical age for this behavior to develop.

DIFFICULTIES IN STUDYING CHILDREN WITH DISABILITIES

Despite the relevance of studying children with disabilities for our understanding of development, there are a number of difficulties associated with their study. One of the main problems is that many children have more than one disability and, in such children, it is often difficult to separate out the effects of each disability on development. If one of our aims is to understand how particular problems affect psychological development, then it is crucial that we examine children with single disabilities. In reality, of course, this is almost impossible. And yet it should be our aim. Once we understand how a particular disability affects development, then we should be in a much better position to begin to understand how a combination of disabilities might influence the development of an individual child. However, sometimes the presence of two disabilities within one child may actually lead to new hypotheses about the origins of certain difficulties, as we shall see later in the case of visual impairment and **autism**.

If we want to ensure that our study of development in children with disabilities has implications for our understanding of the effect of a particular disability, we may need to restrict our study to particular children with that disability. Consider children who are registered blind. Blindness might seem a fairly straightforward disability since just one sense is affected. However, most children who are registered blind can see something and it is well known that even very limited experience of vision can have a marked effect on development, in that the development of such children is usually closer to that of sighted children than to the development of children who can see nothing. Therefore, if we want to understand the effect of not being able to see on development, we must restrict our study to children who have been unable to see anything since birth. In this chapter I use the term **profound visual impairment (PVI)** to describe being unable to see anything more than shades of light and dark. I shall use the term **severe visual impairment (SVI)** to include children with PVI and children who have some limited visual perception of form and shape.

However, even if we restrict our study to children with PVI, a further complication arises. This is that many children who cannot see anything have additional learning difficulties. While it may be that some of these children have learning difficulties as a result of their PVI, it is often difficult to eliminate other causes. Therefore, if our aim is to study the effect of not being able to see on development, we need to focus on children who have never had any vision and have no other disability, including learning difficulties.

Unfortunately, even if we restrict our studies to children with single, relatively clear-cut disabilities, it still may be difficult to reach conclusions about how each disability affects psychological development. The main reason for this is that different children, even if they have the same disability, vary. Just as there is variability in the ways in which children without disabilities develop, so there is variation in how children with the same disability develop. In studies of children without disabilities, this variation is usually dealt with by studying large numbers of children in order to try to eliminate the effects of individual variation; in studies of children with disabilities, this may be difficult, if not impossible, because of the relatively low incidence of certain conditions.

THREE DISABILITIES: PROFOUND VISUAL IMPAIRMENT, AUTISM, AND DOWN'S SYNDROME

There are many disorders of development and it is clearly not possible to consider them all. In the sections which follow, I shall examine the development of children with three very different disabilities – a sensory impairment (PVI), a specific disorder (autism), and a general learning difficulty (Down's syndrome). These different types of disorder shed light on development from different perspectives.

The first are children with PVI who have been unable to see anything from birth. Study of these children can help elucidate the contribution of one of our main senses, vision, to development. Second, I shall look at children with autism. Although many children with autism have learning difficulties, they also have specific difficulties in several areas of development and a number of different explanations have been proposed to explain the pattern of their difficulties. Finally, I shall consider children with **Down's syndrome (DS)**. Children with DS have learning difficulties. However, unlike children with autism where quite specific explanations have been proposed to explain their difficulties, the development of children with DS has been described by some as similar to that of typically developing children but delayed, although others argue that their development is different. In each case I shall describe some of the main effects of each disability on development and then relate this to our understanding of developmental processes.

The incidence of children with SVI and children with autism within the population is very low. About 1 in 10,000 children have SVI, although most of these children will be able to see *something*, about half will have had SVI from birth, and about half will have an additional disability. Obviously children with PVI from birth represent just a fraction of these children. The incidence of autism is about twice that of SVI, that is, about 2 to 3 per 10,000, although recently there is evidence of its incidence increasing. Given that children with SVI and children with autism form only a small proportion of the one in six children who are identified as having some sort of disability at some point in their development, it could be argued that they have attracted a disproportionate amount of attention from developmental psychologists. However, SVI is of particular interest because we think of vision as such a significant sense and yet it is clearly not crucial, since many people with SVI (including people with PVI) are highly competent. Autism presents rather a different picture, since it is the distinctive

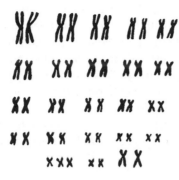

Figure 19.1 Most people with Down's syndrome have an extra number 21 chromosome (trisomy).

pattern of behavioral difficulties which characterize autism and the difficulties in explaining them that have captivated the interest of researchers.

In contrast, children with DS are the largest group of children with learning difficulties, with an incidence of about 16 to 17 in every 10,000 births. There are a number of physical features associated with DS which are often apparent from birth, although not all children with DS will have all of these features. The features include reduced muscle tone, a smaller nose with a flattened bridge, almond-shaped eyes which slant upwards, broad hands and short fingers with a single crease running from side to side across the palm. Because of these physical characteristics, children with DS are usually identified at birth, or very shortly after.

Children with DS also have a different pattern of **chromosomes** from other children: about 97 percent have an additional number 21 chromosome (see figure 19.1) and the others have chromosomal patterns in which part of a number 21 chromosome has fused with part of another chromosome. These distinct chromosomal patterns mean that a diagnosis of DS based on clinical features can be confirmed by chromosomal analysis. They also mean that DS can be detected before birth through various tests, the most common of which is an **amniocentesis**. In this test, a sample of the amniotic fluid surrounding the fetus, which contains fetal and maternal cells, is removed and the chromosomes of the cells in the fluid examined. Such prenatal testing is not routine but is usually restricted to women who have an increased risk of having a child with DS, for example older women. The fact that children with DS can be identified early in development, often before any learning difficulties are apparent, and their clinical identification can be confirmed chromosomally, has meant that of all children with learning difficulties, children with DS have attracted much research.

 Children with Profound Visual Impairments

In this section I shall focus on children with PVI from birth. Such children may be able to perceive areas of light and dark but cannot perceive visually any forms or shapes. Fraiberg, in her excellent book *Insights from the Blind* (1977), points out that children who can see nothing and are not thought to have any other disability develop differently from sighted children. However, perhaps rather surprisingly, unless a child has something visibly wrong with her eyes at birth, even a PVI may not be diagnosed for several months. This is because in the first few months after birth the behavior of infants with PVI may seem fairly similar to that of sighted babies: they may quieten when they hear a sound, they may smile selectively at their parents (though they are obviously smiling at the voice rather than the face of their parent), they can be comforted by being jiggled up and down, and so on. Indeed, in the first 6 months or so babies with PVI and their parents appear to interact in much the same way as sighted babies and their parents (e.g., Preisler, 1991). However, after the first few months, differences become more obvious.

KNOWING THAT OBJECTS AND PEOPLE ARE THERE

Probably the major challenge facing the baby with PVI is to understand that she is surrounded by objects and people. The sighted baby who sees a toy a few meters away from her "knows" that a toy is there. She does not need to understand anything about the permanence of toys – that objects continue to exist even when out of sight – to "know" this (**object permanence** is discussed in chapter 5). But the situation is very different for the baby with PVI. Unless she is holding a toy or can hear the noise it is making (and knows that this noise is associated with this particular toy), her senses will not tell her that the toy is there. And, although it is commonly assumed that when one sense is missing the other senses are heightened or even that such people might have a sixth sense, there is no evidence to support this.

In order for the baby with PVI to "know" that there is a toy a few meters away from her, she needs to have felt it, or heard it, *and* understood that it still exists even though she can no longer feel it or hear it. And, even when the baby with PVI does realize that there are objects and people in her environment, when she is not in contact with them, either tactually or auditorily, her experience of the environment will necessarily be different from that of a baby or young child who has the ability to perceive the form and shape of objects visually, even if his or her vision is not perfect. So how does this difference affect development?

A sighted baby typically begins to reach out for toys or toward her parent at around 4.5 months. In contrast, the baby with PVI may not show these behaviors until she is 10–11 months old, or in some cases even older (e.g., Bigelow, 1986). To reach out, the baby with PVI needs to "know" that there is something there, that the toy she was holding and dropped must be nearby, or that the footsteps she hears indicate that her parent is approaching her cot. This delay in reaching, or more importantly, the difficulty the child with PVI has in appreciating that there are things and people around her, has a number of consequences.

Children with PVI are often older than sighted children when they first show distress when their parent leaves the room they are in. Sighted children characteristically show this behavior first between 6 and 9 months of age, whereas children with PVI are usually 12 months on average before they first protest at a parent's departure (e.g., Tröster & Brambring, 1992). They are also delayed in self-initiated movements such as crawling and walking, which are likely to be motivated in the sighted child by the sight of something or someone on the other side of the room (e.g., Adelson & Fraiberg, 1974). If the child with PVI does not "know" what there is around her, why should she move from where she is? As a result, infants with PVI are often observed to be fairly passive in their movements, perhaps manipulating the things they feel around them, such as their own clothing, bodies, bedding, or floor covering. This may mark the beginning of stereotyped, repetitive behaviors (sometimes called **blindisms**) which can persist well into childhood and beyond. The most prevalent of these observed in children with PVI are eye poking, body rocking, repetitive hand and finger movements, and repetitive manipulation of objects (Tröster, Brambring, & Beelmann, 1991).

The delay in the child with PVI appreciating that there are objects and people around her affects the nature of her interaction with others. Prior to 9 months, sighted babies tend to interact with either people or objects but do not involve both in the same interaction. However, from about 9 months a sighted baby begins to involve others in her interactions with objects. She may see an object, point to it, look toward her parent, make a noise, initiating a preverbal vocal exchange, and through this involve her parent in her interaction with an object. Such exchanges indicate that she understands that both she and another can attend to the same object and that she can direct her parent's attention. As a result of this understanding, the young sighted baby and her parent can engage in give-and-take routines. Such understanding, described as **secondary intersubjectivity**, was not observed by Preisler (1991) in children with PVI until they were about 21 months, when they began to share their environment with others through language.

DIFFERENCES IN UNDERSTANDING THE ENVIRONMENT

If the experience of the young child with PVI of her environment is restricted because she cannot see the things that surround her, it might be expected that her **cognitive development** will be impaired. For example, it has been argued that her understanding of space, of visual terms, and even of what it means to be able to see will be impaired (e.g., Bower & Wishart, 1979). However, others (e.g., Landau, 1991) have argued that children with PVI do develop an understanding of such concepts although, because their understanding is based on senses other than vision, there may be differences. This is an important point because it suggests that the cognitive development of children with SVI is not impaired or **developmentally delayed**, only different in certain respects, because it is based on nonvisual information. Certainly, in terms of intellectual ability, provided that tests are used that do not require vision or ask questions that rely on visual experiences, the average **IQ scores** for children with and without sight do not differ (e.g., Kolk, 1977).

A number of observations will serve to illustrate that children with PVI do develop an understanding of their environment that may differ from sighted children because of the difference in their modality of experience. Urwin (1981) gives a nice example of a 4.5-year-old with PVI who did not want to go into the coal shed because, she said, "It's dark in there." She was asked what she meant by dark and said, "Sort of still. And cold. Like when it's raining." Surely this is as rich an understanding of darkness as a sighted person could have, albeit drawing on different experiences?

Further intriguing observations were made by Bigelow (1988, 1991, 1992) in a series of studies exploring the understanding that two brothers, both of whom had PVI, had of what others could see. These boys, who were 4 and 6 years old at the outset of this **longitudinal study**, realized that when asked to show their brother a toy they had to give it to him, but seemed to think that objects had to be within about 5 feet of a sighted person in order for that person to be able to see it. If an object was more than 5 feet from a sighted person, the boys brought it closer so it could be "seen." If an object couldn't be moved to within 5 feet, the boys thought that it couldn't be seen. When hiding a toy or themselves, they often only partially hid, using their hands or on other occasions just rolled up small and kept quiet. Further, when asked to position a toy so one part could be seen by another person, they often just touched the relevant part, rather than orienting the toy appropriately. Bigelow's observations are consistent with these boys having made sense of the concept of "seeing" through their experience of touch.

This conclusion is also supported by an observation made of a 3-year-old with PVI by Landau and Gleitman (1985). When asked to look up, this child reached her arms above her head, whereas blindfolded sighted children tilted their heads back. Interestingly, Mills (1988) pointed out that words that are very visually oriented, such as "see" and "look," may not only be interpreted tactually by the child with a PVI. For example, she observed children with PVI using "see" as if it meant "hear," and suggested that the interpretation of a particular word may depend upon the context and possibly on the child's individual preferences for particular modalities.

Dᴇᴠᴇʟᴏᴘᴍᴇɴᴛ ᴏғ ᴘʀᴇᴛᴇɴᴅ ᴘʟᴀʏ

A number of studies have reported that children with PVI are delayed in their play. For example, Hughes, Dote-Kwan, and Dolendo (1998), based on observations of 3- to 4-year-old children with PVI, reported that few of the children engaged in **pretend play** (such as pushing a brick along the floor as if it were a car being driven along; see chapter 13), and most of the play observed was exploratory or **sensorimotor** in nature. In this sense their play was more like the play of 1-year-old sighted children. However, despite these and other observations, some children with PVI can produce pretend play at the same age as sighted children. Lewis, Norgate, Collis, and Reynolds (2000) assessed the pretend play of 13 children aged between 2 and 7 years with SVI but no other problems, of whom 7 had PVI, using the Test of Pretend Play, and found they were able to pretend at the same level as sighted children of similar chronological age. This latter study also demonstrated a clear relationship between the amount of pretend play produced and assessments of both **expressive language** and **comprehension**, replicating findings in sighted children (e.g., Lewis, Boucher, Lupton, & Watson, 2000).

Lᴀɴɢᴜᴀɢᴇ ᴅᴇᴠᴇʟᴏᴘᴍᴇɴᴛ

Although children with PVI seem to reach the main language milestones in terms of vocabulary size at much the same age as sighted children (e.g., Mulford, 1988), there are differences in the content of the earliest vocabularies of children with and without PVI (e.g., Bigelow, 1987; Dunlea, 1989; Pérez-Pereira & Castro, 1992), differences which can be understood in terms of their different experience of the environment. Thus, compared to sighted children, the early vocabularies of children with PVI are likely to contain more labels for specific objects and fewer labels for general categories of objects, more words referring to their own actions and fewer referring to what others are doing, fewer words qualifying the nature of objects (e.g., "big" cat), and no words describing the function of objects. Thus, children with PVI tend to use words to describe what they are doing and restrict their use of particular words to the context in which they were first heard, in comparison to sighted children who will comment on what others are doing and things they see, make demands for things, and so on.

Sighted children are able to attract their parents' attention in many nonverbal ways, such as looking, waving, pointing, turning toward and moving in the direction of a desired object, and so on. This is obviously not possible for children with PVI and they also show a restricted repertoire of facial expressions (Tröster & Brambring, 1992). However, once they have acquired some language, they may use this means to attract their parents' attention, perhaps asking incessant questions or repeating something that someone else has said.

Understanding pronouns

Many children with PVI, like sighted children, have difficulties using and understanding pronouns such as "I" and "you" correctly. Thus, they may refer to themselves as "you" or by name, rather than "I." They may also make mistakes in understanding to whom a pronoun refers: for example, if her parent asks, "Where's my mouth?," the child may point to her own rather than to her parent's. In sighted children these difficulties tend to be resolved around the age of 2 to 2.5 years, whereas for some children with PVI the difficulties may persist much longer, even beyond the age of 5 years. In the absence of vision, it takes far longer for a child to realize that the "I" she talks about is the same as the "you" that other people talk about.

REPRESENTATIONAL ABILITY

Many of the findings already discussed can be understood in terms of how the child with PVI represents the environment. **Representational ability** is necessary for pretense (e.g., imagining that a brick is a car) in much the same way as language is (e.g., realizing that the word "car" stands for a car). Similarly, understanding that objects and people continue to exist even when not in contact with her requires that the child with PVI has a representation of the object or person. But why should children with PVI show delays in behaviors that are dependent on representational ability? Is representational ability dependent on vision? Clearly this cannot be the case since most children with PVI eventually demonstrate these abilities. It just takes longer. But why?

It seems likely that vision facilitates the development of representational ability to a greater extent than the other senses. In particular, vision enables links to be made between different experiences in different modalities more easily than any other sense. For example, in the first month, a sighted baby lying in her cot might experience the following: she hears a noise (= her parent talking in another room), the noise continues and then she sees a set of coordinated movements (= her parent entering the room), sees that movements of part of the form (= her parent's mouth) coincide with the noise (= her parent's voice), sees the form getting larger and the noise gets louder (= her parent approaches), and then she feels something (= her parent's hands) touch her body and her view of the world suddenly changes and she loses contact with the cot surface. The young baby with PVI in this situation would experience the following: she hears a noise (= her parent talking in another room), the noise continues and gets louder (= her parent approaches), and then she feels something (= her parent's hands) touch her body and suddenly she loses contact with the cot surface. In such a situation the sighted baby has many opportunities through the visual input, which is more continuously available than information from the other modalities, to discover how the different experiences are linked and so to build up a representation of her parent that involves auditory (her parent's voice), visual (what her parent looks like), and tactual (how her parent holds her) information. Without vision it seems very likely that it is harder for the child with PVI to link the different experiences and so develop a representation of her parent and other objects and people. It is harder, but clearly it is not impossible, as testified by the many children and adults with PVI who are demonstrably able to represent people and objects and make sense of their environment. Thus, it seems clear that although the development of children with PVI may be different from that of sighted children, it is not necessarily impaired or inferior.

AUTISTIC BEHAVIORS

However, while many children with PVI and no other disability develop into competent and effective adults, some children with PVI experience profound difficulties which they never seem to overcome. In particular, a significant proportion present quite marked behavioral difficulties that share many of the same characteristics as evident in children with autism. Clearly, it is not necessary to have PVI in order to have autism, since most children with autism can see. However, the fact that some children with PVI show such behaviors has led to some interesting speculation about the primary problem in autism. And this in turn has led to speculation about the developmental prerequisites of certain developments in sighted children, notably, theory of mind. I shall return to this at the end of the next section, which considers the development of children with autism.

Children with Autism

WING'S TRIAD OF IMPAIRMENTS

Autism was first described by Kanner in 1943 and consists of a set of clinical behaviors, characterized by **Wing's triad of impairments** (Wing, 1976) in: (1) social behavior;

(2) communication; and (3) behavior that is characterized by the presence of stereotyped, repetitive actions. In addition, the majority of children with autism have learning difficulties, with over half having IQs below 50, and with their verbal ability being more severely affected than nonverbal ability. Consequently, it is important to demonstrate that the behaviors which are characteristic of autism are found across the ability range, in the most able as well as in the least able; if this were not the case, then the behaviors could be a consequence of the learning difficulties. Because of this, much research has focused on relatively able children with autism. And to ensure that any learning difficulties that such children may have cannot account for their autistic behaviors, studies often compare the behavior of children with autism to the behavior of children who also have learning difficulties but not autism.

Over the years numerous theories have been put forward to account for the main impairments seen in children with autism and many different causes have been proposed. As yet, no single theory has been put forward that can adequately account for the range of difficulties observed and no specific cause or causes have been identified. One of the problems is that although children with autism will all show difficulties in specified areas, the extent and exact nature of their difficulties vary from relatively mild to extreme. In this section I shall describe the main characteristics of autism, and then outline some explanations that have been put forward.

Social aloofness

Autism is not usually diagnosed before the age of 2 or 3 years, although some retrospective accounts from parents suggest that children subsequently diagnosed as autistic may have behaved differently from birth. Home videos of infants in the age range 9–12 months who were later diagnosed with autism support this suggestion (Baranek, 1999), and a screening device for detecting infants with autism is now available (Baron-Cohen, Allen, & Gillberg, 1992; Charman et al., 2000). Some of the early differences reported include not lifting arms up in response to a parent's approach, not responding to a parent's voice, not pointing to draw another person's attention to something. All these are indicative of problems interacting with other people, and Kanner originally pointed to *social aloofness* as being the primary characteristic of autism.

However, many children with autism do interact with others and may demonstrate **attachment behaviors** (see chapter 6). Nevertheless, the nature of their interaction is likely to appear rather odd. They may show very little interest in other people or what they are doing, and fail to share their own interests with others, and instead endlessly engage, without any sign of boredom, in some apparently meaningless activity such as repeatedly twiddling a small object or piece of paper or just rocking backwards and forwards on the spot. They seldom initiate interactions with others. Their ability to recognize familiar people is impaired (e.g., Boucher, Lewis, & Collis, 1998), and they may show little or no reaction to the emotions of another person, or even respond inappropriately such as smiling when someone is clearly upset (e.g., Dissanayake, Sigman, & Kasari, 1996; Sigman, Kasari, Kwon, & Yirmiya, 1992). This all gives a very odd feel to their behavior.

Communication problems

Kanner also originally identified the absence of any intention to communicate meaningfully with other people as a further characteristic of autism. This is evident in both their nonverbal and verbal behaviors. About 50 percent of all children with autism never acquire any useful speech, and even those who do may not use either speech or nonverbal means to communicate specific things to others. The faces of children with autism often show little expression and they do not use gaze direction or gestures to indicate to another person that they are interested in something or someone. They may cry or scream, and this may signal that they want something, but they may give no indication as to what it is they want. Interestingly, with age, some children with autism may indicate what they want, but they may go about this in a very different way from children without autism. They may guide their parent's hand to the desired object, or they may actually point, but the point will not be accompanied by looking toward their parent to convey their intention to communicate something (e.g., Leekam, Baron-Cohen, Perrett, Milders, & Brown, 1997). This is in contrast to the typically developing child who, even before she has acquired any language, will gesture toward a desired object and look backwards and forwards between the object and her parent.

The absence of an intention to communicate is also apparent in those children with autism who speak. The onset of language is almost always delayed and this delay may be the first clear indication that something is wrong. Children with autism can develop a reasonable vocabulary and even adequate **syntax** (e.g., Tager-Flusberg, 1993). However, their language shows extreme **pragmatic** abnormalities. These show themselves as stilted and pedantic speech, abnormal **prosody**, **turn-taking** difficulties, inappropriate interruptions, and so on. The child with autism may repeat words or phrases she has heard others say in a meaningless and repetitive way, a behavior known as **echolalia**. She may say little else.

For children with autism who do talk spontaneously, rather than simply echoing what others have said, their conversations are very different from those of children without autism. They may talk nonstop about their particular interest, but fail to take account of what anyone else may say or indicate nonverbally. They do not seem to appreciate the two-way nature of conversations and contribute little by way of keeping the conversation going. They may have persisting difficulties using personal pronouns correctly (e.g., Lee, Hobson, & Chiat, 1994), difficulties which typically developing children also show but grow out of. Their language often focuses on concrete things and is literal, with idiom, metaphor, and allusion being noticeably absent. Similarly, they have difficulties understanding metaphor and irony (Happé, 1993).

Repetitive and stereotyped behavior

The third impairment of Wing's triad is repetitive and stereotyped behavior. This has already been alluded to in the examples given so far – the rocking, the twiddling of a small object, the echolalia. Children with autism are often fascinated by regular patterns of objects and may collect and arrange objects they find in a very systematic and repetitive way, but for no apparent reason. Yet they may show great distress if these arrangements are disturbed. Related to this, they seldom play spontaneously, instead simply manipulating the toys and not engaging with them in any meaningful way.

ISLETS OF ABILITY: SAVANT SKILLS

In addition to this triad of impairments, there are other behaviors which are shown by a number of children with autism, although not necessarily all. Many children with autism are often particularly good at visual-spatial tasks. For example, they are often good at locating shapes embedded in a drawing (e.g., Shah & Frith, 1993), can complete jigsaw puzzles when the picture is face down, i.e., not visible, and are not susceptible to **visual illusions** (Happé, 1996). A few children with autism are exceptionally gifted artistically (e.g., Wiltshire, 1987) or in some other way, despite having a very low IQ. These isolated skills, associated with low IQ, have been labeled **savant skills**. Happé (1994b) has suggested that up to 10 percent of children with autism have such an **islet of ability**, whether in art, in music, or in calculating the day of the week of a particular date (e.g., O'Connor & Hermelin, 1988). They may also have exceptionally good rote memories, though what they remember may be of no obvious relevance.

EXPLANATIONS OF AUTISM

As can be seen from the above account, autism is a very complex disorder, with many aspects of development being affected. Perhaps, therefore, it is not surprising that an explanation of why these behaviors are manifest together has been evasive. However, recently, a number of explanations have emerged that go some way toward explaining many, though not all, of the behaviors. I shall now consider these explanations.

Theory of mind deficit

The first proposal stemmed from a study showing that about 80 percent of children with autism have difficulties understanding that the beliefs they hold may differ from those of others (Baron-Cohen, Leslie, & Frith, 1985). Such an understanding is referred to as a **theory of mind**, and chapter 10 gives an account of how typically developing children acquire this ability. The difficulties experienced by the child with autism can be demonstrated in tasks in which the child has to decide what a character, who holds a belief that is false, will do in a particular situation. In one version of this task, there are two dolls, Sally and Anne, together in a room with a basket, a box, and a marble. Sally hides the marble in the basket and then leaves the room. While Sally is out of the room, Anne takes the marble out of the basket and puts it in the box. Sally then returns, and the child's task is to say where Sally will look for the marble. The crucial point is that Sally was out of the room when the marble was moved from the basket to the box, and therefore she has a **false belief** since she believes, wrongly, that the marble is in the basket.

Most children with autism, and typically developing children of less than 4 years, say that Sally will look in the box. While this is where the marble actually is, it is not where Sally *believes* it to be. This finding has been confirmed in many subsequent studies, using a variety of different, and often ingenious, paradigms and focusing on a wide range of behaviors that are thought to depend on an understanding of minds. It led to a proposal that a difficulty with understanding minds is the primary deficit in autism. As an account, it is particularly good at explaining two of Wing's triad of impairments, specifically the impairments in social behavior and in communication. The argument is that if a child with autism is unable to comprehend what another person is thinking, feeling, believing, and so on, the child is very likely to behave inappropriately since appropriate behavior is dependent upon our understanding of others.

However, there are several limitations to this account. The first is that some children with autism, notably those with good verbal skills, do demonstrate an understanding of minds, albeit at an older age than typically developing children. To get around this limitation, it has been suggested that these children may solve so-called theory of mind tasks using strategies other than understanding what is going on in the minds of others. For example, Happé (1994b) suggests that the Sally–Anne task described earlier could be solved correctly if the child simply formed a person–object–place association (i.e., Sally–marble–basket) and drew on this information when answering the question. Such a strategy would not depend on the child appreciating Sally's belief about the marble's location.

Weak central coherence

A second limitation to the theory of mind account is that it cannot explain the third impairment of Wing's triad, the repetitive and stereotyped behavior that is characteristic of autism. However, this has been circumvented by arguing that children with autism have a difficulty in understanding minds *plus* a difficulty in drawing together different bits of information in order to construct an overall understanding of what is perceived. This latter difficulty has been described as **weak central coherence** (e.g., Frith, 1989). A consequence of this proposed weak central coherence is that children with autism pay more attention to the parts of, for example, a picture or an event, rather than to the whole. In other words, they see the individual trees but not the forest. If children with autism have a fragmented, as opposed to a coherent, view of the world, it is likely that their behavior will also be fairly meaningless, consisting of actions which are not integrated in any meaningful way. In addition, if their actions are responses to particular discrete perceptions and neither the perceptions nor actions are integrated in any way, their behavior is likely to be repetitive.

This idea of weak central coherence can also account for some of the islets of ability found in children with autism, such as their good visual-spatial skills. For example, I mentioned earlier that children with autism are often good at locating shapes embedded in a drawing. In this task the shapes do not represent a particular object, whereas the whole drawing is of a particular object. Weak central coherence argues that, unlike children without autism, children with autism do not attend to the overall meaning of the drawing; rather, they focus on the separate lines and shapes that make up the drawing. As a result, they are good at locating **embedded shapes**.

Deficit in executive functioning

A rather different challenge to the theory of mind account has come from studies indicating that children with autism have difficulties both disengaging from reality and inhibiting responses that are inappropriate to achieving a specified goal (e.g., Hughes, Russell, & Robbins, 1994; Ozonoff, Pennington, & Rogers, 1991). For example, if there are two boxes, one containing a chocolate, the other empty, and if the child only gets the chocolate if she points to the empty box, typically developing children very quickly learn to point to the empty box, whereas children with autism persist in pointing to the box containing the chocolate. Children with autism seem unable to inhibit this inappropriate behavior despite not getting any chocolate.

Thus, in the false belief task, it has been argued that children with autism say Sally will look in the box because that is where the marble *is* hidden. In other words, children with autism answer the question about where Sally will look on the basis of reality, i.e., where the marble really is, rather than on the basis of where Sally believes the marble is hidden. This difficulty is described as a deficit in **executive functioning**. Executive functioning enables the child to plan how to achieve a particular goal. Planning requires that current activity is put to one side and replaced by new activity. If children with autism lack executive control, then their attention may be captured by an object, or some aspect of an object or an action, and they will be unable to shift from this. Thus they point to the box containing the chocolate or say that Sally believes that the marble is where it actually is.

One of the attractions of the executive function account of autism is that as well as being able to account for many of the social and communicative difficulties associated with autism, it can also explain the repetitive and stereotyped behaviors. It is as though the child is locked into a simple activity or focused on a particular part of an object and cannot plan a way to move on to something else. Therefore, the behavior is repeated over and over again.

However, the executive function account has one major drawback. This is that deficits in the area of executive functioning are not confined to autism but are found in children with other disorders, notably children with damage to the frontal lobes (e.g., Pennington & Ozonoff, 1996). While the behavior of such children may be similar in some respects to that of children with autism, these children are not autistic. An executive function deficit on its own cannot therefore account for the specific nature of autism.

Deficit in social interaction

At the end of the section considering children with visual impairments I indicated that a number of children with PVI show behaviors that are reminiscent of autism. This raises the interesting question as to whether PVI and autism are independent in these children, or whether the two disorders are related. On the basis of the association of PVI and autism in some children, Hobson (e.g., 1993) has argued that the primary deficit in autism is not a difficulty in understanding that other people have minds. Rather, he has argued that a basic impairment in the biological capacity to engage in social interaction may be the primary difficulty in autism, proposing that if interaction with others is impaired from early on, children with autism will have fewer opportunities to develop an understanding that other people have minds. As we have already seen, PVI poses problems for social interaction, particularly early on in development. If impairments in social interaction are the cause of autistic behavior, children with PVI who fail to discover about people and objects through other modalities and, consequently, do not interact with others, might be expected to show autistic behaviors.

One of the difficulties with this account is that although autism may be associated with the absence of certain social behaviors in the first couple of years, it is not usually associated with *severe* social difficulties from birth. Nevertheless, understanding the nature of the association between PVI and autism is important since the answer could well throw light on the role of vision in development, as well as the nature of autism.

Children with Down's Syndrome

Plate 19.1 shows a child with Down's syndrome (DS). Much research on the development of children with DS has been concerned with the question of whether their learning difficulties result from their development being similar to that of typically developing children and just slower, or because their development is actually different. The former view implies that similar processes underlie the development of both typically developing children and children with DS; the latter implies that the processes are different. If the former is correct, then study of children with DS would illustrate psychological development in slow motion and could therefore be used to elucidate relationships between different developments that may appear to coincide in typically developing children; on the other hand, if the underlying processes are different, this may suggest alternative routes to development. However, in reality, it is very difficult to distinguish between delay and difference.

DEVELOPMENT OF CHILDREN WITH DS

The development of most children with DS is delayed, in terms of the ages at which particular milestones are attained, from early on. Alongside marked *hypotonia*, or muscular floppiness, the time scale of the emergence and disappearance of certain reflexes is delayed, as well as the ages of gross **motor milestones** such as holding the head steady and sitting without support, and finer motor developments such as reaching, and building a tower of bricks (e.g., Cunningham, 1982). Children with DS also show delays in making eye contact, smiling, laughing, and vocalizing. As they get older, they show further delays in walking, in recognizing their reflection in a mirror, and in reacting to their parent leaving the room. They are slow to talk and, in general, their reactions tend to be less intense and they react more slowly than children without DS.

The slower reactions of children with DS have led to the suggestion that they may take longer to process information than children without DS. Certainly children

Plate 19.1 Despite their delayed, and different, cognitive development, children with Down's syndrome are usually very sociable.

with DS under 1 year of age look at objects and people and listen to auditory material for longer before responding than children without DS of a similar developmental level (e.g., Glenn & Cunningham, 1982; MacTurk, Vietze, McCarthy, McQuiston, & Yarrow, 1985). Further, Wishart (1991) has shown that children with DS under 2 years old take longer to learn a contingency, for example between something they do, such as reaching toward a desired object, and something that happens in the environment as a result of their action, such as their parent retrieving the object and giving it to them. Discovering about such contingencies is an important part of making sense of what is going on in the environment. Taking longer to respond and learn are assumed to be due to children with DS taking longer to process information and, it is argued, this slower processing of information results in their developmental delay.

One of the consequences of the slower reactions of infants with DS is that their interactions with adults seem to go less smoothly than when children do not have DS, with many more overlaps or clashes occurring between the child's vocalizations and the parent's vocalizations (e.g., Berger, 1990).

Delays in the cognitive development of children with DS become more marked as the children get older (e.g., Carr, 1994), and this seems to be particularly noticeable in boys. Thus, in the first year, the mean **intelligence quotient (IQ)** of children with DS may be over 70, falling to just over 50 at 2 years and around 40 by the age of 11 years. Nevertheless, although the children's IQ is falling with age, this does not mean that their development is regressing. This is because IQ is a measure of the relationship between a child's developmental or **mental age** (equivalent to the age at which a child without DS would be expected to be showing the same developments) and the child's actual or **chronological age**. It is often expressed as

$$IQ = \frac{mental\ age}{chronological\ age} \times 100$$

If a child's mental age is going up but not keeping pace with her chronological age, the child will be developing as reflected by her increasing mental age, although her IQ will be falling. Thus, it has been demonstrated that young people with DS, despite falling IQs, continue developing certain skills, such as reading, well into their teenage years. (See box 3.1 in chapter 3 for a fuller account of IQ tests and the concepts of IQ and mental age.)

However, there is great variation in the ages at which children with DS achieve different developmental milestones. Cunningham reports an age range for walking of 13 to 48 months, in comparison to 9 to 17 months for typically developing children. Thus, while some children with DS begin walking some 2.5 years after the most delayed typically developing child, others achieve this motor milestone within the range observed for typically developing children. Similarly, Beeghly, Weiss-Perry, and Cicchetti (1990) examined the language development of 41 children with DS aged between 20 and 82 months and reported marked variability in the ages at which certain language milestones were observed. Four of the children, aged 20–30 months, had no spoken language; seven children, aged 24–66 months, had single words; 19 children, aged 26–74 months, were beginning to combine words; eight children, aged 60–82 months, were combining words fairly consistently; and three children, aged 61–76 months, were consistently combining words. In other words, among the children aged 61 months or more, language ability ranged from single words to words being combined most of the time.

INTELLIGENCE TEST SCORES

Wide variability in levels of intelligence achieved has also been noted for children and young people with DS. Carr (1988) reported a range of about 60 points in IQ at each age she studied from infancy through to adulthood, with an upper level in early adulthood of about 70. Interestingly, as well as variability in the cognitive ability of children with DS, it also appears that individual children with DS vary in what they are able to do on different occasions. Thus, Wishart and Duffy (1990) found that when children with DS were tested on the same developmental test on two occasions, one or two weeks apart, the total number of items passed by each child on each occasion did not vary a great deal, but there was considerable variability in which items each child passed. In other words, the children with DS were not consistent in the items they passed and failed each time, passing some items on one occasion and failing them on the next, and vice versa. This observation suggests that children with DS may be more competent than their overall scores suggest; they just vary in the extent to which they engage with the tasks, engaging with certain items more on some occasions than on others. In fact, Wishart (1993) reported that, if performance was based on test items passed at least once over several test sessions, no decline in **developmental quotient** was found.

DELAYED OR DIFFERENT DEVELOPMENT?

These findings also suggest that the way in which children with DS develop may be different from children without DS, rather than simply delayed. Items within developmental tests are generally ordered from the easiest to the most difficult, based on the performance of typically developing children. If children with DS are failing some easy items and succeeding on some difficult items, this indicates that different processes may underlie their development. This is supported by evidence that children with DS do not pass Piagetian object permanence tasks in the same sequence as typically developing children and, in addition, they may fail tasks that they previously passed (e.g., Wishart & Duffy, 1990). This raises questions about Piaget's account of the sensorimotor period, since this assumed that development proceeds through a series of stages, each stage characterized by success on particular tasks, and success at each stage being prerequisite for the next stage (see chapter 2 for a full account of Piaget's theory of development).

Further evidence of possible differences in how children and young people with DS develop has come from studies of reading. In typically developing children, there is a well-demonstrated relationship between their **phonological skills** and reading ability. However, when children and young people with DS were compared with typically developing children who were reading at a similar level, it was found that the phonological skills of the children with DS were inferior to those of the typically developing children (Cossu, Rossini, & Marshall, 1993). Related to this, Buckley (1993) has suggested that children with DS may learn to read by linking print and meaning, rather than by linking print and sound. Support for this view comes from evidence that whereas the early reading errors of typically developing children are mostly phonological (e.g., reading "sun" for "bun"), those of children with DS are usually either visual, confusing words that look similar (e.g., reading "dog" for "bag"), or **semantic**, confusing words with similar meanings (e.g., reading "many" for "lots"). In further support of this idea, there is evidence that phonological **working memory** is limited in children with DS (Hulme & MacKenzie, 1992).

As well as showing evidence of delay overall, the language of children with DS, once acquired, is different in several ways from that of typically developing children. In particular, their **lexical** and **pragmatic skills** are considerably in advance of their

syntactic skills (e.g., Fowler, 1990). Thus, children with DS tend not to combine words until they have acquired about 100 words, whereas in typically developing children combinations usually start to appear once a vocabulary of about 50 words has been achieved. And although the syntactic skills of children with DS do develop, their language remains less mature than that of children with similar-sized vocabularies. Similarly, the pragmatic, or conversational, skills of children with DS have been found to be superior to those of typically developing children producing similar-length utterances.

In this brief overview I have suggested that the development of children with DS should not just be described as being delayed. Rather, the evidence indicates that they may develop in different ways from typically developing children. In particular, compared to typically developing children, children with DS take longer to process information, they progress through object permanence tasks in a different order, they make different reading errors, and the relationships between aspects of their language are different.

Summary and Conclusions

In this chapter I have considered the consequences of three very different disabilities for development – profound visual impairment, autism, and Down's syndrome. In the absence of vision it is much more difficult for the young child to discover that there is a world of objects and people around her, and this has a marked impact on her early development. Nevertheless, this understanding can be gained through modalities other than vision, although this may result in the child with PVI having a different understanding of certain concepts. Children with autism present a rather different picture. They show a distinct pattern of behaviors which is difficult to explain. However, the evidence points strongly to the fact that they have difficulties planning their behavior and understanding that other people have minds. DS is characterized by learning difficulties. However, we have seen that children with DS have specific learning difficulties, rather than being delayed in all aspects of development. Although the evidence is not yet conclusive, it seems likely that the processes underlying the development of children with DS and typically developing children are different.

Consideration of the three disabilities discussed in this chapter indicates that much can be learned by studying the development of children with disabilities. Such studies can contribute to our understanding of the processes underlying development in general. Thus, study of children with PVI has helped to illuminate the role of vision in development and has indicated that there are alternative routes to development that do not require vision. Study of children with autism has demonstrated that having an understanding of minds is probably a critical achievement for typical development. Finally, study of children with DS has demonstrated that there may be a range of different processes underlying development.

Such understanding does not only have implications for our understanding of development in general. It also impacts on practice and intervention with children with disabilities, and this is particularly important. Effective therapies or interventions need to be premised on an understanding of how particular disabilities affect development, and this is a further reason for studying the development of children with disabilities.

DISCUSSION POINTS

1 Why is it relevant to understand how particular disabilities affect certain aspects of psychological development?
2 How do children with profound visual impairments know that there are people and objects in the environment? How do they understand space?
3 Children with autism are socially aloof, have problems communicating, and display repetitive and stereotyped behaviors. Can you think of examples of these behaviors?
4 What explanations have been put forward to account for autism?
5 What sort of problems do children with profound visual impairments, and those with autism, sometimes have in common?
6 Is the development of children with Down's syndrome delayed or different from that of typically developing children?

SUGGESTIONS FOR FURTHER READING

Burack, J. A., Charman, T., Yirmiya, N., & Zelazo, P. R. (Eds.) (2001). *The development of autism: Perspectives from theory and research.* London: Erlbaum.

Lewis, V. (2003). *Development and disability.* Cambridge, MA, and Oxford: Blackwell.

Pérez-Pereira, M., & Conti-Ramsden, G. (1999). *Language development and social interaction in blind children.* Hove: Psychology Press.

Weeks, D. J., Chua, R., & Elliott, D. (Eds.) (2000). *Perceptual-motor behavior in Down syndrome.* Champaign, IL: Human Kinetics.

Glossary

A

A not B error   An object-searching error that is often made by 8–12-month-olds. Infants making this error will look for an object where they have most often found it (location A) rather than where they last saw it (location B).

Abstraction principle   The principle that the number in a set is independent of any qualities of the members in that set, so it doesn't matter if you are counting the number of butterflies or the number of different animals, the counting principles will be the same.

Accommodation   The cognitive process through which children adapt to new experiences by modifying their preexisting **schemas**. An important process in Piaget's theory. See **assimilation** and **functional invariants**, and also **visual accommodation**.

Affect   Emotional state or feelings. Contrast with behavior (what one does in a situation) and **cognition** (how one thinks about a situation).

Affective process   A process that deals with an individual's emotional state.

Age-cohort design   See **sequential design**.

Alleles   Genes for the same characteristic located in the same place on a pair of **chromosomes**.

Alphabetic script   A writing system in which written symbols (letters) correspond to spoken sounds; generally, individual **phonemes** represent the individual letters of an alphabetic script.

Ambiguous figure   A figure that can be perceived in two (or more) different ways.

Amniocentesis   A medical procedure that removes fetal cells from the amniotic sac (the fluid that protects the fetus) for analysis. This procedure is usually carried out between the fourteenth and sixteenth week after conception and can diagnose fetal genetic and developmental disorders.

Analogical reasoning   Resolving a problem by comparing it to a similar problem that has been solved previously.

Animism   A characteristic of children's thinking in Piaget's **preoperational stage** in which they tend to attribute life and life-like qualities to inanimate objects, particularly those that move and are active, such as the wind and the clouds, and sometimes toys and other objects.

Antisocial behavior   Any behavior that shows scant concern about other people's feelings and needs. There is little morality associated with this behavior.

Appearance–reality distinction   An awareness that things are not always what they appear to be. Young children often fail to make this distinction and when shown an object that looks like something else (e.g., a sponge that looks like a rock), they will often give either **phenomenism** answers and report the appearance ("it's a rock"), or **realism** answers and report the reality of the object ("it's a sponge").

Assimilation The process through which children incorporate new experiences into their preexisting **schemas** – that is, they *assimilate* the new to their already-existing schemes of thought. An important process in Piaget's theory. See also **accommodation** and **functional invariants**.

Associative activity An activity in which children interact with one another, performing similar tasks.

Assortative mating The tendency for spouses or partners to be similar in biological and/or psychological characteristics, for instance in height, attractiveness, intelligence.

Attachment behavior Any behavior that helps to form or establish an emotional bond between two individuals. Strong attachment bonds are usually formed between an infant and his or her caregiver. Children with **autism** typically display few, and odd, attachment behaviors.

Attainment targets Descriptions of the knowledge that a child should have acquired as she works her way through the education system.

Attention deficit disorder (ADD or ADHD) A disorder that is characterized by an inability to concentrate on one task at a time and a pervasive impulsivity, which often results in severe behavioral problems and **developmental delay**. Hyperactivity commonly accompanies this disorder, hence ADHD.

Attributions The belief one holds as to why people carry out a particular action or behavior.

Authoritarian parenting Authoritarian parents are high on demandingness and low on responsiveness. They value obedience as a virtue and favor punitive, forceful means to curb the self-will of their offspring. They do not foster their children's autonomy, but rather try to restrict independent behavior. In contrast with children raised by authoritative parents, children raised by authoritarian parents are less socially skilled, less self-assured, less curious, more dependent, and more passive. See also **authoritative parenting**, **indulgent parenting**, and **neglectful parenting**.

Authoritative parenting Authoritative parents are high on responsiveness and demandingness. They set clear standards of behavior for their children that take into account the child's developing capabilities and needs. These parents are considered warm and responsive to the needs of their children. Children raised by authoritative parents tend to be more socially competent, self-reliant, self-controlled, more responsible, creative, and intellectually curious than their **peers**. See also **authoritarian parenting**, **indulgent parenting**, and **neglectful parenting**.

Autism A disorder that affects a person's ability to relate to others. Autistic individuals typically have problems with communication, forming attachments with other people (**attachment behavior**), and lack a **theory of mind**. Autistic people usually avoid social contact and may seek a monotony of environment and action (resulting in repetitive stereotyped movements) which appear to provide some comfort. These problems are often referred to as **Wing's triad of impairments**. Occasionally, some autistic individuals demonstrate extreme talents (**savant skills**) in certain activities (e.g., the ability to accurately draw a building, or to mentally compute seven-figure prime numbers); however, these talents are uncommon. Autism is a rare condition (approximately 4 per 10,000 live births) that is usually inherited but can result from brain damage.

Autonomous stage of moral reasoning A stage of moral reasoning described by Piaget, found in children from about age 10. Obligations, rights, and rules are no longer felt to be one-way or unilateral (as in the earlier **heteronomous stage**), but reciprocal. Children and adults in this stage take actors' intentions into account when judging moral actions.

Autonomy Being in complete control of one's life.

Autosomal genetic disorders   Disorders resulting from a mutation in a gene in one of the nonsex **chromosomes**. Well-known examples are cystic fibrosis (a recessive type) and achondroplasia (dwarfism, a dominant type).

Autosomes   The 22 pairs of human **chromosomes**, with the exception of the sex chromosomes. See also **autosomal genetic disorders**.

Axon   The tail-like part of a **neuron** which transmits impulses (the actual message) away from the cell body.

B

Babbling   The first types of controlled vocalizations produced by infants typically between the ages of 4 and 9 months. See also **canonical** and **modulated babbling**.

Baby biographies   Diaries detailing an infant's development, usually kept by the infant's parents or caregiver. Charles Darwin's biography of his eldest son's development is a well-known example.

Baseline group   Another term for **control group**.

Behavior genetics   The study of how genetic factors influence behavior and, more generally, differences between individuals.

Behaviorism   The theoretical view, associated with J. B. Watson and B. F. Skinner, that sees directly observable behavior as the proper focus of study, and which sees the developing child as a passive respondent to conditioning, reinforcement, and punishment. Emphasizes the role of learning (**nurture**) in causing development rather than inherited factors (**nature**).

Blindisms   Stereotyped repetitive behaviors that are commonly observed in children with **profound visual impairment**. The most common of these behaviors are eye poking, body rocking, repetitive hand and finger movements, and repetitive manipulation of objects.

Bottom-up structures   Bottom-up structures are data driven and the output does not depend on prior knowledge and experience. Compare with **top-down structures**.

Bullying   Term used to define an individual's repeated exposure to negative actions by one or more other students. There are two types of bullying, direct and indirect. **Direct bullying** refers to cases where there are open attacks on the victim that are often physical in nature but also include taunting or verbal abuse. **Indirect bullying** refers to cases where individuals are socially isolated and intentionally excluded from a group. See **provocative victim** and **passive or submissive victim**.

C

Canonical   The usual, normal, or natural appearance of things. *Canonical babbling* refers to **babbling** sounds made by the infant around 6–10 months, when vowels and consonants are combined in such a way that they sound like words. However, there is no evidence that infants actually attach meaning to these sound combinations. See also **modulated babbling**.

Cardinality   The numerical principle that states that any set of items with a particular number is equal in quantity to any other set with the same number of items in it. Therefore, a set of four cars and a set of four buttons may look very different, but cardinality states that there is the same number in each set despite obvious visual differences.

Castration complex   See **Oedipus complex**.

Catharsis hypothesis   The argument that watching aggressive tendencies in others will reduce your own feelings of aggression.

Central coherence   The ability to combine several pieces of information to form an overall understanding of an issue or of what is perceived.

Centration   The focusing or centering of attention on one aspect of a situation to the exclusion of others.

Cephalocaudal trend   Motor development that proceeds in infancy from head to foot along the length of the body – that is, control of the head is first, then the arms and trunk, and finally control of the legs. See also **proximodistal trend**.

Cerebral cortex   The area of the brain that is associated with complex tasks such as memory, language, and thoughts and the control and integration of movement and the senses.

Chemosensory development   Encompasses both the gustatory (taste) and olfactory (smell) senses.

Childhood amnesia   See **infantile amnesia**.

Chromosomes   Strands of DNA (deoxyribonucleic acid) and protein that contain the genes and provide the genetic blueprint for the animal or plant. In humans there are 23 pairs of chromosomes, 22 **autosomes** and one pair of sex chromosomes, the latter often referred to as X and Y genes.

Chronological age (CA)   A person's actual age, as opposed to his or her **mental age**.

Circadian rhythm   Bodily cycles within the body that occur on a 24-hour cycle, such as patterns of sleeping/waking.

Class inclusion   The ability to coordinate and reason about parts and wholes simultaneously in recognizing relations between classes and subclasses.

Classical conditioning   A method of learning first investigated by the Russian physiologist Ivan Pavlov in the early part of the twentieth century. In this form of conditioning, certain behaviors can be elicited by a neutral (normally unstimulating) stimulus because of its learned association with a more powerful stimulus. In Pavlov's experiments dogs learned to salivate at the sound of a bell. An important form of learning in **behaviorism**; see also **operant conditioning**.

Clinical method   Research method first used by Piaget whereby natural behavior is observed and then the individual's environment is changed in order to understand better the behavior of interest.

Cluster effect   Memory for test items is significantly improved if the items can be grouped together according to some category or principle, e.g., items of furniture; cutlery used to eat with; animals, etc.

Cochlea   The inner ear, a structure encased in bone that contains the receptors for sound.

Cognition   Mental activity, such as attention, memory, problem-solving, thinking, intelligence.

Cognitive adaptations   Children's developing cognitive awareness of the world. As a result of cognitive adaptations they become better able to understand their world.

Cognitive conflict   Cognitive conflict arises when there are two or more competing solutions to a situation or problem.

Cognitive development   The development of behaviors that relate to perception, attention, thinking, remembering, and problem-solving.

Cognitive functioning   See **cognition**.

Cognitive processes   Mental activities and processes. See **cognition** and **information processing**.

Cohort   A group of people who were raised in the same environment or who share certain demographic characteristics, for example a group of people born at approximately the same time.

Collaborative learning   Any learning that occurs when two or more people work together on a problem or situation.

Combinatory thought   Before a child can pass a **conservation task**, he or she must possess combinatory thought, i.e., he or she must be able to take more than one factor into consideration. For example, when given the conservation of continuous quantity task where water is poured from one beaker to a different-sized beaker, the child must consider both the height and the width of the beakers before making judgments about the volume of water contained within them.

Comprehension In language development, the language children can understand, distinguished from *production*, which is the language they can produce. Comprehension almost always exceeds production.

Conceptual shift A large qualitative change in an individual's **cognitive processes**.

Concrete operations stage The third Piagetian stage of development in which reasoning is said to become more logical, systematic, and rational in its application to concrete objects. However, abstract thinking is still not fully developed. The concrete operations stage is characteristic of children between about 7 and 11 years of age. See also **conservation** and **reversibility**.

Conditional spelling rules Rules that need to be learned in order to spell certain words; for example, the final "e" that lengthens and changes the quality of the preceding vowel ("hop" as opposed to "hope"). Another example is the way that consonants are doubled in order to shorten the preceding vowel ("hopping" as opposed to "hoping").

Conduct disorder General term used to describe serious behavioral problems in children, including **antisocial** and rule-breaking behavior.

Cones and rods See **rods and cones**.

Configurational processing Any processing that pays particular attention to the overall configuration of the smaller elements within the object being perceived rather than the individual features or elements. Attention to the individual elements is known as **featural processing**. See also **encoding switch hypothesis**.

Congenital Present from birth.

Connectionism A modern theoretical approach that developed from **information-processing** accounts in which computers are programmed to simulate the action of the brain and nerve cells (**neurons**). The programs create so-called artificial **neural networks**. Connectionist models have been applied to many areas of child development, e.g., perception, attention, learning, memory, language, problem-solving, and reasoning.

Conservation The recognition that certain properties of objects (such as number, liquid [or continuous quantity], length, mass [or weight], and volume) are not altered by superficial transformations in appearance, such as changes in length or shape. Children become able to conserve in Piaget's **concrete operations stage**. See also **conservation tasks**.

Conservation tasks These are tasks that examine children's ability to understand that physical attributes of objects, such as their mass and weight, do not vary when the object changes shape. An example would be to show a child two identical beakers containing equal volumes of water. The content of one beaker is then poured into a smaller but broader beaker. One beaker's water level is now much higher, but obviously they both contain the same amount of water. A child who understands the fact that the volume has not changed, despite its change in appearance, will tell you both beakers contain the same amount of water, whereas a child who does not have this knowledge will point to one of the beakers thinking that one has the most water.

Constructivism Piaget's theoretical view that infants are not born with knowledge about the world, but instead gradually construct knowledge and the ability to represent reality mentally.

Continuity in social development Some behaviors show a very strong consistency throughout development, for example the tendency for children to be aggressive shows considerable continuity: the child who fights with other children a lot is likely to be the adolescent who is judged by **peers** to be aggressive.

Continuity versus discontinuity Whether development is *continuous*, and therefore an accumulation of "more of the same," or *discontinuous* and marked by qualitative changes. Piaget's theory is an example of a *discontinuous* theory of development.

Continuous function – decreasing ability Behavior that gets worse as we age. For example, young infants can initially distinguish non-native speech sounds very easily; however, for many sounds they lose this ability after their first year of life. See also **continuous function – increasing ability, discontinuous (step) function**, and **U-shaped functions**.

Continuous function – increasing ability   Behavior that improves with age. For example, during the first year of life the precision with which infants reach for objects increases. See also **continuous function – decreasing ability, discontinuous (step) function**, and **U-shaped functions**.

Control group   In order to evaluate the effectiveness of a particular treatment or manipulation, the control group is that group of individuals in an experiment who do not receive the treatment. Their behavior is then compared with that of the **experimental group**, which does receive the treatment.

Cooperative activity   An activity in which children interact together in complementary ways; for example, one child gets blocks out of a box and hands them to another child, who builds a tower.

Core knowledge   A basic store of information about the world, particularly knowledge about the physical properties of objects, available to the very young infant and probably an **innate mechanism**.

Correlation coefficient   A statistical measure ranging from +1.00 to −1.00 that indicates the strength, as well as the direction, of the relationship between two variables. A correlation coefficient varies between +1 (high positive correlation) through zero (no relationship) to −1 (high negative correlation).

Correlational study   A study that examines whether two variables vary systematically in relation to each other, e.g., as height increases, will weight reliably increase also?

Critical period   A limited period, usually early in an animal's life, in which the young have to be exposed to a particular skill or experience in order for it to be learned. **Imprinting** was thought to occur only during a brief critical period, but it is now known that this can be extended and the concept of **sensitive period** is often used instead.

Cross-cultural study   A study which aims to examine differences that arise purely from culture. An example would be to examine whether there are different **developmental milestones** in different regions of the world.

Cross-sectional design   A study where children of different ages are observed at a single point in time. Compare with **longitudinal design**.

Crystallized intelligence   The store of information, skills, and strategies acquired through education and prior experience. Knowing the capital cities of every country is an example of crystallized intelligence. See also **fluid intelligence**.

Cultural tools   Any tools that help us to calculate, produce models, make predictions, and understand the world more fully, e.g., abacuses, slide rules, calculators, and computers.

Curriculum   A specific course of academic studies.

D

Deceptive box task   This task involves showing children a characteristic box that they will have had some experience with before (e.g., a Smarties tube or M&Ms box that usually contains sweets/candies). The child must say what she thinks is in the box. Usually she will reply "Smarties"/ "M&Ms." She is then shown that the box actually contains pencils. The child is then asked, "What did you originally think was in the box?" Children under the age of 4 will typically say, "Pencils." This task is used to determine whether a child possesses a **theory of mind** or not. See also **posting version of the deceptive box test, state change test**, and **unexpected transfer test**.

Deductive reasoning   The outcome of a specific example is calculated from a general principle, that is, deductive reasoning involves drawing specific conclusions from general premises. See also **inductive reasoning**.

Defense mechanisms   In Freud's theory, if an individual's rational thought (**ego**) is threatened by his or her basic desires (**id**) or his or her conscience (**superego**), then various defense mechanisms are available which mean that, for the short term, the individual does not have to deal with the internal conflict. An example of a defense mechanism is repression, whereby an unpleasant thought or memory is blocked and the individual has no memory of the problem. See also **ego**, **id**, and **superego**.

Demand characteristics   Cues that are perceived as telling participants how they are expected to behave or respond in a research setting, i.e., social factors that "demand" a certain sort of response. Demand characteristics include the tendency of participants to behave in the way they think the experimenter expects them to behave.

Dependent variable   The behavior that is measured or observed in a study. Changes in the behavior are dependent on, that is, caused by, changes to the **independent variable**.

Deprivation dwarfism   A small stature and delayed physical development that is often found in children who lack adequate psychological interaction, even though they receive adequate nutrition.

Derivational constancy   The process whereby new words are generated from ones with similar meanings. For example, "health" is derived from the word "heal," and this relationship is captured in the spelling of the derived word because its stem preserves the spelling of "heal," even though the vowel sound in the two words is different.

Developmental delay   Any delay experienced in a child's development relative to the average child's development. For example, if a child does not reach a **developmental milestone** within the normal range, she can be viewed as having some form of developmental delay; however, this does not necessarily indicate a lasting problem.

Developmental functions   Typical trends in development; for example, we typically get more intelligent as we age. See **continuous function – decreasing ability**, **continuous function – increasing ability**, **discontinuous (step) function**, **stage-like changes in development**, and **U-shaped functions**.

Developmental milestones   Past research has identified the average age at which children start to exhibit certain behaviors; these are termed developmental milestones. For example, the average age that a child stands alone is 11 months. See also **motor milestones**.

Developmental quotient (DQ)   An index of children's development, calculated in the same way as **intelligence quotient (IQ)**. DQ is usually based on perceptual and motor performance rather than on general intellectual development.

Differential psychology   The branch of psychology that deals with individual differences between people.

Diffusion of responsibility   When acting within a group, individuals do not feel as responsible for their behavior as they would when acting alone. Therefore, a group of individuals can perform an action that none of the individual members would ordinarily carry out.

Direct bullying   See **bullying**.

Discontinuous (step) function   Development that takes place in a series of stages or steps. Each new stage is qualitatively different from the preceding and following stages. The **moral judgment stages** described by Piaget and Kohlberg are examples of a discontinuous (step) function. See **continuous function – decreasing ability**, **continuous function – increasing ability**, and **U-shaped functions**.

Discovery learning   Encouraging children to learn by discovering information for themselves. Often teachers will tailor the child's environment in order to maximize this type of learning.

Dishabituation   See **habituation**.

Distributive justice   Ensures that rewards and allocations are distributed fairly amongst the members of a group.

Dizygotic (fraternal) twins Individuals who are conceived at the same time but result from two eggs being fertilized by different sperm. Thus, they are like regular siblings and share half of their genes. Compare with **monozygotic twins**.

Domain-general Knowledge that can be applied to many different situations across many domains. See also **domain-specific**.

Domain-specific Knowledge that can only be applied to specific situations that fall within the same domain. See also **domain-general**.

Dominance Getting one's own way or influencing others in interpersonal encounters.

Dosage-response relationship A relationship existing between the **independent** and the **dependent variables** of a study.

Down's syndrome (DS) A **congenital** (present at birth) condition which is characterized by a flattened face, extra folds of skin on the eyelids, stubby fingers, unusual fold of skin on the soles and palms, and an overlarge tongue. DS is a **chromosomal** abnormality that is caused by faulty cell division soon after fertilization, and people with this disorder typically will have severe learning difficulties. The incidence of DS is about 16 to 17 in every 10,000 births, and the incidence rises with the age of the mother.

d-structure (or deep structure) The abstract representation of a sentence, or the actual meaning that the sentence is trying to convey. See also **s-structure**.

Dynamic systems theory A theoretical approach applied to many areas of development which views the individual as interacting dynamically in a complex system in which all parts interact. As applied to motor development in infancy, dynamic (or dynamical) systems theory views every new developing ability or skill as being jointly influenced by nervous system development, the movement capabilities of the body, and environmental supports for the task or skill the child wants to accomplish.

E

Echolalia The repetition of words and phrases previously heard, often in a repetitive and meaningless way. This behavior is common in individuals with **autism**, and the term has also been applied to infants' early vocalizations at around 9 to 12 months when they appear to be "playing with sounds" and show some comprehension of simple words.

Ecological validity The results obtained from a study are ecologically valid if they are meaningful in the real world.

Ego In Freud's theory, the ego can be thought of as the rational thought that evolved to control the urges of the **id** in order that they meet the demands of reality and maintain social approval and esteem. See also **id**, **defense mechanisms**, and **superego**.

Egocentric An egocentric child is one who finds it difficult to see things from another person's point of view. Not to be confused with egotistical.

Egocentrism The difficulty or inability of young children to distinguish between their own perspective and that of others. A major characteristic of children's thinking in the **preoperational stage** in Piaget's theory. Widely investigated under the topic of **theory of mind**.

Elaboration A memory **mnemonic** that works by making connections between items that have to be remembered. For example, if a child has to remember the pair *fish–fork* in a **paired-associate memory task**, she might imagine eating the fish with a fork. The spontaneous use of this strategy does not appear until adolescence.

Electra complex See **Oedipus complex**.

Embedded shapes Complete shapes that have been used to form part of a different, larger shape. For example, four triangles can be arranged to form a square. Initially we may just perceive the square, but closer inspection will reveal the triangles also. The Embedded Shapes Test is used to test individuals' visuo-spatial skills.

Embryo   In human **prenatal development**, the organism 2–12 weeks after conception.

Emotion   Emotion ranges from simple emotions such as happiness, sadness, fear, and anger, to more complex emotions such as self-consciousness and jealousy.

Emotion regulation   Adjusting one's emotional state to a suitable level of intensity. This prevents emotional "overload" and allows one to function in a consistent manner.

Empiricism   The belief that psychological abilities are acquired primarily through experience. Contrast with **nativism**, and see **nature–nurture issue**.

Encoding switch hypothesis   In face perception, this hypothesis argues that different information about faces is represented in memory by children at different ages. It is suggested that young children rely on information about individual features (e.g., eyes, nose, mouth) in recognizing faces, whereas older children and adults use information about the configuration of the features, that is, the spatial layout. See also **configurational processing** and **featural processing**.

Encoding   The first stage in the memory system. Information that is attended to gets placed (*encoded*) in the memory storage system. Encoded information enters the **short-term memory** store.

Environmentalism   The hypothesis that people learn to be the way they are, that the person we become is a consequence of the experiences we have had throughout life. Compare with **genetic determinism** and see **nature–nurture issue**.

Environmentality   The extent to which variations within a population are caused by environmental factors. Contrast with **heritability**. Often expressed as e^2.

Environment–gene correlation   See **gene–environment correlation**.

Epigenetic principle   The belief that all living things grow according to a design plan or "blueprint" of psychological development. This design is comprised of a few basic "building blocks" that develop into more complex structures through interactions between themselves and the environment.

Episodic memory   Memory for specific personally experienced events, including their temporal and spatial contexts. Thus, the episodic memory for "market" would represent the trips to the market and where you can buy (for instance) the best cheese; remembering your first lecture/class is another example of an episodic memory.

Equilibrium   In Piagetian theory, a state in which children's **schemas** are in balance and are undisturbed by conflict.

Ethnic identity   An awareness of which racial, national, linguistic, or religious group one belongs to.

Ethological approaches   Approaches which emphasize the evolutionary origins of many behaviors that are important for survival, such as **imprinting**.

Event sampling   An **observational study** which records what happens during particular events. Events studied include playing, bathtime, feeding, reading, and so on.

Executive functioning   The process whereby behavior is planned in order that the desired goal will be achieved.

Experimental group   The group of individuals who receive a particular treatment or manipulation. In order to measure the effectiveness of the treatment, their results are compared with those from a **control group** that does not receive the treatment.

Experimental methods   Experimental methods control an individual's environment in systematic ways in an attempt to identify which variables influence the behavior of interest.

Explicit memory   Memory for an experience or event that is easily accessible.

Expressive language   Language that is particularly expressive in its nature and which uses many social words. A child who has an expressive language style has a tendency to use people's names, words for actions, and strings of words.

Extraversion   A personality variable. Someone who scores highly on an extraversion scale will typically be an outgoing and confident person. See also **introversion**.

F

False belief   Incorrectly believing something to be the case when it is not. Often used in **theory of mind** research.

False positive   Believing something to be true, when in fact it is false.

Familial resemblance   The resemblance between relatives whose genetic relationship to each other is known.

Featural processing   In face perception, this refers to a tendency to process the separate features of the face, as opposed to perceiving the relationship between the parts, or **configurational processing**. See also **encoding switch hypothesis**.

Fetus   In human **prenatal development**, the organism 12 weeks after conception until birth.

Field theory   Lewin's theory that behavior results from the interaction between a person (his or her genetic influences) and that person's environment (**nurture**).

Fluid intelligence   Intellectual ability that cannot be taught easily, general ability to grasp new concepts and to think and reason abstractly. This type of intelligence is said to be culture-free since it does not depend upon previous experience. See **crystallized intelligence**.

Folk theories of development   Ideas held about development that are not based upon scientific investigation.

Formal operations stage   The fourth Piagetian stage in which the individual acquires the capacity for abstract scientific thought. This includes the ability to theorize about impossible events and items. This stage, which appears from around 11 years, sees the beginnings of **hypothetico-deductive reasoning**, **propositional thought**, and improvements in the capacity for **combinatory thought**.

Fraternal twins   See **dizygotic twins**.

Frontal cortex   One of the four main lobes of the **cerebral cortex** (the others being parietal, temporal, and occipital), located behind the eyes and forehead. The frontal cortex is involved in emotional experiences and many cognitive abilities, such as problem-solving, planning, and judgment.

Functional invariants   Processes that do not change during development, such as **accommodation** and **assimilation** in Piaget's theory. What do change are the cognitive structures (often called **schemas**) that underlie **cognitive development** and allow the child to comprehend the world at progressively higher levels of understanding.

G

g   The term used to denote general intelligence. Note that it is always written as g and never G.

Gametes   Male or female reproductive cells, sperm and ova, each of which contains one-half the number of **chromosomes** found in the other cells of the body. See also **meiotic cell division**.

Gender constancy   The awareness, in early childhood, that one is either a boy or a girl, and that this is unchangeable – once a girl (boy), always a girl (boy).

Gender development   The developing understanding that a child is either a girl or a boy and that there are gender-appropriate behaviors associated with this difference.

Gender identity   The awareness that one is a boy, or a girl.

Gene–environment correlation   The ways in which a child's genetic inheritance affects the environment he or she experiences, and vice versa (also known as **environment–gene correlation**).

Generalizations   See **overgeneralizations**.

Genetic determinism   The hypothesis that people become who they are as a consequence of their genetic code. Contrast with **environmentalism** and see **maturation** and **nature–nurture issue**.

Genetic predisposition   Any behavior or physical characteristic that is present within an individual's genetic code. These characteristics may not be activated yet, but there is a potential for them. For example, a person may have a genetic predisposition to having a heart problem later in life: this problem will not definitely emerge, but it is more likely to than in someone who does not have such a genetic predisposition.

Genitive   A possessive word, for example the apostrophe + "s" in "the boy's jumper" indicates that the jumper belongs to the boy.

Genotype   The genetic composition of the individual. Contrast with **phenotype**.

H

Habituation   The process by which a response to a stimulus gradually declines over time. For example, infants will initially be very interested in an auditory or visual stimulus and will spend a lot of time attending to it; however, over time they will become bored with the stimulus and their attention to it will decrease. Recovery of attention to a novel stimulus is called **dishabituation**.

Hardware   A computer term meaning the size or capacity of its processing units, sometimes used to refer to the child's capacity to comprehend amounts of information. See also **software**.

Head Start   A federally supported program in the United States with five components: (1) preschool enrichment education; (2) health screening and referral services; (3) nutrition education and hot meals; (4) social services; and (5) parent education and involvement. Research has indicated that a child's cognitive and language development is enhanced during the period that he or she is participating in a Head Start program. The British equivalent is called Sure Start.

Heritability   The extent to which variations within a population are genetically determined. Estimates of heritability range between 0 and 1 – values close to 1 indicate a strong genetic contribution. Often expressed as h^2. Contrast with **environmentality**.

Heteronomous stage of moral reasoning   One of Piaget's stages of moral development. Children in this stage demonstrate a blind obedience to any authority figure, and judge actions by the amount of damage caused rather than in terms of the intentions of the actors. Children in this stage view rules as fixed and rigid, and since they have been laid down by authority figures, they must be obeyed. This is followed by the **autonomous stage** of moral reasoning.

Hierarchy of needs   Stages of needs or desires in Abraham Maslow's **humanistic theory** which go from the basic physiological needs for food and water to the ultimate desire for **self-actualization** or the desire to fulfill one's potential.

Horizontal décalage   Refers to the nonsynchronous development of children on Piagetian tasks (e.g., cases in which children may succeed on conservation of number tasks but not on conservation of continuous quantity).

Human rights and social welfare morality   Kohlberg's final stage of **moral judgment**, also called the **social contract orientation stage**. Individuals who have reached this stage make use of ethical principles to guide moral judgments. Moral decisions are made with reference to the rules one would like to see in an ideal, as opposed to the real, world. Therefore, stealing is acceptable if it is the only way to save another person's life.

Humanistic theory   Theory which assumes that growth in the developing child is influenced by the fulfillment of a set of basic needs that constitute a hierarchy, and that higher needs appear when lower, more compelling ones are satisfied. It is argued that healthy children have satisfied their lower, basic needs (for life, safety, love, and esteem) and are motivated by trends toward **self-actualization**.

Hunter-gatherer tribe   A tribe of people who live in the traditional fashion of hunting and gathering. In such tribes, it is typical that the individual members will live in small communities and they depend upon one another for survival. Typically, the males will leave the home base periodically to hunt wild animals, while the females, children, and infirm stay close to the base and gather various fruits and berries for eating also.

Hypothetico-deductive reasoning The ability to develop theories in an attempt to explain certain phenomena, generate hypotheses based on these theories, and systematically devise tests to confirm or refute these hypotheses.

I

Id In Freud's theory, a primitive collection of urges with which an individual begins life. The id is responsible for an individual's "primitive" instincts, such as eating and reproducing. See also **defense mechanisms**, **ego**, and **superego**.

Identical twins See **monozygotic twins**.

Idiots savants Individuals with low intelligence who display an isolated cognitive skill (an **islet of ability**). Such skills include drawing, arithmetic, calculating days of the year, feats of memory, and others. Sometimes found in individuals with **autism**.

Implicit memory Memory for events that we cannot *consciously* remember.

Imprinting A period soon after birth or hatching in which the young of **precocial species** of animals (which includes ducks, geese, sheep, horses) follow the first moving objects they see. Since this is usually the mother, a parent–infant bond is formed and the following response is adaptive (adds to survival value) because it leads to a physical proximity between parent and offspring. The term is also used in Bowlby's theory of attachment to refer to the formation in the early months of the human infant–mother bond.

Independent variable A factor or variable in a study or experiment which can be systematically controlled and varied by the experimenter to see if there are changes in the child's response. The behavior that changes is called the **dependent variable**.

Indirect bullying See **bullying**.

Inductive reasoning Creating a general principle or conclusion from specific examples, that is, drawing a general conclusion from specific premises. See also **deductive reasoning**.

Indulgent parenting Indulgent parents are high on responsiveness, but low on demandingness. They interact with their children in a benign and passive manner and avoid the use of power when dealing with matters of discipline. They make few maturity demands on the children's behavior and allow them a high degree of **autonomy**. Children from indulgent homes are less mature, less responsible, more easily influenced by their **peers**, and less able to take on leadership roles. See also **authoritarian parenting**, **authoritative parenting**, and **neglectful parenting**.

Infant-directed speech The speech that adults and children over 4 years old use when addressing an infant. When compared to speech directed to adults, infant-directed speech has shorter sentences, a higher pitch, more exaggerated pitch contours, a larger pitch range, and is more rhythmic in nature. It is thought that this type of speech helps infants to segment the **speech stream** into individual words. Also known as **motherese**.

Infantile amnesia Inability to remember events during early childhood (first 3 years). Also called childhood amnesia.

Information processing The view that **cognitive processes** are explained in terms of inputs and outputs and that the human mind is a system through which information flows, i.e., information is received and processed by the brain, which then determines how that information will be used. Information processing is a term borrowed from computer programming.

Innate mechanism A mechanism or ability that does not need to be learned, something we are born knowing.

Insecure-avoidant   A particular type of **attachment behavior** exhibited in the **strange situation** measure. Insecure-avoidant infants appear indifferent toward their caregiver, and treat the stranger and caregiver in very similar ways. They show very little, if any, distress at being left with the stranger. See also **insecure-resistant** and **securely attached**.

Insecure-resistant   A particular type of **attachment behavior** exhibited in the **strange situation** measure. Insecure-resistant infants are overinvolved with the caregiver, showing attachment behavior even during the preseparation episodes, with little exploration or interest in the environment. These infants become very distressed upon separation, but the overactivation of their attachment systems hampers their ability to be comforted by the caregiver upon reunion. See also **insecure-avoidant** and **securely attached**.

Instinct   (1) Behavior that is genetic in its origin, e.g., human sexual desire. (2) A feeling or **emotion** that has no basis in fact, e.g., "My instinct tells me he's not to be trusted."

Instrumental morality   The second of Kohlberg's **moral judgment stages**. In this stage individuals (usually children) become aware that other people have intentions and desires, and that there are two sides to every argument. Moral decisions are made by referring to the side that provides the greatest benefit. Therefore, if someone is very helpful to you, it is acceptable to steal in order to save that person's life.

Intelligence quotient (IQ)   An IQ score gives an indication of an individual's intelligence compared with other individuals of the same **chronological age**. Originally, IQ was calculated in children by dividing a child's **mental age** by his or her chronological age and multiplying by 100, although a slightly different calculation is now used. **Intelligence test** scores stabilize in adolescence and a different calculation is used for older children and adults. A score of 100 denotes a person as having average intelligence for his or her age.

Intelligence tests   Any test that aims to measure an individual's intellectual ability. These tests have traditionally concentrated on **intelligence quotient (IQ)**, but modern tests now examine both **crystallized** and **fluid intelligence**.

Intermental ability   **Cognitive** knowledge that has been learned through individual attainment. Compare with **intramental ability**.

Interpersonal normative morality   This third stage of Kohlberg's **moral judgment stages** is sometimes referred to as the "good boy/good girl orientation." Individuals in this stage seek to be viewed as "good" and feel guilt when it is likely that others will condemn their behavior. Therefore, an action is acceptable if it can be said that someone's heart was in the right place, even if that person breaks rules. For example, stealing to save your wife's life is acceptable as long as you want to be a good husband.

Intersubjectivity   Taking account of other people's intentions, thoughts, emotions, and feelings in deciding what to do. When this involves shared attention with both objects and another person(s), it is termed **secondary intersubjectivity**.

Intervention group   Another term for **experimental group**.

Intonation   The rhythmic pattern of speech. For example, the meaning of a sentence is changed when the ending has a raised pitch, e.g. "He didn't come" versus "He didn't come?"

Intramental ability   Cognitive knowledge that has been learned through group involvement. Compare with **intermental ability**.

Intrasyllabic units   These are units of speech that are smaller than **syllables** but larger than **phonemes**. **Onset** and **rime** are two examples of intrasyllabic units.

Introspectionism   An approach to psychology common in the nineteenth century in which observers were asked to reflect on their thoughts, feelings, and perceptions.

Introversion   A personality variable. Someone who scores highly on an introversion scale will typically be very quiet and reserved. See also **extraversion**.

Intuitive psychology   The awareness some people have regarding others' desires, motives, and beliefs; they appear able to anticipate others' reactions and behavior.

Intuitive scientists   The idea that we are all capable of constructing commonsense theories to explain how the world works, and are able to conduct "experiments" to test them.

Invariance, principle of   As used in connection with **conservation**, the principle that quantities remain unchanged if nothing is added or subtracted.

IQ test   See **Intelligence test**.

Islets of ability   See **idiots savants**.

K

Key stages   Each key stage represents one British school year, and a number of **attainment targets** are set for each key stage.

L

Last-number-counted principle   The principle that the last number counted represents the value for that set.

Law of effect   Law or rule devised by the American psychologist Edward Lee Thorndike which states that the likelihood of an action being repeated is increased if it leads to reward, and decreased if it leads to punishment.

Letter–sound associations   Where one letter represents one sound or **phoneme**.

Lexical skills   The understanding of what constitutes acceptable speech and language, including understanding words and grammar.

Libidinal forces   Sexual desires. Freud thought these were under the control of the **id**.

Life space   Lewin argues that a person's environment can be divided into regions that are separated by more or less permeable boundaries that correspond to the individual's characteristics, needs, and perceptions of the environment. The person and the environment represent inseparable constructs, which together constitute the life space.

Longitudinal design   A study where repeated observations of the same group of children are made at different points in their development. Compare with **cross-sectional design**.

Long-term memory   Items stored in the long-term memory have passed through the **short-term memory** and are now stored for an extended period of time.

M

Maternal deprivation   A term to describe the deprivation an infant experiences as a result of long-term separation from his or her mother, or from being orphaned.

Maturation   Aspects of development that are largely under genetic control, and hence largely uninfluenced by environmental factors. Not to be confused with maturing, which means development into the mature or adult state, however caused.

Maturational unfolding   A pattern of growth which is genetically predetermined (see **genetic determinism**) and which unfolds during childhood.

Mechanistic world view   The idea that a person can be represented as being like a machine (such as a computer), which is inherently passive until stimulated by the environment. This viewpoint argues that a child's development is controlled only through environmental input and is little influenced by genetics. **Behaviorism** is an example of this world view. See also **organismic world view**.

Meiotic cell division   The type of cell division that occurs in sexually reproducing organisms which halves the number of **chromosomes** in reproductive cells (sperm and ova), leading to the production of **gametes**.

Mental age (MA)   The level of mental skills that is average for a particular age group. If a child has a **developmental delay**, then her mental age will be lower than her **chronological age**, and vice versa for bright children.

Meta-analysis   An analysis of many studies on the same topic in order to draw general or overall conclusions.

Metacognition   Knowledge of one's state of mind, reflective access to one's cognitive abilities, thinking about how you are feeling or thinking.

Metamemory   Understanding one's own memory and having an awareness of the ways in which memory works and can be improved.

Microgenetic studies   Studies of development that observe individual children in great detail from the time they first attempt a new skill, such as walking or crawling, until it is performed effortlessly.

Mnemonic strategy   Any strategy that helps to improve one's own memory. Mnemonic strategies include **elaboration**, **organization**, and **rehearsal**.

Modulated babbling   This is the final period of babbling and language play and appears from around 10 months on. This period is characterized by a variety of sound combinations, stress and **intonation** patterns, and overlaps with the beginning of meaningful speech. Modulated babbling may play an important role in the acquisition of the intonation patterns that are important for the infant's native language. See also **babbling** and **canonical**.

Monotropy   The view that the infant has a basic need to form an attachment with one significant person, usually the mother. A central claim in Bowlby's early theory of attachment formation.

Monozygotic (identical) twins   Genetically identical twins, developed from one ovum and one sperm which divides into two shortly after conception. Such twins have the same genetic make-up. Compare with **dizygotic twins**.

Mora   A rhythmic unit in languages like Japanese and Tamil that can be either a syllable or part of a syllable. In English a mora roughly corresponds to a consonant–vowel syllable with a short vowel, e.g., "the" as opposed to "thee," which has a long vowel, or to "them," which ends with a consonant. "Thee" and "them" each consist of two moras.

Moral dilemmas   Situations in which people must choose and justify a course of action or reasoning with respect to a moral issue. Hypothetical moral dilemmas are often used as research tools to examine the development of moral reasoning.

Moral judgment stages   Piaget described two stages in the development of moral reasoning, the **heteronomous stage** and the **autonomous stage**. Kohlberg described five stages, the earlier of which overlap with Piaget's. The five stages are **punishment and obedience orientation**, **instrumental morality**, **interpersonal normative morality**, **social system morality**, and **human rights and social welfare morality**.

Moratorium   Period in an individual's life when they identify with a string of different values, beliefs, and ideologies owing to the lack of a stable and consistent self-image.

Morpheme   The smallest unit of sound that carries meaning. The past verb "cooked" has two morphemes, the stem "cook" and the /t/ sound at the end, which tells you that it is about a past action. The plural "dogs" also has two morphemes, "dog" and "s."

Motherese   Another name for **infant-directed speech**.

Motor milestones   The basic motor skills acquired in infancy and early childhood, such as sitting unaided, standing, crawling, walking.

Myelin   A fatty insulator which prevents leakage of the messages traveling along the nerves, and increases the speed of neural transmission.

Myelination   The process by which **myelin** is formed around the **neurons**. Myelination begins in the sixth month of life in the **fetus** but continues through childhood.

N

National Curriculum The **curriculum** that is followed in all schools in the UK. The government sets the particulars of the subjects covered by the National Curriculum.

Nativism The belief that psychological abilities are the product of genetic inheritance – we are simply the product of our genes. Nativism argues that attributes such as intelligence or personality are inherited, and therefore cannot be changed. Contrast with **empiricism**, and see also **maturation** and **nature–nurture issue**.

Nature–nurture issue Ongoing debate on whether development is the result of an individual's genes (nature) or the kinds of experiences they have throughout their life (**nurture**). See also **empiricism, environmentalism, environmentality, genetic determinism, heritability, nativism**.

Neglectful parenting Neglectful parents are low on responsiveness and demandingness. They try to minimize the amount of time and energy required to raise their children. They know little about their children's lives, interact sparingly with them, and do not include them in making decisions that affect the family. Children from neglectful homes are often impulsive and more likely to be involved in delinquent behaviors such as precocious experimentation with sex, alcohol, and drugs. See also **authoritarian parenting, authoritative parenting**, and **indulgent parenting**.

Neo-cortex In evolutionary terms, the most recently developed areas of the **cerebral cortex**.

Neural networks Artificial computer programs that are intended to simulate the action of the brain and nerve cells. A central concept in **connectionism**.

Neuron Nerve cells within the central nervous system which transmit messages between cells.

Neuropsychological deficits A disorder that stems from the brain which affects a person's behavior or **cognitive functioning**.

Norm referencing Tests that give the average scores for the population, and hence provide a reference point to indicate how individual children perform relative to the scores of other children.

Nurture The belief that psychological abilities are the product of our environment. See **nature–nurture issue**.

O

Object permanence The ability to understand that even if an object is no longer visible, it continues to exist.

Object unity Perceiving an object as complete despite the fact that parts of it cannot be seen.

Observational learning Situation in which people (especially children) learn by observing others and then copying (imitating) the observed acts. Imitation is often influenced by vicarious reinforcement, which is seeing if others are rewarded for producing the behaviors or acts that are observed. A key concept in **social learning theory**.

Observational studies Studies in which behavior is simply observed and recorded, and the researcher does not attempt to influence the individual's natural behavior in any way.

Oedipus complex An important stage of development in Freud's **psychoanalytic theory**. This expression derives from the Greek myth in which Oedipus became infatuated with his mother. In the Freudian account, the young boy develops sexual feelings toward his mother but realizes that his father is a major competitor for her (sexual) affections. He then fears castration at the hands of his father (the castration complex), and in order to resolve this complex he adopts the ideals of his father and the **superego** (the conscience) develops. For young girls the **Electra complex** is when they develop feelings toward their father and fear retribution at the hands of their mother. They resolve this by empathizing with their mother, adopting the ideals she offers, and so the girl's superego develops.

One-to-one correspondence   Two sets are in one-to-one correspondence if each object in one set has a counterpart in the other set. If the objects in two sets are in one-to-one correspondence, they are equal in number.

One-to-one principle   The principle that when counting a set of objects, each object must be counted once and once only.

Onset   The onset of a **syllable** is the consonant, cluster of consonants, or vowel at the beginning of a syllable. The onset of "hat" is "h," and "st" is the onset of "stair." See also **rime**.

Ontogeny   The personal growth of an individual living being from conception. Contrast with **phylogeny**.

Operant conditioning   A form of conditioning investigated by B. F. Skinner. The training, or shaping, of an animal or human by rewarding him/her for producing the desired behavior (or a close approximation to it) and/or either ignoring or punishing undesirable behaviors in order to stop them. An important form of learning in **behaviorism**, and see also **classical conditioning**.

Order irrelevance principle   The principle that it does not matter in which order members of a set are counted: if one person starts at the top and works down, she should get the same result as someone who starts at the bottom and works up.

Ordinality   The numerical principle that states that numbers come in an ordered scale of magnitude: 2 is more than 1, and 3 is more than 2, and as a logical consequence 3 is more than 1.

Organismic world view   The idea that people are inherently active and continually interacting with the environment, and therefore helping to shape their own development. Piaget's theory is an example of this world view. See also **mechanistic world view**.

Organization   A **mnemonic strategy** that works by organizing items into meaningful categories. See **cluster effect**.

Orthography   A writing system. Orthography is used to describe any aspect of print or, more loosely, spelling.

Overextension   Extending the meaning of a word too broadly, for example using the word "bird" to refer to birds, airplanes, and hot-air balloons. See also **underextension**.

Overgeneralization   Creating a new verb by treating a noun as if it were a verb, for example "I am ballereening," meaning "I am dancing like a ballerina."

Overregularization   The name given when a previously learned rule is applied in the wrong situation. For example, a child learning English might say "thinked" rather than "thought" because the child is using the regular past tense rule (attach "-ed" to the end of the verb) rather than the correct exception to the rule ("thought").

P

Paired-associate task   A memory test in which participants must remember pairs of unrelated items. For example, the participant is told to link the picture of a house with the picture of an elephant. During the testing phase, they are shown the elephant picture, and their task is to link this to the house. See also **elaboration**.

Paradigm   A philosophical system of ideas that serves to organize a set or family of scientific theories and associated scientific methods.

Parallel activity   A type of activity where children play near each other with the same materials, but do not interact much.

Parental style   The different ways in which parents raise their children. Generally, different styles are measured according to the degrees of parental responsiveness and parental demandingness. See **authoritarian parenting**, **authoritative parenting**, **indulgent parenting**, and **neglectful parenting**.

Passive or submissive victim Passive or submissive victims are individuals who are not aggressive or teasing in their behavior, and who are often cautious, sensitive, and quiet. They usually react to bullying by crying or withdrawing from the situation, often do not have any friends, and have a very negative attitude toward violence and the use of violent means. See **bullying** and compare with **provocative victim**.

Pedagogy Any activity that is specifically designed to teach.

Peer Companion of approximately the same age and developmental level.

Percentile Location of an individual's development or achievement along a percentage scale. For example, if an individual is at the 60th percentile on height, she is taller than 60 percent of her peers.

Performance limitations Limitations that are associated with the task being asked, rather than a deficiency in competence. For example, it can be argued that a child's failure on the **deceptive box task** is due to performance limitations, since the same child can give the correct response when tested using the **posting version of the deceptive box test**.

Perseveration See **response perseveration**.

Personality trait Facet of a person's character that is relatively stable. Examples of personality traits include shyness, **extraversion**, and confidence.

Perspective-taking Young children tend to be **egocentric** and often have difficulty in understanding a situation from someone else's point of view.

Phenomenism Knowledge that is limited to appearances such that, in tasks that involve distinguishing reality from appearance, children report only appearance. See **appearance–reality distinction** and contrast with **realism**.

Phenotype The apparent, observable, measurable characteristics of the individual. Contrast with **genotype**.

Phoneme A set of sounds that are not physically identical to one another, but which speakers of a language treat as equivalent sounds. So whilst the sound "ba" will sound very different if spoken by a man and a woman, English speakers will still perceive both instances as examples of the same phoneme. The phoneme is also the smallest unit of speech that constitutes a change in meaning, for example "rate" and "late" only differ in one phoneme, yet these words have very different meanings.

Phonological skills An awareness of sounds at the phonetic level, being able to detect the individual sounds (or **phonemes**) in words. Phonology is the aspect of language that is concerned with the perception and production of sounds that are used in language. In order for effective communication to occur, children must learn which sounds are important in the language that they hear.

Phylogeny The evolutionary growth and development of a species. Contrast with **ontogeny**.

Play hierarchy A scheme used for coding children's activities, based on social participation and level of play.

Posting version of the deceptive box test A version of the **deceptive box task** where the child posts what she thinks is in a box. See **state change test**, **theory of mind**, and **unexpected transfer test**.

Postnatal development The development of a human individual after he or she is born, particularly during early infancy.

Pragmatic system The cognitive and social skills that enable us to communicate effectively. For example, the abilities involved in **turn-taking**, initiating new topics and conversations, sustaining a dialogue, and repairing a faulty communication are all important aspects of the pragmatic system. See also **pragmatics**.

Pragmatics The communicative side of language, the intentions expressed in utterances as opposed to the actual words being used. For example, "Would you like to sit at the table?" could actually mean "Come and sit down now."

Precocial species   Those species of animals where the young are able to locomote almost immediately after birth or hatching. These include ducks, geese, sheep, and horses. The young will often **imprint** on and follow their mother, an instinctive response which has clear survival value for the young. See also **critical period**.

Prenatal development   The development of a human individual before he or she is born.

Preoperational stage   A stage of development described by Piaget in which children under the age of approximately 7 years are unable to see enough aspects of problems in order to solve them. Preoperational children fail **conservation tasks** and display **animism** in their thinking.

Pretend play   "Make-believe play" in which the child may pretend to be other people or act out real-life situations, e.g., playing "mommies and daddies," or may pretend that one object (e.g., a banana) is another (e.g., telephone). Sometimes called **symbolic play**.

Preterm   Born prematurely. A human infant is regarded as preterm if he or she is born before 38 weeks of pregnancy.

Primary caregiver   The individual, usually but not always the mother, who satisfies the baby's biological and psychological needs. See also **monotropy**.

Primary drives   Basic needs which include hunger, thirst, and the need for warmth. Bowlby and others have argued that an infant's need for attachment is also a primary drive.

Procedural skills   Applying certain routines or procedures in order to solve certain problems and tasks, such as counting the number of objects in a set.

Profound visual impairment (PVI)   An inability to see anything more than shades of light and dark. See also **blindisms** and **severe visual impairment**.

Projective techniques   Personality tests which attempt to identify **personality traits** through the use of subjective measures. Examples of these would be asking an individual to write a story, draw a picture, or say what she sees in inkblots. The theory is that the individual expresses aspects of her personality through her writing, drawing, or interpretations.

Propositional thought   The ability to express relationships in terms of symbolic (and hence abstract) propositions.

Prosocial behavior   Any behavior that is enacted in order to benefit others.

Prosody   The intonations, stress, and rhythm of speech that are used to communicate meanings, e.g., "this is correct" becomes a question as opposed to a statement when "correct?" ends in a raised inflection.

Protoconversations   Interactions between adults and infants in which the adults tend to vocalize when the infants are not vocalizing, or after the infant has finished vocalizing. Protoconversations may be important precursors to the **turn-taking** observed in early conversations.

Protodeclarative   A protodeclarative occurs when an infant uses pointing or looking to direct an adult's attention toward an object. See also **proto-imperatives**.

Proto-imperative   A proto-imperative occurs when an infant points to an object and then alternates her gaze between the object and the adult until she obtains the desired object. See also **protodeclarative**.

Prototypical face   The face that is produced when many different faces are averaged. For example, the distance between the eyes on the prototypical face will be the average distance between the eyes of all the faces used.

Provocative victim   Provocative victims are individuals who are both anxious and aggressive in their behavior. They often have problems concentrating and they behave in ways that causes irritation and tension around them. They can often be characterized as hyperactive and their behavior often provokes other students, thus resulting in negative reactions from their **peers**. See **bullying** and compare with **passive or submissive victim**.

Proximodistal trend   The development of motor control in infancy which is from the center of the body outwards to more peripheral segments – that is, the head, trunk, and pelvic girdle are brought under control before the elbow, wrist, knee, and ankle joints, which leads to finer control over the hands and fingers. See also **cephalocaudal trend**.

Pseudo-word   A nonexistent but pronounceable nonword, such as "tibudo" or "wug," often used in psychological experiments. Pseudo-words are used to test for spelling, grammar, or other aspects of understanding language where we can be sure that the participants have not heard the "words" before.

Psychoanalysis   The theoretical view, first developed by Sigmund Freud, that much of our behavior is determined by unconscious factors. According to this view, the child goes through **psychosexual stages** of development – oral, anal, phallic, latency, and genital.

Psychoanalytic theory   Most prominently associated with Sigmund Freud. Freud suggested that there are three main personality structures. The **id** is present in the newborn infant and consists of hidden impulses, emotions, and desires. It demands instant gratification of all its wishes and needs. Since this is impractical, the **ego** develops to act as a practical interface or mediator between reality and the desires of the **id**. The final structure to develop is the **superego**, which is the sense of duty and responsibility – in many ways the conscience. See also **psychosexual stages**.

Psychological tests   Instruments for the quantitative assessment of some psychological attribute or attributes of a person. The developmental psychologist will use such testing to measure such things as motor development, motivation, reading ability, or general intelligence.

Psychopathology   A psychological imbalance such that the individual has difficulties in functioning in the real world.

Psychosexual stages   Freud argued that there were five stages of human development. All but the latency stage are centered around the stimulation of an erogenous zone. The stages develop in the following order: oral (0–1 year), anal (1–3 years), phallic (3–5 years), latency (5 years–adolescence), and genital (adolescence onwards).

Psychosocial stages   Stages of development put forward by Erik Erikson. The child goes from the stage of "basic trust" in early infancy to the final stage in adult life of maturity with a sense of integrity and self-worth. There is little empirical evidence for these stages, and it is more a matter of belief than fact (as is the case for **psychoanalytic theory**).

Punishment and obedience orientation   This is the first of Kohlberg's **moral judgment stages** and is very similar to Piaget's **heteronomous stage**. This stage is characterized by an unquestioning belief that something is wrong if a law or an authority figure prohibits it.

R

Racial prejudice   A negative evaluation of someone as a consequence of his or her being in a certain racial or ethnic group.

Reaction formation   A term used in **psychoanalytic theory**. The individual may react, often unconsciously, to negative aspects of her personality so that, for example, the person whose upbringing destines her to become a miser may react against this and become generous.

Realism   In Piagetian theory, characteristic of children who are **egocentric** and assume that others share their own perspective. Also used to refer to children's responses in appearance–reality tasks (e.g., in tasks that involve distinguishing appearance from reality, children report only reality). See **appearance–reality distinction** and contrast with **phenomenism**.

Recall   After witnessing an event, or learning test items, a participant is asked to describe anything about the event or the test items that he or she can remember, where the event or test items are no longer present. See also **recognition**.

Recapitulation   To "go over" and repeat again. The expression "**ontogeny** recapitulates **phylogeny**" refers to the repetition of evolutionary stages in the growth of the fetus and young mammal.

Recognition   After witnessing an event, or learning test items, a participant is shown a list of items and asked to identify (*recognize*) any that were present during the event or initial learning. See also **recall**.

Reductionism   The claim that complex behaviors and skills such as language and problem-solving are formed from simpler core processes, such as neural activity and conditioning, and can ultimately be understood in these simpler terms.

Reflexive vocalizations   The first sounds produced by infants, including cries, coughs, burps, and sneezes.

Rehearsal   A **mnemonic strategy** that involves the repetition of the items or information that have to be remembered. An example is repeating a telephone number so as not to forget it before dialing.

Representational ability   The ability to form a mental representation of an event or an object.

Response perseveration   Repeating a previously learned response usually when it is not appropriate. For example, when infants incorrectly search at location A when making the **A not B error**, they may be repeating the previously successful response to search at A.

Retinal image size   The size of a visually perceived object on the retina of the eyes. This image will vary depending on the real size of the object and its distance from the observer.

Retrieval demands   Cognitive demands made when attempting to remember information. Retrieval demands are greatest in **recall** tasks, and easiest in **recognition** tasks where the task provides retrieval cues by showing the items to be recognized.

Retroactive interference   The finding that information received after an event can interfere with and alter one's memory for the event.

Reversibility   The ability to imagine a series of steps in both forward and reverse directions. Characteristic of thinking in Piaget's **concrete operations stage**.

Rhyme   Words rhyme with each other when they share a **rime** – "cat" and "hat" rhyme because they have the **rime** "at" in common.

Rime   The vowel sound of a **syllable** plus any consonants that follow. The rime of "hat" is "at," and the rime of "stair" is "air." See also **onset**.

Rods and cones   Light-sensitive cells found in the retina of the eye which translate light into electrical signals that are then transferred to the brain so that the image can be interpreted.

Rooting reflex   The reflex that causes a newborn baby to respond to one of her cheeks being touched by turning her head in that direction. This reflex helps the infant to find a nipple with her mouth.

Rouge test   A test to examine an infant's self-concept. A small amount of rouge (or some other color) is placed on the infant's nose before she is placed in front of a mirror. If the infant touches her own nose, as opposed to the reflection in the mirror, she is said to have acquired a self-concept.

Rough-and-tumble play   A friendly type of play that involves play-fighting with a partner.

S

Savant skills   See **idiots savants**.

Scaffolding   The process whereby adults structure and simplify a child's environment in order to facilitate his or her learning. Scaffolding may occur in a variety of contexts, for example by pointing out the next piece in a jigsaw puzzle or offering the child a sock rolled down to make it easier to put on.

Schemas   Mental structures in the child's thinking that provide representations and plans for enacting behaviors. See also **accommodation** and **script**.

Script   A generalized framework for commonly experienced events or situations, with a stored representation of what one would expect to happen in such situations. An example of an event that would typically have a stored script would be going to a restaurant.

Secondary drive   A term used in **behaviorism** to refer to the fact that objects can acquire reinforcing properties by being associated with the satisfaction of an individual's **primary drives**. It is thought that many fetishes can be acquired this way.

Secondary intersubjectivity   Involving both objects and other people in one's interaction with the world. For example, a 9-month-old infant will begin to share the experience of a new object with other people, she may point to the object or make vocalizations in order to direct another's attention toward it. This behavior indicates that the infant understands that both she and another can attend to the same object, and that she can influence and direct another person's attention. See also **intersubjectivity**.

Second-order analogy   An analogy that requires the use of **crystallized intelligence**. In order to make the connections, one must be able to derive a relationship that is not inherent within the analogy. An example of a second-order analogy is (Bert and Ernie):friendship:: (Romeo and Juliet):love. Note that understanding the analogy requires that the relationships of *Sesame Street*'s Bert and Ernie, and Shakespeare's Romeo and Juliet, be derived: only then does the analogy reduce to "friends are to friendship as lovers are to love."

Securely attached   Descriptive of a child who finds comfort and consolation in the presence of a parent or caregiver, and who seeks comfort from that person after a separation or other aversive event. Whilst the caregiver is present, the securely attached infant uses him or her as a secure base to explore the environment. See **insecure-avoidant**, **insecure-resistant**, and **strange situation**.

Selective attention   The ability to allocate attentional resources and to focus on (a) specific topic(s).

Self-actualization   Fulfillment of needs beyond those deemed necessary for survival. When the need for life, safety, love, and esteem is being met, individuals are free to seek the fulfillment of higher needs, such as pursuing talents and dreams. See also **humanistic theory**.

Self-concept   One's awareness and evaluation of one's self.

Self-socialization   The idea that children attend to and imitate same-sex models, and follow sex-appropriate activities, because they realize that this is what a child of their own sex usually does.

Semantic memory   **Long-term memory** of all of our world knowledge, including concepts, algorithms, definitions of words and the relations between them. The semantic memory for "market," for example, includes the knowledge that it is a place for buying and selling goods.

Semantic system   A system that categorizes words in relation to their meaning.

Sensitive period   A period of development, usually early in life, during which the individual is most sensitive to certain types of experience or learning. Refers to a period of time that is more extended than a **critical period**.

Sensorimotor stage   In Piaget's theory, the first stage of **cognitive development**, whereby thought is based primarily on action and internalized thinking is largely absent. This stage is characteristic of infants from birth to about 2 years old.

Sequential design   A longitudinal study that examines the development of children from different age **cohorts**. Additionally, a cross-section of ages is also examined in order that any cohort effects may be identified. Sometimes called age-cohort design. See also **cross-sectional design** and **longitudinal design**.

Severe visual impairment (SVI)   Whilst still having very poor vision, individuals with SVI do have some limited visual perception of form and shape. See also **profound visual impairment**.

Sex-role stereotypes   Beliefs held about what is most appropriate for one sex or the other.

Shape constancy   Understanding that an object remains the same shape even though its **retinal image size** changes when it is viewed from different angles. Therefore, when we view a square tilted on one axis, we do not perceive the shape as a rectangle but as a square tilted away from us. See also **size constancy**.

Short-term memory   **Encoded** events enter the short-term memory first, and can then progress to the **long-term memory**. Short-term memory can typically only hold a limited number of items (about seven) for a short period of time. Also called **working memory**.

Size constancy   Understanding that an object remains the same size despite its **retinal image size** changing as it moves closer to or away from us. Therefore, when we see a car driving down the road away from us, we do not see it as shrinking despite the fact that its retinal image size decreases. See also **shape constancy**.

Social cognition   The comprehension of social situations.

Social contract orientation stage   See **human rights and social welfare morality**.

Social learning theory   Associated with Albert Bandura. The application of **behaviorism** to social and cognitive learning that emphasizes the importance of **observational learning**, that is, learning by observation and then copying (imitating) the observed acts.

Social policy   Actions, rules, and laws aimed at solving social problems or attaining social goals, in particular intended to improve existing conditions.

Social referencing   Infants and young children look to their caregiver for "advice" when faced with a difficult or uncertain situation and seek social cues (such as smiling or frowning) to guide their actions.

Social signaling devices   Devices such as smiling and crying that signify someone's emotional state.

Social system morality   The fourth of Kohlberg's **moral judgment stages**, also called the **law and order orientation stage**. In this stage individuals recognize that all members of society have intentions and pursue goals, but they understand that rules and laws are necessary in order for society to function and to prevent anarchy. It is therefore necessary for them to always side with whoever is more within the law, even if this causes great regret. Therefore, it is never acceptable to steal since this is against the law; however, one may still feel sympathy for a man who steals in order to save his wife.

Sociocognitive conflict   A **cognitive conflict** that arises as a result of a social interaction, e.g., two **peers** having a different understanding of a mathematical problem.

Sociodramatic play   **Pretend play** involving social role-playing in an extended story sequence.

Socioeconomic status (SES)   A scale that gives an indication of someone's social class and income bracket.

Sociometric status   A categorization of children as popular, controversial, rejected, neglected, or average, according to whether they are high or low on positive and negative nominations.

Sociometry   A picture of the social structure in a group, derived from observation, questionnaire, or interview.

Software   A computer term referring to the variety and effectiveness of the strategies or programs that allow the computer to use and manipulate information. See also **hardware**.

Spatial cognition   An understanding of the three-dimensional world and symbols, and that one thing (the symbol or model) can stand for another (the real thing).

Speech stream   The undifferentiated series of words that are produced when we communicate. In order to understand the meaning conveyed when someone speaks, we must first break the speech stream into the individual words contained within it.

Speed of processing   The time it takes for the brain to either receive or output information, or the speed with which a mental calculation can be carried out.

s-structure (or surface structure)   The **syntax** of a sentence. However, one s-structure can have more than one meaning. In order to understand the intended meaning of a sentence, one must examine the **d-structure**.

Stability versus change   The question of whether individuals are stable in the sense of maintaining their rank order across age, e.g., does the bright 2-year-old become a bright 10-year-old?

Stable order principle   The principle that number words must be produced in a set order: if you count 1–2–3 on one occasion, you must never then count 3–2–1 on another.

Stage-like changes in development   Changes in development that can be categorized into qualitatively different stages, so that a child's abilities will remain relatively stable and then, often suddenly, move up to the next stage. Development of this kind is usually nonreversible; once a child has reached a particular stage, she does not fall back to the previous stage's thinking or behavior. A major characteristic of Piaget's theory of intellectual development.

Stages of moral reasoning   See **moral judgment stages**.

Standard deviation   Statistical term that indicates the average spread of scores from the mean. A high standard deviation would indicate that there is a large variability within the data. A low standard deviation indicates that there is little variability in the data, i.e., many of the scores have values that are very close to the overall mean.

Standardization   The development of a test or procedure by administering it to a large group of individuals in order to develop uniform instructions and group norms. A **standardized test** is one that can be given to children (or adults) to compare their performance with that of others of the same age or background.

Standardized score   A score that has been converted to fit a distribution with a given mean and **standard deviation**. Standardized scores make it easy to compare two individuals, since their scores are being converted in the same manner and are therefore relative to each other. **Intelligence tests** use standardized scoring.

Standardized test   A test of a psychological characteristic, such as personality, aptitude, or intelligence, that has been **standardized** on a representative sample of the population.

State change test   Used in **theory of mind** research. A variation of the **deceptive box task**. The child is shown a Smarties tube or M&Ms box and has to guess what it contains. The box is then opened and the child sees the Smarties/M&Ms being removed and replaced by a pencil. The box is then closed again. The question asked is, "When you first saw the box, before we opened it, what did you think was inside?" Using this method, a much larger percentage of 3- and 4-year-old children give the correct response of "Smarties/M&Ms" (80 percent versus 40 percent in the original deceptive box task). See also **posting version of the deceptive box test** and **unexpected transfer test**.

Still-face procedure   This procedure is used to examine how changes to an infant's social surroundings affect his or her behavior. Mothers are asked not to respond to their infants as they normally would, but to remain silent and expressionless. Infants respond to this situation with signs of distress, they gaze warily at their mother, give brief smiles followed by sobs, look away for long periods of time, and eventually become very withdrawn and distressed.

Strange situation   Measure, devised by Ainsworth, of the level of attachment a child has with his or her parent. It is typically conducted when the infant is between 1 and 2 years of age and assesses infants' responses to separation from, and subsequent reunion with, their mother, and their reactions to an unfamiliar woman (the so-called stranger). See also **insecure-avoidant**, **insecure-resistant**, and **securely attached**.

Stranger anxiety   Unhappiness felt by many infants when they encounter an unfamiliar person. Stranger anxiety begins to emerge at around 7 months of age.

Structured observation   An **observational study** in which the **independent variable** is systematically controlled and varied, and the investigator then observes the child's behavior. Similar to an experiment but the degree of control is less precise than in a laboratory setting.

Subitizing   The ability to perceive directly a small number of items without consciously counting them or using another form of calculation. This ability only applies to very small numbers.

Subjective contours   When the corners of an object only are presented, the remaining contours are "filled in" in order that the complete shape can be perceived. The lines that are "filled in" are referred to as subjective contours since they are not really there.

Suggestibility   A child's (or adult's) tendency to change his or her memories and beliefs, often in response to interrogation. This is likely to result in inaccurate recall of events.

Superego   In Freud's theory, a collection of ideals, an individual's morality. This is what we refer to as our conscience and it is often in conflict with our **id**. See also **defense mechanisms** and **ego**.

Sure Start   See **Head Start**.

Syllabary   The name given to a language that relies heavily on **syllables** for meaning.

Syllable   The smallest unit of a word whose pronunciation forms a rhythmic break when spoken.

Syllogism   Comprises two statements (called premises) and a conclusion that is derived from the previous statements. For example: If A is a subset of B, and B is a subset of C, A must also be a subset of C.

Symbolic play   See **pretend play**.

Synapse   The connections between **neurons** which enable them to pass messages.

Synaptogenesis   The building of connections (**synapses**) between nerve cells.

Syntactic skills   An understanding of the basic grammar of a language, understanding which order to place words in a sentence.

Syntax   The manner in which words and parts of words are related to one another to produce grammatical sentences: the production of sentences is governed by grammatical structures and rules.

Synthetic models   Naive and immature models or theories that are often replaced by mature models that better represent reality.

T

Theory of development   A scheme or system of ideas that is based on evidence and attempts to explain, describe, and predict behavior and development.

Theory of mind   The understanding that different people may have different emotions, feelings, thoughts, and beliefs from one's own.

Time sampling   An **observational study** that records an individual's behavior at frequent intervals of time.

Top-down structures   Where prior knowledge and experience help us to make sense of what we experience. As an example, **scripts** are top-down structures in that they lead to the automatic generation of expectations about the structure of an event we will experience in the future. Compare with **bottom-up structures**.

Transitive inference   The relation between two (or more) premises (e.g., A > B, B > C) that leads to an inference that is logically necessary (A > C). See also **transitivity task**.

Transitivity task   A task that examines a person's ability to infer a relationship between two or more items that usually cannot be directly compared. For example, the relationship between A and D can be calculated if one knows that A > B, B > C, and C > D, namely, that A > D. See also **syllogism**.

Transnatal learning   Learning that occurs during the **prenatal** period which is remembered during the **postnatal** period.

Trimester   A period of three months. The course of human pregnancy is divided into three trimesters.

Turn-taking   The understanding that during a communicative exchange each participant takes turns to communicate in an alternating fashion.

U

Underextension   Extending the meaning of a word to too few instances, as when a child restricts his or her use of a word like "duck" to situations in which the child is playing with a toy while in the bath, therefore failing to refer to the animals at the park as "ducks." See also **overextension**.

Unexpected transfer test   A third-person version of the **deceptive box task** as a measure of **theory of mind**. In this test a child sees "Maxi" hide a chocolate bar and then leave the room. Maxi's mother then enters the room and moves the chocolate bar from the cupboard to the fridge. The child is then asked where Maxi will search for the chocolate when he returns. Those children who fail the **deceptive box task** are more likely to fail this test also and say that Maxi will search in the fridge. See also **posting version of the deceptive box test** and **state change test**.

Universal counting principles   These are a set of principles that must be obeyed in order for our number system to work. These principles are the **abstraction principle**, the **last-number-counted principle**, the **one-to-one principle**, the **order irrelevance principle**, and the **stable order principle**.

U-shaped functions   Behavior where ability is initially very good, then decreases, and then increases again follows a U-shaped function of development. An inverted U-shaped function follows the opposite trend, initially poor, then getting better, and then becoming poor again.

V

Vestibular system   The system that controls a person's sense of balance. It is found within the ear.

Violation of expectation technique   This technique is used to examine whether infants have any expectations about the world around them. They are typically familiarized with an event sequence, and then presented with two test trials that are variants on the original, one involving a possible event and the other involving an impossible event. If the infants look longer at the impossible event, this is taken as evidence that they have detected the impossibility of the event sequence.

Visual accommodation   The ability to focus on objects irrespective of their distance from the eye. Therefore, as an object moves closer toward us, it does not appear to go in and out of focus.

Visual acuity   The ability to make fine discriminations between the elements in the visual array.

Visual cliff   A piece of apparatus used to study depth perception in infants. The apparatus consists of a glass table with a checkerboard pattern beneath it. At one half of the table the checkerboard pattern is directly below the glass (the "solid" half). At the other half the checkerboard is several feet below the glass top (the "deep" half). Infants are placed on the "solid" half and encouraged by their mothers to crawl to the end of the "deep" half. Infants crawl to the edge of the "solid" half, but usually refuse to crawl on to the "deep" half (although in reality it would be perfectly safe to do so). This indicates that infants perceive (and fear) depth from visual information alone.

Visual illusion   A visual display that is either ambiguous in nature, or that "tricks" the brain into believing something about the display that is not true.

Visual preference technique   This technique is used to examine whether infants have preferences for certain stimuli. Infants are shown two objects (usually 2-D pictures) side by side,
and the amount of time they spend looking at each one is then compared.

W

Wing's triad of impairments   Impairments of (1) social relationships, (2) communication, and
(3) imagination characteristic of **autistic** behavior.

Working memory   **Short-term memory** store in which mental operations such as **rehearsal**
and categorization take place.

Z

Zeitgeist   The thought or feeling peculiar to a generation or period – as in "the prevailing
Zeitgeist" or "the spirit of the age."

Zone of proximal development   The difference between what children can do on their own, and
what they can do under adult guidance or in collaboration with more able **peers**.

References

Abdel-Rahim, A. R., Nagoshi, C. T., & Vandenberg, S. G. (1990). Twin resemblance in cognitive abilities in an Egyptian sample. *Behavior Genetics*, 20, 33–43.

Aboud, F. (1988). *Children and prejudice*. Oxford: Blackwell.

Abrams, R. M., Gerhardt, K. J., & Peters, A. J. M. (1995). Transmission of sound and vibration to the fetus. In J. LeCanuet, W. Fifer, N. Krasnegor, & W. Smotherman (Eds.), *Fetal development: A psychobiological perspective* (pp. 315–30). Hillsdale, NJ: Erlbaum.

Adelson, E., & Fraiberg, S. (1974). Gross motor development in infants blind from birth. *Child Development*, 45, 114–26.

Adolph, K. E., & Avolio, A. M. (2000). Walking infants adapt locomotion to changing body dimensions. *Journal of Experimental Psychology: Human Perception and Performance*, 26, 1148–66.

Adolph, K. E., Vereijken, B., & Denny, M. A. (1998). Learning to crawl. *Child Development*, 69, 1299–1312.

Ahmed, A., & Ruffman, T. (1998). Why do infants make A not B errors in a search task, yet show memory for the location of hidden objects in a nonsearch task? *Developmental Psychology*, 34, 441–53.

Ainsworth, M. D. (1963). The development of infant–mother interaction among the Ganda. In B. M. Foss (Ed.), *Determinants of infant behavior* (Vol. 2). London: Methuen; New York: Wiley.

Ainsworth, M. D. S. (1967). *Infancy in Uganda: Infant care and the growth of love*. Baltimore: Johns Hopkins University Press.

Ainsworth, M. D. S., Bell, S. M., & Stayton, D. J. (1971). Individual differences in strange situation behavior of one-year-olds. In H. R. Schaffer (Ed.), *The origins of human social relations*. New York: Academic Press.

Ainsworth, M. D. S., Bell, S. M., & Stayton, D. J. (1974). Infant–mother attachment and social development: Socialization as a product of reciprocal responsiveness to signals. In M. P. M. Richards (Ed.), *The introduction of the child into a social world*. London: Cambridge University Press.

Ainsworth, M. D. S., Blehar, M. C., Waters, E., & Wall, S. (1978). *Patterns of attachment: Assessed in the strange situation and at home*. Hillsdale, NJ: Erlbaum.

Ainsworth, M. D. S., & Marvin, R. S. (1995). On the shaping of attachment theory and research: An interview with Mary D. S. Ainsworth (Fall 1994). Caregiving, cultural, and cognitive perspectives on secure-base behavior and working models: New growing points in attachment theory and research (pp. 3–21). *Monographs of the Society for Research in Child Development*, 60 (2–3, Serial No. 244).

Ainsworth, M. D. S., & Wittig, B. A. (1969). Attachment and exploratory behavior of one-year-olds in a strange situation. In B. M. Foss (Ed.), *Determinants of infant behavior* (Vol. 4). New York: Barnes & Noble.

Alárcon, M., Plomin, R., Fulker, D. W., Corley, R., & DeFries, J. C. (1999). Molarity not modularity: Multivariate genetic analysis of specific cognitive abilities in parents and their 16-year-old children in the Colorado Adoption Project. *Cognitive Development*, 14, 175–93.

Alimo-Metcalf, B. (2001). Maslow: A different view. *The Psychologist*, 14, 179–80.

Alsaker, F. D., & Flammer, A. (1999). Time use by adolescents in an international perspective: The case of necessary activities. In F. Alsaker & A. Flammer (Eds.), *The adolescent experience: European and American adolescents in the 1990s*. Mahwah, NJ: Erlbaum.

American College of Obstetricians and Gynecologists (1997). Smoking and women's health [Bulletin].

Amsterdam, B. (1972). Mirror self-image reactions before age two. *Developmental Psychology*, 5, 297–305.

Andres, R. L. (1996). The association of cigarette smoking with *placenta previa* and *abruptio placentae*. *Seminars in Perinatology*, 20, 154–9.

Andrews, G., & Halford, G. S. (1998). Children's ability to make transitive inferences: The importance of premise integration and structural complexity. *Cognitive Development*, 13, 479–513.

Anisfeld, M., Turkewitz, G., Rose, S. A., Rosenberg, F. R., Sheiber, F. J., Couturier-Fagan, D. A., Ger, J. S., & Sommer, I. (2001). No compelling evidence that newborns imitate oral gestures. *Infancy*, 2, 111–22.

Antell, S. E., & Keating, D. P. (1983). Perception of numerical invariance in neonates. *Child Development*, 54, 695–701.

Archer, J., & Lloyd, B. (1986). *Sex and gender*. Cambridge: Cambridge University Press.

Arnett, J. J. (1999). Adolescent storm and stress, reconsidered. *American Psychologist*, 54 (5), 317–26.

Ashmead, G. G., & Reed, G. B. (Eds.) (1997). *Essentials of maternal and fetal medicine*. New York: Chapman & Hall.

Averill, L. A. (1982). Recollections of Clark's G. Stanley Hall. *Journal of the History of the Behavioral Sciences*, 18, 341–6.

Avis, J., & Harris, P. (1991). Belief-desire reasoning among Baka children: Evidence for a universal conception of mind. *Child Development*, 62, 460–7.

Babson, T., & Benda, G. (1976). Growth graphs for the clinical assessment of infants of varying gestational age. *Journal of Pediatrics*, 89, 814–20.

Bahrick, H. P., Bahrick, P. O., & Wittlinger, R. P. (1975). Fifty years of memory for names and faces: A cross-sectional approach. *Journal of Experimental Psychology: General*, 104, 54–75.

Baillargeon, R. (1986). Representing the existence and the location of hidden objects: Object permanence in 6- and 8-month-old infants. *Cognition*, 23, 21–41.

Baillargeon, R., & DeVos, J. (1991). Object permanence in young infants: Further evidence. *Child Development*, 62, 1227–46.

Baillargeon, R., Spelke, E. S., & Wasserman, S. (1985). Object permanence in five-month-old infants. *Cognition*, 20, 191–208.

Baker, L. (1994). Fostering metacognitive development. In H. W. Reese (Ed.), *Advances in child development and behavior* (Vol. 25, pp. 201–39). San Diego: Academic Press.

Baker, L., Fernandez-Fein, S., Scher, D., & Williams, H. (1998). Home experiences related to the development of word recognition. In J. L. Metsala & L. C. Ehri (Eds.), *Word recognition in beginning literacy* (pp. 263–87). Hillsdale, NJ: Erlbaum.

Balaban, M., & Waxman, S. (1997). Do words facilitate object categorization in 9-month-old infants? *Journal of Experimental Psychology*, 16, 139–54.

Ball, D., Hill, L., Eley, T., Chorney, M., Chorney, K., Thompson, L. A., Detterman, D. K., Benbow, C., Lubinsky, D., Owen, M., McGuffin, P., & Plomin, R. (1998). Dopamine markers and general cognitive ability. *Neuroreport*, 9, 347–9.

Bandura, A. (1969). Social learning theory of identificatory processes. In D. A. Goslin (Ed.), *Handbook of socialization theory and research* (pp. 213–62). Chicago: Rand McNally.

Bandura, A. (1973). *Aggression: A social learning analysis*. Englewood Cliffs, NJ: Prentice-Hall.

Baranek, G. T. (1999). Autism during infancy: A retrospective video analysis of sensory-motor and social behaviors at 9–12 months of age. *Journal of Autism and Developmental Disorders*, 29, 213–24.

Barber, B., Olsen, J., & Shagle, S. (1994). Associations between parent psychological and behavioral control and youth internalized and externalized behaviors. *Child Development*, 65, 1120–36.

Barberie, J. S., & Light, P. H. (1992). Interaction, gender and performance on a computer-based problem solving task. *Learning and Instruction*, 2, 199–214.

Bargh, J. A., & Chartrand, T. L. (1999). The unbearable automaticity of being. *American Psychologist*, 54, 462–79.

Barker, D. J. (1995). Fetal origins of coronary heart disease. *British Medical Journal*, 311, 171–4.

Baron-Cohen, S. (1989). The autistic child's theory of mind: A case of specific developmental delay. *Journal of Child Psychology and Psychiatry*, 30, 285–97.

Baron-Cohen, S., Allen, J., & Gillberg, C. (1992). Can autism be detected at 18 months? The needle, the haystack and the CHAT. *British Journal of Psychiatry*, 161, 839–42.

Baron-Cohen, S., Leslie, A. M., & Frith, U. (1985). Does the autistic child have a "theory of mind"? *Cognition*, 21, 37–46.

Barrera, M. E., & Maurer, D. (1981). The perception of facial expressions by three-month-olds. *Child Development*, 52, 714–16.

Barrett, K. C., & Campos, J. J. (1987). Perspectives on emotional development II: A functionalist approach to emotions. In J. D. Osofsky (Ed.), *Handbook of infant development* (pp. 555–78). New York: Wiley.

Barrett, M. D. (1986). Early semantic representations and early word-usage. In S. Kuczaj & M. D. Barrett (Eds.), *The development of word meaning* (pp. 39–67). New York: Springer.

Barrett, M. D. (1999). An introduction to the nature of language and to the central themes and issues in the study of language development. In M. D. Barrett (Ed.), *The development of language* (pp. 1–24). Hove: Psychology Press.

Barry, H., III, Bacon, M. K., & Child, I. L. (1957). A cross-cultural survey of some sex differences in socialization. *Journal of Abnormal and Social Psychology*, 55, 327–32.

Barton Evans, F., III. (1996). *Harry Stack Sullivan: Interpersonal theory and psychotherapy*. London: Routledge.

Bateson, M. (1975). Mother–infant exchanges: The epigenesis of conversational interaction. *Annals of the New York Academy of Sciences*, 263, 101–13.

Baumrind, D. (1967). Child care practices anteceding three patterns of preschool behavior. *Genetic Psychology Monographs*, 75, 43–88.

Baumrind, D. (1978). Parental disciplinary patterns and social competence in children. *Youth and Society*, 9, 239–76.

Bayley, N. (1949). Consistency and variability in the growth of intelligence from birth to eighteen years. *Journal of Genetic Psychology*, 75, 165–96.

Beeghly, M., Weiss-Perry, B., & Cicchetti, D. (1990). Beyond sensorimotor functioning: Early communicative and play development of children with Down syndrome. In D. Cicchetti & M. Beeghly (Eds.), *Children with Down syndrome: A developmental perspective* (pp. 329–68). Cambridge: Cambridge University Press.

Behrend, D. A. (1995). Processes involved in the initial mapping of verb meanings. In M. Tomasello & W. Merriman (Eds.), *Beyond names for things: Young children's acquisition of verbs* (pp. 251–73). Hillsdale, NJ: Erlbaum.

Beilin, H. (1992). Piaget's enduring contribution to developmental psychology. *Developmental Psychology*, 28, 191–204.

Belsky, J., Spritz, B., & Crnic, K. (1996). Infant attachment security and affective-cognitive information processing at age 3. *Psychological Science*, 7, 111–14.

Bendixen, M., & Olweus, D. (1999). Measurement of antisocial behavior in adolescence and preadolescence: Psychometric properties and substantive findings. *Criminal Behavior and Mental Health*, 9, 323–54.

Benoit, D., & Parker, K. (1994). Stability and transmission of attachment across three generations. *Child Development*, 65, 1444–56. Reprinted in D. Muir & A. Slater (Eds.) (2000), *Infant development: Essential readings* (pp. 319–39). Cambridge, MA, & Oxford: Blackwell.

Berger, J. (1990). Interactions between parents and their infants with Down syndrome. In D. Cicchetti & M. Beeghly (Eds.), *Children with Down syndrome: A developmental perspective* (pp. 101–46). Cambridge: Cambridge University Press.

Berko, J., & Brown, R. (1960). Psycholinguistic research methods. In P. Mussen (Ed.), *Handbook on research methods in child development* (pp. 517–57). New York: Wiley.

Bertenthal, B. J., Campos, J. J., & Haith, M. M. (1980). Development of visual organization: The perception of subjective contours. *Child Development*, 51, 1075–80.

Besag, V. (1989). *Bullies and victims in schools*. Milton Keynes: Open University Press.

Best, D. L., & Ornstein, P. A. (1986). Children's generation and communication of mnemonic organization strategies. *Developmental Psychology*, 22, 845–53.

Beuhring, T., & Kee, D. W. (1987). Developmental relationships among metamemory, elaborative strategy use, and associative memory. *Journal of Experimental Child Psychology*, 44, 377–400.

Bever, T. (1970). The cognitive basis for linguistic structures. In J. Hayes (Ed.), *Cognition and the development of language* (pp. 279–352). New York: Wiley.

Bigelow, A. E. (1986). The development of reaching in blind children. *British Journal of Developmental Psychology*, 4, 355–66.

Bigelow, A. E. (1987). Early words of blind children. *Journal of Child Language*, 14, 47–56.

Bigelow, A. E. (1988). Blind children's concepts of how people see. *Journal of Visual Impairment and Blindness*, 82, 65–8.

Bigelow, A. E. (1991). Hiding in blind and sighted children. *Development and Psychopathology*, 3, 301–10.

Bigelow, A. E. (1992). Blind children's ability to predict what another sees. *Journal of Visual Impairment and Blindness*, 86, 181–4.

Bigelow, B. J., & La Gaipa, J. J. (1980). The development of friendship values and choice. In H. C. Foot, A. J. Chapman, & J. R. Smith (Eds.), *Friendship and social relations in children* (pp. 15–44). Chichester: Wiley.

Binet, A. (1905). La science du témoignage [The science of testimony]. *Année Psychologique*, 15, v–vii.

Bjaalid, I., Hoien, T., & Lundberg, I. (1996). The contribution of orthographic and phonological processes to word reading in Norwegian readers. *Reading and Writing*, 8, 189–98.

Bjorklund, D. F., Coyle, T. R., & Gaultney, J. F. (1992). Developmental differences in the acquisition and maintenance of an organization strategy: Evidence for the utilization deficiency hypothesis. *Journal of Experimental Child Psychology*, 54, 434–48.

Bjorklund, D. F., & Schneider, W. (1996). The interaction of knowledge, aptitude, and strategies in children's memory performance. In H. W. Reese (Ed.), *Advances in child development and behavior* (Vol. 26, pp. 59–89). San Diego: Academic Press.

Björkqvist, K., Ekman, K., & Lagerspetz, K. (1982). Bullies and victims: Their ego picture, ideal ego picture and normative ego picture. *Scandinavian Journal of Psychology*, 23, 307–13.

Blake, J., O'Rourke, P., & Borzellino, G. (1994). Form and function in the development of pointing and reaching gestures. *Infant Behavior and Development*, 17, 195–203.

Blank, M., & Franklin, E. (1980). Dialogue with preschoolers: A cognitively based system of assessment. *Applied Psycholinguistics*, 1, 127–50.

Blasi, A. (1980). Bridging moral cognition and moral action: A critical review of the literature. *Psychological Bulletin*, 88, 1–45.

Blaye, A., Light, P. II., Joiner, R., & Sheldon, S. (1991). Collaboration as a facilitator of planning and problem solving on a computer-based task. *British Journal of Developmental Psychology*, 9, 471–83.

Bloom, L. M. (1973). *One word at a time: The use of single-word utterances before syntax*. The Hague: Mouton.

Bloom, L. M. (1991). *Language development from two to three*. New York: Cambridge University Press.

Bloom, L., Margolis, O., Tinker, E., & Fujita, N. (1996). Early conversations and word learning: Contributions from child and adult. *Child Development*, 67, 3154–75.

Bloom, P. (1990). Syntactic distinctions in child language. *Journal of Child Language*, 17, 343–55.

Bloom, P. (1994). Possible names: The role of syntax-semantic mappings in the acquisition of nominals. In L. Gleitman & B. Landau (Eds.), *The acquisition of the lexicon* (pp. 297–329). Cambridge, MA: MIT Press.

Bloom, P., & Kelemen, D. (1995). Syntactic cues in the acquisition of collective nouns. *Cognition*, 56, 1–30.

Blos, P. (1972). The child analyst looks at the young adolescent. In J. Kagan & R. Coles (Eds.), *12 to 16: Early adolescence*. New York: W. W. Norton.

Bock, R. D., & Vandenberg, S. G. (1968). Components of heritable variation in mental test scores. In S. G. Vandenberg (Ed.), *Progress in human behavior genetics* (pp. 233–60). Baltimore: Johns Hopkins University Press.

Bouchard, T. J. (1998). Genetic and environmental influences on adult intelligence and special mental abilities. *Human Biology*, 70, 257–79.

Bouchard, T. J., Lykken, D. T., McGue, M., Segal, N. L., & Tellegen, A. (1990). Sources of human psychological differences: The Minnesota Study of Twins Reared Apart. *Science*, 250, 223–8.

Bouchard, T. J., Jr., & McGue, M. (1981). Familial studies of intelligence: A review. *Science*, 250, 223–38.

Boucher, J., Lewis, V., & Collis, G. (1998). Familiar face and voice matching and recognition in children with autism. *Journal of Child Psychology*, 39, 171–81.

Boulton, M. J., & Smith, P. K. (1993). Ethnic and gender partner and activity preferences in mixed-race schools in the UK: Playground observations. In C. H. Hart (Ed.), *Children on playgrounds* (pp. 210–37). New York: SUNY Press.

Boulton, M. J., & Smith, P. K. (1994). Bully/victim problems among middle school children: Stability, self-perceived competence, and peer acceptance. *British Journal of Developmental Psychology*, 12, 315–29.

Bower, G. H. (1970). Organizational factors in memory. *Cognitive Psychology*, 1, 18–46.

Bower, T. G. R., & Wishart, J. G. (1972). The effects of motor skill on object permanence. *Cognition*, 1, 165–72.

Bower, T. G. R., & Wishart, J. G. (1979). Toward a unitary theory of development. In E. B. Thoman (Ed.), *Origins of the infant's social responsiveness* (pp. 65–94). Hillsdale, NJ: Erlbaum.

Bowerman, M. (1981). Cross-cultural perspectives on language development. In H. C. Triandis & A. Heron (Eds.), *Handbook of cross-cultural psychology* (Vol. 4, pp. 93–185). Boston: Allyn & Bacon.

Bowey, J., Cain, M. T., & Ryan, S. M. (1992). A reading-level design study of phonological skills underlying fourth-grade children's word reading difficulties. *Child Development*, 63, 999–1011.

Bowlby, J. (1952). *Maternal care and mental health*. Geneva: World Health Organization.

Bowlby, J. (1958). The nature of the child's tie to his mother. *International Journal of Psycho-Analysis*, 41, 350–73.

Bowlby, J. (1969). *Attachment and loss. Vol. 1. Attachment*. London: Hogarth Press.

Bowlby, J. (1980). *Attachment and loss. Vol. 3. Loss*. London: Hogarth Press.

Bowler, D. M. (1992). "Theory of mind" in Asperger's syndrome. *Journal of Child Psychology and Psychiatry*, 33, 877–93.

Boysson-Bardies, B., de Sagart, L., & Durand, C. (1984). Discernible differences in the babbling of infants according to target language. *Journal of Child Language*, 11, 1–15.

Bradley, L., & Bryant, P. E. (1983). Categorising sounds and learning to read: A causal connection. *Nature*, 301, 419–521.

Braine, M. D. S. (1971). The acquisition of language in infant and child. In C. Reed (Ed.), *The learning of language*. New York: Appleton-Century-Crofts.

Brainerd, C. J., Kingma, J., & Howe, M. L. (1985). On the development of forgetting. *Child Development*, 56, 1103–19.

Brainerd, C., Reyna, V. F., Howe, M. L., & Kingma, J. (1990). The development of forgetting and reminiscence. *Monographs of the Society for Research on Child Development*, 55 (3–4, Serial No. 222).

Bratko, D. (1996). Twin study of verbal and spatial abilities. *Personality and Individual Differences*, 21, 621–4.

Bremner, J. G. (2001). Cognitive development: Knowledge of the physical world. In J. G. Bremner & A. Fogel (Eds.), *Blackwell handbook of infant development* (pp. 99–138). Cambridge, MA, and Oxford: Blackwell.

Bremner, J. G., & Knowles, L. S. (1984). Piagetian stage IV errors with an object that is directly accessible both visually and manually. *Perception*, 13, 307–14.

Brennan, M., & Brennan, R. (1988). *Strange language*. Wagga Wagga, NSW: Riverina Muury Institute of Higher Education.

Bretherton, I., & Beeghly, M. (1982). Talking about internal states: The acquisition of an explicit theory of mind. *Developmental Psychology*, 18, 906–21.

Bretherton, I., McNew, S., & Beeghly-Smith, M. (1981). Early person knowledge as expressed in gestural and verbal communication: When do infants acquire a "theory of mind"? In M. E. Lamb & L. R. Sherrod (Eds.), *Infant social cognition*. Hillsdale, NJ: Erlbaum.

Bretherton, I., & Waters, E. (Eds.) (1985). Growing points of attachment theory and research. *Monographs of the Society for Research in Child Development*, 50 (1–2).

Brinton, B., & Fujiki, M. (1984). Development of topic manipulation skills in discourse. *Journal of Hearing and Speech Research*, 27, 350–8.

Brinton, B., Fujiki, M., Loeb, D., & Winkler, E. (1986). Development of conversational repair strategies in response to requests for clarification. *Journal of Hearing and Speech Research*, 29, 75–81.

Bronfenbrenner, U. (1979). *The ecology of human development*. Cambridge, MA: Harvard University Press.

Brown, A. L., & Smiley, S. S. (1978). The development of strategies for studying texts. *Child Development*, 49, 1076–88.

Brown, B. B. (1990). Peer groups and peer cultures. In S. S. Feldman & G. R. Elliott (Eds.), *At the threshold* (pp. 171–96). Cambridge, MA: Harvard University Press.

Brown, B. B. (1999). "You're going out with who?": Peer group influences on adolescent romantic relationships. In W. Furman, B. B. Brown, & C. Feiring (Eds.), *The development of romantic relationships in adolescence* (pp. 291–329). New York: Cambridge University Press.

Brown, J. R., & Dunn, J. (1996). Continuities in emotion understanding from three to six years. *Child Development*, 67, 789–802.

Brown, R. W. (1973). *A first language: The early stages*. Cambridge, MA: Harvard University Press.

Brown, R. W., & Hanlon, C. (1970). Derivational complexity and order of acquisition. In J. R. Hayes (Ed.), *Cognition and the development of language* (pp. 11–54). New York: Wiley.

Bruce, D. J. (1964). The analysis of word sounds. *British Journal of Educational Psychology*, 34, 158–70.

Bruck, M., & Ceci, S. J. (1999). The suggestibility of children's memory. *Annual Review of Psychology*, 50, 419–39.

Bruck, M., Ceci, S. J., Francoeur, E., & Barr, R. J. (1995). "I hardly cried when I got my shot!": Influencing children's reports about a visit to their pediatrician. *Child Development*, 66, 193–208.

Bruck, M., Ceci, S. J., Francoeur, E., & Renick, A. (1995). Anatomically detailed dolls do not facilitate preschoolers' reports of a pediatric examination involving genital touch. *Journal of Experimental Psychology: Applied*, 1, 95–109.

Bruner, J. S. (1966). On the conservation of liquids. In J. S. Bruner, R. R. Olver, & P. M. Greenfield (Eds.), *Studies in cognitive growth*. New York: Wiley.

Bruner, J. S. (1983). *Child's talk: Learning to use language*. Oxford: Oxford University Press.

Bruno, J. E. (1996). Time perceptions and time allocation preferences among adolescent boys and girls. *Adolescence*, 31 (121), 109–26.

Bryant, P. E. (1990). Empirical evidence for causes in development. In G. Butterworth & P. Bryant (Eds.), *Causes of development*. Brighton: Harvester Wheatsheaf.

Bryant, P. E. (1992). Arithmetic in the cradle. *Nature*, 358, 712–13.

Bryant, P. (2001). Children's thoughts about reading and spelling. *Scientific Study of Reading*, 5.

Bryant, P., & Cavendish, M. (2001). Two hypotheses about the phonological connection with reading. Paper presented to the Meeting of the Society for the Scientific Study of Reading, Boulder, Colorado, USA (July).

Bryant, P., Devine, M., Ledward, A., & Nunes, T. (1997). Spelling with apostrophes and understanding possession. *British Journal of Educational Psychology*, 67, 93–112.

Bryant, P., MacLean, M., & Bradley, L. (1990). Rhyme, language, and children's reading. *Applied Psycholinguistics*, 11, 237–52.

Bryant, P. E., MacLean, M., Bradley, L. L., & Crossland, J. (1990). Rhyme, alliteration, phoneme detection and learning to read. *Developmental Psychology*, 26, 429–38.

Bryant, P., Nunes, T., & Aidinis, A. (1999). Different morphemes, same spelling problems: Cross-linguistic developmental studies. In M. Harris & G. Hatano (Eds.), *Learning to read and write: A cross-linguistic perspective* (pp. 112–33). Cambridge: Cambridge University Press.

Bryant, P. E., & Trabasso, T. (1971). Transitive inference and memory in young children. *Nature*, 232, 256–458.

Buchanan, C., Eccles, J., & Becker, J. (1992). Are adolescents the victims of raging hormones? Evidence for activational effects on mood and behavior at adolescence. *Psychological Bulletin*, 111, 62–107.

Buckley, S. (1993). Language development in children with Down's syndrome. *Down's Syndrome: Research and Practice*, 1, 3–9.

Bullying. (1996). Video. South Carolina Educational Television, Columbia, SC 29211, United States.

Burks, B. S. (1928). The relative influence of nature and nurture upon mental development: A comparative study of foster parent–offspring child resemblance and true parent–true child resemblance. *Yearbook of the National Society for the Study of Education, Pt. I*, 219–316.

Bushnell, I. W. R. (2001). Mother's face recognition in newborn infants: Learning and memory. *Infant and Child Development*, 10, 67–74.

Bushnell, I. W. R., Sai, F., & Mullin, J. T. (1989). Neonatal recognition of the mother's face. *British Journal of Developmental Psychology, 7,* 3–15.

Butterfield, E., & Siperstein, G. N. (1974). Influence of contingent auditory stimulation upon non-nutritional suckle. In J. Bosma (Ed.), *Oral sensation and perception.* Springfield, IL: Charles C. Thomas.

Butterworth, B. (1999). *The mathematical brain.* London: Macmillan.

Butterworth, G. (1974). The development of the object concept in human infants. Unpublished D.Phil. thesis, University of Oxford.

Butterworth, G. (1977). Object disappearance and error in Piaget's stage IV task. *Journal of Experimental Child Psychology, 23,* 391–401.

Butterworth, G. (1995). Origins of mind in perception and action. In C. Moore & P. J. Dunham (Eds.), *Joint attention: Its origins and role in development.* Hillsdale, NJ: Erlbaum.

Butterworth, G. E., & Grover, L. (1988). The origins of referential communication in human infancy. In L. Weiskrantz (Ed.), *Thought without language* (pp. 5–24). Oxford: Oxford University Press.

Butterworth, G., & Grover, L. (1990). Joint visual attention, manual pointing, and preverbal communication in human infancy. In M. Jeannerod (Ed.), *Attention and performance XIII.* Hillsdale, NJ: Erlbaum.

Cairns, R. B., Cairns, B. D., Neckerman, H. J., Gest, S. D., & Gariépy, J. L. (1988). Social networks and aggressive behavior: Peer acceptance or peer rejection? *Developmental Psychology, 24,* 815–23.

Call, J., & Tomasello, M. (1994). Production and comprehension of referential pointing by orangutans (*Pongo pygmaeus*). *Journal of Comparative Psychology, 108,* 307–17.

Campos, J. J., Anderson, D. I., Barbu-Roth, M. A., Hubbard, E. M., Hertenstein, M. J., & Witherington, D. (2000). Travel broadens the mind. *Infancy, 1,* 149–219.

Canter, S. (1973). Personality traits in twins. In G. Claridge, S. Canter, & W. I. Hume, *Personality differences and biological variation* (pp. 21–51). New York: Pergamon.

Capon, N., & Kuhn, D. (1979). Logical reasoning in the supermarket: Adult females' use of a proportional reasoning strategy in an everyday context. *Developmental Psychology, 15,* 450–2.

Capron, C., & Duyme, M. (1989). Assessment of effects of socio-economic status on IQ in a full cross-fostering study. *Nature, 340,* 552–4.

Cardon, L. R., & Fulker, D. W. (1994). Genetics of specific cognitive abilities. In R. Plomin & G. E. McClearn (Eds.), *Nature and nurture and psychology* (pp. 99–120). Washington, DC: American Psychological Association.

Carey, S. (1978). The child as a word learner. In M. Halle, J. Bresnan, & G. Miller (Eds.), *Linguistic theory and psychological reality* (pp. 264–93). Cambridge, MA: MIT Press.

Carey, S., & Diamond, R. (1977). From piecemeal to configurational representation of faces. *Science, 195,* 312–14.

Carlson, E. A. (1998). A prospective longitudinal study of attachment disorganization/disorientation. *Child Development, 69,* 1107–28.

Carlson, V., Cicchetti, D., Barnett, D., & Braunwald, K. (1989). Disorganized/disoriented attachment relationships in maltreated infants. *Developmental Psychology, 25,* 525–31.

Caron, A. J., Caron, R. F., & Myers, R. S. (1982). Abstraction of invariant face expressions in infancy. *Child Development, 53,* 1008–15.

Carpenter, G. C. (1974). Mother's face and the newborn. *New Scientist, 61,* 742–4.

Carpenter, M., Nagell, K., & Tomasello, M. (1998). Social cognition, joint attention, and communicative competence from 9 to 15 months of age. *Monographs of the Society for Research in Child Development, 63* (4, Serial No. 255).

Carr, J. (1988). Six weeks to twenty-one years old: A longitudinal study of children with Down's syndrome and their families. *Journal of Child Psychology and Psychiatry, 29,* 407–31.

Carr, J. (1994). Long-term outcome for people with Down's syndrome. *Journal of Child Psychology and Psychiatry*, 35, 425–39.

Carr, M., Kurtz, B. E., Schneider, W., Turner, L. A., & Borkowski, J. G. (1989). Strategy acquisition and transfer: Environmental influences on metacognitive development. *Developmental Psychology*, 25, 765–71.

Caruso, D. R. (1983). Sample differences in genetics and intelligence data: Sibling and parent–offspring studies. *Behavior Genetics*, 13, 453–8.

Case, R. (1974). Structure and strictures: Some functional limitations on the course of cognitive growth. *Cognitive Psychology*, 6, 544–73.

Case, R. (1985). *Intellectual development: Birth to adulthood*. New York: Academic Press.

Caspi, A., Henry, B., McGee, R. O., Moffitt, T. E., & Silva, P. A. (1995). Temperamental origins of child and adolescent behavior problems: From age three to fifteen. *Child Development*, 66, 55–68.

Cassidy, J. (1994). Emotion regulation: Influences of attachment relationships. In N. Fox (Ed.), The development of emotion regulation: Biological and behavioral constraints (pp. 228–50). *Monographs of the Society for Research in Child Development*, 59 (2–3, Serial No. 240).

Cattell, R. B. (1941). Some theoretical issues in adult intelligence testing. *Psychological Bulletin*, 38, 562.

Cattell, R. B. (1971). *Abilities: Their structure, growth, and action*. Boston: Houghton-Mifflin.

Ceci, S. J. (1991). Some overarching issues in the child suggestibility debate. In J. L. Doris (Ed.), *The suggestibility of children's recollections* (pp. 1–9). Washington, DC: American Psychological Association.

Ceci, S. J. (1996). *On intelligence: A bioecological treatise*. Cambridge, MA: Harvard University Press.

Ceci, S. J. (1997). False beliefs: Developmental and clinical implications. In D. L. Schacter, J. T. Coyle, G. D. Fischbach, M. M. Mesulam, & L. E. Sullivan (Eds.), *Memory distortion*. Cambridge, MA: Harvard University Press.

Ceci, S. J., & Bronfenbrenner, U. (1985). Don't forget to take the cupcakes out of the oven: Prospective memory, strategic time-monitoring, and context. *Child Development*, 56, 150–65.

Ceci, S. J., & Bruck, M. (1993). The suggestibility of the child witness: A historical review and synthesis. *Psychological Bulletin*, 113, 403–39.

Ceci, S. J., Crotteau-Huffman, M., Smith, E., & Loftus, E. W. (1994). Repeatedly thinking about non-events. *Consciousness and Cognition*, 3, 388–407.

Ceci, S. J., & DeSimone, M. (1992). "I know that you know that I know who broke the toy": Recursivity in three-year-olds. In S. J. Ceci, M. DeSimone, & M. Putnick (Eds.), *Cognitive and social factors in preschoolers' deception*. Hillsdale, NJ: Erlbaum.

Ceci, S. J., DeSimone, M., Putnick, M., Lee, J. M., & Toglia, M. (1990). Motives to lie. Paper presented at the Biennial Meeting of the American Psychology/Law Society, Williamsburg, VA (March).

Ceci, S. J., & Friedman, R. D. (in press). The suggestibility of children: Scientific research and legal implications. *Cornell Law Review*.

Ceci, S. J., Leichtman, M. D., & Putnick, M. (1992). *Cognitive and social factors in early deception*. Hillsdale, NJ: Erlbaum.

Ceci, S. J., & Liker, J. K. (1986). A day at the races: A study of IQ, expertise, and cognitive complexity. *Journal of Experimental Psychology*, 115, 255–66.

Ceci, S. J., Ross, D., & Toglia, M. (1987). Suggestibility of children's memory: Psycholegal implications. *Journal of Experimental Psychology: General*, 116, 38–49.

Chaney, C. (1992). Language development, metalinguistic skills and print awareness in 3-year-old children. *Applied Psycholinguistics*, 15, 485–514.

Chapman, M., & McBride, M. (1992). Beyond competence and performance: Children's class inclusion strategies, subordinate class cues, and verbal justifications. *Developmental Psychology*, 28, 319–27.

Charman, T., Swettenham, J., Baron-Cohen, S., Cox, A., Baird, G., & Drew, A. (2000). An experimental investigation of social-cognitive abilities in infants with autism: Clinical implications. In D. Muir & A. Slater (Eds.), *Infant development: The essential readings* (pp. 343–63). Cambridge, MA, and Oxford: Blackwell.

Cherny, S. (1994). Home environmental influences on general cognitive ability. In J. C. DeFries, R. Plomin, & D. W. Fulker (Eds.), *Nature and nurture during middle childhood* (pp. 262–80). Cambridge, MA, and Oxford: Blackwell.

Cherny, S. S., Cardon, L. R., Fulker, D. W., & DeFries, J. C. (1992). Differential heritability across levels of cognitive ability. *Behavior Genetics*, 22, 153–62.

Chi, M. (1978). Knowledge structures and memory development. In R. S. Siegler (Ed.), *Children's thinking: What develops?* (pp. 73–96). Hillsdale, NJ: Erlbaum.

Chi, M. T. H., & Ceci, S. J. (1987). Content knowledge: Its role, representation, and restructuring in memory development. In H. W. Reese (Ed.), *Advances in child development and behavior* (Vol. 20, pp. 91–142). San Diego: Academic Press.

Chipuer, H. M., Rovine, M., & Plomin, R. (1990). LISREL modeling: Genetic and environmental influences on IQ revisited. *Intelligence*, 14, 11–29.

Chisholm, K. (1998). A three-year follow-up of attachment and indiscriminate friendliness in children adopted from Romanian orphanages. *Child Development*, 69, 1092–1106.

Chomsky, N. (1957). *Syntactic structures*. The Hague: Mouton.

Chomsky, N. (1972). *Language and mind*. New York: Harcourt Brace Jovanovich.

Chomsky, N. (1975). *Rules and representations*. Oxford: Blackwell.

Chomsky, N. (1981). *Lectures on government and binding*. Dordrecht: Foris.

Chomsky, N. (1982). *Some concepts and consequences of the theory of government and binding*. Cambridge, MA: MIT Press.

Chomsky, N. (1986). *Knowledge of language: Its nature, origins and use*. New York: Praeger.

Chomsky, N. (1987). Language in a psychological setting. *Working Papers in Linguistics*, No. 22. Tokyo, Japan.

Chomsky, N. (1988). *Language and problems of knowledge: The Nicaraguan lectures*. Cambridge, MA: MIT Press.

Christie, J. F., & Johnson, E. P. (1985). Questioning the results of play training research. *Educational Psychology*, 20, 7–11.

Chukovsky, K. (1963). *From two to five*. Berkeley: University of California Press.

Chung, M., & Thomson, D. M. (1995). Development of face recognition. *British Journal of Psychology*, 86, 55–87.

Cillessen, A. H. N., van IJzendoorn, H. W., van Lieshout, C. F. M., & Hartup, W. W. (1992). Heterogeneity among peer-rejected boys: Subtypes and stabilities. *Child Development*, 63, 893–905.

Clark, A. H., Wyon, S. M., & Richards, M. P. M. (1969). Free-play in nursery school children. *Journal of Child Psychology and Psychiatry*, 10, 205–16.

Clark, E. V. (1973). What's in a word? On the child's acquisition of semantics in his first language. In T. F. Moore (Ed.), *Cognitive development and the acquisition of language* (pp. 65–110). New York: Academic Press.

Clark, E. V. (1993). *The lexicon in acquisition*. Cambridge: Cambridge University Press.

Clark, P. M., Atton, C., Law, C. M., Shiell, A., Godfrey, K., & Barker, D. J. (1998). Weight gain in pregnancy, tricept skinfold thickness, and blood pressure in offspring. *Obstetrics and Gynecology*, 91, 103–7.

Clearfield, M. W., & Mix, K. S. (1999). Number vs. contour length in infants' discrimination of small visual sets. *Psychological Science*, 10, 408–11.

Cloninger, S. C. (1993). *Theories of personality: Understanding persons*. Englewood Cliffs, NJ: Prentice-Hall.

Cohen, L. B., & Younger, B. A. (1984). Infant perception of angular relations. *Infant Behavior and Development, 7*, 37–47.

Coie, J. D., & Dodge, K. A. (1998). Aggression and antisocial behavior. In N. Eisenberg (Ed.), *Handbook of child psychology* (5th ed.). *Vol. 3. Social, emotional, and personality development* (pp. 779–840). New York: Wiley.

Coie, J. D., Dodge, K. A., & Coppotelli, H. (1983). Dimensions and types of social status: A cross-age perspective. *Developmental Psychology, 18*, 557–70.

Colby, A., & Damon, W. (1995). The development of extraordinary moral commitment. In M. Killen & D. Hart (Eds.), *Morality in everyday life: Developmental perspectives* (pp. 342–70). New York: Cambridge University Press.

Colby, A., Kohlberg, L., Gibbs, J., & Lieberman, M. (1994). A longitudinal study of moral judgment. In B. Puka et al. (Eds.), *New research in moral development. Moral development: A compendium* (Vol. 5, pp. 1–124). New York: Garland.

Cole, P. M. (1986). Children's spontaneous control of facial expression. *Child Development, 63*, 314–24.

Collaer, M. L., & Hines, M. (1995). Human behavioral sex differences: A role for gonadal hormones during early development? *Psychological Bulletin, 118*, 55–107.

Colley, A., Griffiths, D., Hugh, M., Landers, K., & Jaggli, N. (1996). Childhood play and adolescent leisure preferences: Association with gender typing and the presence of siblings. *Sex Roles, 36* (3/4), 233–45.

Collis, G. M., & Schaffer, H. R. (1975). Synchronization of visual attention in mother–infant pairs. *Journal of Child Psychology and Psychiatry, 16*, 315–20.

Committee on Communications. (1995). Children, adolescents, and television. *Pediatrics, 96*, 786–7.

Committee on Public Communications. (2001). Children, adolescents, and television. *Pediatrics, 107*, 423–6.

Commons, M. L., Miller, P. M., & Kuhn, D. (1982). The relation between formal operational reasoning and academic course selection and performance among college freshmen and sophomores. *Journal of Applied Developmental Psychology, 3*, 1–10.

Comstock, G. C., & Strasburger, V. C. (1993). Media violence: Q & A. *Adolescent Medicine, 4*, 505–9.

Connolly, J., & Goldberg, A. (1999). Romantic relationships in adolescence: The role of friends and peers in their emergence and development. In W. Furman, B. B. Brown, & C. Feiring (Eds.), *The development of romantic relationships in adolescence* (pp. 266–90). New York: Cambridge University Press.

Copeland, R. W. (1979). *How children learn mathematics*. New York: Macmillan.

Corsale, K., & Ornstein, P. A. (1980). Developmental changes in children's use of semantic information in recall. *Journal of Experimental Child Psychology, 30*, 231–45.

Cossu, G., Rossini, F., & Marshall, J. C. (1993). When reading is acquired but phonemic awareness is not: A study of literacy in Down's syndrome. *Cognition, 46*, 129–38.

Covell, K., & Abramovitch, R. (1987). Understanding emotion in the family: Children's and parents' attributions of happiness, sadness, and anger. *Child Development, 58*, 985–91.

Cowan, R., & Daniels, H. (1989). The children's use of counting and guidelines in judging relative numbers. *British Journal of Educational Psychology, 59*, 200–10.

Cowen, E. L. (1984). A general structural model for primary program development in mental health. *Personnel and Guidance Journal, 62*, 485–90.

Cowie, H., Smith, P. K., Boulton, M., & Laver, R. (1994). *Cooperative group work in the multi-ethnic classroom*. London: David Fulton.

Crick, N. R., Casas, J. F., & Mosher, M. (1997). Relational and overt aggression in preschool. *Developmental Psychology*, 33, 579–88.

Crick, N. R., & Dodge, K. (1994). A review and reformulation of social-information processing mechanisms in children's social adjustment. *Psychological Bulletin*, 115, 74–101.

Crick, N. R., & Ladd, G. W. (1990). Children's perceptions of the outcomes of aggressive strategies: Do the ends justify being mean? *Developmental Psychology*, 26, 612–20.

Cronin, V., & Carver, P. (1998). Phonological sensitivity, rapid naming and beginning reading. *Applied Psycholinguistics*, 19, 447–61.

Crook, C. K. (1994). *Computers and the collaborative experience of learning.* London: Routledge.

Csikszentmihalyi, M., & Larson, R. (1984). *Being adolescent.* New York: Basic Books.

Culley, L. (1993). Gender equity and computing in secondary schools. In J. Benyon & H. McKay (Eds.), *Computers into classrooms.* London: Falmer Press.

Cummings, E. M., Pellegrini, D. S., & Notarius, C. I. (1989). Children's responses to angry adult behavior as a function of marital distress and history of intraparent hostility. *Child Development*, 60, 1035–43.

Cummings, E. M., Zahn-Waxler, C., & Radke-Yarrow, M. (1981). Young children's response to expressions of anger and affection by others in the family. *Child Development*, 52, 1275–82.

Cummings, E. M., Zahn-Waxler, C., & Radke-Yarrow, M. (1984). Developmental changes in children's reactions to anger in the home. *Journal of Child Psychology and Psychiatry*, 25, 63–74.

Cunningham, C. C. (1982). *Down syndrome: Introduction for parents.* London: Souvenir Press.

Damon, W. (1977). *The social world of the child.* San Francisco: Jossey-Bass.

Damon, W. (1999). The moral development of children. *Scientific American*, 281, 72–9.

Daniels, J., Holmans, P., Williams, N., Turic, D., McGuffin, P., Plomin, R., & Owen, M. J. (1998). A simple method for analyzing microsatellite allele image patterns generated from DNA pools and its application to allelic association studies. *American Journal of Human Genetics*, 62, 1189–97.

Darwin, C. (1872). *The expression of emotions in man and animals.* London: John Murray.

Darwin, C. (1877). A biographical sketch of an infant. In A. Slater & D. Muir (Eds.) (1999), *The Blackwell reader in developmental psychology* (pp. 18–26). Cambridge, MA, & Oxford: Blackwell.

Dasen, P. R., & Heron, A. (1981). Cross-cultural tests of Piaget's theory. In H. Triandis & A. Heron (Eds.), *Handbook of cross-cultural psychology. Vol. 4. Developmental psychology.* Boston: Allyn & Bacon.

Davey, A. (1983). *Learning to be prejudiced: Growing up in multi-ethnic Britain.* London: Arnold.

Davidson, R. G., & Zeesman, S. (1994). Genetic aspects. In G. Koren (Ed.), *Maternal-fetal toxicology* (pp. 575–600). New York: Marcel Dekker.

Davis, A. M. (1991). Piaget, teachers and education. In P. Light, S. Sheldon, & M. Woodhead (Eds.), *Child development in social context. Vol. 2. Learning to think.* London: Routledge.

DeCasper, A. J., & Fifer, W. P. (1980). Of human bonding: Newborns prefer their mothers' voices. *Science*, 208, 1174–6.

DeCasper, A. J., LeCanuet, J.-P., Bunuel, M.-C., Granier Deferre, C., & Maugeais, R. (1994). Foetal reactions to recurrent maternal speech. *Infant Behavior and Development*, 17, 159–64.

DeCasper, A. J. & Prescott, P. A. (1984). Human newborns' perception of male voices: Preference, discrimination, and reinforcing value. *Developmental Psychobiology*, 17 (5), 481–91.

DeCasper, A. J. & Sigafoos, A. D. (1983). The intrauterine heartbeat: A potent reinforcer for newborns. *Infant Behavior and Development*, 6, 19–25.

DeCasper, A. J., & Spence, M. J. (1986). Prenatal maternal speech influences newborns' perception of speech sounds. *Infant Behavior and Development*, 9, 133–50.

Deese, J. (1993). Human abilities versus intelligence. *Intelligence*, 17, 107–16.

DeFries, J. C., Corey, R. P., Johnson, R. C., Vandenberg, S. C., & Wilson, J. R. (1982). Sex-by-generation and ethnic group-by-generation interactions in the Hawaii Family Study of Cognition. *Behavior Genetics*, 12, 223–30.

DeFries, J. C., Johnson, R. C., Kuse, A. P., McClearn, G. E., Polovina, J., Vandenberg, S. G., & Wilson, J. R. (1979). Familial resemblance for specific cognitive abilities. *Behavior Genetics*, 9, 23–43.

Dehaene, S. (1997). *The number sense.* London: Penguin.

DeLaguna, G. (1927). *Speech: Its function and development.* Bloomington: Indiana University Press.

De Lisi, R., & Staudt, J. (1980). Individual differences in college students' performance on formal operations tasks. *Journal of Applied Developmental Psychology*, 1, 201–8.

DeLoache, J. S. (1987). Rapid change in the symbolic functioning of very young children. *Science*, 238, 1556–7.

DeLoache, J. S. (1991). Symbolic functioning in very young children. *Child Development*, 62, 736–52.

DeLoache, J. S. (2000). Dual representation and young children's use of scale models. *Child Development*, 71, 329–38.

DeLoache, J. S., Miller, K. F., & Rosengren, K. S. (1997). The credible shrinking room: Very young children's performance with symbolic and nonsymbolic relations. *Psychological Science*, 8, 308–13.

Deloache, J. S., Pierroutsakos, S. L., Uttal, D. H., Rosengren, K. S., & Gottlieb, A. (1998). Grasping the nature of pictures. *Psychological Science*, 9, 205–10.

Deluty, R. H. (1983). Children's evaluations of aggressive, assertive, and submissive responses. *Journal of Clinical Child Psychology*, 12, 124–9.

DeMarie-Dreblow, D., & Miller, P. H. (1988). The development of children's strategies for selective attention: Evidence for a transitional period. *Child Development*, 59, 1504–13.

Demont, E., & Gombert, J. E. (1996). Phonological awareness as a predictor of recoding skill and syntactic awareness as a predictor of comprehension skills. *British Journal of Educational Psychology*, 66, 315–32.

Dennis, W. (1973). *Children of the creche.* New York: Appleton-Century-Crofts.

Deregnier, R. A., Nelson, C. A., Thomas, K. M., Wewerka, S., & Georgieff, M. K. (2000). Neurophysiologic evaluation of auditory recognition memory in healthy newborn infants and infants of diabetic mothers. *Journal of Pediatrics*, 137 (6), 777–84.

Desforges, A., & Desforges, G. (1980). Number-based strategies of sharing in young children. *Educational Studies*, 6, 97–109.

Desrochers, S., Morissette, P., & Ricard, M. (1995). Two perspectives on pointing in infancy. In C. Moore & P. J. Dunham (Eds.), *Joint attention: Its origin and role in development* (pp. 85–101). Hillsdale, NJ: Erlbaum.

Detterman, D. K. (1978). The effect of heartbeat sound on neonatal crying. *Infant Behavior and Development*, 1, 36–48.

De Woolff, M. S., & van IJzendoorn, M. H. (1997). Sensitivity and attachment: A meta-analysis on parental antecedents of infant attachment. *Child Development*, 68, 571–91.

Diamond, A. (1985). Development of the ability to use recall to guide action, as indicated by infants' performance on A not B. *Child Development*, 56, 868–83.

Diamond, A. (1988). Abilities and neural mechanisms underlying A performance. *Child Development*, 59, 523–7.

Diamond, M., & Sigmundson, H. K. (1999). Sex reassignment at birth. In S. J. Ceci & W. M. Williams (Eds.), *The nature–nurture debate: Essential readings* (pp. 55–80). Cambridge, MA, & Oxford: Blackwell.

Diamond, R., Carey, S., & Back, K. J. (1983). Genetic influences on the development of spatial skills during early adolescence. *Cognition*, 13, 167–85.

DiPietro, J. A., Hodgson, K. A., Costigan, S. C., & Johnson, T. R. B. (1996). Development of fetal movement–fetal heart rate coupling from 20 weeks through term. *Early Human Development*, 44, 139–51.

Dissanayake, C., Sigman, M., & Kasari, C. (1996). Long-term stability of individual differences in the emotional responsiveness of children with autism. *Journal of Child Psychology and Psychiatry*, 37, 461–7.

Dodge, K. A., Pettit, G. S., Bates, J. E., & Valente, E. (1995). Social information processing patterns partially mediate the effect of early physical abuse on later conduct problems. *Journal of Abnormal Psychology*, 104, 632–43.

Dodge, K. A., Pettit, G. S., McClaskey, C. L., & Brown, M. M. (1986). Social competence in children. *Monographs of the Society for Research in Child Development*, 51 (2).

Dodge, K. A., Schlundt, D. C., Shocken, I., & Delugach, J. D. (1983). Social competence and children's sociometric status: The role of peer group entry strategies. *Merrill-Palmer Quarterly*, 29, 309–36.

Dodge, K. A., & Somberg, D. R. (1987). Hostile attributional biases among aggressive boys are exacerbated under conditions of threats to the self. *Child Development*, 58, 213–24.

Doise, W., & Mugny, G. (1984). *The social development of the intellect*. Oxford: Pergamon.

Donahoe, P. K., & Hendren, W. H. I. (1976). Evaluation of the newborn with ambiguous genitalia. *Pediatric Clinics of North America*, 23, 361–70.

Douglas, J. D., & Wong, A. C. (1977). Formal operations: Age and sex differences in Chinese and American children. *Child Development*, 48, 689–92.

Dowker, A. (1989). Rhymes and alliteration in poems elicited from young children. *Journal of Child Language*, 16, 181–202.

Draghi-Lorenz, R. (1997). Jealousy in the first year: Evidence of early interpersonal awareness. Paper presented at the British Psychological Society Developmental Section Conference, Loughborough.

Dromi, E. (1999). Early lexical development. In M. Barrett (Ed.), *The development of language* (pp. 99–132). London: Psychology Press.

Dubowitz, L., Mercuri, E., & Dubowitz, V. (1998). An optimality score for the neurologic examination of the term newborn. *Journal of Pediatrics*, 133 (3), 406–16.

Dubowitz, L. M., Mushin, J., Morante, A., & Placzek, M. (1983). The maturation of visual acuity in neurologically normal and abnormal newborn infants. *Behavioral Brain Research*, 10 (1), 39–45.

Duenholter, J. H., & Pritchard, J. A. (1976). Fetal respiration: Quantitative measurements of amniotic fluid inspired near term by human and rhesus fetuses. *American Journal of Obstetrics and Gynecology*, 125, 306–9.

Dumas, J. E. (1989). Treating antisocial behavior in children: Child and family approaches. *Clinical Psychology Review*, 9, 197–222.

Dunlea, A. (1989). *Vision and the emergence of meaning*. Cambridge: Cambridge University Press.

Dunn, J., Brown, J., & Beardsall, L. (1991). Family talk about feeling states and children's later understanding of others' emotions. *Developmental Psychology*, 27, 448–55.

Dunn, J., Brown, J., Slomkowski, C., Tesla, C., & Youngblade, L. (1991). Young children's understanding of other people's feelings and beliefs: Individual differences and their antecedents. *Child Development*, 62, 1352–66.

Dunn, J., & Kendrick, C. (1982). *Siblings: Love, envy and understanding*. Oxford: Blackwell.

Dunphy, D. (1963). The social structure of urban adolescent peer groups. *Sociometry*, 26, 230–46.

Durrett, M. E., Otaki, M., & Richards, P. (1984). Attachment and mother's perception of support from the father. *International Journal of Behavioral Development*, 7, 167–76.

Duyme, M. (1988). School success and social class: An adoption study. *Developmental Psychology*, 24, 203–9.

Dworetsky, J. P. (1995). *Human development: A lifespan approach*. New York: West.

Eckerman, C. O., & Oehler, J. M. (1992). Very-low birthweight newborns and parents as early social partners. In S. L. Friedman & M. D. Sigman (Eds.), *The psychological development of low birthweight children*. Norwood, NJ: Ablex.

Ehri, L. C. (1995). The emergence of word learning in beginning reading. In P. Owen & P. Pumfrey (Eds.), *Children learning to read: International concerns* (pp. 9–31). New York: Falmer Press.

Eibl-Eibesfeldt, I. (1989). *Human ethology*. New York: Aldine de Gruyter.

Eilers, R. E., Gavin, W. J., & Oller, D. K. (1982). Cross-linguistic perception in infancy: Early effects of linguistic experience. *Journal of Child Language*, 9, 289–302.

Eimas, P. (1985). The perception of speech in early infancy. *Scientific American*, 252, 46–61.

Eimas, P. D., Siqueland, E. R., Jusczyk, P. W., & Vigorito, J. (1971). Speech perception in infants. *Science*, 171, 303–6.

Eisenberg, N., & Fabes, R. (1998). Prosocial development. In N. Eisenberg (Ed.), *Handbook of child psychology* (5th ed.). *Vol. 3. Social, emotional, and personality development* (pp. 779–840). New York: Wiley.

Eisenberg, N., Fabes, R. A., Schaller, M., Carlo, G., & Miller, P. A. (1991). The relations of parental characteristics and practices to children's vicarious emotional responding. *Child Development*, 62, 1393–1408.

Eisenberg, N., Fabes, R. A., Shepard, S. A., Guthrie, I. K., Murphy, B. C., & Reiser, M. (1999). Parental reactions to children's negative emotions: Longitudinal relations to quality of children's social functioning. *Child Development*, 70, 513–34.

Ekblad, S., & Olweus, D. (1986). Applicability of Olweus' aggression inventory in a sample of Chinese primary school-children. *Aggressive Behavior*, 12, 315–25.

Ekman, P. (1973). Cross-cultural studies of facial expression. In P. Ekman (Ed.), *Darwin and facial expression*. New York: Academic Press.

Ekman, P., & Friesen, W. (1971). Constants across culture in the face and emotion. *Journal of Personality and Social Psychology*, 17, 124–9.

Elkind, D. (1967). Egocentrism in adolescence. *Child Development*, 38, 1025–34.

Elkind, D., Koegler, R. R., & Go, E. (1964). Studies in perceptual development. II: Part–whole perception. *Child Development*, 35, 81–90.

Elkind, D., & Scott, L. (1962). Studies in perceptual development. I: The decentering of perception. *Child Development*, 33, 619–30.

Elliott, M. (Ed.) (1991). *Bullying: A practical guide to coping for schools*. Harlow: Longman.

Ellis, H. D., & Gunter, H. L. (1999). Asperger syndrome: A simple matter of white matter? *Trends in Cognitive Sciences*, 3, 192–200.

Ellis, N., & Large, B. (1987). The development of reading: As you seek so shall you find. *British Journal of Developmental Psychology*, 78, 1–28.

Epstein, H. T. (1979). Correlated brain and intelligence development in humans. In M. E. Hahn, C. Jensen, & B. C. Dudek (Eds.), *Development, and evolution of brain size: Behavioral implications*. New York: Academic Press.

Erickson, J. R. (1978). Research on syllogistic reasoning. In R. Revlin & R. E. Mayer (Eds.), *Human reasoning* (pp. 39–50). Washington, DC: Winston.

Erikson, E. H. (1959). Identity and the life cycle: Selected papers. *Psychological Issues*, 1 (Monograph 1). New York: International Universities Press.

Erikson, E. H. (1963). *Childhood and society* (2nd ed.). New York: W. W. Norton.

Erlenmeyer-Kimling, L., & Jarvik, L. F. (1963). Genetics and intelligence: A review. *Science*, 142, 1477–9.

Escher-Graeub, D., & Grossmann, K. E. (1983). *Attachment security in the second year of life: The Regensburg cross-sectional study* (Research report). Regensburg: University of Regensburg.

Eslea, M., & Smith, P. K. (2000). Pupil and parent attitudes towards bullying in primary schools. *European Journal of the Psychology of Education*, 15, 207–19.

Eswaran, H., Wilson, J., Preissl, H., Robinson, S., Vrba, J., Murphy, P., Rose, D., & Lowery, C. (2002). Magnetoencephalographic recordings of visual evoked brain activity in the human fetus. *Lancet*, 360, 779–80.

Evans, W. F. (1973). The stage IV error in Piaget's theory of object concept development. Unpublished dissertation, University of Houston.

Fabes, R. A., Eisenberg, N., Jones, S., Smith, M., Guthrie, I. K., Poulin, R., Shepard, S. A., & Friedman, J. (1999). Regulation, emotionality, and preschoolers' socially competent peer interactions. *Child Development*, 70, 432–42.

Fagan, J. F., & Singer, L. T. (1983). Infant recognition memory as a measure of intelligence. *Advances in Infancy Research*, 2, 31–78.

Fagot, B. I. (1985). Beyond the reinforcement principle: Another step toward understanding sex role development. *Developmental Psychology*, 21, 1097–1104.

Falbo, T., & Polit, D. F. (1986). Quantitative review of the only child literature: Research evidence and theory development. *Psychological Bulletin*, 100, 176–89.

Falconer, D. S. (1990). *Introduction to quantitative genetics*. New York: Longman.

Fantz, R. L. (1961). The origin of form perception. *Scientific American*, 204, 66–72.

Farrar, M. J., & Goodman G. S. (1992). Developmental changes in event memory. *Child Development*, 63, 173–87.

Farrington, D. (1993). Understanding and preventing bullying. In M. Tonry (Ed.), *Crime and justice: A review of research* (Vol. 17). Chicago: University of Chicago Press.

Farwell, C. (1975). The language spoken to children. *Human Development*, 18, 288–309.

Fayol, M., Thenevin, M.-G., Jarousse, J.-P., & Totereau, C. (1999). From learning to teaching to learning French written morphology. In T. Nunes (Ed.), *Learning to read: An integrated view from research and practice* (pp. 43–64). Dordrecht: Kluwer.

Federal Interagency Forum on Child and Family Statistics. (1999). *America's children: Key national indicators of well-being* (NECS Report No. 1999–019). Washington, DC: US Government Printing Office.

Federman, J. (1998). *National television violence study* (Vol. 3). Thousand Oaks, CA: Sage.

Feiring, C. (1996). Concepts of romance in 15-year-old adolescents. *Journal of Research on Adolescence*, 6, 181–200.

Ferguson, C. A. (1989). Individual differences in language learning. In M. Rice & R. Schiefelbusch (Eds.), *The teachability of language*. Baltimore: Brookes.

Fernald, A. (1982). Acoustic determinants of infant preference for "motherese." Doctoral dissertation, University of Oregon, *Dissertation Abstracts International*, 43, 545B.

Ferreiro, E., & Teberosky, A. (1983). *Literacy before schooling*. Exeter, NH: Heinemann Educational Books.

Field, T. (1987). Affective and interactive disturbances in infants. In J. D. Osofsky (Ed.), *Handbook of infant development* (2nd ed., pp. 972–1005). New York: Wiley.

Field, T., Cohen, D., Garcia, R., & Greenberg, R. (1984). Mother–stranger face discrimination by the newborn. *Infant Behavior and Development*, 7, 19–26.

Field, T., Woodson, R., Greenberg, R., & Cohen, D. (1982). Discrimination and imitation of facial expressions by neonates. *Science*, 218, 179–81.

Fielder, A. R., & Moseley, M. J. (2000). Environmental light and the preterm infant. *Seminars in Perinatology*, 24, 291–8.

Fifer, W. & Moon, C. (1989). Psychobiology of newborn auditory preferences. *Seminars in Perinatology*, 13 (5), 430–3.

Fifer, W. & Moon, C. (1995). The effects of fetal experience with sound. In J.-P. LeCanuet, N. Krasnegor, W. Fifer, & W. Smotherman (Eds.), *Fetal development: A psychobiological perspective* (pp. 351–66). New York: Erlbaum.

Finkel, D., & McGue, M. (1993). The origins of individual differences in memory among the elderly: A behavior-genetics analysis. *Psychology of Aging*, 8, 527–37.

Finkel, D., Pedersen, N. L., McGue, M., & McClearn, G. E. (1995). Heritability of cognitive abilities in adult twins: Comparison of Minnesota and Swedish data. *Behavior Genetics*, 25, 421–31.

Finkelstein, N. W., & Haskins, R. (1983). Kindergarten children prefer same-color peers. *Child Development*, 54, 502–8.

Fischhoff, B. (1975). Hindsight is not equal to foresight: The effect of outcome knowledge on judgment under uncertainty. *Journal of Experimental Psychology: Human Perception and Performance*, 1, 288–99.

Flammer, A., Alsaker, F. D., & Noack, P. (1999). Time use by adolescents in an international perspective: The case of leisure activities. In F. Alsaker & A. Flammer (Eds.), *The adolescent experience: European and American adolescents in the 1990s*. Mahwah, NJ: Erlbaum.

Flanagan, O. (1992). Other minds, obligations, and honesty. In S. J. Ceci, M. DeSimone, & M. Putnick (Eds.), *Cognitive and social factors in preschoolers' deception* (pp. 111–26). Hillsdale, NJ: Erlbaum.

Flannagan, T., & Hess, D. (1991). Developmental differences in children's abilities to utilize scripts in promoting their recall for scenes. Paper presented at the Biennial Meeting of the Society for Research in Child Development, Seattle, WA (April).

Flavell, J. H. (1963). *The developmental psychology of Jean Piaget*. Toronto, New York, & London: Van Nostrand.

Flavell, J. H. (1970). Developmental studies in mediated memory. In H. W. Reese & L. P. Lipsitt (Eds.), *Advances in child development and behavior* (Vol. 20, pp. 91–142). New York: Academic Press.

Flavell, J. H. (1993). The development of children's understanding of false belief and the appearance–reality distinction. *International Journal of Psychology*, 28, 595–604.

Flavell, J. H. (1996). Piaget's legacy. *Psychological Science*, 7, 200–3.

Flavell, J. H., Beach, D. R., & Chinsky, J. M. (1966). Spontaneous verbal rehearsal in a memory task as a function of age. *Child Development*, 37, 283–99.

Flavell, J. H., Green, F. L., & Flavell, E. R. (1986). Development of the appearance–reality distinction. *Monographs of the Society for Research in Child Development*, 51 (Serial No. 212).

Flavell, J. H., Miller, P. H., & Miller, S. A. (1993). *Cognitive development* (3rd ed.). Englewood Cliffs, NJ: Prentice-Hall.

Flavell, J. H., & Wellman, H. M. (1977). Metamemory. In R. V. Kail & J. W. Hagen (Eds.), *Perspectives on the development of memory and cognition* (pp. 3–33). Hillsdale, NJ: Erlbaum.

Flieller, A. (1999). Comparison of the development of formal thought in adolescent cohorts aged 10 to 15 years (1967–1996 and 1972–1993). *Developmental Psychology*, 35, 1048–58.

Flin, R. H. (1985). Development of face recognition: An encoding switch? *British Journal of Psychology*, 33, 123–34.

Flynn, J. R. (1984). The mean IQ of Americans: Massive gains 1932 to 1978. *Psychological Bulletin*, 95, 29–51.

Flynn, J. R. (1987). Massive IQ gains in 14 nations: What IQ tests really measure. *Psychological Bulletin*, 101, 171–91.

Flynn, J. R. (1998). Searching for justice: The discovery of IQ gains over time. *American Psychologist*, 54, 5–20.

Fodor, J. A. (1992). A theory of the child's theory of mind. *Cognition*, 44, 283–96.

Fonagy, P., Redfern, S., & Charman, A. (1997). The relationship between belief-desire reasoning and a projective measure of attachment security (SAT). *British Journal of Developmental Psychology*, 15, 51–63.

Fonagy, P., Steele, H., & Steele, M. (1991). Maternal representations of attachment during pregnancy predict organization of infant–mother attachment at one year of age. *Child Development*, 62, 891–905.

Fonzi, A., Schneider, B. H., Tani, F., & Tomada, G. (1997). Predicting children's friendship status from their dyadic interaction in structured situations of potential conflict. *Child Development*, 68, 496–506.

Foster, S. H. (1986). Learning discourse topic management in the preschool years. *Journal of Child Language*, 13, 231–50.

Fowler, A. E. (1990). Language abilities in children with Down syndrome: Evidence for a specific syntactic delay. In D. Cicchetti & M. Beeghly (Eds.), *Children with Down syndrome: A developmental perspective* (pp. 302–28). Cambridge: Cambridge University Press.

Fraiberg, S. (1977). *Insights from the blind*. London: Souvenir Press.

Franco, F., & Butterworth, G. (1996). Pointing and social awareness: Declaring and requesting in the second year. *Journal of Child Language*, 23, 307–36.

Freeman, F. N., Holzinger, K. J., & Mitchell, B. C. (1928). The influence of environment on the intelligence, school achievement, and conduct of foster children. *Yearbook of the National Society for the Study of Education, Pt. I*, 102–217.

Fried, P. A., & Watkinson, B. (2000). Visuoperceptual functioning differs in 9–12-year-olds prenatally exposed to cigarettes and marihuana. *Neurotoxicology and Teratology*, 22, 11–29.

Fried, P. A., Watkinson, B., & Gary, R. (1992). A follow-up study of attentional behavior in 6-year-old children exposed prenatally to marihuana, cigarettes, and alcohol. *Neurotoxicology and Teratology*, 14, 299–311.

Frith, U. (1989). *Autism: Explaining the enigma*. Oxford: Blackwell.

Frydman, O., & Bryant, P. E. (1988). Sharing and the understanding of number equivalence by young children. *Cognitive Development*, 3, 323–39.

Frye, D., Braisby, N., Lowe, J., Maroudas, C., & Nicholls, J. (1989). Young children's understanding of counting and cardinality. *Child Development*, 60, 1158–71.

Fuligni, A., & Eccles, J. (1993). Perceived parent–child relationships and early adolescents' orientation toward peers. *Developmental Psychology*, 29, 622–32.

Fulker, D. W., Cherny, S. S., & Cardon, L. R. (1993). Continuity and change in cognitive development. In R. Plomin & G. E. McClearn (Eds.), *Nature, nurture, and psychology*. Washington, DC: American Psychological Association.

Furman, W., & Buhrmester, D. (1985). Children's perceptions of the personal relationships in their social networks. *Developmental Psychology*, 21, 1016–22.

Furman, W., & Wehner, E. A. (1994). Romantic views: Towards a theory of adolescent romantic relationships. In R. Montemayor, G. R. Adams, & G. P. Gullota (Eds.), *Advances in adolescent development. Vol. 6. Relationships during adolescence* (pp. 168–95). Thousand Oaks, CA: Sage.

Furman, W., & Wehner, E. A. (1997). Adolescent romantic relationships: A developmental perspective. In S. Shulman & W. A. Collins (Eds.), *Romantic relationships in adolescence: Developmental perspectives* (pp. 21–36). San Francisco: Jossey-Bass.

Furrow, D., & Lewis, S. (1987). The role of the initial utterance in contingent query sequences: Its influence on responses to requests for clarification. *Journal of Child Language*, 14, 467–79.

Fuson, K. C. (1988). *Children's counting and concepts of number*. New York: Springer.

Gallagher, T. (1977). Revision behaviors in the speech of normal children developing language. *Journal of Speech and Hearing Research*, 20, 303–18.

Gallagher, T. (1981). Contingent query sequences within adult–child discourse. *Journal of Child Language*, 8, 51–62.

Galotti, K. M., Komatsu, L. K., & Voelz, S. (1997). Children's differential performance on deductive and inductive syllogisms. *Developmental Psychology*, 33 (1), 70–8.

Galton, F. (1869). *Hereditary genius: An inquiry into its laws and consequences.* London: Macmillan.

Garvey, C. (1975). Requests and responses in children's speech. *Journal of Child Language,* 2, 41–63.

Garvey, C., & Hogan, R. (1973). Social speech and social interaction: Egocentrism revisited. *Child Development,* 44, 562–8.

Gathercole, V., & Min, H. (1997). Word meaning biases or language-specific effects? Evidence from English, Spanish, and Korean. *First Language,* 17, 31–56.

Gattis, M. (2001). Reading pictures: Constraints on mapping conceptual and spatial schemas. In M. Gattis (Ed.), *Spatial schemas in abstract thought* (pp. 223–45). Cambridge, MA: MIT Press.

Gauze, C., Bukowski, W. M., Aquan-Assee, J., & Sippola, L. K. (1996). Interactions between family environment and friendship and associations with self-perceived well-being during early adolescence. *Child Development,* 67, 2201–16.

Gellatly, A. (1995). Colourful Whorfian ideas: Linguistic and cultural influences on the perception and cognition of color, and on the investigation of them. *Mind and Language,* 10, 199–225.

Gelman, R. (1982). Accessing one-to-one correspondence: Still another paper about conservation. *British Journal of Psychology,* 73, 209–20.

Gelman, R., & Gallistel, C. R. (1978). *The child's understanding of number.* Cambridge, MA: Harvard University Press.

Gelman, R., & Meck, E. (1983). Preschoolers' counting: Principles before skill. *Cognition,* 13, 343–60.

Gelman, R., Meck, E., & Merkin, S. (1986). Young children's numerical competence. *Cognitive Development,* 1, 1–30.

George, C., Kaplan, N., & Main, M. (1985). The Berkeley Adult Attachment Interview. Unpublished protocol, Department of Psychology, University of California, Berkeley.

Gerber, S. (1985). Stimulus, response and state variables in the testing of neonates. *Ear Hearing,* 6 (1), 15–19.

Gesell, A., & Ames, L. (1940). The ontogenetic organization of prone behavior in human infancy. *Journal of Genetic Psychology,* 56, 247–63.

Ghim, H. R. (1990). Evidence for perceptual organization in infants: Perception of subjective contours by young infants. *Infant Behavior and Development,* 13, 221–48.

Gibbons, J. L., Lynn, M., & Stiles, D. A. (1997). Cross-national gender differences in adolescents' preferences for free-time activities. *Cross-Cultural Research: The Journal of Comparative Social Science,* 31, 55–69.

Gibson, E., & Spelke, E. (1983). The development of perception. In P. H. Mussen, J. H. Flavell, & E. M. Markman (Eds.), *Handbook of child psychology. Vol. 3. Cognitive development* (pp. 1–76). New York: Wiley.

Gibson, E. J., & Walk, R. D. (1960). The "visual cliff." *Scientific American,* 202, 80–92.

Glachan, M., & Light, P. H. (1982). Peer interaction and learning. In G. Butterworth & P. Light (Eds.), *Social cognition.* Brighton: Harvester Press.

Gleason, J., & Weintraub, S. (1978). Input language and the acquisition of communicative competence. In K. E. Nelson (Ed.), *Children's language* (Vol. 1). New York: Gardner Press.

Gleitman, L., & Wanner, E. (1982). The state of the art. In E. Wanner & L. Gleitman (Eds.), *Language acquisition: The state of the art* (pp. 3–50). Cambridge: Cambridge University Press.

Glenberg, A. M. (1997). What memory is for. *Behavioral and Brain Sciences,* 20, 1–55.

Glenn, S. M., & Cunningham, C. C. (1982). Recognition of the familiar words in nursery rhymes by handicapped and nonhandicapped infants. *Journal of Child Psychology and Psychiatry,* 23, 319–27.

Glueck, S. (1982). *Family environment and delinquency.* Littleton, CO: F. B. Rothman.

Gnepp, J., McKee, E., & Domanic, J. A. (1987). Children's use of situational information to infer emotion: Understanding emotionally equivocal situations. *Developmental Psychology, 23,* 114–23.

Godden, D. R., & Baddeley, A. D. (1975). Context-dependent memory in two natural environments: On land and underwater. *British Journal of Psychology, 66,* 325–31.

Golding, J. (1997). Sudden infant death syndrome and parental smoking: A literature review. *Paediatrics and Perinatal Epidemiology, 11,* 67–77.

Goldin-Meadow, S., & Mylander, C. (1984). Gestural communication in deaf children: The effects and noneffects of parental input on early language. *Monographs of the Society for Research in Child Development, 49* (3–4, Serial No. 207).

Goldin-Meadow, S., Mylander, C., & Butcher, C. (1995). The resilience of combinatorial structure at the word level: Morphology in self-styled gesture systems. *Cognition, 56,* 195–262.

Golinkoff, R. M. (1983). Infant social cognition: Self, people, and objects. In L. Lieben (Ed.), *Piaget and the foundations of knowledge* (pp. 57–78). Hillsdale, NJ: Erlbaum.

Golinkoff, R. M. (1986). "I beg your pardon?": The preverbal negotiation of failed messages. *Journal of Child Language, 13,* 455–63.

Golinkoff, R. M., & Hirsh-Pasek, K. (1995). Reinterpreting children's sentence comprehension: Toward a new framework. In P. Fletcher & B. MacWhinney (Eds.), *The handbook of child language* (pp. 430–61). Oxford: Blackwell.

Golinkoff, R. M., Hirsh-Pasek, K., Mervis, C., Frawley, W., & Parillo, M. (1995). Lexical principles can be extended to the acquisition of verbs. In M. Tomasello & W. Merriman (Eds.), *Beyond names for things: Young children's acquisition of verbs* (pp. 185–221). Hillsdale, NJ: Erlbaum.

Golinkoff, R. M., Shuff-Bailey, M., Olguin, R., & Ruan, W. (1995). Young children extend novel words at the basic level: Evidence for the principle of categorical scope. *Developmental Psychology, 31,* 494–507.

Golombok, S., & Fivush, R. (1994). *Gender development.* Cambridge: Cambridge University Press.

Goodman, G., & Aman, C. (1990). Children's use of anatomically detailed dolls to recount an event. *Child Development, 61,* 1859–71.

Goodman, G. S., Batterman-Faunce, J. M., & Kennedy, R. (1992). Optimizing children's testimony: Research and social policy issues concerning allegations of child sexual abuse. In D. Cicchetti & S. Toth (Eds.), *Child abuse, child development, and social policy.* Norwood, NJ: Ablex.

Goodman, G. S., & Clarke-Stewart, A. (1991). Suggestibility in children's testimony: Implications for child sexual abuse investigations. In J. L. Doris (Ed.), *The suggestibility of children's recollections* (pp. 92–105). Washington, DC: American Psychological Association.

Goodman, G. S., Rudy, L., Bottoms, B., & Aman, C. (1990). Children's concerns and memory: Issues of ecological validity in the study of children's eyewitness testimony. In R. Fivush & J. Hudson (Eds.), *Knowing and remembering in young children* (pp. 249–84). New York: Cambridge University Press.

Goodman, N. (1983). *Fact, fiction, and forecast.* Cambridge, MA: Harvard University Press.

Goodsit, J., Morgan, J. L., & Kuhl, P. K. (1993). Perceptual strategies in prelingual speech segmentation. *Journal of Child Language, 20,* 229–52.

Gopnik, A. (1993). How we know our minds: The illusion of first-person knowledge of intentionality. *Behavioral and Brain Sciences, 16,* 1–14.

Gopnik, A., & Astington, J. W. (1988). Children's understanding of representational change, and its relation to the understanding of false belief and the appearance–reality distinction. *Child Development, 59,* 26–37.

Gopnik, A., & Choi, S. (1995). Names, relational words, and cognitive development in English and Korean speakers: Nouns are not always learned before verbs. In M. Tomasello & W. E. Merriman (Eds.), *Beyond names for things: Young children's acquisition of verbs* (pp. 63–80). Hillsdale, NJ: Erlbaum.

Gopnik, A., & Meltzoff, A. (1997). *Words, thoughts, and theories*. Cambridge, MA: MIT Press.

Gordon, W. R., & Caltabiano, M. L. (1996). Urban–rural differences in adolescent self-esteem, leisure boredom, and sensation-seeking as predictors of leisure-time usage and satisfaction. *Adolescence*, 31 (124), 883–901.

Goren, C., Sarty, M., & Wu, P. (1975). Visual following and pattern discrimination of face-like stimuli by newborn infants. *Pediatrics*, 56, 544–9.

Goswami, U. (1986). Children's use of analogy in learning to read: A developmental study. *Journal of Experimental Child Psychology*, 42, 73–83.

Goswami, U., & Mead, F. (1992). Onset and rime awareness and analogies in reading. *Reading Research Quarterly*, 27, 153–71.

Gottfredson, G. D. (1987). Peer group interventions to reduce the risk of delinquent behavior: A selective review and a new evaluation. *Criminology*, 25, 187–20.

Granger, D. A., Weisz, J. R., & Kauneckis, D. (1994). Neuroendocrine reactivity, internalizing behavior problems, and control-related cognitions in clinic-referred children and adolescents. *Journal of Abnormal Psychology*, 103, 267–76.

Greaney, K. T., Tunmer, W., & Chapman, J. W. (1997). Effects of rime-based orthographic analogy training on the word recognition skills of children with reading disability. *Journal of Educational Psychology*, 89, 645–51.

Greco, P. (1962). Quantité et quotité: Nouvelles recherches sur la correspondance terme-à-terme et la conservation des ensembles. In P. Greco & A. Morf (Eds.), *Structures numériques élémentaires: Etudes d'épistémologie génétique* (Vol. 13, pp. 35–52). Paris: Presses Universitaires de France.

Greeley, A. (1997). The other civic America: Religion and social capital. *The American Prospect*, 32, 68–73.

Greenhoot, A. F., Ornstein, P. A., Gordon, B. N., & Baker-Ward, L. (1999). Acting out the details of a pediatric check up: The impact of interview condition and behavioral style on children's memory reports. *Child Development*, 70, 363–80.

Grice, H. P. (1975). Logic and conversation. In P. Cole & J. L. Morgan (Eds.), *Syntax and semantics. Vol. 3. Speech acts* (pp. 41–58). New York: Academic Press.

Grigorenko, E. L. (in press). Other than g: The value of persistence. In R. J. Sternberg & E. L. Grigorenko (Eds.), *The general factor of intelligence: Fact or fiction*. Mahwah, NJ: Erlbaum.

Grigorenko, E. L., & Carter, A. S. (1996). Co-twin, peer, and mother–child relationships and IQ in a Russian adolescent twin sample. *Journal of Russian and East European Psychology*, 34 (6), 59–87.

Grinder, R. E. (1969). The concept of adolescence in the genetic psychology of G. Stanley Hall. *Child Development*, 40 (2), 355–69.

Groome, L. J., Swiber, M. J., Holland, S. B., Bentz, L. S., Atterbury, J. L., & Trimm, I. R. F. (1999). Spontaneous motor activity in the perinatal infant before and after birth: Stability in individual differences. *Developmental Psychobiology*, 35, 15–24.

Grose, J., & Harding, G. F. A. (1990). The development of refractive error and pattern reversal VEPs in pre-term infants. *Clinical Vision Sciences*, 5, 375–82.

Grossmann, K. E., Grossmann, K., Huber, F., & Wartner, U. (1981). German children's behavior towards their mothers at 12 months and their fathers at 18 months in Ainsworth's strange situation. *International Journal of Behavioral Development*, 4, 157–81.

Grossmann, K., Grossmann, K. E., Spangler, G., Suess, G., & Unzner, L. (1985). Maternal sensitivity and newborns' orientation responses as related to quality of attachment in northern Germany. In I. Bretherton & E. Waters (Eds.), Growing points in attachment theory and research (pp. 233–68). *Monographs of the Society for Research in Child Development*, 50 (1–2, Serial No. 209).

Gustafson, G. E., Green, J. A., & West, M. J. (1979). The infant's changing role in mother–infant games: The growth of social skills. *Infant Behavior and Development*, 2, 301–8.

Haeselager, G. J. T., & van Lieshout, C. F. M. (1992). Social and affective adjustment of self- and peer-reported victims and bullies. Paper presented at the European Conference on Developmental Psychology, Seville, Spain (September).

Hagen, J. W. (1967). The effect of distraction on selective attention. *Child Development*, 38, 685–94.

Haight, W. L., & Miller, P. J. (1993). *Pretending at home: Early development in a sociocultural context*. Albany: SUNY Press.

Haith, M. M. (1998). Who put the cog in cognition? Is rich interpretation too costly? *Infant Behavior and Development*, 21, 167–79.

Hanewinkel, R., & Knaack, R. (1997). *Mobbing: Gewaltprävention in Schule in Schleswig-Holstein*. Report. Landesinstitut Schleswig-Holstein für Praxis und Theorie der Schule.

Hansen, J., & Bowey, J. A. (1994). Phonological analysis skills, verbal working memory and reading ability in 2nd grade children. *Child Development*, 65, 938–50.

Happé, F. G. E. (1993). Communicative competence and theory of mind in autism: A test of relevance theory. *Cognition*, 48, 101–19.

Happé, F. G. E. (1994a). *Autism*. London: University College Press.

Happé, F. G. E. (1994b). Current psychological theories of autism: The "theory of mind" account and rival theories. *Journal of Child Psychology and Psychiatry*, 35, 215–29.

Happé, F. G. E. (1995). The role of age and verbal ability in the theory of mind task performance of subjects with autism. *Child Development*, 66, 843–55.

Happé, F. G. E. (1996). Studying weak central coherence at low levels: Children with autism do not succumb to visual illusions. A research note. *Journal of Child Psychology and Psychiatry*, 37, 873–7.

Harlow, H., & Zimmerman, R. R. (1959). Affectional responses in the infant monkey. *Science*, 130, 421–32.

Harris, J. R. (1995). Where is the child's environment? A group socialization theory of development. *Psychological Review*, 102, 458–89.

Harris, J. R. (1998). *The nurture assumption*. London: Bloomsbury.

Harris, P. L. (1973). Perseverative errors in search by young infants. *Child Development*, 44, 28–33.

Harris, P. L. (1974). Perseverative search at a visibly empty place by young infants. *Journal of Experimental Child Psychology*, 18, 535–42.

Harris, P. L. (1983). Children's understanding of the link between situation and emotion. *Journal of Experimental Child Psychology*, 36, 490–509.

Harris, P. L. (1989). *Children and emotion*. Cambridge, MA, and Oxford: Blackwell.

Harris, P. L. (1991). The work of the imagination. In A. Whiten (Ed.), *Natural theories of mind* (pp. 283–304). Oxford: Blackwell.

Harris, P. L. (2000). On not falling down to earth: Children's metaphysical questions. In K. Rosengren, C. Johnson, & P. L. Harris (Eds.), *Imagining the impossible: The development of magical, scientific and religious thinking in contemporary society* (pp. 157–78). Cambridge: Cambridge University Press.

Harris, P. L., Donnelly, K., Guz, G. R., & Pitt-Watson, R. (1986). Children's understanding of the distinction between real and apparent emotion. *Child Development*, 57, 895–909.

Hart, D. (1988a). A longitudinal study of adolescents' socialization and identification as predictors of adult moral judgment development. *Merrill-Palmer Quarterly*, 34, 245–60.

Hart, D. (1988b). Development of personal identity in adolescence: A philosophical dilemma approach. *Merrill-Palmer Quarterly*, 34, 105–14.

Hart, D., Atkins, R., & Ford, D. (1998). Urban America as a context for the development of moral identity in adolescence. *Journal of Social Issues*, 54, 513–30.

Hart, D., & Fegley, S. (1995). Prosocial behavior and caring in adolescence: Relations to self-understanding and social judgment. *Child Development*, 66, 1346–59.

Hart, D., Hofmann, V., Edelstein, W., & Keller, M. (1997). The relation of childhood personality types to adolescent behavior and development: A longitudinal study of Icelandic children. *Developmental Psychology*, 33, 195–205.

Hart, D., & Yates, M. (1997). The interrelation of self and identity in adolescence: A developmental account. In R. Vasta et al. (Eds.), *Annals of child development: A research annual* (Vol. 12, pp. 207–43). London: Jessica Kingsley.

Harter, S. (1982). A cognitive-developmental approach to children's understanding of affect and trait labels. In F. C. Serafica (Ed.), *Social-cognitive development in context* (pp. 27–61). New York: Guilford.

Harter, S. (1983a). Children's understanding of multiple emotions: A cognitive-developmental approach. In W. F. Overton (Ed.), *The relationship between social and cognitive development* (pp. 147–94). Hillsdale, NJ: Erlbaum.

Harter, S. (1983b). Developmental perspectives on the self-system. In C. M. Hetherington (Ed.), *Handbook of child psychology. Vol. 4. Socialization, personality, and social development*. New York: Wiley.

Hartup, W. W. (1996). The company they keep: Friendships and their developmental significance. *Child Development*, 67, 1–13.

Haselager, G. J. T., Hartup, W. W., van Lieshout, C. F. M., & Riksen-Walraven, J. M. A. (1998). Similarities between friends and nonfriends in middle childhood. *Child Development*, 69, 1198–1208.

Hastie, R. (1981). Schematic principles in human memory. In E. T. Higgins, C. P. Herman, & M. P. Zanna (Eds.), *Social cognition: The Ontario Symposium* (Vol. 1, pp. 39–88). Hillsdale, NJ: Erlbaum.

Hauser, M. (1996). *The evolution of communication*. Cambridge, MA: MIT Press.

Hawkins, J., Pea, R. D., Glick, J., & Scribner, S. (1984). "Merds that laugh don't like mushrooms": Evidence for deductive reasoning by preschoolers. *Developmental Psychology*, 20, 584–94.

Hayvren, M., & Hymel, S. (1984). Ethical issues in sociometric testing: Impact of sociometric measures on interaction behavior. *Developmental Psychology*, 20, 844–9.

Hayward, C., Killen, J. D., Kraemer, H. C., & Taylor, C. B. (2000). Predictors of panic attacks in adolescents. *Journal of the American Academy of Child and Adolescent Psychiatry*, 39, 207–14.

Hazan, C., & Shaver, P. (1987). Romantic love conceptualized as an attachment process. *Journal of Psychology and Social Psychology*, 52, 511–24.

Hazan, C., & Zeifman, D. (1994). Sex and the psychological tether. In K. Bartholomew & D. Perlman (Eds.), *Advances in personal relationships. Vol. 5. Attachment processes in adulthood* (pp. 151–80). London: Jessica Kingsley.

Henrik Peters, U. (1985). *Anna Freud, a life dedicated to children*. New York: Schocken Books.

Hepper, P. G. (1988). Adaptive fetal behavior: Prenatal exposure affects postnatal preferences. *Animal Behavior*, 36, 935–6.

Hepper, P. G. (1992). Fetal psychology: An embryonic science. In J. Nijhuis (Ed.), *Fetal behavior: Developmental and perinatal aspects* (pp. 129–56). New York: Oxford University Press.

Hepper, P. (1997a). Fetal habituation: Another Pandora's Box? *Developmental Medicine and Child Neurology*, 39, 274–8.

Hepper, P. (1997b). Memory *in utero*? *Developmental Medicine and Child Neurology*, 39, 343–6.

Hertz-Lazarowitz, R., Feitelson, D., Zahavi, S., & Hartup, W. W. (1981). Social interaction and social organization of Israeli five-to-seven-year olds. *International Journal of Behavioral Development*, 4, 143–55.

Hill, J. (1980). The family. In M. Johnson (Ed.), *Toward adolescence: The middle school years* (79th year-book of the National Society for the Study of Education). Chicago: University of Chicago Press.

Hinshaw, S. P., Lahey, B. B., & Hart, E. L. (1993). Issues of taxonomy and comorbidity in the development of conduct disorder. *Development and Psychopathology*, 5, 31–49.

Hirano, K. (1992). Bullying and victimization in Japanese classrooms. Paper presented at the European Conference on Developmental Psychology, Seville, Spain (September).

Hirsh-Pasek, K., Treiman, R., & Schneiderman, M. (1984). Brown and Hanlon revisited: Mother's sensitivity to ungrammatical forms. *Journal of Child Language*, 11, 81–8.

Hobson, R. P. (1993). *Autism and the development of mind*. Hove: Erlbaum.

Hofer, M. A. (1981). *The roots of human behavior*. San Francisco: W. H. Freeman.

Hoff-Ginsberg, E. (1990). Maternal speech and the child's development of syntax: A further look. *Journal of Child Language*, 17, 337–46.

Hood, B., & Willatts, P. (1986). Reaching in the dark to an object's remembered position: Evidence for object permanence in five-month-old infants. *British Journal of Developmental Psychology*, 4, 57–65.

Hoogsteder, M., Maier, R., & Elbers, E. (1996). Adult–child interaction, joint problem solving and the structure of co-operation. *Learning and Instruction*, 6 (4).

Hooker, D. (1952). *The prenatal origin of behavior*. Kansas: University of Kansas Press.

Horn, J. L. (1970). Organization of data on life-span development of human abilities. In L. Goulet & P. Baltes (Eds.), *Life-span development psychology: Research and theory*. New York: Academic Press.

Horn, J. L. (1978). Human ability systems. In P. B. Baltes (Ed.), *Life-span development and behavior* (Vol. 1). New York: Academic Press.

Horn, J., & Cattell, R. B. (1967). Redefinement and test of the theory of fluid and crystallized intelligences. *Journal of Educational Psychology*, 57, 268–70.

Horn, J. L., Donaldson, G., & Engstrom, R. (1981). Apprehension, memory, and fluid intelligence decline in adulthood. *Research on Aging*, 3, 33–84.

Horn, J. M. (1988). Thinking about human abilities. In J. R. Nesselroade & R. B. Cattell (Eds.), *Handbook of multivariate psychology* (pp. 645–85). New York: Academic Press.

Horn, J. M., Loehlin, J. C., & Willerman, L. (1979). Intellectual resemblance among adoptive and biological relatives: The Texas Adoption Project. *Behavior Genetics*, 9, 177–207.

Horn, J. M., Loehlin, J. C., & Willerman, L. (1982). Aspects of the inheritance of intellectual abilities. *Behavior Genetics*, 12, 479–516.

Horta, B. L., Victora, C. G., Menezes, A. M., Halpern, R., & Barros, F. C. (1997). Low birthweight, preterm births and intrauterine growth retardation in relation to maternal smoking. *Pediatrics and Perinatal Epidemiology*, 11, 140–51.

Houston, D., Jusczyk, P. W., & Tager, J. (1997). Talker-specificity and the persistence of infant's word representations. Paper presented at the 22nd Annual Boston University Conference on Language Development, Boston (November).

Howe, C., & Tolmie, A. (1999). Productive interaction in the context of computer-supported collaborative learning in science. In K. Littleton & P. Light (Eds.), *Learning with computers: Analysing productive interaction*. London: Routledge.

Howe, M. L. (1991). Misleading children's story recall: Reminiscence of the facts. *Developmental Psychology*, 27, 746–62.

Howes, C., & Matheson, C. C. (1992). Sequences in the development of competent play with peers: Social and pretend play. *Developmental Psychology*, 28, 961–74.

Hsu, L. Y. F. (1998). Prenatal diagnosis of chromosomal abnormalities through amniocentesis. In A. Milunsky (Ed.), *Genetic disorders and the fetus: Diagnosis, prevention, and treatment* (pp. 179–248). Baltimore: Johns Hopkins University Press.

Hudson, J., & Nelson, K. (1986). Repeated encounters of a similar kind: Effects of familiarity on children's autobiographic memory. *Cognitive Development*, 1, 253–71.

Hughes, C., Adlam, A., Happé, F., Jackson, J., Taylor, A., & Caspi, A. (2000). Good test-retest reliability for standard and advanced false-belief tasks across a wide range of abilities. *Journal of Child Psychology and Psychiatry*, 41, 483–90.

Hughes, C., Dunn, J., & White, A. (1998). Trick or treat? Uneven understanding of mind and emotion and executive dysfunction in "hard-to-manage" preschoolers. *Journal of Child Psychology and Psychiatry*, 39, 981–94.

Hughes, C., Russell, J., & Robbins, T. W. (1994). Evidence for executive dysfunction in autism. *Neuropsychologia*, 32, 477–92.

Hughes, M. (1986). *Children and number: Difficulties in learning mathematics*. Oxford: Blackwell.

Hughes, M. (1996). Parents, teachers and schools. In B. Bernstein & J. Brannen (Eds.), *Children, research and policy*. London: Taylor & Francis.

Hughes, M., Dote-Kwan, J., & Dolendo, J. (1998). A close look at the cognitive play of preschoolers with visual impairments in the home. *Exceptional Children*, 64, 451–62.

Hughes, M., Wikeley, F., & Nash, P. (1994). *Parents and their children's schools*. Oxford: Blackwell.

Hulme, C., & MacKenzie, S. (1992). *Working memory and severe learning difficulties*. London: Erlbaum.

Hultsch, D., & Deutsch, F. (1981). *Adult development and aging: A life-span perspective*. New York: McGraw-Hill.

Humphrey, G., Dodwell, P., Muir, D., & Humphrey, D. (1988). Can blind infants and children use sonar sensory aids? *Canadian Journal of Psychology*, 42, 94–119.

Humphreys, A., & Smith, P. K. (1987). Rough and tumble, friendship and dominance in school children: Evidence for continuity and change with age. *Child Development*, 58, 201–12.

Hunt, J. McV. (1969). The impact and limitations of the giant of developmental psychology. In D. Elkind & J. H. Flavell (Eds.), *Studies in cognitive development: Essays in honor of Jean Piaget* (pp. 3–66). New York: Oxford University Press.

Hutchins, E. (1993). Learning to navigate. In S. Chaiklin & J. Lave (Eds.), *Understanding practice: Perspectives on activity and context. Learning in doing: Social, cognitive, and computational perspectives* (pp. 35–63). New York: Cambridge University Press.

Hyams, N. M. (1989). The null-subject parameter in language acquisition. In O. Jaeggli & K. Safir (Eds.), *The null-subject parameter*. Dordrecht: Kluwer.

Ingram, D. (1986). Phonological development: Production. In P. Fletcher & M. Garman (Eds.), *Language acquisition* (2nd ed., pp. 223–39). Cambridge: Cambridge University Press.

Ingram, R. (1992). Review of S. Pinker, *Learnability and cognition: The acquisition of argument structure*. *Journal of Child Language*, 19, 205–11.

Inhelder, B., & Piaget, J. (1958). *The growth of logical thinking from childhood to adolescence*. New York: Basic Books.

Isabella, R. A. (1993). Origins of attachment: Maternal interactive behavior across the first year. *Child Development*, 64, 605–21.

Iskol'dsky, N. V. (1988). *Vliyanie social'no-psikhologicheskikh factorov na individual'nye osobennosti bliznetsov i ikh vnutriparnoe skhodstvo po psikhologicheskim parametram* [The role of social-psychological factors in individual and dyadic twin development]. Unpublished dissertation. Moscow: Psychological Institute of the Russian Academy of Education.

Iso-Ahola, S. E. (1980). *The social psychology of leisure and recreation*. Dubuque, IA: Brown.

Iso-Ahola, S. E., & Crowley, E. D. (1991). Adolescent substance abuse and leisure boredom. *Journal of Leisure Research*, 23 (3), 260–71.

Istvan, J. (1986). Stress, anxiety and birth outcomes: A critical review of the evidence. *Psychological Bulletin*, 100 (3), 331–48.

Izard, C. E. (1994). Innate and universal facial expressions: Evidence from developmental and cross-cultural research. *Psychological Bulletin*, 115, 288–99.

Izard, C. E., Huebner, R. R., Risser, D., McGinnes, G. C., & Dougherty, L. M. (1980). The young infant's ability to produce discrete emotional expressions. *Developmental Psychology*, 16, 132–40.

Izard, C. E., & Malatesta, C. Z. (1987). Perspectives on emotional development I: Differential emotions theory of early emotional development. In J. D. Osofsky (Ed.), *Handbook of infant development* (pp. 495–553). New York: Wiley.

Jenkins, J. M., & Astington, J. W. (1996). Cognitive factors and family structure associated with theory of mind development in young children. *Developmental Psychology*, 32, 70–8.

Jenkins, J. M., & Smith, M. A. (1991). Marital disharmony and children's behavior problems: Aspects of a poor marriage that affect children adversely. *Journal of Child Psychology and Psychiatry*, 32, 793–810.

Jensen, A. R. (1969). How much can we boost IQ and scholastic achievement? *Harvard Educational Review*, 39, 1–123.

Jespersen, O. (1922). *Language: Its nature, development, and origin*. London: Allen & Unwin.

Johnson, C. N., & Harris, P. L. (1994). Magic: Special but not excluded. *British Journal of Developmental Psychology*, 12, 35–51.

Johnson, S. P., & Aslin, R. N. (1995). Perception of object unity in 2-month-old infants. *Developmental Psychology*, 31, 739–45.

Jones, M. C. (1957). The later careers of boys who were early- or late-maturing. *Child Development*, 28, 113–28.

Jones, M. C. (1965). Psychological correlates of somatic development. *Child Development*, 36, 899–911.

Judge, N. E. (1997). The physiology of pregnancy. In G. G. Ashmead (Ed.), *Essentials of maternal fetal medicine* (pp. 26–40). New York: Chapman & Hall.

Juel-Nielsen, N. (1980). *Individual and environment: Monozygotic twins reared apart*. New York: International Universities Press.

Junger, M. (1990). Intergroup bullying and racial harassment in the Netherlands. *Sociology and Social Research*, 74, 65–72.

Jusczyk, P. W. (1997). *The discovery of spoken language*. Cambridge, MA: MIT Press.

Jusczyk, P. W., & Aslin, R. N. (1995). Infant's detection of sound patterns of words in fluent speech. *Cognitive Psychology*, 29, 1–23.

Jusczyk, P. W., Cutler, A., & Redanz, N. (1993). Preference for the predominant stress patterns of English words. *Child Development*, 64, 675–87.

Jusczyk, P. W., Pisoni, D. B., Reed, M., Fernald, A., & Myers, M. (1983). Infants' discrimination of the duration of a rapid spectrum change in nonspeech signals. *Science*, 222, 175–7.

Kahn, P. H. (1999). *The human relationship with nature: Development and culture*. Cambridge, MA: MIT Press.

Kail, R. V. (1989). *The development of memory in children* (2nd ed.). New York: W. H. Freeman.

Kaiser, M. K., McCloskey, M., & Proffitt, D. R. (1986). Development of intuitive theories of motion: Curvilinear motion in the absence of external forces. *Developmental Psychology*, 22, 67–71.

Kaiser, M. K., Proffitt, D. R., & McCloskey, M. (1985). The development of beliefs about falling objects. *Perception and Psychophysics*, 38, 533–9.

Kandel, E. R., Schwartz, J. H., & Jessell, T. M. (2000). *Principles of neural science*. New York: McGraw-Hill.

Kanner, L. (1943). Autistic disturbances of affective contact. *Nervous Child*, 2, 217–50.

Kaplan, L. J. (1996). The stepchild of psychoanalysis, adolescence. *American Imago*, 53 (3), 257–68.

Karmiloff-Smith, A. (1992a). *Beyond modularity: A developmental perspective on cognitive science.* Cambridge, MA: MIT Press.

Karmiloff-Smith, A. (1992b). From meta-processes to conscious access: Evidence from children's metalinguistic and repair data. *Cognition, 23,* 95–147.

Karmiloff-Smith, A. (1999). The connectionist infant: Would Piaget turn in his grave? In A. Slater & D. Muir (Eds.), *The Blackwell reader in developmental psychology* (pp. 43–52). Cambridge, MA, & Oxford: Blackwell.

Karmiloff-Smith, A., & Inhelder, B. (1975). If you want to get ahead, get a theory. *Cognition, 3* (3), 195–212.

Kaye, K. (1977). Toward the origin of dialogue. In H. R. Schaffer (Ed.), *Studies of mother–infant interaction* (pp. 89–117). New York: Academic Press.

Kaye, K., & Fogel, A. (1980). The temporal structure of face-to-face communication between mothers and infants. *Developmental Psychology, 14,* 454–64.

Kazdin, A. E. (1987). Treatment of antisocial behavior in children: Current status and future directions. *Psychological Bulletin, 102,* 187–203.

Keating, D. P. (1980). Thinking process in adolescence. In J. Adelson (Ed.), *Handbook of adolescent psychology.* New York: Wiley.

Keating, D. P. (1990). Adolescent thinking. In S. S. Feldman & G. R. Elliott (Eds.), *At the threshold: The developing adolescent* (pp. 54–89). Cambridge, MA: Harvard University Press.

Keating, D. P., & Bobbitt, B. L. (1978). Individual and developmental differences in cognitive processing components of mental ability. *Child Development, 49,* 155–67.

Keenan, E. O. (1974). Conversational competence in children. *Journal of Child Language, 1,* 163–83.

Keenan, E., & Klein, E. (1975). Coherence in children's discourse. *Journal of Psycholinguistic Research, 4,* 365–78.

Keil, F. C. (1989). *Concepts, kinds, and cognitive development.* Cambridge, MA: MIT Press.

Kelley, H. H. (1991). Lewin, situations, and interdependence. *Journal of Social Issues, 47,* 211–33.

Kellman, P. J., & Spelke, E. R. (1983). Perception of partly occluded objects in infancy. *Cognitive Psychology, 15,* 483–524.

Kessler, B., & Treiman, R. (1997). Syllable structure and the distribution of phonemes in English syllables. *Journal of Memory and Language, 37,* 295–311.

Kimble, G. E. (1994). Evolution of the nature–nurture issue in the history of psychology. In R. Plomin & G. E. McClearn (Eds.), *Nature, nurture and psychology* (pp. 3–26). Washington, DC: American Psychological Association.

Kisilevsky, B. S., Muir, D. W., & Low, J. A. (1992). Maturation of human fetal responses to vibroacoustic stimulation. *Child Development, 63,* 1497–1508.

Kitzinger, S. (1990). *The complete book of pregnancy and childbirth.* New York: Alfred A. Knopf.

Klahr, D., & Robinson, M. (1981). Formal assessment of problem-solving and planning processes in preschool children. *Cognitive Psychology, 13,* 113–48.

Kleiber, D., Larson, R., & Csikszentmihalyi, M. (1986). The experience of leisure in adolescence. *Journal of Leisure Research, 18* (3), 169–76.

Kline, P. (1991). *Intelligence: The psychometric view.* London: Routledge.

Klinnert, M. D. (1984). The regulation of infant behavior by maternal facial expression. *Infant Behavior and Development, 7,* 447–65.

Kochanska, G. (1991). Socialization and temperament in the development of guilt and conscience. *Child Development, 62,* 1379–92.

Kohlberg, L. (1966). A cognitive-developmental analysis of children's sex-role concepts and attitudes. In E. E. Macoby (Ed.), *The development of sex differences* (pp. 81–173). Stanford, CA: Stanford University Press.

Kohlberg, L. (1981). *The philosophy of moral development: Moral stages and the idea of justice.* San Francisco: Harper & Row.

Kohlberg, L. (1984). *The psychology of moral development: The nature and validity of moral stages.* San Francisco: Harper & Row.

Kolk, C. J. V. (1977). Intelligence testing for visually impaired persons. *Journal of Visual Impairment and Blindness,* 71, 158–63.

Korner, A. F., Schneider, P., & Forrest, T. (1983). Effects of vestibular-proprioceptive stimulation on the neurobehavioral development of preterm infants: A pilot study. *Neuropediatrics,* 14, 170–5.

Kornfield, J. R. (1971). Theoretical issues in child phonology. In the Proceedings of the Seventh Annual Meeting of the Chicago Linguistic Society (pp. 454–68). Chicago: University of Chicago.

Kreutzer, M. A., & Charlesworth, W. R. (1973). Infants' reactions to different expressions of emotion. Paper presented at the meeting of the Society for Research in Child Development, Philadelphia.

Kreutzer, M. A., Leonard, C., & Flavell, J. H. (1975). An interview study of children's knowledge about memory. *Monographs of the Society for Research in Child Development,* 40 (1), 1–60.

Kuczaj, S. (1975). On the acquisition of a semantic system. *Journal of Verbal Learning and Verbal Behavior,* 14, 340–58.

Kuczaj, S. (1977). The acquisition of regular and irregular past tense forms. *Journal of Verbal Learning and Verbal Behavior,* 16, 589–600.

Kuczaj, S. (1978). Why do children fail to overgeneralize the progressive inflection? *Child Development,* 5, 167–71.

Kuczaj, S. (1982a). Language play and language acquisition. In H. Reese (Ed.), *Advances in child development and child behavior* (Vol. 17, pp. 197–233). New York: Academic Press.

Kuczaj, S. (1982b). The acquisition of word meaning in the context of the development of the semantic system. In C. Brainerd & M. Pressley (Eds.), *Progress in cognitive development research. Vol. 2. Verbal processes in children* (pp. 95–123). New York: Springer.

Kuczaj, S. (1982c). On the nature of syntactic development. In S. Kuczaj (Ed.), *Language development. Vol. 1. Syntax and semantics* (pp. 37–71). Hillsdale, NJ: Erlbaum.

Kuczaj, S. (1983). "I mell a kunk!" Evidence that children have more complex representations of word pronunciations which they simplify. *Journal of Psycholinguistic Research,* 12, 69–73.

Kuczaj, S. (1990). Constraining constraint theories. *Cognitive Development,* 5, 341–4.

Kuczaj, S. (1999a). Is an evolutionary theory of language play possible? *Current Psychology of Cognition,* 17, 135–54.

Kuczaj, S. (1999b). The world of words: Thoughts on the development of a lexicon. In M. Barrett (Ed.), *The development of language* (pp. 133–60). London: Psychology Press.

Kuczaj, S., & Borys, R. (1988). The overgeneralization of morphological forms as a function of experience. *Language Sciences,* 10, 111–22.

Kuczaj, S., Borys, R., & Jones, M. (1989). On the interaction of language and thought: Some thoughts and developmental data. In A. Gellatly, D. Rogers, & J. Sloboda (Eds.), *Cognition and social worlds* (pp. 168–89). Oxford: Oxford University Press.

Kuczaj, S., & Daly, M. (1979). The development of hypothetical reference in the speech of young children. *Journal of Child Language,* 6, 563–80.

Kuczaj, S., & Kirkpatrick, V. (1993). Similarities and differences in human and animal language research: Toward a comparative psychology of language. In H. Roitblat, L. Herman, & P. Nachtigall (Eds.), *Language and communication: Comparative perspectives* (pp. 45–64). Hillsdale, NJ: Erlbaum.

Kuhl, P. (1992). Speech prototypes: Studies on the nature, function, ontogeny and phylogeny of the "centers" of speech categories. In Y. Tohkura, E. Vatikiotis-Bateson, & Y. Sagiska (Eds.), *Speech perception, production and linguistic structure.* Tokyo: Ohmsha.

Kuhl, P., & Miller, J. (1975). Speech perception by the chinchilla: Voiced–voiceless distinction in alveolar plosive consonants. *Science,* 190, 69–72.

Kuhl, P., & Padden, D. (1982). Enhanced discriminability at the phonetic boundaries for the voicing feature in macaques. *Perception and Psychophysics,* 32, 542–50.

Kuhl, P., & Padden, D. (1983). Enhanced discriminability at the phonetic boundaries for the place feature in macaques. *Journal of the Acoustic Society of America,* 73, 1003–10.

Kuhn, D. (1989). Children and adults as intuitive scientists. *Psychological Review,* 96, 674–89.

Kuhn, D., Amsel, E., & O'Loughlin, M. (1988). *The development of scientific thinking skills.* San Diego: Academic Press.

Kuhn, D., Langer, J., Kohlberg, L., & Haan, N. (1977). The development of formal operations in logical and moral judgment. *Genetic Psychology Monographs,* 95, 97–188.

Kyrklund-Blomberg, N. B., & Cnattingius, S. (1998). Preterm birth and maternal smoking: Risks related to gestational age and onset of delivery. *American Journal of Obstetrics and Gynecology,* 179, 1051–5.

Ladd, G. W. (1983). Social networks of popular, average and rejected children in school settings. *Merrill-Palmer Quarterly,* 29, 283–307.

Lagerspetz, K. M., Björkqvist, K., Berts, M., & King, E. (1982). Group aggression among school children in three schools. *Scandinavian Journal of Psychology,* 23, 45–52.

Laible, D. J., & Thompson, R. A. (1998). Attachment and emotional understanding in preschool children. *Developmental Psychology,* 34, 1038–45.

Lamborn, S. D., Mounts, N. S., Steinberg, L., & Dornbusch, S. M. (1991). Patterns of competence and adjustment among adolescents from authoritative, authoritarian, indulgent, and neglectful families. *Child Development,* 62, 1049–65.

Lampl, M., Veldhuis, J., & Johnson, M. (1992). Saltation and stasis: A model of human growth. *Science,* 258, 801–3.

Landau, B. (1991). Knowledge and its expression in the blind child. In D. P. Keating & H. Rosen (Eds.), *Constructivist perspectives on developmental psychopathology and atypical development* (pp. 173–92). London: Erlbaum.

Landau, B., & Gleitman, L. R. (1985). *Language and experience: Evidence from the blind child.* Cambridge, MA: Harvard University Press.

Landers, W. F. (1971). The effect of differential experience on infants' performance in a Piagetian stage IV object concept task. *Developmental Psychology,* 5, 48–54.

Langlois, J. H., Ritter, J. M., Roggman, L. A., & Vaughn, L. S. (1991). Facial diversity and infant preferences for attractive faces. *Developmental Psychology,* 27, 79–84.

Lapsley, D. (1996). *Moral psychology.* Boulder, CO: Westview.

Law, C. M., de Swiet, M., Osmond, C., Fayers, P. M., Barker, D. J. P., Cruddas, A. M., & Fall, C. H. D. (1993). Initiation of hypertension *in utero* and its amplification throughout life. *British Medical Journal,* 306, 24–7.

Lazar, I., & Darlington, R. (1982). Lasting effects of early education: A report from the consortium for longitudinal studies. *Monographs of the Society for Research in Child Development,* 47 (2–3).

Leahy, A. M. (1935). Nature–nurture and intelligence. *Genetic Psychology Monographs,* 17, 236–308.

LeCanuet, J. S. B. (1996). Fetal sensory competencies. *European Journal of Obstetrics and Gynecology and Reproductive Biology,* 68, 1–23.

LeCanuet, J.-P. (1998). Foetal responses to auditory and speech stimuli. In A. Slater (Ed.), *Perceptual development: Visual, auditory and speech perception in infancy* (pp. 317–55). Hove: Psychology Press.

Lee, A., Hobson, R. P., & Chiat, S. (1994). I, you, me and autism: An experimental study. *Journal of Autism and Developmental Disorders, 24,* 155–76.

Lee, M., & Larson, R. (2000). The Korean "examination hell": Long hours of studying, distress and depression. *Journal of Youth and Adolescence, 29,* 249–71.

Leekam, S., Baron-Cohen, S., Perrett, D., Milders, M., & Brown, S. (1997). Eye-direction detection: A dissociation between geometric and joint attention skills in autism. *British Journal of Developmental Psychology, 15,* 77–96.

Leichtman, M. D., & Ceci, S. J. (1995). The effects of stereotypes and suggestions on preschoolers' reports. *Developmental Psychology, 31,* 568–78.

Lenneberg, E., Rebelsky, F., & Nichols, I. (1965). The vocalizations of infants born to deaf and hearing parents. *Human Development, 8,* 23–47.

Lerner, R. (1986). *Concepts and theories of human development* (2nd ed.). New York: Random House.

Leslie, A. M. (1987). Pretense and representation: The origins of "theory of mind." *Psychological Review, 94,* 412–26.

Leslie, A. M., & Thaiss, L. (1992). Domain specificity in conceptual development: Neuro-psychological evidence from autism. *Cognition, 43,* 225–51.

Lester, B. M., Hoffman, J., & Brazelton, T. B. (1985). The rhythmic structure of mother–infant interaction in term and preterm infants. *Child Development, 56,* 15–27.

Lever, J. (1978). Sex differences in the complexity of children's play and games. *American Sociological Review, 43,* 471–83.

Levine, L. V., Tuber, S. B., Slade, H., & Ward, M. J. (1991). Mothers' mental representations and their relationship to mother–infant attachment. *Bulletin of the Menninger Clinic, 55,* 454–69.

Lewin, K. (1939). Field theory and experiment in social psychology. *American Journal of Sociology, 44,* 868–897.

Lewin, K. (1944). The dynamics of group action. *Educational Leadership, 1,* 195–200.

Lewin, M. A. (1998). Kurt Lewin: His psychology and a daughter's recollections. In G. A. Kimble, M. Wertheimer, et al. (Eds.), *Portraits of pioneers in psychology* (pp. 105–18). Mahwah, NJ: Erlbaum.

Lewis, C., Freeman, N. H., Kyriakidou, C., & Maridaki-Kassotaki, K. (1996). Social influences on false belief access: Specific sibling influences or general apprenticeship. *Child Development, 67,* 2930–47.

Lewis, C., & Osborne, A. (1990). Three-year-olds' problems with false belief: Conceptual deficit or linguistic artefact? *Child Development, 61,* 1514–19.

Lewis, M., & Brooks-Gunn, J. (1979). *Social cognition and the acquisition of self.* New York: Plenum.

Lewis, M., Young, G., Brooks, J., & Michalson, L. (1975). The beginning of friendship. In M. Lewis & L. Rosenblum (Eds.), *Friendship and peer relations* (pp. 27–65). New York: Wiley.

Lewis, V., Boucher, J., Lupton, L., & Watson, S. (2000). Relationships between symbolic play, functional play, verbal and non-verbal ability in young children. *International Journal of Language and Communication Disorders, 35,* 117–27.

Lewis, V., Norgate, S., Collis, G., & Reynolds, R. (2000). The consequences of visual impairment for children's symbolic and functional play. *British Journal of Developmental Psychology, 18,* 449–64.

Liberman, I. Y., Shankweiler, D., Fischer, F. W., & Carter, B. (1974). Explicit syllable and phoneme segmentation in the young child. *Journal of Experimental Child Psychology, 18,* 201–12.

Liberman, I. Y., Shankweiler, D., & Liberman, A. (1989). The alphabetic principle and learning to read. In D. Shankweiler & I. Y. Liberman (Eds.), *Phonology and reading disability* (pp. 1–34). Ann Arbor: University of Michigan Press.

Lidster, W., & Bremner, G. (1999). Interpretation and construction of coordinate dimensions by 4- to 5-year-old children. *British Journal of Developmental Psychology*, 17, 189–201.

Light, P. H. (1997). Computers for learning: Psychological perspectives. *Journal of Child Psychology and Psychiatry*, 38, 1–8.

Light, P. H., Buckingham, N., & Robins, A. H. (1979). The conservation task in an interactional setting. *British Journal of Educational Psychology*, 49, 304–10.

Light, P., Littleton, K., Messer, D., & Joiner, R. (1994). Social and communicative processes in computer-based problem solving. *European Journal of Psychology and Education*, 9, 93–109.

Lillard, A. S. (1993). Pretend play skills and the child's theory of mind. *Child Development*, 64, 348–71.

Lindberg, M. (1991). A taxonomy of suggestibility and eyewitness memory: Age, memory process, and focus of analysis. In J. L. Doris (Ed.), *The suggestibility of children's recollections* (pp. 47–55). Washington, DC: American Psychological Association.

Littleton, K., & Light, P. (Eds.) (1999). *Learning with computers: Analysing productive interaction*. London: Routledge.

Littleton, K., Light, P., Joiner, R., Messer, D., & Barnes, P. (1995). Gender and software effects in computer-based problem solving. *Newsletter of the European Association for Research on Learning and Instruction*.

Lobel, M. (1994). Conceptualizations, measurement, and effects of prenatal maternal stress on birth outcomes. *Journal of Behavioral Medicine*, 17 (3), 225–72.

Lobel, M., Dunkel-Schetter, C., & Scrimshaw, S. C. (1992). Prenatal maternal stress and prematurity: A prospective study of socioeconomically disadvantaged women. *Health Psychology*, 11 (1), 32–40.

Locke, J. L. (1983). *Phonological acquisition and change*. New York: Academic Press.

Locurto, C. (1990). The malleability of IQ as judged from adoption studies. *Intelligence*, 14, 275–92.

Loeber, R. (1985). Patterns and development of antisocial behavior. *Annals of Child Development*, 53, 1431–46.

Loeber, R., & Dishion, T. (1983). Early predictors of male delinquency: A review. *Psychological Bulletin*, 94, 69–99.

Loeber, R., & Stouthamer-Loeber, M. (1986). Family factors as correlates and predictors of conduct problems and juvenile delinquency. In M. Tonry & N. Morris (Eds.), *Crime and justice* (Vol. 7). Chicago: University of Chicago Press.

Loeber, R., & Stouthamer-Loeber, M. (1998). Development of juvenile aggression and violence: Some common misconceptions and controversies. *American Psychologist*, 53, 242–59.

Loehlin, J. C. (1989). Partitioning environmental and genetic contributions to behavioral development. *American Psychologist*, 44, 1295–1302.

Loehlin, J. C., & DeFries, J. C. (1987). Genotype–environment correlation and IQ. *Behavior Genetics*, 17, 263–77.

Loehlin, J. C., Horn, J. M., & Willerman, L. (1989). Modeling IQ change: Evidence from the Texas Adoption Project. *Child Development*, 60, 993–1004.

Loehlin, J. C., Horn, J. M., & Willerman, L. (1997). Heredity, environment, and IQ in the Texas adoption study. In R. J. Sternberg & E. L. Grigorenko (Eds.), *Heredity, environment, and intelligence* (pp. 105–25). New York: Cambridge University Press.

Loehlin, J. C., & Nichols, R. C. (1976). *Heredity, environment, and personality*. Austin: University of Texas Press.

Loehlin, J. C., & Vandenberg, S. G. (1968). Genetic and environmental components in the covariation of cognitive abilities: An additive model. In S. G. Vandenberg (Ed.), *Progress in human behavior genetics* (pp. 261–85). Baltimore: Johns Hopkins University Press.

Longeot, F. (1966). Expérimentation d'une échelle individuelle du développement de la pensée logique [Experimentation of an individual scale of logical thought development]. *BINOP*, 22, 306–19.

Lourenço, O., & Machado, A. (1996). In defense of Piaget's theory: A reply to 10 common criticisms. *Psychological Review*, 103, 143–64.

Lundberg, I., Olofsson, A., & Wall, S. (1980). Reading and spelling skills in the first school years predicted from phoneme awareness skills in kindergarten. *Scandinavian Journal of Psychology*, 21, 159–73.

Lynn, R., & Hattori, K. (1990). The heritability of intelligence in Japan. *Behavior Genetics*, 20, 545–6.

Lyons, J. (1977). *Semantics. Vol. 1*. Cambridge: Cambridge University Press.

Lyons-Ruth, K., Repacholi, B., McLeod, S., & Silva, E. (1991). Disorganized attachment behavior in infancy: Short-term stability, maternal and infant correlates and risk-related subtypes. *Development and Psychopathology*, 3, 377–96.

Maccoby, E. E. (1986). Social groupings in childhood: Their relationships to prosocial and anti-social behavior in boys and girls. In D. Olweus, J. Block, & M. Radke-Yarrow (Eds.), *Development of antisocial and prosocial behavior*. New York: Academic Press.

Maccoby, E. E. (1998). *The two sexes: Growing up apart, coming together*. Cambridge, MA: Harvard University Press.

Maccoby, E. E., & Jacklin, C. N. (1974). *The psychology of sex differences*. Stanford, CA: Stanford University Press.

Maccoby, E. E., & Jacklin, C. N. (1980). Sex differences in aggression: A rejoinder and reprise. *Child Development*, 51, 964–80.

Maccoby, E. E., & Martin, J. A. (1983). Socialization in the context of the family: Parent–child interaction. In C. M. Hetherington (Ed.), *Handbook of child psychology. Vol. 4. Socialization, personality, and social development* (4th ed., pp. 1–101). New York: Wiley.

McClearn, G. E., Johansson, B., Berg, S., Pedersen, N. L., Ahern, F., Petrill, S. A., & Plomin, R. (1997). Substantial genetic influence on cognitive abilities in twins 80 or more years old. *Science*, 278, 1560–3.

McCloskey, M., & Zaragoza, M. (1985). Misleading postevent information and memory for events: Arguments and evidence against the memory impairment hypothesis. *Journal of Experimental Psychology: General*, 114, 1–16.

McGarrigle, J., & Donaldson, M. (1974). Conservation accidents. *Cognition*, 3, 341–50.

McGough, L. S. (1994). *Child witnesses: Fragile voices in the American legal system*. New Haven, CT: Yale University Press.

McGraw, M. (1945). *Neuromuscular maturation of the human infant*. New York: Hafner.

McGue, M., Bouchard, T. J., Iacono, W. G., & Lykken, D. T. (1994). Behavioral genetics of cognitive ability: A life-span perspective. In R. Plomin & G. E. McClearn (Eds.), *Nature and nurture and psychology* (pp. 59–76). Washington, DC: American Psychological Association.

Macken, M., & Ferguson, C. A. (1983). Cognitive aspects of phonological development: Model, evidence, and issues. In K. Nelson (Ed.), *Children's language*. Hillsdale, NJ: Erlbaum.

McLaughlin, S. (1998). *Introduction to language development*. San Diego, CA: Singular Publishing Group.

McNamara, J. (1982). *Names for things: A study of human learning*. Cambridge, MA: MIT Press.

McTear, M. F. (1985). *Children's conversations*. Oxford: Blackwell.

MacTurk, R., Vietze, P., McCarthy, M., McQuiston, S., & Yarrow, L. (1985). The organization of exploratory behavior in Down syndrome and non-delayed infants. *Child Development*, 56, 573–87.

Magnusson, D., Stattin, H., & Dunér, A. (1983). Aggression and criminality in a longitudinal perspective. In K. T. van Dusen & S. A. Mednick (Eds.), *Prospective studies of crime and delinquency*. Boston: Kluwer-Nijhoff.

Main, M., & Hesse, E. (1990). Parents' unresolved traumatic experiences are related to infant disorganized attachment status: Is frightened and/or frightening parental behavior the linking mechanism? In M. T. Greenberg, D. Cicchetti, & E. M. Cummings (Eds.), *Attachment in the preschool years* (pp. 161–82). Chicago: University of Chicago Press.

Main, M., & Solomon, J. (1986). Discovery of a disorganized/disoriented attachment pattern. In T. B. Brazelton & M. W. Yogman (Eds.), *Affective development in infancy*. Norwood, NJ: Ablex.

Main, M., & Solomon, J. (1990). Procedures for identifying infants as disorganized/disoriented during the Ainsworth strange situation. In M. T. Greenberg, D. Cicchetti, & E. M. Cummings (Eds.), *Attachment in the preschool years* (pp. 121–60). Chicago: University of Chicago Press.

Mainous, A. G., & Hueston, W. J. (1994). Passive smoke and low birth weight: Evidence of a threshold effect. *Archives of Family Medicine*, 3, 875–8.

Malatesta, C. Z., Culver, C., Tesman, J. R., & Shepard, B. (1989). The development of emotion expression during the first two years of life. *Monographs of the Society for Research in Child Development*, 54 (1–2, No. 219).

Malik, N., & Furman, W. (1993). Problems in children's peer relations: What can the clinician do? *Journal of Child Psychology and Psychiatry*, 34, 1303–26.

Manger, T., & Olweus, D. (1985). Tilbakemelding til skulane. *Norsk Skoleblad* (Oslo, Norway), 35, 20–2.

Mann, V. A. (1986). Phonological awareness: The role of reading experience. *Cognition*, 24, 65–92.

Maratsos, M. P. (1983). Some current issues in the study of the acquisition of grammar. In J. Flavell & E. Markman (Eds.), *Handbook of child psychology. Vol. 3. Cognitive development* (pp. 707–86). New York: Wiley.

Maratsos, M. P. (1999). Some aspects of innateness and complexity in grammatical acquisition. In M. Barrett (Ed.), *The development of language* (pp. 191–228). Hove: Psychology Press.

Maratsos, M. P. (2000). More overregularizations after all: New data and discussion of Marcus, Pinker, Ullman, Hollander, Rosen, and Xu. *Journal of Child Language*, 27, 183–212.

Mares, M. L. (1996). Positive effects of television on social behavior: A meta-analysis. Unpublished manuscript, the Annenberg Public Policy Center, Philadelphia. Downloaded from the World Wide Web on April 4, 2001 (http://www.appcpenn.org/appc/reports/rep3.pdf).

Mareschal, D. (2000). Connectionist modeling and infant development. In D. Muir & A. Slater (Eds.), *Infant development: Essential readings* (pp. 53–65). Cambridge, MA, & Oxford: Blackwell.

Markman, E. M. (1981). Two different principles of conceptual organization. In M. E. Lamb & A. L. Brown (Eds.), *Advances in developmental psychology* (Vol. 1, pp. 199–236). Hillsdale, NJ: Erlbaum.

Markman, E. M. (1990). Constraints children place on word meanings. *Cognitive Science*, 14, 57–77.

Marquis, D. M. (1941). Learning in the neonate: The modification of behavior under three feeding schedules. *Journal of Experimental Psychology*, 29, 263–82.

Marschark, M. (1993). *Psychological development of deaf children*. New York: Oxford University Press.

Marsh, G., & Desberg, P. (1983). The development of strategies in the acquisition of symbolic skills. In D. R. Rogers & J. A. Sloboda (Eds.), *The acquisition of symbolic skills* (pp. 149–54). New York: Plenum.

Marsh, G., Friedman, M. P., Welch, V., & Desberg, P. (1980). The development of strategies in spelling. In U. Frith (Ed.), *Cognitive processes in spelling*. London: Academic Press.

Martin, C. L., Fabes, R. A., Evans, S. M., & Wyman, H. (1999). Social cognition on the playground: Children's beliefs about playing with girls versus boys and their relations to sex-segregated play. *Journal of Social and Personal Relationships*, 16, 751–71.

Martin, N. G., & Eaves, L. J. (1977). The genetical analysis of covariance structure. *Heredity*, 38, 79–95.

Martin, N. G., Jardine, R., & Eaves, L. J. (1984). Is there only one set of genes for different abilities? A reanalysis of the National Merit Scholarship Qualifying Test (NMSQT) data. *Behavior Genetics*, 14, 355–70.

Masataka, N. (1996). Perception of motherese in a signed language by 6-month-old deaf infants. *Developmental Psychology*, 32, 874–9.

Masi, W. (1979). Supplemental stimulation of the premature infant. In T. M. Field (Ed.), *Infants born at risk* (pp. 367–88). New York: Scientific Publications.

Masur, E. F. (1983). Gestural development, dual-directional signaling, and the transition to words. *Journal of Psycholinguistic Research*, 12, 93–109.

Masur, E. F. (1995). Infants' early verbal imitation and their later lexical development. *Merrill-Palmer Quarterly*, 41, 286–306.

Masur, E. F., & Rodemaker, J. E. (1999). Mothers' and infants' spontaneous vocal, verbal, and action imitation during the second year. *Merrill-Palmer Quarterly*, 45, 392–412.

Matheny, A. P., Wilson, R. S., Dolan, A. B., & Krantz, J. Z. (1981). Behavioral contrasts in twinship: Stability patterns of differences in childhood. *Child Development*, 52, 579–88.

Maurer, D., & Barrera, M. (1981). Infants' perception of natural and distorted arrangements of a schematic face. *Child Development*, 52, 196–202.

Maurer, D., & Salapatek, P. (1976). Developmental changes in the scanning of faces by young infants. *Child Development*, 47, 523–7.

Mayes, L. C., & Cohen, D. J. (1996). Anna Freud and developmental psychoanalytic psychology. *The Psychoanalytic Study of the Child*, 51, 117–41.

Mayes, L. C., Klin, A., Tercyak, K. P., Cicchetti, D. V., & Cohen, D. J. (1996). Test-retest reliability of false belief tasks. *Journal of Child Psychology and Psychiatry*, 37, 313–19.

Mazur, J. E. (1990). *Learning and behavior* (2nd ed.). Englewood Cliffs, NJ: Prentice-Hall.

Mehler, J., Jusczyk, P., Lambertz, G., Halsted, N., Bertoncini, J., & Amiel-Tison, C. (1988). A precursor of language acquisition in young infants. *Cognition*, 29, 143–78.

Meins, E., Fernyhough, C., Russell, J., & Clark-Carter, D. (1998). Security of attachment as a predictor of symbolic and mentalising abilities: A longitudinal study. *Social Development*, 7, 1–24.

Meltzoff, A. N., & Moore, M. K. (1977). Imitation of facial and manual gestures by human neonates. *Science*, 198, 75–8.

Meltzoff, A. N., & Moore, M. K. (1983). Newborn infants imitate adult facial gestures. *Child Development*, 54, 702–9.

Mercer, N., & Fisher, E. (1998). How do teachers help children to learn? An analysis of teachers' interventions in computer-based activities. In D. Faulkner, K. Littleton, & M. Woodhead (Eds.), *Learning relationships in the classroom*. London: Routledge.

Merriman, C. (1924). The intellectual resemblance of twins. *Psychological Monographs*, 33, 1–58.

Merriman, W., Marazita, J., & Jarvis, L. (1995). Children's disposition to map new words onto new referents. In M. Tomasello & W. Merriman (Eds.), *Beyond names for things: Young children's acquisition of verbs* (pp. 147–83). Hillsdale, NJ: Erlbaum.

Mervis, C. B. (1987). Child-based object categories and early lexical development. In U. Neisser (Ed.), *Concepts and conceptual knowledge* (pp. 201–33). Cambridge: Cambridge University Press.

Mervis, C. B., Golinkoff, R. M., & Bertrand, J. (1994). Two-year-olds readily learn multiple labels for the same category. *Child Development*, 65, 1163–77.

Messinger, D. S., & Fogel, A. (1998). Give and take: The development of conventional infant gestures. *Merrill-Palmer Quarterly*, 44, 566–90.

Michels, K. B., Trichopoulos, D., Adami, H. O., Hsieh, C., & Lan, S. J. (1996). Birthweight as a risk factor for breast cancer. *Lancet*, 348, 1542–6.

Michie, S. (1984). Why preschoolers are reluctant to count spontaneously. *British Journal of Developmental Psychology*, 2, 347–58.

Miller, C. A. (1956). The magical number seven, plus or minus two: Some limits on our capacity for processing information. *Psychological Review*, 63, 81–97.

Miller, K. (1984). The child as the measurer of all things: Measurement procedures and the development of quantitative concepts. In C. Sophian (Ed.), *Origins of cognitive skills* (pp. 193–228). Hillsdale, NJ: Erlbaum.

Miller, K. E., Smith, C. N., Zhu, J., & Zhang, H. (1995). Mathematical competence: The role of number-naming systems. *Psychological Science*, 6, 123–54.

Miller, K. F., & Stigler, J. W. (1987). Counting in Chinese: Cultural variation in a basic skill. *Cognitive Development*, 2, 279–305.

Miller, P. H. (1993). *Theories of developmental psychology* (3rd ed.). Englewood Cliffs, NJ: Prentice-Hall.

Miller, P. H., & Weiss, M. G. (1981). Children's attention allocation, understanding of attention, and performance on the incidental learning task. *Child Development*, 52, 1183–90.

Miller, P. M., & Seier, W. L. (1994). Strategy utilization deficiencies in children: When, where, and why. In H. W. Reese (Ed.), *Advances in child development and behavior* (Vol. 25, pp. 107–56). San Diego: Academic Press.

Miller, W. R., & Ervin, S. (1964). The development of grammar in child language. In U. Bellugi & R. Brown (Eds.), The acquisition of language (pp. 9–34). *Monographs of the Society for Research in Child Development*, 29.

Mills, A. (1988). Visual handicap. In D. Bishop & K. Mogford (Eds.), *Language development in exceptional circumstances* (pp. 150–64). London: Churchill Livingston.

Milunsky, A., & Milunsky, J. (1998). Genetic counseling: Preconception, prenatal, and perinatal. In A. Milunsky (Ed.), *Genetic disorders and the fetus: Diagnosis, prevention, and treatment* (pp. 1–52). Baltimore: Johns Hopkins University Press.

Mirmiran, M., & Swaab, D. F. (1992). Effects of perinatal medicine on brain development. In J. Nijhuis (Ed.), *Fetal behavior: Developmental and perinatal aspects* (pp. 112–28). New York: Oxford University Press.

Mitchell, P. (1997). *Introduction to theory of mind: Children, autism and apes*. London: Arnold.

Mitchell, P., & Lacohee, H. (1991). Children's early understanding of false belief. *Cognition*, 39, 107–27.

Mitchell, P., Robinson, E. J., Isaacs, J. E., & Nye, R. M. (1996). Contamination in reasoning about false belief: An instance of realist bias in adults but not children. *Cognition*, 59, 1–21.

Miura, I. T., Kim, C. C., Chang, C.-M., & Okamoto, Y. (1988). Effects of language characteristics on children's cognitive representation of number: Cross-national comparisons. *Child Development*, 59, 1445–50.

Miura, I. T., Okamoto, Y., Kim, C. C., Chang, C.-M., Steere, M., & Fayol, M. (1994). Comparisons of children's cognitive representation of number: China, France, Japan, Korea, Sweden and the United States. *International Journal of Behavioral Development*, 17, 401–11.

Mix, K. S., Levine, S. C., & Huttenlocher, J. (1997). Numerical abstraction in infants: Another look. *Developmental Psychology*, 35, 423–8.

Mix, K. S., Levine, S. C., & Huttenlocher, J. (2001). *Quantitative development in infancy and early childhood*. New York: Oxford University Press.

Miyake, K., Chen, S., & Campos, J. J. (1985). Infant temperament, mother's mode of interaction, and attachment in Japan: An interim report. In I. Bretherton & E. Waters (Eds.), Growing points in attachment theory and research (pp. 276–97). *Monographs of the Society for Research in Child Development*, 50 (1–2, Serial No. 209).

Mobility, K. E. (1989). Meanings of recreation and leisure among adolescents. *Leisure Studies*, 8, 11–23.

Moffitt, T. E., Caspi, A., Dickson, N., Silva, P. A., & Stanton, W. (1996). Childhood-onset versus adolescent-onset antisocial conduct problems in males: Natural history from ages 3 to 18 years. *Development and Psychopathology*, 8, 399–424.

Moffitt, T. E., Lynam, D. R., & Silva, P. A. (1994). Neuropsychological tests predicting persistent male delinquency. *Criminology*, 32, 277–300.

Mohn, G., & van Hof-van Duin, J. (1985). Preferential looking acuity in normal and neurologically abnormal infants and pediatric patients. *Documenta Ophthalmolgia*. Special issue.

Molenaar, P. C. M., Boomsma, D. I., & Dolan, C. V. (1999). The detection of genotype–environment interaction in longitudinal genetic models. In M. C. LaBuda & E. L. Grigorenko (Eds.), *On the way to individuality: Current methodological issues in behavior genetics* (pp. 53–70). Commack, NY: Nova Sciences.

Molina, J. C., Chotro, M. G., & Dominguez, H. D. (1995). Fetal alcohol learning resulting from contamination of the prenatal environment. In J. LeCanuet, W. Fifer, N. Krasnegor, & W. Smotherman (Eds.), *Fetal development: A psychobiological perspective* (pp. 419–38). Hillsdale, NJ: Erlbaum.

Molloy, R., Brownell, H. H., & Gardner, H. (1990). Discourse comprehension by right-hemisphere stroke patients. In Y. Joanette & H. H. Brownell (Eds.), *Discourse ability and brain damage: Theoretical and empirical perspectives* (pp. 113–30). New York: Springer.

Money, J., & Ehrhardt, A. A. (1972). *Man and woman/boy and girl*. Baltimore, MD: Johns Hopkins University Press.

Monk, C., Fifer, W. P., Sloan, R. P., Myers, M. M., Trien, L., & Hurtado, A. (2000). Maternal stress responses and anxiety during pregnancy: Effects on fetal heart rate. *Developmental Psychobiology*, 36, 67–77.

Monteil, J. M. (1992). Towards a social psychology of cognitive functioning. In M. Von Granach, W. Doise, & C. Mugny (Eds.), *Social representation and the social bases of knowledge*. Bern: Hubert.

Montemayor, R., Brown, B., & Adams, G. (1985). Changes in identity status and psychological adjustment after leaving home and entering college. Paper presented at the Biennial Meetings of the Society for Research in Child Development, Toronto.

Moon, C., Bever, T. G., & Fifer, W. P. (1992). Canonical and non-canonical syllable discrimination by two-day-old infants. *Journal of Child Language*, 19, 1–17.

Moon, C., Cooper, R., & Fifer, W. (1993). Two-day-olds prefer their native language. *Infant Behavior and Development*, 16 (4), 495–500.

Moon, C., & Fifer, W. P. (1990). Syllables as signals for two-day-old infants. *Infant Behavior and Development*, 13, 377–90.

Moore, E. G. J. (1986). Family socialization and the IQ test performance of traditionally and transracially adopted black children. *Developmental Psychology*, 22, 317–26.

Moore, V. M., Cockington, R. A., Ryan, P., & Robinson, J. S. (1999). The relationship between birth weight and blood pressure amplifies from childhood to adulthood. *Journal of Hypertension*, 17, 883–8.

Morais, J., Bertelson, P., Cary, L., & Alegria, J. (1986). Literacy training and speech segmentation. *Cognition*, 24, 45–64.

Morais, J., Cary, L., Alegria, J., & Bertelson, P. (1980). Does awareness of speech as a sequence of phones arise spontaneously? *Cognition*, 7, 323–31.

Morency, N. L., & Krauss, R. M. (1982). Children's nonverbal encoding and decoding of affect. In R. S. Feldman (Ed.), *Development of nonverbal behavior in children*. New York: Springer.

Morford, J. P., & Goldin-Meadow, S. (1997). From here and now to there and then: The development of displaced reference in homesign and English. *Child Development*, 68, 420–35.

Morgan, I., Damber, L., Tavelin, B., & Hogberg, U. (1999). Characteristics of pregnancy and birth and malignancy in the offspring. *Cancer Causes Control*, 10, 85–94.

Mosier, C. E., & Rogoff, B. (1994). Infants' instrumental use of their mothers to achieve their goals. *Child Development*, 65, 70–9.

Mueller, E., & Brenner, J. (1977). The origins of social skills and interaction among playgroup toddlers. *Child Development*, 48, 854–61.

Muir, D., Humphrey, D., & Humphrey, K. (1994). Pattern and space perception in young infants. *Spatial Vision*, 8, 141–65.

Muir, D. W., & Nadel, J. (1998). Infant social perception. In A. Slater (Ed.), *Perceptual development: Visual, auditory and speech perception in infancy* (pp. 247–85). Hove: Psychology Press.

Mulford, R. (1988). First words of the blind child. In M. D. Smith & J. L. Locke (Eds.), *The emergent lexicon: The child's development of a linguistic vocabulary* (pp. 293–340). London: Academic Press.

Muller, E., Hollien, H., & Murry, T. (1974). Perceptual response to infant crying: Identification of cry types. *Journal of Child Language*, 1, 89–95.

Murooka, H., Koie, Y., & Suda, D. (1976). Analyse des sons intrautérins et de leurs effets tranquillisants sur le nouveau-né. *Journal de Gynécologie Obstétrique et de Biologie de la Reproduction*, 5, 367–76.

Murphy, C. M., & Messer, D. J. (1977). Mothers, infants and pointing: A study of a gesture. In H. R. Schaffer (Ed.), *Studies in mother–infant interaction* (pp. 325–54). London: Academic Press.

Murray, L., & Trevarthen, C. B. (1985). Emotional regulation of interactions between 2-month-olds and their mothers. In T. M. Field & N. A. Fox (Eds.), *Social perception in infants*. Norwood, NJ: Ablex.

Muter, V., Hulme, C., Snowling, M., & Taylor, S. (1998). Segmentation, not rhyme, predicts early progress in learning to read. *Journal of Experimental Child Psychology*, 71, 3–28.

Naslund, J. C., & Schneider, W. (1996). Kindergarten letter knowledge, phonological skills and memory processes: Relative effects on early literacy. *Journal of Experimental Psychology*, 62, 30–59.

Nathwar, S., & Puri, P. (1995). A comparative study of MZ and DZ twins on level I and level II mental abilities and personality. *Journal of Indian Academy of Applied Psychology*, 21, 87–92.

National Center for Educational Statistics. (1991). *Education in States and Nations: Indicators Comparing U.S. States with Other Industrialized Countries in 1991* (NCES Report No. 96–160). Washington, DC: US Government Printing Office.

Nazzi, T., Bertoncini, J., & Mehler, J. (1998). Language discrimination by newborns: Toward an understanding of the role of rhythm. *Journal of Experimental Psychology*, 24 (3), 1–11.

Neale, M. C., & Cardon, L. R. (Eds.) (1992). *Methodology for genetic studies of twins and families*. Dordrecht: Kluwer Academic Press.

Nelson, C. A., & Bloom, F. E. (1997). Child development and neuroscience. *Child Development*, 68, 970–87.

Nelson, K. (1988). Constraints on word learning? *Cognitive Development*, 3, 221–46.

Nelson, K. (1996). *Language in cognitive development*. New York: Cambridge University Press.

Nelson, K. E., & Gruendel, J. M. (1979). At morning it's lunchtime: A scriptal view of children's dialogues. *Discourse Processes*, 2, 73–94.

Nesselroade, J., Schaie, K., & Baltes, P. (1972). Ontogenetic and generational components of structural and quantitative change in adult behavior. *Journal of Gerontology*, 27, 222–8.

Neugebauer, R., Hoek, H. W., & Susser, E. (1999). Prenatal exposure to wartime famine and development of antisocial personality disorder in early adulthood. *Journal of American Medical Association*, 282, 455–62.

Neville, H. J., Coffey, S. A., Lawson, D. S., Fischer, A., Emmorey, K., & Bellugi, U. (1997). Neural systems mediating American Sign Language: Effects of sensory experience and age of acquisition. *Brain and Language*, 57, 285–308.

Newcomb, A., & Bagwell, C. (1995). Children's friendship relations: A meta-analytic review. *Psychological Bulletin*, 117, 306–47.

Newcomb, A. F., & Bagwell, C. (1996). The developmental significance of children's friendship relations. In W. W. Bukowski, A. F. Newcomb, & W. W. Hartup (Eds.), *The company they keep: Friendship in childhood and adolescence*. New York: Cambridge University Press.

Newcombe, N., & Huttenlocher, J. (1992). Children's early ability to solve perspective-taking problems. *Developmental Psychology*, 28, 635–43.

Newman, D. L., Caspi, A., Moffitt, T. E., & Silva, P. A. (1997). Antecedents of adult interpersonal functioning: Effects of individual differences in age 3 temperament. *Developmental Psychology*, 33, 206–17.

Newman, D., Tellegen, A., & Bouchard, T. J. (1998). Individual differences in adult ego development: Sources of influence in twins reared apart. *Journal of Personality and Social Psychology*, 74, 985–95.

Newman, H. H., Freeman, F. N., & Holzinger, K. J. (1937). *Twins: A study of heredity and environment*. Chicago: University of Chicago Press.

Newport, E. L., Gleitman, L. R., & Gleitman, H. (1975). A study of mother's speech and child language acquisition. Paper presented at the 7th Child Language Research Forum, Stanford University, Stanford, CA (September).

Nichols, R. C. (1978). Twin studies of ability, personality, and interests. *Homo*, 29, 158–73.

Nijhuis, J. G. (1992). The third trimester. In J. Nijhuis (Ed.), *Fetal behavior: Developmental and perinatal aspects* (pp. 26–40). New York: Oxford University Press.

Ninio, A., & Snow, C. (1996). *Pragmatic development*. Boulder, CO: Westview.

Nunes, T., & Bryant, P. (1996). *Children doing mathematics*. Oxford: Blackwell.

Nunes, T., Bryant, P., & Bindman, M. (1997). Morphological spelling strategies: Developmental stages and processes. *Developmental Psychology*, 33, 637–49.

Ochs, E., & Schieffelin, B. (1984). Language acquisition and socialization: Three developmental stories and their implications. In R. Shweder & R. LeVine (Eds.), *Culture theory*. Cambridge: Cambridge University Press.

Ockleford, E., Vince, M., Layton, C., & Reader, M. (1988). Responses of neonates to parents' and others' voices. *Early Human Development*, 18, 27–36.

O'Connor, N., & Hermelin, B. (1988). Low intelligence and special abilities. *Journal of Child Psychology and Psychiatry*, 29, 391–6.

Ojito, M. (1997). School officials skeptical of sexual assault charges. *New York Times*, October 22, B3.

Oller, D. (1980). The emergence of speech sounds in infancy. In G. Yeni-Komshian, J. Kavanaugh, & C. Ferguson (Eds.), *Child phonology* (pp. 93–112). New York: Academic Press.

Oller, D., & Eilers, R. (1988). The role of audition in infant babbling. *Child Development*, 59, 441–9.

Olson, D. R. (1994). *The world on paper*. Cambridge: Cambridge University Press.

Olson, D. R. (1996). Towards a psychology of literacy: On the relations between speech and writing. *Cognition*, 60, 83–104.

Olson-Fulero, L., & Conforti, J. (1983). Child responsiveness to mother questions of varying type and presentation. *Journal of Child Language*, 10, 495–520.

Olweus, D. (1973a). *Hackkycklingar och översittare. Forskning om skolmobbning*. Stockholm: Almqvist & Wicksell.

Olweus, D. (1973b). Personality and aggression. In J. K. Cole & D. D. Jensen (Eds.), *Nebraska Symposium on Motivation 1972*. Lincoln: University of Nebraska Press.

Olweus, D. (1977). Aggression and peer acceptance in adolescent boys: Two short-term longitudinal studies of ratings. *Child Development*, 48, 1301–13.

Olweus, D. (1978). *Aggression in the schools: Bullies and whipping boys*. Washington, DC: Hemisphere Press.

Olweus, D. (1979). Stability of aggressive reaction patterns in males: A review. *Psychological Bulletin*, 86, 852–75.

Olweus, D. (1980). Familial and temperamental determinants of aggressive behavior in adolescent boys: A causal analysis. *Developmental Psychology*, 16, 644–60.

Olweus, D. (1981). Bullying among school-boys. In N. Cantwell (Ed.), *Children and violence*. Stockholm: Akademilitteratur.

Olweus, D. (1983). Low school achievement and aggressive behavior in adolescent boys. In D. Magnusson & V. Allen (Eds.), *Human development: An interactional perspective*. New York: Academic Press.

Olweus, D. (1984). Aggressors and their victims: Bullying at school. In N. Frude & H. Gault (Eds.), *Disruptive behavior in schools*. New York: Wiley.

Olweus, D. (1985). 80.000 barn er innblandet i mobbing. *Norsk Skoleblad* (Oslo, Norway), 2, 18–23.

Olweus, D. (1986). Aggression and hormones: Behavioral relationship with testosterone and adrenaline. In D. Olweus, J. Block, & M. Radke-Yarrow (Eds.), *Development of antisocial and prosocial behavior*. New York: Academic Press.

Olweus, D. (1987). Bully/victim problems among schoolchildren. In J. P. Myklebust & R. Ommundsen (Eds.), *Psykologprofesjonen mot år 2000*. Oslo: Universitetsforlaget.

Olweus, D. (1988). Vad menar man med termen mobbning? *Psykologtidningen*, 7, 9–10.

Olweus, D. (1989). Prevalence and incidence in the study of antisocial behavior: Definitions and measurement. In M. Klein (Ed.), *Cross-national research in self-reported crime and delinquency*. Dordrecht: Kluwer.

Olweus, D. (1990). The Olweus Bully/Victim Questionnaire. Unpublished. Bergen: Research Center for Health Promotion (HEMIL), University of Bergen, N-5015 Bergen, Norway.

Olweus, D. (1991). Bully/victim problems among schoolchildren: Basic facts and effects of a school-based intervention program. In D. Pepler & K. Rubin (Eds.), *The development and treatment of childhood aggression*. Hillsdale, NJ: Erlbaum.

Olweus, D. (1992a). Bullying among schoolchildren: Intervention and prevention. In R. D. Peters, R. J. McMahon, & V. L. Quincy (Eds.), *Aggression and violence throughout the life span*. Newbury Park, CA: Sage.

Olweus, D. (1992b). *Mobbning i skolan: Vad vi vet och vad vi kan göra*. Stockholm: Almqvist & Wiksell.

Olweus, D. (1993a). Victimization by peers: Antecedents and long-term outcomes. In K. H. Rubin & J. B. Asendorf (Eds.), *Social withdrawal, inhibition, and shyness in childhood*. Hillsdale, NJ: Erlbaum.

Olweus, D. (1993b). *Bullying at school: What we know and what we can do*. Oxford: Blackwell.

Olweus, D. (1994). Bullying at school: Long-term outcomes for the victims and an effective school-based intervention program. In L. R. Huesmann (Ed.), *Aggressive behavior: Current perspectives*. New York: Plenum.

Olweus, D. (1996). The Revised Olweus Bully/Victim Questionnaire. Unpublished. Bergen: Research Center for Health Promotion (HEMIL), University of Bergen, N-5015 Bergen, Norway.

Olweus, D. (1999a). *Olweus' core program against bullying and antisocial behavior: A teacher handbook*. Bergen: Research Center for Health Promotion (HEMIL), University of Bergen, N-5015 Bergen, Norway.

Olweus, D. (1999b). Noen hovedresultater fra Det nye Bergensprosjektet mot mobbing og antisosial atferd. Manuscript. Bergen: Research Center for Health Promotion (HEMIL), University of Bergen, N-5015 Bergen, Norway.

Olweus, D. (1999c). Sweden. In P. K. Smith, Y. Morita, J. Junger-Tas, D. Olweus, R. Catalano, & P. Slee (Eds.), *The nature of school bullying: A cross-national perspective* (pp. 7–27). London: Routledge.

Olweus, D. (1999d). Norway. In P. K. Smith, Y. Morita, J. Junger-Tas, D. Olweus, R. Catalano, & P. Slee (Eds.), *The nature of school bullying: A cross-national perspective* (pp. 28–48). London: Routledge.

Olweus, D. (n.p.). Unpublished interview data from Greater Stockholm study.

Olweus, D., & Alsaker, F. D. (1991). Assessing change in a cohort longitudinal study with hierarchical data. In D. Magnusson, L. Bergman, G. Rudinger, & B. Törestad (Eds.), *Problems and methods in longitudinal research*. New York: Cambridge University Press.

Olweus, D., & Limber, S. (1999). Bullying prevention program. In D. S. Elliott (Series Ed.), *Blueprints for violence prevention*. Boulder, CO: Center for the Study and Prevention of Violence, Institute of Behavioral Science, University of Colorado.

O'Moore, M. (2000). Critical issues for teacher training to counter bullying and victimisation in Ireland. *Aggressive Behavior, 26*, 99–111.

O'Moore, M., & Brendan, H. (1989). Bullying in Dublin schools. *Irish Journal of Psychology, 10*, 426–41.

O'Neill, D., & Atance, C. M. (2000). "Maybe my daddy give me a big piano": The development of children's use of modals to express uncertainty. *First Language, 20*, 29–54.

Ornstein, P. A., Naus, M., & Liberty, C. (1975). Rehearsal and organizational processes in children's memory. *Child Development, 26*, 818–30.

Oster, H., Hegley, D., & Nagel, L. (1992). Adult judgments and fine-grained analysis of infant facial expressions: Testing the validity of a priori coding formulas. *Developmental Psychology, 28*, 1115–31.

Overton, W. F., Ward, S. L., Noveck, I. A., Black, J., & O'Brien, D. P. (1987). Form and content in the development of deductive reasoning. *Developmental Psychology, 23*, 22–30.

Ozonoff, S., & Miller, J. N. (1996). An exploration of the right-hemisphere contributions to the pragmatic impairments of autism. *Brain and Language, 52*, 411–34.

Ozonoff, S., Pennington, B. F., & Rogers, S. J. (1991). Executive function deficits in high-functioning autistic individuals: Relationship to theory of mind. *Journal of Child Psychology and Psychiatry, 32*, 1081–1106.

Pal, S., Shyam, R., & Singh, R. (1997). Genetic analysis of general intelligence "g": A twin study. *Personality and Individual Differences, 22*, 779–80.

Palincsar, A. S., & Brown, A. L. (1984). Reciprocal teaching of comprehension-fostering and monitoring activities. *Cognition and Instruction, 1*, 117–75.

Palincsar, A. S., & Brown, A. L. (1989). Classroom dialogues to promote self-regulated comprehension. In I. J. Brophy (Ed.), *Advances in research on teaching* (Vol. 1, pp. 35–67). Greenwich: JAI Press.

Pan, B. A., & Snow, C. E. (1999). The development of conversational and discourse skills. In M. Barrett (Ed.), *The development of language* (pp. 229–49). Hove: Psychology Press.

Parker, J. G., & Asher, S. R. (1987). Peer relations and later personal adjustment: Are low-accepted children at risk? *Psychological Bulletin, 102*, 357–89.

Parten, M. B. (1932). Social participation among preschool children. *Journal of Abnormal and Social Psychology, 27*, 243–69.

Patrick, J., Campbell, K., Carmichael, L., Natale, R., & Richardson, B. (1982). Patterns of gross fetal body movements over 24 observation intervals in the last 10 weeks of pregnancy. *American Journal of Obstetrics and Gynecology, 136*, 471–7.

Patterson, G. R. (1982). *Coercive family process*. Eugene, OR: Castalia Publishing.

Patterson, G. R. (1986). Performance models for antisocial boys. *American Psychologist, 41*, 432–44.

Patterson, G. R., Littman, R. A., & Bricker, W. (1967). Assertive behavior in children: A step toward a theory of aggression. *Monographs of the Society for Research in Child Development*, 32 (5), 1–43.

Patterson, G. R., & Stouthamer-Loeber, M. (1984). The correlation of family management practices and delinquency. *Child Development*, 55, 1299–1307.

Pears, R., & Bryant, P. (1990). Transitive inferences by young children about spatial position. *British Journal of Psychology*, 81, 497–510.

Pedersen, N. L., Plomin, R., Nesselroade, J. R., & McClearn, G. E. (1992). A quantitative genetic analysis of cognitive abilities during the second half of the life span. *Psychological Science*, 3, 346–53.

Pegg, J. E., Werker, J. F., & McLeod, P. J. (1992). Preference for infant-directed over adult-directed speech: Evidence from seven-week-old infants. *Infant Behavior and Development*, 15, 325–45.

Pellegrini, A. D. (1994). The rough play of adolescent boys of differing sociometric status. *International Journal of Behavioral Development*, 17, 525–40.

Pellegrini, A. D., & Smith, P. K. (1998). Physical activity play: The nature and function of a neglected aspect of play. *Child Development*, 69, 577–98.

Pennington, B. F., & Ozonoff, S. (1996). Executive functions and developmental psychopathology. *Journal of Child Psychology and Psychiatry*, 37, 51–87.

Pepler, D., Craig, W. M., & O'Connell, P. (1999). Understanding bullying from a dynamic systems perspective. In A. Slater & D. Muir (Eds.), *The Blackwell reader in developmental psychology* (pp. 440–51). Cambridge, MA, and Oxford: Blackwell.

Pérez-Pereira, M., & Castro, J. (1992). Pragmatic functions of blind and sighted children's language: A twin case study. *First Language*, 12, 17–37.

Perner, J. (1991). *Understanding the representational mind*. Cambridge, MA: MIT Press.

Perner, J., Frith, U., Leslie, A. M., & Leekam, S. R. (1989). Exploration of the autistic child's theory of mind: Knowledge, belief and communication. *Child Development*, 60, 689–700.

Perner, J., Ruffman, T., & Leekam, S. R. (1994). Theory of mind is contagious: You catch it from your sibs. *Child Development*, 65, 1228–38.

Perret-Clermont, A. N. (1980). *Social interaction and cognitive development in children*. London: Academic Press.

Perry, D. G., Kusel, S. J., & Perry, L. C. (1988). Victims of peer aggression. *Developmental Psychology*, 24, 807–14.

Petrill, S. A., Ball, D., Eley, T., Hill, L., Plomin, R., McClearn, G. E., Smith, D. L., Chorney, K., Chorney, M., Hershz, M., Detterman, D. K., Thompson, L. A., Benbow, C., & Lubinski, D. (1998). Failure to replicate a QTL association between a DNA marker identified by EST00083 and IQ. *Intelligence*, 25, 179–84.

Petrill, S. A., Johansson, B., Pedersen, N. L., Berg, S., Plomin, R., Fran, A., & McClearn, G. E. (2001). Low cognitive functioning in nondemented 80+-year-old twins is not heritable. *Intelligence*, 29, 75–83.

Pezdek, K., & Roe, C. (1995). The effect of memory trace strength on suggestibility. *Journal of Experimental Child Psychology*, 60, 116–28.

Philipp, S. F. (1998). Race and gender differences in adolescent peer group approval of leisure activities. *Journal of Leisure Research*, 30 (2), 214–32.

Piaget, J. (1926). *The language and thought of the child*. London: Routledge & Kegan Paul.

Piaget, J. (1929). *The child's conception of the world*. London: Routledge & Kegan Paul.

Piaget, J. (1932). *The moral development of the child*. London: Routledge.

Piaget, J. (1950). *The psychology of intelligence*. London: Routledge & Kegan Paul.

Piaget, J. (1951). *Play, dreams and imitation in childhood*. London: Routledge & Kegan Paul.

Piaget, J. (1952). *The child's conception of number*. London: Routledge & Kegan Paul.

Piaget, J. (1953). How children form mathematical concepts. *Scientific American*.

Piaget, J. (1954). *The construction of reality in the child*. (Trans. M. Cook). New York: Basic Books.

Piaget, J. (1960). *The child's conception of the world*. London: Routledge.

Piaget, J. (1962). The stages of the intellectual development of the child. *Bulletin of the Menninger Clinic*, 26, 120–8. Reprinted in A. Slater & D. Muir (Eds.) (1999), *The Blackwell reader in developmental psychology* (pp. 35–42). Cambridge, MA, & Oxford: Blackwell.

Piaget, J. (1970). Piaget's theory. In P. H. Mussen (Ed.), *Carmichael's manual of child psychology* (Vol. 1, pp. 703–31). New York: Wiley.

Piaget, J. (1977). *Science of education and the psychology of the child*. Harmondsworth: Penguin.

Piaget, J. (2001). *Studies in reflecting abstraction*. (Trans. R. Campbell). Hove: Psychology Press.

Piaget, J., & Inhelder, B. (1956). *The child's conception of space*. New York: W. W. Norton.

Piaget, J., & Inhelder, B. (1966). *Mental imagery in the child*. London: Routledge & Kegan Paul.

Piaget, J., & Inhelder, B. (1974). *The child's construction of quantities*. London: Routledge & Kegan Paul.

Piaget, J., Inhelder, B., & Szeminska, A. (1960). *The child's conception of geometry*. London: Routledge & Kegan Paul.

Pillemer, D. B., Picariello, M. L., & Pruett, J. C. (1994). Very long-term memories of a salient preschool event. *Applied Cognitive Psychology*, 8, 95–106.

Pinker, S. (1984). *Language learnability and language development*. Cambridge, MA: Harvard University Press.

Pinker, S. (1987). The bootstrapping problem in language acquisition. In B. MacWhinney (Ed.), *Mechanisms of language acquisition* (pp. 399–441). Hillsdale, NJ: Erlbaum.

Pinker, S. (1989). *Learnability and cognition: The acquisition of argument structure*. Cambridge, MA: MIT Press.

Plomin, R. (1986). *Development, genetics, and psychology*. Hillsdale, NJ: Erlbaum.

Plomin, R. (1988). The nature and nurture of cognitive abilities. In R. Sternberg (Ed.), *Advances in the psychology of human intelligence* (Vol. 4). Hillsdale, NJ: Erlbaum.

Plomin, R. (1994). *Genetics and experience: The developmental interplay between nature and nurture*. Newbury Park, CA: Sage.

Plomin, R. (1995). Genetics and children's experiences in the family. *Journal of Child Psychology and Psychiatry*, 36, 33–68.

Plomin, R. (1997). Identifying genes for cognitive abilities and disabilities. In R. J. Sternberg & E. L. Grigorenko (Eds.), *Intelligence, heredity, and environment* (pp. 89–104). New York: Cambridge University Press.

Plomin, R. (1999). Genetics and general cognitive ability. *Nature*, 402, C25–C29.

Plomin, R. (2001). Genetic factors contributing to learning and language delays and disabilities. *Child and Adolescent Psychiatric Clinics of North America*, 10, 259–77.

Plomin, R., & Bergeman, C. S. (1991). The nature of nurture: Genetic influence on "environmental" measures. *Behavioral and Brain Sciences*, 14, 373–86.

Plomin, R., & DeFries, J. C. (1979). Multivariate behavioral genetic analysis of twin data on scholastic abilities. *Behavior Genetics*, 9, 505–17.

Plomin, R., DeFries, J. C., & Fulker, D. W. (1988). *Nature and nurture during infancy and early childhood*. Cambridge: Cambridge University Press.

Plomin, R., DeFries, J. C., & Loehlin, J. C. (1977). Genotype–environment interaction and correlation in the analysis of human behavior. *Psychological Bulletin*, 84, 309–22.

Plomin, R., DeFries, J. C., & McClearn, G. E. (1990). *Behavioral genetics: A primer*. New York: W. H. Freeman.

Plomin, R., & McClearn, D. L. (Eds.) (1993). *Nature and nurture*. Washington, DC: American Psychological Association.

Plomin, R., McClearn, G. E., & Smith, D. L. (1994). DNA markers associated with high versus low IQ: The IQ QTL Project. *Behavior Genetics*, 24, 107–18.

Plomin, R., McClearn, G. E., & Smith, D. L. (1995). Allelic associations between 100 DNA markers and high versus low IQ. *Intelligence*, 21, 31–48.

Plomin, R., & Neiderhiser, J. M. (1991). Quantitative genetics, molecular genetics, and intelligence. *Intelligence*, 15, 369–87.

Plomin, R., & Petrill, S. A. (1997). Genetics and intelligence: What is new? *Intelligence*, 24, 53–78.

Plowden Report. (1967). *Children and their primary schools*. London: HMSO.

Plunkett, K. (2000). Development in a connectionist framework: Rethinking the nature–nurture debate. In K. Lee (Ed.), *Childhood cognitive development: Essential readings* (pp. 63–90). Cambridge, MA, & Oxford: Blackwell.

Poole, D., & White, L. (1991). Effects of question repetition on the eyewitness testimony of children and adults. *Developmental Psychology*, 27, 975–86.

Poole, D., & White, L. (1993). Two years later: Effects of question repetition and retention interval on the eyewitness testimony of children and adults. *Developmental Psychology*, 29, 844–53.

Posner, S., Baker, L. A., & Martin, N. G. (1994). Genetics of social class in Australian twins. *Behavior Genetics*, 24, 525.

Povinelli, D. J. (1993). Reconstructing the evolution of mind. *American Psychologist*, 48, 493–509.

Powers, S. I. (1983). Family interaction and parental moral development as a context for adolescent moral development: A study of patient and non-patient adolescents. *Dissertation Abstracts International*, 43 (11-B), 3753.

Preisler, G. (1991). Early patterns of interaction between blind infants and their sighted mothers. *Child: Care, Health and Development*, 17, 65–90.

Pressley, M., & Levin, J. R. (1977). Task parameters affecting the efficacy of a visual imagery learning strategy in younger and older children. *Journal of Experimental Child Psychology*, 24, 53–9.

Pulkkinen, L., & Tremblay, R. E. (1992). Patterns of boys' social adjustment in two cultures and at different ages: A longitudinal perspective. *International Journal of Behavioral Development*, 15, 527–53.

Pumpian-Mindlin, E. (1966). Anna Freud and Erik H. Erikson: Contributions to the practice of psychoanalysis and psychotherapy. In F. Alexander, S. Eisenstein, & M. Grotjahn (Eds.), *Psychoanalytic pioneers*. New Jersey: Transaction.

Pye, C. (1986). Mayan speech to children. *Journal of Child Language*, 13, 85–100.

Querleu, D., Lefebvre, C., Titran, M., Renard, X., Morillion, M., & Crepin, G. (1984). Réactivité du nouveau-né de moins de deux heures de vie à la voix maternelle. *Journal de Gynécologie Obstétrique et de Biologie de la Reproduction*, 13, 125–34.

Quine, W. V. (1960). *Word and object*. Cambridge, MA: MIT Press.

Radford, A. (1990). *Syntactic theory and the acquisition of English syntax*. Oxford: Blackwell.

Radke-Yarrow, M., McCann, K., DeMulder, E., Belmont, B., Martinez, P., & Richardson, D. T. (1995). Attachment in the context of high-risk conditions. *Development and Psychopathology*, 7, 247–65.

Read, C. (1986). *Children's creative spelling*. London: Routledge & Kegan Paul.

Reddy, V. (1999). Prelinguistic communication. In M. Barrett (Ed.), *The development of language* (pp. 25–50). Hove: Psychology Press.

Reddy, V. (2000). Coyness in early infancy. *Developmental Science*, 3, 186–92.

Reissland, N., & Harris, P. L. (1991). Children's use of display rules in pride-eliciting situations. *British Journal of Developmental Psychology*, 9, 431–5.

Rheingold, H. L., & Adams, J. L. (1980). The significance of speech to newborns. *Developmental Psychology*, 16, 397–403.

Rice, C., Koinis, D., Sullivan, K., Tager-Flusberg, H., & Winner, E. (1997). When 3-year-olds pass the appearance–reality test. *Developmental Psychology*, 33, 54–61.

Rice, T., Corey, R., Fulker, D. W., & Plomin, R. (1986). The development and validation of a test battery measuring specific cognitive abilities in four-year-old children. *Educational and Psychological Measurement*, 46, 699–708.

Rich-Edwards, J. W., Stampfer, M. J., Manson, J. E., Rosner, B., Hankinson, S. E., Colditz, G. A., Willett, W. C., & Hennekens, C. H. (1997). Birthweight and the risk of cardiovascular disease in adult women. *British Medical Journal*, 315, 396–400.

Richie, W. C., & Bhatia, T. K. (Eds.) (1999). *Handbook of child language acquisition*. San Diego, CA: Academic Press.

Rigby, K., & Slee, P. (1991). Victims in school communities. *Journal of the Australasian Society of Victimology*, 25–31.

Riggs, K. J., Peterson, D. M., Robinson, E. J., & Mitchell, P. (1998). Are errors in false belief tasks symptomatic of a broader difficulty with counterfactuality? *Cognitive Development*, 13, 73–90.

Ringel, B. A., & Springer, C. J. (1980). On knowing how well one is remembering: The persistence of strategy use during transfer. *Journal of Experimental Child Psychology*, 29, 322–33.

Robinson, A., Linden, M. G., & Bender, B. G. (1998). Prenatal diagnosis of sex chromosome abnormalities. In A. Milunsky (Ed.), *Genetic disorders of the fetus* (pp. 249–85). Baltimore: Johns Hopkins University Press.

Rochat, P., Neisser, U., & Marian, V. (1998). Are young infants sensitive to interpersonal contingency? *Infant Behavior and Development*, 21, 355–66.

Rogoff, B., & Gardner, W. (1984). Adult guidance in cognitive development. In B. Rogoff & J. Lave (Eds.), *Everyday cognition: Its development in social context* (pp. 95–116). Cambridge, MA: Harvard University Press.

Rohwer, W. D., & Bean, J. P. (1973). Sentence-effects and noun-pair learning: A developmental interaction during adolescence. *Journal of Experimental Child Psychology*, 15, 521–33.

Roscoe, B., Diana, M. S., & Brooks, R. H. (1987). Early, middle, and late adolescents' views on dating and factors influencing partner selection. *Adolescence*, 22, 59–68.

Rose, S. A., & Blank, M. (1974). The potency of context in children's cognition: An illustration through conservation. *Child Development*, 45, 499–502.

Rosner, B. & Doherty, N. (1979). The response of neonates to intra-uterine sounds. *Developmental Medicine and Child Neurology*, 21, 723–9.

Rotterman, M. J., & Gentner, D. (1998). The effect of language on similarity: The use of relational labels improves children's performance in a mapping task. In K. Holyoak, D. Gentner, & B. Kokinov (Eds.), *Advances in analogy research*. Sofia: New Bulgarian University.

Rowe, D. C. (1994). *The limits of family influence: Genes, experience, and behavior*. New York: Guilford Press.

Rozin, P. (1976). The evolution of intelligence and access to the cognitive unconscious. In J. M. Sprague & A. N. Epstein (Eds.), *Progress in psychobiology and physiological psychology* (Vol. 6, pp. 245–80). New York: Academic Press.

Rubin, K. H., Watson, K. S., & Jambor, T. W. (1978). Free-play behaviors in preschool and kindergarten children. *Child Development*, 49, 534–6.

Ruble, D., & Brooks-Gunn, J. (1982). The experience of menarche. *Child Development*, 53, 1557–66.

Rudy, L., & Goodman, G. S. (1991). Effects of participation on children's reports: Implications for children's testimony. *Developmental Psychology*, 27, 527–38.

Ruiz, R. O. (1992). Violence in schools. Problems of bullying and victimization in Spain. Paper presented at the European Conference on Developmental Psychology, Seville, Spain (September).

Rutter, M. (1983). School effects on pupil progress: Research findings and policy implications. *Child Development*, 54, 1–19.

Rutter, M., & Madge, N. (1976). *Cycles of disadvantage*. London: Heinemann.

Rutter, M., & Pickles, A. (1991). Person–environment interaction: Concepts, mechanisms, and implications for data analysis. In T. D. Wachs & R. Plomin (Eds.), *Conceptualization and measurement of organism–environment interaction* (pp. 105–41). Washington, DC: American Psychological Association.

Rutter, M., & Quinton, D. (1984). Parental psychiatric disorder: Effects on children. *Psychological Medicine*, 14, 853–80.

Ryan, R., & Lynch, J. (1989). Emotional autonomy versus detachment: Revisiting the vicissitudes of adolescence and young childhood. *Child Development*, 60, 340–56.

Sagi, A., Lewkowicz, K. S., Shoham, R., Dvir, R., & Estes, D. (1985). Security of infant–mother, father, metapelet attachments among kibbutz-reared Israeli children. In I. Bretherton & E. Waters (Eds.), Growing points in attachment theory and research (pp. 257–75). *Monographs of the Society for Research in Child Development*, 50 (1–2, Serial No. 209).

St. James-Roberts, I., & Menon-Johansson, P. (1999). Predicting infant crying from fetal movement data: An exploratory study. *Early Human Development*, 54 (1), 55–62.

Salk, L. (1962). Mothers' heartbeat as an imprinting stimulus. *Transactions of the New York Academy of Sciences*, 24, 753–63.

Salk, L. (1973). The role of the heartbeat in the relations between mother and infant. *Scientific American*, 228, 24–9.

Saltmarsh, R., Mitchell, P., & Robinson, E. J. (1995). Realism and children's early grasp of mental representation: Belief-based judgments in the state change task. *Cognition*, 57, 297–325.

Sants, J., & Barnes, P. (1985). Childhood. Unit 2 of the Open University second-level course, *Personality, development and learning*. Milton Keynes: Open University Press.

Sapp, F., Lee, K., & Muir, D. (2000). Three-year-olds' difficulties with the appearance–reality distinction: Is it real or is it apparent? *Developmental Psychology*, 36, 547–60.

Savin-Williams, R. C., & Small, S. A. (1986). The timing of puberty and its relationship to adolescent and parent perceptions of family interactions. *Developmental Psychology*, 22, 342–7.

Saxe, G. (1979). A developmental analysis of notational counting. *Child Development*, 48, 1512–20.

Saxe, G. (1981). Body parts as numerals: A developmental analysis of numeration among the Oksapmin in Papua New Guinea. *Child Development*, 52, 306–16.

Sayers, J. (1997). Adolescent identity and desire: History, theory and practice. Essays in honor of Paul Roazan. In T. Dufresne (Ed.), *Freud under analysis*. New Jersey: Jason Aronson.

Saywitz, K., Goodman, G., Nicholas, G., & Moan, S. (1991). Children's memory of a physical examination involving genital touch: Implications for reports of child sexual abuse. *Journal of Consulting and Clinical Psychology*, 5, 682–91.

Scarr, S. (1992). Developmental theories for the 1990s: Development and individual differences. *Child Development*, 54, 424–35.

Scarr, S. (1997). Behavior-genetic and socialization theories of intelligence: Truce and reconciliation. In R. J. Sternberg & E. L. Grigorenko (Eds.), *Intelligence, heredity, and environment* (pp. 3–41). New York: Cambridge University Press.

Scarr, S., & McCartney, K. (1983). How people create their own environments: A theory of genotype–environment effects. *Child Development*, 54, 424–35.

Scarr, S., & Weinberg, R. (1977). Intellectual similarities within families of both adopted and biological children. *Intelligence, 1,* 170–91.

Scarr, S., & Weinberg, R. (1978). The influence of family background on intellectual attainment. *American Sociological Review, 43,* 674–92.

Scarr, S., Weinberg, R., & Waldman, I. (1993). IQ correlations in transracial adoptive families. *Intelligence, 17,* 545–55.

Schaal, B., Orgeur, P., & Rognon, C. (1995). Odor sensing in the human fetus: Anatomical, functional and chemoecological bases. In J. LeCanuet, W. Fifer, N. Krasnegor, & W. Smotherman (Eds.), *Fetal development: A psychobiological perspective* (pp. 205–38). Hillsdale, NJ: Erlbaum.

Schacter, D. L. (1987). Implicit memory: History and current status. *Journal of Experimental Psychology: Learning, Memory and Cognition, 13,* 501–18.

Schaefer, M., & Smith, P. K. (1996). Teachers' perceptions of play fighting and real fighting in primary school. *Educational Research, 38,* 173–81.

Schaffer, H. R. (1984). *The child's entry into a social world.* London: Academic Press.

Schaffer, H. R. (1996). *Social development.* Oxford: Blackwell.

Schaffer, H. R., & Emerson, P. E. (1964). The development of social attachments in infancy. *Monographs of the Society for Research in Child Development, 29,* No. 94.

Schagen, I., & Hutchinson, D. (1994). Measuring the reliability of National Curriculum assessment. *Educational Research, 36* (3), 211–21.

Schaie, K., & Strother, C. (1965). A cross-sequential study of age changes in cognitive behavior. *Psychological Bulletin, 70,* 671–80.

Schank, R. C., & Abelson, R. P. (1977). *Scripts, plans, goals, and understanding: An inquiry into human knowledge structures.* Hillsdale, NJ: Erlbaum.

Schauble, L. (1991). Belief revision in children: The role of prior knowledge and strategies for generating evidence. *Journal of Experimental Child Psychology, 49,* 31–57.

Schieffelin, B. B., & Ochs, E. (1983). A cultural perspective on the transition from prelinguistic to linguistic communication. In R. M. Golinkoff (Ed.), *The transition from prelinguistic to linguistic communication* (pp. 115–31). Hillsdale, NJ: Erlbaum.

Schiff, M., & Lewontin, R. (1986). *Education and class: The irrelevance of IQ genetic studies.* Oxford: Clarendon Press.

Schneider, W. (1985). Developmental trends in the metamemory–memory behavior relationship: An integrative review. In D. L. Forrest-Pressley, G. E. MacKinnon, & T. G. Waller (Eds.), *Metacognition, cognition, and human performance* (Vol. 1, pp. 57–109). Orlando, FL: Academic Press.

Schneider, W., & Pressley, M. (1997). *Memory development between two and twenty* (2nd ed.). Mahwah, NJ: Erlbaum.

Schneider, U., Schleussner, E., Haueisen, J., Nowak, H., & Seewald, H. J. (2001). Signal analysis of auditory evoked cortical fields in fetal magnetoencephalography. *Brain Topography, 14* (1), 69–80.

Schoultz, J., Säljö, R., & Wyndhamn, J. (2001). Heavenly talk: Discourse, artifacts, and children's understanding of elementary astronomy. *Human Development, 44,* 103–18.

Schwartz, D., Dodge, K., & Coie, J. (1993). The emergence of chronic peer victimization in boys' play groups. *Child Development, 64,* 1755–72.

Schwartz, G. M., Izard, C. E., & Ansal, C. E. (1985). The 5-month-old's ability to discriminate facial expressions of emotion. *Infant Behavior and Development, 8,* 65–77.

Scullin, M. H., & Ceci, S. J. (2001). A suggestibility scale for children. *Personality and Individual Differences, 30,* 843–56.

Scullin, M. H., & Warren, H. K. (1999). Individual differences and responsiveness to suggestive interviewing techniques in children. Poster presented at the Joint Meeting of the American

Psychology/Law Society and the European Association of Psychology and Law, Dublin, Ireland (July).

Shah, A., & Frith, U. (1993). Why do autistic individuals show superior performance on the Block Design Task? *Journal of Child Psychology and Psychiatry*, 34, 1351–64.

Shahidullah, S. & Hepper, P. (1994). Frequency discrimination by the fetus. *Early Human Development*, 36, 13–26.

Sharabany, R., Gershoni, R., & Hofman, J. (1981). Girlfriend, boyfriend: Age and sex differences in intimate friendship. *Developmental Psychology*, 17, 800–8.

Sharp, S., & Smith, P. K. (1991). Bullying in UK schools: The DES Sheffield Bullying Project. *Early Child Development and Care*, 77, 47–55.

Shatz, M., & Gelman, R. (1973). The development of communication skills: Modifications in the speech of young children as a function of a listener. *Monographs of the Society for Research in Child Development*, 38 (Serial No. 152).

Shaw, S. M., Caldwell, L. L., & Kleiber, D. A. (1996). Boredom, stress and social control in the daily activities of adolescents. *Journal of Leisure Research*, 28 (4), 274–92.

Shields, J. (1962). *Monozygotic twins: Brought up apart and brought up together.* Oxford: Oxford University Press.

Shweder, R. A., Much, N. C., Mahapatra, M., & Park, L. (1997). The "big three" of morality (autonomy, community, divinity) and the "big three" explanations of suffering. In A. M. Brandt & P. Rozin (Eds.), *Morality and health* (pp. 119–69). New York: Routledge.

Siegal, M. (1997). *Knowing children: Experiments in conversation and cognition* (2nd ed.). Hove: Psychology Press.

Siegal, M., & Beattie, K. (1991). Where to look first for children's knowledge of false beliefs. *Cognition*, 38, 1–12.

Siegal, M., Butterworth, G., & Newcombe, P. A. (2002). Culture and children's cosmology. Unpublished manuscript, University of Sheffield.

Siegal, M., & Share, D. L. (1990). Contamination sensitivity in young children. *Developmental Psychology*, 26, 455–8.

Siegal, M., Waters, L. J., & Dinwiddy, L. S. (1988). Misleading children: Causal attributions for inconsistency under repeated questioning. *Journal of Experimental Child Psychology*, 45, 438–56.

Siegler, R. S. (1976). Three aspects of cognitive development. *Cognitive Psychology*, 8, 481–520.

Siegler, R. S. (1981). Developmental sequences within and between concepts. *Monographs of the Society for Research in Child Development*, 46 (2, Serial No. 189).

Siegler, R. S. (1993). *Children's thinking* (3rd ed.). Englewood Cliffs, NJ: Prentice-Hall.

Siegler, R. S. (1995). How does change occur? A microgenetic study of number conservation. *Cognitive Psychology*, 28, 225–73.

Sigman, M. (1998). Change and continuity in the development of children with autism. *Journal of Child Psychology and Psychiatry*, 39, 817–28.

Sigman, M. D., Kasari, C., Kwon, J. H., & Yirmiya, N. (1992). Responses to the negative emotions of others by autistic, mentally retarded, and normal children. *Child Development*, 63, 796–807.

Skinner, A. (1992). *Bullying: An annotated bibliography of literature and resources.* Leicester: Youth Work Press.

Skinner, B. F. (1961). *Cumulative record.* London: Methuen.

Skodak, M. (1950). Mental growth of adopted children in the same family. *Journal of Genetic Psychology*, 77, 3–9.

Skodak, M., & Skeels, H. M. (1949). A final follow-up on one hundred adopted children. *Journal of Genetic Psychology*, 75, 84–125.

Skuder, P., Plomin, R., McClearn, G. E., Smith, D. L., Vignetti, S., Chorney, K., Chorney, M., Kasaesa, S., Thompson, L. A., Detterman, D. K., Petrill, S. A., Daniels, J., Owen, M. J., & McGuffin, P. (1995). A polymorphism in mitochondrial DNA associated with IQ? *Intelligence*, 21, 1–12.

Slater, A., Carrick, R., Bell, C., & Roberts, E. (1999). Can measures of infant information processing predict later intellectual ability? In A. Slater & D. Muir (Eds.), *The Blackwell reader in developmental psychology* (pp. 55–64). Cambridge, MA, and Oxford: Blackwell.

Slater, A., Johnson, S. P., Brown, E., & Badenoch, M. (1996). Newborn infants' perception of partly occluded objects. *Infant Behavior and Development*, 19, 145–8.

Slater, A., Mattock, A., & Brown, E. (1990). Size constancy at birth: Newborn infants' responses to retinal and real sizes. *Journal of Experimental Child Psychology*, 49, 314–22.

Slater, A., Mattock, A., Brown, E., & Bremner, J. G. (1991). Form perception at birth: Cohen and Younger (1984) revisited. *Journal of Experimental Child Psychology*, 51, 395–406.

Slater, A., & Morison, V. (1985). Shape constancy and slant perception at birth. *Perception*, 14, 337–44.

Slater, A., Morison, V., & Rose, D. (1983). Perception of shape by the newborn baby. *British Journal of Developmental Psychology*, 1, 135–42.

Slater, A., Morison, V., & Somers, M. (1988). Orientation discrimination and cortical function in the human newborn. *Perception*, 17, 597–602.

Slater, A., & Muir, D. (Eds.) (1999). *The Blackwell reader in developmental psychology*. Cambridge, MA, & Oxford: Blackwell.

Slater, A., & Quinn, P. C. (2001). Face recognition in the newborn infant. *Infant and Child Development*, 10, 21–4.

Slater, A., von der Schulenburg, C., Brown, E., Badenoch, M., Butterworth, G., Parsons, S., & Samuels, C. (1998). Newborn infants prefer attractive faces. *Infant Behavior and Development*, 21, 345–54.

Slavin, R. E. (1990). *Co-operative learning: Theory, research and practice*. Englewood Cliffs, NJ: Prentice-Hall.

Slobin, D. I. (1979). *Psycholinguistics*. Dallas, TX: Scott, Foresman.

Small, M. Y. (1990). *Cognitive development*. Toronto: Harcourt Brace Jovanovich.

Smigaj, D. (1997). Drug abuse in pregnancy. In G. G. Ashmead (Ed.), *Essentials of maternal fetal medicine* (pp. 185–201). New York: Chapman & Hall.

Smilansky, S. (1968). *The effects of sociodramatic play on disadvantaged preschool children*. New York: Wiley.

Smith, L. B., Thelen, E., Titzer, R., & McLin, D. (1999). Knowing in the context of acting: The task dynamics of the A-not-B error. *Psychological Review*, 106, 235–60.

Smith, M. (1926). An investigation of the development of the sentence and the extent of vocabulary in young children. *University of Iowa Studies in Child Welfare*, 3 (5).

Smith, N. (1973). *The acquisition of phonology: A case study*. Cambridge: Cambridge University Press.

Smith, P. K. (1988). Children's play and its role in early development: A reevaluation of the "play ethos." In A. D. Pellegrini (Ed.), *Psychological bases of early education* (pp. 207–26). Chichester: Wiley.

Smith, P. K. (1991). The silent nightmare: Bullying and victimization in school peer groups. *The Psychologist*, 4, 243–8.

Smith, P. K. (2001). Should we blame the bullies? *The Psychologist*, 14, 61.

Smith, P. K., & Brain, P. (2000). Bullying in schools: Lessons from two decades of research. *Aggressive Behavior*, 26, 1–9.

Smith, P. K., Morita, Y., Junger-Tas, J., Olweus, D., Catalano, R., & Slee, P. (Eds.) (1999). *The nature of school bullying: A cross-national perspective*. London: Routledge.

Smith, P. K., & Sharp, S. (1994). *School bullying: Insights and perspectives*. London: Routledge.

Smith, P. K., & Shu, S. (2000). What good schools can do about bullying: Findings from a survey in English schools after a decade of research and action. *Childhood: A Global Journal of Child Development*, 7, 193–212.

Smith, P. K., Shu, S., & Madsen, K. (2000). Characteristics of victims of school bullying: Developmental changes in coping strategies and skills. In J. Juvonen & S. Graham (Eds.), *Peer harassment in school* (pp. 332–51). New York: Guilford.

Smith, P. K., & Thompson, D. (Eds.) (1991). *Practical approaches to bullying*. London: David Fulton.

Snarey, J. R. (1994). Cross-cultural universality of social-moral development: A critical review of Kohlbergian research. In B. Puka et al. (Eds.), *New research in moral development. Moral development: A compendium* (Vol. 5, pp. 268–98). New York: Garland.

Snidman, N., Kagan, J., Riordan, L., & Shannon, D. C. (1995). Cardiac function and behavioral reactivity during infancy. *Psychophysiology*, 32, 199–207.

Snyder, L. S., Nathanson, R., & Saywitz, K. (1993). Children in court: The role of discourse processing and production. *Topics in Language Disorders*, 13, 39–58.

Soja, N., Carey, S., & Spelke, E. (1991). Ontogenetic categories guide young children's inductions about word meaning: Object and substance terms. *Cognition*, 38, 179–211.

Sophian, C. (1988). Limitations on preschool children's knowledge about counting: Using counting to compare two sets. *Developmental Psychology*, 24, 634–40.

Sorce, J., Emde, R., Campos, J., & Klinnert, M. (1985). Maternal emotional signaling: Its effect on visual cliff behavior of 1-year-olds. *Developmental Psychology*, 21, 195–200.

Spangler, G., & Grossmann, K. E. (1993). Biobehavioral organization in securely and insecurely attached infants. *Child Development*, 64, 1439–50.

Spelke, E. S., Breinlinger, K., Macomber, J., & Jacobson, K. (1992). Origins of knowledge. *Psychological Review*, 99, 605–32.

Spelke, E. S., Kestenbaum, R., Simons, D. J., & Wein, D. (1995). Spatiotemporal continuity, smoothness of motion and object identity in infancy. *British Journal of Developmental Psychology*, 13, 113–42.

Spence, M. J., & DeCasper, A. J. (1982). Human fetuses perceive maternal speech. (Paper presented to the meeting of the International Society for Infants Studies, Austin, Texas).

Spence, M. & Freeman, M. (1996). Newborn infants prefer the maternal low-pass filtered voice, but not the maternal whispered voice. *Infant Behavior and Development*, 19 (2), 199–212.

Spitz, R. (1965). *The first year of life*. New York: International Universities Press.

Spitzer, W. O., Lawrence, V., Dales, R., Hill, G., Archer, M. C., Clark, P., Abenhaim, L., Hardy, J., Sampalis, J., Pinfold, S. P., et al. (1990). Links between passive smoking and disease: A best-evidence synthesis. A report of the Working Group on Passive Smoking. *Clinical and Investigative Medicine*, 13, 17–42.

Spuhler, K. P., & Vandenberg, S. G. (1980). Comparison of parent–offspring resemblance for specific cognitive abilities. *Behavior Genetics*, 10, 413–18.

Stahl, S. A., & Murray, B. A. (1994). Defining phonological awareness and its relationship to early reading. *Journal of Educational Psychology*, 86, 221–34.

Stanger, C., Achenbach, T. M., & Verhulst, F. C. (1997). Accelerated longitudinal comparisons of aggressive versus delinquent syndromes. *Development and Psychopathology*, 9, 43–58.

Stanovich, K. E., Siegel, L. S., & Gottardo, A. (1997). Converging evidence for phonological and surface subtypes of reading disability. *Journal of Educational Psychology*, 89, 114–27.

Stark, R. E. (1980). Stages of speech development during the first year of life. In G. H. Yeni-Komshian, J. F. Kavanagh, & C. A. Ferguson (Eds.), *Child phonology*. New York: Academic Press.

Starkey, P., & Cooper, R. G. (1980). Perception of number by human infants. *Science*, 210, 1033–5.

Starkey, P., Spelke, E. S., & Gelman, R. (1990). Numerical abstraction by human infants. *Cognition*, 36, 97–128.

Statistics Canada. (2001). *Average hours per week of television viewing*. Downloaded from the World Wide Web, April 8, 2001 (http://www.statcan.ca/english/Pgdb/People/Culture/arts23.htm).

Steele, H., Steele, M., & Fonagy, P. (1996). Associations among attachment classifications of mothers, fathers, and their infants. *Child Development*, 67, 541–55.

Steinberg, L. (1981a). Autonomy, conflict, and harmony in family relationship. In S. Feldman & G. Elliot (Eds.), *At the threshold: The developing adolescent* (pp. 255–76). Cambridge, MA: Harvard University Press.

Steinberg, L. (1981b). Transformations in family relations at puberty. *Developmental Psychology*, 17, 833–40.

Steinberg, L. (1987). Bound to bicker: Pubescent primates leave home for good reasons. Our teens stay with us and squabble. *Psychology Today*, 36–9.

Steinberg, L., Lamborn, S., Darling, N., Mounts, N., & Dornbusch, S. (1994). Over-time changes in adjustment and competence among adolescents from authoritative, authoritarian, indulgent and neglectful families. *Child Development*, 65, 754–70.

Steinberg, L. & Silverberg, S. (1986). The vicissitudes of autonomy in early adolescence. *Child Development*, 57, 841–51.

Stern, D. N. (1985). *The interpersonal world of the infant: A view from psychoanalysis and developmental psychology*. New York: Basic Books.

Sternberg, R. J., & Grigorenko, E. L. (1997). Interventions for cognitive development in children 0–3 years old. In M. E. Young (Ed.), *Early child development: Investing in our children's future* (pp. 127–56). Amsterdam & Tokyo: Elsevier.

Sternberg, R. J., & Okagaki, L. (1989). Continuity and discontinuity in intellectual development are not a matter of "either-or." *Human Development*, 32, 158–66.

Sternberg, R. J., & Rifkin, B. (1979). The development of analogical reasoning processes. *Journal of Experimental Child Psychology*, 27, 195–232.

Stevens, R. (1983). *Erik Erikson*. Milton Keynes: Open University Press.

Stoel-Gammon, C., & Otomo, K. (1986). Babbling development of hearing impaired and normally hearing subjects. *Journal of Speech and Hearing Disorders*, 51, 33–41.

Stone, C. A., & Day, M. C. (1978). Levels of availability of a formal operational strategy. *Child Development*, 49, 1054–65.

Stott, D. H., & Latchford, B. A. (1976). Prenatal antecedents of child health, development, and behavior. *Journal of American Academic Child Psychiatry*, 15 (1), 161–91.

Strauss, M. S., & Curtis, L. E. (1981). Infant perception of number. *Child Development*, 52, 1146–52.

Sullivan, H. S. (1953). *The interpersonal theory of psychiatry*. New York: W. W. Norton.

Sundet, J. M., Tambs, K., Magnus, P., & Berg, K. (1988). On the question of secular trends in the heritability of intelligence test scores: A study of Norwegian twins. *Intelligence*, 12, 47–59.

Susser, E. B., Brown, A., & Matte, T. D. (1999). Prenatal factors and adult mental and physical health. *Canadian Journal of Psychiatry*, 44, 326–34.

Sutton, J., Smith, P. K., & Swettenham, J. (1999). Social cognition and bullying: Social inadequacy or skilled manipulation? *British Journal of Developmental Psychology*, 17, 435–50.

Tager-Flusberg, H. (1993). What language reveals about the understanding of minds in children with autism. In S. Baron-Cohen, H. Tager-Flusberg, & D. J. Cohen (Eds.), *Understanding other minds: Perspectives from autism* (pp. 138–57). Oxford: Oxford University Press.

Takahashi, K. (1986). Examining the strange situation procedure with Japanese mothers and 12-month-old infants. *Developmental Psychology*, 22, 265–70.

Tate, C. S., Warren, A. R., & Hess, T. M. (1992). Adults' liability for children's "lie-ability": Can adults coach children to lie successfully? In S. J. Ceci, M. D. Leichtman, & M. Putnick (Eds.), *Cognitive and social factors in early deception* (pp. 69–87). Hillsdale, NJ: Erlbaum.

Tate, C. S., & Warren-Leubecker, A. R. (1990). Can young children lie convincingly if coached by adults? In S. J. Ceci (Chair), Do children lie? Narrowing the uncertainties. Symposium conducted at the Biennial Meeting of the American Psychology/Law Society, Williamsburg, VA (March).

Taylor, M., & Carlson, S. M. (1997). The relation between individual differences in fantasy and theory of mind. *Child Development*, 68, 436–55.

Taylor, M. J., Menzies, R., MacMillan, L. J., & Whyte, H. E. (1987). VEPs in normal full-term and premature neonates: Longitudinal versus cross-sectional data. *Electroencephalography and Clinical Neurophysiology*, 68, 20–7.

Teasdale, T. W., & Owen, D. R. (1984). Heritability and familial environment in intelligence and education level: A sibling study. *Nature*, 309, 620–2.

Templin, M. C. (1957). *Certain language skills in children: Their development and interrelationships.* Minneapolis: University of Minnesota Press.

Thapar, A., Petrill, S., & Thompson, L. A. (1995). The heritability of memory in the Western Reserve twin project. *Behavior Genetics*, 25, 155–60.

Thatcher, R. W. (1992). Cyclic cortical organization during early childhood. *Brain and Cognition*, 20, 24–50.

Thelen, E. (1986). Treadmill-elicited stepping in seven-month-old infants. *Child Development*, 57, 1498–1506.

Thelen, E. (1999). Three-month-old infants can learn task-specific patterns of interlimb coordination. In K. Lee (Ed.), *Childhood cognitive development: Essential readings* (pp. 91–105). Cambridge, MA, & Oxford: Blackwell.

Thelen, E., & Spencer, J. P. (1998). Postural control during reaching in young infants: A dynamic systems approach. *Neuroscience and Biobehavioral Reviews*, 22, 507–14.

Thompson, L. A., Detterman, D. K., & Plomin, R. (1993). Differences in heritability across groups differing in ability, revisited. *Behavior Genetics*, 23, 331–6.

Thurstone, L. L. (1938). *Primary mental abilities.* Chicago: University of Chicago Press.

Tincoff, R., & Jusczyk, P. W. (1999). Some beginnings of word comprehension in 6-month-olds. *Psychological Science*, 10, 172–5.

Tizard, B., Blatchford, P., Burke, J., Farquhar, C., & Plewis, I. (1988). *Young children at school in the inner city.* Hove: Erlbaum.

Tizard, B., & Hughes, M. (1984). *Young children learning.* London: Fontana.

Tizard, B., Mortimore, J., & Burchell, B. (1981). *Involving parents in nursery and infant schools.* London: Grant McIntyre.

Tomasello, M. (1992). *First verbs: A case study of early grammatical development.* Cambridge: Cambridge University Press.

Tomasello, M. (1995). Joint attention as social cognition. In C. Moore & P. J. Dunham (Eds.), *Joint attention: Its origin and role in development.* Hillsdale, NJ: Erlbaum.

Tomasello, M. (Ed.) (1998). *The new psychology of language: Cognitive and functional approaches to language structure.* Mahwah, NJ: Erlbaum.

Tomasello, M., & Brooks, P. (1999). Early syntactic development: A construction grammar approach. In M. Barrett (Ed.), *The development of language* (pp. 161–90). London: Psychology Press.

Tomasello, M., Farrar, M. J., & Dines, J. (1984). Children's speech revisions for a familiar and an unfamiliar adult. *Journal of Speech and Hearing Research*, 27, 359–63.

Tomasello, M., Kruger, A. C., & Ratner, H. H. (1993). Cultural learning. *Behavioral and Brain Sciences*, 16, 495–552.

Totereau, C., Thenevin, M.-G., & Fayol, M. (1997). The development of the understanding of number morphology in written French. In C. A. Perfetii, L. Rieben, & M. Fayol (Eds.), *Learning to spell: Research, theory and practice across languages* (pp. 97–114). Mahwah, NJ: Erlbaum.

Towse, J. N., & Saxton, M. (1997). Linguistic influences on children's number concepts: Methodological and theoretical considerations. *Journal of Experimental Child Psychology*, 66, 362–75.

Trainor, L. J., Austin, C. M., & Desjardins, R. N. (2000). Is infant-directed speech prosody a result of the vocal expression of emotion? *Psychological Science*, 11, 188–95.

Trehub, S. E. (1976). The discrimination of foreign speech consonants by infants and adults. *Child Development*, 47, 466–72.

Treiman, R., Mullenix, J., Bijel-Babic, R., & Richmond-Welty, E. D. (1995). The special role of rimes in the description, use and acquisition of English orthography. *Journal of Experimental Psychology: General*, 124, 107–36.

Tremblay, R. E., Masse, B., Perron, D., Leblanc, M., Schwartzman, A. E., & Ledigham, J. E. (1992). Early disruptive behavior, poor school achievement, delinquent behavior, and delinquent personality: Longitudinal analyses. *Journal of Consulting and Clinical Psychology*, 60, 64–72.

Tremblay-Leveau, H., & Nadel, J. (1996). Exclusion in triads: Can it serve "metacommunicative" knowledge in 11- and 23-month-old children? *British Journal of Developmental Psychology*, 14, 145–58.

Tronick, E. Z. (1989). Emotions and emotion communication in infants. *American Psychologist*, 44, 112–19.

Tröster, H., & Brambring, M. (1992). Early social-emotional development in blind infants. *Child: Care, Health and Development*, 18, 207–27.

Tröster, H., Brambring, M., & Beelmann, A. (1991). The age dependence of stereotyped behaviors in blind infants and preschoolers. *Child: Care, Health and Development*, 17, 137–57.

Tulloch, J., Brown, B., Jacobs, H., Prugh, D., & Greene, W. (1964). Normal heartbeat sounds and the behavior of human infants: A replication study. *Psychosomatic Medicine*, 26, 661–70.

Tulving, E. E. (1983). *Elements of episodic memory*. London: Oxford University Press.

Tulving, E. E., & Watkins, M. J. (1975). Structure of memory traces. *Psychological Review*, 82, 261–75.

Turiel, E. (1998). The development of morality. In N. Eisenberg (Ed.), *Handbook of child psychology* (5th ed.). *Vol. 3. Social, emotional, and personality development* (pp. 863–932). New York: Wiley.

Turkheimer, E. (2000). Three laws of behavior genetics and what they mean. *Current Directions in Psychological Science*, 9, 160–4.

Turkheimer, E., & Gottesman, I. I. (1991). Individual differences and the canalization of human behavior. *Developmental Psychology*, 27, 18–22.

Turner, P. (1991). Relations between attachment, gender, and behavior with peers in preschool. *Child Development*, 62, 1475–88.

Underwood, J., & Underwood, G. (1999). Task effects on co-operative and collaborative learning with computers. In K. Littleton & P. Light (Eds.), *Learning with computers: Analysing productive interaction*. London: Routledge.

United Nations Criminal Justice Information Network. (1993). Fourth United Nations survey of crime trends and operations of criminal justice systems 1986–1990. [4 paragraphs]. *UNCJIN Crime and Justice Letter*, 1. [On-line serial]. Available: http://www.ifs.univie.ac.at/~pr2gq1/85275.html#funsoc [1999, August 29].

Urwin, C. (1981). Early language development in blind children. *The British Psychological Society Division of Educational and Child Psychology Occasional Papers*, 5, 78–93.

Uttal, D., & Perlmutter, M. (1989). Toward a broader conceptualization of development: The role of gains and losses across the life span. *Developmental Review*, 9, 101–32.

van IJzendoorn, M. H., Dijkstra, J., & Bus, A. G. (1995). Attachment, intelligence, and language: A meta-analysis. *Social Development*, 4, 115–28.

van Loosbroek, E., & Smitsman, A. W. (1990). Visual perception of numerosity in infancy. *Developmental Psychology*, 26, 916–22.

Vandenberg, S. G. (1968a). The nature and nurture of intelligence. In D. C. Glass (Ed.), *Genetics* (pp. 3–58). New York: Rockefeller University Press.

Vandenberg, S. G. (1968b). Primary mental abilities or general intelligence? Evidence from twin studies. In J. M. Thoday & A. S. Parke (Eds.), *Genetic and environmental influences on behavior* (pp. 146–60). New York: Plenum Press.

Vellutino, F. R., & Scanlon, D. M. (1987). Phonological coding, phonological awareness and reading ability: Evidence from a longitudinal and experimental study. *Reading Research Quarterly*, 30, 854–75.

Vihman, M. M. (1996). *Phonological development: The origins of language in the child*. Cambridge, MA, and Oxford: Blackwell.

Visser, G. H. A. (1992). The second trimester. In J. Nijhuis (Ed.), *Fetal behavior: Developmental and perinatal aspects* (pp. 17–25). New York: Oxford University Press.

Vosniadou, S. (1994). Capturing and modeling the process of conceptual change. *Learning and Instruction*, 4, 45–69.

Vygotsky, L. S. (1962). *Thought and language*. Cambridge, MA: MIT Press.

Vygotsky, L. S. (1978). *Mind in society*. Cambridge, MA: Harvard University Press.

Vygotsky, L. S. (1981). The genesis of higher mental functions. In J. V. Wertsch (Ed.), *The concept of activity in Soviet psychology*. New York: Sharpe.

Vygotsky, L. S., & Luria, A. R. (1993). *Studies on the history of behavior: Ape, primitive and child*. Hillsdale, NJ: Erlbaum.

Wagenaar, V. A., & Groeneweg, J. (1990). The memory of concentration camp survivors. *Applied Cognitive Psychology*, 4, 77–87.

Wagner, R., & Torgeson, J. K. (1987). The nature of phonological processing and its causal role in the acquisition of reading skills. *Psychological Bulletin*, 1101, 192–212.

Wahlsten, D. (1990). Insensitivity of the analysis of variance to heredity–environment interaction. *Behavioral and Brain Sciences*, 13, 109–61.

Wakeley, A., Rivera, S., & Langer, J. (2000a). Can young infants add and subtract? *Child Development*, 71, 1525–34.

Wakeley, A., Rivera, S., & Langer, J. (2000b). Not proved: Reply to Wynn. *Child Development*, 71, 1537–9.

Wakschlag, L. S., Lahey, B. B., Loeber, R., Green, S. M., Gordon, R. A., & Leventhal, B. L. (1997). Maternal smoking during pregnancy and the risk of conduct disorder in boys. *Archives of General Psychiatry*, 54, 670–6.

Waldman, I. (1997). Unresolved questions and future directions in behavior-genetic studies of intelligence. In R. J. Sternberg & E. L. Grigorenko (Eds.), *Intelligence, heredity, and environment* (pp. 552–70). New York: Cambridge University Press.

Walker, A. G., & Warren, A. R. (1997). The language of the child abuse interview: Asking the questions, understanding the answers. In T. Ney (Ed.), *Allegations in child sexual abuse, assessment and case management*. New York: Brunner/Mazel.

Walker, L., Hennig, K., & Krettenauer, T. (2000). Parent and peer contexts for children's moral reasoning development. *Child Development*, 71, 1033–48.

Walker, L., & Taylor, J. H. (1991). Family interactions and the development of moral reasoning. *Child Development*, 62, 264–83.

Wallace, D. B., Franklin, M. B., & Keegan, R. T. (1994). The observing eye: A century of baby diaries. *Human Development*, 37, 1–29.

Walsh, R. A. (1994). Effects of maternal smoking on adverse pregnancy outcomes: Examination of the criteria of causation. *Human Biology*, 66, 1059–92.

Walton, G. E., Bower, N. J. A., & Bower, T. G. R. (1992). Recognition of familiar faces by newborns. *Infant Behavior and Development*, 15, 265–9.

Walton, P. D. (1995). Rhyming ability, phoneme identity, letter–sound knowledge, and the use of orthographic analogy by prereaders. *Journal of Educational Psychology*, 587–97.

Waltz, J. A., Knowlton, B. J., Holyoak, K. J., Boone, K. B., Mishkin, F. S., Santos, M. M., Thomas, C. R., & Miller, B. L. (1999). A system for relational reasoning in the human prefrontal cortex. *Psychological Science*, 10, 119–25.

Warren, A., Hulse-Trotter, K., & Tubbs, E. (1991). Inducing resistance to suggestibility in children. *Law and Human Behavior*, 15, 273–85.

Watson, J. B. (1970). *Behaviorism*. New York: W. W. Norton.

Waxman, S. (1999). Specifying the scope of 13-month-olds' expectations for novel words. *Cognition*, 70, 35–50.

Waxman, S., & Markow, D. (1995). Words as invitations to form categories: Evidence from 12- to 13-month-old infants. *Cognitive Psychology*, 29, 257–302.

Wechsler, D. (1991). *Wechsler intelligence scale for children* (3rd ed.). San Antonio: Psychological Corporation.

Wehren, A., & De Lisi, R. (1983). The development of gender understanding: Judgements and explanations. *Child Development*, 54, 1568–78.

Welch-Ross, M. K., Diecidue, K., & Miller, S. A. (1997). Young children's understanding of conflicting mental representation predicts suggestibility. *Developmental Psychology*, 33, 43–53.

Wellman, H. M. (1988). Children's early development of memory strategies. In F. E. Weinert & M. Perlmutter (Eds.), *Memory development: Universal changes and individual differences* (pp. 1–29). Hillsdale, NJ: Erlbaum.

Wentzel, K. R., & Asher, S. R. (1995). The academic lives of neglected, rejected, popular, and controversial children. *Child Development*, 66, 754–63.

Werker, J. F. (1989). Becoming a native listener. *American Scientist*, 77, 54–9.

Werner, H., & Kaplan, B. (1963). *Symbol formation*. New York: Wiley.

White, S. H. (1992). G. Stanley Hall: From philosophy to developmental psychology. *Developmental Psychology*, 28 (1), 25–34.

Whiten, A., & Byrne, R. W. (1988). Tactical deception in primates. *Behavioral and Brain Sciences*, 11, 233–73.

Whitney, I., & Smith, P. K. (1993). A survey of the nature and extent of bullying in junior/ middle and secondary schools. *Educational Research*, 35, 3–25.

Wilcox, B. M. (1969). Visual preferences of human infants for representations of the human face. *Journal of Experimental Child Psychology*, 7, 10–20.

Wilcox, T., & Baillargeon, R. (1998). Object individuation in infancy: The use of featural information in reasoning about occlusion events. *Cognitive Psychology*, 37, 97–155.

Willatts, P. (1997). Beyond the "couch potato" infant: How infants use their knowledge to regulate action, solve problems, and achieve goals. In G. Bremner, A. Slater, & G. Butterworth (Eds.), *Infant development: Recent advances* (pp. 109–35). Hove: Psychology Press.

Williams, E. M., & Shuard, H. (1986). *Primary mathematics today*. London: Longman.

Wiltshire, S. (1987). *Drawings*. London: J. M. Dent.

Wimmer, H., & Hartl, M. (1991). Against the Cartesian view on mind: Young children's difficulty with own false beliefs. *British Journal of Developmental Psychology*, 9, 125–38.

Wimmer, H., & Perner, J. (1983). Beliefs about beliefs: Representation and constraining function of wrong beliefs in young children's understanding of deception. *Cognition*, 13, 103–28.

Windham, G. C., Eaton, A., & Hopkins, B. (1999). Evidence for an association between environmental tobacco smoke exposure and birthweight: A meta-analysis and new data. *Paediatrics and Perinatal Epidemiology*, 13, 35–57.

Wing, L. (1976). *Early childhood autism*. Oxford: Pergamon Press.

Wing, L., & Gould, J. (1979). Severe impairments of social interaction and associated abnormalities in children: Epidemiology and classification. *Journal of Autism and Developmental Disorders*, 9, 11–29.

Wishart, J. G. (1991). Taking the initiative in learning: A developmental investigation of infants with Down syndrome. *International Journal of Disability, Development and Education*, 38, 27–44.

Wishart, J. G. (1993). The development of learning difficulties in children with Down's syndrome. *Journal of Intellectual Disability Research*, 37, 389–403.

Wishart, J. G., & Duffy, L. (1990). Instability of performance on cognitive tests in infants and young children with Down's syndrome. *British Journal of Educational Psychology*, 60, 10–20.

Wolff, P. H. (1968). The serial organization of sucking in the young infant. *Pediatrics*, 42, 943–56.

Wolff, P. H. (1969). The natural history of crying and other vocalization in early infancy. In B. M. Foss (Ed.), *Determinants of infant behavior* (Vol. 4, pp. 81–110). London: Methuen.

Wood, D. (1986). Aspects of teaching and learning. In M. Richards & P. Light (Eds.), *Children of social worlds*. Cambridge: Polity.

Wood, D. J., Bruner, J. S., & Ross, G. (1976). The role of tutoring in problem solving. *Journal of Child Psychology and Psychiatry*, 17, 89–100.

Wood, D. J., & Middleton, D. J. (1975). A study of assisted problem solving. *British Journal of Psychology*, 66, 181–91.

Wood, D. J., Wood, H. A., & Middleton, D. J. (1978). An experimental evaluation of four face to face teaching strategies. *International Journal of Behavioral Development*, 1, 131–47.

Woolfolk, A. E. (1998). *Educational psychology*. Boston: Allyn & Bacon.

Wylie, J. (1993). *Family Therapy Networker* (Sept./Oct.), 40–6.

Wynn, K. (1992). Addition and subtraction by human infants. *Nature*, 358, 749–50.

Wynn, K. (1995). Origins of numerical knowledge. *Mathematical Cognition*, 1, 35–60.

Wynn, K. (1998). Psychological foundations of number: Numerical competence in human infants. *Trends in Cognitive Science*, 2, 296–303.

Wynn, K. (2000). Findings of addition and subtraction in infants are robust and consistent: Reply to Wakeley, Rivera, and Langer. *Child Development*, 71, 1535–6.

Youniss, J., & Smollar, J. (1985). *Adolescent relations with mothers, fathers, and friends*. Chicago: University of Chicago Press.

Youniss, J., & Yates, M. (1997). *Community service and social responsibility in youth*. Chicago: University of Chicago Press.

Yussen, S. R. (1974). Determinants of visual attention and recall in observational learning by preschoolers and second graders. *Developmental Psychology*, 10, 93–100.

Zaitchik, D. (1990). When representations conflict with reality: The preschoolers' problem with false belief and "false" photographs. *Cognition*, 35, 41–68.

Zajonc, R. B. (1983). Validating the confluence model. *Psychological Bulletin*, 93, 457–80.

Zaragoza, M. (1991). Preschool children's susceptibility to memory impairment. In J. L. Doris (Ed.), *The suggestibility of children's recollections*. Washington, DC: American Psychological Association.

Zelazo, P. R. (1983). The development of walking: New findings and old assumptions. *Journal of Motor Behavior*, 15, 99–137.

Zelazo, P. R., Weiss, M. J. S., & Tarquinio, N. (1991). Habituation and recovery of neonatal orienting to auditory stimuli. In M. Salomon and P. Zelazo (Eds.), *Newborn attention: Biological constraints and the effect of experience* (pp. 120–41). Norwood: Ablex.

Ziegler, S., & Rosenstein-Manner, M. (1991). *Bullying at school: Toronto in an international context* (Report No. 196). Toronto: Toronto Board of Education, Research Services.

Zimmer, E. Z., et al. (1993). Vibroacoustic stimulation evokes fetal micturition. *Obstetrics and Gynecology*, 81, 178–80.

Index of Names

Subject Index

Note: page numbers in *italics* denote illustrations or tables where separated from textual references